The World Famous Beaverpedia

By

Brian Humek

Dedicated to the loving memory of Tony Dow

NS New Siberian Publishing

2010 Ridgewood St. Irving, TX 75062
http://leaveittobeaverbooks.com

Copyright © 2022 by Brian Humek

Cover design: Keith Miller
Cover photo: (Alamy) Public Domain per U.S. Law. This photo is in the public domain in the United States because it was published in the United States between 1927 and 1977, inclusive, without a copyright notice. Regulations found in Copyright office circular 3.
Back cover photos: Tony Dow and Joe Connelly (courtesy Karen Donovan), Bob Mosher (public domain), Jimmy Hawkins and Tony Dow (courtesy Jimmy Hawkins), Republic Studios (courtesy Jerry Schneider)

ISBN – 9798848078985

Table of Contents

FOREWORD

BY

STU SHOSTAK

Like the author of this book, I too was a big fan of "Leave it to Beaver" growing up; in fact, I'm old enough to remember watching the last two seasons in first run on ABC in the early 1960s! The show had such an impact on me that I'm still an admirer of the series today.

Being a television archivist and a talk show host whose main intention is to preserve the legacy of classic television, it was a goal of mine to set out and have as many members of the "Leave it to Beaver" sitcom on my program as I could. It turned out that this goal was very handily met – once I got acquainted with Frank Bank (Lumpy) and Ken Osmond (Eddie), the others followed in a natural progression since they all kept in touch with one another, lo those many years. Frank was instrumental in getting Jerry Mathers to do the show, and my wife (then girlfriend) Jeanine Kasun happened to meet Tony Dow and his beautiful wife Lauren at a function in Northern California shortly afterward. The rest, as they say, was history.

Not only did each appear on my show many times, but as a result of our chemistry on the air, Jeanine and I developed very close friendships with all of them - Frank, Ken, and especially Tony and Lauren, so much so that when Jeanine suffered a near-fatal brain aneurysm, both Tony and Lauren gave us so much support and were always there for us during the time that when I proposed to Jeanine so I could continue to get her the care she needed as both her husband and Advance Directive, Lauren (a licensed officiator) married us, with Tony standing beside us as my best man.

Let me tell you a little about Tony Dow. What you saw on LITB was the real thing. Tony was Wally Cleaver and Wally Cleaver was Tony. Nobody could ask for a better friend – a smart, sophisticated, extremely loyal, honest, sincere person who would give you the shirt off his back if you needed it. He was not only a wonderful actor, but he was a terrific director and a very talented sculptor. His artwork can be seen in many popular galleries around the world. Moreover, as an individual, he was someone to really look up to – always there with the right advice or to lend a helping hand for whatever situation arose. Calling him a mentor would be an understatement. Everyone should be lucky enough to have a Tony Dow/Wally Cleaver in their life. I don't think he ever realized how iconic his character had become as a result of the thousands of reruns the show has endured over the years. His marriage to Lauren lasted forty-two years – an amazing accomplishment when you think about the divorce rate in Hollywood. Tony and Lauren truly loved and respected one another and when he passed, he left a void that will never be filled, not only for Lauren, but for all of us. Indeed, we've all lost our "big brother."

Tony would have been a bit embarrassed to find that Brian is dedicating this book to him. He was a little taken aback when I told him there could be no other person worthy of being the best man at my wedding to Jeanine than he. That's the kind of guy Tony was – unassuming and with very little ego despite so many talented accomplishments in his lifetime. However, in the end, I think Tony would have also felt very honored by Brian's decision, as I am, that he chose me to write the foreword to this wonderful book.

Stu Shostak,
TV Historian/Host, "Stu's Show"
www.stusshow.com

Jeanine, Stu, Lauren and Tony
October 26, 2014

INTRODUCTION

My fascination with *Leave it to Beaver* began before I ever saw a single episode of the classic TV situation comedy. In the early 1980s, Charlie Rose had an interview program on CBS which aired at 2:00 a.m. One morning, I watched an interview with two child actors, all grown up. Their names were Jay North, who played Dennis the Menace, a show I watched frequently. The other actor was Jerry Mathers, who everyone knew as "The Beaver" from the situation comedy *Leave it to Beaver*, a show I had never seen.

While the questions were basically the same for each actor, their answers were polar opposites. From Jay North, the answers spewed from his mouth with a big dose of bitterness as an exclamation point at the end of each sentence. However, from Jerry Mathers, the answers gently streamed, like the water of a babbling brook flowing into Friend's Lake. A smile accompanied each answer. The difference between the two actors was life changing for me.

After this evening of hearing Jay North complain about how sailors made fun of him while he was in the Navy and all the other trials and travails that happened upon him simply because he was cast as Dennis the Menace, I rarely watched his program again. My feelings were that a person watches a show filled with innocent child characters because of the fun involved in their on-screen ordeals and how the problems are solved. Isn't watching TV, especially classic comedies, supposed to be fun? Watching Jay North, a bitter man in his 30s who had no good memories of *Dennis the Menace*, complain about his experience would make watching the show a reminder of all the complaints I had heard from Jay in this interview. Life should be fun, so right then; I became a *Leave it to Beaver* fan and never turned back.

Only recently, did I find out that Jay North, with the help of a therapist in the 1990s, finally came to terms with his early fame and the abuse he endured from his aunt and uncle because of it. My sincerest prayers go out to Jay and his family. Now, I am a fan of both shows and wish *Dennis the Menace* was as readily available on the airwaves for fans, as is *Leave it to Beaver*.

After that Charlie Rose interview, I soon found *Leave it to Beaver* on Superstation WTBS. Every weekday, I watched both episodes that aired from 4:05 p.m. to 5:05 p.m. central time. As I watched the episodes and the silly situations Beaver found himself a part of, I did sometimes think back on that interview and the great amount of positivity Jerry Mathers exuded while answering the questions from Charlie Rose. The episodes I watched were a week in the life of Jerry Mathers. He had fun making these shows. They weren't his real life, but they were real life situations, many which happened to either the creators of the show, Joe Connelly and Bob Mosher during their childhood, to their children, or the situations were taken from the real lives of other writers' kids.

I have never stopped marveling at Jerry Mathers' attitude about *Leave it to Beaver*. Interviewers and authors are often amazed that he has kept such a positive attitude about his role in this classic TV comedy which first aired over sixty-five years ago. As I was putting the finishing touches on this book, I watched an interview with Jerry, this one with Ken Boxer from February 2014. In the interview, Ken asked Jerry about the pluses and minuses of portraying Beaver Cleaver. Of course, Jerry rattled off as many pluses as he could in the limited time he had. But Ken had also asked him to list some of the negatives. Jerry told him he had not found any negatives yet, but if he did, he'd make sure to come back and let him know.

For Jerry, he may wonder why any actor would not revel in the fact they have brought entertainment into the homes of tens of millions of people for decades and are known all around the world. "Why..." Jerry may ask, "...would I ever be unhappy about that?" If I am right about what Jerry thinks about his fame, something he has pretty much stated outright in numerous TV interviews, I think we have an outstanding mother to thank for his great attitude. No, that wouldn't be June Cleaver, even though she modeled that great attitude too, but the credit should go to Jerry's mother and father. His parents raised him correctly. A big thank you is due Norman Mathers and Marilyn Mathers.

I may have always been destined to find *Leave it to Beaver* on TBS back in the 1980s, but if not for that interview with Jerry Mathers, I may not have become the fan I am today. I love all the actors on the show and was pleased to interview some of them during the writing of this book. While this introduction is a big shout out to Jerry, it's also a big thank you for all actors, writers, directors, producers and those behind-the-scenes people, who helped put the show on the air.

And here's something funny (or sad), and it is proof of my long term *Leave it to Beaver* fascination. The following was found recently in an old journal entry of mine from when I was an unemployed slacker in my early 20s; "Woke up at 1 p.m. watched *Leave it to Beaver*." This wasn't just one journal entry; it was basically a few months' worth of journal entries.

If you are wondering where the inspiration for this book came from, it was my writing a devotional book in 2013 and 2014 called *Leave it to God* which included an actor encyclopedia of season one actors. I figured at the time; I could eventually do that for all six seasons. Then, the idea expanded into an encyclopedia about the entire show. This book is so encyclopedic that I refer to it as a TV history textbook. I hope it becomes one of your favorite references for not only *Leave it to Beaver*, but for classic TV in general.

Sincerely,
Brian Humek
(A *Leave it to Beaver* addict who is not searching for a twelve-step program)

Reading Notes: (1) In many chapters, you will see an episode in parentheses next to some text about a subject. For example, in the chapter about gifts, it mentions that Ward was given a gift of English bath salts ("June's Birthday"). This means that this episode is the one in which that gift is spoken about, not that he was given the gift in that specific episode. That type of reference is seen in almost every chapter. (2) You will notice that when the boys are spoken of doing something for their mother or father, the text will read, for example, "The boys bought Ward a hunting jacket" instead of "The boys bought their father a hunting jacket." (3) You will find some redundancy in a few chapters as there are some topics that are repeated and that is because some readers may use this as a reference work and not read it through from cover to cover. Instead, they may be more interested in looking up certain topics. For example, Ward scoring twenty-three points in a college basketball game is mentioned in the chapter about Ward and the chapter about sports.

Have fun reading!

1

BOB AND JOE

Bob Mosher

Co-creator, producer and writer of *Leave it to Beaver*, Bob Mosher, was born in Auburn, New York on January 18, 1915. He wrote in an autobiographical sketch in 1937, that his birth "…resulted at the same time in the death of my mother."[1]

Auburn, at the time of his birth, had a population of around 25,000 people. The city is located thirty miles west of Syracuse, New York and 260 miles northwest of Manhattan. Mosher's childhood home was located at 53 Lake Avenue in Auburn. If Lake Avenue sounds familiar, it is mentioned in both the "Beaver and Andy" and "Beaver's Cat Problem" episodes. His family were prominent members of St. John's Episcopal Church in Auburn. His father was a partner in the Mosher & Barry Insurance Agency.[2] His stepmother was Marian McCamey, and married Mosher's father in 1920 when Bob was five years old.

As a baby, Bob's father gave him into the safekeeping of his unmarried sister in New York City. She taught English at P.S. (public school) #4 in the Bronx. This is the grade school Mosher attended when he came of school age. While he lived in New York City and had what he called a "plain" life in an apartment building, Mosher said his aunt filled his life with her cultural influences and refinement, "She appreciated good music, books and plays, and instilled in me an appreciation of them."[3] Raised by an English teacher, he was taught to speak and write correctly and to have a high regard for good literature. Each summer, when school ended, Mosher escaped New York City when he and his aunt returned to spend their vacations with his father back in Auburn.

After grammar school, Mosher attended Morris High School in the South Bronx. The school was located on Boston Road at 166th Street. In his own words, Mosher said this about his education there, "The New York School system being what it is, I learned little there, but at least I was somewhat prepared for college."[4]

After graduating from Morris High School, Mosher chose to attend Susquehanna University, a small school in Selinsgrove, Pennsylvania. He attended from 1933 to 1937, majored in English, and while at Susquehanna, was a very active student. Mosher was a member of the Bond and Key Club and worked on the school newspaper, *The Susquehanna*, all four years he attended the university. He was also a class treasurer, yearbook editor and a member of the French Club. While a freshman, he began his work on the school newspaper as a reporter, and in his following years, he became a features writer, managing editor, then co-editor as a senior. He also wrote a weekly column for the paper titled, "Ramblings, the Mental Meanderings of a Mere Male." He proudly stated in his biography, "In four years, I have never missed a deadline."[5]

During summers of his college years, Mosher labored at a few different jobs, all which gave him good experience in his future endeavors as an advertising copywriter, and as a writer for

---

[1] Mosher, Bob. "Autobiographical sketch." *Employment file at the J.W. Thompson Advertising Agency*, 1937.
[2] "Robert Livingston Mosher Sr." https://www.findagrave.com/memorial/65438816/robert-livingston-mosher
[3] Mosher, Bob. "Autobiographical sketch." 1937.
[4] Ibid.
[5] Ibid

radio and television programs. Those jobs included stints as a gas station attendant, a car salesman, and a spray gun operator.

After college graduation, he made his way to New York City where he began work at the J. Walter Thompson advertising agency, one of the largest in the United States at the time. He began as a messenger's apprentice on October 11, 1937, eventually working his way up to copywriter. This is where he met future radio show and TV writing partner Joe Connelly. He and Connelly worked in what they called the "bullpen" along with three other copywriters. While they didn't get paid much, Connelly once commented that the two did not feel exploited.[6] In regard to writing for radio, Connelly explained that on Saturdays he and Mosher worked on a script for Edgar Bergen and W.C. Fields.[7] Both Bergen and Fields worked on the *Chase & Sanborn Hour* radio program until September 1937, when Fields ceased being a regular player. In an article in the Contra Costa Gazette, Connelly said they wrote advertising spots for W.C. Fields during his appearances on *Chase & Sanborn* or as he called it, "The Edgar Bergen Program."[8]

In late January of 1942, Mosher was transferred by the agency to its Hollywood office where he worked on scripts of the *Chase & Sanborn* show on NBC with head writer Joe Bigelow. One of the show's acts was Edgar Bergen and his dummy, Charlie McCarthy.[9] His J. Walter Thompson employment file at the time stated that he not only had been transferred, but he had been added to the payroll of the *Chase & Sanborn* show on January 27th of that year. He worked on the program through 1944. Joe Connelly, who had been sent to Hollywood by J. Walter Thompson in 1942 to work on the *Kraft Music Hall* program, joined Mosher on *Chase & Sanborn* in 1943, replacing Joe Bigelow who had moved to *What's New?* on NBC.[10][11]

From 1944 through the end of the 1940s, Mosher worked on various radio shows, many with his friend from the J. Walter Thompson advertising agency, Joe Connelly. The shows included *Chesterfield Music Shop with Johnny Mercer* (1944), *The Frank Morgan Show* (1945 w/ Connelly), *The Ginny Simms Show* (1946), and *The Fitch Bandwagon* (1946-1947 w/ Connelly). He and Connelly also wrote audition episodes for *Barnaby* (1945) and *The Harry Von Zell Show* (1946).[12] The biggest radio success Mosher experienced with his partner Joe Connelly, was with the Amos 'n' Andy radio series. In the late 1940s, Freeman Gosden and Charles Correll, the creators of Amos 'n' Andy, asked Bob and Joe to write some episodes of their show. The writing duo worked out well, because for the next twelve years, they wrote in excess of 1200 Amos 'n' Andy episodes![13]

Bob Mosher, along with his partner Joe Connelly, turned their sights toward television in the early 1950s. They wrote an episode (possibly more) for *The Alan Young Show,* and they created

[6] Palmer, Zuma. "Radio – Television." *Los Angeles Citizen News*, March 17, 1958.
[7] Ibid.
[8] Danson, Tom. "Ray Milland Plays TV Role to Quiet Insistent Agent." *Contra Costa Gazette*, September 17, 1953.
[9] "Behind the Mike." *Broadcasting*. February 16, 1942, 34.
[10] Ellett, Ryan. *Radio Drama and Comedy Writers, 1928-1962*. McFarland, 2017, 148.
[11] In most accounts of how Mosher and Connelly wound up in Hollywood, the stories say that they left the advertising agency they worked with in New York to branch out into writing radio scripts. However, they were still employed by the J. Walter Thompson advertising agency when they moved to Hollywood. The agency transferred them to Hollywood to work on *The Chase & Sanborn Hour* (Mosher) and *The Kraft Music Hall* (Connelly) in 1942. Their employment files state they were off the company payroll in 1942 after their transfers and on the payrolls of the shows on which they worked.
[12] Ellett. *Radio Drama and Comedy Writers*, 148.
[13] "Worlds of Children, Adults Never Shall Meet – Not Quite." *San Bernadino County Sun*, April 7, 1958.

a program for Ray Milland called *Meet Mr. McNutley*. He also wrote with Connelly, the story for the film, *The Private War of Mr. Benson*, for which he and partner Connelly earned an Oscar nomination. Not long after, they created the most endearing family comedy of all time, *Leave it to Beaver* (1957).

After *Leave it to Beaver* had been on for a few years, a television writer told Mosher that his children loved the show. Mosher told the writer why, at first, they didn't think children would be part of their audience. "We had no cowboys or murders or robberies, all the things nice children go for. But they watched anyhow… One reason I think is that we frequently take the side of the kids against the parents. We often think it's necessary to remind the parents what it's like to be a child."[14]

Looking closer at Mosher's life will show how some things in it have made their way to the small screen in various *Leave it to Beaver* episodes. His childhood home was on Lake Avenue, a street mentioned in "Beaver's Cat Problem" and "Beaver and Andy." Mosher was a member of the Bond and Key Club at Susquehanna University. Its goals were "brotherhood and service" and had as their motto, "Bound as Knights." Sounds a bit like Beaver's group in the "Beaver and Ivanhoe" episode. He attended university in Selinsgrove, PA, about an hour away from Muhlenberg College, the opponent Ward Cleaver scored twenty-three points against with a hook shot while he was in college. Also, in an article, in The Santa Maria Times, Mosher speaks of Mathers and Dow as being "old pros," something we hear coming out of Ward Cleaver's mouth a few times in the series. When asked what it was like working with kids, Mosher said, "To tell the truth, I think it's harder than working with grown-ups, but much more satisfying."[15]

After two decades of creating and writing some of the best television the medium has ever seen, Mosher, a man who truly loved his writing profession, died much too young, in 1971, at the age of 57.

Joe Connelly

Joe Connelly was born in New York City in 1917. Although some newspaper accounts mention he was raised by his grandmother in New York City, these accounts are untrue. When he was five years old, he was sent to live at Ladyciff Academy, a military school. He only lived there for two years, but it made a lasting impression on him. He quickly learned that the ability to get along with his fellow humans was one of the most important steps in life. After leaving Ladycliff, he spent the next ten years living in Ashbury Park, New Jersey with his mother and brother.

Although Joe understood getting along with his fellow humans was a key to life, it is unfortunate that his fellow humans, or in the case of school, his fellow classmates, didn't feel the same about him, at least when it came to his attire. He stated in his biographical sketch when applying to the J. Walter Thompson agency, that he had two ambitions as a young lad. They were to win the half-mile race in the Jersey Championships and to get out of short pants, "The fact that I was kept in short pants until I left grammar school taught me how to scrap."[16] Another of his ambitions was to join the Naval Academy.

Connelly had good marks in high school, except in French class. Despite his doing well in school, he still had time to get into the types of difficulties that his later creation, "Beaver Cleaver"

---

[14] Crosby, John. "Father Has Problems." *Los Angeles Mirror News*, October 17, 1958

[15] "'Beaver' Writers Rely on Their Own Children for Situations." *Santa Maria Times*, July 22, 1961.

[16] Connelly, Joe. "Brief History of My Life." Early 1941.

would endure, in fact, Connelly's were worse. As all *Leave it to Beaver* fans know, Beaver fell out of a boat ("The Boat Builders"). Joe Connelly fell out of a boat too. Let him tell you in his own words from his, *Brief History of My Life* he wrote for his employer J. Walter Thompson: "I remember one summer while fishing in a sailing canoe, some four miles off the Jersey coast, with my brother, we had the misfortune to capsize. It was near dark, and we were almost out of sight of land and in waters noted, that summer, for sharks. After five full hours in the water, we were picked up by market fishermen."[17]

Connelly excelled in track during high school, captaining his team. In his last two years on the track team, he only lost one race. He once ran in the track national championships at Madison Square Garden while sick with the stomach flu. While leading the race, he fell and tumbled onto the wooden track, with parts of the track splintering his body. Fully recovered, and with his ability intact, he earned a track scholarship to the exclusive Roxbury School in Cheshire Connecticut, where he graduated in 1937. Roxbury was a prep school for students who aspired to attend nearby Yale University. However, Yale was not in his future; Connelly wanted to see the world.

Connelly may not have joined the Naval Academy as he had desired, but he did sign up to join the Merchant Marines for a year, becoming a cadet aboard the Santa Clara of the Grace Line in 1938.[18] He was the second youngest crew member on the ship which traveled through the Panama Canal, visited ports in South America and visited Havana, Cuba. This was the ship on which he sailed where some say he met a man, he, or other shipmates, named "Beaver." His experiences on board and in port were priceless, and then there were the traumatic moments too. He witnessed a shipmate fall from the mast to his death. He watched another shipmate drown alongside the ship before he could be saved. He spent a night in a Peruvian jail. He was also almost shot to death when a drunken passenger wanting to commit suicide threatened to take Connelly with him. "A shipmate and I finally got the gun away from him."[19] He had planned on continuing in his effort to see the world. This would have involved shipping out to the Middle East, but while back in New York, waiting for a ship, he took a position working at the 1939 World's Fair.

After obtaining his job with the World's Fair, Connelly fell in love and married Cathryn Scanlan. They were wed in 1940. Almost a year later, in March 1941, he was employed by the J. Walter Thompson Advertising Agency as a radio writer, where he met his future radio and TV writing partner, Bob Mosher. As mentioned earlier, both men were transferred by their company to Hollywood in 1942. Mosher left first for the *Chase & Sanborn Hour* in late January and in late March or early April, Connelly was transferred to Hollywood to work on the *Kraft Music Hour*. In 1943, Connelly joined Mosher on the *Chase & Sanborn Hour* and continued their collaborating for over twenty years. From 1944 through the end of the 1940s, Connelly worked with Mosher on a variety of radio shows and Connelly also wrote for *Maxwell House Iced Coffee Time* in 1944.[20]

As stated above, in addition to their radio work, especially their massive output of *Amos 'n' Andy* scripts, Bob Mosher and Connelly set their goals towards television and the big screen. In addition to the previously mentioned shows, the duo also wrote some for the *Marge and Gower Champion Show* in early 1957 and attempted to create a TV program based on their story idea for *Private War...* but it did not come to fruition. Joe and Bob then created *Leave it to Beaver* (1957) for the George Gobel and David O'Malley owned Gomalco Productions.

When *Leave it to Beaver* was created, the show was written to have the world seen through the eyes of a child. When filming began, Connelly had six children and a lot of the situations he

[17] Connelly, Joe. "Brief History of My Life." Early 1941.
[18] Crew member list of the Santa Clara from August 29, 1938, National Archives Records Administration.
[19] Connelly, Joseph. "Brief History of My Life." Early 1941.
[20] Ibid.

dealt with as a father, unsurprisingly, were similar to the ones Ward had to deal with on the show with Wally and Beaver. Many newspapers in the late 1950s, when the show first aired, all the way up to Connelly's obituary in the New York Times, report that two of Connelly's children, Ricky and Jay, were the models for Beaver and Wally Cleaver.[21] Partner Bob Mosher also had two children about the age of Wally and Beaver, and they too, were models for some of the show's situations.

After *Leave it to Beaver* left the air in 1963, Connelly, along with Mosher, went on to create *The Munsters*, a similar, but also, an entirely different type of family situation comedy. Over the years, during and after *Beaver*, the duo created and wrote many other shows including *Bringing Up Buddy*, *Ichabod and Me*, *Calvin and the Colonel* and *Karen*.

Connelly was a boisterous man, a contrast to his much more reserved partner Bob Mosher, who was a classic car collecting, quiet prankster at heart.[22] This dynamic about the duo is noticed in almost every article involving both Bob Mosher and Joe Connelly. The first one quoted in these articles or columns is Connelly, and later, you'll read words like "Mosher interjected," "Mosher picked up the ball," "Mosher took over the cudgel," or similar such phrases. Theirs, however, was an equal partnership when it came to producing and writing, and the results were often amazing. When it comes to their creation *Leave it to Beaver,* the result so far, has been everlasting enjoyment, as in, never ending. The situation comedy has appeared on a TV station somewhere in America every single week since October 4, 1957.

A final thing to share from the autobiographical sketch Connelly wrote for his employer in early 1941 gives a possible reason for the endearing characters he created for *Leave it to Beaver*. Again, in his own words: "It's always been my policy, wherever I've been, to try to meet and talk to as many people as possible and try to understand how they act, think, and what motivates their daily life. I feel that in this way I have come to know a little of human nature, a knowledge that I think is of great value."[23]

Joseph Connelly passed away in 2003 at the age of 85. He left all *Leave it to Beaver* fans a lasting legacy, one we cheerfully watch over and over again and because we watch, we now know some of the human nature that inhabited this great writer.

[21] "Joe Connelly, 85, a Creator of 'Leave It to Beaver' on Television." *New York Times*, February 17, 2003.
[22] Ellett. *Radio Drama and Comedy Writers*, 148.
[23] Connelly, Joe. "Brief History of My Life." Early 1941.

2

... AND *LEAVE IT TO BEAVER*, AS THE BEST SITUATION COMEDY

Leave it to Beaver was a television program that would show the world as seen through the eyes of two children. It was new, unique and would not be filled with slapstick comedy or forced humor, nor have a big name in a starring role. Some experts said the show would never succeed with such a formula.[24] Were the experts wrong? They were monumentally wrong. It may be providence that the show even exists, because if the careers of Connelly and Mosher had gone a bit differently, the pilot may never have been filmed, sold, and turned into the 234 thirty-minute treasures it has become to its fans.

According to movie columnist Louella Parsons, a new television series was set to debut in December 1956. It would feature Buddy Ebsen and be written by the duo of Joe Connelly and Bob Mosher and directed by Leo McCarey.[25] If this series had happened, American TV and movie fans may have lost two very important Hollywood treasures. First, Mosher and Connelly would not have created *Leave it to Beaver* and director McCarey would not have filmed *An Affair to Remember*.[26]

The idea for *Leave it to Beaver* was first inspired by Connelly and Mosher's success with the film *The Private War of Major Benson*. The story idea for that film came from an incident Connelly witnessed personally as he took his son to school.[27] After the film's success, the duo knew they had to write what they knew. They each had children; Connelly had six, and Mosher two. They had all that source material, and they had their own childhoods which they remembered fondly. The source for some of their scripts for *Leave it to Beaver*, a show that was modern for its time, but still reminded some critics of *Penrod and Sam* or *Huckleberry Finn*, came from their own childhood. Bob Mosher told a reporter in 1958, "We often recall our own experiences as kids. We have bull sessions. Then something hits a familiar chord, and there's the storyline."[28] Connelly stated in the same interview that they never embellish on any of the memories they use for storylines, saying it wasn't necessary.

Connelly and Mosher took their time in creating *Leave it to Beaver*. Over a one-year period, the two would meet for lunch at a local restaurant, three or four times a week, and discuss their families and the exploits of their children. Of course, they also discussed their craft of scriptwriting. Combining them both, they had the idea of a family situation comedy and the only real dilemma they had was whether to make up situations for their new characters or to rely upon their own kids and their kids' friends for ideas. They chose the latter approach. Soon after the pilot was filmed, so-called experts said the pilot would not sell because it did not go for big laughs or have a big-name star.[29] The biggest problem for experts seems to have been that it wouldn't have the big laughs one might see from popular late night comics in their monologues, like those of Jay Leno in the 1990s or Greg Gutfeld today, or even the big laughs that would be seen on *The Dick Van Dyke Show* a couple years after *LITB* debuted, which interestingly enough, was a comedy

---

[24] Rich, Allen. "Listening Post and TV Review." *The Valley Times*, February 8, 1960.

[25] "Buddy Ebsen Wanted for New TV Series." *San Francisco Examiner*, November 20, 1956.

[26] McCarey created the story, co-wrote the screenplay, directed and produced the film and without him, most likely, An Affair to Remember would not have happened.

[27] McLellan, Dennis. "Joe Connelly, 85, Helped Create 'Leave it to Beaver." *Los Angeles Times*, February 14, 2003.

[28] "Worlds of Children, Adults Never Shall Meet – Not Quite." *San Bernadino County Sun*, April 7, 1958.

[29] Rich, Allen. "Listening Post and TV Review."

about writers of a TV show.

The pilot episode, "It's a Small World," was directed by Jerry Hooper, the man who directed the film *The Private War of Major Benson*, whose story was developed by Mosher and Connelly. On June 10, 1957, *Broadcasting* announced the pilot had been sold to CBS for $4,000,000 for 52 weeks (39 shows with 13 reruns). Jerry Mathers and Paul Sullivan were the listed stars.[30] The pilot was probably shot in mid-March as it aired on April 23, 1957 on *Heinz Studio 57*. It took about six weeks for the pilot to sell, but that was long enough for actor Paul Sullivan to grow 3 ½ inches.[31] Once Connelly and Mosher saw how he had grown, they began looking for a new "Wally." The re-casting of his part, and that of Ward Cleaver, must have finished no later than the end of July, as filming began at Republic Studios in the first week of August 1957.[32]

The show was called *Wally and Beaver* in July by the TV editor for the *The Daily Independent Journal* in San Rafael,[33] and as late as August 8, 1957 in newspapers like the *Redwood City Tribune* and *The Napa Valley Register*, in their TV news section talking about the new Friday night show on CBS. [34] Many people may have believed there was a new children's show featuring a boy and his pet beaver. However, a blurb in *Broadcasting* magazine from July 1, 1957, states the obvious when it announced that Harry Ackerman had been brought on as the executive producer. "The series, whose title will be changed to one more appropriate for a situation comedy and not so suggestive of a children's program, which this is not, will begin on CBS Oct. 4 in the Friday night 7:30 – 8:00 p.m. time period."[35] Jerry Mathers mentioned to Stu Shostak that a few years earlier there had been a movie titled, *Leave it to Blondie*, so the new title may have come from there.[36] If one looks at the movie poster for that film, you'll find the same font used for the season two opening of *Leave it to Beaver*. As early as the first week of August 1957 when shooting began, it may have finally been settled to ditch the *Wally and Beaver* name when it was announced in *Broadcasting* magazine that Remington Rand had become a sponsor of *Leave it to Beaver*.[37]

The week before *Leave it to Beaver* debuted, Mosher and Connelly did not know what type of response it would receive. In fact, they spoke of their direct and simple approach with a show that could be considered "slow comedy" to Mirror-News TV editor Hal Humphrey. "We May die the death of a dog with this kind of show, but we're going to stick with our original premise." Connelly said. "We're not going to hoke it up or strain for laughs."[38] *Broadcasting* magazine said of the first episode, "Connelly and Mosher have avoided any trace of slapstick in this new series. If the opening sequence is typical, *Leave It to Beaver* will be equal parts of humor and sentiment, with lots of smiles and chuckles and a few nostalgic tears, but not many belly laughs."[39] *Leave it to Beaver* was cited by a mass media forum in 1960 as "true to life, wholesome and presenting positive ideals with a desired emphasis."[40] A UPI television critic wrote about season two – "Writers Bob Mosher and Joe Connelly have scribbled their way through an elegant season. It's the

---

[30] "Gomalco Sells 'Wally & Beaver.'" *Broadcasting*, June 10, 1957.
[31] Seymour, Gene. "How 2 in 'Beaver' Pilot Crashed and Lived." *Philadelphia Daily News*, November 18, 1988.
[32] "Gomalco Engages Ackerman." *Broadcasting*, July 1, 1957.
[33] Foster, Bob. "Pay Television Seems Several Years Away." *The Daily Independent Journal*, July 19, 1957.
[34] Walker, Ellis. "Sarnoff is planning 'Specials' for NBC." *Redwood City Tribune*, August 8, 1957.
[35] "Gomalco Engages Ackerman." *Broadcasting*, July 1, 1957.
[36] Stu's Show November 8, 2008.
[37] "Eager for 'Beaver.'" *Broadcasting*, August 12, 1957.
[38] Humphrey, Hal. "Amos n' Andy Writers Try for New Laughs." *Los Angeles Mirror-News*, September 30, 1957.
[39] "In Review." *Broadcasting*, October 7, 1957.
[40] "Youth Conference Rakes Over TV." *Broadcasting*, April 4, 1960.

only family TV comedy rooted in reality."[41] Syndicated TV columnist John Crosby said, "*Leave it to Beaver* is not great art, but it is charming and sincere." This is high praise from a columnist who obliterated Connelly and Mosher for their previous TV effort, *Meet Mr. McNutley*[42]

If wondering about what type of money was involved in the selling and making of *Leave it to Beaver*, industry trade magazine, *Broadcasting*, as mentioned previously, announced in their June 10, 1957 issue that Gomalco sold the show to CBS for $4,000,000 for fifty-two weeks, which included thirty-nine episodes and thirteen reruns, with options for three additional years.[43] In their October 7 issue, they mention the first episode cost $40,000 to produce. In August 1961, Gomalco, who owned 50% interest in the *Leave it to Beaver* show, sold its interest to Revue Productions for $1,000,000.[44] When speaking about having writers script episodes of *Leave it to Beaver* or for their other productions, Connelly mentioned they paid 2,000 per episode.[45]

For those who may remember watching the series during its initial run from 1957 to 1963, there may have been times you had to search for the show. There were many changes regarding the day it was shown, its time slot, and even network. The show debuted on CBS October 4, 1957, at 7:30 p.m. – 8:00 p.m. on Friday nights. It competed against *Saber of London* on NBC and *The Adventures of Rin Tin Tin* on ABC. The first schedule change for *LITB* occurred in March 1958 when it moved to Wednesday nights at 8:00 p.m. going against *Wagon Train* on NBC and the *Disneyland* program on ABC. When the show moved to ABC the following year, it aired originally on Thursdays at 7:30 p.m. and its competition was *I Love Lucy* on CBS and *Jefferson Drum* on NBC. It aired in the 9:00 p.m. timeslot for summer reruns. During seasons three through five (1959-1962) it aired on Saturday nights at 8:30 p.m. and ran against *Wanted Dead or Alive* on CBS and *The Man and the Challenge* on NBC (1959-1960), *Checkmate* on CBS and *The Tall Man* on NBC (1960-1961), *The Defenders* on CBS and *The Tall Man* on NBC (1961-1962). For the 1962-1963 season, *LITB* made a move to Thursday nights at 8:30 p.m. to compete against the final half hour of *Perry Mason* on CBS and the first half hour of *Dr. Kildare* on NBC. In its final season, *Leave it to Beaver* was part of a blockbuster night of comedy on ABC with *The Adventures of Ozzie and Harriet*, *The Donna Reed Show*, *My Three Sons* and *McHales's Navy*.

As for the move from CBS to ABC, their original network was not thrilled with the ratings which could have been one reason for the move. Jerry Mathers said in a 2008 interview that ABC had given advertisers a better deal. This was when Ralston Purina came on to be a sponsor, along with Miles Labs (Alka Seltzer)[46] Another advertiser was Peter Paul Inc. the candy company who made Mounds and Almond Joy bars.[47] Plymouth also sponsored the show and provided new Plymouth Fury automobiles for Ward Cleaver to drive. In addition to moving networks, the show also switched studios. *Leave it to Beaver was* filmed at Republic Studios for seasons one and two. The filming then moved a couple miles east to Universal Studios for seasons three through six. One of the possible reasons for the move was due to Republic exiting the movie business and their renting out parts of their backlot to independent filmmakers, possibly making the Cleaver home exterior unavailable. No definitive reason had ever been given for the move.

In TV history, shows with only decent ratings, but great fan appeal, are sometimes moved to different days or timeslots, to find the perfect audience. Here are some mentions of ratings

[41] "Ewald's TV Review." Press Democrat, February 6, 1959.
[42] Crosby, John. "Film Stars Flock to TV for Mostly Inadequate Roles." *The Sacramento Bee*, September 30, 1953.
[43] Allen. "Listening Post and TV Review," June 6, 1957.
[44] "Lonesome George Picks Up a Bundle." *Broadcasting*, August 28, 1961.
[45] Connolly, Mike. "Jackie Has Clearance." *The Desert Sun*, May 14, 1960.
[46] "Business briefly…" *Broadcasting*, June 2, 1958.
[47] " Business briefly..." *Broadcasting*, June 26, 1961

during a few years of the show, none of them spectacular. At the beginning of season four, *LITB* was beat by the drama *Checkmate* on CBS but beat *Tall Man*, a western, on NBC. In April 1961, toward the conclusion of season four, the show ranked #8 in the 6-11 age group with a Q rating of 67. This ranked it just ahead of *The Andy Griffith Show*. The Q rating meant that 67% of all children aged 6-11 called *Leave it to Beaver* one of their favorite programs.[48] However, it wasn't nearly as popular in any other age group, which is why it never ranked in the top twenty in any of its six broadcast seasons. In September 1961, at the beginning of season five, the show came in last place in the Saturday 8:30 p.m. ratings against *The Defenders* and *Tall Man*, receiving only a 23% share of the audience.[49]

Frank Bank (Lumpy) said, when interviewed in 2008, that on Friday afternoons, the cast would go to the little gray bungalow that belonged to Connelly and Mosher and pick up their script for the following week. They were to read it over the weekend. "Well, I read it Monday morning on the way to the studio, hoping to remember my lines."[50] Jerry Mathers, during the same interview, added some details about the production week, saying that they would do table reads of the script on Monday mornings. They would go over the script four or five times. Jerry said that the script was typed on white paper originally, then the revision would be on pink paper and on blue paper if another revision was needed. They were done on Mondays with reading by 2:30 p.m. On Tuesdays, the cast would block the entire show (go through the details of how the scenes will play out in relation to the camera). That would occur from 8:00 a.m. to 4:30 p.m. when the writers would come down and watch the cast run through the entire show, from beginning to end. They took notes while they watched. Shooting would start the next morning. Scenes would be shot out of order. All the scenes in the living room, all the scenes in the boys' room would be shot together "We'd usually do the outside stuff on Wednesdays," said Mathers.[51] They would start with master shots, then close ups and the kids would only work until 5:00 p.m., which included three hours of school. After a dinner break from 5:00-6:00 p.m., the adults would come back and work from 6:00-11:00 p.m.[52]

Another interesting tidbit provided by Connelly in an article, decades earlier, was about the laugh track used on the show. He told a reporter, "We run each show to an audience of eighteen people and then put in our laugh track to their cues. We don't believe in pumping laughter into the show. We put our laughs only where our audience cues them, and we keep them at low level."[53]

Of course, fans know the names Billingsley, Beaumont, Dow and Mathers, but every actor has stand ins. They stand where actors are to be while scenes are lit. They also take the place of a principal actor for rehearsals, camera blocking, and shot composition. Some who have been stand ins say it was pretty low on the Hollywood totem pole back in the 1950s and 1960s, but then again, others have enjoyed the job, and being on a Hollywood set. On *Leave it to Beaver*, at the beginning, there were four stand ins whose names are known. One was former *Our Gang* actor and Bronze Star winner in WW II, Mickey Scott (a stand in for Tony Dow), another was Hazel Rosmonda (Jerry Mathers' stand in)[54] and Rory O'Connor (another Jerry Mathers stand in). Rory

[48] "Who Likes What Television Program." *Broadcasting*, April 10, 1961.

[49] "More ratings for the new television season." *Broadcasting*, Oct. 9, 1961

[50] Stu Show November 8, 2008.

[51] Ibid.

[52] Ibid.

[53] Johnson, Erskine. "Television Fans Still 'Leave it to Beaver.'" *Progress-Bulletin*, November 11, 1959.

[54] "Once 'Our Gang' Member, Actor, 41, is Kid Again, in Little Beaver Series." *The Roberts News*, Nov. 24, 1957.

went on to work behind the scenes, winning six Emmys for technical achievements. Later, Patrick Curtis, was a stand in for Tony Dow and also worked on the set in other capacities. One of his duties was taking actors like Jerry Mathers, Rich Correll, and Stephen Talbot out for lunch to Bob's Big Boy in Burbank on occasion. There were most likely, many other stand ins over the years, but their names may never be known.

There were a few times when Joe Connelly probably wished he had his own stand in. The best time for one of those would've been during those terrible controversial moments of the show when organized groups came after he and his partner. Yes, it's hard to believe there would be any controversy that would involve *Leave it to Beaver*. While in the late 1950s and early 1960s when many shows featured violence in crime shows and in westerns, there was a lot of protest against the TV networks and *Leave it to Beaver* was like a safe harbor in a storm for many parents and school organizations. But the show wasn't without its own detractors.

Connelly bemoaned the existence of those who would protest the show for what he deemed very nonsensical matters. Sixty years before cancel culture and woke culture came to invade comedy in our current decade of the 2020s, Joe Connelly and Bob Mosher were fighting against organized groups in the late 1950s. One instance was a laundry association or lobby who complained about the show's content when in the season two episode, "Beaver's Hero," Beaver mentions that Larry is sick because something the laundry put in his shirt gave him an allergic reaction. Also, if you remember, "The Paper Route," episode, that one made the California Newspaper Boy Association extremely mad because the boys worked for a mean newspaper man, the infamous "Old Man Merkel." They didn't like his portrayal and caused so much trouble, Connelly and Mosher had to add a character in a later show from that same newspaper who wasn't portrayed in such a manner. Connelly complained to TV critic Hal Humphrey, saying, "Everybody is organized, and it is rapidly killing TV as a medium for comedy." [55] He also had a few more choice words to groups that caused dialect humor to be banned a few years earlier and for the NAACP who had the *Amos 'n' Andy* show cancelled.

Leave it to Beaver was a show that had enough popularity to continue beyond 1963, when it left the ABC airwaves. In a November 2008 interview with Stu Shostak, Jerry Mathers had the following to say about how the show ended and spoke of ABC approaching Connelly and Mosher:

> The network came to us in 1962 … ABC wanted to start having color shows… the problem was, color took a lot longer to light… and Connelly and Mosher felt that they had had six good years in black and white… and what the studio was proposing was instead of having our two days, one day of reading and one day of rehearsal, we would start on Monday morning filming, and film five days, because that's what the extra lighting and doing color would've taken and they felt that they had six good years, and they could've squeezed out two or three more… in color, but the show wouldn't have been the same… and they said, "no, we're just going to wrap it now."

Frank Bank and Ken Osmond, on another episode of Stu's Show, echoed similar sentiments. Bank said the network (he mentioned it was NBC) didn't just want color, they wanted to make it one hour. Osmond said, "I remember the color…" and added "They couldn't come up with one-hour scripts… It was the writers who said no… but put that with other factors like Jerry

---

[55] Humphrey, Hal. "Joke Vigilantes are killing What's Left of TV's Humor." *Los Angeles Mirror*, July 30, 1960.

wanting to leave…" [56]

      After *Leave it to Beaver* left ABC as a first run show, it immediately went into syndicated reruns on television stations around the United States. The following were the first stations to show *LITB* daily: KRLD -TV Dallas -Ft. Worth; WHTN -TV Huntington, WV; WJZ -TV Baltimore; WFMY Greensboro, NC; KBTV Denver; KVII Amarillo; WDSU New Orleans; WBTW Florence, SC and WTIC Hartford, CT. *Leave it to Beaver* was popular in the U.S., but also around the world.

      There's not a lot of documentation of where *Leave it to Beaver* has run in syndication worldwide. Jerry Mathers has said in interviews that the show has played in over 100 countries and been translated into ninety languages. A reporter with *The Morning Call* in Allentown, Pennsylvania, writing about the *Still the Beaver* movie, reported that the original show, in 1983, was still playing in Australia, Japan and parts of Africa.[57] Other evidence is only anecdotal. In 2022, when the question was posed to the "Leave it to Beaver Fanclub" Facebook group, of where people have seen the show outside the U.S., answers ranged from Australia, Canada, England, Turkey, Germany (on German television) and Bratislava, Slovakia, dubbed in Czech. Ken Osmond even once mentioned getting fan mail from Poland.

---

[56] Stu's Show March 5, 2008.
[57] Lawler, Sylvia. "Should Jerry Mathers Have Left it to 'The Beaver?'" *The Morning Call,* March 18, 1983.

3

WHO IS STU SHOSTAK?

There are two types of *Leave it to Beaver* fans. The two types are those who are very familiar with television historian / broadcaster Stu Shostak, and the other type are those who are not familiar with him. If you count yourself among that second group…. allow me to introduce you to Mr. Stu Shostak.

From reading the foreword, those fans who are in the second group have learned a bit about Stu. He was a good friend of Tony Dow, and he is the host of the *Stu's Show* program where he interviews anyone and everyone who has been a part of TV history. But how did Stu get in such a position to know everyone in television? How did he begin his career and why is he an important part of *Leave it to Beaver* history? His story is definitely an interesting journey.

Stu Shostak was born November 7, 1956, in San Francisco. His family moved to southern California in 1960. By the time he was eight or nine years old, Stu realized he was destined to work in the TV industry. His love for television was such that the worst punishment he ever suffered was his parents taking his television privileges away from him.[58] His parents tried discouraging him from the pursuit of a career in television. His father was a customs lawyer and had hopes of his son following in his footsteps, also becoming a lawyer. That desire of his dad's was totally dashed the summer he made Stu work in his office to help earn money for a car. After that, Stu knew for certain, he'd never be an attorney, especially a customs attorney.[59]

During high school, after he finally bought his car, Stu would attend school for half a day, then drive his car to Hollywood and attend tapings of *Truth or Consequences* with host Bob Barker. It was one of the easier shows to get tickets to and he had a plan to get noticed. After about three months, he was noticed by Jerry Jacobious, the man who was in charge of giving out tickets. He needed someone to assist him and that was Stu's first job in Hollywood. He was to hawk tickets to game shows like *Joker's Wild* and *Concentration* and other productions. Stu has mentioned in numerous interviews that this wasn't as easy of a job as many might think.

Wanting to work in the television industry, Stu took his general education classes at UCLA, and had a desire to enter the television department to finish up his degree. There were two things he admitted to podcaster Jeff Dwoskin that worked against him, his grades, and affirmative action, "I told them, 'I'm Jewish does that…' " Before he could finish his question, they told him, "Nah, get out of here."[60] Of course, they probably said it a bit more diplomatically than that. He did get out of there and with the reluctant blessing of his parents, he transferred into Cal State Northridge, and entered their television department. Even with the 1950s TV equipment in its classrooms, Stu jumped in headfirst, and it was a 180 degree turn from his time at UCLA. He devoured classes such as *Directing a Documentary*, *FCC Regulations*, *Aesthetics of Television*, and *Writing for Television*. During this time, he continued his work at studios in Hollywood, including

---

[58] Pastis, Steve. "'Stu's Show' Celebrates Classic Television Programs." *The Good Life.* July 24, 2002.https://www.thegoodlifesv.com/story/2022/07/01/entertainment/stus-show-celebrates-classic-television-programs/719.html
[59]Dwoskin, Jeff "#128 You're Gonna Love Stu's Show with Stu Shostak." *Jeffisfunny.com.* https://jeffisfunny.com/2022/05/128-youre-gonna-love-stus-show-with-stu-shostak/
[60] Ibid

a stint at *One Day At a Time* where he became friends with Mackenzie Phillips (still friends to this day) and was also friendly with Valerie Bertinelli, Pat Harrington, Bonnie Franklin and a crusty old director named Herb Kenwith, who had honed his directing chops on the soap operas *Valiant Lady* in the 1950s and *Return to Peyton Place* in the early 1970s. Kenwith had also directed quite a few episodes of *Here's Lucy* from 1969-1970. Kenwith allowed Stu to sit in the booth with him while the actors blocked their scenes. "He was nice to me because he saw potential in me, a young guy interested in behind-the-scenes stuff."[61]

It was in 1977, while Stu attended Cal State Northridge, that the school hired Lucille Ball to teach the *Aesthetics of Television* class on Monday nights. This was the same *Aesthetics of Television* class, RTVF 210, Stu had previously taken. His college counselor spoke to him about taking the class. It seemed they were afraid they wouldn't fill the large, almost 300 seat auditorium they had put Lucille Ball in to teach the class. They had opened the class up to non-majors and maybe the encouragement for Stu to take the class and promising to turn those credit hours into an elective, was so they would have an additional TV major in the class.[62] [63]

Stu had a dilemma about taking the class. It wasn't that he had already taken it. That was easily fixed with a promise from his counselor to turn it into an elective. His dilemma about the class was a warning from director Herb Kenwith. He knew Stu was a big Lucy fan and he told him if he didn't want to have his bubble burst about Lucy, that he shouldn't take the class. He said Lucy was not anything like the Lucy Ricardo from the *I Love Lucy* show. Kenwith went on to relate a few war stories he had from directing her, stories Stu later figured were far from the truth,[64] probably as far from the truth as Aaron Sorkin's *Being the Ricardos* script. Stu's counselor, a former TV director, gave him the following words of wisdom, "I've been in the business a long time myself, and I learned never to judge anybody until I see how that person is for myself."[65] Stu admits that was the best thing anybody has ever told him. He signed up for the class and it forever changed his life.

Each class began with an episode of *I Love Lucy*. This helped create questions for the Q&A session that followed. Not satisfied with just asking questions during class, Stu would speak with Lucille Ball during their ten-minute breaks on the hour. He'd discuss TV with her while she had a cigarette and drank coffee,[66] and talk about his family and friends.[67] It didn't take long for her to know who Stu Shostak was and he left an indelible mark on her. During the class with Lucille Ball, he was also taking his TV Documentary class and his class project was a documentary on the *I Love Lucy* show. He edited it together with two Betamax machines and had the nerve to give a rough cut to Lucy. She took it home, and she and her husband Gary Morton watched it. The next class session, Gary Morton was a guest and he and Stu spoke afterward. Gary had loved the documentary. That was the first time Stu broached the subject of one day working with he and Lucy. Gary replied, "We'll keep you in mind." It may have sounded like a Hollywood nicety to Stu, but Gary did keep him in mind.[68]

[61] Dwoskin, Jeff. "#128 You're Gonna Love Stu's Show with Stu Shostak." *Jeffisfunny.com*. https://jeffisfunny.com/2022/05/128-youre-gonna-love-stus-show-with-stu-shostak/
[62] "Stu Shostak" Hey Alexandra podcast. April 18, 2022. https://www.youtube.com/watch?v=iILn3bfbSGk
[63] Dwoskin, Jeff.
[64] Ibid
[65] *Stu's Show*. Directed by C.J. Wallis. Canada: FortyFPS Productions / Margrette Bird Pictures, 2022.
[66] Ibid
[67] *Stu's Show*, 2022.
[68] *Stu's Show*. Directed by C.J. Wallis. Canada: FortyFPS Productions / Margrette Bird Pictures, 2022.

Lucy had recently signed with NBC for a variety show and while promoting it, she went to many TV talk shows, including Johnny Carson, Dinah Shore, John Davidson, and Stu would often go to the shows and sit in the audience, to support his new friend and future employer. One such time was an appearance on *The Merv Griffin Show*. During that taping, Lucy pointed out Stu to Merv and said about him, "That's an enterprising young man who gets out and does for himself the type of thing that I talk about to students." [69]

While waiting for Gary Morton and Lucy to "keep him in mind," Stu continued another pursuit, becoming an audience warm up guy. This is the guy who works for producers, to keep the energy level of the television audiences high. That was necessary because the producers wanted laughs from the audience during all retakes if they happened. They had to be the same laughs the audience laughed the first time they saw a scene or the fifth or sixth time. That was part of Stu's job warming up audiences for such shows as *Diff'rent Strokes*, *The Jeffersons*, and *Mama's Family*. His longest tenure was on *Silver Spoons*, where he successfully entertained the studio audience from 1983-1985. He would warm up the crowd, interact with them, more than talk at them, and introduce the cast before the show began. He would also entertain if there was ever a break in the filming. He mentioned in an interview with Jeff Dwoskin that when he began his work warming up audiences in the early 1980s, the tapings were about ninety minutes at the longest, but by the time he ended studio warm up work about 2000 or 2001, he said it was rare that he would get out of the studio before midnight. [70]

About two and a half years after his last Monday night class with Lucy, her publicist Howard McClay passed away. Lucille Ball and her husband Gary Morton asked Stu to work with her archives. This was just one of the positions held by McClay. Stu worked as Lucille Ball's archivist for about ten years. He was with her at the time she was lured back into television by ABC to work on the *Life of Lucy* TV show. One night, as he was driving Lucy home, he got the nerve to ask her if he could have a part in one of the episodes. She didn't hesitate to say yes. In fact, when they arrived at her house, Lucy had him get writer Madelyn Davis on the phone. Moments later, Lucy told Stu he'd have a part in the next week's show. [71] [72] That episode was "Lucy's Green Thumb," in which Stu plays a photographer.

Stu went from warming up audiences of situation comedies, to speaking to audiences via audio on the internet about classic TV. His program *Stu's Show* was one of the first podcasts to feature talk about Classic TV of the 1950s, 60s and 70s. *Stu's Show* debuted in 2006. The show became an internet TV show in 2017 when his shows left audio behind and went directly to a video format. Think *The Larry King Show*, but more interesting if you're a fan of classic TV. When counting audio and video formats, he has done over 600 episodes over the past sixteen years. If you're a fan of his show, then you definitely know Stu's wife Jeanine.

Stu met the love of his life, Jeanine Kasun ("Jeanine from Petaluma") through their common enjoyment of classic TV, and especially their interest in Lucille Ball. Another of Jeanine's loves is *Leave it to Beaver*. Stu has spoken about her love of *Leave it to Beaver* in interviews with the show's cast members. She has said as much when she was in the studio with Stu when he recorded his first *Stu's Show* episode featuring Frank Bank (Lumpy) and Ken Osmond (Eddie) in

---

[69] *Stu's Show*, 2022.

[70] Dwoskin, Jeff. "#128 You're Gonna Love Stu's Show with Stu Shostak." *Jeffisfunny.com*. https://jeffisfunny.com/2022/05/128-youre-gonna-love-stus-show-with-stu-shostak/

[71] "Stu Shostak" Hey Alexandra podcast, April 18, 2022. https://www.youtube.com/watch?v=iILn3bfbSGk

[72] *Stu's Show*, 2022.

2008. In fact, for all the early cast member interviews of *Leave it to Beaver* actors, Jeanine was there in the Chatsworth studio. It is the story of her later health problems and how Stu fought to get her back to health after a brain aneurysm she suffered on November 19, 2013, that is the subject of the CJ Wallis documentary *Stu's Show*. Search for the show on YouTube or any streaming platform and watch. It is well worth your time and as Stu says about the lesson to be learned from the documentary, "You can beat the system. You can fight the medical industry, even when they say no, if you push hard enough. You can emerge victoriously."[73] Fair warning, you will cry when you watch the documentary. No matter how callous of an individual you may be, there's no stopping the tears. And if you're a very emotional person, go buy some stock in Kleenex before watching. There is so much more that could be said about the documentary, but it is best that you watch it for yourself.

Of the interviews done on his internet TV program, *Stu's Show*, and before that, with his audio podcast, Stu has interviewed many *Leave it to Beaver* actors. They include multiple shows with Frank Bank, Ken Osmond, Tony Dow and his lovely wife Lauren and one show with Jerry Mathers. He also has interviewed director Rich Correll, who played Beaver's friend Richard Rickover, twice (a total of almost ten hours). He has also interviewed writer / director Brian Levant who spearheaded the revival of *Leave it to Beaver* with the 1983 TV movie, *Still the Beaver* and the resulting series, *The New Leave it to Beaver*.

Stu met Ken Osmond (Eddie) and Frank Bank (Lumpy) in 2008 at the Hollywood Heritage Museum where Jon Provost was signing his new book. It was book signings like this and autograph shows where Stu met many actors who became guests on his *Stu's Show* program and eventually became his friends. The most unique things about Stu are his friendliness, outgoing nature and his bubbly (and quite boisterous) personality. He is infectious, and that's meant in a good way.

He's become friends with interviewees, some still living, some not. These friends of his include the cast of *My Three Sons*, some of the cast of *Leave it to Beaver*, especially Ken Osmond, Frank Bank, Tony Dow (and wife Lauren), Michael Cole from *Mod Squad*, Ed Asner, Dick Van Dyke and many more could be added to this short list. As you read in the foreword, he became so close to Tony and Lauren Dow that when he and Jeanine decided to get married, Lauren Dow officiated the wedding and Tony Dow was Stu's best man. Those are close friendships. It was through the interviews and eating together (Stu typically takes guests on his show out to eat before or after their interviews), where the friendships grew. It's the interviews that Stu has done where some great information has been shared about the *Leave it to Beaver* program. Any fan of *Leave it to Beaver* should sign up to become a VIP member of the *Stu's Show* program (stusshow.com) and you will then have access to all of his shows, including those that feature *Leave it to Beaver* actors.

In 2009, Stu began working as a co-producer with *Shout! Factory*. This company has released some of the greatest DVD collections ever and are the go-to company for classic TV shows on DVD. For Shout! Factory, Stu first licensed two of his "Stu's Show" audio broadcasts with Alan Young and Connie Hines for the release of the second and third seasons of *Mr. Ed*. Then, in 2010, he wrote, produced, and directed the thirty-minute documentary, "Ken Osmond and Frank Bank Remember," for the "Leave it to Beaver - The Complete Series" DVD set, a set of DVDs fans had been yearning for and would often ask about whenever Stu would interview any cast members pre-2010. Later in 2010, Shostak co-produced the "Dennis the Menace" TV series on DVD. He appears on camera interviewing former stars of the show, Gloria Henry (Alice Mitchell)

[73] "Stu Shostak" Hey Alexandra podcast, April 18, 2022. https://www.youtube.com/watch?v=iILn3bfbSGk

and Jeannie Russell (Margaret).

Besides the work Stu has done with Shout! Factory, Stu, as mentioned earlier, has interviewed anyone and everyone who has been involved in classic television, both in front of and behind the cameras. His interviews are both entertaining and enlightening. Once you watch your first Stu interview, you'll be hooked on his *Stu's Show* program. You can find his shows, which air bi-weekly, at stusshow.com. If you want to dive deep into TV history, you can do so on his website as it contains the archives of the over 600 shows produced so far.

In addition to the interviews he's conducted over the years on "Stu's Show", Stu also offers a classic television channel at shokusvideo.com. Shokus Video was a leader in providing 1950s television programming to the home video marketplace (starting in 1979) and this new channel highlights over thirty-six continuous hours of content from that era - everything from *Jack Benny* and *Burns and Allen* to *Dragnet* and *Love That Bob*. Viewers with either a Roku device or Roku television can also take advantage of an official Roku Stu's Show TV channel, available at no cost from the online Roku Store. Simply search "Stu's Show" and then add the channel to your menu lineup. Both Stu's current interview channel as well as the Shokus Video Classic Television channel are accessible there, as well as over forty "on demand" previous Stu's Show interview programs, all at no cost.!

Warning!

Beginning on the next page, you will learn more about the content of *Leave it to Beaver* episodes than you ever thought possible.

4

GEE

There are a number of ways this book on *Leave it to Beaver* could have begun. However, I decided to combine trivia with a word of dialogue for which the show and its characters are most well-known… and that word is "gee." The series is filled with its use in lines by Theodore "Beaver" Cleaver and his brother Wally, and even Eddie Haskell. If you ask any nominal fan of this TV show to recite a line from *Leave it to Beaver*, they most likely would say something similar to one of the following, "Gee, Mrs. Cleaver, you look nice today" or "Gee Wally, do you think Dad knows?" or "Gee Beaver, you're gonna get it."

Over the years, whenever I read a news article or saw a report on TV about *Leave it to Beaver*, the reporter or the writer would typically begin with the word "gee." This was a word I knew was used a lot on the show, but I never thought it was used as much as they made it seem. This one word came to symbolize the simplicity and sweetness of the late 1950s / early 1960s, and this TV show in particular. However, after months of research, and dissecting all 234 episodes and the pilot, all I can say is, "gee," everybody, I was wrong.

So, here is the trivia question… Which character was the first to use the word "gee," on the *Leave it to Beaver* TV show? Think about that for a moment. And bonus points if you can also name to whom it was said and in which episode it was used first. No, you're not getting the answer now, you'll find it at the end of this chapter. But if you want to channel your inner Eddie Haskell and peek, there's no "wardens" around to stop you.

This chapter comes with a warning, and it goes out to all but the most diehard of *Leave it to Beaver* fans, because diehard LITB fans will appreciate what they find in this chapter. Here's the warning: Every single chapter of this book will include some of the most minute details about the show, but this chapter may go overboard with some graphs and charts too. Get ready, 'cause here come all those details on the word "gee."

It will probably be a surprise to no one that Theodore "Beaver" Cleaver said the word "gee" more than any other character on the show. He said it most often to Ward, and typically, when wondering about life or explaining his actions, and it was even used when showing gratitude to Ward for some act of kindness. For example, in "Beaver Takes a Walk," he asks Ward, "Gee, you mean when I'm grown up, I'll forget about today being such a bad day?" Then, in the episode, "Beaver Runs Away," he uses the word when explaining how the holes were drilled into the garage wall. Beaver tells Ward, "But Gee, Dad, I didn't mean it to happen, it just happened." And in one of the more sentimental moments in the series, in the episode, "Beaver's Short Pants," Beaver tells Ward, after he rescues Beaver from another day of ridicule at school, "Gee, thanks Dad, you're almost like one of the fellas."

Was the word "gee" a bit overused on the series? We may have different opinions on that, but in six seasons, it was used almost 2000 times (see chart A). From the chart, you can see that the writers were just getting into the groove of using the word in season one and its usage stayed quite steady in seasons two through five and in the final season, its usage dropped by about 35%. I think it's safe to assume that "gee" was used less often in season six because the boys were growing up, one about to enter high school, and the other in college. But as Ward and June did say "gee" on occasion, over the run of the series, it wasn't totally taboo for adults to use the word in Mayfield.

Some interesting tidbits about the word "gee" include it being used the most in "Wally's

New Suit." This is the episode in which Wally wanted to assert his independence and show his maturity by purchasing his own suit, without parental supervision. Wally explains it quite simply to Ward and June, "Gee, I'm in high school now, well, how about if I just bought my own suit?" And how could *Leave it to Beaver* fans ever forget the times when Eddie used the word in partnership with a compliment to June Cleaver? He did this in "The Clubhouse," episode, not just once, but twice. "Gee, Mrs. Cleaver, your hair looks nice." She replies to the compliment with a gracious, "Thank you Eddie." A little while later, before leaving for home, Eddie doubles down on the insincerity and says, "Gee, Mrs. Cleaver, your hair really does…" and before he can finish, she interrupts, "You said that Eddie."

If you ever wondered how the writers could jam in so many "gee" words in a single episode, consider the "Beaver and Henry" episode in which during one conversation between Ward and Wally, the elder son of the family uses "gee" four times in only seventeen seconds! The talent of the writers shines brilliantly here because using the word that many times in that short of a time span, doesn't even seem unnatural when watching that scene of the boys in the garage with Ward discussing their new rabbit.

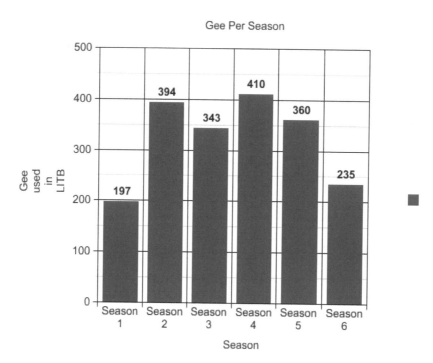

The World Famous Beaverpidia

Let's dive a bit deeper into the use of the word "gee" on the *Leave it to Beaver* show… and you thought we had already done that? No, we've just been wading in the kiddie pool. When it comes to Beaver's use of the word, he did use it most of the time when speaking to Ward, but let's look at the usage breakdown in Chart B.

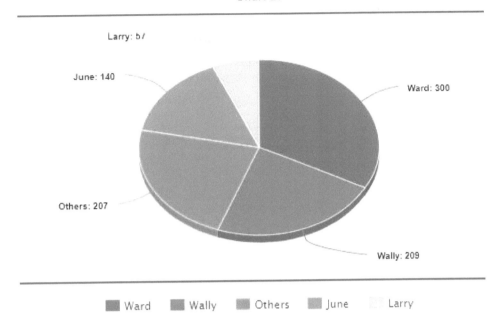

Beaver Cleaver Gee Usage
Chart B.

Larry: 57

June: 140

Ward: 300

Others: 207

Wally: 209

Ward   Wally   Others   June   Larry

This chart may change the way you've always thought about how many times Beaver would say to his brother, "Gee, Wally…" While the research done for this book, did not look specifically at that usage, it is reliable to say it was not said in a majority of the interactions between Beaver and Wally. In fact, most of the time, when the word "gee" is used by a character, it is without acknowledging the person to whom the character is talking. While there are plenty of times we hear "Gee, Wally…" or "Gee, Mrs. Cleaver…" or "Gee, Dad…" and "Gee, Eddie…" for the most part, those were exceptions to the rule, not the rule itself.

Gee usage changes a little bit for Wally. For instance, the number of times he uses the word with June is nearly 100% more often than Beaver uses it. Of all uses of "gee," for Wally, 29% of the time it is when speaking with June. However, Beaver, only uses it 15% in conversations with June. Also, Ward, June and Beaver rank one to three when Wally uses the word "gee" but when Beaver uses it, Ward, Wally and Others rank one to three. Chart C shows the breakdown for Wally by number of uses and percentages.

There is, among users of the word "gee," a group of "others." Who makes up this group and why are they using Beaver and Wally's word? The writers of the show liked to spread around its use outside of the main characters. This group of others is made up of thirty-four characters, including everyone's favorite, "unidentified boy," and his friend "unidentified "girl." It also includes scoundrels like Kenneth Purcell who stole items from school lockers and gave them to Beaver in "Beaver and Kenneth," and the unidentified bicycle thief in "Beaver's Bike." But let's not forget Roger Delacy who conned Beaver and Larry out of $3.00. He used "gee" twice when pulling his con.

There are plenty of actors that made one-time appearances on *Leave it to Beaver* who were given "gee" as part of their dialogue. The most well-known celebrity at the time to make one of those appearances and utter the word "gee" was Los Angeles Dodgers pitcher Don Drysdale. In the episode, "Long Distance Call," Alan, Gilbert and Beaver are left alone at Beaver's house, and they begin playing with the phone, making crank calls and then coming up with the great idea to call Don Drysdale at Dodger Stadium. When Don Drysdale finally gets out of the shower and picks up the phone, Gilbert tells him they're calling from Mayfield. Drysdale responds, "Well, gee, that's quite a distance to be calling from." This proves that big tough athletes can use the word "gee," and helps viewers who like to debate the location of Mayfield figure out that the city is quite a ways from Los Angeles.

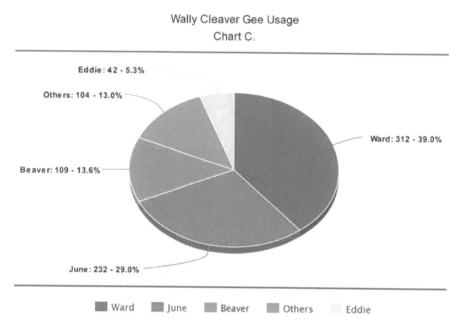

Wally Cleaver Gee Usage
Chart C.

Eddie: 42 - 5.3%
Others: 104 - 13.0%
Ward: 312 - 39.0%
Beaver: 109 - 13.6%
June: 232 - 29.0%

■ Ward ■ June ■ Beaver ■ Others ▨ Eddie

Going back to the trivia question… can you name the character who first said the word "gee" on *Leave it to Beaver*? Well, if you guessed Beaver, you would be wrong. The first character to use "gee" on *Leave it to Beaver* was June Cleaver in "Beaver Gets 'Spelled." It occurs when June goes to the school after Mrs. Rayburn had requested to speak with her. The scene at the school begins with Mrs. Rayburn saying goodbye after their meeting had ended. She tells June that she hopes Beaver is not too upset and that he is back in school the next day. This surprises June as Beaver had earlier left to go to school…that's when she says it, "Gee, that was over two hours ago."

Unless you're listening for it, and maybe even if you are listening for it, you may just miss her saying "gee." I had to confirm this with transcripts of the show and closed captioning. It's there. Believe me. Only a little over 1900 times more do we get to hear the word "gee" on the show until "The Family Scrapbook," six years later, closes out the run of one of the most wonderful family friendly, life affirming, TV shows ever to appear on American television.

5

BATHS, SHOWERS, AND OTHER GROOMING HABITS

If Beaver and Wally were anything, they were clean . . . eventually. Let's start right now and dive into the depths of the (bath) water and see what the boys, especially Beaver, think of taking baths, showering, washing and their other grooming habits.

Baths

In the first episode, "Beaver Gets 'Spelled," Wally is shown expressing a negative attitude toward baths, one of the few times, and he does so, by his actions. After the boys are told to take a bath, Wally runs the bath water as he talks to Beaver about the note Miss Canfield sent home with him. The tub fills, and before they leave the bathroom, after not taking a bath, Wally asks Beaver for some of his turtle dirt. He throws it into the tub and tells Beaver, "It'll leave a ring." That's funny. However, not nearly as funny as when Beaver asks Wally if they should open the note and Wally replies, "Of course not. That'd be dishonest." Another time Wally expresses a negative thought about baths is in "Happy Weekend." When examining the cabin, he's thankful there's not a bathtub. Then, in "Blind Date Committee," Ward implies Wally takes very few baths when he's asked by Wally if he'd ever tell anyone who calls him, that he was taking a bath. Ward says with the amount of baths Wally takes; it'd be doubtful anyone would ever call while he was taking one.

Beaver speaks of his displeasure with baths in a few different episodes. In "Captain Jack," Wally says they could keep their alligator in the bathtub, but they couldn't take baths. Beaver says that's one good thing about owning an alligator. When Wally says in high school guys take showers every day in gym class, Beaver asks if there's any way to get out of it. In "Beaver Makes a Loan," Beaver refers to taking a bath as punishment, when he explains Larry's late arrival to pay him back money he owes. He says, "Well, something could've happened to him. His mother might have made him clean his room or take a bath or some other punishment." Another negative comment from Beaver about baths is when told by June to take a bath in "Mother's Day Composition." Beaver says, "You'd think with all my other problems, at least I wouldn't have to take a bath."

Other interesting bath moments include in "Beaver and Poncho," when Beaver gives the dog a bath in their bathroom sink. In "Beaver's Monkey," Beaver says he and Larry are going to give the mouse he brought home a bath. June is surprised in "The Boat Builders" when she hears the tub running and Wally confirms Beaver is taking a bath. "On a Saturday morning without anyone making him?" She should have known something was up. Beaver tells Larry in "Larry Hides Out," that he cannot hide in his bathtub forever because someone will have to take a bath or shower eventually. In what is probably one of the last baths Wally takes, Beaver mentions to Evelyn Boothby in "Wally's Chauffeur," that Wally spent a lot of time in the bath and he's running late because of that. Who can forget the tramp named Jeff who takes a bath in Ward and June's bathroom in "Beaver's Good Deed?" Now, the bath of all baths, is one not taken. It's found in the episode, "Beaver Takes a Bath." He doesn't take a bath in this episode, only prepares to take one. The water overflows, flooding the bathroom and ruining the kitchen ceiling.

Showers

Although Beaver takes a shower, in "Beaver, the Bunny," when Wally tells him, "Go take a shower and hop off to bed," Beaver's shower taking outside this episode is extremely limited. Wally takes his first shower in "Beaver and Poncho" late in season one, but Wally continues to take baths into season three. Showers become something Wally takes, almost exclusively, beginning in season four, the exception to that as mentioned earlier, is in "Wally's Chauffeur."

Other Grooming Habits

Wally spends a lot of time looking in the mirror, combing his hair. Occasionally, Beaver combs and grooms his hair too, but those times are rare. Hair combing is the number one grooming habit seen in the Cleaver boys' room. Other than combing hair, adding something to the hair to help it sit better, stay in place, or not fall out, is also a big activity for Wally in many episodes and for Beaver in a few. Wally uses Groomwell for the fastidious man on his hair in "Wally's Girl Trouble," something Beaver calls "goop." Wally adds something different to his hair in "Wally's Pug Nose." In this episode, he applies gel made from sheep fat to his hair to keep it from falling out. In "Wally's Hair Comb," he puts gunk on his hair that is "solider" and guaranteed not to bend his hair when he goes to bed, no sticky spots either. It's supposed to dry out, and get hard, like cement. Wally adds lilac hair tonic or regular hair tonic to his hair in "Teacher's Daughter," "Beaver Goes in Business," "Kite Day," "Wally's Weekend Job," and "Wally's Chauffeur." Wally also spends time unnecessarily shaving in two episodes, "The Shave" and "In the Soup." He tries to make it look like he shaves in "Chuckie's New Shoes," actually shaves before a date in "Wally Goes Steady," and in "Beaver's Laundry," tries figuring out if needs to shave regularly.

Beaver, being a few years younger than Wally, has nowhere near the problems trying to keep up his appearance as Wally does. This is because Beaver doesn't care about his appearance until the later seasons. It's obvious in season one that Beaver doesn't care about his appearance in the first half of the "Cleaning Up Beaver" episode. But after Ward compliments Wally on his fine appearance, Beaver wants to try to look good too. Beaver begins to care a lot about his appearance in "Beaver's Freckles," where he tries to cover up his freckles with June's make up and in "Beaver, the Sheep Dog," he uses Glama-Spray Miracle Mist, Herron's Hair Oil, Slick-O, and Crew Stay to keep his hair from falling in front of his eyes.

Eddie, when visiting the Cleavers, also likes to look at himself in the mirror to make sure he looks good. In "The Hypnotist," Eddie stands in front of it running his fingers through his hair as he sings Nat King Cole's, "Baby Won't You Please Come Home." One other time, in "Beaver Goes in Business," Eddie is in the boys' room and looks in the mirror, brushes his hair, and looks closely at his teeth while singing and humming. Then, in "The Silent Treatment," Eddie grooms his hair in his car's sideview mirror in the Cleaver driveway and remarks, "Boy, you doll, you."

In addition to grooming hair and shaving, we also find the Cleaver boys (most often, it's Wally) using aftershave or cologne. Wally is seen doing so in numerous episodes, but Beaver uses aftershave a few times, these include "Beaver Sees America," "Brother vs. Brother," and "Don Juan Beaver." But Eddie too, uses aftershave lotion. In "Cleaning Up Beaver," after arriving at the Cleaver home, he asks June if he looks good, and she says he does, then remarks that he smells good too. He discloses that he smells good because he's put on aftershave lotion. When asked if he shaves, Eddie tells her he doesn't, and says, "But I like to smell like I do."

6

EDDIE AND COMPLIMENTS

Here's a chapter for all of you that love Eddie Haskell like I do. This will be fun to read. While there's just a little over twenty episodes in which Eddie spouts his sometimes-insincere compliments, it seems like he's buttering up June much more often. That could be because almost half of his compliments come in season one. You could also chalk that up to Ken Osmond's great acting and how well his part was written. It never was that he complimented so often, but that his acting ability made his lines so memorable. This list will include the episode in which he made a compliment, the compliment, and any remarks or reactions by the person he compliments if their remark or reaction is memorable.

"New Neighbors" – Eddie's first compliment ever is aimed toward June. "Good morning Mrs. Cleaver, that's a very pretty dress." Then, later in the episode, maybe an hour later just before she tells him he has to go home, Eddie says, "Gee, Mrs. Cleaver, that's a nice dress." Her reply: "I know Eddie. I know."

"The Clubhouse" – Eddie gives a compliment soon after he gets to the Cleaver house, "Gee, Mrs. Cleaver, your hair looks nice." Then, when June goes upstairs to tell the boys she's making lunch, Eddie says, "Gee, Mrs. Cleaver, your hair really does look . . ." She cuts him off and tells him, "You said that Eddie."

"Voodoo Magic" – "Gee, Mrs. Cleaver, you even look pretty in an apron." (June rolls her eyes, looks at Ward and replies) "Thank you very much Eddie."

"Lonesome Beaver" – "Gee, Mrs. Cleaver, you sure do look nice. My mother says you must spend all of your time in the beauty shops." June replies, "Well, thank you very much Eddie. And say thank you to your mother too." In this reaction, June seems just as insincere as Eddie does.

"Cleaning Up Beaver" – Eddie compliments Ward about his painting the kitchen door, "You're doing a real neat job there."

"The Perfect Father" – "Hello Mrs. Cleaver, Gee, that's a nice sweater."

"Next Door Indians" – "You're all right Beaver." Eddie tells Beaver this because he's the one who is responsible for Eddie and the other big guys finding the garnets and for making them rich.

"New Doctor" – "Gee, your kitchen always looks so clean..." (well thank you Eddie) "My mother says it looks as if you never do any work in here." June sneers after he leaves the kitchen.

"Cat Out of the Bag" – "It was awfully nice seeing you again Mrs. Cleaver."

"Beaver and Chuey" – "Gee, that sure is a neat looking apron." (Thank you Eddie)
"Wally's New Suit" – "Oh, that's a very nice phonograph." Later in the episode when he sees the new suit Wally has bought on his own, Eddie exclaims, "That's the best suit I ever saw in my

whole life." This is what seems to be one of the few sincere compliments Eddie utters in the entire six seasons of *Leave it to Beaver*.

"Wally's Present" – When Eddie sees Wally's birthday cake he says, "Gee, that's a very nice cake Mrs. Cleaver ... It almost looks like you bought it in a store."

"Blind Date Committee" – In this episode Eddie does double duty with the compliments. First, he compliments June's attire, "Gee, that's a very nice sweater Mrs. Cleaver." He then compliments Ward's yard, "Gee, Mr. Cleaver, your front lawn sure looks nice."

"Wally's Election" – In an effort to try to give Wally some confidence about his chances to become sophomore president, Eddie fires off a list of compliments, "You've got letters in three sports, the teachers like you, and I heard Mary Ellen Rogers say you look like Lloyd Bridges."

"Beaver Finds a Wallet" – "Gee, Mrs. Cleaver, your hair looks real pretty today." In her reply, she references what he just mentioned to Wally about nobody being home and how they should call up some girls and pretend they're talent scouts, "Well, you should know Eddie, being a talent scout."

"The Spot Removers" – While June cooks, Eddie waits in the kitchen for Wally to return home. After annoying June, she tells him he could go wait upstairs with Beaver. On his way out of the kitchen, he tells her, "Smells delicious... whatever it is." Upstairs, catching Beaver trying to paint over bleach stains he got on Wally's suit, Eddie compliments Beaver, "You're getting to be a pretty good little sneak."

"Beaver, the Model" – Eddie tells Beaver, "You're not the ugliest kid in the world."

"Wally and Dudley" – "You're looking very well Mr. Cleaver." When Eddie goes upstairs, June says, "Well, that was very nice of Eddie. "Yes, wasn't it?" replies Ward. June says, "You say that as if you mean the opposite." Ward then utters a witty truism, "I do dear."

"Stocks and Bonds" – Although June doesn't think so, Eddie seems to be laying it on kind of thick with his compliment in this episode. He walks in and sees the Cleavers and looks stunningly at June and says, arms extended, "Mrs. Cleaver, you've done something new to your hair." June then messes with her hair a bit and says, "Not a thing." Eddie continues, "Oh, it looks very nice." After Eddie goes upstairs Ward makes an admission, "Sometimes that kid gets under my skin." June has a different thought, "Sometimes, I think he's a very nice boy."

"Eddie, the Businessman" – "Oh, Mrs. Cleaver, that dress is very attractive. That color is most becoming." After Eddie leaves, June tells Ward, "Wasn't that nice of him to say that?" Ward comes back with, "I thought you just said his charm was phony." Her reply, "Well, I didn't say all the time."

"The Parking Attendants" – "Oh, have you been redecorating?" (No, not recently). "Oh, everything looks so nice and fresh. I guess it's just the way you keep house."

    You can read more about compliments by visiting http://leaveittobeaverbooks.com. While there, don't forget to sign up for free *Leave it to Beaver* gifts that will be given away after every 100th sale of *The World Famous Beaverpedia!*

7

OTHER COMPLIMENTS

Compliments can be a device used to cheer a soul or to manipulate a person into granting a wish or desire. There are those who use compliments to butter people up, and sometimes, they are used in a twisted way to insult someone. All of these uses are seen throughout the six seasons of *Leave it to Beaver*. When it comes to insincere insults, we all know who had a monopoly on those… that would be Eddie Haskell, and you just read them all. This chapter will consist of a sample of the other compliments on the show. There will also be a discussion about a few of the compliments found here, i.e. who said them and why they were said if there seems to be an ulterior motive for them.

As for how the compliments were dished out… the top five recipients of compliments, in order, were Wally (27.7%), Beaver (16.9%), June (15.7%), Ward (15.7%) and Eddie (7.1%).

Compliments to Beaver

"You know, you're not as creepy as I thought." Wally sure knows how to give a compliment. He gives this compliment after he finds out Beaver stuffed a spring-loaded snake in Miss Canfield's desk ("Beaver's Crush").

"Beaver, your new home is just lovely." and *"You're the nicest boy I ever knew."* If there's one thing Judy Hensler knows how to do, that is lay it on thick. These two compliments may be sincere, but considering the source, they sure do seem insincere. She wants Beaver to tell her how he got back on the bus after being kicked off of it by the driver ("School Bus").

"You're the nicest boy in our whole class." and *"That Beaver Cleaver is the nicest looking boy in dancing school."* are two of the most insincere compliments to ever come out of a girl's mouth. The first is from Penny and told to Beaver in the hall after class. The second is something she says she told her mom. Don't believe it. She only wants one thing… his vote for her to be Junior Fire Chief. When he tells her no, she goes back to calling him names ("Junior Fire Chief").

"You know young man, I think you're a very fine young gentleman." The shoe store clerk told that to Beaver when he saw how he handled Chuckie. When Beaver was complimented by the clerk, he wasn't too keen on accepting the compliment. He told the salesman that he didn't have to say that since he already bought the shoes ("Chuckie's New Shoes").

"You were just terrific in the game yesterday." Charlene tells Beaver that he did amazing in the football game when he caught the winning touchdown. It wasn't just her; Donna, Terry and others also complimented him. Beaver got a big head. These were compliments that eventually hurt him and got him suspended from the team for a week ("Beaver, the Hero").

Compliments to Wally

"You're a wonderful brother." Beaver says this when Wally is fixing his hair ("Beaver's Haircut").

"Wally, you certainly look great tonight, so neat and clean." Ward has an ulterior motive with this compliment. He wants Beaver to want to be cleaner ("Cleaning up Beaver").

"I think this young man deserves some credit. After all, you took your brother all the way up to Crystal Falls on the bus, saw that the Peyton's picked him up, came all the way back on the bus without a hitch." In one of the longer compliments you'll hear, Ward let's Wally know how proud he is of his oldest son. Too bad, Wally later has to burst his pride bubble and tell him what really happened, how he lost Beaver and all the rest of the problems ("The Bus Ride").

"Wally, I think you're the nicest boy I ever met." Jill Bartlett isn't joking. While sitting at the malt shop, she tells this to Wally and when Wally says she's joking, she admits she doesn't know how to joke. She feels it was nice of Wally to pay his friends to dance with her and to take her out himself when he couldn't find anyone to go with her ("Blind Date Committee").

"You ran around very nicely between the halves." In one of the silliest compliments doled out on the show, and I'm sure Wally thought it silly at the time, June gave him this one after she and Ward went to watch him play football. The only time she got to see him was at halftime. At this point in the show, he had yet to become a first-string player ("Borrowed Boat").

"Isn't it wonderful that you have such an important job?" Gloria Cusick says this when she sees Wally selling Igloo Bars near her house. At first, it seems like just a little exaggeration on her part. But she knew from the moment she approached him that she didn't have the money to pay for the number of Igloo Bars she wanted. She had an ulterior motive the entire time.

"Yeah, but you drink it neater, than any guy I've ever seen." Beaver tells Wally he's a great milk drinker. Oh yeah, he wants something. He wants Wally to take he and his friends camping. Once he asks him about it in front of his parents, it works ("A Night in the Woods").

"Nice game Wally." Ted, a Mayfield High School alum, and current player on the State University / College baseball team, tells Wally he had a nice game, probably one of Wally's favorite compliments because it came from a peer and someone he respected ("Wally and the Fraternity").

Compliments to June

"You really are pretty...for a mother." At bedtime, Beaver let's out this amazing compliment to June. He was looking at her, as Ward says, through the eyes of a trash man's son ("The Grass is Always Greener").

"I'm not gonna marry any silly girls, I'm gonna marry a mother." While Beaver may not have meant these words as a compliment, June definitely took them as such ("Dance Contest").

"Oh, dear, I think I'll just save the pedestal and put you up on it." Earlier in this episode, Ward was furious about Beaver allowing his autographed baseball to get destroyed. He mellowed out at

the end and was able to give June this wonderful comment about the pedestal that used to display the baseball ("Ward's Baseball").

"You're getting prettier every day. Right now, you look like the middle of next week." Uncle Billy sure has a way with words. ("Uncle Billy's Visit").

Compliments to Ward

"Yeah, your dad's all right. My pop says he's an all-right guy." Pete Fletcher, the son of the trash man comes over to the Cleaver house with his brother and spends the day. They give the Cleaver boys a new outlook on their family, and it begins with this compliment ("The Grass is Always Greener").

Sure, what do you think dad is, a monster or something? While this may not sound like a compliment, Ward thanks Wally for his words to June after she says to be gentle with Beaver when he speaks with him ("Beaver's Old Buddy").

"There's a lot worse fathers around than you." Wally is the master of backhanded compliments. Ward says he took these words as a compliment ("Larry Hides Out").

"You really understand kids. You're a real neat father." Beaver's friends know a good father when they see one. And for Larry, who rarely sees his own father, he might be happy with any father that is just present. ("Larry Hides Out.")

"Golly, Mr. Cleaver, you sure are good to Beaver." Again, Beaver's friends know a good father when they see one. Gilbert pays this compliment because Ward will buy Beaver a typewriter. When told by Ward his father is a good father too, Gilbert says, "Well, that's what he's always telling me, but I haven't noticed it."

Compliments to Eddie

"Why, yes, you look very nice." June says to Eddie after he fishes for a compliment. She then catches a whiff of him, and she says, "Smell quite nice too." When he tells her that's his after-shave lotion, she asks him if he shaves. "No, But I like to smell like I do." That conversation is one of the best of all 234 episodes ("Cleaning Up Beaver").

"You're a real neat guy." Beaver gives Eddie that compliment after he helps Beaver out of a jam with Wally. Eddie warns him not to start slobbering over him or he'll slug him. ("The Spot Removers").

"I love that blue in your sweater, it brings out the blue in your eyes," Caroline (pronounced Carolyn) Shuster is one of the most insincere young women seen in the entire series. She is using Eddie so she will have something to do on the weekends while her boyfriend is grounded. She talks bad about Eddie and laughs at him behind his back. Wally overhears her viciousness and tells Eddie about her. Eddie wasn't too pleased….with Wally ("Eddie's Double-Cross").

There are many more compliments and these are just a sample of some of the better ones doled out on the series. For more, visit http://leaveittobeaverbooks.com.

8

LOST AND FORGOTTEN

When was that last time you went a week without losing or forgetting something? Okay, can't think back that far? Let me edit that question. When was the last time you went one day without forgetting or losing something? The truth is we often forget and lose things. We often forget to take out the trash, or we forget our wedding anniversaries, birthdays, and to be thankful for the good things in our lives, and sometimes we forget if we've taken our daily doses of medicine. But we never forget to watch *Leave it to Beaver*, do we? We sometimes lose things like our keys, our wallets, our shoes and with the world the way it is today, we sometimes lose our minds… then we watch some *Leave it to Beaver* to regain our sanity. So, when we watch our favorite show, we should cut Beaver some slack when he loses his haircut money or not be too hard on Ward when he forgets the kite for Kite Day or the paint for Wally to paint the garbage cans. We need to offer them some grace, and we do.

Below, you'll see details on the various items the characters in *Leave it to Beaver* lose or forget. Before you look at the details, you may like to know who the three biggest losers on *Leave it to Beaver* are…. When you hear that term, you might think of Roger Delacy who stole Beaver and Larry's cookie fund money. You might think about the bad guy who stole Beaver's bicycle or the crook of a salesman who gypped Beaver with the wrong size ice skates. No, when I mention the three biggest losers, I mean the three characters who are mentioned in the most episodes as losing some sort of item. Those would be Beaver who is mentioned in 58% of all episodes that mention something being lost, far and away above Ward in second place and Wally in a distant third. When it comes to the three biggest forgetters, those would be Ward, Beaver and Wally.

Things Lost

As noted, Beaver is really good at losing things. Sometimes those items are bigger than others. Looking at the smaller, less important items, Beaver loses his shoe, but quickly finds it in the wastepaper basket in their room ("Party Invitation"). His shoelaces are lost in another episode which features Linda Dennison ("Her Idol"). He explains that they just came out when he was playing, something which sounds very unlikely. He loses a shoe once again after Ward announces the family will spend a weekend up at Shadow Lake ("Happy Weekend"). It is mentioned that previously, Beaver had misplaced one of Ward's screwdrivers ("Beaver's Cat Problem"). And on a day where everyone has lost something, Beaver can't find his gym socks ("Tennis, Anyone?")

Some of the more serious lost items include money, and that's always a bad thing to lose. The first time this occurs is when Beaver loses his haircut money. This causes a big problem because Wally helps cut Beaver's hair, and that has a disastrous outcome ("The Haircut"). In that same episode he's repeatedly lost his lunch money and he went hungry at school for a few days too. When Beaver goes through the neighborhood with Gilbert soliciting money for the local Community Chest, all is fine until he and Gilbert buy some ice cream cones. After that, Beaver doesn't hear the can jingling with change and realizes he lost the money. He lost an entire can of money and Ward will replace it, but he must go back and find out how much each person gave. Everyone feels sorry for Beaver and replace their own money. One lady even admonishes his father for this punitive action ("Community Chest").

There are some things Beaver loses that would be classified somewhere between shoelaces and a can filled with change. One of these would be a note sent home with him from Miss Canfield requesting he play Smokey Bear in the fire prevention pageant ("Beaver Gets 'Spelled"). Another is his old teddy bear, Billy ("Beaver's Old Friend") who wasn't really lost but put in a hiding place and taken by the garbage man. When looking for Billy, Beaver tells the garbage man he "losted" something. Other similar mildly important items include the combination to his locker at school ("Ward's Problem") and what is probably an imaginary pocketknife he uses as an excuse to go over to Gilbert's house ("Beaver and Gilbert").

Wally is mentioned as losing very few items. They include his arithmetic book which is found in the wastepaper basket moments after Beaver finds his shoe in the same basket ("Party Invitation"). He also can't find his tennis racquet ("Tennis, Anyone?") and of all things, loses his own brother on the way to drop him off at his friend's farm in Crystal Falls ("The Bus Ride").

Ward loses a little bit more than Wally, but nowhere near as much as Beaver. Some of his lost items include his claw hammer ("Beaver and Chuey"), the bucket he uses to wash the car ("The Boat Builders"), his car key ("Wally's Election"), his fountain pen ("Beaver and Violet"), his wristwatch ("Tennis, Anyone?"). Actually, Ward really never loses anything outright but misplaces his items. In each episode, his things are found, except the claw hammer, and the missing bucket was taken by the boys for their boat.

June is such an organized mother; she's mentioned only once as possibly losing or misplacing something and that would be her scissors and that was only used by the writers to advance the plot, as the next scene begins with the clipping of scissors ("The Haircut").

Things Forgotten

Since Ward is mentioned as forgetting things more often than others, he gets the honor of going first in this category. Like losing items, forgetting has its various levels of importance. One of the more important of Ward's forgetful moments is when moving from the old Cleaver house, Ward forgot to take the tree they had given Beaver as a gift. Beaver sure didn't forget about it after Miss Landers read that poem about trees ("Beaver's Tree"). Ward's other forgetful moments are not nearly as important except to those who were relying on him to have a good memory. This was the case when he forgot the paint for Wally to paint trash cans ("Wally's Job"), when he forgot to get the materials to help Beaver make a kite ("Kite Day") and when June, who wasn't planning to cook asks him where the Chinese food is he was supposed to bring home after work ("The Dramatic Club").

Rating not very important are the times when Ward forgot his briefcase and had to come back home mid-morning to retrieve it ("The Last Day of School"), when he forgot to buy flashlight batteries ("Wally, the Lifeguard") and when he forgot Beaver had taken his rake to Miss Lander's house ("Miss Landers' Fiancé"). See, nothing very important among these items, but having to make a second trip, as in the case of the briefcase and flashlight batteries, is always a tedious task.

Two other times the topic of forgetting is mentioned do not concern Ward forgetting, but Beaver wondering whether or not Ward will forget something. In these two cases, Beaver wonders if Ward and June will forget to buy him presents for his birthday since he doesn't want a party ("Beaver's Birthday") and if Ward will forget to bring home a diary for him which Ward had suggested was a good way for Beaver to begin his desired writing career ("Beaver's Secret Life").

When Beaver forgets something, there's a big chance it is some type of clothing item. He forgets his jacket outside and leaves it draped over a camellia bush ("Beaver Goes in Business"). He forgets his hat on a few occasions ("Voodoo Magic" / "Beaver and Henry" / "The Price of Fame") and forgets his sneakers for the field day activities ("Beaver Gets Adopted"). He also forgets about being invited to David Manning's birthday party ("Forgotten Party") and he mentions forgetting in an abstract way when he talks about forgetting about all the problems he has at school by the time he gets home each day ("Wally's Test").

As for June, she has a pretty good mind on her despite a forgetful moment or two.

9

ACTIVITIES

What in the world do Wally and Beaver do to occupy their time in Mayfield? This chapter will look at the activities of Wally, Beaver, and their friends, but there will also be some attention paid to adults. While Wally, Beaver and the others spend time watching workers of all sorts, from the jingling belt lady in "The Black Eye" to the guys changing a billboard on Grant Avenue in "Farewell to Penny," such times as those will not be mentioned here as they have their own chapter. The same goes for school activities which are included in the "School" chapter. Here, we will proceed season by season and witness together the change in the types of activities the boys spend their time on as they grow up through the six seasons of *Leave it to Beaver*.

Season One

Beaver and Johnny Cooper look for four leaf clovers ("Beaver Gets 'Spelled").
Beaver spits off a bridge on his way to see Violet Rutherford ("The Black Eye").
Wally and Beaver play Chinese checkers and go fishing ("Brotherly Love").
Wally and his friends trade marbles and build a clubhouse ("The Clubhouse").
Ward practices putting inside the house ("The Clubhouse").
Ward goes golfing ("Wally's Girl Trouble").
Wally and Beaver go fishing for bullheads each Saturday ("Wally's Girl Trouble").
June attends Women's Club meetings ("The Perfume Salesmen").
Wally builds and paints a model airplane ("Part Time Genius").
Ward and June play cards with the Rutherfords ("Lumpy Rutherford").
Ward plays solitaire waiting for the Rutherfords to arrive ("Lumpy Rutherford").
Wally and Beaver play checkers ("Lumpy Rutherford").
Wally and Beaver polish the #7 fire truck on occasion ("Child Care").
Beaver plays with electric trains ("The Bank Account").
Beaver plays near the railroad tracks in town and flattens coins ("The Bank Account").
Wally, Tooey and Eddie join the Boy Scouts and go camping ("Lonesome Beaver").
Chester and some of his friends play baseball ("Lonesome Beaver").
Beaver and Larry go down to the "old tunnel" to listen to their echoes ("Cleaning Up Beaver").
Wally and Beaver go to the Sportsman Show with Mr. Dennison ("The Perfect Father").
Wally and his friends play basketball at the Cleaver and Dennison homes ("The Perfect Father").
June knits a dog sweater ("Beaver and Poncho").
Wally and Beaver make a go-cart ("The State vs. Beaver").
Wally and friends play baseball in the street ("The Broken Window").
The family goes for a picnic at Crystal Falls ("The Broken Window").
Wally and Beaver and friends spend all day at the movies ("Tenting Tonight").
Wally and Beaver camp in the back yard ("Tenting Tonight").
Ward and Wally play catch in a vacant lot ("Music Lesson").
June sews in the living room ("The Music Lesson").
Beaver and his friends look for empty pop bottles on trash day ("Beaver's Old Friend").
Beaver and Larry play with toy soldiers and play Go Fish card game ("Beaver's Guest").

Season Two

Beaver pretends to shoot an imaginary rifle ("Beaver's Poem").
Beaver and Larry trade marbles ("Beaver's Poem").
Wally plays with a squirt gun ("Ward's Problem").
Wally and Eddie pretend to fish in the back yard ("Ward's Problem").
Beaver and Chuey play with electric trains, toy soldiers and marbles ("Beaver and Chuey").
Wally plays with a gasoline powered toy airplane ("The Lost Watch").
Wally goes fishing ("The Lost Watch").
Wally and his friends play a game of sandlot baseball ("The Lost Watch").
Larry and Whitey dig a hole ("Her Idol").
Linda Dennison climbs a tree and looks at bird's eggs, with Beaver and then Larry ("Her Idol").
Chester and Eddie go to the auto junkyard to look at a couple new wrecks ("Wally's New Suit").
The boys go to North St. to watch people get tickets at new parking meters ("The Visiting Aunts").
The family goes to the carnival in Garden Grove and eat at the Chuckwagon ("The Visiting Aunts").
Wally and Beaver make a raft to float to a deserted island ("Happy Weekend").
Ward takes the boys fishing at a stocked pond ("Happy Weekend").
Beaver plays in a trash dump ("The Grass is Always Greener").
Wally and his friends build a genuine Eskimo boat ("The Boat Builders").
The boys read Tom Sawyer ("The Garage Painters").
Ward plays catch with Wally after work ("The Tooth").
The boys participate in Field Day at the city park ("Beaver Gets Adopted").
Gilbert, Larry, Whitey and Beaver play football ("Beaver and Gilbert").
Beaver and Larry search for four leaf clovers ("The Price of Fame").
Wally and Chester go to the dance studio to watch Tooey take his lesson ("The Price of Fame").
Ward completes the daily crossword puzzle ("A Horse Named Nick").
Beaver and Larry play checkers ("Beaver's Newspaper").
Ward plays golf ("Beaver's Sweater").
Beaver and Larry go to the carnival, Wally and Tooey go later ("Found Money").
Eddie and Wally go to Metzger's Field to play a game of touch football ("Beaver's Prize").

Season Three

Beaver and Larry go to the movies ("Beaver's Prize").
Beaver and Larry go to Friend's Lake and skip rocks ("Borrowed Boat").
Ward plays golf ("Beaver's Tree").
Beaver plays by himself in the yard ("Beaver Makes a Loan")
Ward plays golf ("Beaver Makes a Loan").
Ward tosses football with Wally and Beaver in front yard ("Tire Trouble").
Larry's sister goes to the museum with a friend ("Larry Hides Out").
Beaver plays with a toy gun by himself ("Larry Hides Out").
Lumpy and Eddie go to Mary Ellen Roger's house to play records ("Wally's Test").
Wally goes to Eddie's to shoot baskets ("Beaver and Andy").
Beaver walks in the mud on Lake Avenue ("Beaver and Andy").
Fred, Lumpy and Wally go to see a mud slide on Crest Highway ("The Hypnotist").
Wally plays tennis with Alma Hanson ("Wally and Alma").
Beaver and Larry play tic tac toe in the street downtown ("Beaver's Bike").
Ward and June go for a walk after supper ("Ward's Baseball").

Beaver and Larry go to the zoo ("Beaver's Monkey").
Wally and Eddie go jumping at the trampoline place ("Beaver Finds a Wallet").
Beaver and Larry play with army men ("Mother's Day Composition").
The family goes to Friend's Lake with the Rutherfords ("Beaver and Violet").
Wally goes to a party ("The Spot Removers").
Richard and Beaver go fishing ("The Spot Removers").
Beaver and Whitey duel in the backyard with sticks and garbage can lids ("Beaver and Ivanhoe").
Beaver pretends to be on a nuclear submarine going to the North Pole ("Wally's Play").
Beaver and friends play football at Metzger's Field ("Beaver's Team").

Season Four

Wally and Beaver go fishing ("Beaver Becomes a Hero").
Eddie, Mary Ellen and Alma enjoy a day at Friend's Lake ("Wally, the Lifeguard").
Miss Landers and Tom Brittingham play tennis ("Miss Landers' Fiancé").
Wally and Eddie go ice skating ("Chuckie's New Shoes").
Wally plays basketball and then to play touch football ("Teacher's Daughter").
Beaver makes a model, and plays "Korea" and darts with his friend Jackie ("Beaver's Old Buddy").
Wally and his friends attend a party at Christine Staples' house ("Wally and Dudley").
Wally and Eddie play chess ("Eddie Spends the Night").
Beaver and Gilbert play baseball ("Beaver's Report Card").
Family goes on a picnic with Ginny Townsend ("Wally's Dream Girl").
Wally goes to various houses to listen to records ("In the Soup").
Richard and Gilbert go roller skating ("Beaver's Frogs").
Ward and Fred Rutherford play golf each Saturday ("Kite Day").

Season Five

Tom Henderson plays touch football on Saturdays at Metzger's Field ("Wally Goes Steady").
Wally and Evelyn Boothby go to the Hendersons for dinner, TV, and cards ("Wally Goes Steady").
Beaver and friends go to the Piedmont St. bridge to get their feet jiggled ("No Time for Babysitters").
Beaver and Judy play checkers ("No Time for Babysitters").
Ward plays golf ("Wally's Car").
Beaver goes fishing ("Beaver's Cat Problem").
Ward goes golfing ("Beaver's Cat Problem").
Beaver and Gilbert ride coasters down the sidewalk ("Beaver's Doll Buggy").
Wally plays touch football at Metzger's Field ("Beaver Takes a Drive").
Beaver goes ice skating with friends ("Beaver's Ice Skates").
Ward plays golf ("Ward's Golf Clubs").
Gilbert and Beaver play with electric trains ("Beaver's Electric Trains").
Gilbert, Beaver and Whitey go bike riding ("Beaver's Electric Trains").
Ward and June play cards at the Blakes' house ("Beaver's Long Night").
Beaver plays a small pinball game in living room ("Beaver's Long Night").
Beaver, Wally, and his friends go to the Bellport Amusement Park ("Beaver's Fear").
Beaver, Whitey, and Gilbert work on models ("Eddie Quits School").
Wally and Beaver make a model ("Lumpy's Car Trouble").
Wally and Beaver play checkers ("The Younger Brother").

Beaver and Mary Tyler play Monopoly ("Brother vs. Brother").
Ward and Beaver play catch ("Sweatshirt Monsters").
Wally takes Beaver and his friends camping ("A Night in the Woods").

Season Six

Ward and June play cards ("Wally's Dinner Date").
Beaver and Ward play checkers ("Double Date").
Ward plays golf ("Eddie, the Businessman").
Wally and Lumpy play chess ("Bachelor at Large").
Wally and Lumpy toss the football in front yard (Bachelor at Large").
Beaver and Gilbert listen to records ("Beaver Joins a Record Club").
Wally throws a party ("The Party Spoiler").
Beaver and Gilbert go to the carnival and so do Wally and Eddie ("More Blessed to Give").
Ward takes the boys to the Sportsman's Show (Beaver's Good Deed").
Beaver in living room plays checkers by himself ("The Credit Card").
Beaver plays darts ("Beaver the Caddy").
Ward plays golf ("Beaver the Caddy").
Ward and June play cards ("Box Office Attraction").
Ward and Beaver play checkers ("The Silent Treatment").
Beaver and Gilbert play tennis ("The Silent Treatment").
Beaver plays baseball at Metzger's Field ("Beaver's Prep School").
Wally goes to Eddie's house to play records, play monopoly and out to eat pizza ("The Poor Loser").
Beaver listens to music in his room and dances ("Don Juan Beaver").
Beaver throws darts in his room ("Beaver's Graduation").
Wally and Ward play gin rummy ("Beaver Sees America").

There's more about activities you can read about if you want over at the website http://leaveittobeaverbooks.com.

10

BOYS LEFT ALONE

Over the six seasons of *Leave it to Beaver,* Theodore "Beaver" Cleaver gets into trouble quite often. If he didn't have some sort of conflict, the episodes would have been a lot shorter in length and a lot less interesting. Think back on your own childhood for a moment, was it easier to get into trouble when your parents were home, or when you were alone because they were out shopping together, or at a dinner party, or somewhere else? I bet you just said it was when you were home alone. Heck, wasn't there a series of movies made in the 1990s about such a situation?

The boys are left alone over thirty different times. Sometimes it is both Wally and Beaver. Those are typically the times when Ward and June are going to visit friends out of town or travel with friends out of town for the weekend. A few times, the boys are left alone when Ward and June go out to eat locally or visit the Rutherfords. Then, there are those times when Beaver is left all by himself. There are many times when Beaver is left home alone. Now, of the times that Beaver is left home alone, he doesn't do something wrong on every single occasion, but let's look closer at some of those times just to make sure.

"The State vs. Beaver" - Yes. Beaver does something wrong in this episode when he is home alone. He was told to not take the go-cart for a ride by himself. Larry convinces him that he's not alone because he is with him. Beaver ends up getting a ticket for driving without a license.

"Beaver's Bad Day" – Yes. Beaver does something wrong in this episode when he is home alone. He was told to change his nice pants before going out. Again, Larry convinces him to do something his parents told him not to do… two things in fact. He gets in trouble again

"Eddie's Girl" – No. Beaver doesn't do anything wrong in this episode when he is left alone. He does crush stuff which he can only do when everybody is gone. But apparently, it's not against the rules, just something that is frowned upon.

"The Pipe"- Yes. Beaver does something terribly wrong in this episode. With Larry's urging he smokes the pipe Fred Rutherford sent Ward as a gift from his travels to Germany.

"Dance Contest" – Yes. Beaver does something wrong when left alone. He messes with Wally's stuff. In this instance, it's Wally's cha-cha practice record. He and Larry are playing it and when Wally gets home, the record gets broken. If only he hadn't touched Wally's stuff.

"Beaver and Andy" – Yes. Beaver does something wrong. One afternoon, the alcoholic painter named Andy asks Beaver for something to drink. He offers him some juice, but Andy is looking for something with a little more kick. He prods Beaver and eventually gets some of Ward's Brandy for a drink. He falls off the wagon and has to give up the painting job.

"Ward's Baseball" – Yes. Beaver does something wrong when left alone. He also gets into a lot of trouble after playing with Ward's baseball which is autographed by numerous Major League baseball players. Larry throws it into the street, and it is run over by a truck.

"Kite Day" – Yes. Beaver does something wrong. He listened to Gilbert. And by doing so, is convinced to go fly the kite even though the glue has not dried long enough. The kite breaks and all that hard work of Ward went to waste.

"The Spot Removers" – Yes. Something bad happens when Beaver is home alone in this episode. However, it's mostly Richard's fault. He's the one who spills oil on Wally's suit that just came back from the cleaners. Believe it or not, it's Eddie Haskell who saves the day for Beaver.

"Ward's Golf Clubs" – Yes. Beaver does something wrong when alone in the house. He is convinced by Gilbert to use a club to hit a golf ball Gilbert found. Beaver swings the club and believes he broke it. He didn't, but he doesn't know that. He goes to great lengths to cover it up.

"Beaver's Long Night" – No. Beaver doesn't do anything wrong. But maybe for the time and place, he may have been a bit overzealous in calling the police on two strange men who were parked outside the Cleaver house. The call resulted in Bill Scott and Lumpy being taken in by the police, and let's just say, Fred Rutherford was not very pleased.

"Beaver's Jacket" – No. Beaver doesn't do anything wrong here because he's alone. He and Richard are a bit sneaky in this episode but do nothing inherently wrong.

"Wally Stays at Lumpy's" – No. Beaver did not do anything necessarily wrong in this episode. This is an evening when Gilbert and Beaver *get* the Cleavers on a technicality and Gilbert stays over at Beaver's house when he was explicitly told to not spend the night. Wally does practically the same thing over at the Rutherfords.

"Beaver's Laundry" – No. Beaver did not do anything wrong in this episode, but he did mess something up. Also, he wound up home alone, but was not left alone at home. Beaver left home to help Richard take his family laundry to the cleaners to have it washed. Richard loses his money, and they decide to ask Beaver's mom to wash the laundry. When June isn't home, they do it themselves. The washing machine overflows with soap suds and causes a big mess. But everything ends up well and the Cleavers end up with a spotless, newly mopped kitchen floor.

"Long Distance Call" – Yes. Beaver does something wrong here when left alone. Boys should not play with the telephone. Beaver and his friends first make crank phone calls and then decide to call Dodger Stadium in Los Angeles to talk with Don Drysdale. They swear to keep it a secret, but someone always opens their big mouth, don't they?

"Wally's Car Accident" – No. Beaver doesn't do something wrong in this episode when left alone. He does lie to his parents by omission when they call while Wally is out, but this episode is definitely more about what Wally does wrong.

"Beaver's Good Deed" – Yes. Beaver did something wrong. Alone in the house, he let a "tramp" come in and have something to eat. Then, the man takes a bath in Ward and June's bathroom. He steals a suit of clothes from Ward. This was a dangerous thing to do, even back in the early 1960s.

The Book Report" – Yes. Beaver does something wrong in this episode. He winds up watching *The Three Musketeers* on TV and uses it as the basis for his book report and not the book itself. Not sure if you can chalk it up to him being alone, but maybe if his parents had been home, he may not have been doing homework down in Ward's den. He definitely wouldn't have been doing his homework while watching television.

Well, there you have it. Most of the time when Beaver was left home alone, the writers used it as a formula for creating conflict and having Beaver do something wrong. His being alone made for some amazing episodes. But What about Wally? Was he ever left alone? From what I have found, he was specifically left alone in "Part-Time Genius" when Ward and June take Beaver to visit the Hawthorne School. On other occasions he may be alone, but not specifically left alone after June and Ward announce they are going to be elsewhere.

When Beaver and Wally are left by themselves, there are a few times the writers use this too for conflict and problems that make for entertaining television. I think the best example of this is found in "Beaver Takes a Bath." One can't say that Beaver overflowing the bathtub wouldn't have happened if June or Ward had been home, but in all those times June had him take a bath when she was home, it never did happen. Other times that their being alone was the impetus for a problem include "The Yard Birds," "The Broken Window," and "Chuckie's New Shoes."

If you want to read more about all the times Wally and Beaver were left alone, visit http://leaveittobeaverbooks.com.

11

DANCING AND PARTIES

I often pass by the Arthur Murray Dance studio in Grapevine, Texas. It's nestled between an In-N-Out Burger and a Chic-fil-A and is right across the street from an Arby's. These are some of my favorite fast food joints. Each time I pass that Arthur Murray dance studio I can't help but think of *Leave it to Beaver*. It reminds me of the dancing class episodes but also "Price of Fame," in which Wally and Chester go down to the dance studio to make faces at Tooey while he takes a lesson. That place also reminds me of the time in "Dance Contest" when Ward takes Wally for a thirty-minute cha-cha lesson at a local dance studio. These days, there doesn't seem to be much interest in sending kids to dancing school… well, I do know one woman who does, and she's quite a pearl.

Dancing School

Back in the 1950s and early 1960s, dancing school seems to have been a big part of suburban life. Early in the series, Beaver and Wally are both against attending dancing school ("Wally's Girl Trouble"). Ward and June patiently await their newest excuse and when they come downstairs to leave, they do so willingly, and almost happily. Ward and June are surprised. That's because the boys plan to skip out on class in the middle of it and go fishing. Well, until the new girl Penny Jamison catches Wally's eye. Wally thinks she's pretty, but Beaver thinks she has a face like a flounder. That was the first time viewers see the bad taste dancing school can leave in the mouth of a young child.

There are many references to dancing school made in *Leave it to Beaver* that are never seen. For example, Larry talks about winning a prize in dancing school ("Beaver's Poem"). Beaver asks if he won it for dancing and Larry tells him, "No…for being the only one to go to all the classes." Wally talks about attending dancing school while trying on suits ("Wally's New Suit"). One of the suits reminds him of one he wore to dancing school. Wally tells his parents that Beaver is upstairs moping like when they used to make him go to dancing school ("Beaver's Old Buddy"). In the episode where Beaver is at that awkward age when he's ugly and repulsive (according to Richard), Ward and June are looking at a cute picture of Beaver on his first day at dancing school ("Nobody Loves Me"). Penny Woods, when she's trying to butter up Beaver to get his vote for Junior Fire Chief, says that she told her mom he was the cutest boy at dancing school ("Junior Fire Chief").

Beaver typically enjoys getting a letter in the mail. But when that letter is an invitation to a series of dances, that one is not enjoyed nearly as much as when Uncle Billy sends him $10.00. While Beaver is sitting at the dinner table thinking of some way to get out of going to the Mayfield Cotillion dances, Wally tells him that if he doesn't know how to dance by the time he gets to be his age, he'll feel like a creep "(Beaver's Dance"). That's not much of a comfort to Beaver. Even though he is told Larry will also be attending, Beaver still says he doesn't want to go.

While Wally may not have skipped out on dancing class with Beaver, Larry is more than willing to do so after the first dance of the Mayfield Cotillion series of dances. In this episode, moments after arriving for the first dance, Larry says something that is a bit surprising for such a wholesome show. When Mrs. Prescott goes down the line of seated boys and girls, calling the boys to go to a girl to ask for their hand, Beaver mumbles, "I wish I was dead." Larry then surprises viewers by saying, "I wish she was." That line was both surprising and brilliant. They skip out on the dance the following week and meet up with a girl who wants to grow up to be a cowboy. The actress is Karen Sue Trent, but in this episode, she is not playing Penny Woods, but an unnamed girl on a horse. She allows Beaver and Larry to ride her horse and they get back home filthy and with horsehair on their suits. When asked how he got hair on him, Beaver says, "Gee, mom, maybe some of the girls were shedding." This is by far, one of the best episodes of *Leave it to Beaver*.

Dances

Dancing school eventually leads to dances. The first dance mentioned in *Leave it to Beaver* is when Mary Ellen uses Beaver to get Wally to take her to the eighth-grade dance ("My Brother's Girl"). The second instance is seen near the beginning of season two when Caroline Cunningham wants to have Wally go with her to a dance at the country club ("Eddie's Girl"). Wally wouldn't mind going with her, but he doesn't know her, and besides, she's Eddie's girl. That's what Beaver tells June after she mentions she's accepted an invite from Mrs. Cunningham for Wally to take Caroline to the dance. Wally's not having any of it and yells at the top of his lungs he's not going, even if it means he has to spend the rest of his life in his crummy old room as a punishment. But… he ends up going with her, because as he explains to Beaver, it's because Eddie's his friend. Needless to say, Beaver is confused because that's why he thought Wally didn't want to go with her in the first place.

Wally attended quite a few dances, whether they were school related (most of them) or social events at the country club (a few), dancing school paid dividends for him. Although he planned to take Mary Ellen Rogers to a Saturday night dance ("Wally's New Suit"), he, Eddie and the guys end up taking no dates. In another episode, Wally doesn't want to, but winds up taking Mary Ellen Rogers to the Mayfield Cotillion at the country club. She even signs him up for the cha-cha contest ("Dance Contest"). Wally also attends the school sophomore dance with Myra ("Wally's Orchid"). Wally, again, does not want to attend a dance when Kitty Bannerman's mom arranges for him to go with Kitty to a dance at the country club ("Wally's Glamour Girl"). Mary Ellen Rogers is his date at another Saturday night dance ("Beaver's Frogs"), the last one of season four.

In season five, the school year begins with a couple dances in the first month or so, and with a new school year, he gets a new girl to dance with. He goes with a girl named Susan to the first school dance of the year out at the lake ("No Time for Babysitters"). About a month later in Mayfield time, the guys at Mayfield High must ask girls from Riverside High to go to a dance. Wally ends up with a very tall girl, but at the dance, she's not nearly as tall as when he first met her. It's amazing what wearing one's hair down and flats will do for height ("Wally's Big Date").

The series finishes up with three dances for Wally in season six with a fancy dance at the country club where Wally wears a tuxedo ("Beaver's Football Award"), the school prom at the country club ("Wally's Car Accident") and the all-night graduation party which had eating, dancing, more eating and even more dancing ("All-Night Party").

As a younger guy, Beaver didn't attend many dances, but in "Beaver's First Date," he goes with a new girl from dancing class named Betsy. She's really the first girl he's ever liked and as he explains it to Wally, it's because she's new. She's the only girl he's ever known that wasn't always there. When he asks her to a dancing school sponsored dance, Beaver is a bit awkward. Then, at the dance, more awkwardness ensues when she dances with another guy and he's surprised or shocked. She then asks him, "Didn't you ask any other girls to dance with you?" He says no and then she goes and dances with Billy McKinzie. Poor Beaver. He then meets up with Richard and Whitey and shows them some new sounds he can make.

Another dance Beaver has the chance to attend is the Eighth Grade Graduation Dance ("Don Juan Beaver"). He agrees to go with his classmate Peggy McIntosh. Then, a transfer student shows interest in Beaver. Her name is Melinda Nielson. She's pretty and her southern accent even makes her seem prettier to Beaver. She wants Beaver to take her to the dance. So, what is he to do? He's got one dance and two girls who want him to take them to it. He heeds Eddie Haskell's advice to play a game he calls, "Ditching the Dodo." He is as rude as possible to Peggy in the hope that she will drop him, and he'll be free to go with Melinda. Things don't go as planned and as a shock to Beaver, he ends up with no date for the dance and stays home on Saturday night and watches television.

Parties

Parties are festive events. Early in season one there are a couple parties worth mentioning. One is the tea party thrown by Tooey's mom ("Water, Anyone?") in which she chooses to serve soft drinks instead of buying water from Beaver. The other is Linda Dennison's all-girl birthday party which Beaver ran away from and into a room full of guns that belong to her father. Beaver ends up having a grand old time with Mr. Dennison at the party. Parties are fun and sometimes even lead to dancing. Let's look closer at some of those parties which also include some dancing.

One of the first parties we see with dancing is one thrown at the home of Christine Staples. Eddie invites Wally's new "friend" Dudley to the party. Wally knows it's just to make fun of Dudley. Wally takes it upon himself to help Dudley learn how to dance. When party night arrives, the guys all dance until the record player stops working. That's when Dudley sits at the piano and plays them some music ("Wally and Dudley").

Another party, one where we don't know if there was dancing or not, was a masquerade party thrown at Mary Ellen Roger's house ("Beaver's Long Night"). Wally was going to go to the party and get a ride with Lumpy and Bill Scott, but because of Beaver, the police took them in after Beaver called the police on them. Wally, Bill and Lumpy missed Mary Ellen's party. It couldn't have been much fun without them.

It was big news in Mayfield, or at least at Ward's office and in the Cleaver house, when Lumpy was given permission to throw a party ("Wally Stays at Lumpy's"). When talking with Wally after the party was over and the guests had gone home, we hear a few details about the party. There was dancing, but we're not sure if everybody danced or only Fred Rutherford danced. One time, for certain, Fred came downstairs and did a dance for the girls he called, "The Apple." Lumpy says he thinks the girls got a kick out of it. Wally mentions that his dad only came downstairs about eight times. He even showed color slides. Lumpy finishes the conversation with one big admission, "At least my party was different."

Talk about different, Wally has a party at his house, and it too could also be classified as "different." But it's not Ward coming down and interrupting the party with a crazy dance or showing color slides that makes his party different. It's Beaver that makes it different. Whether it's everyone dancing to music from the record player, then the power turning off, then turning back on, then off again to rubber slices of cheese, and bugs in the ice cubes, Wally's party seems more like a kiddie party instead of one for mature teens like Lumpy and Eddie. It takes him a few minutes, but Beaver finally admits to all the childish pranks. He did so because Wally refused to invite him to the party until the last moment…. after he had already put all the pranks into action.

The final party, where there is dancing and eating and more eating and then more dancing is the all-night party after Wally's high school graduation. Lots of fun is had until everyone is on their way home and outside the country club an older drunk man pushes Wally's date into the water fountain. Mr. Gregory, his date's father, is furious when he sees his daughter come home soaking wet. Wally tries to explain, but to no avail. Eventually, Wally does get to explain, and he does so sort of forcefully.

12

LOCATIONS

While the location of Mayfield is the biggest question that *Leave it to Beaver* fans will probably ever ask, something that is similarly interesting is what locations are mentioned throughout the series? These "locations" can be what viewers would consider local to Mayfield or its vicinity or those that are further away from Mayfield, somewhere else in America or even other countries.

Some of the more exotic locations include Zanzibar ("The Merchant Marine"), Morocco ("Beaver's Autobiography"), and the Sahara Desert ("The Black Eye"). A few of the closer by locales include Lynwood, Metzger's Field, Friend's Lake, Bellport and Miller's Pond. Some locations are mentioned as places a character has gone, would go to soon, runway to, or travel to in their dreams.

Let's look at all locations mentioned. They will be listed in three categories. The first will be those locations that are within minutes to hours of Mayfield. The second will consist of those locations that are in another state, or what seems to be another state by the way the place is spoken of within the conversation in which it is mentioned. The final category, since we probably all believe Mayfield is located within one of the fifty American states, will be places in foreign countries. These locations will be listed in order they are mentioned throughout the series and if they are mentioned more than once, they will only be listed the first time they appear in the series.

Minutes to hours from Mayfield

Miller's Pond	Indian Caverns	Wagner's Cave
Metzger's Field	Elmhurst	Lake Crescent
Friend's Lake	Hadley City	Lagoon Bay
The Sandhills	Burns Junction	Medford
Crystal Falls	Madison	Lynbrook
Riverside	Fairfield Park	Porterville
Bellport	Freeport	Willoughby's Meadow
Garden Grove	Lynwood	Shaker Heights
Moosehead Point	Mount Grover	Shadow Lake

Out of State (or so it seems)

Binghamton	Des Moines, Iowa	Oklahoma
California	Honolulu	St. Louis, Missouri
New York	Hawaii	Pittsburgh
Chicago	Yellowstone National Park	Baltimore
Arizona	Princeton	San Francisco
Sequoia National Park	Cleveland, Ohio	New Jersey
West Point	Alaska	Pennsylvania
Grand Canyon	Wyoming	Texas
Middlesex County, MA	Kansas City	Fort Knox
Niagara Falls	New Mexico	Los Angeles, California

New England
Charleston
Juneau, Alaska
The Alamo

Atlanta
Williamsburg
Mt. Vernon
Grant's Tomb

Washington Monument
Carlsbad Caverns
Albuquerque, New Mexico

Far, Far Away

Sahara Desert
Damascus, Syria
Persia
Haiti
Peru
Chimborazo
Acapulco, Mexico
South America
Egypt
India
Frankfurt, Germany
England
China

Wake Island
Guadalcanal
Europe
Fiji Islands
Belgium
Mexico
Argentina
Australia
Bolivia
Brazil
Canada
Jutland
The Balkans

Versailles
France
Africa
Nile River
Canada
Sheffield, England
The Moon
Zanzibar
Spain
Windsor Castle
Japan
Paris
The Orient

13

JOBS AND MAKING MONEY

Money is important. Everybody needs it, even young boys the age of Beaver and Wally. There are plenty of things they need to have a happy life, or so they, and every other child believes. There are baseball gloves and bicycles to be bought, popsicles and ping pong paddles to be purchased. There's all kinds of things Beaver and Wally want to buy, and they often expect Ward to pull a wad of bills from his pocket or they want him to pick some bills off the magical money tree he has hidden somewhere in the backyard, so they can have their needs fulfilled. No, they're not that bad or greedy, but one question from Beaver is quite revealing.

"Where else are you going to get money if you don't get it from your father?"
– Beaver Cleaver

Ward replies "… work."

We see in multiple episodes that the boys did get a good work ethic from their father. They also have a bit of an entrepreneurial spirit, especially Beaver. Below, you will see the many ways Beaver, Wally and even Eddie, earn money for the various things they want or need.

Both Wally and Beaver

Wally and Beaver buy an alligator from an ad in a comic book. When their gator arrives, it is about six inches long. After the gator grows a little, Wally and Beaver give alligator shows to their friends for ten cents per person ("Captain Jack").

Wally and Beaver send away for Flower of the Orient perfume to sell door to door ("The Perfume Salesmen").

Wally and Beaver go down to the local newspaper, the Sun Courier, to get a job delivering newspapers. They must talk to Old Man Merkel to get the job. He's also very mean. They get the job, but eventually get fired, but by no fault of their own ("The Paper Route").

Ward talks about Wally and Beaver wanting $1.00 to wash their car ("Child Care").

The boys get paid fifty cents per hour to babysit Puddin' Wilson ("Child Care").

In a job that may have been one in which they were underpaid, they receive fifty cents a day for taking care of the Donaldson's cat over the weekend. They also have to water their lawn and pick up the newspapers. They get paid the same amount for this job as for taking care of Puddin' for two hours. In the end, they refuse to take money from Mr. Donaldson because they lost Puff-Puff for an evening ("Cat Out of the Bag").

The boys are told they will receive ten dollars each for two days of work at a traveling carnival at Metzger's Field. Instead of the money, they get an old, tired horse as payment. This payment is for their efforts carrying water, sweeping up, rubbing down horses, cleaning animal cages, and picking up after people leave the carnival ("A Horse Named Nick").

Beaver Making Money

Beaver sells water to Wally and his friends. He later adds squeezed lemons and sugar because he figures he can charge more if he calls it lemonade ("Water, Anyone?").

Beaver receives fifty cents for catching the Donaldson's parakeet ("Train Trip").

Beaver receives fifty cents a day to walk Miss Cooper's dog, although it does take a while for him to accept that she is not a witch ("Haunted House").

Beaver starts his own newspaper with Larry. Beaver says this is the neatest job he's ever had. He makes money by selling ads and papers. The paper is defunct after two issues ("Beaver's Newspaper").

Beaver has a job, along with Whitey, raking leaves for Miss Landers ("Miss Landers' Fiancé").

Beaver wants to make money for a used canoe. Ward tells him if he earns half the money, he will pay for half. Richard tells him about a man who pays twenty-five cents for frogs. He croaks them for medical research ("Beaver's Frogs").

Beaver goes into business with Gilbert to cut lawns. After getting yelled at a couple times, Gilbert gives up, but Beaver presses on. He finds a woman who needs her lawn cut and agrees to $5.00 for the front and back ("Beaver Goes in Business").

Beaver babysits for Pat Murdock, chuckie's older sister ("Beaver the Babysitter").

Beaver wants to get a job as a paper boy because after hearing a newspaper man in a school assembly, he wants to be in the newspaper business. He doesn't get the job ("The Late Edition").

After seeing an advertisement for modeling in New York City, Beaver thinks he can make $100 a day being a model ("Beaver, the Model").

Beaver and Gilbert get jobs caddying at the country club. Beaver receives a $5.00 tip from the cheater Mr. Langley ("Beaver the Caddy").

Beaver speaks of his upcoming summer job delivering newspapers ("Summer in Alaska").

Wally Making Money

Wally mows the lawn and other miscellaneous yard work for twenty-five cents per hour ("Water, Anyone?").

Wally wonders how a guy can get a bike if their dad doesn't give it to them ("Paper Route").

Wally gets paid for taking care of Beaver for the weekend when Ward and June are out of town for his business meeting ("Beaver Takes a Bath").

Wally agrees with a handshake to paint trash cans for fifty cents each. Beaver and Wally wind up each painting one and then June finishes the job on her own ("Wally's Job").

Wally sells Igloo ice cream bars ("Wally, the Businessman").

Wally gets a job at Friend's Lake as a lifeguard. The pay is $10.00 a day. He winds up not being able to take the job because the required age was recently raised to eighteen and Wally is only seventeen years old. Not all is lost because there is an opening for a candy butcher ("Wally, the Lifeguard").

Wally is employed by June to polish the door knocker, the mailbox, and other areas around the house for fifty cents an hour ("Beaver's Freckles").

Wally gets a job on weekends to work the soda fountain at Mr. Gibson's drug store ("Wally's Weekend Job").

Wally says he will be working at the soda fountain during the upcoming summer ("Summer in Alaksa").

Eddie / Wally & Eddie

Eddie and Wally went to the home show to get a job counting people but didn't get the job since applicants had to be college graduates ("Beaver the Magician").

Eddie tells Alma he may work his way over to Europe on a ship, maybe as a purser or as a companion to a millionaire ("Wally and Alma").

Eddie and Wally get a job at the Mayfield Dairy with the help of Ward ("Eddie, the Businessman").

Eddie gets a job at the local pet store. He gets fired. ("Big Fish Count").

Eddie gets a job at Thompson's Garage for $80 per week. He quits before he gets fired ("Eddie Quits School").

Eddie and Wally get a job parking cars for the Langley Wedding ("Parking Attendants"); $5.00 each.

Eddie has a job interview with the captain of a commercial fishing boat. He does not take the job. ("Summer in Alaska").

Lumpy

Lumpy says his dad got him a job handing out towels in the country club locker room for the summer before college. His dad says he'll meet the cream of society and that his dad went over the membership list with him and checked off all the big shots ("Summer in Alaska").

14

FEAR

Fear can be a terrible emotion, but also a much needed one. If not for fear, we could get ourselves into some of the most dangerous of situations. As long as fear doesn't consume a person, it's a good feeling to have. I think with Beaver and Wally, fear kept them out of trouble, at least once in a while. I like the way Wally talks about fear in "Wally's New Suit" when Beaver asked him why they make kids suits so stiff looking. Wally replies, "I guess just to scare you so while you're in them, you won't do anything bad." That's pretty good logic because that's exactly what being scared can do to a person, keep them from doing bad.

In this chapter, we'll look at many occasions when Beaver has a fear, which sometimes is justified and other times, nothing to be worried about at all. Also, we'll look at Wally and a few times this brave big brother is afraid. Their friends also are afraid at times, and they will be examined a little bit too. To finish off, some other generic mentions of fear will be discussed.

Beaver's Fears

The entire *Leave it to Beaver* series begins with Beaver and fear. The first episode aired was "Beaver Gets 'Spelled," and in this episode, Beaver is given a note to take home to his parents. The episode includes some of the funniest and most clever dialogue in the entire series. Beaver is afraid that he will be expelled from school. His friends tell him that's what the note is all about. When talking with Wally around the bathtub before bed, Beaver goes over all the scenarios that may be the reason for his mysterious upcoming expulsion from school. He eventually finds out that it wasn't a note about something bad he had done, but a note asking if he could be Smokey Bear in the upcoming fire prevention pageant.

Being afraid happens for so many different reasons. However, when a child is afraid of their own father… things may be going a bit too far. In "The Black Eye," June confronts Ward at the dinner table, "You're frightening him." Beaver sure looks scared. Ward raised his voice when he found out Beaver ran away when he got into a fight at school. Unknown to Ward, the kid who gave Beaver a black eye was a girl. Beaver was being a gentleman by not hitting a girl back after being hit by her. So, fear sometimes comes from the unlikeliest of places.

Did you ever happen to notice that Beaver had a tendency to lose things? This is seen very plainly in "The Haircut." It was good parenting by Ward to give him another chance after losing his lunch money once again. The second chance he gives Beaver is handing over money for a haircut. June is surprised he would trust him with the money for a haircut. The entire episode is centered around the haircut Beaver gives himself, with a little help from Wally. The deception the boys use to hide the awful home haircut is almost brilliant in its planning and in how it is carried out. But their ruse is discovered, and as June says near the end of the episode, the only reason it happened was because Beaver was afraid of Ward and what would happen if he admitted he lost the haircut money. Ward feels a bit guilty and admits to June, "One of the problems of being a parent is that you love your kids so much that you scare the pants off of them." When a child is young, I guess they are more likely to fear their parents than they are to be afraid of the dark.

The first time anyone on *Leave it to Beaver* is given "the business" is in the "New Neighbors" episode. This was also the first appearance of Eddie Haskell, and yes, he is the first one to give anybody "the business." Beaver is his target after he sees Mrs. Donaldson, the new neighbor, give Beaver a kiss of thanks on the cheek after Beaver gives her flowers from June. Eddie tells Beaver that bad things happen to guys who kiss another guy's wife. Beaver says he didn't kiss her. "She kissed me." That doesn't stop Eddie from giving him "the business" again and again throughout the show. To say Beaver is scared is a gross understatement. This may be the most fear he has in the series until "The Haunted House" episode in season two.

Once again, Eddie Haskell is the cause of Beaver's fear. In "Voodoo Magic," Eddie convinces Beaver and Wally to go with him to see *Voodoo Curse* instead of *Pinocchio*, which is what their mother wants them to see. At a very tense moment in the film, Eddie pokes Beaver and almost scares him out of his seat. That is the first time in the episode Beaver is scared. The second time is when Eddie is sick. But why should Beaver be scared because Eddie is sick? Well, it's because he thinks the voodoo doll he made of Eddie is working. Laughter ensues and eventually the psychosomatic symptoms Eddie experiences go away after Ward sends Beaver over to Eddie's with a curse remover incantation to recite over him.

Fear and girls is a theme that runs through a few episodes. This is first highlighted in "Party Invitation" when Beaver is invited to Linda Dennison's birthday party. He eventually escapes from the girls and finds himself in Mr. Dennison's den. He asks Beaver if he's afraid of Girls. "Kinda sorta," he answers. In "The Dramatic Club," Beaver isn't scared to perform in the school play but becomes scared after finding out he has to kiss Victoria Bennett. This is a combination of fear and embarrassment. He'll do it but says he doesn't want his family to watch. Then, in "Beaver's First Date," Beaver admits his fear to Wally who has a great response, although not very helpful to Beaver, when he says, "You're supposed to be scared." In an episode that features Eddie, "Eddie Quits School," Beaver looks back at some fear he had in the past. He mentions that he once told the guys he was going to kiss Angela Valentine. He was scared and pretended to be sick for two days. This theme of fear and girls continues in "Double Date." Beaver pretends to be hip and mature when Wally asks him to double date with him. However, he's simply hiding his fear. His date, Susan, is so scared she cancels, and the date is off. Beaver calls her and tries to convince her to go. He asks her if she's scared. She says she is, and he admits he's scared too. They are both happier after those admissions of fear. Maybe one day, they say, they'll see each other when they aren't scared. Yes, girls can be scary sometimes.

Beaver finds himself in "Lonesome Beaver" walking home alone at night in the midst of what seems like a coming storm. The winds are howling, and a coyote is too. This is one of the rare night scenes we see in *Leave it to Beaver*. Walking at night would be frightening enough, but the wind, and the creaking gates, it's all too much for a little boy all alone.

"The State Versus Beaver" shows Beaver afraid of two different things. He violates a rule his father put down when he helped Wally and Beaver build their go-cart. The rule was no one is to take out the go-cart alone. Larry did not count as a second person. Ward meant Beaver couldn't take it out without him or Wally nearby and watching. Beaver did so, drove on the street, and received a ticket from the police. Beaver was afraid to tell Ward what had happened because he had disobeyed him. He later must go to traffic court and was afraid of the judge. It's a good thing the judge was very understanding, and all works out well when the judge expunges the citation from Beaver's record.

When a person does something wrong, they typically fear being caught or discovered. This is exactly how Beaver's fear manifests in "Train Trip." Aunt Martha lets the boys buy their own train tickets and before they do, they spend most of their money on junk food. With not enough money to buy a ticket to Mayfield, they buy a ticket to Bellport and plan to ride all the way home. But when the conductor begins taking tickets, Beaver starts to fear what will happen when they are caught. Many comedic lines are provided by Beaver and Wally and eventually they tell the truth and make a deal with the conductor to pay him back if he takes care of their tickets now. The lesson to learn here is that you have less fear when you do the right thing.

Medically, Beaver is afraid of a doctor a few times and a dentist once in various episodes. These episodes are "New Doctor" in which Beaver is lying about being sick and is afraid he'll be found out, "Beaver's Tonsils," when he's afraid of having his tonsils taken out, which turns out to be a temporary fear, "Beaver's Ring," when he fears the doctor cutting his finger off, and "The Tooth," in which Lumpy scares him into thinking a filling is the worst thing in the world.

In both "Beaver's Bad Day," and "Beaver and Henry," his fear concerns animals. In the first, Beaver is afraid of Eddie's big attack dog when they are at the construction site. The dog eventually bites him when he visits the site a second time. The second animal fear Beaver has is when he thinks a bunch of little rats have knocked over their rabbit Henry and are biting him. He is screaming at the top of his lungs in this episode, maybe the loudest screams by anyone in the entire series.

Here are some other names of people Beaver is specifically afraid of throughout the series. Lumpy Rutherford (twice), Miss Cooper and Sonny Cartwright. The two episodes in which Lumpy scares him are "The Lost Watch" and "Wally's Track Meet." These are two very different episodes when it comes to how the writers deal with Beaver's fear of Lumpy. In the first, Lumpy is being his typical season one and season two bully self. Similar to the "Lumpy Rutherford" episode in season one, here, in "The Lost Watch" he tries to force Beaver to pay for a watch he lost, making Beaver think he's the one who lost it. He even threatens to call the police on him. In "Wally's Track Meet," Beaver is scared of Lumpy but still goes to his house to tell him he's a rat and calls him Lumpy Dumpy to his face because he got Wally in trouble when he was really the one to blame. He tells Wally that he was scared but says if you don't let a big guy know how scared you are, you forget he's such a big guy.

The other two people Beaver fears, Miss Cooper and Sonny Cartwright, are found in the episodes, "The Haunted House," and "Beaver's Fortune." The first is a woman who wants Beaver to walk her dog, but living in the old Cooper house, Beaver thinks she's a witch, and he doesn't want to be turned into a dog or suffer some fate worse than that. The second is a school bully that is scheduled to fight Beaver in the park at 3 p.m., thanks to Larry and his big mouth. Sonny never shows and Beaver survives to live another day. Sonny even shows Beaver some respect their next day in school. Larry, on the other hand, gets punched right in the stomach by Sonny.

In another instance of Eddie giving Beaver "the business," we find Beaver scared that Eddie is going to really jump into a body of water after Beaver tells him to go jump in a lake ("The Hypnotist"). You see, Beaver just hypnotized Eddie, or so he thinks, and he is unsuccessful in bringing Eddie out of his trance. Beaver also has a nightmare in which he wakes up terrified. In his nightmare, he has Eddie about to jump into a volcano.

Beaver gets into trouble and gets scared once again when he goes against his father's wishes. He is told that the letter he receives from the modeling agency in "Beaver, the Model," is a gyp, a real come on. He sends in a letter approving their entering his photo in their modeling directory and agrees to their charge for doing so. Beaver never pays and the lawyers for the modeling agency go after him. Beaver winds up going to a lawyer friend of Ward's and when asked if he was afraid, he tells Wally, "Of course I was scared. I'm always scared of guys in offices."

Wally tells a story from the past about fear, about one of Beaver's childhood fears. In "Beaver's Electric Trains," Wally tells him that when he was little, he feared going down into the basement. The reason? Beaver thought the furnace was a monster with red eyes and teeth. He thought the pipes were the arms reaching out to get him.

To end this partial list of Beaver's fears, we must do so with the episode, "Beaver's Fear." That would only be appropriate, no? Here, Beaver is going to hang out with the big guys at the amusement park on Saturday and the Big Dipper roller coaster is the ride everyone wants to experience. Well, everyone except Beaver wants to experience it. Wally explains to him that roller coasters are supposed to be scary. Beaver seeks help from Gus, the Fireman, a friend who has always had words of wisdom for the Beave. When Beaver explains to Gus the fear he has about riding the Big Dipper, Gus surprises Beaver with a story about one of his own fears. When Gus was a rookie fireman, he had to go up on a tall tower and jump into a net. Gus figured that other men jump into the net, and he didn't believe they were any braver than he was, and then he realized what was really wrong with him. He was just afraid of being afraid. Gus tells Beaver that after he climbed up that ladder and jumped off the building, he had never been happier with himself than he was then. He encourages Beaver to just think of "Gus and the net" when he's up in that roller coaster. It turns out that the only one afraid of the rollercoaster was Eddie, the guy who gave Beaver "the business" about being afraid.

Wally's Fears

Beaver is not the only Cleaver to experience fear. Wally does too in quite a few episodes. The first time we see Wally experience fear on his own (outside of the "Lumpy Rutherford" episode where both boys are afraid of getting on Lumpy's bad side), is in "The Shave." In this episode, Wally shaves for the first time and as he is about to put the razor to his skin, his hand is trembling in fear. It's a good thing the razor wound up not having a blade in it.

Wally is very popular with parents. Alma's parents are no exception to that rule. Alma's mother becomes very enamored with Wally in "Wally and Alma" after he eats dinner at the Hanson's house one evening. She arranges many Alma and Wally get togethers. It gets to be annoying for Wally and he wants to stop hanging out with Alma. Beaver tells Ward that Wally is afraid of Alma's mother. Eventually, Wally gets Alma interested in some other guys and he's set free from the grasp of Alma's mother.

Reading above, you realize Wally is not exempt from fearing females. In the case of "Wally and Alma," he was afraid of a mother. However, in "Wally's Orchid," Beaver is afraid of a girl in his class. He wants to ask Myra to the sophomore dance and he's afraid to ask her. Eddie helps him out by taking her friend away so it's just he and Myra alone. Wally conquers his fear and asks her out and is quite surprised when she says yes. Good for Wally for conquering his fear.

In "Substitute Father," Wally admits to Ward that he is a little scared, but not of a person or an object. He is frightened of something more abstract, the responsibility of being in charge at home while Ward is out of town on a business trip to St. Louis. He does very well as the man of the house while Ward is gone, even having a parent / teacher meeting with Miss Landers after Beaver gets in trouble at school.

Both Beaver and Wally

There are times when both Beaver and Wally are equally afraid of someone. Two occurrences to mention are in "Lumpy Rutherford" and "The Paper Route. The first is when the boys are afraid of running into the big bully, who they call Lumpy Dumpy. He stops them from walking home down the street to their house. The second is when they get a paper route, delivering the Courier Sun newspaper. There's one terrifying thing about delivering newspapers in Mayfield, and that's Old Man Merkel.

Outside the Cleaver family

In "Eddie Spends the Night," there are two times Eddie is afraid. He tells Wally he's afraid of Ward, basically, because he feels he doesn't like him. He tells Wally that when he opens the door it looks as if his father would be happier to see Khrushchev at the door instead of him. The other thing Eddie fears is staying at home alone. It seems to petrify him, although he plays it off when Wally visits his house to ask him to come back to his to spend the night. Later, when alone with Beaver, he admits that he is afraid to stay home by himself.

As shown above, Beaver is afraid of girls, kissing them, talking to them, just everything about them creeps him out. Wally is afraid too at times as seen with his interactions with Myra in "Wally's Orchid." Then there's Dudley McMullen, the son of June's friend Ruth. He's new to Mayfield High and Wally is tasked by June to befriend Dudley in "Wally and Dudley." He admits to Wally he's scared of girls and Wally says he used to be until he found out that girls are afraid of boys too. Dudley also admits this to Mary Ellen Rogers at a party attended by everyone late in the episode.

Both Richard and Gilbert are afraid when after Richard throws a rock and breaks a window of an abandoned house, the police stop and give chase to them. Gilbert gets away, but Richard is caught and questioned by the police officer. He tells Beaver later, that he was scared when the officer caught him and that's why he gave him Beaver's name and address. He apologies for doing so and they remain good friends, despite Richard's lapse in judgement.

Sometimes, fear is a good motivator. We've looked at some examples of fear seen throughout the series and there's plenty more examples that can be examined and if you want to see some of those, just visit http://leaveittobeaverbooks.com.

15

KISSES

While not a romantic comedy, *Leave it to Beaver* does have its share of on screen kisses. There's nothing too explicit, except for that scene where Marlene jumps Wally when he parks the car in "Box Office Attraction." Shocked by her behavior, Wally pushes her away. That's as racy as the kisses get. Then, there was that time in "Captain Jack," where Ward stands behind June in the kitchen while she's cooking and holds her very close.

This is the chapter where we examine as many of the kisses on the show as possible. There's bound to be a few that are missed, so your grace and mercy will be much appreciated if you find a kiss I miss. We'll fist examine kisses between June and Ward. Then, there will be a look at Beaver's kisses and those that involve Wally. Finally, there will be talk of other kisses, most all of those will be kisses spoken about, not seen.

June and Ward

Most every time Ward and June exchange a kiss, it is before Ward leaves for work, or after Ward returns home from work. Of all the episodes when Ward comes home from work, he and June exchange a kiss in 61% of them. Of those kisses, 91% are a kiss on the lips. When it comes to the entire series, the husband and wife kiss (on the lips, cheek, forehead, or neck) in 104 episodes or 44.4% of the shows. They share a kiss on the lips in 76% of those episodes.

June and the Boys

As a loving mother, June also kisses her children. She kisses Beaver the most, typically with a kiss goodbye or kiss goodnight, in thirty-one episodes or 13.2% of all episodes. She kisses Wally in only sixteen episodes or 6.8% of all episodes. The final time she kisses Beaver is in "The Silent Treatment," and the final episode in which she kisses Wally is "Wally's Car Accident." Both episodes are from season six.

Beaver and Wally Kissing Others

Other than the characters of Ward and June Cleaver, the character who is kissed the most is Beaver. There are those times he's kissed by June in the thirty-one episodes mentioned above and then there are the seven times Ward kisses him or he kisses Ward. But then you must add Aunt Martha's kisses, Miss Hathaway, Mrs. Donaldson, Miss Thompkins, whose wallet he found, Violet Rutherford, Victoria Bennett and the irresistible Donna Yeager. That's a lot of kisses for a young boy. But for Wally, his non-June kisses only include Aunt Martha and Marlene ("Box Office Attraction").

Other Kisses

There are only a few other kisses seen in the show, one is when Don and Carole kiss at the tennis courts in "Tennis, Anyone?" The others are the two times Mrs. Mondello kisses Larry ("Found Money" / "Beaver's Guest"). Bengie's mother also kisses her son in "Beaver, the Magician."

Kisses Spoken About

There are numerous episodes in which kisses are spoken about. A lot of this talk occurs in "The

Dramatic Club." Wally tries to convince Beaver he shouldn't be afraid of kissing Victoria Bennett in the play in which he has the lead part. He tells Beaver he's kissed Aunt Martha and Aunt Helen. Then Beaver admits he's even kissed Uncle Billy, but he doesn't want to kiss a girl, especially in front of people. In "New Neighbors," Beaver asks Ward if he's ever kissed any other married women. Wally tells Beaver in "Party Invitation" about a time he went to a party where he was forced to play kissing games. Wally says in "Wally's New Suit," how terrible it is to be seen in public being kissed by one's father. In "Beaver and Gilbert," Larry mentions he saw a movie and the main character was named Gilbert and he was always kissing a lady. Then, Beaver agrees with Larry in "Beaver's Prize," that the Jungle movie they watched was pretty good, but it had too much kissing and not enough apes.

There are many other episodes in which kisses are spoken about, but as usual, just visit http://leaveittobeaverbooks.com to get more info and sign up for updates and free *Leave it to Beaver* prizes.

16

CITY OF MAYFIELD

I always wanted to be a cartographer. If you're not familiar with the word, a cartographer is someone who makes maps. If I had the ability and enough information, I would create a map of Mayfield, USA. That would be a stunning contribution to this *Leave it to Beaver* encyclopedia. Unfortunately, there's not nearly enough information to make a complete map of the town or city of Mayfield. We can figure out from certain episodes which streets run perpendicular to one another. Right off the top of my head, one such episode is "Wally and Dudley." This occurs when Wally is walking Dudley to school and he suggests going down Filbert Street, and he says it goes the same direction as the street they are on, which is Pine Street. He was trying to avoid anyone seeing him walk with Dudley.

Instead of creating a map of Mayfield, the next best thing and the next next best thing is what you'll read about in this chapter. The first is a list of every street mentioned in Mayfield. Grant Avenue is probably mentioned the most times throughout the series, but there are many other streets, and you'll know them all in a matter of minutes. The next thing you'll read in this chapter will be a list of every business that is mentioned, seen or alluded to in Mayfield. This will be as exhaustive of a list as you'll ever find. So, let's get started… streets first.

Streets

4th Street – Location of the Zesto Soup billboard ("In the Soup")

10th Street – The cross street with Grant Avenue where Beaver finds a wallet ("Beaver Finds a Wallet")

40th Street – Vacant lot where Eddie and Lumpy dump trash ("Yard Birds")

Camelback Cutoff – The shortcut from Bellport to Mayfield

Crestview Avenue – The Ritterhoffs live on this street ("Wally Stays at Lumpy's")

Dock Street – Location of a 5&10 store downtown Mayfield ("Beaver's Fortune")

Elm Street – A street where the boys deliver newspapers ("The Paper Route"); a street where Wally stands around with a girl ("Beaver's Rat"); a street where Beaver and Gilbert collect for the Community Chest ("Community Chest")

Elmhurst Rd. – Home of a woman buying Flower of the Orient Perfume ("Perfume Salesmen")

Euclid St. – A street on the poor side of town, where the town dump is located ("The Grass is Always Greener")

Fairview St. - Vacant lot where Eddie and Lumpy dump trash ("Yard Birds")

Filbert St. – A street that is perpendicular to Pine St. and is named after some dead guy named Filbert according to Wally ("Wally and Dudley"); Also, the street where Gilbert and Beaver begin collecting for the Community Chest ("Community Chest"); Beaver goes there to find fire code violations ("Junior Fire Chief")

Glen Haven St. – The Wendovers live on this street ("Wally Stays at Lumpy's")

Grand Street – Location of Mayfield Specialty Store at the corner of Main and Grand ("Beaver's Typewriter")

Grant Avenue – Where Grant Avenue school is located

Highway 7 – The direct route to Bellport to and from Mayfield

Highway 39 – The road that leads out of town toward Indian Caverns ("The Visiting Aunts")

Hudson Ave. – Eddie found a quaint little bakery there ("Bachelor at Large")

Jefferson St. – One of the streets where Beaver and Gilbert collect for the Community Chest ("Community Chest")

Juston St. – Where Marlene, the girl who works at the Madison Theater lives ("Box Office Attraction")

Lake Avenue – This is the name of a street that co-creator / producer / writer Bob Mosher lived on in Auburn, New York ("Beaver and Andy") ("Beaver's Cat Problem")

Lakeview Avenue – Location of new Cleaver house until the deal falls through ("Most Interesting Character")

Lakeview Terrace – A street where the boys deliver newspapers ("The Paper Route")

Madison St. – Location of a new house being built ("Beaver's Jacket")

Main St. – Where Spear Pharmacy is located; Cut-Rate Sporting Goods is located at 513 Main ("Eddie's Double-Cross") ("Beaver's Ice Skates") ("Sweatshirt Monsters")

Mapleton – Where the Cleavers lived in seasons one and two

Metzger's Avenue – Location of the Metzger's Avenue school ("Beaver and Ivanhoe")

North St. – Wally and Beaver are to meet Tooey and Chester there ("The Visiting Aunts")

Oak St. – Location of the Zesto Soup billboard ("In the Soup")

Piedmont St. – There is a bridge on Piedmont ("No Time for Babysitters")

Pine – Where the Cleavers lived in seasons three through six

Prospect Avenue – Location where a lot of new houses are being built ("Beaver's Electric Trains")

State St. – Location of the State Street Bridge ("Beaver's Secret Life")

Stevens St. – Location where Eddie and Wally park cars ("The Parking Attendants")

Vanderbush Ave. – Where Wally and the guys hit each other in the arm ("Eddie's Double-Cross")

Vista Drive – A street where the boys deliver newspapers ("The Paper Route")

Mayfield Businesses (by season)

Season 1 – Candy shop, travel agency, Conway Vibrator Scientific Reducing shop, ice cream shop, barber shop, bowling alley, Elks Lodge, Thermal Products Company, Briarcliff Country Club, Kennebec Motel, Blue Moon Tavern & Grill, Antonio's Shoe Repair, drug store with lunch counter, Miss Spencer's School of the Dance, a gift and novelty store, goodwill donation box, Courier Sun Newspaper, City Cab Company, People's Security and Trust Bank, Texaco Gas Station, Abernathy Potts Sporting Goods, Henny's Hardware Store, Oddfellows Lodge, Mac's Garage, Cotton's Lumberyard, an unnamed restaurant downtown, The Globe Movie Theater, The Valencia Theater, The Palace Theater

Season 2 - Citizen's Trust & Savings Bank, Olympic Movie Theater, The Prep Store, Sweet Shop, medical offices, The Chuckwagon Restaurant (in or near Mayfield), Antique Shop, Newsstand, Henry's Refuse Company, at least two unnamed supermarkets, unnamed paint store, Claxton's Pet Store, Margaret Manning Adoption Society, Continental Travel Bureau, unnamed riding stable, Hoskins Real Estate, Thompson-Baker Real Estate, Walter Dean Insurance Agency, Frozen Stick Ice Cream trucks, Kirby's Clothing Store, Judson's Toy Store, unnamed photography store, Circle Garage, Jackson Realty

Season 3 - unnamed miniature golf course, Village Hardware Store, Jean's Photo Studio, Simpson's Paint Store, First National Bank, unnamed appliance store, Canton Chinese Restaurant, Park Drug Store, Ritz Hotel, Gilbert's Pharmacy, Uncle Artie's Magic Shop, Allen's Pet Store, Hadyn Memorial Library, Sweet's Malt Shop, Carter Drugs, unnamed dry cleaner, unnamed flower shop, Mayfield Zoo, unnamed insurance office, unnamed book store, Carter's Market, Coronado Savings & Loan Company, Summer's Drugs, Mason's Mortuary, Pool Hall, Farrago's Dry Goods, Compton and Bennett Attorneys at Law, Hampshire House restaurant, The Mayfield Theater

Season 4 - Thornton's Department Store, Terrence University, Spear Pharmacy, unnamed sign shop, unnamed ice skating rink, Buster Brown Shoe Store, unnamed bakery, Briggs Sporting Goods, Clair's Fine Candies, unnamed bookstore, unnamed shoemakers shop, Colonial House Restaurant, South Bay Shopping Center, Mr. Paley's Record Shop, Parker's Pet Store, Gorman's Department Store, Gaylord Electric Appliance Store, two unnamed dry cleaners, Army surplus store, unnamed TV Shop, unnamed drive-in restaurant, The Malt Shop, Martin's Soda Fountain, Jeanne's Lingerie Store, unnamed lumber yard, unnamed hobby shop, unnamed penny arcade, Bozart Theater, unnamed adult movie theater, The Orpheum, unnamed drive-in theater

Season 5- Mayfield Hobby and Toy Shop, Mr. Gibson's Soda Shop / Mayfield Drugs, Cut Rate Sporting Goods, The Ice Palace, golf driving range, The Book Nook, State Bank, Dorman's Store, Mayfield Realty, Thompson's Garage, unnamed laundromat, Uncle Sidney's Toys, Foster's Sporting Goods or Shoe Store, Mayfield Specialty Store, Olson Manufacturing, Jackson & Co. Importers, unnamed museum, Planters Insurance Agency, Tilden's Sporting Goods, unnamed tattoo parlor, Benson's Meat Market, Mayfield Power & Electric, Mayfield-Ross Oil Company

Season 6 - The White Fox, Mayfield Motor Vehicle Department, Mayfield Dairy, Mayfield Sport Track (motorsports), Liberty Café, YMCA, Al's Service Station, Roberts Malt Shop, Dobson's Market, unnamed bicycle shop, Mayfield Campus Shop Clothing Store, Kenneth R. Langley

Investment Broker, Hank's Place, The Red Top, The Birdcage, The Green Door, Monahan's, Mayfield Stadium (baseball field), unnamed Italian restaurant, Arctic Fish Company.

That's a lot of businesses. Of course, with multiple mentions of malt shops, drug stores, and hardware stores, there is always the possibility that they co-existed or one or two may have gone out of business and been replaced. Whatever. We know it's a fictional town with fictional businesses, but it is interesting to have this list to browse over. I hope you've enjoyed it.

As there is always something more to say about the streets or businesses, please visit http://leaveittobeaverbooks.com to read more. The website will be updated every few weeks and don't forget to sign up for updates and free prizes.

17

TALKING ABOUT PARENTS

In his 1998 autobiography, Jerry Mathers spoke of the unique nature of the *Leave it to Beaver* TV show. He said, "It presented a child's view of the world."[74] This is noticed throughout the series in how Wally and Beaver encountered many of life's experiences and the people in their world. Think about some of the situations they found themselves in when sending away for something through the mail. There was that giant alligator that was only about six inches long. Also, the people from Acme Products were a bit unscrupulous when they sent the boys twenty-four bottles of *Flower of the Orient* perfume. That perfume should've been called *Flower of Gutter Water*, or *Essence of Old Catcher's Mitt*. Talk about a gyp. Let us not forget the problems Beaver experienced with the accordion, the model directory, and the record club. Am I missing anything? Maybe, but you see the point…and may wonder why they ever wanted to deal with adults after those experiences.

Wally and Beaver also experienced the world of adults with some good moments too, ones that would leave them learning good lessons from those adults. Gus the fireman is one example. He was always around to help Beaver whether it was with a broken typewriter, teaching him the value of rocks (or lack of value), helping him with a rabbit, a horse, or in how to get over a fear. The experiences Beaver had with police officers may have been traumatic in the beginning of each situation, but in end, the experiences were helpful for Beaver learning right and wrong or mercy and justice. In "The State vs. Beaver," the police officer encounter wasn't nearly as frightening to Beaver as was the judge encounter, but that judge showed mercy and grace to Beaver and Beaver came away a better person because of it.

The adults that Beaver and Wally interacted with most often were, of course, their parents Ward and June. This led to many conversations about their parents. Why did they act in certain ways? For instance, showing them mercy ("The Haircut"), or not following through with a punishment. How did parents know certain things like Ward knowing their trouble with the train conductor ("The Train Trip") or about the Camelback Cutoff ("Lumpy's Car Trouble"), and about the broken headlight ("Wally's Car Accident"). In "Lumpy's Car Trouble," Beaver says, "Wally isn't it spooky how parents always find out what a guy does?" These are the things they would sometimes ponder when they were alone in their room. Typically, it was Wally who had the wisdom about such things, and he would impart it to his younger brother, who would then agree with him.

The bits of wisdom seen in the dialogue are very insightful such as this line from Wally in "The Haircut" episode in the first season, "You know, they go along nice and easy and smiling, but all the while, they're getting ready to jump on you." Kind of cynical, don't you think? Here's another slightly cynical way Wally had of looking at parents, "They're always sayin' mean things like that so, well, you'll be too scared to do somethin' wrong." And clearly, Eddie is a cynic when it comes to parents. He tells Wally in "Wally's New Suit," that parents going with a kid to buy their clothes is just another way for them to keep them under their control. In "Wally's License," Beaver even chimes in with some cynicism of his own, "Parents promise you a lot of stuff when you're little. They figure it will keep you quiet and you'll forget about it."

One of the most swell things about Wally and Beaver is the way they stick up for their dad, especially when Eddie tries to lump in Ward Cleaver with other fathers, like his own. Eddie took a

---

[74] Mathers, Jerry. *And Jerry Mathers as the Beaver* (New York: Berkley Boulevard, 1998), 5.

shot at his own father in "Tenting Tonight," speaking about how fathers will promise something and not follow through on that promise. "My pops the same way. He promises you something to keep you quiet. Saturday comes along, you remind him of it, he acts like you got rocks in your head." Wally tells Eddie their dad is not anything like that and when he makes a promise, he keeps it. Unfortunately, Ward did have to beg out of going camping with the boys, but it sure wasn't the way Eddie described such ordeals with his father. Ward Cleaver, here, was quite remorseful.

This is the same episode in which Eddie says it's good Wally and Beaver have a dad who doesn't care about them and lets them stay out in the backyard, camping in the rain. After Eddie leaves the room, Beaver asks Wally if that was true. Wally assures him it wasn't and says, "Who do you think left the back door unlocked?" This was an act which allowed the boys to sneak into the house when the rain came down hard and sneak back out when it was over. Beaver, happy, to be assured that his father loved them, goes with Wally to catch up with Eddie and walk to church.

If there's one thing that Wally and Beaver do understand about their parents, they understand their behavior can be confusing. When they expect to get yelled at, they sometimes get treated to something special instead ("The Haircut"). This happens on quite a few occasions. In "Price of Fame," after Beaver makes himself "conspicuous" for a second time, he expects to get yelled at or something worse. That doesn't happen. Instead, he is given the Ward Cleaver "you can always come to me" talk and everything is fine after that. When Larry wonders if he got in trouble, Beaver tells him what happened, and says, "You know Larry, you never can tell what they're going to do." That wisdom about parents is not original with Beaver as he seems to have picked that up from Wally when he said in "The Haircut," about their parents, "You just can't ever figure 'em out."

Wally tells a story to Beaver in "The Boat Builders" episode about Larry getting lost on a camping trip. When the scoutmaster told Larry's parents that they found him, they were happy. Then, when he got home, his mom yelled at him, and his dad hit him. Beaver and Wally are both confused on how a parent can be happy with a kid and yell at them at the same time. Wally surmises, "I don't know. I guess you gotta be a parent to do that." Wally admits to more confusion about parents when he says in "Beaver's Bike," that "Sometimes when you think he'll say no, he says yes, and sometimes when you think he'll say yes, he says no. I think that's got something to do with being a father." On top of these two examples, Wally confirms his confusion about parents when he says in "Beaver's Ice Skates," "Boy, you know mom, sometimes I can't figure you and Dad out."

Wally and Beaver's friends have quite a few thoughts about parents. In "Beaver's Bike," Larry tells Beaver, "My father's never said anything was his fault his entire life." He then adds, "My mother said if he was home more, he'd understand me better." His thoughts are not only about his father, but about Beaver's too. Reacting to Beaver being grounded in "Ward's Baseball," Larry looks up to Beaver's window from outside and tells him, "You know, you got a real scrooge for a father."

Eddie Haskell has a parental philosophy that I do not believe Wally and Beaver shared. In "Wally's Glamour Girl," Eddie says to Wally, "I told you before Sam, we got to stick together or we're going to lose this Cold War against the adults." Eddie believes the parent child relationship is one of two things. The first, being a war in which the children are the freedom loving patriots who want their liberty, and the parents are the Communist overlords. The second is that the children are prisoners, sometimes being held in solitary confinement, by their oppressive prison wardens, their parents. In "Tell it to Ella," Eddie reiterates his kids vs. parents philosophy, "I'm with you 100% in this battle against the enemy."

In "Beaver's Long Night," Wally's friend Bill Scott says about parents, "They're all the time being polite so they can find out what you're up to." Gilbert says, in "Three Boys and a Burro," that kids can't really save enough money on their own. He reasons, "If any kid ever saved up $30.00, his parents would take it away from him." Here's a question for *LITB* fans, did that ever happen to you when you were a child?

In "Junior Fire Chief," Beaver and his parents have a discussion about whether he will become the Junior Fire Chief for his class. They tell him, as he says in his words, "not to always be a nothing." It's interesting to hear what his friends Harry and Richard say about that. "I thought only my parents said stuff like that," said Harry. Richard then tells Beaver and Harry, "My parents even say it to me and look what a big shot I am."

Over the years, in my interactions with many *Leave it to Beaver* fans, there's a constant theme in what many say, "I wish I had a father like Ward Cleaver." This was also seen in some characters of *Leave it to Beaver*. The character named Scott (later Bill Scott) in "Weekend Invitation," said it well. "Just once, I wish my old man would care enough for me to tell me not to do something." And lest we forget how encouraging words (or discouraging ones) make a difference in a boy's life. An exchange between Beaver and Whitey in "Beaver's Ice Skates," is a good illustration. "My parents think I have good sense," says Beaver. Whitey is surprised and tells Beaver, "No foolin'? My parents are always telling me how dumb I am. Sometimes they tell me so much, I really think I am dumb." Whitey definitely could've used a Ward Cleaver in his life.

Wally sums up parents best in "Mother's Helper." He tells Beaver, "You know, Beav, you might not think so, but most of the time, parents know what's best for a guy."

Check out some other wisdom Wally and Beaver have about their parents and what other characters think about theirs, by visiting http://leaveittobeaverbooks.com.

18

DISTANCES

As a fan, I have always been intrigued when any distance was mentioned in an episode of *Leave it to Beaver*. Sometimes, I figure, this will help me determine where Mayfield is located. Other times, I think a distance will help me get a better sense of the town of Mayfield. There aren't a lot of times distances are mentioned, but I did try to catch all of them. One thing you'll notice in the following list is a lack of continuity in the show. This occurred because many different writers were employed to write scripts for *Leave it to Beaver*. Sometimes a place is only a couple miles away, and in a different episode it could be fifty miles away. That was just life in 1950s and 1960s television. Here are the distances… enjoy!

The Cleavers live six blocks away from dancing school ("It's a Small World").

Linda Dennison's house is only a few blocks away from the Cleavers ("Party Invitation").

Friend's Lake is fifty or sixty miles away from their home per Ward Cleaver ("Lonesome Beaver").

Mayfield to Bellport is ¾ the distance it is from Mayfield to Riverside. This is determined because the fare from Bellport to Mayfield is ¾ the price as a ticket from Riverside to Mayfield ("The Train Trip").

Ward refers to Larry Mondello's house as being "way over there" but Beaver walks over there quite often ("Beaver Runs Away").

Crystal Falls is sixty miles away from Mayfield per Wally ("Ward's Problem").

Garden Grove, the town which is hosting a carnival is far enough away for the boys to need to take a bus or get a ride ("The Visiting Aunts").

Indian Caverns is hours away from Mayfield. This is determined by June saying she hopes Aunt Martha and her friend arrive before dark and they are leaving at 2:15 p.m.

Shadow Lake is four hours away from Mayfield. If they average 40-50 m.p.h. on the way there, including any bathroom breaks, this would mean the lake is 160-200 miles away from Mayfield ("Happy Weekend").

Crystal Falls is ninety miles away per Ward. He also says it's a three-hour trip. The bus driver stops for one big lunch break, or he drives mighty slow ("The Bus Ride").

The Cleaver house is three or four miles from the downtown Mayfield bus station IF one looks at the cost of the taxi ride which was $1.65. Going by New York City cab fares of the time, the distance would've been three or four miles, and if one considers the fares are cheaper in Mayfield, the distance would be further. This shows the distance is not realistic as the boys would've not walked normally three or four miles or further from their home to downtown, and definitely not in the time span often shown in various episodes.

Madison, a town where the Cleavers may buy a house, and a town in which Mayfield High competes against in sports is according to Wally far away. He mentions, "… way over to Madison." And Beaver says his friend Larry could visit them because he knows how to take the bus ("Beaver Says Good-Bye").

David Manning lives five to six blocks away from the Cleaver house. The question arises, "Why does he now go to a different grammar school and never seen among Beaver's friends in the show?" ("Forgotten Party").

Freeport may be two to three hours away from Mayfield. Ward mentions he would like to leave at 4 p.m. so they could miss traffic and get there before dark ("Beaver Takes a Bath"). Freeport is also long distance and Ward refers to it as "up there," so it is possibly north of Mayfield ("Eddie Spends the Night").

The Cleaver house, beginning in season three, is closer to Judy Hensler's and Larry Mondello's houses ("School Bus").

Mayfield to Lynwood is a thirty-minute drive (possibly twenty miles) ("Beaver's Prize").

Mayfield to Friend's Lake seems to be some distance as they speak of going "up to" Friend's Lake ("Beaver and Violet").

Eddie Haskell's house from the Cleaver house, according to Wally, "It must have been a mile and a half…" ("Beaver's Doll Buggy").

Mary Ellen Roger's house is around the corner from the Cleaver house according to Lumpy ("Wally's Weekend Job").

Ward reminds Wally that the city park is only three blocks away. Ward reminds Beaver that Gilbert only lives around the corner ("Beaver Takes a Ride").

The lake Wally is invited to by Scott is two hours away and its direction is referred to as "up." This distance corresponds with Friend's Lake in an early episode of the series ("Weekend Invitation").

The Murdock family live only a couple minutes away from the Cleavers ("Beaver the Babysitter").

Lynbrook is approximately forty miles away from Mayfield. This is determined because Lumpy says it will take 75 cents worth of gas to get there. His 1940 Ford automobile at the best, gets 17 mpg. Gas costs 31 cents per gallon on average at that time ("The Credit Card").

Mayfield to the beach is at least two miles, but probably not much further since Lumpy's car can only go a couple miles before the radiator erupts. He mentions they went to the beach and people thought a beached whale had spouted ("The Credit Card").

Malt shop from the Cleaver house is only a couple blocks per Wally ("The Credit Card").

Beaver's friend Alan lives two blocks from the Cleaver house ("The Book Report").

I hope you have enjoyed this "distance" chapter as much as I have. It's always fun to find out some new information about my favorite TV show. If you want more detailed info on distances, please visit http://leaveittobeaverbooks.com.

19

SENTIMENTAL MOMENTS

When it comes to emotions or feelings, no two people are exactly the same. So, when it comes to a chapter which will list some of the most sentimental moments found throughout the six seasons of *Leave it to Beaver,* this list is very subjective. Now, if you don't think the moment when Ward almost begins to cry when he opens the box with his hunting jacket in it is sentimental, you may be insensitive, but everyone can have their own opinion. The list below will take a closer look at the moments from the show that most people may think are sentimental. Most of these moments occur during the first four seasons.

"Beaver's Short Pants" – Aunt Martha arrives in town to take care of the Cleavers. Almost immediately she traumatizes Beaver by buying him some short pants and making him wear them to school. Wally gets Ward to help keep Beaver from getting beat up two days in a row. Ward does this by hiding in the garage and catching Beaver before he leaves for school. He has a change of clothes for him. Beaver changes and responds, "Gee, thanks, dad, you're almost like one of the fellas." Ward tells him, "Well Beaver, I think that's one of the nicest things you've ever said to me." Ward then says, "It looks a little like rain today. I better take this (referring to his umbrella)." Beaver then shakes Ward's hand and when Ward bends down, Beaver hugs and gives him a kiss.

"The Bank Account" – Ward is all about saving money. He brings the boys home a piggy bank. They save money for weeks and finally decide to spend their money on two baseball gloves. Ward says maybe they should put it in their school bank account. They later tell him they have decided to deposit the money in their account. They take the money to school, but instead of depositing it in their account, they withdraw some money. When Ward finds out the boys have spent all that money at the most expensive sporting goods store in town, Abernathy Potts, Ward is quite upset. After the package arrives, he orders the boys to come downstairs. He shows them the package and tells them, they're going to open this together and decide whether it was a waste of money or not. And if it was, they will return it. He opens the package, and his demeanor changes. He lifts a brand-new men's hunting jacket… looks at it admiringly, he pauses… he looks at the boys and says softly, "Me?" And they nod "yes." A moment ago, I had to look at the scene again to get that quote correct . . . and yes, I had tears in my eyes.

"Cleaning Up Beaver" – Beaver is a mess. He's a slob. Wally is growing up and wants to be clean. They can no longer co-exist. That is why Beaver moves into the guest room. He doesn't want to share a room with a clean guy like Wally. June laments the boys growing apart. It's like an end of an era for her, having the boys no longer sharing a room. Thank goodness for fear. Beaver, in his first night out of the bunkbeds, hears creepy noises, cats yowling, and sees shadows lurking and it all leads to a fearful crescendo that has Beaver running back to his bedroom for protection from Wally. Beaver bravely asks Wally if he's okay and not scared. They talk for a moment or two and Wally tells Beaver, before he leaves, that if he needs anything, to just holler. Beaver says the same to him. Then Wally comes up with the good idea that Beaver should just stay because it could save a lot of hollering. Beaver gets excited and jumps in bed with Wally. They then discuss why Beaver got mad and moved out. Beaver says it was because Wally got neat, called him a pig and then kidded him. They come to an agreement for Wally to be a little sloppier and for Beaver to be a little bit neater and Beavers says, "It might just work out." June was quite happy to see Beaver back in his room.

"Music Lesson" – Ward voices his pleasure with Wally for becoming the first-string pitcher on his baseball team. In contrast, Beaver must tell his dad he is not a good player, and he was not allowed to be on the team. Beaver is a bit sad he can't really do anything good. The next school day, Beaver decides to go out for the band. He finds out soon enough, he's not good enough for baseball or band. He pretends to be in the band and carries on that charade all the way up to their first recital. Beaver, worried about what is going to happen, even puts on a suit on the evening of the performance and continues the charade. Wally goes to Ward and tells him and June about what happened and how Beaver didn't want to disappoint him again, so he pretended to still be in the band. Beaver comes down a moment later and Ward says that something had come up that would prevent them from going to the performance at school. Beaver goes back upstairs. June tells Ward to imagine what Beaver's gone through the previous few weeks just so he would still be proud of him. That's when Ward shares this wonderful piece of advice, "We'd be a lot better parents if we didn't wait 'til they did something good to let them know we're proud of them… every once in a while, just for no reason at all, we ought to tell them we love them."

"Boarding School" – Oooh, that Eddie Haskell. If not for him, Wally would not be in the bathroom washing his face, because he was crying. A moment later, Beaver is on the stairway as Ward starts going up to talk to Wally. Beaver asks, "Dad, why don't you like Wally anymore?" That prompts a deep conversation and Ward is now fully prepared to talk with Wally. June sees Beaver and tells him she's going up to talk to Wally too. But Beaver says, "That's okay mom, I think me and dad just took care of it." She looks thoughtfully at him and sits down next to him to hear him explain.

"Beaver Runs Away" – When Ward was a child, he ran away from home. His dad just let him go and didn't do anything to try to stop him. It did not make him feel wanted or loved. It was like he was dispensable. But when Beaver threatens to run away, he treats Beaver the same way. Why? Well, in the closing moments of the episode, Beaver asks him that same question and Ward responds with these words after taking a moment to gather his thoughts: "Well, I guess I made a mistake Beaver. I guess I was so anxious to be right that I kind of forgot what it felt like when I was a little boy." Beaver listens intently and when Ward finishes, Beaver reaches to shake Ward's hand and says, "Good night dad," and walks upstairs to bed. All is forgiven.

"The Visiting Aunts" – Apologies are oftentimes very sentimental. In this episode, Beaver and Wally go to the kitchen to apologize for their actions during Aunt Martha's visit. Wally gives a touching apology when he says, "Sure, we wanted to go the carnival, but gee, there's a lot of carnivals, but a guy doesn't get to have too many mothers." June really appreciates their apology and things turn out just fine when the entire family goes over in the evening to enjoy the carnival, and "doggie" burgers at The Chuckwagon.

"Beaver Gets Adopted" – Beaver is looking for new parents. He gets the idea from Ward, but Ward didn't actually mean he should go out and get new parents. But that's exactly what Beaver does when he visits the local adoption agency. After talking to Mrs. Brady, the woman in charge of the office, she tells him she'll be back in a few moments. The longer Beaver waits, the more it looks like he's having second thoughts. She calls the Cleavers with a plan and has them come down to the agency. Mrs. Brady then talks to Beaver as she waits for Ward and June to arrive. He expresses even more second thoughts, but she assures him this set of parents is the perfect couple and are looking for a boy just like him. When Ward and June walk in, she tells Beaver, "I think these are the people I talked to." Beaver turns to see his parents and has a look of shock on his face…which quickly turns into a huge hug and smile, as he wraps his arms around June. Whew, that was a close one. Beaver without Ward and June would've been terrible.

"Most Interesting Character" – Stupid Judy is writing her "most interesting character" essay about her father. Beaver dismisses the idea of writing about his own father almost immediately. But Wally convinces him that Ward would like to have an essay written about him. He reasons with Beaver, "If you were a father and you had a kid, well, you'd like it if the kid liked you." That's when Beaver decides to write his essay about Ward. But after not finding anything interesting to write, and one attempt at lying about his dad in the essay. He tries again with something more authentic. Here's that essay in its entirety: "The most interesting character I have ever known is my father, Mr. Ward Cleaver. He does not have an interesting job. He just works hard and takes care of all of us. He never shot things in Africa or not saved anybody that was drowning, but that's alright with me because when I am sick, he brings me ice cream, and when I tell him things, or ask him things, he always listens to me, and he will use up a whole Saturday to make junk with me in the garage. He may not be interesting to you or someone else because he's not your father, just mine." Beaver says he doesn't know if it sounds too good, but it sure made him feel good to write it. Ward agrees and says it made him feel good to read it. Okay, pass the tissues.

"Wally's Glamour Girl" – In this episode, it's Wally who has a problem. He has a date with a girl he corresponded with while he was away at camp. He told her a bunch of lies about how popular and rich he was in order to keep her writing him back during camp. Now, his untruths are about to come home to roost. She's in town and her mother has asked June if Wally will take her to a dance at the country club. He comes clean and tells Ward about his problem. Of course, Ward has a solution. Just go over there and tell her the truth. Ward must drive him since Wally doesn't really have his own car as he told her he did. He asks that Ward park the car down the street for a few minutes so he can tell Kitty what a nothing he is without anyone being around to see. Ward says if he wants, he'll wait twenty minutes. After coming clean to Kitty about his lack of a car and admitting to the other untruths, she says, "You said you didn't have a car, Wally. Is that one of your friends out there waiting to drive us to the dance?" Wally looks the direction of his dad's car and says, "You know… um… I never thought much about it before, but, I guess he's probably one of the best friends I've got."

"Nobody Loves Me" – Beaver is at that awkward age when he thinks no one loves him. He's gangly and clumsy and his voice is changing and everything else that goes along with puberty. Wally comes down near the end of the episode and says Beaver's been in the bathroom and thinks he's been crying. Ward and June are determined to go up and say the right thing, but June wonders what exactly they will say. "I think somehow we'll know what to say, if we just remember that a boy Beaver's age needs more assurance of love and understanding than he ever has before." They then go up with that in mind and see Beaver lying on his bed. He says he feels sick. Ward and June make a fuss over him and even take his temperature. As it is being taken, Ward discusses with June, a co-worker and his child who is about Beaver's age. The father is having problems because his son doesn't think he's loved any longer just because he's going through changes. Ward comments that the boy is not very bright and can't understand that his parents still love him and maybe show it in different ways. Beaver is listening intently to their conversation. Ward takes the thermometer and looks at it and says, "Absolutely normal." Then looks down at Beaver and adds, "Normal in every way." Beaver's smile is probably the largest it's been since he won the sports car in "Beaver's Big Contest."

"Beaver's Football Award" – Beaver has a tendency to give into peer pressure and believe some of the wildest things his friends or classmates say. In this episode, the quarterback of his team says he's not wearing a coat and tie to the awards banquet. Other teammates agree not to wear a coat and tie either. That causes trouble in the Cleaver house on the night of the banquet. Beaver is bound to win the "Most Inspirational Player" award and he insists on not wearing a coat and tie. That would be embarrassing. Despite the protestations of June and Ward… Ward eventually allows him to just go in a shirt and sweater. He tells Beaver he'll pull the car around and to be downstairs in a few minutes. They go to the awards banquet and beaver is surprised to see Terry and the other players all wearing coats and ties. A few moments later, he asks Ward if they can leave to go home because he's feeling sick. He gets out to the car and Ward brings out a coat and tie and from the car trunk. Beaver feels much better. This is reminiscent of "Wally's Suit." Most of the time, parents do know best.

"Wally Buys a Car" – Respect can be sentimental, especially to a father when that respect is given by a son who is growing up and showing maturity. Wally is maturing and it's time for him to buy his first car. He could've wound up with a real clunker, but Ward prevents that from happening. In this episode, Wally gives his father due respect with just a few simple words. They occur in the final scene after they come home from eating out and being chauffeured by Wally in his new $180 car. "Boy, if you hadn't come along with me, I could've really been taken. It really meant a lot to me," says Wally. Ward pats him on the arm and replies, "Well, it means a lot to me to hear you say that." No other words were needed. The scene is a wonderful portrayal of mutual respect between a father and a son. A job well done by director David Butler.

"The Silent Treatment" – This episode has always been one of my least favorite and from comments by *Leave it to Beaver* fans in various Facebook groups, it is not a favorite of many people. However, after watching for research purposes while writing this book, I came to have a newfound appreciation for it. One must get through the tough parts i.e. Beaver treating his mom terribly because he is mad at her and get to the end where she is very much needed by Beaver. He gets stung by a bee and of course, he runs straight to the caring mother after all episode ignoring her. Their conversation while June is doctoring him up is very touching and needs to be watched in its entirety, a few quotes here would not do it justice. It highlights the care that a mother has for their child and speaks of how a mother knows when a child his hurt or unhappy with the child not having to say anything at all. Beaver winds up telling her he's no longer mad at her and he admits he's happy that the bee stung him. She returns that gratitude with a hug and a kiss.

I think the above examples are the best of the sentimental moments found in *Leave it to Beaver's* six seasons. Among them, there must be a couple you simply adore. If you want to read about some more sentimental moments from the show, visit http://leaveittobeaverbooks.com.

20

NEWSPAPERS

The era in which the Cleavers lived (1957-1963), was before the massive decline in newspaper readership we see today. It was in this time that a majority of news was gathered from either a morning or an afternoon newspaper. Due to a lack of continuity in some episodes of *Leave it to Beaver*, sometimes Ward read the daily newspaper in the morning instead of his usual early evening read after work. The episode, "The Book Report," is one example of a weekday morning reading. But whether Ward and June read the paper in the morning or the evening, one thing is for certain, the newspaper was a big part of their everyday lives. It was such a big part that it was read in the Cleaver house, by either Ward, June, Wally or Beaver, (and Uncle Billy once) in 48% of all episodes.

Newspaper Names

Were there many different newspapers in Mayfield? If you look at the episodes in which you can identify the papers themselves, that's a definite, "yes." Let's look at that list of newspapers:

1) *Mayfield Press* (36)

2) *Press Herald* (2)

3) *Daily Dispatch* (2)

4) *Courier Sun* (2)

5) *Maple Drive News (Beaver's Paper)* (1)

6) *The Bulletin* (1)

7) *The Daily Chronicle* (3)

8) *The Ledger* (1)

9) *Capital City Times* (2)

In the case of the *Press Herald* and the *Courier Sun*, the names of those papers seemed to have come about due to newspaper mergers. There are real life examples of such mergers and newspaper names, you can probably think of some on your own. Here are two examples of such mergers. The *Birmingham Post-Herald*, a newspaper in Alabama that went out of business in 2005, went through a merger in 1950 when the *Age-Herald* merged with the *Birmingham Post*.[75] The Los Angeles Herald Examiner was also a product of a merger. In 1962, the *Los Angeles Herald-Express* merged with the *Los Angeles Examiner*.[76] So, the same

---

[75] "Scripps Closing 'Birmingham Post-Herald,' Dissolving JOA." *Editor and Publisher*, September 22, 2005.
[76] Pasternak, Judy Pasternak and Thomas B. Rosenstiel. "Herald Examiner Will Halt Publishing Today," *Los Angeles Times*, November 2, 1989.

probably happened with the *Press Herald* and with the *Sun Courier* where the boys worked as paper boys ("The Paper Route") and where they placed a classified ad for a lost dog ("Beaver and Poncho").

The above newspapers are the only ones with complete names shown on the front pages, or in the case of *The Ledger*, mentioned as a newspaper. Fred Rutherford mentions *The Ledger* to Mr. Langley in "The Parking Attendants." We can only make assumptions to what some of the other complete names are, so here, try to fill in the blanks:

1) _____ *Herald (could be the Press Herald)*

2) _____ *Bulletin*

3) *The* _____ *Globe*

Headlines

What has always been interesting to this *Leave it to Beaver* fan and to many others is to find out any information possible about the town in which the Cleavers reside. What better way to do that than to scour the Mayfield newspapers for information. Since we're unable to physically turn the pages of any of the above-mentioned newspapers, the best we can do is look at the headlines, or stories seen on interior pages. Let's look at some of the headlines:

Heat Wave Mounts; No Relief in Sight ("Water Anyone?)

HIGH WINDS SWEEP CITY ("Lonesome Beaver")

Limited Farm Bill Favored ("Lonesome Beaver")

American Racing Legend ads British Citizenship ("Lonesome Beaver")

New Tax Bill May Be Needed ("Lonesome Beaver")

Engineer is killed as Limited Crashes ("Lonesome Beaver")

Paroled Murderer (partial headline) ("Beaver's Cat Problem")

Thompson Williams Sign Title Bout Today ("Beaver's Poem")

Wanted for Murder (partial headline) ("Forgotten Party")

Jury Awards $45,000 Judgement Against Cab Company ("Beaver Takes a Walk")

Publisher's Daughter, Editor, Rescued from Kidnaping Gang ("Beaver Makes a Loan")

MURDERESS STRIKES AGAIN ("The Spot Removers")

After the fourth season began, two things related to newspapers changed. First, the newspaper seen in shows was the Mayfield Press 94% of the time. No more random newspaper names. Second, no more headlines are seen other than that of "Paroled Murderer" in "Beaver's Cat Problem" (S5 EP 5). However, there are two news stories seen in the interior pages of the

Mayfield Press in the later seasons and those were about North Mayfield having a new sewer line built ("Wally's Dinner Date") and construction starting on a new hospital in Mayfield ("Wally's License"). One thing that stands out if one were to take seriously the headlines, believing they were actually from a newspaper in Mayfield, instead of just props, is the fact that there was a lot of crime in Mayfield. In the above-mentioned headlines from eight papers, 37% of them concern murder. Gee, that's a lot of murder in Mayfield.

Beaver in the News

"Price of Fame"

Beaver is gullible. Maybe the best example of this is seen in "Price of Fame" when he believes Larry's lie about Mrs. Rayburn having a spanking machine in her office. Beaver winds up getting locked in the office with no way to call for help. He pulls the fire alarm and is rescued. The firemen drop him off at home in the fire truck. That's a lot of fun for a young boy, but embarrassment for the family. On top of everything, the newspaper writes up a story about Beaver being driven home in the fire truck. But Wally tells his parents that Chester said it was just a small hunk of a story.

"Beaver Becomes a Hero"

In this episode, Wally and Beaver are fishing and find a canoe floating in the lake. Beaver rescues the canoe. There's no one in the canoe and he didn't go out far to rescue it. However, when the kids finish spreading the story to others and Miss Landers hears it, Beaver has rescued a girl and the canoe has turned into a speedboat. Judy tells Miss Landers that the local paper pays $25 for an interesting news item, and she submits it to *Mayfield Press,* and they print it.

"Beaver's Football Award"

Beaver refuses to wear a coat and tie to a football awards banquet ceremony. He believes all the other kids will be going casual, thanks to Terry, the big mouth quarterback. Ward saves the day by having Beaver's coat and tie in the trunk and allowing Beaver to change after he's embarrassed that everyone else is dressed up and he is wearing a sweater instead of a coat. Good thing he changed because the award winners that evening had their picture taken for the next morning's paper. Beaver had his picture taken with former football star Mule Saunders.

"Tell it to Ella"

Tell it to Ella is the name of an advice column for the local newspaper. Beaver has a beef with his parents about staying out on school nights. Eddie Haskell convinces Beaver to write Ella and to get her to side with him against his parents. While it doesn't work out the way he wants, and his letter uses the anonymous name of "Prisoner," nevertheless, here's another time Beaver makes it into the local newspaper.

"Beaver the Hero"

We all know Beaver is a pretty levelheaded kid, but even a levelheaded kid can get thoughts of grandeur stuck in his head if enough people continuously tell him he's amazing. That's what happens in this episode, and if teammates telling him he's amazing was not enough, having a picture of him catching a winning touchdown pass, sealed the deal. Beaver's head grew big and it's a wonder he could fit through a doorway. He was so full of himself by the end of the episode that he believed he was so important that he did not have to go to football practice. Well, he gets suspended from team because of that belief. This was the biggest news event that put Beaver in the pages of the local Mayfield newspaper.

The *Leave it to Beaver* era is captured perfectly with how the writers and set decorators used newspapers in the individual episodes. From Ward bringing in the newspaper after work to the kids asking to read the Sunday comics, the series is splashed with reality from newspaper history. Sometimes, fans long to go back to the more simple days, an easy way to start would be to subscribe to your local newspaper.

Check out http://leaveittobeaverbooks.com for more information on newspapers in the show and see the actual headlines.

21

INSULTS

In *Leave it to Beaver*, insults were heard quite often, and they were equally doled out by all of the characters, Beaver to Wally, Wally to Beaver, Wally to Eddie, Lumpy to Beaver. Believe it or not, Ward Cleaver even insulted Fred Rutherford in one episode, although Fred was his usual oblivious self and didn't even realize he was being insulted. And Fred Rutherford's son was always an easy target, as Fred, on more than one occasion, told Lumpy he was a "big oaf" and Lumpy's friend Eddie Haskell in "Wally's Test" told Lumpy he was a "dope."

Over fifty years after Eddie first insulted his friend Lumpy, the actors who portrayed Eddie and Lumpy were friends in real life and Eddie was still insulting Lumpy, or rather, Frank Bank, the actor who portrayed Lumpy. When they were interviewed by Stu Shostak for an episode of Stu's Show back in 2008, Stu stumbled a bit over Frank Bank's introduction and in true Eddie Haskell fashion, Ken pipes up with, "It's hard to say something good about him." A little friendly insult to start the show. In an earlier Stu Shostak interview (March 5, 2008), Frank is talking about being at Trader Joe's in the healthy food section and Ken chimes in with, "What do you know about the section with healthy foods Frank?" (a little insult about Lumpy/Frank's weight). So, fifty years later, Eddie can still dish out insults as if Connelly, Mosher, MacLane and Conway were writing them for him.

I think we can we all agree that insults are rather fun. Of course, not so much if we are the target of one. But to listen to them either in person, if they are said jokingly, like in a game called the "dozens," or when one of our favorite characters says one on a TV show or in a movie, can be quite amusing.

As mentioned above, all the characters on *Leave it to Beaver* are good at handing out insults. Some are one-word insults that simply consist of calling someone a name, like "rat" and then repeating it multiple times like Beaver would do on quite a few occasions. But other times, the insults were more complex and of everyone on the show, Eddie Haskell had the type of character one would think should be the master of insults. He did have a few zingers: "Gnaw down any trees today?" (Eddie to Beaver in "Beaver the Model?"). "Shut up fat boy!" (Eddie to Larry in "Beaver's Bad Day"). "Why don't you do your family a favor and get lost?" (Eddie to Beaver in "More Blessed to Give.")

Insulting the athletic skills of a person can be pretty demeaning too, especially if the person being insulted is a good athlete. This occurred in "Eddie's Double-Cross" when Wally takes the advice of Ward and tells Eddie that Caroline (pronounced Carolyn) Shuster, thought Eddie was a conceited creep and that she was using him so she would have something to do while her real boyfriend was grounded. Eddie gets upset and tells Wally he was just trying to get Caroline for himself and some other nonsense and then, as he stormed out of the room, said, "And you're a crummy basketball player too."

Sometimes insults on the show are just simple and to the point as when Beaver finds out in "Beaver's Team," that Penny told the Tigers of the secret play the Lightning Eleven were going to use to win the football game. Beaver just plainly and calmly told Penny, "You're a real dumb girl." Judy, who was the mean girl in Beaver's class, prior to Penny's arrival, was good with a simple insult too as she demonstrated in the "Music Lesson" episode. After listening to Beaver play the clarinet, she states, "You're awful."

Now, you may be like me, and think of Eddie as a guy with a sharp sense of humor and the ability to insult with impunity, but while researching every episode, I found that while Eddie could sometimes dish out the insults, they were nothing compared to what Wally says to Beaver in "Beaver's First Date." In this episode, Wally is trying to help Beaver with his dancing ability since he has a date with Betsy from dancing school class in a few days. Wally feels Beaver is utterly helpless and lets him know it. "You dance like a duck, your shirt tail is hanging out, you haven't had a bath in two days and your hair's full of sand." Talk about being hard on a brother.

Wally dishes the insults out to his brother numerous times. If all you had to go on was insults, one might assume Wally doesn't think Beaver is the brightest rodent in the animal world. Here's just a small list:

What a goof! ("The Haircut")

You and Larry are little babies. ("The Haunted House")

You're throwing like a girl. ("Beaver's Prize")

Hey, you dumb little creep. ("Beaver Becomes a Hero")

You're a dumb little kid. ("Chuckie's New Shoes")

You're a dumb little kid. ("Ward's Millions") five episodes later

Boy, Beaver, you must be the dumbest kid in your whole school ("Beaver's Report Card")

Sometimes I think you're a real dumb kid. ("Weekend Invitation")

You know something Beaver... You're sickening. ("Silent Treatment")

When it came to Beaver and insults, it was always his involvement with a girl when the most insults were hurled in an episode. This occurred in "Beaver, the Sheepdog," "Beaver's Autobiography," and "Farewell to Penny." These are the three most insult-laden episodes of the entire series. In the latter episode, Penny and Beaver exchange their typical insults in the classroom and in the hallway. Beaver had forgotten his presidents when asked in class to name them and Penny is right there to tell him he's a dummy. Whitey even insults Beaver after class, saying, "It doesn't pay to be stupid." Beaver then perfectly recites the presidents and says it's all because of Penny that he messed up. He claims she put a hex on him with her creepy face and calls her a zombie. She tells Beaver he's "a stupid little rat" and he retaliates with, "You're a funny looking goat!" She comes back with a classic, "You're a goony hunk of nothing," one of the best insults on the show.

Later, when Beaver finds out Penny is moving away. He comes to realize he will miss her, even her insults. Penny and Beaver, at her going away party, share their mutual attraction toward each other. They admit they will miss each other and like each other, but only because it is safe to do so because they will no longer see one another. Then, everything changes when Penny gets to stay until the end of the year by moving in with her grandmother. When Beaver finds out, he's upset and finds her in the hallway before school the next day to say he didn't mean any of the goofy stuff he had said about her, such as that he liked her and would miss her. She promptly calls him a "creepy little rat" and he responds with, "Funny looking spook!" And she finishes with, "Stupid little goof," and then turns to enter the classroom. Beaver stands at the doorway admiring her anger, and his skill for insults that caused it.

In "Beaver, the Sheepdog," one of the funniest episodes of the sixth season, Beaver's classmate Shirley calls Beaver a sheepdog, an insult referencing his messy hair. He eventually wants to get her back and insult her in such a way that will leave her dazed and not able to respond. Eddie Haskell to the rescue. He provides Beaver with the following insults:

Hey, you, I've seen better looking faces on iodine bottles.

Hey, I remember you, you're the cover girl for Mad Magazine.

She started to have her face lifted, then saw what was underneath it, so they put it back down.

Hi ugly, is that your face, or are you breaking it in for a monkey?

Is that your nose, or are you eating a banana?

While those are good, Beaver uses the following two insults the next day, "Halloween's over, why don't you take off your mask?" and "Hey ugly, the last time I saw a face like that, it was on a clock, and a cuckoo came out of it." Shirley immediately breaks down in tears and Beaver immediately gets in trouble when Shirley's friends tell Mr. Bailey that Beaver was picking on Shirley.

The writers of *Leave it to Beaver* got even with Beaver Cleaver a few months later when they gave a grammar school vixen named Melinda Nielsen, a transfer student from Savannah, Georgia, the following line: "You're nothing but a miserable cotton-picking little creep!" That insult worked perfectly when combined with her soft, and syrupy sweet southern accent.

As mentioned earlier in the chapter, Wally had a way with insults, but his best insult, by far, was reserved for his best friend Eddie Haskell in the episode, "The Parking Attendants." After messing up the entire afternoon by parking Fred Rutherford's car in a no parking zone and getting it towed away and impounded, and then saying some silly remarks, Wally gives Eddie a much-needed dose of reality, "Eddie, did anyone ever tell you that you're a big dumb stupid loudmouth?"

The biggest surprise about this insult was Eddie's response, "Gee, no, Wally, why would anybody do that?"

Talk about being oblivious….

Here's a few more insults from the series you may enjoy:

"You're the meanest guy in the whole class." (Beaver to Larry in "Beaver's Guest").

"Usted tiene una cara como puerco." (Eddie teaches this to Beaver in "Beaver and Chuey").

"Violet Rutherford drinks gutter water." (Sign on Violet Rutherford's back in "The Black Eye").

"You're a smelly old ape." (Beaver to Linda Dennison in "Her Idol").

"I bet you were a real homely baby." (Judy to Beaver in "Baby Picture").

As with all chapters, feel free to visit http://leaveittobeaverbooks.com to enjoy more content.

22

ALCOHOL & TOBACCO

It's always interesting to see how more mature topics are addressed or how often they are mentioned in shows that feature child actors and storylines that are told from the view of children. In *Leave it to Beaver*, the world is shown as how a child might see it. In the beginning, these children, Beaver and Wally, are in second grade and eighth grade respectively.

So, when it comes to alcohol, how often is it mentioned specifically or alluded to in the episodes? What about tobacco? This chapter will examine these two vices, which are found in many more *Leave it to Beaver* episodes than you might think. Before we begin, you probably have noticed that when it comes to the pilot episode, "It's a Small World," I rarely reference it in any of the lists found in this book, although it is included in the episode guide. But since that episode has one of the best lines about alcohol use, I felt compelled to include it here.

Alcohol

Sometimes, in the episodes of *Leave it to Beaver* which mention or allude to alcohol use, the effects of drinking are what the characters speak about. This is seen in the pilot episode, "It's a Small World." In this episode, Ward is having a conversation with Mr. Baxter from the Franklin Milk Company and wonders why he would give his boys a bicycle if their company was not sponsoring a contest giving away a bicycle. Mr. Baxter (Richard Deacon) is at a loss for words, that's when Ward (Max Showalter) gives his best line of the pilot episode, "I know you work for a milk company, but there are indications of a much stronger beverage here."

In "Captain Jack," after the character Captain Jack (Edgar Buchannan) tells the boys that putting a bit of brandy in the milk they feed their baby alligator makes it healthy and happy, Ward begins noticing that the brandy bottle is steadily losing some of its contents. After hearing their maid Minerva happily singing while doing the laundry, Ward begins to suspect she has been taking nips of the brandy. When she comes running out of the basement yelling in fright that she's seen an alligator, it removes all of Ward's doubts.

Similar to "Captain Jack," which had two references to alcohol, the same goes for the "Water Anyone" episode. The first reference is when Ward hears banging sounds. June remarks it sounds like someone walking up the side of the house. Ward shakes off that suggestion saying, "No, that only happens on New Year's Eve." Later, June asks, "Ward, wasn't there a Cleaver way back in your family who sold guns to the Indians?" He tells her, "No, that was whiskey. He just got them in the mood to buy guns."

When the Cleavers go to a wedding with the Wilsons in the "Child Care" episode, Ward offers Janet Wilson another glass of punch. She refuses, saying the last one went straight to her head and she's feeling "absolutely giddy." When her husband tells her it was only pineapple juice, she then says, it must be all the excitement getting to her.

In "Beaver, the Bunny," after running into a telephone booth, Beaver calls the police. His problem is that there's barking dogs surrounding him. They think he's a bunny and he tells the officer his name is Beaver. The police officer remarks to a fellow officer, "Boy, we usually don't get calls like this so far before New Year's." Eventually all turns out well and Beaver is picked up by the police and taken to school so he can be in the pageant.

As Wally grows up, Ward knows he will have to make decisions about what kind of person he is to become. Knowing bad company corrupts good character, Ward does worry a bit when he finds out Wally and Eddie have been recruited to join the Barons. In this episode, "One of the

Boys," Ward finds out they are a social club made up of entitled, well to do students who do not care about their education. Wally soon finds out that the club is not made up of good guys. He gets an inkling of that at lunch, only hours before the big membership meeting that evening. Ward never tells Wally what to think about the club and finds out after Wally returns home from the meeting that it wasn't necessary for him to do so. Wally says the guys played pool, but he says, "Most of the time, they just sat around and knocked stuff. You know, the school, other people. Just about everything." He later tells Ward the guys wanted to go somewhere for beer and he and Eddie just walked back to Eddie's house for a while. Wally knows how to make good choices.

In "All-Night Party," the Mayfield High graduating class is having an event held at the local country club. Food, dancing and per the ground rules set out by a group of parents which included Ward and June, no beer or liquor. Wally heartily agrees. Now, if he can only get Kathy Gregory's dad to let her go to the party. After meeting Wally, Mr. Gregory says he'll allow Kathy to go with him. That's great news for Wally and Kathy. But then, after the party is over, some drunk man comes out of nowhere and bumps Kathy into the fountain in front of the country club. Her dad has a fit. Wally comes to her rescue when he finds out she's been grounded. Wally explains everything to Mr. Gregory and defends Kathy, proving Wally is indeed turning into a very mature and caring young man and soon to be college man.

The above two mentioned episodes which reference alcohol center on high school students and whether or not they will make decisions to drink, but what about adults? The first episode to mention in this section is "Box Office Attraction," which spans high school age with post high school age when Wally expresses interest in a girl who works at the Madison Theater. Her name is Marlene and Beaver's seen her around. Yes, Beaver saw her in a bar smoking a cigarette and drinking a beer. Wally has no idea what he's in for, especially when she has him park the car as they go out on their date. She jumps him and tries to start kissing Wally. He's shocked and pushes her away. Then she suggests going to a bar, and even other bars. Wally finds out on his own that he's out of her league and he really doesn't want anything to do with that league. He leaves her at Hank's Place and goes home. He ends up telling Ward that he and Marlene just didn't dig each other.

There are some moral dilemmas found in "Beaver, the Caddy." The most evident one is when Mr. Langley makes a $500.00 bet with Art Howard and has Beaver write down wrong scores so he would win the bet. Yes, that's the big moral dilemma in the episode. But when trying to explain why he cheated, Mr. Langley tells Beaver he'd had a few drinks when discussing the bet with Art Howard and he says to Beaver, "You know how that is..." and Beaver says he doesn't know. He's most likely talking about being buzzed or drunk and making a bad decision while being in such a state. Then, to top it off, Mr. Langley asks Beaver to caddy for him and cheat again so he loses and can give back the money to Art Howard. Do two wrongs make a right? No, they don't.

The most well know episode of *Leave it to Beaver* which speaks about alcohol is "Beaver and Andy." The subject matter of alcoholism was not common fodder of situation comedies in 1960. The episode begins with Beaver telling his father a man is outside wanting to speak with him. It's Andy, a painter who once worked for the Cleavers years earlier. Ward and Andy exchange some niceties and then Andy asks Ward for a job. When asked about his "trouble," Andy tells Ward that he hasn't had that trouble for five or six months and then gives Ward a couple references he can call if he wants. Ward says that won't be necessary and gives him a date to start. Beaver asks about Andy's *trouble* and Ward says, "it's nothing." If only he'd been honest with Beaver, maybe Beaver wouldn't have given him some brandy a few days later, when Andy comes into the kitchen shaking and needing something to drink. Later, Andy winds up needing Wally and Ward to help him get into Ward's car so Ward could take him wherever he lived. Beaver says he had no idea what was wrong with Andy and Ward says they were trying to protect him, but June chimes in and says they can't always protect the boys from the truth. That's a lot of wisdom from June Cleaver.

Other alcohol references include Ward speaking about drawing a beer advertisement with horses ("Beaver's Poster") and Beaver's classmate Harry says a Shirley Temple is something you drink while your father's having an Old Fashioned, both are mixed drinks, but the Shirley Temple is non-alcoholic ("The Dramatic Club"). Alcohol is one of two vices spoken about on *Leave it to Beaver* and tobacco is the other.

Tobacco

Public sentiment towards smoking has changed significantly since the year 1957 when *Leave it to Beaver* first aired. It may seem strange for us as viewers today to see smoking in a situation comedy. To be fair, smoking is only seen a few times, and spoken of or alluded to in a couple other episodes. By far, the most well-known episode which mentions tobacco use is "The Pipe." After Fred Rutherford sends Ward a Meerschaum pipe from Germany as a souvenir, it's placed on a shelf in the Cleaver living room for display. When Larry comes over to visit, he sees it and suggests he and Beaver smoke it. Beaver hesitates after Larry tries smoking it with coffee. The next day, Larry brings a bunch of cigarette butts he found at home after a party and the two friends smoke the pipe after filling it with tobacco. Larry and Beaver have never been so sick. Ward and June mistakenly believe Wally is the guilty party until Beaver finally admits what he had done.

The remaining tobacco allusions or references are very minor in comparison to Beaver smoking a pipe. They include other pipe references such as the one in which Beaver talks about Miss Hildebrand, the woman Wally had a crush on at the lake, marrying the guy with the pipe ("Beaver's Crush"). After talking to Wally and Beaver about buying June a present for her birthday, June asks why Ward was upstairs. He says he was looking for his pipe, but she remarks that he doesn't smoke a pipe ("June's Birthday). And the last pipe reference is when Wally asks whether Ward would come downstairs during his party looking for his pipe and other things ("The Party Spoiler").

The final references to mention are Uncle Billy's visit when he's holding a cigarette when he meets the boys ("Uncle Billy"), when Ward fills the cigarette lighters in the house ("Baby Picture") and when Beaver meets a transient in the city park wearing a sandwich board who sits on the park bench with him and lights a cigarette ("The Clubhouse").

You can read more about alcohol, tobacco and more by visiting the website http://leaveittobeaverbooks.com. Don't forget to sign up for free *Leave it to Beaver* gifts that will be given away after every 100th sale of *The World Famous Beaverpedia!*

23

PRICES

Below, you will find one of the few non-exhaustive lists in these chapters. There are certainly a few things with prices that are omitted. If you find any that have been omitted, you can send them to the website, and I'll add them as soon as possible to the "Prices" chapter page at http://leaveittobeaverbooks.com.

One thing a lot of fans do is find an online calculator that estimates the price of something in dollars back during *Leave it to Beaver* days and calculate how much it would be in today's inflation ravaged economy. A word of warning, not every type of item inflates at the same rate. So, those prices that are calculated are sometimes wrong. For example, a pound of ground beef the Cleavers would've bought in 1957 (73/27 fat %) was 85¢ then but is not $9.00 now – it may get that expensive if inflation keeps up, but it's not there yet. While ground beef may be overpriced by the inflation calculator, a child's movie ticket at 30¢ in 1957 is not $3.19 today. So, things like movie tickets may be underpriced by the calculator. And another very underpriced item is first class postage which was 3¢ in 1957 and the inflation calculator says that would be 32¢ today. But I would say, for the most part, the calculations are correct.

So here you go, a hunk of prices from the show for you to devour.

Food and drink

Dogie Burgers at the Chuckwagon Restaurant 18¢
Chuck roast 85¢ per pound
New potatoes 6 for 25¢
Whole uncooked chicken $1.85
Crock of two quarts of pickles $4.75

White Fox prices:

Coffee 40¢ soup 80¢ Guinea Hen $7.50 Squab Au Cresson $7.50
Lamb Cutlets Marechale $7.50 Cote de Veau Chatelaine $7.00
Calves Liver Grille Americaine $8.00 Chateau Briand A La Moelle (for two) $14.00
Sirloin Steak (for one) $8.00 Fillet of sole de Almondine $6.25

1962-1963 Menu prices at Hank's Place: Hamburger 65¢ Cold Cuts 30¢ Hot Roast Beef 75¢
Chili & Beans 40¢ Grilled Cheese 65¢ Club Sandwich 60¢ Ice Cream 20¢ Milk 10¢ Coffee 10¢

Desserts / Snacks

Double Deck Ice Cream Cone 10¢
Root Beer Float 40¢
Ice cream sodas 22¢ each (1957)
Ice cream sodas 35¢ (1958)
Banana Split 40¢
Lemonade Frost 10¢
Malted Milkshake 20¢
Strawberry Flip 35¢

Igloo ice cream bar 15¢
Quart of ice cream 60¢ each
Limeade 15¢
Giant Malts 35¢
College special - Banana Split 44¢
Movie popcorn 10¢
Ice cream soda 45¢ (1963)

Toys / Sports Related costs

Tomahawk used at Custer's Last Stand $1.98
Pogo stick $3.00
Bow and arrow set $6.50
Genuine Oriental Magic set $2.30
Model race car gasoline powered $9.38
Model airplane $2.00
Store bought kite $1.00
Baseball uniform $3.98

Football helmet $6.00
Catcher's glove for Wally $8.00
Fielders' mitt for Beaver $5.98
Brand new baseball 50¢
Professional Racing Skates $12.95
Speed flash driver golf club $13.00
Skate rental at the Ice Palace 50¢

Clothes

Ward's hunting jacket $45.12
Wally's letterman's sweater $19.00
Eddie's sports jacket $45.00
Eddie's dress shoes $16.50
Wedding dress $200
Women's blouse with Parisian landmarks $1.98
Gym socks 50¢

Sportscoat $42.00
Beaver's Sweater $12.98
Ice skates $12.95
Laundry costs 11¢ per pound at laundromat
Beaver's Jacket $23.76

House

Fixing leak in the basement $280
Hinges $3.75
Stack chairs $3.69
Exterminator $7.50 per month

Memberships

Secret club membership $1.00
Bloody Five membership 25¢
Membership in Beaver's Knighthood club 10¢
Record Club membership cost Gilbert's sister 87¢ a week

Services

Mowing a medium sized lawn, front and back $5.00
Dry Cleaning shirts 89¢ Dresses 99¢
Selling advertising space on Beaver's sandwich board 50¢ front; 75¢ back
Mr. Peck charges $5-$6 for a load of trash to take to the dump
Washing Ward's car $1.00 (for Wally and Beaver)
Shoeshine at train station 25¢
Tutor prices are $3.00 an hour
Walking the dog of a witch 50¢
Reward for lost dog $1.00 for boys from Mrs. Bennett
Reward for finding Bootsy the cat $1.00 per time

Animals

Dead frog 25¢
Half interest in a two-foot garter snake that Gilbert found 15¢
Parakeet 99¢
Parrot rental overnight $10.00
Cat food (not sure if can, bag, or multiple cans) 17¢
Stable a horse on a farm $10.00 per month
Parrot $200
White rat 50¢

Entertainment

Movie price ("Beaver's Sweater") 30¢ Beaver / 60¢ Wally
Movie admission 35¢
Mayfield Theater admission for children 40¢
Hoopla game on carnival midway 5 hoops per 10¢
Film projector $30.00
Admission to a personal baby alligator show 10¢
Price to watch teacher eat dinner 25¢ per student
Broadway or off-Broadway play (with Helen Hayes) $4.00
One hour of fishing at Shadow Lake $1.00
  - Cleaning fish 50¢ each
  - Fish at Shadow Lake $1.00 each
  -

Reading Materials

Large hard cover books $2.75
Magazine 35¢
3 used books for $1.00
Millionaire book for Ward $2.98
Daily Newspapers cost 5¢
Overdue library book fee 5¢

Automotive Related

Gallon of gas costs 32¢
New battery, lowest quality $15.00
Parts and labor to fix headlight and edge of hood $18.00
Second moving violation in traffic court $25.00
Reckless driving violation $50.00 or 10 days in jail
Gas and oil for car, $4-$5 a week
Car parts:
Horn $1.00
Taillight and rear-view mirror $1.25
Manifold $1.00
Rear wheels $3.50
Spare tire $3 -$4

Grooming

Small bottles of Flowers of the Orient perfume $1.00
Lilac fragrance hair tonic 69¢ a bottle
Adult haircut $2.25
Shampoo $1.50
Shave $1.00
Children's Haircut $1.50

School Related

Nice ink pen $1.00
Fountain pen 59¢
School music lesson $5.00
Protractor and notebook $1.25
Student activity card $2.00
School notebook 25¢

Misc.

Postage for first class mail 3¢
Braces / orthodontist work $800
Plant food $1.25 per pound
Bicycle $52.98
Brand new Canoe $200
Cross country trip two months for Wally $130
Package of pins 21¢
Taxi ride from bus station to 485 Mapleton $1.65
Photo finishing $1.25
Telescope $16.98
Orthodontic work on Jackie Waters in "Beaver's Old Buddy" $1200
Raffle tickets $1.00 each
Carbon and paper $1.25 enough for twenty-four one-page newspapers Maple Drive News
Local bus ride 10¢
Disappearing coin trick 15¢
Tie pin 25¢
Gift wrap box 25¢
120 Feet of pipe $80
Shipping a monkey from Mayfield to South America $80
Alarm clock / radio $16.95

Interested in more information on prices, visit http://leaveittobeaverbooks.com.

24

ANIMALS / PETS

You may have wondered, "How many pets did Wally and Beaver have?" That would make a rather short chapter. However, listing all animals mentioned in the show is an entirely different matter. That will take some space and time to write about and it's an interesting topic.

What animal was mentioned the most in *Leave it to Beaver* episodes? That's easy, it's that rodent called a rat. Now, that's not speaking about a pet rat, or a white rat, or a rat that lives in a junkyard. Those mentions of a rat include Beaver, Wally, Eddie, and others. The word, "rat," is used in many episodes as an insult. A lot of times, it's used by Beaver to describe girls. So, if you have to say what type of animal is mentioned the most, it is a rat. But, if we leave rats out of the equation, what are some of the other most mentioned animals on the series? Let's look season by season at the animals mentioned. This list will include animals seen and those that are only mentioned, and each section will begin with a list of all past or current pets that are mentioned during the season. Let's go!

Season One

Mentions of past or current pets: alligator, pigeons, turtle, fish, dog, rabbit, frog

All Animals Mentioned: Cat, fish, turtle, alligator, puppy, Airedale dog, canary, gorilla, silver foxes, dog, frog, dog, gopher, catfish, beetles, bugs, frogs, worms, dog, tiger, ducks, elephant, pig, worms, lions, cats, chihuahua dog, dog, cows, parakeet, gopher, buffaloes, jack rabbits, grizzly bears, turtles, goldfish, sharks, horse, worms, eagle, dog, dog, dog, horse, gopher, rat, rabbit, pigeons, caterpillar, kangaroo, white Rat, seagull, cat, dog, lion

Season Two

Mentions of past or current pets: multiple fish, goldfish, pigeons, rat, hamsters, horse

All Animals Mentioned: Birds, bear, ducks, skunk, fish, frog, fish, pigeon, oyster, lion, snakes, toads, lizards, tiger, canary, worms, trout, bears, mountain lions, fish, deer, alligator, rats, terrier dog, walrus, polar bear, rat, cow, monkey, pig, pigeons, hamsters, cat, goldfish, dog, burro, cow, pigs, dog, horse, dog, rabbit, ants, dog, cat, sheepdog, polar bear, panther, dog, dog, horse, rat

Season Three

Mentions of past or current pets: rabbit, pigeons, goldfish, parrot, hamster, dog, mouse, monkey

All Animals Mentioned: Owls, gopher, monkey, bugs, parrot, ape, grizzly bears, lion, parakeet, chinchillas, elephant, nightcrawlers, rabbit, Pekinese dog, Weimaraner dog, cat, homing pigeons, white rat, hamster, frog, eagle, dog, horse, gopher, sheep, cat, rabbit, mouse, monkey, rat, dog, cat, lion, tiger, kittens, chickens, dog, cat, fish, worms, fish, bulldog dog, pigs, dog, bear, fox, frog, bulldog

Season Four

Mentions of past or current pets: goldfish, frog

All Animals Mentioned: Dog, goldfish, worms, dog, monkey, frog, lion, frogs, dog, grizzly bear, worms, butterflies, lizards, pig, rats, fish, horses, collie puppy, monkeys, rat, bugs, frog

Season Five

Mentions of past or current pets: burro

All Animals Mentioned: Pig, cat, dog, lion, garter snake, bloodhound dog, bunny, zebra, kangaroo, snake, butterfly, pig, dogs, grizzly bear, gopher, horse, duck, rabbit, frog, burro, mule, donkey, dog, dog, rat, grizzly bear, snake

Season Six

Mentions of past or current pets: none

All Animals Mentioned: Sheepdog, gopher, camels, hippopotamus, frog, dog, sheepdog

As you can see by the lists above, the number of animals mentioned shrunk dramatically in seasons four, five and six. Possibly this is due to Beaver getting older and finding and bringing home less animals, or the writers exhausted their use of animals. There's no telling why the use of animals diminished, but interesting to see that it did lessen over time. Another thing to note is the top three animals mentioned in our list include #1 Dogs #2 Birds #3 Fish. Other interesting things this research has uncovered are that in season four, only butterflies, and a collie are animals mentioned that had not been mentioned before. In season six, the only new animals mentioned are a hippopotamus and camels.

Alphabetical list of animals mentioned or seen

Alligator, Airedale, ants, ape, bear (generic), beetles, birds (generic), Bloodhound, buffalo, bugs, bulldog, burro, butterflies, camels, canary, cat, caterpillar, catfish, chickens, chihuahua, chinchillas, Collie puppy, cow, deer, dog (generic), donkey, ducks, eagle, elephant, fish (generic), fox (generic), frog, garter snake, goldfish, gopher, gorilla, grizzly bears, hamsters, hippopotamus, homing pigeons, horse, jackrabbit, kangaroo, kittens, lion, lizards, monkey, mountain lions, mouse, mule, nightcrawlers, owls, oyster, panther, parakeet, parrot, Pekinese dog, pig, pigeons, polar bear, puppy, rabbit, rat, seagull, sharks, sheep, sheepdog, silver foxes, skunk, snakes, terrier dog, tiger, toads, trout, turtle, walrus, Weimaraner dog, white rat, worms, zebra

List of all Cleaver pets (mentioned or seen)

Alligator, burro, dog, fish, frog, hamsters, horse, monkey, mouse, pigeons, rabbit, rat, turtle

To see even more information on the animals in *Leave it to Beaver*, visit the website http://leaveittobeaverbooks.com and while there, sign up for the newsletter and for free *Leave it to Beaver* prizes.

25

NICKNAMES USED

Nicknames are sometimes used as a term of endearment. In the following list, you'll see that to be the case when used by Fred Rutherford and the few occasions Ward uses "Old Pro" and the one-time June uses "Papa" to refer to Ward. But when teens use them, there's a tinge of an insult that goes along with them, but for Eddie who uses them on any occasion, his nicknames are sort of neutral, neither insulting nor endearing. While one or two may have been missed throughout the six seasons, most all nicknames in the show will be listed below.

Nicknames Used by Eddie

Men i.e. "Hello Men"
Rock i.e. "Cut it out Rock" (Hudson)
Junior
The Lump
Sam
Muscles
Kid
Lover
Captain Igloo of the Eskimo Navy
Doc
Queen of the Dance Hall Girls
Tarzan
Champ
Doll
Buddy Boy
Short Stuff
Moe
Isabel
Brother Wolf
Little Red Riding hood and her friends
Rover
Sir Waldo the Great
Lancelot
Charlie
Gretchen
Davy Crockett
Maisie
Daniel Boone
Rover Boys
Rodney
Irma
Br'er Rabbit
Little Orphan Annie
Daddy Warbucks

Lover Boy
Lord Beaverbrook
Gilbert the Goon
Big Daddy
Jack
Junior Lawncutters of America
right-type boys
Orville
Moritmer
Elwood
Claude
Agnes
Clyde
Chum
Homer
Jeff
Fat Stuff
Smokey the Bear
Babykins
Alvin
Gwendolyn
Gertrude
Cornelius
Gladys
Chicken Little
Big Champ
Crazy Legs
Lionel
Duncan Hines
Leroy
Sam Benedict
Stella
Mr. Peepers

Nicknames Used by Wally

Hi Men	All-American	Crazylegs
Lump	Rockefeller	Don Juan
Sam	Goldilocks	Joe Pro

Used by Lumpy

Baby Face	Tiger
Gertrude	Elvis Presley of Mayfield High
Freckles	

Used by Fred Rutherford

Old Slugger	Men	Big Champ
Old Bruiser	Junie	Ole Boy
Old Man	Mrs. C.	

Used by Beaver

Men	Mad Bomber
Loverboy	The Goon Brothers
Moby Dick	

Used by Misc. People

Wise Guys – Mr. Merkel
Sis – Gus, the Fireman
Old Boy – Duke
Freckles – Whitey / Larry / Lumpy
Peachy – Carolyn Schuster
Bunny Boy – Whitey
Floppy – Whitey
Fabian – Gilbert
Cottontail – Richard
Block of Granite – Newspaper about Lumpy
Casanova - Julie Foster
Teddy - Mary Margaret Matthews / Tom Brittingham
Gilly - Mary Margaret Matthews

26

MAYFIELD AT NIGHT

Something not seen very often in episodes of *Leave it to Beaver* are scenes that take place in the evening or at night. We'll talk about plenty of them in this chapter, but they are rare. Jerry Mathers mentioned in his Archives of American Television interview that there was one time when he remembered filming at night. As state law prohibited children filming at studios after 5:00 p.m., this was one time there had to be special permission given for the filming. It occurs in season one when Beaver goes home after the scoutmaster in "Lonesome Beaver" tells him he can't be present while he "oaths" the boys in, as Beaver had asked to watch after finding out he was too young to join.

The scene in which Beaver traverses through an almost stormy night to get home, is filled with fright for him. The wind is howling, a gate on a picket fence is slamming over and over again due to the wind, and after hearing a howling coyote or wolf, he runs in fear all the way home, first going the wrong direction, turning around, losing his hat, picking it up and finally getting home to Ward opening the door for him. The look on his face when he gets inside makes it seem as if he's been terrorized.

There are plenty of other scenes in *Leave it to Beaver* which take place at night or early evening, but none of the others were filmed at night. That honor belongs only to "Lonesome Beaver." We'll examine these night scenes per season in this chapter. Also, not every night scene in the series is mentioned here, but these are some good examples.

Season One

"New Neighbors" – In this episode, in which the Eddie Haskell character makes his debut and gives Beaver "the business," Beaver is invited to the next-door neighbor's house for a get together with their niece. Beaver goes for a few moments, but quickly returns home, afraid that Mr. Donaldson may kill him because earlier in the day his wife had kissed his cheek after taking her flowers from June.

"Beaver's Crush" – This is the episode in which Beaver proves to his friends, who had teased him about being a teachers' pet, that he isn't one and does so by placing a spring snake into Miss Canfield's desk. Wally and Beaver sneak out of the house at night and sneak into the school to remove the snake. After a big dog inside the school scares them away, they get back home just in time to sneak back in their room before Ward catches them.

"The Perfume Salesmen" – Wally and Beaver are out selling perfume in the neighborhood. Ward and June anxiously await their arrival and they don't get home until after dark.

"The Paper Route" – One time, Wally comes home while it's dark and raining. Ward then takes him in the car to deliver the rest of the papers.

"Party Invitation" – Ward and June are in the kitchen as they wait for Beaver to return from the all-girl party Ward forced him to attend. Ward looks outside into the dark back yard and remarks that it is getting kind of late. Bever returns a few moments later.

"Tenting Tonight" – The boys are outside in the backyard, and it is dark at 6:45 p.m. They are spending the night in their tent since Ward was unable to take them camping as he had promised.

"Beaver Runs Away" – While not pitch dark when he leaves home right before supper, it is when he comes back home after June and Wally pick him up at Larry's house.

"Cat Out of the Bag" – When the boys take a job caring for the neighbor's cat Puff Puff, Ward is unsure they are responsible enough for the job. They prove him correct when the cat gets away and they find it in the middle of the night in a tree in their yard. Not only does Puff Puff get stuck in the tree, so does Beaver.

Season Two

"The Price of Fame" – While Beaver is trapped inside Mrs. Rayburn's office, looking for a non-existent spanking machine, the exterior of the school is shown at night. The fire department soon comes to rescue Beaver and take him home.

"Beaver's Hero" – Ward arrives home at night, late from work, and wonders why the light is on in the garage.

"Beaver, the Athlete" – In the front yard after supper, Ward teaches Beaver how to tumble. It's practically dark when they come inside. In another scene later in the episode, Beaver is very late coming home from school. Ward and Wally find him at the baseball field, with a light on, hitting baseballs at night.

Season Three

"Teacher Comes to Dinner" – Miss Landers is invited over for dinner by Mrs. Cleaver. By the time they begin eating, it is night. They eat outside on the patio and Larry, Gilbert and Whitey watch while perched in a tree.

"Pet Fair" – Ward goes out at night to visit the owner of the pet store and rent a parrot for Beaver.

Season Four

"Wally's Glamour Girl" – Wally is dreading his date with Kitty Bannerman. Ward drives him to her house the night of their date and waits in the car for them. When asked if that's a friend in the car waiting for him, Wally thinks for a moment and says, "You know, I never thought much about it before, but, I guess he's probably one of the best friends I got."

"Ward's Millions" – Beaver is upset that Ward doesn't think much about the book he gave him with all sorts of ideas on how to become a millionaire. Beaver is upset enough that he leaves the house around dusk, almost night, and climbs up a tree to be alone and feel bad for himself.

"Eddie Spends the Night" – After a fight about a chess game, Eddie leaves the Cleaver's house where he is supposed to be spending the night. He goes home and after Ward finds out from Eddie's father that the Haskells are away for the night, takes Wally over to retrieve him. After some convincing, Eddie goes back to spend the night with Wally.

"In The Soup" – Curious Beaver gets stuck in a bowl of soup on a billboard at night. All of Wally's friends are late getting to Wally's party because they're at the scene of embarrassment looking at the kid being rescued by the fire department.

Season Five

"Beaver's Long Night" – When Gilbert is allowed to spend the night, he and Beaver spend their time watching a gangster movie in the den. Not long after it ends, they see a car parked in the street outside. It's dark, Beaver doesn't recognize the car and the two shadowy characters in the car frighten Beaver, especially after watching that gangster film. Beaver calls the police and they come and haul the driver and passenger down to the police station. Beaver didn't realize the driver, who wore a mask, was Lumpy. Boy, does Fred Rutherford give Ward an earful on the telephone later.

"A Night in the Woods" – Wally takes Beaver and his friends camping. Lumpy and Eddie want Wally back in Mayfield so they can all go on their planned triple date. The only way to make that happen, figures Eddie, is to scare Beaver and friends the first night of the camping trip. He tries, but it's Eddie that winds up scared and then in peril after falling down to a ledge in the middle of the night.

Season Six

"The Late Edition" – Beaver wants a job in the newspaper industry and wants to begin by being a paper boy. He wants the route that delivers to his house. The papers are arriving to their house later each day and eventually, Ward decides he must talk to the new paper boy. Beaver waits outside to tell him his father wants to talk to him. The paper boy arrives and doesn't want to go inside and Bever knocks him off his bike when trying to drag him inside. But the paper boy is a girl and moments later, she's inside the den in tears.

"Tell it to Ella" – Near the end of this episode, Ward and Beaver come into the house very late at night. In fact, "it's practically Sunday morning."

"Eddie's Sweater" – Wally has been going over to Cindy Andrews' house for quite a few nights helping model a sweater she is making for her boyfriend Eddie. When Lumpy tells Eddie he's being two-timed, they go out one night to stake out the house and see if Wally is going over there behind Eddie's back. They see Wally and Cindy together and, in the shadows, it looks like they're hugging or maybe even kissing. Eddie is angry, but not so angry that he'll go confront Wally immediately. He waits until the next day at school to do that.

While there's not much else to say about nighttime scenes in *Leave it to Beaver* episodes, there will be a couple tidbits to add over at http://leaveittobeaverbooks.com. Don't forget to sign up to win free *Leave it to Beaver* prizes which will be given away after every 100th sale of *The World Famous Beaverpedia!*

27

POCKETS

Pockets have been around a long time. What we consider the modern pocket, one that is sewn into clothing such as pants, first appeared in the 17th century.[77] If it weren't for this modern fashion invention, where would Beaver have been able to put everything from turtle dirt ("Beaver Gets 'Spelled") to a dead goldfish ("Beaver's Short Pants") to a glass doorknob and lead soldiers ("The Haircut")?

Beaver's pants or jeans aren't the only pockets in which he keeps his goods. His jackets and shirts also make for good junk receptacles. Let's look at a statistical pocket breakdown. For Beaver, there's four places where the pockets are located… front pants pockets (50%), jacket pockets (31.3%), shirt pockets (12.5%) and rear pants pockets (6.2%).

Most of the time, the contents of Beaver's pockets are benign. They typically have no relevance on the episode in which they are found. However, there are a couple episodes in which the contents do have some bearing on the individual episode.

In the "Music Lesson" episode, June is going through the dirty laundry and finds the following in a pair of Beaver's pants: a horse tooth, dead worms, and a notice for a band concert. This is a band concert that Beaver has never mentioned. He was not chosen for the band after tryouts. He simply did not play the clarinet well enough. He pretended for about two weeks to still be part of the band. Ward and June get ready for the band concert at school and so does Beaver. Wally finally tells his parents what happened and when Beaver comes down to leave for school, Ward tells him they are unable to go the concert. Beaver was very relieved. The charade would've continued if June had not found the notice for the concert in his pants pocket.

In "Beaver Won't Eat," Beaver tries hiding his Brussels sprouts in his shirt pocket, but June is too clever for Beaver and finds them. She continues to insist that he eat his vegetables. He refuses. If she hadn't found him hiding his unwanted veggies in his shirt pocket, she may have thought he had eaten them and hence, the entire episode would've been over in five minutes.

Here's a list of everything I found in my research that was found in Beaver's pockets: turtle dirt ("Beaver Gets 'Spelled"), glass doorknob, lead soldiers ("The Haircut"), a dead goldfish ("Beaver's Short Pants"), old worms, horse tooth, band concert notice ("Music Lesson"), permission slip ("Ward's Problem"), coins ("Beaver's Newspaper"), an apple in a jacket pocket ("School Bus"), three crackers with deviled ham ("Beaver's Monkey"), worms in shirt pocket ("Beaver and Violet"), minnows in jacket ("The Spot Removers"), Brussels sprouts in shirt pocket ("Beaver Won't Eat"), frog in jacket pocket ("Beaver's I.Q."), Community Chest can in rear pants pocket ("Community Chest"), dirt in jacket pocket ("Beaver Goes in Business"), twenty-five cents ("Wally's Weekend Job"), melted candy bar ("Beaver's Jacket").

Wally and his pockets were also a big thing in *Leave it to Beaver*. Don't believe me? Just think back to the "Wally's New Suit" episode. Wally exclaims to Beaver in the menswear shop, "Boy, look at all these pockets!" That was a huge selling point for the suit. For the life of me, I can't even think what he'd put in all those pockets. He was much too old for turtle dirt,

---

[77] Summers, Chelsea. "The Politics of Pockets," *Vox.com* Sept 19, 2016.

that's for sure. An episode in which the contents of Wally's pockets launch a storyline is in "Wally and Alma." June finds Alma Hanson's phone number in one of Wally's pockets and gets Ward to find out some info on her. It turns out innocent enough but does begin a great story. Another example of an episode that would've been over in five minutes if June had not found the contents of a pocket.

Here's a list of everything in the series that is mentioned or seen from Wally's pockets: cookies ("Beaver's Poem"), a half-eaten carrot ("Her Idol"), a grilled cheese sandwich ("Price of Fame"), Alma Hanson's phone number ("Wally and Alma"), picture of Kitty Bannerman at camp ("Wally's Glamour Girl"), peanuts and candy ("In the Soup").

Now, food, as you can see with Wally in a few episodes and Beaver in a couple, gets a full-blown treatment with Larry and his pocket contents. My research shows that in the series, in twelve episodes, Larry has something in his pockets. Of these episodes Larry has food in his pockets in ten of them. In one episode, "Forgotten Party," Larry has an apple in one coat pocket, a banana in another coat pocket, and later in the episode, he has a candy bar in his pocket while at the park.

In the episode, "Beaver's Bad Day," Larry is the character with something in his pocket that if not shown, may have taken away from the overall plot. He shows Beaver some slugs he has in his pocket that he found where the new house is being built. He encourages Beaver to go over there with him to find more slugs. Beaver is not supposed to go over there, but Larry talks him into it. There is only one other non-food item found in Larry's pockets throughout the series ("Beaver's Long Walk"), and that is his watch, which he kept in his pocket.

Here is Larry's pocket contents in the series: an apple ("Wally's Girl Trouble"), apple in shirt pocket ("Cleaning Up Beaver"), slugs ("Beaver's Bad Day"), unidentified food ("Beaver and Henry"), apple ("Beaver Runs Away"), unidentified food ("The Lost Watch"), candy bar ("Wally's Present"), apple, banana and candy bar ("Forgotten Party"), crackers ("Beaver Takes a Bath") a watch ("Beaver Takes a Walk"), an apple ("Borrowed Boat") and a bologna sandwich ("Beaver's Dance").

In the series, Wally had several jobs, and in "Wally's Weekend Job," Beaver tells his friends Gilbert and Richard about Wally working at the soda fountain and invites them for free ice cream. He assumes Wally will give him and his friends ice cream at no cost. He assumed wrong. When they tell Wally they thought it would be free, he threatens to call the police if they don't cough up the dough. They rifle through their pockets in search of change, and they empty everything on the counter. Richard had a beat-up golf ball, a locker key, a gruesome looking hand, a toy Indian figure, a piece of chalk and eleven cents. Beaver had twenty-five cents, Gilbert had six cents and some baseball cards. The baseball cards which can be identified are 1959 Topps cards #437 Ike Delock, a pitcher with the Boston Red Sox; # 418, Gino Cimoli, a pitcher with the St. Louis Cardinals, #392 Whitey Herzog, Kansas City Athletics Outfielder, #416 Haywood Sullivan, Boston Red Sox Catcher and #383 Words of Wisdom, Larsen and Stengel.

For even more content to enjoy about pockets of the characters on *Leave it to Beaver*, there are pictures and a little bit more to say over at http://leaveittobeaverbooks.com.

28

POLICE AND CRIME

Wouldn't you want to live in Mayfield? It's an idyllic place. It's peaceful, friendly, they have a good school system. Mayfield is the place to be. But wait a minute. The newspaper headlines seem to scream a very different story and even the pilot episode, "It's a Small World" foreshadows what could become a vicious crime scene in the city. In that pilot episode, Wally and Beaver provide the first example of crime in Mayfield when they steal milk bottle caps off recently delivered milk to their neighbors' porches. Crime and the police response is something that should be investigated… let's do that now.

The first thing one may notice are the blaring headlines. In "The Spot Removers," Ward is reading the local newspaper and we see these words on the front page, "MURDERESS STRIKES AGAIN!" Then there are those partial headlines that are seen in "Forgotten Party" and "Beaver's Cat Problem." They read "…WANTED FOR MURDER" and "Paroled Murderer…" Wow! After reading those headlines, would you still want to live in Mayfield?

Those headlines could be fake news, after all, they were created by the prop department. But what about the police in the show? Were they seen very often? Did Beaver have any interactions with the police? He sure did. Below, we'll look at every police interaction on the show. This will be fun.

Season 1

We know that the premise of *Leave it to Beaver* was the world being seen through the eyes of a child. It's often repeated, especially in this book. This is shown immediately in the opening montage of the first episode filmed, "Captain Jack." In case you don't remember, the early season one episodes featured various clips of characters from *Leave it to Beaver*, some that are never seen in actual show footage, along with a narration from Hugh Beaumont about the week's episode. In "Captain Jack," Hugh Beaumont begins the narration, "Children and adults look at the world through different eyes. When you're young, a policeman stands ten feet tall." While reciting those words, a camera pans upward at a tall policeman, looking stoic, while swinging his billy club. This opening is brilliant directing by Norman Tokar. This is the first time we see a policeman on *Leave it to Beaver*.

We don't have to wait long to see the police appear in a *Leave it to Beaver* episode, and the wait is even less to hear them referenced. In "The Black Eye," a girl yells, "They called the cops" on the kids fighting over at Metzger's Field. Fred hears that and he's very concerned about his daughter's safety. The next reference to the police also involves the Rutherford family. In "Lumpy Rutherford," the boys place barrel hoops in Lumpy's driveway and try to lure him out to fall down while walking on them. Instead of Lumpy, Fred comes out and immediately falls and hurts himself. Later at home, Beaver wonders if the police are still checking the barrel hoops for fingerprints. Fred asks Ward if he should take a baseball cap he found at the scene down to the police. Ward says he should.

Beaver's first interaction with the police is seen in "The State vs. Beaver." Ward lays down the law with the boys about a go-cart he helped them build. Do not take the go-cart out by yourself. Larry comes over one afternoon and finds Beaver pretending to drive the go-cart. He then convinces Beaver to take the car out. When told he can't go by himself, Larry says he won't be because he'll be with him. Beaver chooses not to fight that logic and off they go. They go about a block before a motorcycle policeman drives slowly by them and tells Beaver to pull over. When asked if he has a license, Beaver says he has a license for his dog that ran away but admits he does not have a license to drive a motor vehicle. No need to worry, the judge "spunged" the ticket from his record.

There are two more episodes in season one where police are mentioned. In "Tenting Tonight" Ward suggests the boys go to the park and play Mumblety-Peg, a game played with pocketknives. However, Wally says, "They'll arrest you if you do that." The other episode is "Beaver Runs Away," when June suggests they call the police to help find Beaver.

Season 2

Lumpy Rutherford is not the nicest guy in the first couple seasons of *Leave it to Beaver*. Don't believe me? Just watch "The Lost Watch" and see how mean of a guy he can be. He loses his watch. He blames Beaver. He then threatens to call the police on him if he doesn't pay for it. That Lumpy Rutherford sure is a dirty rat. The next reference to a policeman comes in "Wally's Present" when Beaver tells Ward he couldn't return a bow and arrow set he bought for himself because a policeman wouldn't let him cross the street. He lied, but finally admits why he couldn't return the bow and arrow.

In "The Grass is Always Greener," Larry and Beaver are walking through downtown Mayfield and witness a policeman giving a woman a ticket for parking in a no parking zone. She is giving the officer all sorts of grief. She's probably still mad for buying that terrible *Flower of the Orient* perfume. She also played Whitey's mom in "Lonesome Beaver." Beaver mentions to Larry that he once wanted to be a policeman, but after seeing that woman speaking to the officer the way she did, he says he doesn't want to be one any longer.

Ward Cleaver always has great advice for his children. Some parents may think their children don't remember the wise pieces of advice they are given, but oftentimes, they do remember, especially when they encounter some sort of difficulty. This is what occurs in the episode, "Beaver Plays Hooky." This is also an episode in which a policeman is mentioned. The policeman is mentioned when the hooky incident turns into hunger and Beaver and Larry say they are starving. Beaver repeats the wise words of his father saying they should always tell a policeman when they're in trouble. Larry agrees to a point, then blurts out, "But not when you're playing hooky."

There are two police encounters mentioned in season two which happened at some previous time that are not ever seen in *Leave it to Beaver*. I call these such episodes the "Lost Episodes" and they are written about in another chapter. The first one in season two is when Beaver got lost at a football game and ward had to go prove who he was before he could take Beaver home ("Price of Fame"). The second encounter was the last time Mr. Mondello was out of town and Mrs. Mondello could not find Larry. She called the police to help find Larry and he was found asleep in a closet ("Found Money").

Season 3

In this season of *Leave it to Beaver*, we find the most police mentions and interactions out of all six seasons. Twice, these interactions are in response to a theft. The first is seen in "Borrowed Boat," where two boys from Mayfield High give Larry and Beaver a boat for them to use at Friend's Lake. Unknown to Larry and Beaver, the boat was stolen from the Friend's Lake boat house. The second theft in the season is seen in "Beaver's Bike." Can you guess what was stolen in that episode? In "Beaver's Bike," Sgt. Peterson of the Mayfield Police (not the Royal Canadian Mounted Police) visits the Cleaver house to take a report. Ward is mighty sketchy on the details about the bike, but Beaver provides Sgt. Preston with precise detail after precise detail. They eventually find the bike, but it is pretty messed up. Larry even sees the thief one day and the bicycle thief runs away from Larry.

In three episodes, the police are referred to but not seen. June wants to call the police to stop a fight between Beaver and Sonny Cartwright in "Beaver's Fortune." In the episode, "Beaver's Dance," when Beaver and Larry skip the dance, Beaver says that the police may stop them and ask questions if they see two boys walking around in blue suits. Then, in "The Hypnotist," Larry warns Beaver that if after he tells Eddie, who is pretending to be hypnotized, to go jump in the lake and he does drown, that the police will arrest Beaver.

Beaver looks to the police to give him some good news in "Beaver Finds a Wallet." Beaver finds a wallet in a gutter on Grant Avenue and does the right thing by turning it into the police department. If no one claims it in ten days, the wallet and the money inside will be his. Ward suggests placing an ad in the local paper to make it easier for the person who lost the wallet to find it. After doing so, Beaver calls the police a few times during the week to see if anyone has yet claimed the wallet. On the final day, when he arrives at the police station, he meets the woman who lost the wallet. Poor Beaver.

Now, you may not have known it, but Mayfield has two different police forces. There is the regular Mayfield Police Department which takes care of thefts like the stolen boat and stolen bicycle, but there's also the "library" police force. Well, that's what Eddie Haskell told Beaver in another case of him giving the Beave "the business." Beaver goes to the library to plead for mercy and finds out they won't send his dad to jail. They may have sent out an investigator, but not an official library policeman.

Season 4

When a boy is excited about something, he'll do anything, even try to sell a raffle ticket to a policeman. In "Beaver's Big Contest," Beaver receives one free raffle ticket for every book of ten he sells. The more people he can sell to, the better. The police officer he encounters looks very menacing and when asking if he wants to buy a raffle ticket, Beaver tells him he has a card that proves he's not a gypper. After the sale, Beaver apologizes to the officer for interrupting him from being mean to people. It takes a moment, but the officer eventually laughs.

The only other episode in season four in which Beaver has the opportunity to speak with a policeman is in "Mistaken Identity." When Beaver sees that an officer is coming to the house, he gets excited, and it shows when he comes downstairs to meet him. However, the officer looks a bit confused. Richard Rickover, earlier in the day, had been caught breaking a window in an abandoned house by this very officer. He gave the officer Beaver's name and address. The policeman and his superior apologize to Beaver and Mr. and Mrs. Cleaver.

In "Beaver's I.Q.," a policeman is mentioned in regard to the I.Q. test Beaver will soon be taking. Wally explains that a lot of the test is about common sense, like if you saw a lost girl you have to say that you would take her to a policeman. Beaver agrees he could say that, even if he wouldn't do it. In another episode, Beaver tells Ward that the cops should go over to the house of the woman who paid him for lawn mowing with a bad check. He wants them to go over in four squad cars, with machine guns and tear gas. Then, in "Substitute Father," when Beaver is not home when Wally shows up after school, he tells June that he'll go look for him and that there was no reason to call the police.

Season 5

The next reference to the police occurs in "Wally's Weekend Job," when Wally threatens to call the police on Gilbert, Richard and Beaver for not having money to pay their bill at the soda fountain. The boys rummage through their pockets and only find some of the money needed to pay the bill. Mr. Gibson motions to Wally to just let them go without paying the bill.

The most disappointing experience anyone has with the police in *Leave it to Beaver* is seen in "Beaver Takes a Drive." The policeman (badge #146) gives Wally a ticket for driving without a license. Beaver and Gilbert had been playing in the car and it rolled into the street. Wally was just driving it back into the driveway. For goodness sakes, why did the policeman give Wally a ticket? Well, some of us realize, it was just to move the story forward. If there was no ticket given, the episode would've ended right there. Nevertheless, the story does demonstrate the only negative experience a character on the show has with the police.

The only mere mention of police in this season comes in "Beaver's Ice Skates," when Beaver says his dad has a meeting with some policemen. He tells this to the salesman who gypped him with skates three sizes too big. His effort to scare the salesman to give him back his money doesn't work. Later, Ward goes to pay the man a visit and gets Beaver's money refunded.

As mentioned earlier, Lumpy isn't the nicest guy in the world. While he does eventually become a friend of Wally's, he's still able to give Wally a hard time and does so in "Wally's Chauffeur." After a dance at the country club, he blocks Evelyn Boothby's car so she can't get out. She chauffeured Wally to the club, and this was a way to give her and Wally "the business." A policeman comes along at that time and tells Lumpy to move his vehicle. He then cites him for a few violations, parking in a no parking zone, having one headlight out, and illegal pipes. Thank you, officer, for giving Lumpy his comeuppance.

The final two police encounters in season five happen in "Beaver's Bunny" and "Beaver's Long Night." In the former, Beaver calls the police from a pay phone when dogs are surrounding him, and he needs help. Again, here is Beaver heeding Ward's advice. He gets dropped off at school in time for the play, dressed as a bunny, in a police car. The latter episode has Beaver calling the police on Lumpy and Bill Scott, who are parked outside the house waiting for Wally to return from a basketball game. Beaver is home alone with Gilbert and due to them watching a gangster movie, are now afraid the mysterious car contains some thugs out to get them. The police come and take away Lumpy and Bill. Needless to say, Fred Rutherford is rather upset.

Season 6

Members of the Rutherford family seem to pop up in a few episodes when the police are mentioned or seen. This time, in "The Parking Attendants," it happens once again. But it's all Eddie's fault as he parked Mr. Rutherford's car in a no parking zone. This mishap is the reason Wally and Eddie do not get paid for a hard day of work. Wally refuses the pay and tells Mr. Langley to put it towards the impound bill for Mr. Rutherford. This isn't the only episode in which Mr. Langley is mentioned in connection with the police. A few episodes later in season six, Mr. Langley has Beaver help him win a bet, although Beaver didn't know that is what was happening at the time ("Beaver the Caddy"). Beaver confronts Mr. Langley at his office and after telling Wally what he did, his big brother says Mr. Langley could've called the police and had Beaver arrested for defamation.

Two more episodes during this season refer to the police. In "Beaver's Good Deed," a tramp named Jeff is allowed inside by Beaver. He winds up taking a bath in Ward and June's bathroom and then he steals a suit from Ward. Wally comes home and a search for Jeff ensues.

Wally tells Beaver if he sees Jeff the tramp, that he should call the cops. The final police reference occurs in "All-Night Party," when Fred Rutherford says he has a connection with the Chief of Police and could get some officers assigned to the graduation party. That's Fred Rutherford for you, he's always big on touting and sometimes exaggerating, about the connections he had.

Crime in Mayfield

Above, I wrote a little bit about the headlines seen in the Mayfield Newspapers and the crime they mention in bold print, above the fold. But one may say those papers were from another city and the Mayfield news was only seen in the local section of the nearby big city paper. In seasons one through three, that may be possible. However, in season four, the newspaper was the *Mayfield Press* about 90% of the time.

By just looking at criminal incidents in or near Mayfield, we can determine that Mayfield was a very safe place to live. No crime mentioned or alluded to ever seems to go to a criminal kingpin level. Below, you'll see a list of the crimes with the episodes in which they occur in parentheses. Not every crime, violation or offense is listed here, but enough is provided to give you a good idea that Mayfield was quite safe.

Stolen Tires – Fred Rutherford says a gang of kids stole the tires off their car when they were away on vacation in Mexico ("Lumpy Rutherford").

Fraud – An eighth grader named Roger Delacy fraudulently steals cookie fund money from Beaver and Larry and threatens them with his gang if they say anything about the theft ("The Cookie Fund").

Stolen Boat – Two high school boys steal a boat from the Friend's Lake boat house ("Borrowed Boat").

Stolen Bicycle – Beaver has his bike stolen by a boy outside the malt shop downtown ("Beaver's Bike").

Check Kiting – A customer writes a bad check to the pet shop owner ("Pet Fair").

Vandalism – A boy is arrested after removing glitter from a campaign sign ("Beaver Becomes a Hero").

Theft – A classmate of Beaver's steals items from lockers and gives them to Beaver ("Beaver and Kenneth").

Theft – The shipping foreman and the manager at the Mayfield Dairy are stealing product and selling it to stores on their way home from work.

So, there really isn't a lot of crime in Mayfield, minus the sensational news headlines seen in seasons one through three. If you would like to read more about the police or crime in Mayfield, visit http://leaveittobeaverbooks.com.

29

BRANDS

  Throughout the series, many brand names are seen. Because producers either didn't have permission to use certain brand names or did not want to promote them without being paid by the product, they often covered up brand names to look different than their real name. Other times, a real brand name is seen, but this was rare when compared with the number of times a fictional brand name is shown.

  Of all the products I found in various episodes, there were sixteen episodes in which fictional brand names are used. At least two of the products were altered by the prop department to not show a real brand name. These were a box of Hi Ho Crackers and a box of Kellogg's Corn Flakes. In these sixteen episodes there are twenty different products found:

Flower of the Orient Perfume

Screenmaster Movie Projector

Mohawk Canoes (Real company founded in 1964, seven years after the name appears in *LITB*).

Middies Cigarettes

Morely Coffee

H H Cookies (A box of Hi Ho Crackers Larry eats from in the Cleaver kitchen)

Tantilizing Tasties (Some type of cereal)

S&S Sugar

Oskar's Leather Dressing

Star Soap (seen in three episodes)

EC Thin Crackers

Delight Soda

Generic Corn Flakes

Glama-Spray Miracle Mist

Herrons Hair Oil

Slick-O

Crew Stay

Dry Dock Cigarettes

Arabian Nights After Shave

Buckskin After Shave

For one reason or another, the producers allowed certain brand names to be used on the show. This may have occurred in a few episodes because they believed their placement was in the background and could not be seen. Never in their wildest dreams did they believe there would be a way to freeze a frame fifty or sixty years in the future and dissect each episode and they probably had no idea people would even know what *Leave it to Beaver* was in the 21st century.

Here is a list of real products shown on *Leave it to Beaver*:

Keneth Hopkins Hats	*General Electric Flashbulbs*
Voit Basketball	*Wheat Chex*
Shopsmith Power Tools	*Rice Chex* (two episodes)
Dell Books	*Alka Seltzer* (implied by Gilbert that he saw an ad for the product on TV)

The difference between filming *Leave it to Beaver* in the 1950s and 60s compared to shows filmed today is the concept of product placement. In today's world of television, companies pay to have their products placed in a scene or multiple scenes. When you think of it, with the thorough research done in searching for brand names in *Leave it to Beaver,* it's amazing to have only found twenty-four episodes with twenty-eight products mentioned out of a total of 234 episodes (not counting the pilot). If it were filmed today, I think that number would be much higher.

For more information on brand names used on *Leave it to Beaver* episodes, including various screenshots of products, visit http://leaveittobeaverbooks.com.

30

JUNE LEAVES THE HOUSE

Although there is a reference June Cleaver makes to rarely getting out of her cave in one episode I watched during the research of this book, which I took note of, but now cannot place, June Cleaver wasn't always trapped at home in the kitchen or keeping house. She had many duties she took care of outside of the home. There are times she drove Ward to work and kept the car to run errands and attend meetings. There are times when she magically drives somewhere after Ward leaves to go to work with the car. Of course, we can assume she took the cab on those occasions, although no cab or taxi is called or appears. Or we can chalk those times up to the little inconsistences that appear from time to time in scripts of all classic television shows. The point is that there were two different times June left the house, those times on her own, or with one of the boys, and those times when she left the house with Ward. Let's look at both of those in this chapter.

Leaving the House **<u>WITHOUT</u>** Ward

Starting in season one, very early on, we see June leave the house to visit Mrs. Rayburn about the confusion concerning Ward's illness and the note Beaver was to bring home to his parents about being in the school play ("Beaver Gets 'Spelled"). A few episodes later, she leaves not only the house, but town, when she visits her sister Peggy after she has a baby ("Beaver's Short Pants"). June goes grocery shopping on a Saturday while Ward is at home and Beaver is out at the barber shop, not getting a haircut ("The Haircut"). She goes shopping again while Ward is putting up a basketball backboard on the garage ("The Perfect Father"). She mentions going to the market and seeing Mrs. Sutton ("My Brother's Girl"). She also goes shopping when specifically told by Ward she could have the car ("Beaver's Bad Day"). When Ward arrives home to see her in a rush to make supper, she mentions she had just returned from a meeting ("The Bank Account"). Other meetings she has include an unidentified club meeting ("The State vs. Beaver"), and a meeting at school about an upcoming dance ("My Brother's Girl"). The other times in season one when she leaves the house without Ward are when she drops the boys off at the movies ("Tenting Tonight"), delivers papers with Beaver, goes to buy Wally a model for him to make while sick in bed ("New Doctor"), and when she takes Wally out to find Beaver when he runs away ("Beaver Runs Away").

In the second season, the number of times June leaves the house drops tremendously. Of the six times, four are without Ward and three of those are for shopping. She leaves for groceries with Wally and gets the car washed ("The Grass is Always Greener"), talks about meeting Mrs. Cooper at the market ("The Haunted House"), and is out shopping while Beaver is home alone. This happens a second time in the same episode when she goes downtown to meet Ward for birthday present shopping for Beaver ("The Pipe") and June also goes to Judson's to get a toy for David Manning's party ("The Forgotten Party"). She only leaves the house for one meeting this season and that is when she goes to Mayfield High to meet with the principal Mr. Haller about Wally's hair ("Wally's Haircomb"). June also leaves to visit the school nurse when Beaver gets his ring stuck on his finger ("Beaver's Ring") and takes Beaver to the store to buy a sweater ("Beaver's Sweater").

For June, season three is a breakthrough season for leaving the house. She does so on her own like she has in the previous two seasons, but here, she's also shown or spoken of leaving the house quite often with Ward. Of the times she leaves the house, she does so on her own at least four times. She does so twice in one episode, going shopping and later picking up Ward from work ("Beaver and Andy"), she goes to the Mother's Club tea where she doesn't wear the "ghastly" blouse given to her by Beaver ("June's Present") and June visits Mrs. Rayburn about the fictional story of her life told in Beaver's composition ("Mother's Day Composition").

When season four comes, we find June again leaving the house more often, without Ward, than with him. Her journeys to the grocery store are the least of any season so far, with only one time when she goes by herself to the market ("Junior Fire Chief"). She also goes to a store on a weekday to buy Beaver poster board after he messes up the one he has been using ("Beaver's Poster"). Her other excursions away from her domicile include taking Beaver to the dentist twice ("Mother's Helper" / "Beaver's Report Card"), taking Beaver to the bank to cash the $5.00 check he received for mowing a yard ("Beaver Goes into Business"), and going to the school twice, once for an open house ("Community Chest") and once for a Mother's Club meeting ("Beaver and Kenneth").

In season five, June seems to get back into grocery shopping on her own. She's seen putting up food when Wally comes home from school ("Beaver's Ice Skates") and mentions going to the market twice ("Eddie Quits School" / Beaver's Birthday"). Another time, she goes shopping with her friend Marge downtown. She tells Ward she'll only be window shopping, but then asks where Ward put the checkbook ("Sweatshirt Monsters"). She also attends a Mother's Club meeting at Beaver's school, and she learns about Beaver's typewriter needing a repair from his teacher ("Beaver's Typewriter").

In the final season of the show, June's out of the house schedule hearkens back to the first season when she goes shopping quite often. She's putting away groceries when Ward arrives home from work ("Beaver the Caddy"), she speaks of having seen Mrs. Bellamy at the market ("Beaver's Good Deed"), she arrives home just before the boys with groceries ("Tell it to Ella") and is putting away groceries after school ("Beaver, the Sheep Dog"). She also has a Women's Club meeting at Mayfield High ("The Poor Loser"), must take Beaver to the dentist ("The Poor Loser"), go to the hair salon ("The Silent Treatment") and the woman of mystery that she is, June comes home on a Saturday afternoon dressed very well, which includes her donning a hat and gloves. This must have been some type of meeting, but it is never identified and Ward, when he comes in soon after her, never asks why she was dressed so well on a Saturday afternoon, or where she had been. His only concern was whether dinner was ready or not. Obviously, it wasn't ("Eddie, the Businessman").

Leaving the House **WITH** Ward

This section will cover those times June left the house with Ward to go places like shopping for groceries, household goods like drapes or patio furniture, playing cards with friends, and a variety of other times. The episodes listed do not include times she went with Ward and both boys, or one of the boys, for example in "Wally's Suit" when the entire family went back to the store to have the coat altered.

Of all the times June leaves 485 Mapleton in season one, she only does so with Ward on a few occasions. The first is seen when she and Ward decide to help the boys with delivering their newspapers, although they deliver the wrong papers ("The Paper Route"). June is next seen in public by everyone attending the wedding of the Clarkson's oldest daughter ("Child Care"). Later in the season, June and Ward go out looking at lots with Willis "Corny" Cornelius, leaving the boys at home to get in trouble ("The Broken Window").

June's season two outings with Ward alone are very limited. Basically, she goes with Ward just once this season anywhere with him alone. This outing is to a barbecue given by the Andersons. This planned barbecue is the reason why Ward cannot take Beaver to Crystal Falls to see his friend Billy Peyton. Instead, Wally volunteers to take him to Crystal Falls on the bus while Ward and June enjoy the barbecue.

Season three begins with a bang when June first leaves the house, but, that bang turns out to be a big splash. She and Ward go out of town for a business conference. Ward's company likes spouses to go along too. The boys get to experience life on their own, no wardens (i.e. parents, babysitters or any adult for that matter). Wally tells Beaver to take a bath while he's making hamburgers. When he calls Beaver down to supper, Beaver forgets to shut off the tub and it floods the bathroom and does damage to the kitchen ceiling ("Beaver Takes a Bath"). The other times June leaves the house with Ward during season three are a lot less traumatic or damaging. Well, if you don't include the time Ward and June go to see Wally play football in Lynwood and Beaver stays behind and winds up at the police station accused of stealing a boat ("Borrowed Boat") and the time they went shopping for porch furniture and Beaver and Larry destroy a prized possession belonging to Ward ("Ward's Baseball").

The other less traumatic or damaging times include going to spend time with friends, first with the Suttons in Lynwood ("Beaver's Prize") and then with the Rutherfords for an afternoon get together ("Beaver's Tree"). June goes shopping with Ward a couple times ("The Spot Removers" and "Larry Hides Out") and out to eat dinner ("Beaver, the Model") and shopping at the drug store and stopping at the soda fountain for a couple black and whites ("School Sweater").

The number of times June and Ward go out alone together diminishes in season four. The first time we see is when they visit Mrs. Thompson and her new baby in the hospital ("Chuckie's New Shoes"). It is implied by Beaver that she went out one evening when he tells her in the morning before school that she must have stayed out late because she still had her hat on, but she tells him she's going to school for a meeting ("Beaver and Kenneth"). June and Ward also go out shopping once this season ("Eddie Spends the Night").

The next season, Ward and June spend more time with friends or being entertained. They first go to the McBride anniversary party ("No Time for Babysitters"), then it's playing bridge at the Blakes ("Beaver's Long Night"), six weeks later, they go over to the Ritterhoffs and the Wendovers for two parties in one evening and their festivities end for the season when they go spend an afternoon with the Graysons. They also do some shopping, first for groceries at the supermarket ("Ward's Golf Clubs") and then for drapes ("Beaver's Jacket") and finish off with some good old generic shopping in downtown ("The Yard Birds"). The other two times they go out are when she has an appointment at the beauty parlor and Ward goes to get a haircut while she's being beautified ("Beaver's Laundry") and when they go see the school play in which Beaver plays a bunny ("Beaver, the Bunny").

The final season sees Ward and June leave town twice with friends. Their first trip is with the Haneys. Ward hopes to get in a round of golf with Mr. Haney while they're away ("Wally's Car Accident"). They also go out of town and spend time at the Miller's lake house. Uncle Billy stays with Wally and Beaver while Ward and June are away on this trip ("Uncle Billy's Visit"). In one episode, June and Ward enjoy a nice lunch at the country club while a tramp enjoys a nice bath in their tub ("Beaver's Good Deed"). To round out their times taking a break from the toil of the household, Ward and June enjoy a relaxing night at the movies ("Beaver's Book Report").

31

UNDERWEAR AND SOCKS

Of all the struggles Beaver faced during six seasons of *Leave it to Beaver* episodes, having to change his socks must be near the top of the list. Second on that list might be having to change his underwear. Throughout the 234 episodes, socks or underwear are mentioned in fifty of them, and a majority of those mentions have to do with physically changing either socks or underwear or the reluctance to do so. To be more precise, thirty-one of the episodes mention socks, sixteen mention underwear and three combine both items. I know all *Leave it to Beaver* fans have been waiting their entire lives for someone to take a closer look at this sock and underwear issue. It is an honor to be able to present a closer look at the issue in this chapter.

Not every episode in which socks or underwear are mentioned deal with June having an issue with Beaver changing or not changing either item. In some episodes, socks or underwear are hidden, lost, found, played with, mended, or used for alternative uses. In fact, the beforementioned list makes up 46% of all sock and underwear mentions.

One of my favorite underwear stories is when Beaver tells Wally how much fun they had on Wally's twelfth birthday when he received a kite for a gift. They cut up a pair of Beaver's old underwear and used it for a tail. His underwear flew all around town ("Wally's Present"). Twice, characters are spoken about being in their underwear, Gilbert's father ("Beaver and Gilbert") and Wally ("Beaver's Report Card"). Underwear is purchased or is mentioned being purchased in a few episodes ("Last Day of School"), ("Beaver's Jacket") and ("Beaver Sees America"). A pair of underwear is thrown under the bed ("The Lost Watch"), and one pair is lost ("Beaver's Sweater").

References of underwear needing changed are seen a few times. Once is when Beaver had to change his underwear because he had it on backwards ("Beaver Plays Hooky"). Another instance is when Larry mentions he had to change his underwear when he was getting ready for dancing school ("Beaver's Dance"). Beaver and Richard discuss the school doctor and the one day warning the school gives students before he comes to school, giving everyone a chance to change their underwear ("Beaver's English Test"). Wally also gets into the act of changing underwear and Beaver shares the disturbing news with Ward, "He's putting on clean underwear just to play touch football." Ward relays the info to June in a more elegant manner. He tells her he's put on clean "underclothes" ("Teacher's Daughter"). Ward is the topic of one underwear mention. Wally says that when Ward was a kid, he too, was probably told to put on clean underwear ("Wally's Chauffeur").

I don't know what it is about socks, but they just don't seem as exciting or as thrilling as the subject of underwear. I mean, as a child, if you received socks as a Christmas gift, that is nowhere near as terrible as receiving underwear for Christmas. It's true, isn't it? And if you lose your sock (or socks), that's not as big a deal as if you lose your underwear, as Beaver did in gym class. Beaver ought to be grateful he never did receive underwear for Christmas. Now about the socks...

There is only so much a person can write about socks, but I will provide a list of the times June told Beaver to change his socks or was concerned about whether or not he did change socks.

"Beaver's Short Pants" (June warns him to change socks while she's away)

"Train Trip" (Boys only washed their feet while visiting Aunt Martha, didn't change their socks)

"Eddie's Girl" (Ward speaks to June about Wally still needing to be told to change his socks.)

"Beaver's Ring" (June tells Wally to go upstairs and change his fluorescent socks.)

"The Visiting Aunts" (Beaver tells Wally he won't change his socks "until mom makes me.")

"Forgotten Party" (Beaver's socks are mismatched and he has to change them.)

"Beaver Takes a Bath" (June laments forgetting to tell Beaver to change his socks.)

"Beaver the Magician" (When Ward calls Aunt Martha, Beaver had just put on clean socks.)

"Beaver, the Model" (Instead of putting on clean socks, he turns his dirty ones inside out.)

"Beaver's House Guest" (Chopper didn't take his socks off when sleeping in Wally's bed.)

"Wally's Glamour Girl" (Beaver puts sock on other foot so hole won't be on big toe.)

"Beaver and Kenneth" (Wally says his mom asked coach to make sure he wore clean sweat socks.)

"Wally's Dream Girl" (Beaver didn't change his socks for an entire week the previous summer.)

"Community Chest" (Wally still needs to be told to change his socks.)

"Beaver Goes Steady" (Beaver says Wally has been putting on clean socks, shirts, and shaving.)

"No Time for Babysitters" (When asked for a favor, Wally tells June he already put on clean socks.)

"Beaver's Ice Skates" (Beaver tells salesman he changed only one sock in the morning.)

"Double Date" (Beaver had one blue and one brown sock on and had to change them.)

"Wally's Car Accident" (While away on a trip, June forgets to ask Beaver if he has on clean socks.)

I'd leave you with the wrong impression, if you thought every sock reference in *Leave it to Beaver* was June griping at Beaver about putting on clean socks. Ward and June even have a conversation about socks in "Lonesome Beaver" as June sits in the living room mending a few pairs. Ward compliments June on her sock mending ability and explains to her that boys have a knack of wearing out socks with alternative uses. One such use is carrying marbles in them as seen in "Price of Fame" when Larry is sent to the principal's office for wearing only one sock, because he was using the other one to carry his marbles. In "Wally's Present," Beaver saves up money for a gift for Wally's birthday. He takes the entire $6.98 rolled up in a sock to buy a camera for his brother.

As for dirty socks, they're found behind a dresser ("Nobody Loves Me"), under the bed ("Larry's Club"), and underneath Wally's mattress ("Beaver's Old Friend"). One sock is found under a cushion, but Ward never mentions if it is a clean sock or a dirty one ("Captain Jack").

And we can't forget to add that in "Wally's Suit," he invites Tooey and Eddie to check out something special to go along with the suit he had just purchased, "Come up to my room, I'll show you the crazy socks I got to go with it."

Please visit http://leaveittotbeaverbooks.com for more information on underwear and socks. While there, don't forget to sign up for the chance to win free *Leave it to Beaver* prizes.

32

SONGS, MUSIC AND POEMS

One of the things we find in many episodes of *Leave it to Beaver* is the use of music, songs, and poems. Sometimes the songs are obvious as when the class sings "Row Your Boat" in "Teacher Comes to Dinner" or when Beaver sings "Jingle Bells" in "Beaver Becomes a Hero." At other times, a lot of research is undertaken, especially for someone like me who is unfamiliar with many songs which would be sung in a TV series that aired between 1957 and 1963. Not every song, piece of music and poem from the show is listed here, but most of them are. I hope you enjoy this list.

Songs and Music

Beaver sings "The Monkeys Have no Tails in Zamboanga." The song is featured in the movie *They Were Expendable*, a 1945 film starring John Wayne, Donna Reed, Robert Montgomery, and Ward Bond. Zamboanga is a city in the Philippines ("Lonesome Beaver").

"America," "Mary Had a Little Lamb," and "Minuet in G" by Beethoven are played for band tryouts by Beaver, Thomas, and Judy Hensler ("Music Lesson").

"Twinkle, Twinkle, Little Star" is played on a violin by a student in the school festival ("School Play").

"Juanita" is sung by Ward at the cabin at Shadow Lake. The song was published by Caroline Norton in 1855 ("Happy Weekend").

"Goodbye Beaver" is sung by Miss Landers and his classmates when he tells everyone that he is moving away ("Beaver Says Good-Bye").

Wally plays an unidentified cha-cha song on a record ("Dance Contest").

"Row, Row Your Boat," is sung by Beaver's class ("Teacher Comes to Dinner").

Larry sings "You Always Hurt the One You Love" as he is on his way to Beaver's house to repay a loan. The song was made popular by The Mills Brothers and sung by Connie Francis and many others.

June sings along to "I'll Never Smile Again," which is playing on the radio as she cuts potatoes in the kitchen. At the time of the filming of this episode, the song had been performed by many artists including Tommy Dorsey, The Ink Spots, Anne Shelton, and Frank Sinatra ("Pet Fair"). In this episode a parrot also sings "Over There," by George M. Cohan.

Beaver sings, "Oh My Darling Clementine" ("Beaver and Andy").

Eddie Haskell sings "Baby, Won't You Please Come Home?" in the boys' bedroom ("The Hypnotist"). This blues song was written in 1919 by Charles Warfield and Clarence Williams, although Warfield claimed he was the sole composer.[78] The first hit version was released in 1923 by Bessie Smith.[79] Versions popular around the time *Leave it to Beaver* aired were those recorded by Ricky Nelson, Billie Holiday, Della Reese and Frank Sinatra. Eddie also sings this song in an episode when he visits the Cleaver house and sees Wally and Beaver sitting on the bench outside their front door ("Wally's Play").

Beaver sings "She'll Be Coming Around the Mountain." This song was first published in 1899 in a book of hymns called, "Old Plantation Hymns."[80] Carl Sandburg reported that the song was a Negro Spiritual that was adapted by railroad workers in the 1890s.[81]

While not confirmed, a slightly sped up instrumental version of the song "Heart and Soul" written by Hoagy Carmichael is likely what is heard at dancing school when the boys and girls begin dancing ("Beaver's Dance") and what is heard in the background in the restaurant when Beaver is confronted with Brussels Sprouts ("Beaver Won't Eat").

Beaver sings "Jingle Bells" as he and Wally are fishing. Wally wonders why since it is nowhere near Christmas ("Beaver Becomes a Hero").

June plays "Chi mi frena in tal momento" from the 1835 opera *Lucia di Lammermoor* written by Gaetano Donizetti on the record player in the living room ("Beaver's Big Contest").

Beaver sings "Alouette" ("Teacher's Daughter").

Beaver sings "Jeanie with the Light Brown Hair" but changes the name to Margie ("Mother's Helper"). The song was written by Stephen Foster and published in 1854.

Penny Woods sings "Buffalo Gals" which is originally credited to minstrel performer John Hodges ("Dramatic Club").

A classmate of Beaver's sang "Indian Love Call" in a school assembly ("Kite Day"). The song was from a Broadway musical titled "Rose-Marie." It was later made into a movie starring Jeanette MacDonald and Nelson Eddy.

Eddie Haskell leaves Wally's room signing *Come On-a My House*, a song made popular by Rosemary Clooney, Della Reese and many others ("Bachelor at Large").

The fictional records "Thump, Thump, Thump, My Heart is Marching," "Theme from the Three-Eyed Monster," "Rachmaninoff Concerto #2" by the Harmonica Rascals, "Crying and Sighing and Dying for You" by Billy Baxter, "My Wild Irish Geisha," and "You're Driving Me Ape, You Big Gorilla" are records Beaver receives via mail when he joins a record club in season six ("Beaver Joins a Record Club").

Jeff, the tramp, sings "Asleep in the Deep" ("Beaver's Good Deed"). This song was written by Arthur J. Lamb and Henry W. Petrie in 1897.

---

[78] Jasen, David A. and Gene Jones: *Spreadin' Rhythm Around: Black Popular Songwriters, 1880–1930.* Routledge, 2005.

[79] "Jazz Standards Songs and Instrumentals (Baby Won't You Please Come Home)". Jazzstandards.com.

[80] Waltz, Robert B.; Engle, David G. (2012). "She'll Be Coming Around the Mountain". California State University, Fresno

[81] Sandburg, Carl (1927). The American Songbag. New York: Harcourt, Brace & company. p. 372.

Lumpy Rutherford hums what could be a rendition of the Louis Prima song Angelina ("The Book Report").

Poems

Whitey Whitney recites a few lines from "The Wreck of the Hesperus" by William Wadsworth ("Beaver and Poncho").

Ward writes a poem for Beaver titled, "I Would Like to Be a Bear." After Ward confesses to Mrs. Rayburn, she allows Beaver to write his own poem. He writes a poem titled, "The Duck."

Miss Landers has the class memorize the poem, "The Heart of a Tree," by Henry Cuyler Bunner ("Beaver's Tree").

Judy reads a welcome back poem to Miss Landers ("Beaver and Ivanhoe").

Victoria Bennett recites the poem "Foreign Children" by Robert Louis Stevenson ("Dramatic Club").

Harry recites the poem "Casey at the Bat," by Ernest Lawrence Thayer ("Dramatic Club").

Gilbert recites some of "An Incident of the French Camp" by Robert Browning ("Dramatic Club").

Beaver recites "Concord Hymn" by Ralph Waldo Emerson ("Dramatic Club").

Penny recites a poem to her classmates ("Farewell to Penny")

Lori Ann, a girl Wally likes, recites lines from "The Flight" by Lord Alfred Tennyson ("Un-Togehterness").

For more information on songs, music and poems that appear on *Leave it to Beaver*, including full text and recordings, please visit http://leaveittotbeaverbooks.com.

33

CARS

It was not very long ago that I first saw a video of a Ford automobile advertisement from 1960 which featured Tony Dow and Jerry Mathers. The advertisement showed the 1960 models of the Galaxie, Starliner, Country Sedan station wagon, Thunderbird and Falcon. As Beaver says in the commercial, "And in my whole life, I never knew there were so many Fords." Wally says he didn't even know that when he was Beaver's age.

Ward's Cars

One would think that with the boys filming an ad for Ford, that Ward would drive a Ford on *Leave it to Beaver*, but he didn't, not when this ad was filmed. The cars driven by Ward include a 1957 Ford Fairlane in season one, actually two of them, one was a two door (unknown license) and the other a four door (License # MPF 713). An example of the two door is seen in "The Black Eye," and the four door Ford Fairlane is seen in "The Clubhouse," "The Party Invitation," "The Paper Route," "The Perfect Father," and "The Broken Window" episodes. It looks like the producers figured out the Cleavers needed a four door after only one episode showing them with a two door Fairlane. For the following seasons (two through six), Ward drives a new Plymouth Fury each year.

Cars as a Plot or Plot Moving Device

In *Leave it to Beaver* episodes, cars play a very integral part on many occasions. We see this first in "The Paper Route." Ward drives Wally in the rain to deliver some papers even after agreeing not to help the boys too much with their job. Then, both Ward and June help way too much when they find leftover newspapers in the garage on a Saturday. They think the boys forgot about their job and decide to deliver the papers themselves. That maneuver gets the boys fired from their job since those were extra papers from the previous week.

The entire "State vs. Beaver" episode hinges upon the use of a car. In this case, the illegal use of a car, a one lunger go-cart used by Beaver. Egged on by his trouble causing best friend Larry Mondello, Beaver proves he knows how to drive it and he takes the car for a cruise down the street, until a police officer stops him and writes Beaver a ticket.

After being warned about playing ball near the house by Ward in "The Broken Window," the boys promise to never do it again. Left by themselves the next morning, Beaver asks Wally to throw him a pitch by the garage. He felt it was a safe thing to do since he never hits the ball…. until now. *Craassh… tinkle…. tink….* There it is, another broken window, the second in two days. This time it's the car window and for the rest of the episode, the boys try to find money to fix the window but come up short. They end up following Eddie's advice to roll the window down so their father won't notice it. He doesn't, but they eventually tell on themselves accidentally.

In "Tire Trouble," a car plays a prominent role in two different ways. The boys make a mess in the garage where they are making cages for the chinchillas they want to purchase. They give up and the mess keeps Ward from parking his car inside. This happens two days in a row. He then demands they spend their Saturday cleaning the mess. They find Ward has driven over a board with a nail in it because of their not cleaning the garage and driveway. They sneak the tire to a service station to have it fixed and their sneakiness is eventually discovered.

Wally buys his own car, even before he has a license in "Wally's Car." Talk about a jalopy, it's doubtful this 1936 Coupe even qualifies for that low class of car. His dad explains the costs of owning a car with insurance, registration and other fees and tells him he cannot keep it to work on until he gets his license. Having to sell it, he can't find any of his friends who want the whole car, but when he begins selling it part by part, it goes fast. The funniest thing about this episode was when Wally tells Beaver that when a kid turns fifteen, he automatically knows everything about cars.

Two cars are cause for concern in "Wally's Chauffeur." The first is Lumpy's car which will be full of couples going to the country club dance. This is how Wally plans to take Evelyn to the dance. But Ward puts a damper on things when he tells him it's not safe to have all those kids in one car and June says it's not considerate to put Evelyn in that situation as her dress and corsage would get ruined. Mr. Boothby's car is the second automotive concern in this episode. Evelyn comes up with a great idea, but she doesn't tell Wally about it until she arrives at his house on the night of the dance. She will drive them in her father's car. To say Wally is upset is understating things just a tad.

When Gilbert and Beaver play in Ward's car in "Beaver Takes a Drive," the two boys pretend to be parents with misbehaving children, and the dialogue provides plenty of laughs to go around…until the gear shift gets kicked out of place and the car rolls down the driveway into the street. Soon, cars get backed up, horns start honking and Gilbert leaves Beaver there all alone to deal with the frustrated adults. Wally comes to save the day by moving the car back into the driveway with an extra key he finds under the seat, but a police officer on the scene is not thankful. Instead, he gives Wally a ticket for driving without a license.

In "Lumpy's Car Trouble," Wally needs a ride to an out-of-town track meet. His father must work and Lumpy comes over and announces his car is out of service. He needs a new water pump. The only other option is if Lumpy borrows Mr. Cleaver's car and drives Wally and Beaver to the track meet. Of course, one wonders why June doesn't offer to drive them, but then this episode would've only been five minutes long if she had. Ward gives Lumpy permission and gives Wally some rules for the drive up there, like stick to the highway and no other guests in the car. That second rule is broken first when they pick up Eddie and the first rule is broken on the way back home when they take a shortcut via the Camelback Cutoff. There is a big problem after that escapade, but the boys think if they fix it on their own that no one will be the wiser. They thought wrong.

In Mayfield, back in the early 1960s, a kid couldn't get a license until he turned seventeen. Some enterprising detective could use this information found in "Wally's License" to help figure out where Mayfield is located. But let's not go there yet, that's for another chapter. So, on the day Wally turns seventeen, he's ready to start drivers' education and get his license. June does not want that to happen. But Ward promised, and so it's off to learn how to drive a car. He takes his classes using a Plymouth Belvedere automobile. Wally's not such a keen driver when he first starts, but he improves, and you can see his confidence grow with each new day behind the wheel. On the day he goes to take his test, Beaver even says a prayer that he passes the road test… and Wally passes with flying colors.

There's nothing more frustrating than getting a scrape or a dent on a new car and few things more frightening than letting your teenage son drive your new car, with his nearly new license. In "Wally's Accident," Ward gives permission for Wally to use his new car to take Shirley to the prom. Things go fine until Eddie convinces Wally to give Lumpy's heap a push. A headlight is broken, and some body damage occurs, and Wally must get it fixed before his father comes home from out of town. He fixes it, but like usual, gets caught, this time thanks to Lumpy's big mouth.

The final episode that is centered around a car is appropriately named, "Wally Buys a Car." You can't get much more of a car-centric *Leave it to Beaver* episode than this one. It has a teenager wanting to buy car, almost getting gypped, a caring father with valuable advice about buying cars, and respect paid to a father from a son. Wally comes up with many reasons why he should get his own car. He's saved $180 and can buy it himself, he could take Beaver to school and save the bus fare, he could charge Beaver's friends for a ride to school, he can get eight cents a mile for taking members of school teams to events, and he could drive June to the beauty parlor. Beaver suggests that if Ward's car breaks down on a Sunday, they could use Wally's car to get to church. Ward admits that it is possible that their car may break down on a Sunday, but admonishes Beaver, saying, "Now son, don't you think it's a little unfair to bring up the religious issue in this campaign?" Wally gets a good deal on an adequate car, a 1953 Chevrolet 210 Convertible, after he and Ward visit an honest car dealer. Wally finds out those aren't the easiest thing to find, whether one lives in Mayfield, Lynwood, Bellport, or even Euless, Texas. It's a good thing he had Ward along to help.

Car Repairs

The above-mentioned episodes are the ones where cars are central to the plot or move the plot forward, but there are plenty of other episodes where cars are mentioned. For example, sometimes, Ward must take the car to the service station to get fixed. He takes it to Mac's Garage to have the brakes looked at because "someone" had been driving the car with the emergency brakes on ("The Broken Window"). Hmmm, who could that have been? June is not happy with his insinuation. Ward tells Larry their car is at the garage being "greased" when he explains why he can't take him to his grandmother's house ("Beaver's Guest"). Ward has a fanbelt replaced in the car when his old one is loose ("Most Interesting Character").

Lumpy, Eddie and Wally also had their cars repaired at various times. Often, the guys would do the work themselves. For Lumpy's car, he sometimes needed little fixes like a flat tire ("Beaver the Bunny") or fenders needing replaced ("Beaver's Long Night"), replacing a fanbelt, or adding a quart of oil he steals from his father's car ("Eddie Quits School"). Lumpy also gets a new water pump and a radiator ("Lumpy's Car Problem") and Wally helps him replace the springs in his car ("Beaver's Good Deed").

Eddie has a car too, but it's seen or spoken of must less often than Lumpy's car. Wally helps him install an FM radio in his car and Beaver was going to help until June makes him go to the store instead ("The Silent Treatment"). Eddie has problems with his car that need fixing which include fixing the back seat because the springs come through the seat ("Beaver, the Hero"), his driver side doors are tied together with a rope ("Wally's Practical Joke") and he installed a tachometer, a device used to measure the speed of an engine, but he complains that his engine doesn't go fast enough to register ("Wally's Practical Joke").

June Using the Car

Other mentions of the car include times when June must use the car. She's seen in the car driving it very rarely, and possibly only once, as is seen in "The Perfect Father" when she pulls up in the driveway as Ward is installing a backboard on the garage. There are many mentions of her driving the car, and they typically occur on weekdays when Ward would be using the car to go to work. This seems to have been one of the little inconsistences that are found in the episodes, the idea of her using the car for something and Ward having already gone to work. This is seen in "New Doctor," when she kisses Ward goodbye, and he walks out the front door to drive to work and she mentions to Beaver that she will drive Wally to school if the doctor comes over and says he's okay. A couple episodes later, in "Beaver's Bad Day," Ward specifically tells June she can have the car because Fred Rutherford is picking him up. This confirms what Beaver says about their car situation in "The Grass is Always Greener" when beaver says they only have one car. Then there's that reference in "Most Interesting Character," when Ward tells June that the people interested in buying their house are offering a pick-up truck as a down payment. He says, "Well, here's your chance, dear. You always wanted a car of your own."

Other instances of this confusion include June being reminded by Wally in "Beaver's Ring," that Ward has the car when she's notified about Beaver's problem at school. Then, in "Beaver Plays Hooky," there's a bit of confusion when June tells Wally she has to go to the market to get Beaver," and he reminds her the doctor is coming, but doesn't tell her Ward has the car. When she calls Ward at work to ask if he'll get Beaver, he wonders why she can't go down to get him. Who has the car? They both must think the other one has it. In "Wally's Election," Ward is looking for the key to the car before going to work. He leaves and when Beaver tells June he needs a cake for school, she says she'll go to the market for one, but Ward has the car. It's hard to imagine she took the taxi everywhere she went. Just another little inconsistency.

In "The Last Day of School," we find June taking Ward to work for the first time. June also picks Beaver up at school a couple other times, once in "Beaver Goes into Business," to take him to the bank, and another time is when he has a dentist appointment in "Beaver's Report Card."

There are many other references to cars you can find within the episodes and from time to time, they will be added to the following website – http://leaveittobeaverbooks.com. Also, don't forget to sign up for updates and you'll be eligible to win LITB prizes after every 100th copy of *The World Famous Beaverpedia* is sold.

34

THE CLEAVER HOMES

Let's start off this chapter with a trivia question. Put your thinking caps on… okay, ready? In how many houses did Theodore "Beaver" Cleaver live? If you said anything other than "Three" or "At least three," then according to Beaver, in "Beaver's Old Friend," you have the wrong answer. At least in that episode, Beaver says he remembers when the family lived at the "other" house, referring to one before their present home which was at 485 Mapleton. He says to Wally that when they lived there, Aunt Martha gave him Billy Bear, his old stuffed bear he had just found in the garage. Beaver was sick with the measles and Billy Bear helped him get though that bad time. According to June, in "Beaver's Autobiography," he had the measles when he was six years old. If you take her words from that episode and Beaver's words from this one, a viewer might surmise that the Cleavers have only been at the 485 Mapleton address for a couple years. But you know what this means, that during the years of filming, there were over forty writers and no series bible for writers to read before crafting their individual thirty-minute masterpieces (or twenty-two minutes with commercials). So, the correct answer appears to be "three," but the judges would also count "at least three" as a correct answer too since we don't know if the Cleavers lived somewhere before the "other" house Beaver mentions in "Beaver's Old Friend."

Now that we got their third house, or their first house, out of the way, let's concentrate on the two houses seen in the 234 episodes of *Leave it to Beaver*. These are the homes located at 485 Mapleton (or Maple in an episode or two) and at 211 Pine Street /Avenue. A close look at the boys' bedroom, the kitchen, living room and garage will be taken for the 485 Mapleton house. Those areas, plus the den will be looked at closer for the 211 Pine house, minus the garage.

Different Studios…Different Houses

The first two seasons of *Leave it to Beaver* were filmed at Republic Studios at 4024 Radford Avenue in Studio City, CA. This studio produced many "B" Westerns and other similar films in different genres and also produced television shows such as *Wagon Train, The Rifleman, M Squad* and many others. In terms of the type of studio it was regarding its strength, it was considered a *mini-major* studio.[82] The production of *Leave it to Beaver* moved to Revue Studios or the current Universal Studios for seasons three through six. A reason mentioned for the move was that the exterior façade used for the Cleaver House would no longer be available to use, meaning some other television production would be using it since Republic would no longer be making feature films. If the lack of an exterior façade is what happened, it could have been it was included in what was rented out to independent producers as that was one way Republic used to remain profitable. [83] It all worked out well. The Cleavers only had to move a few miles east down Ventura Blvd. and not to Madison, as Wally was dreading might happen ("Good-Bye Beaver").

Leave it to Beaver may have been shot at Republic the first two seasons because this was a studio where Connelly and Mosher were a known entity. They had created *The Ray Milland Show / Meet Mr. McNutley* in 1953 and seventy-seven episodes were filmed at Republic. It may be that

---

[82] Dixon, Wheeler Winston. *Death of the Moguls: The End of Classical Hollywood (illustrated ed.)*. Rutgers University Press, 2012, 67.

[83] Scheuer, Philip K.. "Film Making to Be Ended by Republic: Studio Will Step Up Efforts to Rent Lot Use to Independents." *Los Angeles Times*. April 2, 1958, p. B1.

Connelly and Mosher were happy to have the pilot greenlit for production and agreed to take whatever exterior façade of a house that Republic Studios had to give them. It also could have been familiarity that led them to that façade. The house exterior used for the main character in *The Ray Milland Show / Meet Mr. McNutley* was the exact same exterior used as the Cleaver home for the first two seasons of *Leave it to Beaver*. From the oftentimes incorrect IMDB, it shows that nine actors and two writers used for their *Ray Milland* production were also used for *Leave it to Beaver*.

So, what about the implied reasons for the Cleaver move to a much nicer home at a new studio? Was it a plan by the producers to show their upward mobility? Was it planned at all? Could it have been the producers' familiarity with the house on the Republic lot from their previous series that caused them to keep it for the first two seasons? Maybe it's true that the façade was not going to be available for their third season due to the changes at Republic. Sometimes the simplest answer is the correct one.

A Closer Look at 485 Mapleton (or Maple Drive)

Well, how is this for a description of the Cleaver's first home? "A charming three-bedroom house with a den, on beautifully landscaped ground, modern dream kitchen, patio, spacious, airy, the ultimate in suburban living, near schools and transportation." That's how the Jackson Realty Company advertised their house in the newspaper. June says after reading the ad, "It almost sounds too good to leave." Then she wonders where the den is located, and Ward tells her it's that little space behind the living room that they have never figured out what to do with ("Most Interesting Character."

The first Cleaver home can be better described as a very modest abode. It was probably built anywhere from the 1930s to the late 1940s. It has three bedrooms, and a small garage. There is a small dining room, a cellar (or basement) and it does not include a den, no matter what Jackson says at his realty company. The areas most often shown in the seventy-eight episodes in which it is featured, are the room belonging to Beaver and Wally, their bathroom, the kitchen, dining room, living room and garage. Okay, basically, every room is featured except Ward and June's room, the guest room (seen once) and the cellar (seen once).

Starting the tour in the boys' room, you'll notice bunk beds. The boys having their beds in this manner only lasts through episode thirty ("Music Lesson"). When Beaver asks Wally why their parents took the beds apart, Wally answers, "Grown people always get a kick out of moving furniture around ("New Doctor"). Although bunk beds are always more fun, as the guy up top is well, up top and the guy below, has his very own fort, one could easily understand how for shooting a TV show with a lot of dialogue between characters in a bedroom, having the beds apart would be easier for production.

In looking at episodes throughout seasons one and two, you will find the boys' room is decorated with pennants, pictures and posters of all sorts. Some items in their room are present for every episode like the desk, various pennants, the toy strength meter and their wooden chest. Other items like a cowboy painting above Beaver's top bunk disappear, and the lamp between their beds changes from a lamp base decorated with train engines to a faux oil lamp like one on their desk. Items also move from time to time, like the Lyndale pennant on the right side of the mirror on their dresser in "Beaver's Old Friend," to just above Wally's bed in "Beaver's Guest," which aired just six episodes later. The mirror above their clothes dresser with four rows of drawers is small in the early episodes, noticeable in "Captain Jack," but in later episodes of season one, it is replaced with a much larger mirror.

Here is a list of what we find in the boys' room in seasons one and two: (1) electric lamp with trains painted on its base (1) painting with a cowboy riding a horse above their wooden chest and between the two windows (1) desk (1) poster featuring Indians of North America (1) short medium sized stool (1) wooden chest (1) toy strength meter similar to what one might see at a carnival which they are seen using in "The Clubhouse" episode (1) small "D" pennant (1) small "P" pennant (1) small "H" Pennant (1) hat hanging on the left side of their clothes dresser mirror (1) small globe which is sometimes on their chest and sometimes on their desk (1) four drawer high clothes dresser (1) radio on their clothes dresser (2) horseshoes, pointing down, hanging on their wall (1) Lyndale pennant (1) faux oil lamp electric lamp on their desk and then later (2) faux oil lamp electric lamps, one on the desk and one between their beds on a night stand (1) painting of a small town street with houses and large trees above the tall dresser (1) tall dresser on the right side of Beaver's bed (1) basketball on top of the tall dresser (1) strange painting above Beaver's bed which sort of looks like an angelic figure floating (1) tennis racquet and (1) baseball bat standing in the corner next to Beaver's bed (1) very small and short stool (1) painting of a cowboy herding horses in a canyon above Beaver's bunk bed (1) typewriter on the desk (1) jet airplane toy on their small dresser (1) canoe paddle or boat oar standing in the corner next to Beaver's bed .

The kitchen is pretty basic even though Jackson Realty says it's a modern dream kitchen. Back in the late 1950s, I think every dream kitchen included a dishwasher and the Cleavers had no dishwasher. This kitchen is quite roomy as it holds a china cabinet, a small table with four chairs for breakfast and lunch, plenty of countertops, shelves with glass windows, obviously, so guests will know where to look for a plate or a bowl and not need to ask which cabinet. They have a large electric mixer on the far end of the counter and in some episodes, you can see a silver waffle iron or waffle maker. There is also a creepy looking (by today's standards) clown cookie jar. This cookie jar is usually found in the kitchen in most episodes, but then sometimes, it suddenly disappears, or it moves. June has pans hanging on the wall above the stove, and in some episodes, there's also a toaster on the counter between the mixer and waffle iron. As in the boys' bedroom, sometimes items disappear or move locations.

Early in season one, the following are found in the Cleaver living room: (1) fireplace (2) lamps (non-matching) (2) end tables (1) couch / sofa (1) desk and chair (1) telephone on an end table (1) ornate clock hanging on the wall (1) large painting of a pastoral scene above the fireplace (2) urns or vases on the mantle (1) built-in book shelf with four shelves (1) built-in bookshelf with glass doors behind the couch (1) coffee table (1) large upholstered chair. In some later episodes, the shelves behind the couch and Ward's desk are seen and they hold figurines instead of books. Like in the kitchen and in the boys' room, some items are moved, and some items disappear, depending on the episode.

The dining room is nonchalant. They have their large dining room table, a large china cabinet sits behind Ward, a painting of a jar of flowers hangs on the wall near the door, a chest of drawers sits behind June, and it has candlestick holders on top. One thing you will notice about the dining room is how the table shrinks in size. For the first ten episodes of season one, the Cleavers own a large dining room table or maybe it's just that the leaf was inserted in the middle, extending its length. Of those ten episodes, when the family eats a meal in the dining room, the boys sit on the same side of the table for all but one, "The Haircut." Then, beginning with "Beaver's Short Pants," the boys sit on opposite sides of the shortened table until the series ends.

The garage is the scene of many of Beaver and Wally's exploits in the first two seasons. One thing that many fans miss when the Cleavers move to the new house is that the garage is rarely used or seen. When you look at season one, there are many great episodes that show the boys in the garage. Just look at "The Black Eye," which has Ward teaching Beaver how to box in the garage. In "Beaver's Short Pants," the garage is the scene of one of the most touching moments of all *Leave it to Beaver* episodes. In "The Paper Route," the garage plays a prominent role, as it is where June rolls papers with Beaver and the boys do so too. Of course, we can't forget "The Perfect Father," where the backboard is installed on the garage one foot too short, and the boys are playing ball in the driveway with Ward. Then there's "The State vs. Beaver," "The Broken Window," "Next Door Indians," "Beaver's Old Friend," "Wally's Job," "Beaver and Henry," and "Beaver Runs Away," all in season one.

The list continues in season two with episodes like, "Eddie's Girl," where Eddie shows a bit of his humanity to Beaver in the garage at the end of the episode. And what about "Ward's Problem," "Beaver and Chuey," "The Pipe," "The Grass is Always Greener," "The Boat Builders," and obviously, "The Garage Painters." But there are even more… "Beaver's Pigeons," "A Horse Named Nick," "Beaver's Hero," "Beaver's Newspaper," and "Dance Contest," where Lumpy, Chester and Tooey are talking with Wally about going to the dance with Mary Ellen Rogers.

There aren't a lot of things you'll find inside the garage besides some power tools and some other items. As for the power tools found in the Cleaver garage, they are a Dewalt radial arm saw which can now be purchased rebuilt for about $5000 or more, depending on the condition and the market. There is also a Shop Smith lathe. They have lots of old papers and magazines stored, old tires, and miscellaneous other junk. And typically, the garage houses an automobile, except when the boys are inside creating something or using it for some other purpose.

The garage at their 485 Mapleton house has an amazing place in *Leave it to Beaver* history. A lot of big discussions were undertaken in the garage. They kept rabbits, a horse and pigeons in there. They worked hard creating things like a go-cart, a boat, and found things like WW II memories, a typewriter, a globe, a shot put and an old comforting memory in the form of a teddy bear. The garage was a good place to set many scenes of the show and I personally lament they didn't continue using the garage as much in seasons three through six. But I think it is understandable why they didn't. The garage was a place of youth…as the boys grew, there wasn't much more to do in the garage. They weren't going to be building things, especially with Wally's time taken up by sports and girls.

As for the cellar or basement, it is only seen or spoken of on a few occasions, among those are when Minerva the maid finds an alligator in the basement when she's doing the laundry in "Captain Jack." In "The Boat Builders," Wally puts Beavers' wet clothes and boots to dry and they begin to melt on the furnace or water heater. Then, in the "Most Interesting Character" episode, Ward looks for screens and finds them in the basement.

Okay, load up the moving van, we're moving to the new house.

A Closer Look at 211 Pine Street (or Pine Avenue)

The picket fence is gone, the small backyard has been replaced with a much bigger one, and a den has been added to the Cleaver house. This is a brand-new house on a brand-new studio back lot. There's not a lot of talk about their living in a new house. One of the few times is in "Beaver's Tree," when Ward and June talk about whether Beaver's having a hard time adjusting to his new home and the new neighborhood. They find out later, that the only thing he's not adjusting to is living in the new home while knowing the tree they had given him for his birthday, is at their old home.

The boys' room is not much different. Some of the same items are found in this new bedroom, probably because it was the same prop department and of course, a family would move belongings and not throw them away and buy all new stuff. The most obvious items seen in both rooms are an oar or paddle in the corner by Beaver's bed, although it's a different paddle. They have two horseshoes on their wall, under a light fixture, just like in their previous room and they're still pointing down in the early episodes of season three. They also have pennants in their room, but they feature different letters, except for the "H" pennant which still survives. The new ones include an "F" pennant and a "W" pennant. And in what he believes is season six, Bryon Nelson Jr. of the "Leave it to Beaver Fan Club" Facebook group, says there is an "M" pennant on their wall we see momentarily in at least one episode.

There are some new items and upgrades in Wally and Beaver's room. The first thing noticeable is their chest of drawers next to the window which also has bookshelves in which they keep some books, but also some toys. They have a toy plane on one shelf, what looks to be board games on the top shelf, boxing gloves slung over the left corner of the top bookshelf, and in later seasons they have a starfish displayed. They also have a decorative wall hanging which features a cat on the same wall their beds are against, they now have a bigger world globe, they have a new cushioned chair, a lamp with a shade featuring a clipper ship, a hurricane style lamp next to Beaver's bed, a poster featuring basketball players that some have said looks like a page from a school yearbook, but obviously is not due to its size, and beginning with the "June's Birthday" episode, the horseshoes get turned right side up so the luck doesn't run out of them. That's something Eddie Haskell told them would happen and even though Wally doesn't believe in that sort of thing, he turns them around anyway.

As the seasons progress, there are other items that appear on the dresser, shelves and on their walls. These include a sailboat on the dresser, a clown picture by their door on the wall above the light switch, a model covered wagon on the dresser alongside Wally's bed, a framed photo of Wally and Beaver on their dresser, above the dresser near Wally's bed are a framed picture of two dogs and framed pictures of multiple horses, they also have a second clown picture on the left side of their dresser mirror, and starting around the middle of season four, a bulletin board appears next to their book shelf, replacing a poster of basketball players, which was on a different wall in season three but had been moved to between the bookshelf and the desk.

In the living room, there are three new pastoral paintings. The one above the fireplace is larger than the painting above the fireplace at the Mapleton house. To the right of the fireplace, there are two smaller pastoral paintings. Two other paintings featured near the living room, in the entry area, are *The Blue Boy* (c. 1770) by English portrait and landscape painter Thomas Gainsborough and Sir Thomas Lawrence's *Pinkie* (c. 1794).[84] They have a new, what looks to be a white sofa, and a wing chair covered with a chinoiserie print. They have a house plant on the coffee table in front of the sofa, a chest of drawers on the exterior house wall next to the living room window, another pastoral painting above it, two glass figurines on the chest of drawers, and a telephone on the end table next to the chair.

The dining room is larger in the new house, with a double door opening out into the living room. The percentage of times the Cleavers eat in the dining room is less in the new house compared to the old. Behind the large dining room table, next to the doors, is a silver tea set on a small table, small paintings adorn the walls, a chest of drawers sits behind Ward's chair and a large painting hangs above it. Next to the door from the kitchen, there are two small pictures featuring birds. There are four windows behind Wally's chair with a large curtain that can be pulled to cover all of them, although each has their own individual curtain.

---

[84] These two paintings are owned by The Huntington in San Marino, California.

The design of the new house lets in a lot of light to both the dining room and the kitchen. The nook in the kitchen is next to a group of three windows. The appliances include a new refrigerator and an island with a stove top. There's a cabinet and shelf above the kitchen table which holds quite a few figurines. There are cabinets which have a glass front which look as if they hold some of their better dishware, maybe china. There are also other cabinets which are all wood. The oven is built into the wall, next to the second kitchen door. They still have a mixer on the counter, and one constant is a cookie jar, which begins as a mammy style cookie jar and then becomes the pickle crock turned cookie jar in later seasons. The pickle crock is not introduced until Season 3 Episode 35 in "Wally the Businessman." In season four, the crock becomes a cookie jar. One other interesting note about the kitchen is the back door buzzer. I believe the only time it is mentioned or heard in *Leave it to Beaver* is in the "Junior Fire Chief" episode. The next time I personally saw the buzzer at the back door was when Jim Rockford pushed it during an episode of *The Rockford Files* titled "In Hazard." For those of you who are also *Marcus Welby M.D.* fans, you may have seen the buzzer rung on a few occasions. The Cleaver house was used as Welby's in the medical drama.

The new addition to the Cleaver house is the den. This is where Ward does the family bills. It is also where he takes care of work he brings home over the weekend, where he has many talks with Wally and Beaver when they have problems, or when they need a lecture. The den is where the TV is seen in episodes that feature TV watching. Typically, this is Beaver watching TV and on occasion Ward ("Mother's Day Composition), or Ward and June (Wally's Chauffeur). Near the end of season four, the den is home to a game of hide and seek, where in some episodes, a TV can be seen from the living room and the entry, and then in other episodes, the TV is replaced with a large globe. Then, the TV reappears. This happens continuously until the end of the series, but there are stretches in seasons five and six when the TV becomes a regular fixture. As TV historian Scott Hettrick has noted, there are times when the TV changes from one model to another and back to the original model.

Ward's den is furnished with a large desk, with a phone, and a desk clock with a thermometer. There is a large leather chair across from the desk. The desk sits in front of four rows of bookshelves built into the wall. Adorning the walls are a few prints. Two of them on the wall to the right of the desk, when looking at the desk from the front, feature numerous antique cars. Other unidentified pictures are on the wall across from Ward's desk. Also across from Ward's desk is a reproduction print of the Declaration of Independence. There is also one table lamp which sits next to the leather chair.

As for the cellar or basement, it's only mentioned a few times in the new house. In "Beaver Takes a Bath," after cleaning up the mess in their bathroom, Wally suggests they throw the wet towels in the cellar. June, in "The Spot Removers," says that Beaver got his watercolor set from the basement. In "Beaver's Team," June tells Ward about some things she needs fixed or replaced around the house, one of those is the basement light which burned out.

I still wish we knew more about that house they lived in before moving to Maple Drive.

35

WARD CLEAVER FAMILY AND MEMORIES

"You know, Ward, I don't believe half the stories you tell about your boyhood" – June

Ward Cleaver b. 1923; m. June Bronson 1944; Children: Wallace b. 1945 and Theodore b. 1949 (all years are approximate)

When describing a character on *Leave it to Beaver*, one should understand that anyone researching a character will find numerous inconsistencies while they comb through various episodes. One need look no further than Ward Cleaver's immediate family. In most episodes that mention siblings, he has only one unnamed brother. There is a younger brother mentioned in "Boarding School" and an older brother mentioned in "Beaver Becomes a Hero," but other than those episodes, he usually remarks, "My brother…." with the exception of "Ward's Baseball," where he mentions having two brothers. The other big inconsistency is the age at which he met June. In "Wally's Fraternity, she's mentioned as meeting Ward at State, the institution of higher learning where they studied after high school. However, there are mentions of him buying her an orchid when she was sixteen ("Wally's Orchid") and of their first date happening while he still lived under his parent's roof ("Un-Togetherness"). As long as you can grasp and come to accept there are inconsistencies (because over forty different writers wrote the scripts over six seasons), we can delve deeper into Ward's childhood and other aspects of Ward Cleaver (pre-marriage).

Ward's Family

Ward Cleaver had a loving mother who was with him and comforted him when he had his tonsils taken out ("Beaver's Tonsils"), and a very strict father who also loved him. Ward spoke of his father many times, and often, those times had to do with a punishment Ward received and how his father often set down the law. Ward got a taste of the "strap" ("Broken Window"), speaks of getting taken to the woodshed ("Beaver Gets Adopted"), got it with the "strap" after breaking off the key in the ignition of their car ("Beaver Takes a Bath"), he would take a walk with his father to the toolshed and that scared him ("The Silent Treatment"), and his father made him do a lot of chores ("Beaver's Freckles"). When he was old enough, he went hunting with his father ("Boarding School").

We hear about other relatives throughout the series and sometimes they are only mentioned for one moment on one episode. For example, his grandfather is mentioned once ("The Clubhouse") and Ward made a profit off of him by charging friends to see him while he slept. Ward made eighty cents and all because his grandfather had a beard. His grandmother is mentioned a couple times and there is not much substance to those mentions. He says she had a water pump in her sink at home ("The Happy Weekend") and she gave him a nasty tasting tonic when he was sick as a child ("Miss Landers' Fiancé").

While grandparents are rarely mentioned on *Leave it to Beaver*, aunts and uncles are, especially Aunt Martha and Uncle Billy. There are many other aunts and uncles mentioned, at least in one episode. These include his Uncle Frank ("Ward's Baseball"), Uncle Tom, who lives in Florida ("Beaver's Birthday"), an uncle some assume (like Wikipedia) is Ward's brother, and an Uncle Harry ("Brotherly Love"). Ward has four uncles on his father's side ("Uncle Billy"). An

Uncle Henry ("Beaver's Tree") is mentioned as being deceased and is not identified as being Ward or June's uncle. In addition to June's Aunt Martha, other aunts mentioned include Ward's Aunt Emma ("Beaver, the Hero"), an unidentified aunt of Ward's who gave him a red velvet jacket he was forced to wear to Sunday School ("Beaver's Doll Buggy"), and an Aunt Mildred is mentioned by Beaver ("Poor Loser") and Beaver also has an Aunt Helen ("The Dramatic Club") and one of those may be Ward's sister which is mentioned in "Brotherly Love."

Ward's Siblings

As shown above, most often, Ward mentions having a brother, not multiple brothers. He speaks of a sister once and she wasn't very nice to him. In fact, she hit him in the head with a rock and he required five stiches ("Brotherly Love"). His brother or brothers are mentioned multiple times and they took part in many activities which included going fishing ("Beaver Becomes a Hero"), bringing home a duck that was trapped on top of a frozen pond ("Beaver and Poncho") and filling a cardboard box with water ("The Shave").

Ward also mentions that his brother used to walk him to and from church ("Beaver's Fear") and that his brother went away to boarding school ("Beaver's Doll Buggy"). He and his brother were 4H members and entered their prize hog in the 4H show ("Wally and Alma") and they once got a new bike and had to share it ("The Paper Route") and Ward and his brother used to drop a pogo stick they received as a gift, from the barn hayloft, to see how high it would bounce ("Beaver's Electric Trains").

Ward in Shaker Heights

Jerry Mathers, as well as the producers of *Leave it to Beaver*, know very well Mayfield was not located in any specific state. It was always meant to be Anywhere, USA. Nevertheless, some fans (maybe even you) will argue about Mayfield's location ad nauseum. The following six episodes give those fans more than enough ammo to say Mayfield was absolutely located in Ohio. Specifically, somewhere near Shaker Heights. You see, the city of Shaker Heights was mentioned in "Beaver's Accordion," "Wally's Dream Girl," "Kite Day," "Beaver, the Hero," "Beavers Prep School," and "Wally's Practical Joke."

Oftentimes, writers will take something from their life and insert it in scripts they pen. This happened in *Leave it to Beaver* with entire stories. But it also happened with streets. One example is when the street writer/producer Bob Mosher grew up on during the summers (Lake Street in Auburn, NY) was mentioned in a couple episodes. I first noticed this phenomenon in a movie called *Glengarry, Glen Ross* written by David Mamet. The final scene shows Ricky Roma (Al Pacino) talking with a prospective client about a meeting. They give him their address which is 6947 Euclid. What's the significance of that address? After googling his name and the address, I found out that was the address screenwriter/playwright David Mamet lived at in Chicago as a child. That same reference showed he also lived in Park Forest, IL, my hometown. Writers do this sort of thing all the time so it's probably safe to presume that many writers did this in *Leave it to Beaver* too, not just Bob Mosher with the street on which he grew up. So, when looking for a location in which the Cleavers lived and understanding over forty different writers contributed to the series, viewers can find references to many different places, maybe places from the childhood of any of the writers.

As for Shaker Heights, the six episodes in which it is mentioned were written by three different writer teams: Dale and Katherine Eunson, Dick Conway and Roland MacLane, and Joe

Connelly and Bob Mosher. Were any of them from Shaker Heights? Research has shown that is not likely. The first mention of the city was by Connelly and Mosher. They also supervised the scripts of the Eunsons and Conway and MacLane. They are the common denominator. Maybe they threw the name in there to throw off any viewers that thought Mayfield could be identified as being in one particular state. Then again, maybe this right here is way too much thought put into the subject.

As for the references, Ward talks about a girl in Shaker Heights (Beaver's Accordion), he talks about another girl, the "Darling of Shaker Heights" ("Wally's Dream Girl"), he was the best kite maker in the city ("Kite Day"), the Red Grange of Shaker Heights ("Beaver, the Hero"), a Cleaver put in a pipe organ in a Shaker Heights high school ("Beaver's Prep School"), and he was known as the "Shaker Heights Swinger" ("Wally's Practical Joke").

Ward on the Farm

At least twelve times, Ward mentions or is mentioned as living on a farm when he grew up. Here are those twelve references: He says he was "practically brought up on a farm ("Boarding School"). He mentions being a sentimental old farm boy ("A Horse Named Nick"). June tells Beaver that Ward was brought up on a farm ("Most Interesting Character"). He says his parents worked seven days a week on the farm ("Pet Fair"). He talks about his many chores on the farm ("Beaver's Freckles"). He entered a hog in the fair ("The Dramatic Club"). Ward says he grew up on a farm and never saw silk pajamas ("Beaver Finds a Wallet"). He also says he was a boy on a farm ("Beaver, the Model"). June says Ward lived on a farm ("Beaver's Rat"). Ward has memories of the farm when he hears croaking frogs ("Beaver's Frogs"). He again mentions being a boy on the farm ("Beaver's Electric Trains"). Finally, he mentions hiding in the barn when he was mad at his father ("The Merchant Marine").

The Ward Cleaver Childhood

As shown above with the June quote, the stories of Ward's childhood, at times, could be a bit unbelievable. Even Ward admits, "… sometimes I have trouble really believing they happened myself." ("Miss Landers' Fiancé") The unbelievable things were sometimes just exaggerations like how he walked twenty miles a day ("Beaver Takes a Walk"), had at least 100 fights by the time he was in the second grade ("The Black Eye") and watched hundreds of horror movies in the early 1930s at the beginning of the Great Depression ("Voodoo Magic"). But then there were other things like sleeping in a tree in fourth grade ("Tenting Tonight"), shooting rats at the town dump ("The Grass is Always Greener"), fishing for eels off the city bridge ("The Spot Removers"), and reading three to four books a week ("Beaver's Library Book") which are much more believable.

There are things that Ward did as a child that could be classified as adventurous or dangerous, including running away from home ("Beaver Runs Away"), getting in the aforementioned fights ("The Black Eye"), sneaking out of the house at night ("Beaver's Crush"), hunting with his father ("Boarding School"), riding to Chicago by himself on the train ("The Train Trip"), and shooting rats at the dump with his .22 rifle ("The Grass is Always Greener").

Some unique things that Ward did in his boyhood are things today's generation may never experience and even those who were raised in the 1960s or 1970s may have not experienced. They were eating ice off an ice wagon ("Beaver's Old Friend"), going to the train station to watch people rush for trains, watching a fat woman hit a child ("The Train Trip"), and he went to church (something 90% of America no longer does) ("Beaver's Fear" and "Beaver's Doll Buggy").

Other activities that kept Ward occupied as a boy included spending lots of time on the ice in winter ("Beaver's Ice Skates"), he was involved with scouting ("Lonesome Beaver"), fished with his brother ("Happy Weekend"), had his own lawn cutting business ("Beaver Goes in Business"), hung out at carnivals and circuses when they came to town ("A Horse Named Nick"), made his own crystal radio ("School Picture"), and collected stamps ("Wally's Orchid").

One of the other things to mention regarding Ward's boyhood are his ordeals with bullies in school. One bully caused him to take the back alleys to school until he finally faced the bully ("Beaver's Fortune"). Also, he took revenge on another bully by laying out barrel hoops and enticing him out of his house where he walked over them and fell down ("Lumpy Rutherford"). Some final things to mention include Ward having his tonsils removed when he was in the fifth grade ("Beaver's Tonsils"). He went to the State Fair and got gypped by a guy selling a tin whistle ("Beaver's Accordion"). He also owned a canoe ("Beaver's Frogs"), lived on or near Shannon Avenue ("The Grass is Always Greener") and some of the kids at school called him elephant ears ("Wally's Pug Nose" and "Beaver, the Sheepdog").

Ward Cleaver the Athlete

If you ever wondered where Wally got his great athletic ability, we know June was the captain of her school basketball team, but it was Ward who was the most athletic parent. He played baseball, football, track and field, and basketball. There are many episodes in which he talks about his athletic abilities and even one in which June talks about his athletic inability as when he fumbled the ball on the one-yard line in a game ("The Paper Route"). Of the sports he played, Ward was best at basketball as is evidenced by his being a starter on his college team and scoring twenty-three points against Muhlenberg College ("The Perfect Father").

Starting with baseball, Ward speaks of his playing baseball as a boy in the Industrial League ("Beaver Takes a Walk") and that he was a first basemen ("Perfume Salesmen"). He also speaks of playing baseball where the new department store in Mayfield was built ("Teacher Comes to Dinner"). He also had baseball tryouts in second grade, and he tried building up his pitching arm by carrying an unabridged dictionary all week before the tryouts ("Next Door Indians"). He was also a big fan of baseball and some of that may have come from having an uncle who was a major league player, his Uncle Frank. He went to a game when he was seventeen years old, and his Uncle Frank had some of his friends autograph a ball for Ward. One of his favorite players was Kiki Cuyler ("Ward's Baseball"). One final point related to baseball was his forging the signature of a major league baseball player on a baseball. He signed Gabby Hartnett's signature on a baseball and addressed it to himself ("Beaver and Kenneth").

There are also quite a few football references Ward makes in various episodes. He speaks of playing as a kid when Beaver asks for a football helmet, uniform and pants for a new football team he is creating ("Beaver's Team"). He played football in high school while working and keeping up good grades ("Part-Time Genius"), played football either in high school or college ("Wally, the Lifeguard"), played high school football ("Beaver, the Hero") and played college football ("The Paper Route").

In addition to baseball and football experiences, Ward was a very good basketball player and it is seen with his awesome hook shot when he demonstrates it to Wally and his friends. As he demonstrates, he tells the boys how he scored twenty-three points against Muhlenberg College ("The Perfect Father") in Pennsylvania. As of this writing, Muhlenberg is a Division III basketball program. In high school, Ward participated in the shot put and once, came close to setting a school record ("Beaver's Old Friend"). Ward was also a competitive swimmer as a kid ("Beaver's

Team"). I almost forgot to mention, that in second grade, Ward won the Hop, Step and Jump event, something similar to a child's Field Day event.

Ward and Girls

There's no certain timeline to when Ward's girl experiences began, but he says there was a "little" girl in one of his classes that he had a crush on and he began acting strange, at least, that's what his parents thought about his behavior. He acted so sick that they almost took him to the doctor ("More Blessed to Give"). He speaks of other schoolboy crushes which included an eighth-grade girl who had platinum hair, a page boy haircut and braces ("Beaver's Crush"). In sixth grade, he had a crush on a girl named Eleanor Christoph whose father had owned a paint store ("Farewell to Penny"). Whether it was a crush or a real girlfriend, Ward mentions his first love was a girl whose face was "a mass of freckles and she had burnt orange hair and one tooth that was slow coming down" ("Brother vs. Brother").

The following five girls were specifically ones Ward dated or liked in high school. If not specifically mentioned as being in high school, they seem to fit in the context of the episode in which they are mentioned, as being in high school. They include Evelyn Bowdenhouse who told him he looked like Melvyn Douglas ("Beaver's Accordion"), Agnes Fuller, who he took on a date and forgot his wallet. His mom wound up taking it to him while on the date ("Wally's Dinner Date"). Another was Helene Quigley, a girl it took him over a year to get a date with (Beaver the Babysitter), Loretta Misch who was considered the "Darling of Shaker Heights," sort of his dream girl ("Wally's Dream Girl"), and June Bronson, a girl he gave an orchid to when she was just sixteen years old ("Wally's Orchid"). He also skipped out on a regular Sunday afternoon ride with his parents in the country in order to go on his first date with her ("Un-Togetherness").

After high school, maybe during college, Ward went to San Francisco and spent time with a woman there sometime between 1939 and 1944. He recounted the memory to June, but she told him she'd never been to San Francisco… ooops ("Pet Fair"). Another girl around this time was Maude Hegeman, the daughter of his mother's friend and he had to take her to prom in college ("Blind Date Committee"). He also speaks of an unnamed girl in college that liked him, but the feelings weren't mutual ("Wally and Alma").

Cars

Ward had at least two automobiles and maybe more. He mentions that he owned a roadster ("Beaver's Old Friend") and had a car that every time the door was slammed, the headlights went on ("Beaver Plays Hooky"). Family cars, when he was a young boy, included a Model T ("Beaver Takes a Drive") and a Hupmobile ("Ward's Millions"). He tells June that she became his last girlfriend when he found out her dad owned a Hupmobile ("Brother vs. Brother").

School Memories

In Ward's younger school years, he heard a rumor that the school had a machine that would wash out your mouth with soap ("Price of Fame"). He was also forced to wear white stockings to school once ("Beaver's Short Pants"). Ward claims to have been a new boy in school a couple times when speaking to Gilbert's father, but a move is never mentioned as part of his childhood. He may have been referring to when he entered grammar school and when he entered high school ("Beaver and Gilbert").

Ward says he went to prep school ("Cleaning up Beaver"), but that is never mentioned in another episode and a couple high school memories for Ward involve having to wear a collared shirt and tie to school each day ("Beaver's Ring") and joining a group of guys to help carry one of his classmates' small Austin automobile up to the top of the school steps as a practical joke ("Wally's Practical Joke").

In College, Ward worked a job and played sports ("The Paper Route") ("Most Interesting Character"). He was a basketball player, either as a starter or the best sixth man ever. This is determined by his scoring twenty-three points against Muhlenberg College ("The Perfect Father"). Ward performed in a play in college where he had the role of a hula girl and had to wear a grass skirt ("Wally's Play"). He was a member of the Alpha Kappa fraternity ("Wally and the Fraternity") and its president at State ("Wally's Election"). He also cooked for his fraternity brothers ("Mother's Day Composition").

World War II

Ward Cleaver was either drafted or he enlisted in the United States Navy. The Seabees, of which he was a part, is mentioned or alluded to in the following episodes: "The Perfect Father," "Beaver's Hero," "Most Interesting Character," "Double Date," "The Mustache," "Eddie's Sweater" and "Summer in Alaska."

When Ward tells June that he put up 100s of basketball backboards across the South Pacific during the war, June makes a remark about how everyone contributed to the war effort in their own way ("The Perfect Father"). She was making a joke, but someone with thinner skin that Ward, may have been a bit offended by her remark. In another episode, Ward tells Beaver that he was an engineer when he entered the armed services. He says that the government put people where they could be useful and that's how he got into the Seabees ("Beaver's Hero"). When speaking about how a girl or woman can cause a fight between friends like what happened between Eddie and Wally in "Eddie's Sweater," Ward shares that he got in a fight in the Seabees over a poster of Lana Turner. The final time Ward is spoken of being a member of the Seabees is when Eddie Haskell visits the Cleaver house in "Summer in Alaska" and tells Ward that he didn't realize the Seabees were such a nautical outfit.

You can read more about Ward over at http://leaveittobeaverbooks.com.

36

MOVIES AND TV

Our lives today center quite a lot around television and movies. One may say that life centered a lot around TV even back in the 1950s as that is when the TV dinner was invented by Swanson. They sold 10,000,000 dinners the year the TV dinner debuted and 25,000,000 the following year.[85] That was the beginning of the end of the nightly family gathering around the dinner or supper table. If only the selections on TV were as good now as they were then. But at least today, we have the many retro TV networks airing great shows like *Leave it to Beaver*.

In *Leave it to Beaver*, the first season rarely mentions television. It looks to only have been mentioned in "Captain Jack" and "Lonesome Beaver." Season two has the number of mentions of television shows or something said about television at an over 400% higher rate. For each of the following seasons, the number of episodes a TV show or television is mentioned remains in double digits, ranging from eleven to thirteen times per season.

For the most part, movies on *Leave it to Beaver* are simply movies. They are just something to waste some time on a Saturday morning or Saturday afternoon and in later years for Wally, they are a place to take a date like Mary Ellen Rogers or Julie Foster. But occasionally, a plot is centered around a movie, this happens with two fictional movies created by the writers.

The first of these movies is *Voodoo Curse* in the episode, "Voodoo Magic." Watching this movie at Eddie Haskell's suggestion, got Wally and Beaver into some trouble at home. They were caught in a blatant lie to their parents. No more movies for them for a while. Watching this movie didn't just get them in trouble, it gave Beaver a really good idea. He made his very own voodoo doll out of an old Raggedy Andy doll. He stuck Eddie's name on the doll with a piece of tape and stuck a nail in its chest and a pin in its stomach. You've got to love the way Beaver explains the reasoning for doing that… "I stuck the pin in him in case the nail don't get him." There's the first movie of our two that use a fictional film as a device to move the plot forward.

The Mad Hypnotist is the next fictional film to be used in such a way, as seen in "The Hypnotist." Beaver watches this film with Larry and afterward, wants to hypnotize someone, anyone, even the cat from across the street. But he has no willing subjects. Well, the cat may have been a willing subject, but Ward told Beaver to stop bothering the cat before he could successfully hypnotize it. Eddie then decides to really give Beaver "the business." He pretends to be the willing subject that Beaver has been looking for to hypnotize. Eddie puts on the full act for Beaver and walks away before Beaver has an opportunity to bring him out of his hypnotic trance. Eddie carries on this charade for quite a while until Wally puts an end to it. Eddie Haskell winds up flat on the muddy ground, which is absolutely the best place for a snake like him.

Quite a few TV shows are mentioned on *Leave it to Beaver*, but what about watching TV? Where did it happen? Who did the watching? We'll see further below the shows they did watch. For the most part, TV in the Cleaver household was watched in the den in seasons three through six. It was also watched in the boys' room at least twice ("Beaver Plays Hooky") and ("Beaver, the Hero"). Ward and June watched TV together in their room once ("Party Spoiler") and one time, June watches TV in their bedroom with Stanley, the monkey ("Beaver's Monkey"). Most of the time, Beaver is the one seen watching TV the most, while Ward and June speak of watching television at least nine times. Wally is seen watching TV a couple times ("Beaver Plays Hooky") ("Beaver on TV"). He asks or talks about wanting to watch TV three different times and references something he saw on TV a few other times including his great line, "The only fathers who don't

---

[85] Randle, Aaron. "Who Invented the TV Dinner?" *History.com*. February 24, 2021.

yell at their kids are on television." ("Tire Trouble")

Below is a list of the television shows and movies watched, mentioned, or alluded to on *Leave it to Beaver*. Movies are listed in their own categories in alphabetical order and listed under "fictional" or "actual." The actual category are movies that were produced in real life and shown at local movie theaters. A "fictional" movie is one that is made up for the purposes of a particular episode. TV shows will also be listed alphabetically and labeled "fictional" if they were made up for the show, although most every TV series listed was a show produced in real life. Each listing for a movie or TV show will have the name of the *Leave it to Beaver* episode in which it is spoken of or watched in parentheses after its title. Enjoy these lists.

Movies (fictional)

Congarilla at the Bozart Theater ("Beaver's Old Buddy")

Flowers in Spring (adults only) ("Beaver's Old Buddy")

Hot Rod Cuties at the Valencia ("Tenting Tonight")

Island of Fear at the Madison Theater ("Box Office Attraction")

Jungle Fever at the Olympic ("Happy Weekend")

Jungle Massacre at the Orpheum ("Beaver's Old Buddy")

Man Beast From Mars at the Valencia ("Tenting Tonight")

Massacre at Blood River at the Globe Theater ("Voodoo Magic")

Monsters from outer space at the Globe Theater ("Voodoo Magic")

Planet of Doom at the Bozart Theater ("Beaver's Old Buddy")

Rope Justice at the Valencia ("Tenting Tonight")

Spanish Daze at the Palace Theater ("Voodoo Curse")

The Iron Fiend ("Beaver Makes a Loan")

The Mad Hypnotist ("The Hypnotist")

The Thing that Creeps at the Globe Theater ("Voodoo Magic")

Vampires from the Amazon at the Valencia ("Tenting Tonight")

Vampire Valley at the Bozart Theater ("Beaver's Old Buddy")

Voodoo Curse at the Globe Theater ("Voodoo Magic")

Wayward Girls Go to Town at the Orpheum ("Beaver's Old Buddy")

Movies (actual)

Against All Flags w/ Maureen O'Hara ("Brother versus Brother")

How the West Was Won (1963) ("The Poor Loser")

King Kong ("Mother's Day Composition") ("Tennis, Anyone?")

Mutiny on the Bounty ("Summer in Alaska")

Pinocchio at the Valencia ("Voodoo Curse")

Roman Holiday ("Miss Landers' Fiance")

Snow White ("Wally's Dream Girl")

Spartacus ("Teacher's Daughter") ("Uncle Billy's Visit")

Tammy and the Bachelor ("Beaver's Sweater")

The Longest Day ("Wally's Practical Joke")

The Mummy's Curse (1944) starring Lon Chaney (on television)

The Three Musketeers w/ Don Ameche and The Ritz Brothers ("The Book Report")

West Side Story ("Eddie's Sweater")

Movie Theaters

Globe Theater

Madison Theater

Mayfield Theater (40 cents a ticket) ("Beaver's Prize") ("Beaver Makes a Loan")

Olympic Movie Theater

Palace Theater

Unnamed Rated X Theater ("Wally's Glamour Girl")

The Orpheum ("Beaver's Old Buddy")

The Bozart

Unnamed Drive In Theater ("Double Date") ("Chuckie's New Shoes")

Valencia Theater

Television Shows

77 Sunset Strip (reference to the character Kookie in "Larry Hides Out") ("Beaver and Kenneth")

Ben Casey ("Summer in Alaska") ("The Silent Treatment")

Captain Kangaroo ("Beaver on TV") ("The All-Night Party")

Crusader Rabbit - first cartoon made specifically for TV (1950) ("Beaver's Jacket")

Dobie Gillis ("One of the Boys")

Have Gun Will Travel ("Beaver's Tonsils")

Huckleberry Hound ("Wally's Weekend Job")

Huntley & Brinkley (News show) ("Brother versus Brother")

Kiddies' House Party (fictional show) ("The Party Spoiler")

Lassie ("The Big Fish Count")

McHale's Navy ("Summer in Alaska")

Meet the Press ("Beaver on TV")

Men Of Annapolis ("Wally's Track Meet") ("Beaver, the Hero")

Mickey Mouse Club ("Beaver on TV")

Sea Hunt (allusion) ("The Merchant Marine")

Perry Mason ("The Clothing Drive")

Teen Age Forum ("Beaver on TV") (fictional)

The Ed Sullivan Show ("Beaver's Accordion")

The Lone Ranger ("Beaver's Prize")

The Twilight Zone ("Beaver on TV")

The Untouchables ("Wally's Big Date") ("The All-Night Party") ("The Clothing Drive")

Route 66 ("Summer in Alaska")

West Point ("The Visiting Aunts")

Wyatt Earp ("The Garage Painters") ("Beaver's Fortune") ("Beaver's Tonsils")

There's so much more to be said about the movies and TV shows mentioned, seen, or alluded to on *Leave it to Beaver*. If you would like even more information on these topics, please visit http://leaveittobeaverbooks.com.

37

JUNE'S FAMILY AND MEMORIES

June Bronson b. 1925 (approximate)

From gleaning information in episodes of *Leave it to Beaver*, there are many things we can learn about June Bronson before she became a Cleaver. There are different areas we see mentioned, her parents, other relatives, her childhood, including her time at boarding school, after boarding school, college and memories of her and Ward.

Fair warning, there are many contradictions in some of the stories told by June. This is because the series was written by over forty different writers. They did not coordinate with one another. There was no series bible for all writers to study before penning an episode. Sometimes, they just did a job and wrote an episode, possibly without ever seeing a previous episode. That is perhaps why sometimes June's stories change and why any other inconsistencies exist in various episodes. These inconsistencies will be pointed out below, but that won't be a criticism on my part. I find nothing wrong with these inconsistencies, they're unique elements of the overall *Leave it to Beaver* story. Now, let's look at June, her family, and some of her memories.

June's Parents

Aunt Martha is like a mother to June and means the world to her. She asks Ward to please not allow the boys to treat her bad while Aunt Martha stays with them while she is out of town ("Beaver's Short Pants"). She states in this early first season episode that Aunt Martha is like the only mother she knew when she was young. This is similar to co-creator Bob Mosher's life when he lived with his aunt growing up. In the following mentions about June's mother, you'll notice that this is one of those "in this episode" occurrences.

In the third grade, June wanted very badly to buy an opal ring she used to look at in Sutter's Jewelry store window. Her father wouldn't let her get it. Instead, he told her she should buy something more sensible. What in the world could that be for a third grader? He had the answer…galoshes ("Beaver's Sweater"). He sounds like he was a normal father.

June's mother was a good cook, and her father had a good sense of humor. Ward seems to have gone over to her house to eat quite a few times. Her father once mentioned to her mother that they'll know if Ward is ever serious about June if he one day looks at her like he looks at one of her mother's pot roasts ("Beaver's Doll Buggy"). I assume June inherited her skill at cooking pot roast from her mother.

Fans discuss a lot about June's family being high class people with a lot of money. The Bronsons are sometimes looked down upon by fans of the show, and quite unnecessarily. But there is no episode that says her immediate family were the Bronsons. We know Aunt Martha was a Bronson. She may have been June's aunt on her mother's side, but maybe not. But one thing we can make a better assumption about is that June was raised by an affluent family. This is assumed because she attended boarding school (multiple episodes). Her mother also had the money to spend on two Broadway shows or Broadway quality shows in a short period of time, during the Great Depression, both starring Helen Hayes ("Wally and Alma"). Another thing that points to her family having money is that she was able to save enough for an opal ring in the third grade. This could've come from birthday money or other sources, but it's doubtful she earned it from doing chores ("Beaver's Sweater"). I think it's safe to assume her father had a very good job and the family was a bit well to do.

June's mother could also be a bit rough on her daughter. When June told all her friends at boarding school that her mother was a former actress named Laverne Laverne, her mother made her tell the whole school that she had lied ("Pet Fair"). Another boarding school incident that June was not very fond of was when her mom pulled some strings to get her a lead role in a school play. Her mother had recently seen Helen Hayes in a play and decided that June should be an actress. She made June take voice lessons and acting lessons. After her mom saw June perform, she saw Helen Hayes one week later and June says the comparison of the two almost killed her mom ("Wally and Alma"). That was kind of harsh of her mother.

Other Relatives

The first two relatives of June mentioned in the show are her sister Peggy and her Aunt Martha ("Beaver's Short Pants"). It is unknown if her sister Peggy is older or younger, but we can assume she was younger because she needs help from June after having a baby and because June seems to have been married at least twelve to fourteen years at this point in the show.

Aunt Martha is like the mother June never had when she was young. But again, this seems to be only an "in this episode" occurrence because her mother is referenced in many other episodes. We also know from this episode that Aunt Martha is sensitive, old fashioned and never been married. This seems to be consistent all the way up to her final appearance in the season six episode, "Beaver's Prep School." We know quite a few other things about Aunt Martha. She has two brothers ("Train Trip"), one of them is named Theodore ("Beaver's Ring"), the other brother is possibly named Wilbur and Wally looks a lot like him and Wilbur married a French girl ("Beaver's Prep School"). Aunt Martha speaks French ("Community Chest"). We know Aunt Martha is kind because she always gives gifts to the boys such as umbrellas ("Beaver's Ring"), Billy, the teddy bear ("Beaver's Old Friend"), a ring ("Beaver's Ring"), short pants ("Beaver's Short Pants"), and $3.00 ("Beaver's Birthday"). She also knows how to cook eggplant and make milk toast ("Beaver's Short Pants").

Four other relatives of June we never see in any *Leave it to Beaver* episodes include her grandfather who was "almost a genius" and an uncle who has passed away who was a judge ("Beaver's I.Q."). She also has an older cousin named Frankie and an overprotective Aunt Emma ("Beaver the Babysitter"). Yes, both, she and Ward had an Aunt Emma.

School

June attended boarding school. The grades she attended are never mentioned but there are allusions to high school ages as she mentions being the captain of her basketball team and earning a letter ("The Dramatic Club"). She also mentions wanting to be popular at the boarding school she attended ("Beaver and Kenneth"). This may be something more important to girls in junior high or high school than in lower grades. This is not necessarily so, but without more details, the only thing to do is make an assumption here. She learned how to do two practical things in boarding school, and they were mending socks, and how to make a court bow in case she married a foreign diplomat ("Bank Account"). Again, these are things she might learn at an older age. She also played George Washington in a play at boarding school. Since it was an all-girls school, the girls played male roles ("Wally's Play"). This seems like a role for an upper grammar school or high school age. She also mentions sitting in her room and imagining herself as one of the heroines in the books she would read like *Lorna Doone*, *Vanity Fair* and *Little Women.* The first two of these books are best read by the thirteen and over age group and so this also points to June being in high school at boarding school ("Beaver and Ivanhoe"). She also stayed with Aunt Martha in the summer while in boarding school ("Mother's Day Composition").

A few things mentioned about June and school are not spoken of specifically in relation to boarding school. These could have been while she was at boarding school, or the writers may have thought they happened in a regular public school. These include her being the last in her class to wear high heels ("The Shave"), her only dating boys in her own class ("Brother vs. Brother"), she admits she had only average intelligence ("Beaver's Hero"), she told kids her mother was an actress and gave it up to marry her father ("Pet Fair").

After Boarding School

June traveled to New York City and attended an opera with her boyfriend Freddie Rice. She also attended a boxing match at Madison Square Garden. She doesn't mention specifically if this was after boarding school, but it is assumed this wasn't a high school trip with her boyfriend ("Beaver's Big Contest"). June mentions in another episode that she served solders at the USO in Mayfield every Thursday. Since this was during the war, it must have been either after boarding school or during summers, but the latter would contradict her staying at Aunt Martha's during the summers ("Mother's Day Composition").

At College

When helping Beaver folding newspapers the afternoon that Wally is away at a baseball game, Beaver compliments her on her skill. She tells him she used to fold napkins for her sorority house in college ("The Paper Route"). When speaking about her rebellious side in college, she said she demonstrated it by wearing dirty saddle shoes ("Wally and the Fraternity"). In this same episode, it is mentioned that she met Ward at State, the school Wally will be attending.

Early Memories of Ward

In the discussion of her memories of Ward, we see some of the typical inconsistencies found in quite a few episodes. Again, there's nothing wrong with these inconsistencies, they were just a part of being a writer for 1950s and early 1960s television. One of those inconsistencies is Ward giving her an orchid when she was sixteen ("Wally's Orchid") when she says in "Wally's Fraternity" that they met in college. She mentions a specific night that Ward went to her house to eat supper with her family. This was also the first time they ever washed dishes together. He held her hand under the soap suds ("Wally's Glamour Girl"). There's a reference to his going to eat supper at her house when she mentions her father talking about him enjoying her mother's pot roast ("Beaver's Doll Buggy"). June spoke one time about how she used to wait around for Ward to call her. Because of that memory, she doesn't want Wally to make Alma wait for him to call her ("Wally and Alma").

If you want to read more about June's memories, visit http://leaveittobeaverbooks.com. While there, don't forget to sign up for updates so you will be eligible for our future giveaways of autographed photos and other LITB related merchandise.

38

FIREMEN

A lot of *Leave it to Beaver* fans may overlook that there were three firemen featured as Beaver's firehouse friend in season one. We all know Gus, the fireman, played by actor Burt Mustin. He was brilliant as a friend to the young Beaver. But do you remember Charlie or Pete?

Fireman Charlie

Charlie is seen in only one episode of *Leave it to Beaver*. In "The Clubhouse," Wally, Chester, Eddie and Tooey decide to make a clubhouse. They can charge people to be in their club. Beaver wants to join too, and Eddie tells him he can be in the club, and they'll only charge him $3.00. In his effort to make money, Beaver begins walking through town wearing a sandwich board, selling advertising to make money. He goes to Auxiliary Fire House #7 and asks the fireman on duty if he'd like to advertise. The fireman is asleep when Beaver makes his presence known. Beaver says hello to Charlie. Wait! What happened to Gus? He was just there a few episodes earlier. Well, this Fireman Charlie, played by actor Raymond Hatton, is only around for this episode. Maybe he was too busy with other commitments to continue on with *Leave it to Beaver*. Throughout his career, he had over 400 roles in movies and television. Who knows why he never appeared again? Sometimes, it's just that one actor is a better fit than another.

Fireman Pete

If you need a cat out of a tree, Fireman Pete is the man to call. But what about getting kids out of a bathroom? Yes, he can do that too. Wally and Beaver find themselves in a bit of trouble after Puddin' locks herself in the Cleaver bathroom. Little Bengie Bellamy, in a failed rescue attempt, gets locked in the bathroom too. Wally calls Pete at auxiliary firehouse #7 and he comes to the rescue. The actor who played Pete was veteran B-movie actor Will Wright. He appeared in almost every quality late 1950s TV show after working the 1940s and early 50s in films.

Fireman Gus

You must admit that Gus is the only fireman Mayfield ever needed. He was the perfect companion for Bever Cleaver. His first appearance on *Leave it to Beaver* was in "The Black Eye." His last appearance was in "Beaver's Fear." Gus was there any time Beaver needed help ("Beaver's Newspaper"), needed some advice ("Beaver and Henry" and "A Horse Named Nick"), had a worry ("Beaver's Fear"), and even gave him a dose of reality when necessary ("Next Door Indians" and "Junior Fire Chief").

Beaver often stopped by the fire station to see Gus when he was in trouble ("Beaver Gets 'Spelled'") or when he had some time to spare ("Brotherly Love"), even if Gus didn't have any spare time for Beaver ("Lonesome Beaver). One of the things Beaver enjoyed the most about Gus was his intelligence. He knew a lot of things. When asked why a nozzle was called a nozzle, Gus told him, "Well, I guess 'cause the first fella who ever saw one thought it looked more like a nozzle than anything else." One can't argue with that. When Beaver inherited Wally's typewriter, it wouldn't work, so he and Larry took it down to the fire station ("Beaver's Newspaper"). Gus put a little oil on the keys, and it worked like magic. Beaver marvels at his intelligence and tells him how he could fix about anything, and Gus deflects the compliment by saying, "Well, I can fix clocks and wagons and bicycles... stuff like that. But if a feller come in here from Washington... with one of them satellite gadgets under his arm that was on the blink, I wouldn't even know how to get the cover off."

Gus didn't only know about how to fix things like typewriters, clocks, wagons and bicycles, he knew a lot about animals too. He knew how to disguise the smell of a human on a baby bunny rabbit so its mother would not neglect her ("Beaver and Henry). He also knew that sometimes a horse figures out if you want it to stand up, you might want him to do some work ("A Horse Named Nick).   Gus was a good fireman and a great friend. We are blessed to have had him in as many episodes of *Leave it to Beaver* as we did. If you look at his busy schedule, it's amazing he was even in the fourteen episodes in which he did appear. From 1957-1962, the time period in which he appeared on *Leave it to Beaver*, actor Burt Mustin also worked on forty-five different television shows in sixty-three different episodes. That is in addition to the fourteen episodes he worked on as Gus, the Fireman. That's a lot of work. Kudos to Gus for being the hardest working fireman Mayfield has probably ever seen, that's despite his sometimes taking a nap at Auxiliary Fire House #7 ("The Black Eye," / "Nobody Loves Me").

Beaver encounters other firemen in "The Price of Fame." In this episode, he believes, erroneously, that Mrs. Rayburn has a spanking machine in her office. He and Larry had been cleaning up in Miss Lander's classroom and when they were leaving school, Beaver goes back to the room to get his baseball cap while Larry heads home. The only people in the school are Beaver and the janitor. Beaver decides to go to Mrs. Rayburn's office to look for the spanking machine Larry told him about. The janitor locks the office door on him and the only way for Beaver to get out is to ring the fire alarm. The firemen rescue him and one of them knew his friend Gus.

There is another big rescue firemen make when Beaver finds himself in a troublesome situation. This may be the most famous rescue ever seen in all classic situation comedies. Beaver and Whitey are walking over to Whitey's house when they see a new billboard in Mayfield. The billboard advertises Zesto Soup. Whitey and Beaver disagree on whether there is real soup in the bowl on the billboard. Beaver climbs all the way up and falls into the bowl. After spending a lot of time trying to get out, the fire department comes to rescue Beaver. All of Wally's friends who were supposed to be at the Cleaver house for a party, are there at the billboard watching the rescue. Oh my! Beaver has made himself conspicuous again.

Beaver gets sentimental in the season six episode "Beaver's Prep School." In this episode, Aunt Martha decides to pay Beaver's tuition to Fallbrook, a prep school back east, a school that many Bronsons have attended in the past. When walking home from school one day, while still considering whether he will stay in Mayfield and attend Mayfield High or not, he walks by the old Auxiliary fire station. Beaver walks up to the fire house doors and there is a sign announcing people should call Fire Station #12. This auxiliary station is closed now. This scene is supposed to represent time passing and old memories. Beaver rubs dust off the window and looks inside. This sentimental moment has Beaver longing for days gone by and it is helping him make up his mind about whether to leave Mayfield or not. But for those of us who are sticklers about *Leave it to Beaver* details, you'll notice along with me, that the sign on the outside of this fire station identifies it as "Auxiliary Fire House #5," but Gus worked at Auxiliary Fire House #7 and for that matter, so did Pete and so did Charlie. Oh well, it's just one of those things that sometimes get overlooked.

39

FOOD AND DRINKS

Ever wondered about all the different types of food the Cleavers ate at home either for snacks, lunch or supper? If so, this is the chapter for you. And what about that final meal of the day, was it supper or dinner? We'll also look at the Cleavers and their eating habits outside the house. Did they ever go out for a meal? Did they like fancy restaurants or fast food joints? Let's delve into all the above below by first looking at every food item eaten or mentioned in the 234 episodes over the six seasons of *Leave it to Beaver*.

Foods Eaten (foods eaten multiple times are listed once per season)

Season 1 – tomato, hot dog, eggs, ice cream bar, celery stick, gum, soup, bread, pot roast, potato pancakes, cake, taffy, mint, liverwurst sandwich, eggs, candy bar, chocolate cake, cookies, crackers, unidentified sandwiches, apple, Boston cream pie, milk toast, toast, steak and mushrooms, corn on the cob, lima beans, Waldorf Salad, eggplant, chopped egg sandwiches, popcorn, cutlets, banana, ice cream, cereal, pie, ham, roast beef, hamburgers, hard boiled eggs, scrambled eggs, scrambled egg sandwich, (was going to be fried egg sandwich), lambchops, peas, raisin nut cookies, donuts, pear, bacon, chocolate chip ice cream, Jello, peanuts, tea sandwiches, chocolate mousse, box of raisins, carrot, tuna fish sandwiches, meat loaf, green beans, mashed potatoes, biscuits

Season 2 – bananas, cookies, ice cream, cake, bacon, eggs, bread, cereal, hard boiled eggs, potatoes, apple, toast, carrot, scrambled eggs, chocolate cake, white cake, fried eggplant, deviled ham, hamburger, celery sticks, peanut butter and jelly and lettuce sandwich ("School Play," Ward makes it but doesn't eat it), hot dog, popcorn, unidentified sandwiches, Canadian bacon, fish, cherry pie, candy bar, yellow cake with chocolate icing, Swiss cheese sandwiches, tuna fish sandwiches, lambchops, corn, tomatoes, black licorice, Chocolate Rockets, soft boiled eggs, French toast, peanut butter and jelly, roast, pork chops, sundae, orange, cream cheese and jelly sandwiches, grilled cheese sandwiches, olives, oats and hay (for horse), jam sandwich, peanut butter sandwich, peas, mashed potatoes, broccoli, coconut cake, coleslaw, peanuts, tapioca pudding, candy floss/cotton candy

Season 3 – pickles, potato chips, cookies, hamburgers, peas, biscuits, toast, pancakes, sandwiches, popcorn, ice cream, eggs, roast, apples, olives, salad, steak, onions, peanuts, tuna fish sandwiches, apple pie, cake, bananas, meatloaf, carrots, bread, celery sticks, scrambled eggs, old fashioned pot roast frozen dinner, chicken, soup, crackers, candy, lambchops, chocolate cake, gingerbread man, bologna sandwich (meat on outside of bread), deviled ham, canned corn boiling, leg of lamb, spaghetti, ice cream bar, salami sandwich, pickle, French toast, chopped egg sandwiches

Season 4 – Brussels sprouts, eggs, toast, bacon, cake, olives, potatoes, shrimp cocktails, apple, carrots, canned peaches, ice cream, soup, crackers, cookies, pears, chocolate sundae, peas, potatoes, ice cream bar, waffles, bread, apple pie, celery, salad, ribs, mashed potatoes, licorice, fried eggs, ham and grape jelly sandwich (The Dramatic Club), roast beef, pork chops, fried chicken, stuffed eggs, cheese, nuts, lettuce, ice cream cones

Season 5 – Snap beans, oatmeal, bread, fried eggs, toast, sandwiches, Wheat Chex, hamburgers, pan friend salmon, apples, ice cream (mashed potatoes), cookies, vanilla ice cream, pistachio ice cream, mashed potatoes, peas, Rice Chex, bananas, pancakes, cake, French toast, carrots, bacon, TV dinners, chocolate cake, day old eclairs, scrambled eggs, roast beef, hot dogs, pot roast

Season 6 – Bacon, eggs, bananas, pancakes, toast, candy, cereal, ice cream sundae, pie, sandwich, meatloaf, bread, mashed potatoes, pot roast, peas, apple, chicken salad, tossed green salad, rolls, soup, spare ribs, potato chips, yellow cake, hot dogs, cotton candy, peanuts, chocolate chip cookies, orange, green beans, apple pie, carrots, chocolate cake, French toast, pizza at drive-in restaurant, (Poor Loser), cheese sandwich, fruit cocktail, turnips, strawberry shortcake, corn

List of all foods eaten on *Leave it to Beaver* (Alphabetical Order)

Apple, apple pie, bacon, bananas, biscuits, black licorice, bologna sandwich (meat on outside of bread), Boston cream pie, bread, broccoli, Brussels sprouts, cake, Canadian bacon, candy, candy bar, candy floss/cotton candy, carrots, celery sticks, cereal, cheese, cherry pie, chicken, chicken salad, chocolate cake, chocolate chip cookies, chocolate chip ice cream, chocolate mousse, Chocolate Rockets, chocolate sundae, chopped egg sandwiches, coconut cake, coleslaw, cookies, corn, corn on the cob, crackers, cream cheese and jelly sandwiches, cutlets, deviled ham, donuts, eclairs, eggplant, eggs, eggs (fried), eggs (hard boiled), eggs (scrambled), eggs (soft boiled), fish, French toast, fried chicken, fried eggplant, fruit cocktail, gingerbread man, green beans, grilled cheese sandwiches, gum, ham, ham and grape jelly sandwich (The Dramatic Club), hamburgers, hot dog, ice cream, ice cream bar, ice cream cones, jam sandwich, Jello, lambchops, leg of lamb, lettuce, licorice, lima beans, liverwurst sandwich, mashed potatoes, meat loaf, milk toast, mint, mushrooms, nuts, oatmeal, old fashioned pot roast frozen dinner, olives, onions, orange, pancakes, pan friend salmon, peaches (canned), peanut butter sandwich, peanut butter and jelly sandwich, peanut butter and jelly and lettuce sandwich (school play, makes, but doesn't eat it), peanuts, pears, peas, pickles, pie, pizza at drive-in restaurant, (Poor Loser), popcorn, pork chops, potato chips, potatoes, pot roast, raisin nut cookies, raisins (box of), ribs, Rice Chex, roast, roast beef, rolls, salad, salami sandwich, scrambled egg sandwich (was going to be fried egg sandwich), shrimp cocktails, snap beans, soup, spaghetti, spare ribs, steak, strawberry shortcake, stuffed eggs, sundae, Swiss cheese sandwiches, taffy, tapioca pudding, tea sandwiches, tomatoes, toast, tossed green salad, tuna fish sandwiches, turnips, TV dinners, unidentified sandwiches, waffles, Waldorf Salad, Wheat Chex, white cake, yellow cake with chocolate icing.

Most Eaten Foods

When it comes to snacks or desserts, the most often eaten was an apple (16.2%) followed by cookies (15.8%), ice cream (12.8%) and cakes (10.7%). Apples were eaten in almost forty episodes and of those episodes, Larry was the eater in most of them (47%), more than doubling Wally's apple consumption (23.7%). Beaver comes in third place in the race for the most apples eaten (15.8%). Interesting tidbits about ice cream on the show: In "Wally's Weekend Job," Wally pours pistachio ice cream all over Lumpy. Frank Bank said it was lime yogurt, and said it was a very hot day on the studio lot, about 110 degrees. [86] Actor Stephen Talbot mentioned that once when he and Beaver are eating ice cream cones while walking home, that the scoops of vanilla ice

---

[86] Stu's Show March 5, 2008. According to production code for that episode, it was filmed first in season five. Pamela Beaird, in an interview with author also mentioned it being very hot that day.

cream were really scoops of mashed potatoes, so if multiple takes were needed, the ice cream wouldn't melt.[87]

For breakfast, there are just a little over 100 episodes in which food is shown and can be identified. Eggs are eaten at breakfast in 52% of those episodes. No French toast or pancakes are mentioned or seen in the show until Beaver tells Larry he ate French toast for breakfast, as they sit hiding behind a billboard in "Beaver Plays Hooky." The French toast output seems slight (10.6%), but it's impressive that even one day before church, maybe one of the most hectic mornings of the week, June makes French toast for the family in "Beaver's Old Buddy." Pancakes do make a better showing as a breakfast food in *Leave it to Beaver* episodes (13.5%).

One of the more surprising things about the Cleaver breakfasts first occurs in "Beaver's Cat Problem" (S 5 Ep 5). A box of Chex brand cereal appears on the kitchen counter. In this episode, it was Wheat Chex. Then, in three of the next six episodes, a box of Rice Chex is seen. After these appearances, never again, does a box of Chex cereal appear in any *Leave it to Beaver* episodes.

Supper or Dinner?

In *Leave it to Beaver*, the characters use the terms supper and dinner for the third meal of the day interchangeably. For example, Ward called the meal either supper or dinner in over fifty episodes. In 56% of those episodes, he called the meal supper and dinner 44% of the time. The most interesting thing is that in six episodes, he called the meal both supper and dinner within just a few moments. June referred to the meal as supper or dinner in over seventy episodes. She called it supper 68% of the time and 32% of the time, she called it dinner. In two episodes, she called it both dinner and supper. In "Eddie, the Businessman," June calls the meal supper when talking to Beaver in one line and in her next line to him, she calls it dinner. Wally speaks of the meal in over thirty episodes, with dinner beating supper 68% to 32% while Beaver identifies the meal in over twenty-five episodes with dinner winning at a 71% to 29% margin. The most eaten foods for dinner/supper are not mentioned because with these meals, the food is less easily identified, and the sample would be small.

Eating Out

A look at where and when the Cleavers may have eaten outside the home shows this occurred in about thirty different episodes. This number includes eating at a malt shop, having an ice cream at the drug store, an expensive meal at the *White Fox* or at an unnamed restaurant where they serve Brussels sprouts. In these episodes, Ward and June go on their own 29% of the time. The Cleavers as a family eat out 32% of the time, while some combination of Wally and Ward, Wally and friends, Ward by himself, and Ward with others make up 39% of all times eaten out.

The restaurants where a good meal was had, ranged from *The Chuckwagon* where they serve doggie burgers ("The Visiting Aunts") to the swankiest joint in town, *The White Fox* ("Wally's Dinner Date"). Other restaurants mentioned were *The Colonial House* ("Wally's Track Meet"), where the family didn't eat since Wally was kicked off the team, and *The Hampshire House* where Fred invited Ward to lunch ("Last Day of School").

There's more information on food to be found at the http://leaveittobeaverbooks.com website.

---

[87] Stephen Talbot in an email correspondence with Bryon Nelson Jr. of the "Leave it to Beaver Fan Club" Facebook group. Also mentioned in a post in the group on August 24, 2022.

40

GIFTS AND PRIZES

Throughout the series, someone is always being given a gift. There are gifts given for many different reasons and among them are birthdays, illnesses, people moving away, celebrating great accomplishments, Christmas, souvenirs from vacations, and there are gifts given just for the sake of giving gifts. Let's take a closer look.

Gifts for Beaver (or to both boys)

Sometimes, there are gifts given that are not exactly welcomed or looked upon enthusiastically by their recipients. For Beaver and Wally, this includes soap they receive at Christmas from an unidentified relative and umbrellas from Aunt Martha ("Beaver's Short Pants"). The boys also receive a piggy bank from Ward, an instrument that helps them save money, not a gift for which they have been yearning ("The Bank Account"). Whitey and Judy give Beaver his missed homework assignments when he was home sick from school, a far cry from the magic set Wally was given by his class when he was sick the previous day ("New Doctor"). Aunt Martha strikes again when she gives both Beaver and Wally sweaters ("The Visiting Aunts"). A final unwanted and underappreciated gift is when Ward gives Beaver a hamster for the pet fair after he already lied to Miss Landers, telling her he had a pet parrot ("Pet Fair").

Ward typically gave good gifts. He gave the boys a full-size film projector when the Mason Acme company sent them a hunk of junk ("The Perfume Salesmen"). He gives them a regulation size basketball and basketball goal ("The Perfect Father"). After Beaver is scolded for using Ward's tools, and then runs away, Ward at the end of the episode, gives Beaver and Wally their own toolset ("Beaver Runs Away"). Ward gives Beaver a piece of his childhood, a pedometer, and when it causes Beaver to lose his baseball glove, Ward gives him a new glove to replace the one he lost in a bet ("Beaver Takes a Walk"). When Beaver finds a wallet and the owner promises to send him a gift, she never does. Ward picks up the slack and buys him a clock radio on her behalf ("Beaver Finds a Wallet"). Penny at her farewell party, gives Beaver her pencil box ("Farewell to Penny"). When Beaver's grown too old for birthday parties and toys, Ward and June give him $10.00 ("Beaver's Birthday"). Another fine gift Ward gives, along with June, is a specially inscribed wristwatch ("Beaver's Graduation").

Aunt Martha, best known for umbrellas at Christmas time, also gave good gifts on occasion. She gave Beaver a teddy bear when he had the measles ("Beaver's Old Friend"). She also gave Beaver a 14k gold ring that belonged to his Uncle Theodore ("Beaver's Ring"). She also gave Beaver a savings bond for his birthday ("The Lost Watch"). Then, maybe her best gift ever… short pants… no, that's a joke. No, her best gift was an expensive prep school education at Fallbrook. She was willing to pay for Beaver to go east to school, continuing the Bronson tradition. Beaver declines but does his best not to hurt her feelings ("Beaver's Prep School").

Gifts for Wally

Wally is the recipient of several good gifts. Early in the series, he speaks of receiving an arrowhead from an uncle who had visited Arizona ("Next Door Indians"). When sick in bed, he receives a model from June, and a magic set from his class. On his birthday, he receives $10.00 from Aunt Martha, a watch from his parents, a Microcraft brand microscope from Eddie, a pen and pencil set from Uncle Tom. Along with those good gifts, he also received a paddle and ball toy from Beaver ("Wally's Present"). Uncle Billy gives Wally and Beaver $10.00 each when he comes to visit ("Uncle Billy"). When Wally is tasked to be the man of the house while Ward is on a business trip, he does such a fine job that June asks Ward to bring him something special ("Substitute Father"). On a past birthday, Wally was given a record player by Aunt Martha ("Wally's Dinner Date"). On Wally's seventeenth birthday, he receives a box of handkerchiefs from Beaver and a very nice sweater from Ward and June, and he gets what he wants most, permission to get his drivers' license ("Wally's License"). Uncle Billy brings the boys a gun and a big knife when he comes visiting and gives them money the next morning before they head out for the day ("Uncle Billy's Visit"). Finally, Beaver gives Wally a foul ball he caught at the baseball game he attended, when Wally said he could go since Beaver was acting like such a bad sport ("The Poor Loser").

Gifts for Ward

The first gift Ward receives on *Leaver it to Beaver* is a bouquet of flowers from Miss Rayburn. It's a gift given on false pretenses because Beaver lies about him being sick ("Beaver Gets 'Spelled"). He is sent an ornamental pipe from Fred Rutherford while he's away on a vacation in Germany ("The Pipe"). Ward's Uncle Billy gave him an apron that reads, "Chief cook and bottle washer" ("Teacher Comes to Dinner"). Other gifts Ward receives are English bath salts ("June's Birthday"), a bottle of brandy from Uncle Billy ("Beaver and Andy"), an autographed baseball from Uncle Frank ("Ward's Baseball"), Royal brand shaving lotion ("Beaver's House Guest"), and that wonderful book, *How I Became a Millionaire in 12 Months* that Beaver gives him that will make all his money problems disappear ("Ward's Millions"). The gift that has the biggest impact on Ward, and one he almost had sent back to the store, is the hunting jacket the boys bought him from the fanciest sporting goods store in town, Abernathy & Potts. As the clerk told Wally and Beaver, the jacket they are buying him will last a lifetime ("The Bank Account").

Gifts for June

When Larry spends the night at the Cleavers, his mother gives June a box of candy. Unfortunately, Larry sits on the box and squashes it on the way over to their house ("Beaver's Guest"). June receives flowers from Beaver's friend Chuey's parents ("Beaver and Chuey"). For her birthday, yes, the birthday where Beaver buys her *THAT* blouse, she also receives a monogrammed wallet from Wally and a watch from Ward ("June's Birthday"). Not to be outdone by Beaver when it comes to gifts, one day, for no reason at all, Ward decides to gift June a crock of pickles. He comes home with this surprise, and she has no idea how they'll ever eat them all ("Wally, the Businessman"). June also receives a box of candy from Beaver's friend Chopper ("Beaver's House Guest").

Gifts for Ward and June

As a couple, Ward and June speak of receiving a few different gifts. Ward's Uncle Harry gave them the book *Quotations from the Arabic* on their anniversary. However, Ward was expecting a check from him instead ("Brotherly Love"). Ward and June received a teapot as a wedding present from Beaver's grandmother, maternal or paternal is unknown ("Beaver Says

Good-Bye"). A gift given to Ward and June by Ward's mother were some bowls he thinks look silly, until June tells him they were a gift from his mother ("Teacher Comes to Dinner").

Gifts for Others

Beaver is a good gift giver, except for that one birthday of June's… and that one birthday of Wally's and that David Manning birthday too. Wait, it was June who gave him an inappropriate gift to give to David. Beaver wound up giving him his new camera ("Forgotten Party"). So, honestly, Beaver is a good gift giver most of the time. Just look at the shrunken head he gave Miss Canfield ("Beaver Gets 'Spelled"), along with Wally, he gave away his alligator to the alligator farm ("Captain Jack"), he gave his frog Herbie to Penny Jamison ("Wally's Girl Trouble"), he took flowers to Mrs. Donaldson ("New Neighbor") and did the same for Eddie when he was home sick ("Voodoo Magic"). Beaver also gave Bengie Bellamy his old Teddy bear ("Beaver's Old Friend") because he had the measles. Beaver also did the unthinkable, by giving Miss Landers an inappropriate gift of a slip ("The Last Day of School"). Beaver also gives his electric trains to Jimmy Battson and a $20.00 locket to a girl he likes named Donna Yeager.

Other gifts given throughout the series include Larry buying his father a tie pin for a quarter ("June's Birthday"), Miss Landers is given a fountain pen from Gilbert, a bottle of perfume from Judy and Richard gives her a frog paper weight ("The Last Day of School"), Ward and June give Mrs. Thompson flowers when they visit her in the hospital ("Chuckie's New Shoes"), they also give a gift to Paul and Joanne McBride for their anniversary ("No Time for Babysitters"), Mr. Blair gives Penny Woods a nice fountain pen for a going away present ("Farewell to Penny") and Lumpy receives many gifts at the party celebrating his scholarship ("Lumpy's Scholarship").

Prizes Won

Beaver wins the majority of prizes on *LITB*. His prizewinning begins when his name is drawn at Linda Dennison's party. He wins a lovely toy doll ("Party Invitation"). His winning continues when his ticket is drawn at the Mayfield Theater after Larry talks him into leaving his house and going to the movies even though he's grounded. He wins an English Touring bicycle, but the theater manager calls it a racing bicycle. Beaver's winning ticket was #6487532 ("Beaver's Prize"). The most valuable prize Beaver wins is a $3500 sports car, but Ward forces him to sell it ("Beaver's Big Contest"). He wins a $20 locket playing Hoopla at the carnival. The girl he gives it to, Donna Yeager, does not get to keep it. Her father makes her return it and Donna claims doing so may just give her a trauma ("More Blessed to Give").

Others who win prizes include Angela Valentine winning a box of candy in the class baby picture contest, a contest she suggested. That seems quite fishy ("Baby Picture"). Mary Ellen Rogers is a big winner, not just because she got Wally to go with her to a couple dances, but because she won three records from a DJ on the radio ("Beaver, the Bunny"). Then, there were all the kids who won the collie at Mr. Parker's pet shop because Eddie gave Lumpy the winning number of fish in the tank and he doesn't know how to keep a secret ("Big Fish Count").

The Absolutely Best Ever Gift

Some character on the show would tell me what I'm about to say is corny, but the best gift in regard to the show is the show itself. The show is a gift given to us by its creators Joe Connelly and Bob Mosher, and the forty plus writers who scripted the 234 episodes, along with the many directors and all crew members behind the scenes…and of course, the actors. Thank you everyone!

41

GIRLS

When the *Leave it to Beaver* series begins, Beaver doesn't like girls and Wally is getting to a point where he likes them, but that feeling of semi-affection toward the opposite sex is something new to him. A thorough examination of all the girls, ones that are hated, ones that are liked, and those who are loved is good subject matter for an exhaustive *Leave it to Beaver* book like this one. We'll look at Beaver and his relationship with girls first, then Wally, Eddie and that all important category, "others."

Beaver and Girls

How Beaver feels about girls throughout the series is an appropriate way to begin his section. As you can imagine, it takes a few seasons for Beaver to gain any appreciation for girls. Even by the series' end, his attention span can stray away from a girl somewhat easily, as in taking a cross country trip with his best friend ("Beaver Sees America").

In season one, Beaver's feelings are quite evident when he tells Gus that he's never getting married ("The Black Eye"), admits to Mrs. Donaldson that he doesn't like girls ("New Neighbors"), tells Miss Higgins that girls make him sick ("Wally's Girl Trouble"), tells Wally that Linda Dennison looks awful ("Party Invitation") and ignores Mary Ellen Rogers after she uses him to get a date with Wally ("My Brother's Girl"). He also gives a good reason for his dislike of girls to Miss Canfield when he tells her that little girls don't smell as nice as she does ("Beaver's Crush").

His dislike for girls doesn't stop at the end of season one as we see him say over the next few seasons that he'd rather smell a skunk than go see Eddie's girl ("Eddie's Girl"), tells Linda he never talks to girls ("Her Idol"), says that there is no girl in the entire school someone could pay him to kiss ("School Play"), admits he'd rather take a million hikes than dance with a girl ("The Grass is Always Greener"), tells Wally he'd never change his nose for a girl, even if it was a foot long ("Wally's Pug Nose"), tells June that he won't ever marry a silly girl, instead, he'll marry a mother ("Dance Contest"), surmises that girls mess up guys ("Dance Contest"), says "anything is better than dancing with girls" ("Beaver's Dance"), asks why Wally doesn't sock Frances when she doesn't give his sweater back ("School Sweater"), warns that he won't go to high school if they make guys call girls ("Wally and Alma"), calls girls rats ("Eddies' Double-Cross"), tells Ward that girls give him the creeps ("Teacher's Daughter"), admits to Wally that girls make him sick ("The Dramatic Club"), says he and Richard have a pact to hate girls ("Wally's Chauffeur"). It seems that his utter disdain for girls begins to ebb near the end of season four.

Now, Beaver liking girls is a rare occurrence in the early years, but there are some episodes in which he does mention liking a particular girl. Beaver tells Mrs. Donaldson that he likes Angela Valentine ("New Neighbors"), but that *like* seems more similar to intrigue when he says it is because she has an extra toe. He likes Linda Dennison ("Her Idol") because she climbs trees and doesn't mind getting dirty ("School Sweater"). Beaver eats with Mary Ellen Rogers at school and likes her, but it is because she lets him come over to play with her father's trains ("My Brother's Girl"). When June finds out, he asks her to keep it a secret from Wally because, as he says, "We're supposed to hate girls." Beaver doesn't come out and say he likes Penny when he visits her house ("Beaver's Doll Buggy"), but they seem to tolerate each other and are friendly which is a precursor to his "liking" and admitting he will miss her in "Farewell to Penny."

Beaver liking any girls is quite surprising. In fact, Wally is shocked when he finds out Beaver likes a girl at dancing school ("Beaver's First Date"). Beaver temporarily falls for a new girl in "Brother vs. Brother" until she sees Wally and wants nothing else to do with Beaver. When Wally tells her off and calls her a little girl, she then wants Beaver again, but he tells her to DROP DEAD. A few other girls Beaver ends up liking are the paper girl he beats up and then goes with her to the beach at the end of the episode ("The Late Edition"), Donna Yeager, to whom he gives an expensive locket ("More Blessed to Give), the girl in each of these episodes was played by actress Chrystine Jordan; the Southern Belle Melinda Nielson ("Don Juan Beaver") and Mary Margaret Matthews, a girl who is way too advanced for Beaver ("Beaver Sees America").

Love finds Beaver on a few occasions. The first is when he is in love with his second-grade teacher Miss Canfield ("Beaver's Crush"). This is an episode filled with trouble for Beaver and includes him admitting to Miss Canfield that he'd asked his mom when he would be able to marry her. In his second bout with love, Beaver expresses it with lovesickness when he finds out Miss Landers has a fiancé and is planning to get married, leaving him behind at the proverbial altar ("Miss Landers' Fiancé"). He is later asked by Gilbert if he is in love with Donna Yeager ("More Blessed to Give"), but Beaver isn't sure if he is or not.

Beaver and marriage is something that wouldn't seem too important of a topic due to his age. He, however, does speak about it on various occasions, some of those times are when June warns him that one day, he'll get married. He tells her, "Well Maybe, but I'm not going to marry any silly girls, I'm gonna marry a mother" ("Dance Contest"). While in "Beaver Takes a Bath," Beaver says when he gets married, he's not going to take his wife anywhere and explains that just because a guy gets married, it doesn't mean he has to like girls. After meeting a character played by Karen Sue Trent, a girl dressed in cowgirl garb and riding a horse ("Beaver's Dance"), Beaver and Larry have a deep philosophical talk in which Beaver admits that when he gets married, he's going to marry a girl with a horse. And as mentioned above, his first ever talk of marriage and his object of affection then, was his second-grade teacher Miss Canfield ("Beaver's Crush").

Wally and Girls

There never was a time on *Leave it to Beaver* when Wally was as anti-girl as Beaver was through the first three seasons. When June tells Beaver that Wally has changed his mind and now likes girls, Wally interjects and says, "There's an awful lot of girls that still give me the creeps" ("Blind Date Committee"). But, for the most part, Wally really digs girls, although he never really makes a big deal about his feelings toward girls, especially around his parents.

The following are the names of every girl Wally liked or went out on a date with on *Leave it to Beaver*: Miss Hildebrand, Penny Jamison, Mary Ellen Rogers, Caroline Cunningham, Gloria Cusick, Harriet, Jill Bartlett, Ralph, Marty's sister, Alma Hanson, Myra Barker, Kitty Bannerman, Julie Foster, Margie Manners, Ginny Townsend, Evelyn Boothby, Gail Preston, Carole Martin, Lori Ann, Carolyn Stuart, Shirley, Marlene Holmes and Kathy Gregory.

Let's look at the girls he likes in the early seasons first. After a crush he tells Beaver he had on Miss Hildebrand, the woman who lived next to them up at the lake ("Beaver's Crush"), the girls he likes starts with Penny Jamison ("Wally's Girl Trouble"), a girl Beaver says has a face like a flounder. She also doesn't like grubby little kids. Mary Ellen Rogers makes her first appearance in season one ("My Brother's Girl") when she cozies up to Beaver, eating with him at lunch and inviting him over to her house to play with her father's train set, just so she could get Wally to take her to the school dance. Her last appearance comes in season five ("Wally's Weekend Job") and she continues to be mentioned as a girlfriend, date or close friend into season six ("Beaver's Football Award"). Viewers know that Wally is growing up about the same time Beaver notices this occurrence ("Her Idol"). He tells Wally that he's been walking home with Mary Ellen Rogers, but that he used to throw rocks at her. Now, that's a change in attitude towards a girl.

Other girls Wally likes from the first couple of seasons are Caroline (pronounced Carolyn) Cunningham who shows up in season two when Eddie claims she is his girl ("Eddie's Girl"). The funny thing about Eddie's claim is that when Wally and Eddie visit her home, she doesn't know Eddie. She takes a liking to Wally and her mom calls June to arrange a date for her to the country club dance with Wally. At first, Wally objects, but with Eddie's late in the episode encouragement, he's all for the date with Caroline. A girl named Harriet is one Wally hopes to meet at the roller rink on a Saturday if he gets there in time ("Beaver's Newspaper"), but she is never seen in the show. The girl that may have caused Wally the most trouble, at least initially, is Gloria Cusick. Her saying Wally had a pug nose has Wally searching the word in the dictionary and the definition almost debilitates him ("Wally's Pug Nose"). He later finds out she didn't mean it in a negative sense. She simply likes pug noses.

The character Mary Ellen Rogers takes a temporary hiatus in season three, as she is not spoken of or seen as a girlfriend or date for Wally. Instead of Mary Ellen, Wally's dance card is filled with a few other girls he mentions, likes or dates. These girls include one named Ralph ("Beaver's Fortune"), Marty's sister who may go to the movies with he and Marty ("Larry's Club"), Alma Hanson who he spent a lot of time with at the insistence of her mother, and then there was the anti-Mary Ellen named Myra Barker who Wally takes to the sophomore dance and even buys her an orchid ("Wally's Orchid").

While the character Mary Ellen is absent in season three, she storms back in season four as it is mentioned that Wally takes her to the movies in four different episodes ("Beaver's Freckles" / "Beaver's Big Contest" / "Miss Landers' Fiance" / Chuckie's New Shoes"). She is seen in two episodes during season four. Her first appearance is when she desires to go to the beach to see Wally working as a lifeguard. She also goes with Wally to Christine Staples' party in "Wally and Dudley." In addition to Mary Ellen, Wally also goes to a dance with Kitty Bannerman ("Wally's Glamour Girl") and goes out with Julie Foster ("Teacher's Daughter"), and then gets a big crush on Margie Manners, even neglecting his homework, and his athletic commitments, to hang out with his mother's helper ("Mother's Helper"). And then there's Ginny Townsend, who Eddie says is, "a dream walking." But Wally soon finds out she's anything but a dream. June gets heavily involved in this relationship as a parent and in the end, Wally thanks her ("Wally's Dream Girl").

Wally starts off season five with a bang by going steady with Evelyn Boothby. This comes as a big surprise to Ward and June. A bigger surprise is Wally hanging out with her sister and her husband, the Hendersons. But hanging out with the Hendersons, especially one evening at their apartment, turns out to be a good thing ("Wally Goes Steady"). Mary Ellen appears early in the season and gawks at Wally in his soda jerk outfit ("Wally's Weekend Job"), and is mentioned twice more in the season as Wally does his homework at her house in "Beaver's Typewriter," and is said to have had a fight with Wally and is not giving back his letterman's sweater in "The Merchant Marine." Other girls he dates in season five include Gail Preston ("Wally's Big Date"), Julie Foster ("Beaver's First Date"), Carole Martin ("Tennis, Anyone?"), Lori Ann ("Un-Togetherness"). Well, he didn't really go out with Lori Ann, but he did walk her home a couple times.

In the final season of *Leave it to Beaver*, Wally's main girl interest is Julie Foster, at least according to Ward ("Eddie's Sweater"). True, she does seem to be his main squeeze as she is either seen or mentioned in multiple episodes ("Wally's Dinner Date" / "The Mustache" / "Uncle Billy's Visit" / "Eddie's Sweater" / "The Book Report"). But when looking at the entire season, Wally seems to play the field as is seen when he dates Lori Ann ("Beaver's Football Award"), Carolyn Stuart ("Double Date"), Shirley ("Wally's Car Accident"), Marlene Holmes ("Box Office Attraction"), and Kathy Gregory ("All-Night Party").

Eddie and Girls

Eddie is very interested in girls as he and Wally are going to either talk to some girls, run into some girls or meet some in many different episodes, especially at the movies ("Cleaning Up Beaver" / "Her Idol"). He and Wally also go jumping at the trampoline place where they will meet some girls who hang out there ("Beaver Finds a Wallet").

While Eddie likes girls, he is not nearly as prized of a find for the girls as is Wally. This is seen early on when "his girl" Caroline Cunningham finds Wally more interesting and attractive than Eddie ("Eddie's Girl"). However, Eddie does get some girls to go out with him. He goes on a double date with Wally with an unidentified girl ("Beaver's Team"), a double date with an unidentified girl ("Wally, the Lifeguard"), Belinda McGowan, who decided to go out with Eddie after only one hour of convincing ("Beaver's Big Contest"), Caroline Schuster ("Eddie's Double-Cross"), Dottie Donovan, who Wally says is kinda cute ("Teacher's Daughter"), Christine Staples, played by Marta Kristen ("Wally and Dudley"), and an unidentified girl on a double date with Wally ("Beaver, the Babysitter"). A girl who seemed to be more of a steady girlfriend of Eddie's was Cindy Andrews, the girl who knit him a sweater ("Eddie's Sweater").

Others

Beaver's friend Larry sits in a tree with Linda and looks at Beaver's and Linda Dennison's nest full of eggs after the class is lectured by Miss Landers about how it's natural for boys and girls to like one another. Beaver then gets a bit jealous of Larry ("Her Idol"). But Larry doesn't really like girls as is seen when asked by Beaver what's wrong with Judy Hensler and he replies, "She's a girl" ("The Cookie Fund") and later says he'd rather look at snakes than girls any day ("Baby Picture"). Larry does seem resigned to the fact he will one day marry a girl when he agrees with Beaver that if he must get married, he'll marry a girl who owns a horse ("Beaver's Dance").

Richard makes his feelings about girls very clear. He tells Beaver in "Junior Fire Chief," that he will vote for him for Junior Fire Chief because "... at least he's not a girl." He also says in "Brother vs. Brother" that girls only cause trouble. In this same episode, Gilbert agrees that girls are no good, saying they're not fun because all they do is worry about getting their dresses dirty. Gilbert does offer Beaver some wisdom in "More Blessed to Give." He tells Beaver that if he's in love with Donna, that there's a lot more to being in love than just looking at her. A sure sign that Gilbert is maturing is seen late in season six when he tells Beaver he is going to the eighth-grade dance with Angela Valentine. When Beaver says he thought Gilbert hated her, Gilbert replies, "Well, I used to, but ever since I've been in the eighth grade, it's not as easy to hate girls as it was." Whitey then chimes in that he's been on dates and mentions Dorothy Wainwright ("Don Juan Beaver"). The final girl Beaver and Gilbert are entranced by is Mary Margaret Matthews ("Beaver Sees America"), but Wally warns Beaver that she's too much for him to handle and hitting in the World Series while Beaver is still in the pony league . . . Wow, that sure was a lot of girls!

42

WASHING DISHES

There are a few combinations to washing dishes in *Leave it to Beaver*. But first of all, one has to know that all dishes are washed by hand in the Cleaver household. They have no dishwasher. June does ask for one in "Beaver's Poem," but Ward says, "Dear, if I gave you a dishwasher now,
what would I give you for Christmas?" He never does get her one for Christmas.

So, in the household, who washes dishes the most? And what does washing the dishes mean? Is it just washing the dishes, or does it include washing and drying the dishes and putting them away? For our purposes, the term "washing dishes" will include all aspects of the job, washing, drying, or putting away. If you read that Ward, Wally or Beaver helped wash dishes, it generally means, June put the dishes in soap and water and cleaned them, then she rinsed them and handed them to another family member to dry and put away. The possible dish washing combinations include June and Ward (most often seen), June by herself (second most seen), June and the boys (one or both of them), Wally and Beaver, Beaver by himself, Ward by himself, and Wally by himself.

The dishes are seen being washed fifty-six times in 234 episodes or 24% of the time. Now, since we know that June and Ward did the washing together on most occasions, I would like to first examine those dish washing combinations that occurred the least in the show.

The first would be those that involve either Wally or Beaver, or both of them. Wally is not seen washing dishes on his own in any episode. Wally and Beaver wash dishes together four times and they wash dishes with Eddie once ("Eddie Spends the Night"). In the Eddie episode, this act of kindness from the boys was initiated, believe it or not, by Eddie. Wally thought it was some sort of set up, but it wasn't. Eddie did all the hard work. We see Beaver wash dishes on his own in "Wally's Car Accident." He does this after breakfast as Wally goes to get an estimate on repairing the damage to the car before their parents get home. Beaver also washes one time in season one, but he's not washing dishes. Instead, he washes the pipe that Fred Rutherford sent Ward from Germany, after he and Larry smoked it.

Ward washing dishes with June is a regular kitchen event, at least when you think of drying as part of the washing process. However, Ward washing dishes on his own is quite rare. He takes over for June when Beaver wants to talk with her after supper in the den ("Mother's Day Composition"). He promptly burns himself on the hot water after June warned him it was hot. The next time we see him wash dishes (dipping them in the water and scrubbing them) is in season six, when he washes dishes twice. In "Eddie's Sweater," Ward dons an apron and is in full dish washing mode instead of June. She isn't taking a vacation, but instead, is clearing the dining room table. Then, in "Don Juan Beaver," Ward has an apron on again, and doing the washing and June is drying the dishes. I can only imagine if there had been a season seven, that Ward may have washed dishes even more often.

June and Beaver wash dishes together six times throughout the series. Occasionally, this happens because Wally has Ward occupied in some fashion or another. For example, in "Dance Contest," Ward is occupied taking Wally for a cha-cha lesson. In "Wally's Test" and "The Merchant Marine" episodes, Ward is not available to wash dishes with June because he is busy talking to Wally in his den. Beaver, again, helps June with the dishes in "Beaver's First Date." He goes downstairs to help her while Wally receives help on his homework from Ward. He has an ulterior motive for helping her though. He would like to have a new suit for his upcoming first ever date and he and Wally decided it would be best to ask her about getting him a new suit. The other two times it is just Beaver helping June are because she needs help ("Wally Stays at Lumpy's") and because Wally is out taking his license test. Twice, Wally helps June with the dishes and each of those times it is because Beaver has Ward occupied in his den, with a talk about one of Beaver's problems.

June washes dishes with both boys in two episodes, and each of those feature a party. Ward clears the table and June and the boys wash and dry dishes in "The Party Invitation," and in "Lumpy's Scholarship, the boys help June wash dishes after the party that is thrown in Lumpy's honor.

June, alone, washes and dries dishes in many episodes, about 30% of time. The number of times when Ward and June are both in the kitchen washing dishes (June washing / Ward drying) is about 42% of the time. And in both "The State vs. Beaver" and "Beaver and Gilbert," the entire family is shown in the kitchen washing dishes. Just a few other dishwashing tidbits to round out this chapter include the fact that Ward and June are seen washing dishes together in season three more than in any other season. In "Wally's Glamour Girl," June reminds Ward about the first time they washed dishes together when her mother had invited Ward over for supper at their house before they were married. He held her hand under the soap suds. June also tells Ward once, when he helps her with the dishes, "You know what dear, you're a very helpful husband." Finally, Ward shares an idiom that possibly explains one of the reasons he often helps with the dishes, "Many hands make light work." This idiom, which he shares in the "Beaver's Poem" episode dates from back to the 1300s and initially appeared in a story called *Sir Bevis of Hampton*.

There is even more information to read about dish washing on *Leave it to Beaver* and if you would like to read it, please visit http://leaveittobeaverbooks.com.

43

WATCHING WORKERS

Think back on your own childhood and you may remember a time when you stopped what you were doing to watch a grown up on their job. Maybe they were fixing a city street, fighting a fire, or delivering a package. As a child, it always was quite interesting to watch the world at work around you. Beaver and his friends watched workers quite often and Wally and his friends did too, but to a lesser extent. As you read the list below of the times they did watch or talk to workers (Ward joined in a time or two), see if you can remember any similar times when you were a kid at the ages of Beaver or Wally and enjoyed watching workers.

Wally and Beaver

The boys planned on watching men tar the roof of a business, but neither went due to Wally being punished and Beaver having to go to a party ("Party Invitation").

In the rain, the boys watched a man changing a tire in the mud ("Beaver and Poncho").

Beaver and his friends

On Beaver's way home from school, after receiving a note from Miss Canfield, Beaver made a few stops. One of those stops was watching some men change a tire on a bus ("Beaver Gets 'Spelled").

Beaver and Violet Rutherford are downtown and watch the lady in the jiggle belt in a store window ("The Black Eye").

While Beaver is out selling water, he talks to some men from the water department preparing to dig up a street. They tell him that soon, the water will be turned off to the entire neighborhood ("Water, Anyone?").

Beaver watches a worker painting a bridge. He asks the man who owned the bridge. The man tells Beaver that it belongs to all the citizens of Mayfield, even him ("The Clubhouse").

Ward finds Beaver sitting next to a manhole. He is waiting for Charlie, the electric man, to return from getting coffee. He says Charlie is his friend ("Lonesome Beaver").

Beaver watched some men digging a hole ("Eddie's Girl").

Beaver and Larry watch a policeman give a woman a ticket for parking in a no parking zone ("The Grass is Always Greener").

Beaver and Larry tell June, they won't be late to school again, but wind-up watching men at a construction site on the way to school ("Beaver Plays Hooky").

Beaver and Larry watch a man build a mannequin in a department store window ("Beaver's Sweater").

Beaver and Larry go watch workers on a Saturday. They watch workers fill the municipal pool in the park. They then plan on going to watch men tar the road and then Beaver suggests they go watch a woman make pancakes. They end up doing neither ("Forgotten Party").

Larry suggests he and Beaver go watch the man paint turtles while they wait for Beaver's package ("June's Birthday").

Beaver and Whitey go to Anderson's dump to watch the men bury trash with the bulldozer ("Uncle Billy").

Beaver, Richard and Gilbert toss around some ideas of what they could do. One idea is to go watch some workers knock down walls of a building they are tearing down. Richard and Gilbert decide to go to the old McMahon house instead ("Mistaken Identity").

Beaver and Whitey stop while walking down Grant Avenue to watch some guys change a billboard. They only had half a lady up and wanted to see how she came out ("Farewell to Penny").

Beaver and Whitey watch some firemen do a drill ("Beaver's Autobiography").

If you'd like to read even more on watching workers, you will be able to find some more info over at http://leaveittobeaverbooks.com.

44

SLANG WORDS

As a fan of *Leave it to Beaver*, you will notice that a show of this type from the late 1950s and early 1960s will at times, have its very own vocabulary words. Whitey Whitney tells Beaver in "Beaver's Long Walk" that he wouldn't want everyone to think he's a "boob" by saying something stupid. June has her own slang for someone who goes around acting half-witted or silly when they are infatuated. We hear her slang in "Eddie's Double-Cross," when she says she doesn't want Wally going steady with a girl and "lollydolling" around. The following list is not exhaustive, but it is extensive. Among some of the most used slang in the series are, "creep," "conk," "flaky," "goof," and "warden."

There are a few other words that could be considered slang but are more archaic and they can be found at http://leaveittobeaverbooks.com.

B

baloney (bologna) – n. something false, made up

beef – n. a compliant or a grievance.

belt – v. hit (someone or something) hard. "I ought to belt you."

big freeze – n. ignoring someone or giving somebody the cold shoulder or the silent treatment.

big wheel – n. someone who thinks they are very important.

boob – n. a fool or a foolish person. "A guy wouldn't want to make stuff up like that and look like a boob in front of the whole class." – Whitey Whitney

bunk – a statement of fact that a hearer believes to be untrue or an exaggeration. "Don't give me that bunk."

C

chin-chin – n. casual talk or chatter. "Fred Rutherford wanted some chin-chin."

clod – n. a clumsy or slow-witted person. "Snap into it you clods." - Eddie Haskell

clobbered – v. to defeat someone in a fight or hit something or someone hard. "Some guy clobbered him." – Wally Cleaver

clop – v. to pound or hit something or someone. "I should clop him."

clover – n. money. "You'll be sitting in clover."

clue him in – to inform someone about a situation.

colossal – adj. a descriptive word about a positive trait or skill. "His football skills are colossal."

conk – v. die. "If the monkey gets too cold and wet, he may conk out."

cop – v. to get or take something. "At the game, he managed to cop a foul ball."

cornball – n. something or someone unsophisticated, dumb or silly

crate – n. a dilapidated old car. "We gotta give Lumpy's crate a shove." – Eddie Haskell

creep – n. an obnoxious person or a person who is different from others in a group.

croak – v. death or to die.

crooked it – to steal something. "I wonder if they will catch the guy who crooked it."

crow – n. an ugly person, typically referring to a girl. "Did some crow invite you to a vice versa dance?"

crummy – adj. Something that is subpar or not up to standards

cut it out – to stop an action

D

dandy – adj. a compliment. "The sweater looks dandy."

dibs – n. first rights to an item. "I've got dibs on the baseball glove."

dig – v. to like or enjoy something. "She doesn't dig geometry."

dope – n. dumb. "He's acting like a dope."

dreamy – adj. someone or something that is very nice. "The boy is very dreamy."

dry up – v. stop being a wise guy, stop talking, mind your own business.

F

flaky – adj. acting in a way that is very unusual. "He is acting flaky because of a girl."

flipped – v. having a negative reaction to something. "A girl in class flipped today when we had a test."

fuss – n. a big commotion or causing a scene about something.

G

gee - introductory expletive or expressing surprise or enthusiasm, in Leave it to Beaver, usually the former. "Gee, mom, I don't think the Beaver likes girls yet."

gee whiz - introductory expletive or expressing surprise or enthusiasm, in Leave it to Beaver, usually the former. "Gee whiz, how did dad know?"

giving the business – give someone a hard time, joke around. "You guys giving me the business?"

go ape / going ape – going wild or getting upset. Usage is possibly Air Force slang about troops being unable to leave their barracks i.e. stir crazy originating in the early 1950s.

golly – expressing surprise or wonder

goods, the – n. details, typically about a problem. "I think he has the goods on us."

goof – n. a person who does something dumb or stupid. "He was a real goof."

goofed up – messing up or causing a problem because of some dumb or stupid action.

goofy – adj. an action or an object that is silly or dumb

goofball – n. a person whose behavior is dumb, strange or abnormal

goon – n. an unlikable girl, or person, a person who is thought of negatively.

gyp artist – someone who takes advantage of others in a business transaction.

gypped – v. getting taken advantage of by a person or a business. "Do you think we got gypped?"

H

heap, thanks a – an expression of gratitude

heel – n. a person with little self-worth, someone who is not a good person, "You don't have to make me feel like a heel."

holy mackerel – an expression of surprise or shock.

horse around – playing around, usually when someone should be getting work done

hot dog! – a positive enthusiastic expression, "Hot dog! There's no bathtub"

hunk – n. a piece or small part. "Just a little hunk."

hunk of junk – something that is unworthy of keeping, a piece of trash

J

jazz – n. nonsense or something unbelievable. "Where do you get that kinda jazz?" - Wally

jazz it up / jazzing things up - exaggeration

joshin' – v. pretending or joking. "I was just joshin' Mrs. Cleaver" – Eddie Haskell

K

keen – adj. very good or great. "That is a keen comic book."

knucklehead – n. goofy, childish, or dumb person

knockout – adj. a compliment referring to an object or a person. "She's a real knockout."

kooky – adj. silly or dumb.

L

Lay off – leave me alone. "Lay off of me, will ya?"

Like fun you will – expression of disbelief.

lollydolling – v. – acting aloof, sometimes due to an intense infatuation with a person. "I don't want him to go lollydollying around."

M

malarky – n. nonsense

messing around – hanging out with friends. "You just go someplace and wait for something to happen." – Wally Cleaver.

most – a very high complement, typically, about a girl. "Have you seen her lately? Is she ever the most!" - Tooey Brown.

mooncapping – v. going around half-witted, could be because a person is infatuated with another

murder – n. an intense struggle, a difficult situation. "That history test was murder."

N

natch – rarely heard slang, short for the word naturally.

neat / neato – both words began appearing around season 3 Episode 27 when "neato" was first used. The former word is used more often.

no strain – similar to the phrase, "no problem."

O

on account (of) (a) – interchangeable with "because."

on the string – "I bet you got three or four girls on the string." - Uncle Billy

operator – n. a popular guy with the girls. "Some operator you are..." – Lumpy Rutherford.

P

pipe down – be quiet.

poke – n. a punch with a fist. "I'll take a poke at you."

punk – adj. low quality, cheaply made product. "That's a punk bow."- Larry Mondello

pus, the – mouth. "Did he let you have it across the pus? – Eddie Haskell

putting on the dog – to pretend that one is very stylish or rich. "I hope she doesn't smell these fancy soap suds on me. She might think I'm putting on the dog or something." – Wally Cleaver

R

razz – v. like give the business, joking, giving someone a hard time

red blanket case – a person in physically critical condition, a patient going to an emergency room. "She was a real red blanket case." – Wally Cleaver in "The Late Edition."

S

sailing – v. dancing, moving or grooving to music. "Don't bother me Wally, I'm sailing." – Beaver Cleaver in "Beaver Joins a Record Club."

search me – the same as "don't ask me," said when someone does not know an answer.

sharp – adj. an enthusiastic description of something, typically a piece of clothing or how well someone is groomed. Used in only a few episodes such as "Wally's New Suit," "Eddie Quits School," and "Double Date."

shoving – v. leaving. "Guess I ought to be shoving." - Wally Cleaver in "Tennis Anyone?"

sore – n. upset, mad.

sorehead – n. a person who is upset or mad about something or at someone.

spot – n. a bad place or situation. "I wouldn't leave you in a spot." – Larry Mondello.

square – adj. uncool, out of date. "That suit is square."

squaring it – v. making things better. "Shc's squaring it with him now." Wally Cleaver

swankiest – adj. very nice, elegant. "That's the swankiest restaurant in town."

swell – adj. good, cool, just fine. "He's a swell guy."

swingers – n. guys in school who think they are very important and are very popular. "They usually just take the swingers." Wally Cleaver.

swipe – v. steal or take without permission. "No one will swipe it."

W

warden – Someone of authority to watch over children, a parent or a babysitter. "She's okay if we gotta have a warden." – Wally Cleaver.

wreck – v. to ruin something. "If a guy has a best pal, why wreck it?" – Beaver Cleaver

wise guy – someone who thinks they know everything, a smart aleck

wise him up – Similar to clue him in. To inform someone on a situation.

Y

yummy – similar to other slang words like cool or neat, something that is very good or desirable.

45

SPORTS

Was there ever another family situation comedy in the 1950s or 1960s in which sports was played as much as it was in *Leave it to Beaver*? I don't think so. The top four sports seen or talked about on the show were baseball, football, track, and basketball, in that order.

Baseball

Baseball is the sport seen in action or heard about in *Leave it to Beaver* in more episodes than any other sport.

Wally played baseball in Mayfield, in the street in front of his house, at Metzger's Field, in sandlots, and just out and about in town at unidentified places which could have been anywhere. He also plays for the school teams, and quite possibly, although never stated clearly, he probably plays on a city sponsored league or a team sponsored by a local business. He could have played Pony League Baseball, although that is never mentioned specifically for Wally, but for Beaver, the Pony League is mentioned once.

Wally is seen or spoken of playing baseball with his friends only in seasons one & two. He played baseball with his friends five times in season one and twice in season two. It appears that after he went to high school (beginning in season two), his time was monopolized by league or school baseball teams. The two exceptions were in the episodes, "The Lost Watch" where he played with all the guys in a sandlot and in "Beaver's Pigeons," where he's mentioned as playing baseball with the guys. A look at seasons two through six show Wally playing baseball only three times.

With limited statistics available for Wally, we know that in the four games mentioned in "The State vs. Beaver," "Music Lesson," "The Lost Watch," and "The Haunted House," Wally batted five times with two singles, two homeruns, and a walk. He also pitched one game giving up twelve runs and getting the win against Bellport.

In the show, Beaver is not as athletic as Wally. This is seen in "The Music Lesson" when Beaver tells Ward about his tryout with the "C" team at school. The coach threw him two fly balls and he caught one and the other hit him in the head, but he didn't cry. The coach told him he wasn't good enough for the team. When you think about what happens later in the episode, being told he's not good enough for the band, one must have pity on Beaver.

Beaver plays baseball in gym class in "Beaver the Athlete" and strikes out four times. He goofs off the first day of practice and finally takes things seriously the next day after he sees Judy do so well. At the boys vs. girls baseball game that week, Beaver gets three singles with men on base each time.

In "Ward's Golf Clubs," Beaver tells Ward that he doesn't like baseball. A few episodes later Wally speaks about Beaver's athleticism, saying he made the baseball team at school so he should also try out for the city basketball league. Beaver says in this episode that he's a first basemen. Later, we see he's made a position switch in "Beaver's Prep School," as its stated in this episode that he plays third base in the Pony League. This episode is one of the only times Beaver is said to be out playing baseball with his friends.

Of Wally's friends, Eddie Haskell and Lumpy Rutherford are not very good baseball players. Evidence is found in "Wally's Job" from late in season one. In this episode, Eddie and

Wally are walking home from a baseball game that had just finished and Eddie says he would've got a couple hits if the sun had not been in his eyes. Wally says, "Yeah, sure Eddie. It's just bum luck you struck out six times." In the episode, "The Lost Watch" Lumpy is seen striking out in a sandlot game and he doesn't even come close to getting wood on the ball, the one time he takes a swing.

Other good baseball memories from the show include the boys wanting to start their own baseball team in "Water Anyone?" I love it when Ward brags about Wally as a "natural born shortstop," in the episode "The Perfume Salesmen." This is also when we find out that that Mr. Brown talked the coach into putting Tooey on the baseball team. We're introduced to Gilbert in "Beaver and Gilbert" and it's in this episode that Gilbert tells Beaver his brother plays baseball for the St. Louis Cardinals. Wally also has a game in this episode and his team loses 6-2. He implies it's because his science teacher Mr. Driscoll was umpiring. Maybe, the most memorable baseball related episode, and the most depressing, is "Ward's Baseball." Larry talks Beaver into playing catch with Ward's autographed ball given to him by his uncle. Larry throws it into the street when they're playing catch and it gets destroyed.

There are five Major League Baseball players mentioned throughout the series (outside of the "Ward's Baseball" episode). These players are Mickey Mantle (4), Don Drysdale (3), Roger Maris (2) Ted Williams (1) Babe Ruth (1) and Warren Spahn (1). The players mentioned who signed Ward's baseball include Kiki Cuyler, Babe Ruth, Lou Gehrig, Lefty Grove, Augie Galan, Bill Dickey and Grover Cleveland Alexander. In Eddie's room in "Voodoo Curse," he has a picture of Mickey Mantle on his wall.

Among the professional baseball teams alluded to in the series, we see characters either wearing a hat for a team or talking about a specific team in multiple episodes. For the St. Louis Cardinals, this occurs in "The Visiting Aunts" and "The Lost Watch" in which Chester wears their baseball cap. In "Beaver and Gilbert," Gilbert tells Beaver his brother plays for the team. Beaver asks Ward if the Cardinals will have a good season in "Ward's Golf Clubs." Fred Rutherford, in "Beaver and Violet," wears a Yankees baseball cap on their picnic to Friend's Lake. In "Beaver, the Hero," Eddie tells Beaver how the Yankees signed a former little league champ to a contract.

Basketball

Basketball in *Leave it to Beaver* is mostly Wallycentric. The only times that Beaver is around a basketball court is when he watches Wally, and the older boys play in their driveway in the "The Perfect Father" episode and in "The Younger Brother," when he tries out for the park league and fails miserably. Beaver just isn't a basketball player.

In seven episodes throughout the series, Wally is spoken of as either playing a basketball game (4) or attending a basketball practice (1), shooting baskets with a friend (1) or shown playing basketball (1). In two episodes, Wally speaks about basketball practice being canceled and in "Wally's Glamor Girl," he lies to his parents about an extra Saturday night practice.

From the episodes in which any statistics are revealed, we find Wally is a very good player and got better as he grew older. In season three, we find out in "School Sweater" that Wally scored three points in two minutes and fouled out of the game. In season four, in the "Eddie's Double-Cross" episode, he shares with Caroline (pronounced Carolyn) and Alma that he scored twelve points in a game the previous Thursday night. In "The Younger Brother," Wally says that his high point game was thirty-two points he scored for the Mayfield Crusaders against Taft High School.

He's an impressive athlete.

Ward is a fine athlete too. In season one, "The Perfect Father" episode is centered almost entirely around basketball. The boys are playing basketball quite often at the Dennison house and Ward wants the boys around home. He puts up a basketball hoop on their garage so the boys can play in their own driveway. One afternoon while the boys are playing, Ward decides to give them some pointers. The hook shot is his specialty, and he tells the boys he did very well with it against Muhlenberg College, a school in Allentown, Pennsylvania.

Wally didn't just get his great ball playing skill from his father; he has genes from two good basketball playing parents. June lets him know that when she was in boarding school, she received a letter for playing basketball. Wally is shocked and tells her it's just a bit too much thinking about a guy's mother jumping center.

Football

Both Beaver and Wally love football. They are both very good players. Ward loves football too. June is the only member of the family who seems to dislike the sport. The best example of this is when Wally intercepts a pass in a freshman game and scores a touchdown. She laments that the coach will probably want Wally to play more.

Wally's games and practices are spoken of in seven episodes, three of these are in season two, three in season three and one in season five. The games, one can assume, are typically played on Saturdays. In "Beaver Takes a Walk," the football team is scheduled on the upcoming Saturday to play against Madison. While in "Borrowed Boat," the episode in which Beaver turns down the opportunity to ride with Wally and the team on the bus, Mayfield High plays at Lynwood on Saturday. For this game, Wally is on the third team.

As for his football accomplishments, Wally was captain of the varsity football team his senior year ("All-Night Party"). He was also third-team all-state ("Lumpy's Scholarship.") Beaver begins his football career in the last episode of the third season of *Leave it to Beaver*. Although it is baseball season, he and his friends want to start a football team. The name of the team? The Lightning Eleven. They will be playing against Richard Rickover's team, the Grant Avenue Tigers. Wally is their coach and with Eddie as their assistant coach, what could go wrong? Only one thing goes wrong. They develop a secret play they call "Ole 98." They could've used that play to win their game against the Grant Avenue Tigers if it were not for Beaver's big mouth and Penny's bigger mouth. She reveals the secret to Richard Rickover and one of his teammates.

Beaver does much better as his football career progresses. He is named the most inspirational player for his eighth-grade team at Grant Avenue Grammar School. He also becomes a hero for catching the winning touchdown in a game. He gets a photo of his touchdown reception in the newspaper and the more kids talk about what a great player he is, the bigger his head becomes. They even named a sundae at the malt shop after him called the "Beaver Special." Beaver, although a good player, gets his comeuppance in the end, when he skips practice because he thinks he didn't have to go since he is such a good player. He thought wrong and winds up suspended from the team.

An interesting thing to note is that Lumpy Rutherford was a good football player too. In fact, he scores a full ride athletic scholarship to State in "Lumpy's Scholarship." It's said in this episode that Lumpy had one of the best games of his high school career against Taft High School.

This is the high school Mayfield played basketball against when Wally had his highest scoring game. Taft must have had lousy sports teams.

Professional football is spoken of in a few episodes. In Gilbert's first appearance in *Leave it to Beaver,* he mentions Johnny Unitas of the Baltimore Colts. Beaver almost misses out on going to a Green Bay Packers game in "Beaver Won't Eat." But after making a deal with his parents, he gets to go to the game. The Baltimore Colts are mentioned in "Beaver's Secret Life" when Ward mentions Somerset Maugham. Beaver asks if he's a writer and Wally says he thought with a name like that, he could be a linebacker with the Colts. Both the 49ers and the Rams are mentioned in "Beaver, the Hero." NFL and college football legend Red Grange is also mentioned in this episode as well as Rams running backs Jon Arnett and Glenn Davis, and so is West Point star Doc Blanchard who was drafted in the first round by the Pittsburgh Steelers in the 1947 draft, although he never played for them. In "Uncle Billy's Visit," Uncle Billy asks if the Packers know about Wally and Beaver.

Golf

While baseball, football, and basketball were the big sports on *Leave it to Beaver*, golf is also mentioned quite often. If off the top of your head, you had to make a quick guess of how many times Ward went golfing throughout the series, would you say ten… twenty…. thirty…. forty … or fifty times? If I had not done the research, I would have guessed forty times. But it was only twenty times that he went golfing. How about his golf partners? For the most part, he went with Fred Rutherford, but why? Was it because they were good friends? June asks him why he golfs with Fred in the "Kite Day" episode. He tells her, "If I don't, he'll sulk all week at the office." Over the six seasons of *Leave it to Beaver*, he also golfs with Mr. Cartwright ("The Perfume Salesmen"), Ted Worden ("Eddie, the Businessman"), Mr. Haney ("Wally's Car Accident"), Mr. Miller ("Uncle Billy's Visit"). Two professional players are mentioned in the series, Arnold Palmer and Sam Snead.

Track

Wally also competed in track and field. He is first mentioned as going out for track in the eighth grade in "Beaver's Crush." Later in season one, in "Beaver's Old Friend," we find out that Ward was a shot putter. In "Beaver the Athlete," Wally competes in a track meet and does the 440 in 58 seconds. His coach told him if he cut 13 seconds off his time, he'd have beaten the world record. When this episode was filmed, the world record was 45.2 seconds by American Lou Jones. In "Wally's Track Meet," Wally is scheduled to run the 220 and the 100 but winds up being suspended for throwing a towel in the locker room. At a track meet in Bellport in "Lumpy's Car Trouble," Wally wins the 100 and comes in second in the 220 while Lumpy comes in third in the shot put and sixth in the discus, helping the Mayfield team win. In "Tennis Anyone," we find out that Wally has been in the newspaper in a staged track photo.

Beaver also participates in track and his career in this sport begins a bit bumpy. His first attempt at a track event was in his schools' field day in "The Tooth." He ran the fifty-yard dash but fell down because someone pushed him. Violet Rutherford won the race. In the next episode, "Beaver Gets Adopted," Beaver runs the fifty-yard dash again, this time at the Mayfield Park Field

Day. Beaver forgot his shoes and had to use Larry's which were too big for him, and he fell down, again. In "The Late Edition," Beaver wants to take the job away from the new paper boy. He figured he could build up his legs for track while delivering papers on his bicycle. This episode indicates that he is either going to go out for the track team or was a current member of the team.

As mentioned above, Lumpy competes in the Bellport track meet. Eddie is also on the track team. However, he gets kicked off the team in "Mother's Day Composition" for loosening Pee Wee Logan's starting block. Eddie ends up being the track team manager in "Wally's Track Meet."

Other Sports

Wally also participates in swimming which is mentioned in a few different episodes such as "Beaver's Crush," "Wally's Haircomb," "Wally's New Suit," "Wally, the Lifeguard," and "Lumpy's Scholarship." Other sports mentioned include a bowling league ("The Haircut"), girls' field hockey ("The Shave"), wrestling on TV ("The Garage Painters"), handball ("The Haunted House"), judo and boxing ("Beaver's Fortune"), miniature golf ("Eddie's Double-Cross"), girls volleyball ("Wally and Dudley"), hockey ("Beaver the Babysitter"), tennis ("Tennis, Anyone?" / "Wally and Alma"), auto racing ("Wally's License")

Twice, professionals are mentioned from the "other sports" category. Once is when Eddie asks Beaver, "Who are you, Cassius Clay?" Most people would know him as Muhammad Ali. This occurs in the episode, "Summer in Alaska." Then, in "Tennis, Anyone?" Beaver mentions tennis player Poncho Gonzalez.

If you are craving more sports content from *Leave it to Beaver*, all you need to do is visit http://leaveittobeaverbooks.com.

46

TELEPHONE CALLS

The telephone calls on *Leave it to Beaver* are almost always used to move the plot forward in a story. Of course, there are times when they are trivial or pointless like when Fred Rutherford calls just to talk to Ward about a water softener ("Beaver's Old Friend") or when Larry and Beaver talk on the phone going over spelling words, an important thing to do, but it was not important to the story in that specific episode ("Tire Trouble"). But most of the time, phone calls on *Leave it to Beaver* typically help move a story in a certain direction as when Mrs. Bellamy calls the Cleavers to tell them they have a horse in their garage ("A Horse Named Nick") or June calling Miss Landers to invite her to dinner ("Teacher Comes to Dinner").

Of the telephone calls counted for the research purposes of this book, they include phone calls made or received by the Cleaver family and Fred Rutherford. When multiple phone calls are made by a character like Ward calling twenty-three women in "The Perfume Salesmen," or when June calls "all over town" looking for Beaver in "Beaver's Old Friend" or when Beaver calls multiple friends in "Party Invitation," but they are not named, those phone calls are not counted among the total calls. The total number of phone calls counted were 437.

Of the 437 phone calls made or received during the six seasons of *Leave it to Beaver* by the following characters, the percentages of calls made or received by each one are:

Ward Cleaver: 29.7%

June Cleaver: 29.5%

Wally Cleaver: 19.9%

Beaver Cleaver: 15.2%

Fred Rutherford: 5.7%

A deeper look into the phones calls of these characters reveal some interesting tidbits. Let's look at each character below:

Wally Cleaver –For America's favorite big brother, 64% of his phone calls are between he and his friends or classmates. Of those phone calls, 41% are with eleven different girls, and of that 41% Mary Ellen is in 21% of these calls and Julie Foster 17%. Carolyn ("Double Date") speaks with Wally in 13% of these calls, but they take place in one episode. Of Wally's friends, he speaks on the phone with Eddie the most (23%), then Lumpy (10.7%), and Tooey (5.4%) and Chester (3.6%) comes up at the rear of the pack. Wally and Beaver speak in 8% of Wally's total phone calls.

Beaver Cleaver – As you can see in the stats above, Beaver is not on the phone as often as Wally. For those times he is on the phone, the number of times he's speaking with his friends is much less than when Wally is on the phone at 44% compared to Wally's 64%. The amount of time spent talking to girls when he is talking with friends or classmates is only 13.8% compared to Wally's 41.1%. When it comes to his friends, as one would expect, Larry and Beaver speak on the phone the most (28%), Gilbert is next (24%), and Richard and Whitey (10.7%) bring up the rear.

June Cleaver – June and Ward are on the telephone about the exact number of times throughout the series. The people she speaks to the most on the telephone are Ward, Mrs. Mondello, teachers/principals and Fred or his wives Geraldine or Gwendolyn bring up the rear.

Ward Cleaver – Before making an exact count, I believed Ward would speak with Fred on the phone more than anyone else on the show. After counting, that was an almost correct assumption. Ward speaks with Fred on the phone just a little less than he speaks with June. Rounding out the top three, are his talks with a principal or teacher. Ward also talks with Mrs. Mondello quite a few times and even Mr. Mondello once ("The Pipe").

Fred Rutherford – Obviously, the phone calls here are mostly going to be between Fred and either Ward or June. For the calls to the Cleavers, they were all made to Ward, but at different times, Fred would talk to June because Ward was either busy in the garage ("Beaver's Old Friend"), not home yet ("The Broken Window"), telling June to say he wasn't home ("Beaver's Bad Day") or some other reason kept Ward off the phone. When calling the Cleavers, Fred spoke on the phone with Ward almost entirely (84%) and with June on a few occasions (16%). He also spoke with Lumpy on the phone in "The Parking Attendants" and in "Lumpy's Scholarship."

Unidentified Callers – Of the 437 calls cataloged in the research done for this chapter, only five times does someone call the Cleaver home and viewers are unable to identify who had called. Four of these times it happens when June answers and it occurs with Ward once.

The Cleaver Phone Numbers

The Cleavers had at least two different phone numbers at the house on 211 Pine. Of course, in a real home, they would've only had one phone number for seasons three through six unless Eddie continually prank called the house. Again, chalk it up to different writers. Their phone number was KL5-4763 in "Long Distance Call," but WH1-2738 in "Beaver's Big Contest."

There is more that can and will be shared about phone calls. Visit http://leaveittobeaverbooks.com to sign up for updates and for a chance to win *Leave it to Beaver* prizes!

47

"THE BUSINESS"

Aside from the pilot episode for *Leave it to Beaver*, "It's a Small World," the term, "the business," whether giving it or taking it, was first used by Eddie Haskell in the "New Neighbors" episode. The term "the business" which is usually preceded by the words "give him," "giving him," "give you," or "giving you," is used in only about thirty episodes of *Leave it to Beaver*.

But before we go any further, what exactly is "the business?" Well, from the context in which it's used in various episodes, the business could just be a hard time as in "Her Idol" when Wally tells Beaver, the guys will give him "the business" if they find out he was hanging around with Linda Dennison. It could also be used like it is in "Beaver and Gilbert" where Wally tells Beaver that Gilbert has just been giving him "the business" when it comes to all the things he has told him, like his brother playing for the St. Louis Cardinals. In this case, "the business" simply means lies.

It's easy to see that Eddie Haskell gives others "the business" more than any other character on the series. Remember, he was the first one on the show to use the term in the "New Neighbors" episode. Wally speaks of "the guys" giving Beaver or himself "the business," and Eddie is included in "the guys." But believe it or not, Eddie only gives "the business" to Beaver, Wally and the other guys about 17% of the time.

There are many examples of Eddie giving someone "the business." He does so to Dudley on numerous occasions in "Wally and Dudley." He gives Beaver "the business" in "Beaver Finds a Wallet," "The Hypnotist," and "Beaver Goes into Business." While Eddie may have originated giving someone, "The business," there are plenty of other characters on the show who could dish out "the business" very well.

Beaver seems to be given "the business" the most of any person on the show. Wally told him his classmates would give him the business for wearing short pants to school ("Beaver's Short Pants"). Wally gave Beaver a similar warning when Beaver tells him he was hanging around Linda Dennison over the weekend, specifically, he was up in a tree with her in the park ("Her Idol). Beaver doesn't understand why his classmates would give him "the business" for hanging around a girl since no one gives Wally "the business" for hanging around girls. Wally explains that easily enough and says it's because he's in high school and a guy can do a lot of things in high school without someone giving him "the business."

Fear has a lot to do with "the business." In "The Tooth," Lumpy is purposely trying to scare Beaver about a filling he might need at his next dentist appointment. He lies about the dentist drilling a big hole and making it bigger than he has to just to get paid more money. In "Beaver's Fortune," Larry sees Sonny Cartwright at school a day after he believes Sonny chickened out of a fight with Beaver. He tells Beaver to go give him "the business." Beaver refuses and Larry says he's not going to let Sonny get away with that and goes to give him "the business" for chickening out. We don't see what happened, but Larry comes back to Beaver holding his stomach. Sonny had punched Larry right in his gut. Fear also has Beaver a bit worried about receiving the business from Eddie, Lumpy and Bill Scott when they go to the amusement park in "Beaver's Fear." Wally tells him not to worry about that happening because if they do give him "the business," he'll clobber them. As it turns out, Eddie's the one who received "the business" when he got very sick after riding the roller coaster.

Lumpy is at it again when he wants to give Beaver "the business" in "Beaver's Report Card," if he fails any classes. He also gives Wally "the business" when Evelyn Boothby drives Wally to the dance at the country club in "Wally's Chauffeur." He even encourages the guys to really give Wally "the business" when he comes out after the dance. They refuse to do so because Wally's a good guy and they already gave him a hard time.

While the tern "the business" is used sparingly, as mentioned, only in about thirty episodes, "the business" is given to Beaver, Wally and others all the time, without actually calling what is given to them, "the business." Think about what Lumpy did to Eddie and Wally's cars in "Wally's Practical Joke." And what about Eddie calling Lumpy up in the same episode pretending to be Julie Foster? Think about that time Eddie switched dates with Wally in "Wally's Big Date." That was pretty sneaky, and all of those things could qualify as giving someone "the business."

So, "the business" was a rather routine way of life for the teens of Mayfield, whether or not it was officially referred to as "the business" or not.

To read about more instances of "the business" and just more "business" about "the business" like its possible origin, visit http://leaveittobeaverbooks.com.

48

RELIGION AND AMERICA'S FAVORITE FAMILY SITUATION COMEDY

During the 1950s, religion was still a large piece of the fabric that made up American life. Between 1955-1958, a time that encompassed two years prior to and through the first two seasons of *Leave it to Beaver*, about half of Americans were attending church. That was the largest percentage of Americans up to that time to ever attend church,[88] a percentage that has steadily declined ever since. Regular church attendance was nearly 50% then and religion was not the dirty word it has become in the 21st century.

Leave it to Beaver was not overtly religious, but it didn't shy away from using God's name in a positive light. While the religious feelings of most cast members is unknown, it is highly doubtful any were anti-religious or atheists at the time of the show's filming. The producers and writers occasionally inserted religious references into episodes, whether it was church attendance of the family, especially that of the children, or references to God being all knowing and all seeing.

In season one, the boys are seen getting ready to attend Sunday school with Eddie Haskell in "Tenting Tonight." This is the first episode in which church attendance is mentioned in the show. One would be within the bounds of logical questioning to ask, "What did Eddie Haskell learn at Sunday school?" His character certainly did not demonstrate many obvious Christian behaviors, especially those traits of integrity (Titus 2:7) or sincerity (2 Corinthians 2:17). In the episode "Beaver's Old Friend," Ward and June come home from church while Wally, Beaver and Eddie stay after worship for Sunday school. The Cleavers also attend church in "Beaver's Bad Day," "Beaver and Chuey," "Beaver's Pigeons," (Just Ward and Wally), "Beaver Gets Adopted," (where we find out Larry goes to a different church), "The Hypnotist," "Wally and Alma," "Beaver's Cat Problem," "Ward's Golf Clubs," and "Sweatshirt Monsters." Each of these episodes speaks of the family attending church or the boys attending Sunday School. In these episodes, one can assume that if Ward is wearing a suit, that the entire Cleaver family first attended worship, before leaving the boys there for Sunday school, which followed. Church attendance is also mentioned in a few other episodes including "Wally's Haircomb," "Eddie's Double-Cross," "Beaver Takes a Drive," "Substitute Father," and "Wally Buys a Car." That's eleven episodes in which the Cleaver family members go to church and five other episodes in which church attendance is mentioned. Church attendance at that time was simply a regular part of life for half of America.

In "Beaver's Bad Day," there is a deep discussion about God in a little conversation between Beaver and his mom.

> **June:** Beaver, it's telling lies that gets us into trouble. You'll always be safe If you tell the truth. And anyway, even when you think you're getting away with it, God knows you're lying.
> **Beaver:** How?
> **June:** Oh, because God knows everything, and he sees everything.

Of the actors, this is what is known about their religiosity. Hugh Beaumont (Ward Cleaver) was a minister in the Methodist Church. He graduated from the University of Southern California with a master's degree in theology. He played a minister, pastor, priest, reverend or chaplain ten

---

[88] Tucker, Carol. "The 1950s – Powerful Years for Religion," *USC News*, June 16, 1997. http://news.usc.edu/25835/The-1950s-Powerful-Years-for-Religion/.

times in his career on the small and large screen.[89] During his time filming *Leave it to Beaver*, some of his Sunday mornings were spent preaching at local Methodist churches. [90]

Jerry Mathers came from a conservative Catholic upbringing [91] and was also a product after *Leave it to Beaver*, of Notre Dame High School, a parochial school in Sherman Oaks where his father was once a coach. Jerry has also done fundraising for Catholic education. He was the keynote speaker a number of years ago for the 16th Annual Bishop's Dinner for Catholic Education in his hometown of Sioux City, Iowa.[92] Jerry, whether or not he is a devout Christian today, something we do not know since that is a very personal matter, does display Christian traits. The morality by which he lives his everyday life and his positive attitude demonstrated in numerous interviews, both reflect how Christians should behave.

However, back in 1957, we do know this about Jerry Mathers, he said bedtime prayers each night. One day, he worked with Hugh Beaumont on a short commercial film. Hugh played Jerry's father in the short. Jerry and his mother enjoyed working with Hugh that day. Jerry's mother Marilyn had told Hugh about auditions for the role of Ward Cleaver on a show which had been green lighted for CBS. They needed someone to replace the actor who had portrayed Jerry's father in the pilot. That evening, Jerry said his usual prayers, but added this specific request, "Please God, make the actor I worked with today my father in the new series." A couple months later, Jerry and his mother saw God in action when they walked onto the *Leave it to Beaver* set on day one and Hugh Beaumont greeted them.[93]

Of the other actors on the show that have mentioned religion or Christianity, been mentioned by others in the same context, or had a Christian education, there are a few. Among them are Pamela Beaird who played Wally's love interest Mary Ellen Rogers in five episodes and is mentioned in many others. Years after the show, she went on to college and graduated from Southwestern Assemblies of God University. She and her husband helped plant churches all across America and led gospel singing programs and both were very involved in the Hollywood Christian group in the 1960s.[94] Ken Osmond has always presented himself as a very moral man and Barbara Billingsley commented in her Archives of American Television interview that dinner at his house was preceded by Ken saying grace for those around the table. Something she mused was very un-Eddie like.[95] Stanley Fafara, after his battles with addiction ended, or possibly, because of them, declared his own dependence on Christ as his savior.[96]

There are a few *Leave it to Beaver* episodes that come quickly to mind where God is spoken of directly. They were, "Beaver's Bad Day," "Beaver and Kenneth," and "Beaver's Prize." On the latter episode, Larry and Beaver discuss with their child logic, some very deep theology on the workings of God. In some episodes, prayer is mentioned as in, "The Tooth," where Beaver is in the bathroom praying about his tooth. Prayer is also mentioned in "Beaver Finds a Wallet," "Kite Day," "Wally's License," and in "Beaver and Ivanhoe," when Wally mentions that Beaver prays every night and has lately been including Miss Landers.

While *Leave it to Beaver* was not a religious show in any sense of the term, the producers and writers were definitely not afraid of the Christian religion, like many are today.

---

[89] "Hugh Beaumont," IMDB.com, accessed September 22, 2014.

[90] Barbara Billingsley, interviewed by Karen Herman, Santa Monica, CA, July 14, 2000.

[91] Tony Dow, interviewed by Eric Greenburg, October 6, 2006.

[92] Renee Webb, "Jerry Mathers Keynotes Bishop's Dinner," *Catholic Globe*, October, 2012. http://www.catholicglobe.org/Renee10.18.12b.html.

[93] Marilyn Mathers, "My Mother's Memories of Hugh Beaumont…," jerrymathers.com, February 16, 2013. http://www.jerrymathers.com/my-mothers-memories-of-hugh-beaumont/.

[94] Personal interview with Pamela Beaird, summer 2022

[95] Barbara Billingsley interviewed by Karen Herman.

[96] Stanley Fafara, emailed to Tim Schmitt, August 10, 1998.

49

METZGER'S FIELD

There were a few different places the boys could go to play within Mayfield and its vicinity. There was Miller's Pond, Friend's Lake, the city park, bumming around town, and then there was Metzger's Field. For me, the name Metzger's Field sounds like the name of a dairy that sells some of the best chocolate milk around. I can picture its logo being a field with a couple Jersey cows grazing, and a red barn and a tall silo in the background. What a lovely place to be.

However, the real Metzger's Field is a place where children can have some good clean fun, playing baseball, going to a traveling carnival, watching two school kids fight, playing touch football, or enjoying flying kites and so much more. If I erase the cows, barn and silo from my mind for a moment, I feel Metzger's Field is where I would spend each and every Saturday of my youth. Another thing I feel about Metzger's Field is that it's always partly cloudy with a high of 75 degrees. Some perfect weather for a perfect place in the perfect town of Mayfield. Before you continue reading the rest of this chapter, think for a moment, back to your youth, where was your Metzger's Field?

Metzger's Field is etched firmly in each of our minds because Wally and Beaver spoke about it all the time, right? No, that would be incorrect. For some reason, it may seem like it's spoken of a lot, or visited often, but when you look at the stats, that isn't the case. In fact, Metzger's Field is not even mentioned twenty times out of the show's 234 episodes. If that's true, why does it seem like we hear about it many more times. Could it be due to fact that everything which is done at Metzger's Field is fun stuff? Could it be since it's mentioned more times than Friend's Lake. Whatever it is, Metzger's Field deserves a closer look.

Sports at Metzger's Field

Although the field is run by the city and sports are played on the grounds, it is an all-purpose park with what seems to be a lot of open space. But what about the sports that are played at the park? We know that football and baseball is played at Metzger's Field. Of these two sports, baseball is played at the field by one of the Cleaver boys 29% of the time and football is played 71% of the time. The total number of times sports is mentioned at Metzger's Field is only seven times, but rest assured, they were all fun times, except once, which will be spoken of below.

Baseball is the first sport mentioned of being played at Metzger's Field ("The Broken Window"). Instead of playing ball near the house, in the street, the boys decide to go to the park to play. They can't break another window if they just go to an open field or play where there's a backstop and actual baseball field. We don't know if there was a baseball field at Metzger's Field, but they were going there anyway. But before they go, Beaver gets the bright idea to ask Wally to throw him the baseball and when he does, Beaver smashes it harder than he ever has before, and the result is a broken car window. Their plans to go play baseball are scrubbed right away.

There is one other time mentioned when baseball is to be played at Metzger's Field. After Beaver is presented with an offer from Aunt Martha to send him away to Fallbrook, a prep school in New England, she sends brochures and pamphlets about the school to Beaver ("Beaver's Prep School"). He needs to look them over and make a decision about what he wants to do, go to Fallbrook, or stay and go to Mayfield High? When given the information and asked to take it upstairs with him, he says he was about to go to Metzger's Field and play baseball and wonders if he can make a life decision like whether to go to Fallbrook or not after he gets back home.

For football, Metzger's Field (or Metzger Field as shown on the sign) is the home of the

Lightning Eleven football team ("Beaver's Team"). This is the park where the team holds their practices run by their head coach Wally and assistant coach Eddie. Their home games, well, their one and only home game, is also played at Metzger's Field. In their big game against Richard Rickover and his team, The Grant Avenue Tigers, Beaver's team believes they will destroy them because they have a secret play called "Ole 98." It might have worked if Penny Woods had not told the other team about it, not on purpose, but because she's a stupid girl, according to some of the boys. Also, Beaver should not have played football during baseball season.

Another football mention for Metzger's Field is when Eddie suggests he and Wally go play a game of touch football. This is when Beaver and Wally are tossing the baseball around in the front yard on a day when Beaver is not allowed to leave the yard ("Beaver's Prize"). Wally leaving Beaver alone is not a good idea since Larry comes over soon after and convinces Beaver to leave the yard.

The other times when Metzger's Field is spoken of in regard to football are when Wally is preparing to go see Gloria Cusick at the city park, but mentions that he might go to Metzger's Field to play touch football ("Teacher's Daughter"), Wally mentioning that Tom Henderson plays with Wally and his friends each Saturday at Metzger's Field ("Wally Goes Steady") and when Wally explains to the judge in traffic court that he was going to go to Metzger's Field to play football with Eddie ("Beaver Takes a Drive").

Non-Sports Events at Metzger's Field

Other than sports, sometimes the city rents out the grounds for other events. The first time we see this occur is when Wally and Beaver burst into the living room with really big news ("A Horse Named Nick"). Wally and Beaver have been over at Metzger's Field where there is a travelling carnival setting up for a few days. The boys have got themselves a job and they are excited. After just a couple days of work, they will receive twenty dollars. Ward warns them that sometimes carnivals have been known to leave town without paying their bills, including the wages of workers. That doesn't happen to Wally and Beaver. They get paid, even more than the promised twenty dollars. They get a real live working carnival horse (now retired) named Nick.

The carnival they work is not the only carnival to come to town and set up in Metzger's Field. In Mayfield time, only two and a half months later, there's another carnival and Wally goes to this one with Tooey. But Beaver, after wasting his allowance, can't afford to attend. That all changes after Larry calls and offers to pay for Beaver. When Larry is told he gets no allowance because he had too many charges at the drug store, he must find another way to pay for his buddy Beaver. In a flash of thieving inspiration, Larry decides to take money from his mother's sewing basket and throw it out the window and then find it, since she did say if he found money, he could keep it ("Found Money"). Beaver comes over and Larry invites him to keep any money he finds in his yard. They go to the carnival after it's all found. This, however, is one time Metzger's Field turns out to be no fun, at least for Larry. But for Beaver, he doesn't get in trouble since he believed the money they found in Larry's yard did fall out of an airplane pilot's pocket when he flew upside down, which is what Larry said might have happened.

Another event, not sports, but recreational in nature, was the Father and Sons Kite Day event at Metzger's Field. Sure to be a great time, there will be a lot of prizes given away and the mayor will even be there. Beaver probably will win since his dad was the best kite maker in Shaker Heights when he was a kid. Beaver is stuck making a kite with his dad from a store-bought kit, but it's still a good kite, but the glue must dry first so the day of the contest will be the first day it flies. Well, thanks to peer pressure from Gilbert, it flies a bit sooner, a day too soon. When it crashes to the ground, it really crashes. Beaver reveals this fact on Kite Day and Ward decides they should go down and buy a kite so he can still participate. They wind up winning third place intermediate class, as Beaver says, they fixed it so every kite could win something, sort of akin to our modern-day participation trophies.

Other Happenings at Metzger's Field

We've gone over sports. We've gone over non-sports events. What else happened at Metzger's Field? The first mention in *Leave it to Beaver* of Metzger's Field is when Fred Rutherford and Ward are out looking for Beaver and Violet after Ward is convinced Beaver is out to get revenge for the black eye she recently gave him ("The Black Eye"). While looking for them, they run across two kids who they ask if they've seen any kids fighting. They say no, but then one remarks to the other after Fred and Ward leave, that they're going over to Metzger's Field because that's where all the kids have fights.

Other mentions include Beaver wanting to take Pete and Chris over to Metzger's Field to mess around ("The Grass is Always Greener"), Ward taking the car and driving over to Metzger's Field to look for Beaver ("Forgotten Party"), Ward asking Beaver if he's seen Larry at Metzger's Field ("Larry Hides Out"), Ward drops off Beaver at Metzger's Field to meet up with the Bloody Five ("Larry's Club"), Ward asks June if Wally had come home from Metzger's Field ("Beaver's Accordion") and finally, Beaver finds the Rutherford's dog over by Metzger's Field ("Beaver's Secret Life").

You can see a picture of Metzger's Field by visiting http://leaveittobeaverbooks.com.

50

MONEY

Money makes the world go around, or so the saying goes. That's even the case on *Leave it to Beaver*. The Cleaver household needs money for it to run smoothly, to keep the lights on, keep the gas flowing, pay for garbage collection, there are insurance costs for the home, car and life. They stay well fed by paying for their food. There's all that money they must spend to fix the messes the boys get into, especially Beaver ("Beaver's Accordion") ("The Broken Window") or to pay for the times they were gypped ("Perfume Salesmen") ("Beaver Finds a Wallet") or get them into business ("Wally the Businessman") or providing money that is lost ("The Haircut"). There's also money that the boys earn, spend, save or loan and there's even pretend money ("Beaver's Bad Day"). There are even talks about money as in how hard it is to pay bills or living in the poor house ("The Grass is Always Greener") ("The Train Trip"). A final thing you'll read about in this chapter is money being made by going into business ("Wally's Weekend Job") ("Wally, the Businessman") (Eddie, the Businessman") ("Beaver Goes into Business") ("Water Anyone?") ("The Cookie Fund") and ("The Paper Route"). And as another saying goes… "and so much more." Let's look closer at a bunch of these money mentions.

Loans

The mentions of money come in all shapes, sizes and forms in *Leave it to Beaver*. One of the more often referenced of these comes in the way of loans. The loans given by Ward (or asked to be given) to the boys in the form of advances of their allowance happen in numerous episodes ("Beaver's Accordion" / "Wally's Dinner Date" / "The School Picture" to name a few). Loans are also given or asked to be given by various other characters such as by Wally to Beaver ("Beaver's Accordion"), Beaver to Wally ("Wally, the Businessman"), Wally to Eddie ("Eddie's Double-Cross" / "Beaver's Typewriter" / "Beaver, the Sheepdog"), Beaver to June ("Beaver Joins a Record Club" / "Sweatshirt Monsters"), Wally to Richard ("Beaver's Laundry"), Wally to Chester and Eddie to Chester ("Beaver and Andy") Larry to Beaver ("Beaver Takes a Walk") and probably the most noteworthy loan is when Beaver makes a loan to Larry, although not purposely, in "Beaver Makes a Loan."

Millions of Dollars and Other High Dollar Amounts

A constant refrain from my childhood, one said by my friends and myself, was "I'm going to be a millionaire." That was back in the day when a million dollars was worth something and inflation had not eaten away at its value. But that was the high dollar mark back in the 1950s and 1960s, during *Leave it to Beaver* days. It's mentioned many times and there are also other mentions of lesser, but still high dollar figures.

The references begin in season one when Wally and Beaver send away for twenty-four bottles of Flower of the Orient perfume. They will sell it door to door. When it arrives in the mail, Beaver mentions they will make a hundred million dollars ("The Perfume Salesmen"). One would think that's the highest dollar amount mentioned in *Leave it to Beaver*, no, not even close. That happens in the episode where Beaver falsely claims there had been a skirmish with Indians in the vacant lot across the street from their house ("Next Door Indians"). Instead of finding Indian artifacts, they find rocks, specifically garnets. Tooey says they will all be millionaires, but Beaver tells Gus they will become jillioinaires, that's JILLION with a "J." That is a lot more than the hundred million dollars he said they'd make selling perfume.

The remaining claims of riches are typically just how someone will become a millionaire ("The Haunted House" / "Wally and Alma"/ "Beaver Finds a Wallet" / "Beaver and Violet"/ "Beaver, the Model"), someone will give a million dollars or another amount ("Beaver's Fortune"), bet a million dollars ("Next Door Indians" / "Beaver Takes a Walk"), or how they would give a million dollars for such and such like seeing the expression on Lumpy's face when the axle fell off his car ("Wally's Practical Joke"). Lesser amounts are mentioned too, like making $50,000 for selling chinchillas ("Tire Trouble") and a lady giving Beaver and Larry a $100,000 for saving her by stopping her runaway horse ("Forgotten Party")

Things are a bit different when Ward mentions a million dollars. When he is asked by Beaver if he'll ever be a millionaire, he bursts Beaver's hopes and tells him that he won't become a millionaire ("Ward's Millions). The other time Ward mentions a million dollars is after June tells Ward about Fred Rutherford calling about a water softener. She explains that if he gets five people to buy one, he will get his free. That's when Ward makes the smart remark about if only they could get five people to give them $200,000 each, they would be millionaires.

Paying Bills and Running the Household

A more frustrating aspect of money seen in *Leave it to Beaver* is the money spent on the daily grind of life, paying the bills. This is seen in a few episodes, and it is either shown as just something Ward is doing when Beaver or June speak to him about something else that is pertinent to the plot ("Beaver Says Good-Bye" / "The Paper Route") or as a method to move the plot forward ("Ward's Millions" / "The Grass is Always Greener").

In "Ward's Millions," paying bills begins a conversation about the difficulty of paying bills, how many people worry about them and the fairness of paying for stuff that is "already used up." This conversation gives Beaver the thought that if only his father was a millionaire, all his money worries would disappear. Likewise, in "The Grass is Always Greener," a conversation is started after Ward is paying bills and Beaver does some "listening" in on a conversation Ward has with June. A poorhouse is mentioned and the next day, Beaver asks about poorhouses and the fact that they don't know any poor people. When the garbage man comes by to collect trash, Beaver notices holes in his sweater and asks about him being poor. Paying bills and talking about them becomes a springboard for the entire episode.

Other mentions of money regarding running the house include June speaking of the grocery bill. She does this typically after Ward sees how many groceries she has brought home after shopping as in "The Perfect Father" and "The Haircut," where she talks specifically about the problem of inflation.

Savings and Investments

Whether it is Ward encouraging the boys to put some money into a bank, be it piggy or at the Mayfield Savings and Loan, saving money is mentioned many times on the show. Investments are mentioned too, but to a lesser extent. A closer look will show that many of these mentions move the plots forward in the episodes in which they are referenced.

The boys are encouraged to save money when Ward comes home from work one day with a piggy bank ("The Bank Account"). Beaver says what we may find to be the strangest thing when he sees the piggy bank, he asks, "What is it?" Although Piggy Banks had been around since about the 1300s,[97] they did not come into popular use in America until possibly the 1940s. The boys each put in some money and Ward and June add some too. The boys continue putting money into the bank until they finally decide to take it out and buy themselves each a baseball glove. Ward discourages their inclination and tells them that the next day is bank day at their school. They should deposit it in their accounts at school instead. They agree to do so, until they see Ward's beat up hunting jacket and decide to do something kind for Ward. This is the first example of saving money, piggy banks, and bank accounts on *Leave it to Beaver*. The other mentions of a piggy bank come when the boys want to take money out of their piggy bank to fix the car window they break with a baseball ("The Broken Window") and when Beaver takes money of his bank to buy a monster sweatshirt ("Monster Sweatshirts").

Money is saved by Beaver at other times, but he doesn't keep it in a piggy bank. He saves up $6.98 to buy Wally a birthday present and that money was kept in a sock ("Wally's Present"). In another episode, Wally and Beaver save up $2.00 and $1.00 respectively, but there is no mention of a piggy bank ("Blind Date Committee"). Beaver has thirteen cents saved up to spend at the 5&10 ("Beaver's Fortune") and another time, Wally mentions that Beaver has a whole drawer full of money he's been saving ("Wally, the Businessman").

There are several mentions of money in a brick-and-mortar bank building, Beaver mentions he has $25.00 in his bank account that he could use to buy himself a sweater ("Beaver's Sweater"). Beaver and Wally tell Ward that if they had $200, he'd make them put it in the bank ("Tire Trouble"). Ward suggests Beaver start a bank account when he receives a check for mowing a lawn ("Beaver Goes into Business"). It's strongly suggested by Ward, and later, Wally, that Beaver should put his birthday money into the bank ("Beaver's Birthday").

Investments are not mentioned on *Leave it to Beaver* as much as savings. One of the few mentions include Fred Rutherford telling Ward that he and Gwendolyn have a little "nest egg" saved up ("Tire Trouble"). He doesn't delve into the details of the "nest egg" but it probably included savings and investments. Ward tells the boys that he does own some stocks and bonds and says they are "comfortable" when Beaver asks if they are rich ("Stocks and Bonds"). Ward also tells Wally that he doesn't have to fear not going to State after not receiving a scholarship. He tells Wally they have been saving for years for his college education ("Lumpy's Scholarship").

Money is a Big Responsibility

With handling money comes responsibility. While Ward and June feel their boys are responsible in many areas of their lives, money is not always one of them. While Ward feels Beaver is responsible enough to give money to for a haircut, even after repeatedly losing his lunch money, June does not feel the same ("The Haircut"). Then, when Beaver is given the responsibility of handling his class cookie fund, it is Ward that is doubtful Beaver can handle that responsibility ("The Cookie Fund"). He again expresses doubt, this time regarding Wally, when his eldest son asks if he can have a credit card ("The Credit Card").

Economics

The eminent economist, Thomas Sowell, once wrote a book titled *Basic Economics*. While it is a large book, it is one of the simplest to read and understand on the subject. Surprisingly, a few

---

[97] "The Accidental Invention: The Origin Of Piggy Banks." The Financial Brand. https://thefinancialbrand.com/news/financial-education/history-of-piggy-banks-24204/

of the lessons he teaches are found within episodes of *Leave it to Beaver* and they include the concepts of capitalism ("Water, Anyone?"), the myth of the gender wage gap ("Mother's Day Composition") and 401K plans, pensions, and investments ("Stocks and Bonds"). When an interviewer once asked Dr. Sowell why he didn't have any graphs, charts, and mathematical formulas in his book, *Basic Economics*, he jokingly answered, "Because I wanted people to read it." Let's look at these economic concepts as they are found in *Leave it to Beaver*.

In "Water, Anyone?" Beaver wants to get a uniform for the new baseball team the big guys are forming. Wally and his friends are each given jobs so they can help earn money for uniforms. Despite many pleas from Beaver, his parents and other parents tell him they have nothing for him. Not being able to make money by being given a job, he creates his own business, selling water. Ward tells him later, that it's not correct for him to sell his friends water. Beaver then turns the table on Ward. He asks about Mr. Michaelson, the grocer. Ward says he knows him, grew up with him and admits they are friends. Beaver wonders why Mr. Michaelson doesn't give Ward groceries for free. Good one Beave! Ward says it's because Mr. Michaelson is a businessman and Beaver says he's a businessman too. What's even funnier is that Tooey's mom doesn't understand capitalism, because she calls Ward to complain about Beaver selling water and says this sort of thing leads to communism, an entirely different form of economics.

The gender wage gap theory states that men make much more than women for doing the same exact job. While existence of the gap is true on the surface in many areas, it's looking for the reason why it exists where Thomas Sowell's understanding and explanation are seen in the "Mother's Day Composition" episode of *Leave it to Beaver*.

In this episode, Judy speaks about her mom. She tells Miss Landers that her mother was a head buyer for a department store and was going to be promoted to be general manager, but before she did so, her mom decided to quit and get married, leaving the work force. This is the reason for the "gender pay gap" we saw in the 1950s and even today. Women, more than men, leave the work force for various reasons, such as getting married and raising children, although it is less often now than it was back in Judy Hensler's day. As for a "gender pay gap," today, there is not much of one when it comes to men and women in the same job who have spent the same amount of time in a position with continuous service, the same education and same experience. Thomas Sowell has spent years of study on the subject and demonstrates in many of his books and columns on the subject that if "leaving the workforce" is taken out of the equation, men and woman are basically, paid the same salaries for the same jobs, with the same experience and education [98].

In "Stocks and Bonds" Ward helps the boys get some practical experience in the world of investing. Although it is Wally who needs help understanding this world for his economics class, Ward welcomes Beaver along for the ride and he provides them with $100 to invest in whatever they want. Of course, that means Ward will strongly suggest they invest in something conservative. They wind up investing in Mayfield Power & Light or Mayfield Power and Electric or Mayfield Electric and Power (all depending on who is speaking); it's sort of like "supper vs. dinner."

The boys were considering another stock, a defense contractor named Jet Electro. It's a penny stock, and it looks like it's taking off like a jet. It goes fast and rockets past Mayfield Power and whatever. The boys soon regret buying a rock steady utility company and get Ward to sell their stock and buy Jet Electro. Their new stock continues going up until it doesn't. The boys think they are washed out of Wall Street until Ward tells them he gave his broker a stop limit order on the Jet

---

[98] Sowell, Thomas. Orlando Sun-Sentinel. "Pay disparity for women a true statistical fraud." April 18, 2014.

Electro stock and he put their money back into the utility company with the ever changing name.

Where economics and Thomas Sowell come into the equation is how he states in *Basic Economics* that attacks on "Wall Street" and rich people are nonsensical as we see in "Stocks and Bonds," that Wall Street is made up of regular people, just like Wally and Beaver and Ward and June. It's made up of hard-working employees who have pensions, who happen to work at their own individual "salt mines." They have pension funds; union workers have the same type of funds and most any good job has options to help employees invest. Sowell mentions that attacks on "Wall Street" and the desire to hurt "Wall Street" actually hurt people who live on "Main Street." The attacks hurt your neighbors and may hurt you. As June Cleaver so eloquently says, after Ward explains stockholders, "And in a way, they become part owner of the company. Lots of companies have thousands of stockholders. Isn't that right Ward?" And those stockholders include millions of hard-working American citizens.

Other Money Mentions

Let's turn from economics lessons to looking at the economics of finding lost stuff. Other interesting mentions of money include Beaver receiving monetary rewards for finding a lost dog ("Beaver and Poncho"), finding a lost cat ("Beaver's Cat Problem"), Beaver rescuing a lost canoe ("Beaver Becomes a Hero") and finding a lost wallet ("Beaver Finds a Wallet"). We also see money being given away as a tip for good service at a restaurant ("Wally's Dinner Date") and also for taxi service, once when the taxi was no longer needed ("Beaver's Guest") and the other time when Beaver returns home after a bus ride brought him back home by accident ("The Bus Ride").

There are many other instances of money being mentioned in *Leave it to Beaver* and you can find some of those as they are added regularly to "The Chapters" section at http://leaveittobeaverbooks.com.

51

JUNE'S CHORES

June spent a lot of her time on *Leave it to Beaver* doing various chores. She was a stay-at-home mom and took care of the house very efficiently. The most obvious chore, if one wants to call it that, was cooking. For me, cooking just seems like something that is done every day. It's the more monotonous tasks like sweeping the floor, vacuuming, cleaning cobwebs, mopping and similar jobs that seem to be more like chores. I do many of those things myself and cook occasionally. Cooking can be enjoyable, mopping, never.

This chapter will not be a discussion of how June wore pearls and high heels and dresses when she cleaned. Barbara Billingsley would be disheartened if that occurred here. In her Archive of American Television interview on July 14, 2000, she expressed exasperation about Oprah Winfrey asking such a question, "I thought 'God, I love you and I think your program's great, but couldn't you think of another question besides high heels and pearls?' but anyway…"

Here, we'll just look at her different tasks and at the frequency they occur. For example, June sewed, knitted and embroidered in almost 11% of the 234 *Leave it to Beaver* episodes or 41% of all episodes in which she is doing some type of work around the house besides cooking or gardening. In a few of those episodes, she wasn't knitting a sweater or sewing a shirt or socks, she was simply sewing a name tag onto an article of clothing like Beaver's sweater ("Beaver's Sweater"), or his jacket ("Beaver's Jacket") or onto all his clothing he's about to take on a cross country trip ("Beaver Sees America").

One of her biggest sewing or knitting jobs take place in "Beaver and Poncho" when she knits a small sweater for the dog Beaver brought home. However, when Ward first sees her knitting in the living room, he thinks she's knitting something for a baby and gets a bit frightened. She also has a big job with a community afghan she is working on with a group of women in "The Train Trip." George Haskell brings it over to her since it's her turn to knit the afghan and this gives him a chance to tell Ward about the story his boys told the conductor that afternoon on the train. He was so giddy in telling the story, I thought he was Fred Rutherford. You know Fred would've relished telling that story. She also has important sewing chores to do when she alters Beaver's angel costume ("The Hair Cut") and his canary costume ("School Play").

When it came to mending clothes, June is first seen sewing socks ("The Bank Account"), a skill she learned in boarding school. She sews a shirt ("Tenting Tonight"), sews a button on Ward's shirt ("Wally's Big Date"), sews the lining in her fur stole or coat ("Beaver's First Date"), sews Beaver's pants ("Nobody Loves Me"), sews a button on Beaver's sweater ("Bachelor at Large") and sews a shirt ("Wally and the Fraternity").

An interesting tidbit about June with any kind of needle in her hand is that, unless there's been a big oversight on my part, she doesn't sew, mend, knit, quilt or embroider in any of the season three or season four episodes. Of all instances of her sewing, 64% of them take place in seasons five and six.

There are plenty of other chores she undertakes during the run of the series, the number of times she undertakes them are in parentheses. These include vacuuming (10), dusting (3), laundry (7), polishing silver (3), cleaning windows (2), waxing or cleaning the kitchen floor (4), working on drapes (1), papering kitchen shelves (1) and ironing clothes (2). It's a possibility that these types of chores were done on a Wednesday. The reason for believing these were done on a Wednesday, especially the bigger of these chores, is because in the "Forgotten Party" episode, Beaver tells Larry he can't come inside the house because it was a Wednesday, the day when his mom cleans the house.

Since June cleans the house a little each day, he probably meant it's the day she deep cleans the house as in washing windows, vacuuming, mopping and other duties.

Looking at the percentages, the top five chores on June's to do list break down as follows (if you include sewing chores as only those that include mending an article of clothing): Vacuuming (25%), Sewing (17.5%), laundry, which includes washing, drying and folding clothes (17.5%) and cleaning or waxing the kitchen floor (10%).

When you add the few times she was planting or cutting flowers and all of her cooking, we can firmly say June was hardest working Cleaver in the family. She may not have made the money to pay the mortgage and the electric bill, but she sure gave the family a spark, a spark larger than anything the Mayfield Power and Light company could provide. That's just the kind of thing loving and caring mothers like June Cleaver do for a family.

For more information on June and her chores, visit http://leaveittobeaverbooks.com.

52

MAIL RECEIVED

One of my fondest memories as a child was receiving mail. Sometimes I was surprised by a post card from some faraway place where my own Uncle Billy had traveled. Although, I called him Uncle Bill, his similarities with Uncle Billy were that he traveled a lot and that he was my great uncle. I could hardly wait to find out what exotic place he was going to travel to next. We received postcards from Norway, Argentina, Greece. It thrilled me to get his cards in the mail. His post cards gave me a lifelong love for travel, or more so, a desire to travel. The same thing happened when I lived with my grandparents and each week, I would get a letter from my mom and dad and included with the letter was a package of Topps baseball cards. Those letters helped me become a lifelong baseball card collector. Later, I learned to like junk mail, if it was addressed to me and not just to "resident" or "occupant." That's why when I was young, I sent in a card from a magazine asking for information about the Galena Territory, a residential community in northwestern Illinois. I loved receiving that glossy brochure in the mail.

Wally and Beaver also loved getting letters or packages in the mail. It seems they always got things in the mail that were better than what I received. Think about it for a moment… an alligator ("Captain Jack"), an accordion ("Beaver's Accordion"), a film projector ("Perfume Salesmen"), a ring ("Beaver's Ring"), birthday cards with money in them ("Beaver's Birthday"), records from a record club ("Beaver Joins a Record Club"). They must have loved their mailman.

For the most part, this chapter will cover mail received by Beaver or Wally. But a few items that Ward or June receive will also be mentioned. This will be a season by season look as I try to capture every mail delivery for the boys.

Season 1

Alligator- The boys send off for an 8 ft Everglades alligator. They receive a much smaller one in the mail ("Captain Jack").

Perfume – The boys send away for twenty-four bottles of *Flower of the Orient* perfume. If they sell it all, they will get a free film projector ("Perfume Salesmen"). They receive the perfume in the mail, and they later receive a projector in the mail. Fortunately for them, Ward intercepts the lousy projector the Mason Acme Products company sent them and replaced it with one he bought.

Hunting Jacket – The boys receive a hunting jacket for Ward as a special delivery in one of the most touching episodes on *Leave it to Beaver* ("The Bank Account").

Season 2

Ring – Aunt Martha sends a ring and a letter to Beaver ("Beaver's Ring").

Pipe – Ward receives a pipe as a souvenir from Germany from Fred Rutherford and Fred winds up causing trouble all the way from Europe ("The Pipe").

Nose Flattener – Wally believes Gloria Cusick thinks his nose makes him look like a monkey or a pig, so he sends away for a contraption that will flatten his nose ("Wally's Pug Nose").

Letter from Billy Peyton – Beaver receives a letter from his old friend Billy Peyton who now lives on a farm. He invites Beaver to visit him ("The Bus Ride").

Season 3

Mayfield Cotillion Invite – This is a piece of mail that Beaver Cleaver is not pleased about at all. He and Larry eventually skip out on the second dance and get caught doing so ("Beaver's Dance").

Model Agency Letter(s) – After not sending the money he owes the modeling agency for adding his photo to their modeling catalog, they send their lawyers after Beaver ("Beaver, the Model").

Season 4

Letter from the Bannermans -June receives a letter from her old friend Margaret Bannerman. The Bannermans used to live in Mayfield. Her friend asks if Wally can accompany their daughter Kitty to an upcoming dance at the country club when they visit town the following week ("Wally's Glamour Girl").

Accordion – Beaver receives an accordion on a free trial but must send it back in the allotted time. When he doesn't, the company sends a representative to the Cleaver house to retrieve the accordion or the money to replace it ("Beaver's Accordion").

Season 5

Registered Letter from Uncle Billy - Gilbert finds a notice for a registered letter on the floor at Beaver's house. When they go to the post office to get it, Beaver finds it's a letter from Uncle Billy and he's given him $10.00 for his birthday, albeit a little late.

Penny's Party Invite – The mother of Beaver's classmate Penny sends an invitation to Penny's good-bye party to the Cleaver house. He doesn't want to go. Penny doesn't want him to attend. He goes, and they admit they will miss each other when she is gone. But that mutual affection goes by the wayside when Beaver finds out she is remaining at school until the end of the year ("Farewell to Penny").

Merchant Marine letters – June finds a letter from the Merchant Marines and is worried that Wally wants to leave home. She can't believe that Wally may want to leave home because of a blow up he and Ward had a few nights earlier about Wally coming home late. She feels that there must be something else behind his desire to join the Merchant Marines. She sees a second letter in the mail from the Merchant Marines and becomes more concerned. However, the letters are for Lumpy who is upset about his father taking his car keys away.

Season 6

Records – Beaver receives multiple deliveries of records to the house after he joins a record club. He states in this episode that it is neat to belong to a club. However, he forgets to send in the post cards that tell the company not to send him the full price records. He ends up owing a lot of money ("Beaver Joins a Record Club").

Locket – Donna Yeager's dad sends back to Beaver, the locket he gave her as a gift ("More Blessed to Give").

Special Delivery Letter – The Teen Age Forum TV program sends Beaver a letter inviting him to be on one of their panel discussions ("Beaver on TV")

Junk Mail – Ward receives junk mail offering him a chance to purchase cheap land in Palm Springs. What an opportunity! He then reads further and sees it is in Palm Springs, North Dakota ("Wally and the Fraternity"). In another episode, he also receives junk mail offering to put his poetry to music, but he doesn't write poetry.

There's more that can be said about the mail received at the Cleaver house, but you'll have to visit http://leaveittobeaverbooks.com to learn about it.

53

THE CLEAVER MARRIAGE RELATIONSHIP AND CHILD REARING

The dynamic between Ward and June in their marriage is amazing to watch over the six seasons of *Leave it to Beaver*. Their relationship is full of love and understanding. Some will argue it was misogynistic and demeaning toward June, but to paraphrase Lucille Ball when she had those arguments said against her and the relationship she and Ricky Ricardo had in *I Love Lucy*, "It was a TV show and we were trying to entertain people, not fix all the ills in society." According to TV historian / archivist Stu Shostak, Lucille Ball would often have one such person in an audience for the talks she presented on one of America's most beloved comedy classics.

June was a strong woman and often expressed her opinion. Sometimes her views were expressed quite forcefully. This is especially seen in "Beaver Runs Away," when Ward is stubborn and won't go look for Beaver who may experience all kinds of toil and dangers during his "running away" adventure. June wasn't taking any chances and she and Wally go look for Beaver while Ward sits at home. They don't find Beaver, but after Ward makes a phone call to Mrs. Mondello, Beaver is found. He's enjoying a nice meal at the Mondellos.

This chapter will focus on two areas; the first is the marriage relationship, as it is seen between Ward and June and the understanding of marriage by Beaver and Wally. The second is how Ward and June rear Beaver and Wally and any disagreements they may have on child rearing issues. We'll start here with the marriage relationship.

Marriage and Family

Since *Leave it to Beaver* is billed as a show in which the world is seen through the eyes of a child, actually, two children, this section will begin with the thoughts about marriage and family from the viewpoint of Wally and Beaver. In "The Garage Painters," the boys read in *Tom Sawyer* about him standing on his head in front of a girl. Ward had said he had done a lot of things that Tom did. Beaver wonders if he had done that for their mother. Wally assumes that he may have done it, but after getting married, no longer had to do it. In "Mother's Day Composition," Beaver learns that June was a prize-winning swimmer. Wally comments that when they go to the beach, they can't drag her near the water. Beaver says, "Yeah. I guess that's because when you're married, you don't care about having fun anymore." After hearing his friend Chopper talk, in "Beaver's House Guest," about all the presents he gets because he has two families after a divorce, Beaver begins longing for Ward and June to divorce. Wally tells him how goofy that is, and Wally was right. Beaver eventually figures out how bad divorce can be when his friend must leave to console his crying mother. A big misunderstanding the boys have about marriage is seen in "Mother's Helper." Wally says when he gets married, he'll have his wife do the dishes because girls are supposed to do that kind of stuff. Beaver says he won't get married, instead, he'll use paper plates.

Regarding the family, in "Three Boys and a Burro," Ward decides to take the family out for dinner. Beaver wonders why and Wally tells him, "I think it's on account of togetherness like you read about in the magazines. It's supposed to make us a happy family, and all that kind of junk." After Beaver wonders why they couldn't just be a happy family eating at home, Wally says, "That's no good. You got to go out and show people you're a happy family."

When looking at the Cleaver marriage, it's seen in "Ward's Problem, that the two enjoy a date night once in a while. There are other times that they plan on going out such as in "Beaver's

Poem" and "Mother's Helper." These are evenings that were to be spent at the movies, but due to helping Beaver with his homework, and June not feeling well in the latter episode, they don't go out in either one. Ward, many times, opens the door for June when they get into the car. He pours her coffee in season five ("Beaver's First Date") and washes dishes ("Eddie's Sweater" / "Don Juan Beaver"). June, shows what a wonderful wife she is and her love towards Ward by letting her sons know that she loves her husband in "Beaver's House Guest," and compliments him to Beaver in "Beaver's Graduation." June demonstrates patience in "Beaver and Andy," when Ward thanks her for not saying, "I told you so." She replies, "It was a real effort, but I managed." It's also shown, in "Beaver's Team," that their marriage was what some would call typical when on a lazy Saturday afternoon, Ward is being exactly that… lazy. He's resting on the couch when June comes in with a list of chores to do and he says he can't wait till Monday when he can go back to work and relax. In the "Late Edition," Ward shares a thought on marriage that almost get him in trouble. He compares newspaper delivery to marriage. "The first few weeks the bride is all lipstick and make up. Then one morning, the man comes downstairs and bingo, old housecoat and hair curlers." She says, "I don't think I appreciate the comparison." He says that comparison never applied to her.

When it comes to family, Ward and June speak of it fondly and lament in "Beaver's Doll Buggy" how the boys drift apart as they grow older and instead of being the best friend each has in the world, they just become someone to exchange cards with at Christmas. In "Un-togetherness," June speaks of how much she loves spending time up at Crescent Lake in the summers because the family seems so much closer there. After joking about the cramped quarters, Ward says, "Here, we seem to be going in four different directions. Up there, the pace sort of slows down, and we have a chance to get acquainted with one another." Ward let's Beaver know the importance of family in "All-Night Party," when Beaver wants to skip out on the party Ward and June want to throw Wally in honor of his graduation. "Now, Beaver, this Friday's going to be one of the most important days in Wally's life so far. It's times like this that the family comes first."

Parenting and Child Rearing

This section will discuss how Ward and June raised Wally and Beaver, but will also highlight a couple of their differences on parenting. The first difference happens early in season one when Ward wants to teach Beaver how to fight ("Black Eye"). June doesn't think a father should teach a son to fight. There are other episodes where Beaver is involved in fighting, and we see some insight into their parenting styles in them. When Beaver gets into a fight against Gilbert ("Beaver and Gilbert"), Ward advocates for Beaver growing up and facing his antagonist instead of cowering in fear. In the episode where Beaver has a fight scheduled with Sonny Cartwright ("Beaver's Fortune"), June wants it stopped, but Ward tells her, "Now, June, you mustn't get so upset about this. This is something every boy must go through. It's just a part of growing up." Later in season three ("Beaver and Ivanhoe"), Beaver gets into a couple more fights and June still hasn't learned, and babies him after one of the altercations and Ward just rolls his eyes.

When it comes to responsibilities, Ward talks big about how responsible the boys are to Mr. Wilson, so much so, that Mr. and Mrs. Wilson ask if Wally and Beaver can take care of their daughter Helen while they and the Cleavers attend a wedding ("Child Care"). June feels wary about this responsibility, but the boys come through with flying colors. Ward later makes it clear, a couple times, that he is the one who is wary of the boys taking on too much responsibility when it comes to other people's property or money ("Cat out of the Bag" and "The Cookie Fund"), but likes to give responsibility and does so with Wally when he allows him to accompany Beaver to

Crystal Falls on the bus ("The Bus Ride"). When Beaver buys his own ice skates ("Beaver's Ice Skates"), June is the one who is glad they gave Beaver the responsibility because it's a sign of maturity and growing up and Ward kids her saying, "June, he just bought a pair of ice skates. He didn't propose to them." Ward, after telling Wally he is not allowed to go for the weekend to Scott's lake house without any adult supervision ("Weekend Invitation"), tells Wally they generally like to give him responsibility to go places and do things on his own, but not in this situation. In another episode, June believes the sparkling clean floor in the kitchen Wally says was done just because he and Beaver wanted to clean it, shows a great sense of growing up and being responsible. Ward doubts any kid would grow up to be that responsible ("Beaver's Laundry). Ward is correct, but they say nothing about it to the boys.

Ward says that he's tried hard to be a buddy to the boys, to prove that he is on their side ("The Haircut") and shows it too ("Beaver's Short Pants"). Ward also shows his love and his being on their side when the boys experience some struggle like Wally needing an orchid ("Wally's Orchid"), or when Beaver loses his fielder's glove in a bet he only made because of Ward's exaggeration ("Beaver Takes a Walk"), or when he tries to build up Wally's confidence while at a swanky restaurant ("Wally's Dinner Date"). Ward also builds things with them like a go-cart ("The State vs. Beaver"), a kite ("Kite Day"), and on occasion, Ward even tries too hard to be a buddy ("The Perfect Father") and winds up causing some embarrassment for the boys.

Ward talks a lot about not babying Beaver ("The Tooth") and June does baby him after Gilbert pushes Whitey on him when they are playing football ("Beaver and Gilbert") and when he gets in a fight trying to act like Ivanhoe ("Beaver and Ivanhoe"). In a situation that is a lot less painful than the previous three mentioned, June babies him once again when the store mixes up boxes and she gives him a ladies' slip to give to Miss Landers as a gift. When he comes home at the end of the day, she babies him and admits she didn't do that to him on purpose and that it was an accident ("The Last Day of School"). June also laments about Beaver's feelings being hurt because Lumpy calls him "Freckles." Beaver gets upset and leaves the dinner table and she says, "Poor Beaver" ("Beaver's Freckles"). In an outright admission of wanting to baby him, Ward and June discuss going after him when he runs away from home and Ward says, "All right, if you want to spoil him and give in to him, make a baby out of him." June replies, "That's exactly what I wanna do." Then, in one of the last times we see this blatant babying, Ward tells June, "He's growing up. We can't baby him and hold his hand all his life. June replies, "Well, we're going to baby him and hold his hand through this" ("Beaver, the Sheepdog").

We know Ward is very understanding and a good listener. Even though those two things are true, sometimes his understanding and affability come a bit too late, meaning that sometimes a troublesome situation occurs before he demonstrates his understanding and listening skills. There are numerous examples but let us look at just a few. Beaver is invited to Linda Dennison's birthday party, and he finds out it's an all-girl party ("Party Invitation"). He doesn't want to go. Wally tries to get him out of it by imitating Ward. Beaver gets yelled at. Wally gets in trouble. It's not until Ward forces him into the Dennison house and he gets back home, that Ward finds out about the all-girl party problem and demonstrates his understanding and listening skills to Wally.

Ward shows himself to be very understanding and a good listener when Beaver fears he has too many freckles, but not until after he first totally misses the cues Beaver is giving about his freckle concerns ("Beaver's Freckles"). It wasn't because Ward wasn't understanding or refused to listen to Beaver, it's because Ward didn't think Beaver could be upset about his freckles since he had so few. The thought never crossed his mind when he told Beaver that there was once a guy on the *Our Gang* comedies who made lots of money because everyone would laugh at him because he had so many freckles. Soon after his talk and one with June too, Beaver goes upstairs to try to get rid of his freckles by scraping them with sandpaper and then by putting makeup on to cover his freckles. Ward eventually has a good talk with Beaver and tries to instill in him the importance of inner beauty. It's a good few minutes of listening and understanding, but it's not until Beaver talks to Clyde Appleby that Beaver gets over his anger about having freckles. Afterward, he even wishes he had more.

Ward and June have expectations of their boys. When speaking of expectations, this doesn't mean parents expecting their kids go to college after high school, although that is something Ward and June did expect. Their biggest expectations were that both Wally and Beaver would be well rounded, kind, thoughtful, caring members of their community who had respect for themselves, their friends, girls they would date and elders. Wally and Beaver were very well behaved, very respectful, and well-adjusted young men. As Ward and June speak of them at the end of the final episode, "Family Scrapbook," they say they're not young boys anymore, they're growing up and are "very responsible individuals now." Their maturity and their respect are due to Ward and June having high expectations, and not low expectations. You can always identify in society, the children of parents who have low expectations of their kids, and Wally and Beaver were definitely not them.

There are a number of simple expectations that June and Ward have. One is that the boys be dressed well for dinner. They're told to get changed for dinner or to put a clean shirt on for dinner quite often. When the boys finish with their meals, they ask to be excused. The boys use "yes sir" quite often, but not as often as some children, but more than all their friends combined. Beaver knows to respect the police and understands from what Ward has told him, that the police are who a person goes to when there is trouble ("Beaver Plays Hooky"). You'll notice in many episodes, especially as Wally gets involved with girls, that he is told to respect them, treat them well and when visiting the homes of friends, especially a girl like Alma Hanson, he's told to eat everything that he's given to eat ("Wally and Alma"). June gives Beaver some rules when he visits Larry's for dinner and they include thanking them for the meal, not eating with his elbows on the table, not talking with his mouth full, and eating the food even if he doesn't like it ("Friendship"). And let us not forget how Ward and June had the boys attend dancing school, after all, a boy wouldn't want to grow up to be a wallflower.

June is caring, loving, intelligent, resourceful, hard-working, and protective of her family. Some people like to criticize June, saying she is too overprotective of her children, especially when it comes to her youngest son in the first few seasons of *Leave it to Beaver*. Those who say June is overprotective typically hail from the Baby Boomer generation or from Generation X (people born from 1946-1980) while Millennials or those from Generation Z (people born from 1981-2010) are less likely to believe that. June Cleaver gets a bad rap for being overprotective and I see her as being a very loving mother. In the Lifetime Movie, *The Shoplifting Pact*, when the main evil character is about to kill her prey, she tells her victim, "You think your parents are overprotective? Some of us would kill for that kind of love." I won't tell you how that movie ends in case you're a fan of those types of movies and haven't seen it yet. But she's right, for lots of people, they would have loved to have had a mother that seemed to be or was overprotective, at least when compared to the mother they had while growing up.

One of the ways people say June demonstrates this overprotection is how she gets into the boys' business. When it comes to girls, this is true. She gets involved often in Wally's relationships during the first few seasons of the show. But it's not always her doing. Look at the time Caroline Cunningham's mother calls to arrange a date with her daughter and Wally ("Eddie's Girl"). June was not the instigator. Even when all those mothers asked her if Wally would take their daughter to the eighth-grade dance ("My Brother's Girl"), June had ample opportunity to interfere, but didn't. However, there is that time when she finds Alma Hanson's phone number in Wally's jacket pocket and expresses some worry and quite a bit of interest. That concern melts away when she finds out Wally drew her name and must take her to a school picnic. After that, she's encouraging towards Wally and the dates Alma's mother arranges for them, but June isn't involved in this relationship.

It seems that June expresses a lot of concern and worry more than she gets actively involved in his relationships. There's the finding of Alma's number mentioned above and look at his going out with Evelyn Boothby. In that latter relationship, both her and Ward are concerned, and she does try to interfere through Ward, but it doesn't work ("Wally Goes Steady"). When there's news about Eddie going steady (a season earlier), June is worried Wally will do the same thing ("Eddie's Double-Cross"). June also expresses a lot of concern when she overhears Frances Hobbs speak of Wally as if she's got him wrapped around her little finger ("School Sweater"), but to stick up for June once again, Ward is very concerned about that girl too. June also shows her concern when the family is out shopping downtown and sees Wally and Julie Foster together in the city park, walking hand in hand ("Teacher's Daughter").

Now, if you want to see some interference on her part, you can find it. When they want to hire some help for June around the house, Mrs. Manners sends her daughter Margie over to the Cleaver house. Margie and Wally take an instant liking to one another. It isn't long before Wally is neglecting his homework and track practice. June tries to get Beaver to interfere and eventually gets Mrs. Manners to take over her daughter's duties ("Mother's Helper"). Then, when Wally is floating around the house mooncapping over Ginny Townsend ("Wally's Dream Girl"), Beaver accidentally reveals her name and June winds up inviting her on their family picnic. If you're imitating a football official, you might throw a flag (call a penalty) on that play by June. Oh yeah, it's awkward for Wally, but after a short time of reflection, Wally thanks June for inviting Ginny on the picnic because it saved him from all sorts of trouble down the road.

June is often the voice of wisdom in many of the episodes when she and Ward must come to some tough decision or handle a difficult situation. When Beaver asks June about Ward lying, after Ward had just lectured him about lying, June makes sure Ward remedies the situation and his punishment is having to go play cards with the Rutherfords that same evening ("Beaver's Bad Day"). She convinces Ward to allow Wally to come to them about smoking ("The Pipe") and Ward agrees. Wally doesn't, and Ward gives June a bit of grief about it, but Wally didn't have anything to admit because he didn't smoke the pipe. She is the smart one who figured out a way for Wally to take his atrociously loud suit back to the store and exchange it for a better one. She allows Wally to think it was his idea to get the more acceptable suit ("Wally's New Suit"). June advises Ward that he had neglected the boys a little bit over the weekend when Eddie caused trouble by making Beaver think he had hypnotized him ("The Hypnotist") and June convinces Ward to buy an orchid for Wally's date ("Wally's Orchid") after she shows Ward the orchid, he bought her when she was just sixteen. It was June who reminds Ward they agreed Beaver was growing up and he no longer needed a babysitter ("Beaver's Long Night"). In what is one of the least enjoyed episodes by many fans, June advises Ward to not say anything to Beaver about his ignoring her ("The Silent Treatment"). She says the problem will solve itself, and she's correct. That June Cleaver was a great mother!

54

POP CULTURE / CURRENT AND RECENT PAST EVENTS

At first glance, maybe your first time watching every episode, you may not notice what people call pop culture references. These would be references to various things going on in society at the time the show was being filmed or maybe a few decades earlier, if a character speaking is older. But if you get into the show and watch episodes repeatedly, like many fans do, you'll notice more such references all the time. This will be a season-by-season list. Let's examine how the use of such references flowed throughout the series. Some of these references are repeated.

Season 1

Tab Hunter – Penny Jamison tells Wally he has eyes like the popular actor at the time ("Wally's Girl Trouble").

Happy Hooligan – Ward refers to the popular comic book character drawn by Frederick Burr Opper. It debuted in 1900 and ended in 1932. He says the film in the projector sent to the boys by the Mason Acme Products had a character that looked just like Happy Hooligan ("The Perfume Salesmen").

Bernard Baruch – Ward says about the boys' initiative and getting a paper route is how this great American financier got started. He was one of the most powerful men in America and a presidential advisor for Woodrow Wilson, Franklin Roosevelt and Harry Truman ("The Paper Route").

J. Edgar Hoover – Mrs. Wilson says their little Puddin' would be as safe with Wally and Beaver as she would be with the current FBI Director ("Child Care").

Babe Ruth – Beaver and Wally are looking at an advertisement for a baseball glove said to be the kind the famous baseball player used ("The Bank Account").

Cesar Romero – June mentions the dog Beaver brought home, a chihuahua, as having the same Latin charm as the famous actor ("Beaver and Poncho").

Ted Williams – The famous baseball player is mentioned while the boys play ball in the street in front of their house ("The Broken Window").

Sal Mineo – After finding a vacant lot filled with garnets, Chester says they'll be richer than all the kids in the world, even the actor Sal Mineo ("Next Door Indians")

Rock Hudson – The famous actor of the time is mentioned by Eddie Haskell when Wally wonders why Mary Ellen Rogers was asking about him and made a goofy face when saying, "Give my love to Wally." Eddie says, "Cut it out Rock." ("New Doctor")

Harvey – June asks Ward if he will be staying in the garage talking to his friend Harvey. She is referencing the Jimmy Stewart movie *Harvey* which is about the Stewart character and his imaginary best friend, a rabbit that stands 6'3½" tall ("Beaver and Henry").

Season 2

Superman – After Ward talks about the things Wally and Beaver are planning to do, without them telling him and his having no way to find out, Beaver comments that maybe he has x-ray ears like Superman, the comic book character with all sorts of superpowers, but Beaver is conflating x-ray vision with super hearing ("Her Idol").

Mickey Mantle – A comment is made that Wally does not hold his razor like the famous New York Yankees baseball player ("The Shave").

Adolph Menjou - Ward says the third grade may have just lost another Adolph Menjou, a great actor from silent films to the current time when this episode was filmed. Ward was referencing the actor when told Beaver beat out Claude Bonnefield for the lead role ("School Play").

Clyde Beatty – When Wally and Beaver protest having to take baths each night they come home from the carnival where they got a job, Ward tells the boys Clyde Beatty has the same problem of having to take nightly baths. Clyde Beatty was a world-famous animal trainer who owned and ran his own circus ("A Horse Named Nick").

Cary Grant – When talking about Wally going to the dance with Mary Ellen Rogers, Lumpy says, "Get a load of Cary Grant." Grant was a famous actor who had lead roles in many romantic comedies as well as in a few Hitchcock films ("Dance Contest").

Phone booth stuffing – Mr. Haller, the principal of Mayfield High, discusses with June the new trend of the boys wearing a jellyroll hair style. He says Wally will eventually get over it and do something more mature like stuffing himself in a phone booth with twenty-six other guys. This was a weird fad in the 1950s, but in picture I've seen, it looks like it was a fun fad ("Wally's Haircomb").

Ted Williams – Ward tells Beaver that one of the best hitters ever in Major League Baseball, Ted Williams, even struck out once in a while ("Beaver, the Athlete").

Season 3

Prince of Wales and Mrs. Simpson – Ward says arranging a blind date was probably not the way Prince Edward, the Prince of Wales and Mrs. Wallis Simpson met ("Blind Date Committee").

Walt Disney – Beaver speaks about Mr. Disney having trees in his movies that scream, have feelings and run ("Beaver's Tree").

Dinah Shore – Wally is surprised to find June singing in the kitchen. He says he's never heard of mothers singing. She says Dinah Shore is a mother. She was a singer and actress and attained most of her chart success during the 1940s ("Pet Fair").

Bob Cousy – Wally is standing in front of the mirror practicing poses, trying to look like the star basketball player from the Boston Celtics ("Beaver's Library Book").

Dale Evans – A famous cowgirl who was married to actor and singer Roy Rogers. Actress Karen Sue Trent plays a character who says she's going to be a cowgirl like Dale Evans ("Beaver's Dance").

Fred Astaire and Gene Kelly – Ward announces the return of Larry and Beaver from dancing school by referring to them as two famous dancers at the time who stared in many Hollywood musicals ("Beaver's Dance").

Rod Cameron – An actor who performed in scores of "B" movies in the 1940s and 1950s. His best known role at the time was that of Lt. Rod Blake in *State Trooper* which aired from 1956-1959. Ward references him as having gone to school with the father of one of the members of the Bloody Five ("Larry's Club").

Disneyland – The theme park opened in 1955 in Anaheim, CA. When Ward tells the story of people in France building a castle, a moat and a drawbridge, Beaver says, "Just like Disneyland" ("Larry's Club").

Rock Hudson – A famous actor at the time, well known for his movies made with actress Doris Day. Eddie asks Wally, "Who do you think you are Rock Hudson?" ("The Hypnotist")

Cary Grant – A famous actor known for his brilliant romantic comedies of the 1940s and also his roles in Alfred Hitchcock movies like *North by Northwest* which was released a couple years before this episode was filmed. Ward says that Alma, the girl whose phone number June finds may think Wally is another Cary Grant ("Wally and Alma").

Sal Mineo – A well know actor at the time who had appeared in many television shows and also in the movie *Rebel Without a Cause*. Richard Rickover says his cousin was in the army with Sal Mineo (Mother's Day Composition").

Tony Curtis – An actor at the time who was well known for his roles in *Some Like it Hot*, *Operation Petticoat* and *The Defiant Ones*. Eddie tells Wally they can "play it kinda Tony Curtis" ("The Spot Removers").

Tony Curtis - (same as above) Ward asks, "Whose picture did he send in, Tony Curtis'?" ("Beaver, the Model").

Sal Mineo – Eddie asks Wally, "Why you ripping modeling school for? I think that's the way Sal Mineo got started" ("Beaver, the Model").

Cornel Wilde - Wally says, cut it out, who do you think you are, Cornell Wilde or something? Wilde was an actor with roles in films such as *Hot Blood* and *Beyond Mombasa* ("Beaver and Ivanhoe").

Payola – Beaver says he needs to give Miss Landers a gift, but it can't be too nice, so it doesn't look like payola or anything like that ("Last Day of School"). This episode aired June 18th and disc jockey Alan Freed was indicted for Payola, taking money and other favors to play certain records on the radio, on May 19th, 1960, about the time this episode was filmed.

Season 4

Burt Lancaster – An actor who was well know at the time for his roles in *From Here to Eternity*, *The Rainmaker*, *Run Silent, Run Deep* and *The Unforgiven*. Ward tells Fred that he's noticed how Lumpy is built like Burt Lancaster ("Beaver Becomes a Hero").

Audrey Hepburn – Wally tells Beaver how he had a crush on the actress Audrey Hepburn. She was best known at the time for her roles in *Roman Holiday*, *Sabrina* and *Funny Face* ("Miss Landers' Fiancé").

Broderick Crawford – Wally asks if Eddie is lying like the time he said he saw the actor Broderick Crawford on the bus. Crawford was best known for his role as Dan Matthews in *Highway Patrol* from 1955-1959 ("Eddie's Double-Cross").

Rock Hudson and Doris Day – Best known at the time for their co-starring roles in *Pillow Talk* and *Lover Come Back*. Eddie mentions to Wally that Rock Hudson, in the films, doesn't go up to Doris Day and say, "We've come to look at 'cha ("Eddie's Double-Cross").

Frank Sinatra – Wally tells Kitty Bannerman that his mom knows Frank Sinatra. At the time Frank Sinatra was a very famous singer and actor ("Wally's Glamour Girl").

Captain Kangaroo – The host of a children's television show on CBS beginning in 1955 and lasting until 1984. Eddie asks Wally, "Who do you think you are, Captain Kangaroo?" when he tells Eddie he has to take Chuckie to get shoes ("Chuckie's New Shoes").

John Boles – June says when she was in boarding school, she used to tell people that John Boles, an actor and singer who was popular from the 1920s to the 1940s, was her uncle ("Beaver and Kenneth").

Fabian – A singer from Philadelphia, Fabian Forte became a star in the late 1950s after many appearances on American Bandstand, and later ventured into acting. When Beaver asks Eddie if he thinks he could become a star, Eddie replies, "If it could happen to Fabian, it could happen to anybody" ("Beaver's Accordion").

Robert Horton – Wally is told he has eyes like Robert Horton. He was an actor known for his role as Flint McCullough in *Wagon Train* ("Beaver's Accordion").

Somerset Maugham – An author known for his novels *Liza of Lambeth*, *Of Human Bondage*, *The Moon and Sixpence* and *The Razor's Edge*. He also wrote many plays and short stories. Beaver said he wants to be a writer when he grows up and Ward says the best way to start is to do what Somerset Maugham did, keep a journal ("Beaver's Secret Life").

Susan Hayward – Ward mentions that Jackie Waters' mother looked like the actress Susan Hayward. She was known at the time by her roles in *The President's Lady*, *My Foolish Heart* and *I Want to Live!* ("Beaver's Old Buddy")

Douglas Fairbanks – A major silent film actor in the 1910s and 1920s. When Wally says he held a rope in his teeth and shimmied up a tree, June mentions he was just like Douglas Fairbanks ("Beaver's Old Buddy").

Betsy Wetsy Doll – This was a drink and wet doll invented in 1935 and enjoyed great popularity in the 1950s. Helen mentions that the Martha Washington doll she dressed up was made from a "Wetsy" doll. The actress who portrayed Helen (LeiLani Sorenson) mentioned to me that she thought she had said Betsy Wetsy and that they may have overdubbed it due to that being a brand name.

Shirley Temple – Famous for being an adorable child actress in the 1930s. She later played adult roles and after acting, became a U.S. Ambassador. She is mentioned in this episode by both Gilbert and Penny ("Dramatic Club"). An interesting side note is that Shirley Temple's daughter Lori Black played bass for grunge pioneers the *Melvins* (1988-1993).

John Wayne – Ward mentions to Beaver that this famous American actor who starred in *The Quiet Man*, *The Sands of Iwo Jima*, and *Stagecoach* kissed girls in movies. Beaver shouldn't feel ashamed because he has to kiss one in the Dramatic Club performance ("Dramatic Club").

Gary Cooper – Star in many great movies including *High Noon* and *Pride of the Yankees*. Ward mentions to Beaver that this famous American actor kissed girls in movies and that Beaver shouldn't feel ashamed because he has to kiss one in the Dramatic Club performance ("Dramatic Club").

Sal Mineo - A well know actor at the time who had appeared in many television shows and also in the movie *Rebel Without a Cause*. Eddie wonders if anyone has ever asked Beaver if he looks like Sal Mineo. Beaver tells him no and Eddie says he's not surprised, because he doesn't. ("Eddie Spends the Night"). Also mentioned in "Mother's Day Composition" and "Next Door Indians."

Tony Curtis – Eddie says Wally looks like Tony Curtis and smells like a floor walker ("Wally's Dream Girl").

Floorwalker – Similar to a salesman in a modern department store, a worker with a lot of seniority who would assist customers and supervise salespeople. Jack Benny would often employ a floorwalker as comedic device in his old CBS and NBC radio shows ("Wally's Dream Girl").

Happy Hooligan – A popular comic book character drawn by Frederick Burr Opper. It debuted in 1900 and ended in 1932. When Beaver makes a face in the school picture, Ward says he looks like Happy Hooligan ("The School Picture").

Season 5

Roger Maris and Mickey Mantle – Wally asks Evelyn Boothby's sister if she thinks either New York Yankee will hit sixty home runs during the current season ("Wally Goes Steady").

Sal Mineo – An actor best known at the time for his role in *Rebel Without a Cause*. Beaver mentions a Sal Mineo movie where a car goes off a cliff and he plays a drum, possibly *The Gene Krupa Story*. ("Wally's Car").

Captain Kangaroo – The host of a children's television show on CBS beginning in 1955 and ending in 1984. Beaver surmises that Captain Kangaroo is a child because he talks to animals ("Beaver's Cat Problem").

Rock n' Roll – A type of music Ward does not enjoy. Popular at the time this episode was filmed were Chubby Checker, The Ventures, Elvis Presley, The Everly Brothers and The Hollywood Argyles. Wally mentions an airport once played rock n' roll records to scare birds away from a runway ("Beaver's Cat Problem").

Sandra Dee – A popular actress in the 1950s and 1960s. Eddie says about his date, "She's no Sandra Dee, but we made music together." Sandra Dee was rated #6 in movie star popularity the year this episode was filmed ("Wally's Big Date"). It is interesting to note that she performed at Beverly Hills' Canon Theatre in a stage production of *Love Letters*, a play that Tony Dow performed in at many dinner theaters across the country in the 2010s.

Eliot Ness – The lead character and real-life prohibition agent featured in the TV show *The Untouchables.* Eddie tells Beaver, "Don't start playing Eliot Ness with me" ("Wally's Big Date").

Doris Day and Cary Grant – Actor and actress who starred in *That Touch of Mink* which was released the year this episode aired ("Farewell to Penny").

Natalie Wood – Gilbert says Georgia Batson thinks she looks like Natalie Wood, an actress best known at the time for her roles in *Miracle on 34th Street*, *Rebel Without a Cause* and *West Side Story* ("Beaver's Electric Trains").

Frankie Avalon – A chart topping singer in the late 1950s and an actor known for his series of beach movies with actress Annette Funicello. Wally says Beaver is looking at himself in the mirror like he's Frankie Avalon ("Beaver's Jacket").

Lucius Beebe – A famous American writer and gourmand. Ward says Fred Rutherford thinks Lumpy's first party will make him the next Lucius Beebe ("Wally Stays at Lumpy's").

Tuesday Weld – A stunning young actress who had roles in many TV shows around the time she is mentioned on *Leave it to Beaver* including roles on *The Many Loves of Dobie Gillis, 77 Sunset Strip, The Adventures of Ozzie and Harriet* and in the films *Return to Peyton Place* and *Sex Kittens Go to College*. Eddie exclaims when helping Wally clean a mess in the kitchen caused by Beaver and Richard, "What if Tuesday Weld caught me doing this?" ("Beaver's Laundry")

Fabian – Eddie uses the name of the famous singer and actor as a nickname ("Lumpy's Car Trouble").

Mitch Miller – A choral conductor, A&R man, and television personality. He became popular in the 1950s with a series of sing-along albums. This brought about a TV series titled, *Sing Along with Mitch* in 1961. Eddie asks Beaver who he thinks he is… Mitch Miller ("Lumpy's Car Trouble").

The Rockefeller Foundation – The second oldest philanthropic institution in the United States. Eddie says, "What Am I, the Rockefeller Foundation?" ("Lumpy's Car Trouble")

Bob Cousy – A star basketball player with the Boston Celtics. Fred Rutherford mentions him in regard to Beaver being on the city park league basketball team ("The Younger Brother").

Lloyd Bridges – An American actor known for his role in the series *Sea Hunt*. Wally mentions him when telling Lumpy he should wait until he finishes high school before running off to the sea like Lloyd Bridges ("The Merchant Marine").

Huntley and Brinkley – The NBC news program which aired from 1956-1970. It was officially titled, *The Huntley-Brinkley Report*. Wally tells Beaver that when talking to a girl while you walk with her doesn't have to be Huntley and Brinkley ("Brother Versus Brother").

Maureen O'Hara – An American actress who was well known for her role in *The Quiet Man* with John Wayne. She is mentioned by Gilbert talking about her movie *Against All Flags* ("Brother Versus Brother").

Tony Curtis – American actor. Mary Tyler tells Wally she likes him the same way her sister likes Tony Curtis ("Brother Versus Brother").

Pancho Gonzalez – A world famous tennis player who won thirteen Grand Slam titles in his prime in the 1950s and 1960s ("Tennis, Anyone?"). Beaver mentions the player in this episode.

Vic Tanny – A professional body builder and entrepreneur who owned about 100 fitness centers at the time he was mentioned in *Leave it to Beaver* ("One of the Boys"). When Wally tells Eddie he is going to the gym, Eddie asks, "Who are you, Vic Tanny?"

Pat Boone – Famous singer in the 1950s, also well known for squeaky clean image and for drinking milk ("Long Distance Call"). Alan suggests calling him or John Glenn.

John Glenn – The third American astronaut in space and the first to orbit the earth. Alan suggests calling him or Pat Boone ("Long Distance Call").

Don Drysdale – Baseball pitcher for the Los Angeles Dodgers. Alan, Gilbert and Beaver call him from Mayfield ("Long Distance Call").

Rockefeller – Beaver asks "Is this how Rockefeller started?" referencing buying stocks. He was likely referring to John D. Rockefeller Jr., an American financier, real estate developer and philanthropist ("Stocks and Bonds").

Dear Abby – An advice columnist who began writing her syndicated column in 1956. Wally asks Beaver, "Who are you all of a sudden, Dear Abby?" ("Un-Togetherness").

Season 6

Cesar Romero – An actor who was well known for roles as a Latin lover in a number of romantic films and musicals. Eddie asks Wally if he thinks he's Cesar Romero ("Wally's Dinner Date").

Bobby Darin – An American singer and actor who is best known for his song Mack the Knife. Eddie tells Wally, "If they cause trouble, tell them you're Bobby Darin." ("Wally's Dinner Date")

Rock Hudson – An American actor famous in the 1950s and 1960s. Popular movies included romantic comedies made with Doris Day. Beaver tells his parents Wally has seen Rock Hudson eat in the movies ("Wally's Dinner Date").

Cary Grant – American actor. When Beaver says he's known for years that girls weren't reliable, Ward says he said that with a typical Cary Grant attitude ("Double Date").

Peter Lawford – A British born actor who about the time of *Leave it to Beaver*, was known for his role as Nick Charles in *The Thin Man*. Eddie Haskell is told at his first day on the job at the Mayfield Dairy, "Okay Peter Lawford, there's a smock for you in there," by the company foreman. Probably because he makes a point to tell him he's wearing a $40.00 imported jacket ("Eddie, the Businessman")

Elvis Presley – The King of Rock n' Roll who began his career in the late 1950s. Eddie tries to convince Beaver he is as important as Elvis, Bobby Darin, or Frankie Avalon because he caught the winning touchdown pass in the previous football game ("Beaver, the Hero"). Lumpy refers to Wally as the Elvis Presley of Mayfield High School ("Eddie's Sweater) because he thinks Wally is cheating with Eddie's girl.

Marlon Brando – At the time of his mention on *Leave it to Beaver*, Brando was an actor best known for his roles in *The Wild One*, *On the Waterfront* and *Mutiny on the Bounty*. Wally jokes with Beaver that maybe Marlon Brando will play him when they turn Beaver's autobiography into a movie ("Beaver's Autobiography").

Dorothy Lamour – An American actress known for such films as *Greatest Show on Earth* and *Road to Bali*. When Ward and June are watching TV, they are switching channels and one channel is showing a Dorothy Lamour movie ("Party Spoiler").

Mickey Rooney – Beaver mentions the actor Mickey Rooney and one of his many Andy Hardy movies. He acted with Judy Garland in a few of those films ("The Mustache").

Cesar Romero – A popular Latin actor at the time of this mention in *Leave it to Beaver*. When Beaver looks at Wally with his new mustache, Beaver says Wally is no Cesar Romero ("The Mustache").

Dickens or Fenster – This is a reference to the *I'm Dickens, He's Fenster* television show that debuted in 1962. Eddie throws an insult at Beaver asking which of the characters he is ("The Parking Attendants").

King Kong – A fictional monster that looked like a gorilla which made its first appearance in 1933. Eddie suggests Beaver put a picture of himself and King Kong in the doubled hearted locket he wins at the carnival ("More Blessed to Give").

The Gabor Sisters – Donna Yeager's dad asks if they are raising one of the Gabor sisters. They were Magda, Eva and Zsa, Zsa, three Hungarian sisters who were actresses and socialites. Sister Eva eventually acted on *Green Acres* for six years ("More Blessed to Give").

Our Man Higgins – Beaver makes a reference to the show *Our Man Higgins* when Wally asks him to do him a favor. Higgins was a butler in the show *Our Man Higgins* ("Beaver's Good Deed").

Noel Coward – A British playwright, songwriter and actor. June comments when she sees the clothes the tramp Jeff left in their bedroom, that she didn't think Beaver was entertaining Noel Coward ("Beaver's Good Deed").

Tuesday Weld – An attractive young actress popular at the time. Eddie says, "What did you think I'd do with $15.00, elope with Tuesday Weld?" ("The Credit Card").

Peter Lawford – In referring to a vest he bought with his credit card, he says, "It brings out the Peter Lawford in me." Lawford was an actor popular at the time for his role as Nick Charles in *The Thin Man* ("The Credit Card").

George Sanders – Beaver references the actor who was very active in many films in the 1950s and early 1960s ("Beaver the Caddy").

Bennett Cerf – The founder and publisher of Random House. He was also a panelist on *What's My Line?* ("Beaver on TV").

Captain Kangaroo – The host of a children's television show on CBS beginning in 1955 and lasting until 1984. Wally jokes about Beaver accidentally going to the set of the show instead of to *Teen Age Forum* ("Beaver on TV").

Jack Paar – The second host of NBC's *Tonight Show* replacing Steve Allen in 1957. Wally mentions that Beaver may have got flaky when they turned the camera on him and began bawling worse than Jack Paar ("Beaver on TV").

Twilight Zone – Gilbert says Beaver going on the TV show *Teen Age Forum* but not actually being seen on the TV show is sort of like *The Twilight Zone*, a very popular show on CBS written and hosted by Rod Serling.

Deputy Dawg – Beaver asks if Wally finally received his *Deputy Dawg* badge? *Deputy Dawg* was the main character in a cartoon of the same name, created by Terrytoons. It debuted on CBS in 1960.

Burt Lancaster – An American actor who was well known at the time for his roles in *From Here to Eternity*, *The Rainmaker*, *Run Silent, Run Deep*, *Elmer Gantry* and *The Unforgiven*. When State University did not give Wally a scholarship, Beaver wonders what they want up there, "Burt Lancaster?" ("Lumpy's Scholarship")

Rock Hudson – Eddie mentions actor Rock Hudson when he says he got the idea for installing an FM radio in his car from one of his movies ("Silent Treatment").

Tony Curtis – American actor. Beaver mentions Tony Curtis ("Uncle Billy's Visit").

Tuesday Weld – An American actress popular at the time. Beaver tells Uncle Billy he could tell her hello for Wally if he sees her in California ("Uncle Billy's Visit").

Gidget – Beaver mentions *Gidget*, the movies which featured Sandra Dee in the first installment of the fun summer teen series ("Eddie's Sweater").

West Side Story – Beaver says keeping track of all the people who sacked Rome (his history homework) was harder than keeping track of the gangs in *West Side Story* ("Eddie's Sweater").

Pablo Casals – Eddie asks Lumpy when making some musical sounds, "Who do you think you are Pablo Casals?" Eddie tells him he plays in a combo at the White House. In fact, he was a famous cellist ("Eddie's Sweater").

Jimmy Stewart – When Wally explains how Eddie thinks he's making a move on his girlfriend, Beaver says he saw something like this happen in a Jimmy Stewart movie. Jimmy Stewart was a famous actor known best for his roles in *Winchester '73*, *Harvey*, *It's a Wonderful Life* and *The Man Who Knew Too Much* ("Eddie's Sweater").

Lana Turner – Ward mentions that when he was in the Seabees, he got into a fight over a picture of American actress Lana Turner, who was well known for being a pin up girl for American soldiers during World War II. Her well-known movie roles included *The Postman Always Rings Twice*, *Peyton Place* and *Imitation of Life*.

The Kennedys – The first family of the United States at the time of their mention in *Leave it to Beaver*. June asks Ward what happened to his Kennedy coloring book ("The Book Report").

Frankenstein – Gilbert comes over to the Cleaver house, he knocks on the door and Beaver asks who's there and Gilbert responds, "It's Frankenstein, the monster." Frankenstein is the name of a doctor who created a monster in a book by Mary Shelley.

Don Ameche – An American actor who starred in the comic remake of *The Three Musketeers* movie. Beaver watches it on TV and writes a book report from it ("The Book Report").

The Ritz Brothers – Co-stars in the comic remake of *The Three Musketeers* movie from which Beaver writes his book report ("The Book Report"). The Ritz Brothers made a number of films and if you can catch any of them, check them out. You'll enjoy them. They are very much under appreciated.

Elsa Maxwell – A noted gossip columnist and professional hostess who threw parties for royalty and members of high society. When Ward tells June she's a social butterfly, she replies, "Yes, me and Elsa Maxwell" ("The Poor Loser").

Bobby Darin – American singer and actor. Wally calls Beaver "Bobby Darin" and asks if he was talking to Sandra Dee on the phone ("Don Juan Beaver").

Sandra Dee – American actress (see above).

Marlon Brando – When Eddie is being interviewed by a fishing boat captain, Wally and Lumpy are listening and comment that he's a real Captain Bligh. And then Wally says that Eddie is no Marlon Brando. The reference is to the movie *Mutiny on the Bounty* starring actor Marlon Brando (Summer in Alaska).

Clyde Beatty – Wally tells Beaver he shouldn't slack off at the end of the school year. He says that would be like the famous lion tamer, tiger trainer and circus owner Clyde Beatty turning his back on a cage of tigers and lions ("Beaver's Graduation").

Pat Boone – A pop star in the 1950s and early 1960s who was known for his squeaky-clean image. Wally mentions that he'll have to look like Pat Boone to be able to get permission for Kathy Gregory to go with him to the all -night graduation party ("The All-Night Party").

If you want more details on some of these pop culture references, there will be some found at http://leaveittobeaverbooks.com.

55

PUNISHMENTS

For a television character to get in trouble as often as Beaver Cleaver did, you can only imagine the number of times he was punished and what some of the punishments included. The list below will include many of his punishments over the six seasons and the associated situations that necessitated such punishments. Let's see his most lenient punishments and his most harsh punishments and figure out why Ward and June punished him the way they did.

Of course, Beaver is not the only character on *Leave it to Beaver* to be punished. Wally was punished quite a few times too. But this chapter will also include Eddie, Lumpy, and some of Beaver's friends. It's interesting to see how Wally's and Beaver's friends were punished or disciplined and how those actions are different than those dispensed by Ward and June.

The following list consists of the highlights in the punishment category, or maybe those being punished would call these the lowlights. Either way, this is not an exhaustive list, but merely, quite a few times when each character experienced a punishment or discipline of some sort.

Beaver

When Beaver is teased by the kids at school for being the teacher's pet and for having a crush on Miss Canfield in the "Beaver's Crush" episode, he denies the accusations and they tell him to prove they aren't true. They give him a fake snake toy that would pop up if put in a compact space like a desk drawer and they tell him to put in Miss Canfield's desk. He does. The next day, the kids all try to get Miss Canfield to open her desk drawer. Near the end of the school day, Whitey asks Miss Canfield if he can borrow her ruler. Beaver thinks fast and then reaches across the aisle and pulls one of Judy's ponytails. Beaver gets in trouble, but he prevents Miss Canfield from opening the desk drawer. His punishment? Beaver must write on the chalkboard "I will not pull Judy Hensler's hair." The number of times is not mentioned. Not much of a punishment, and after a long talk about what happened and why, and him telling Miss Canfield he wants to marry her, she tells him he doesn't have to finish the sentences. But he tells her she can't show any favoritism. So, he finishes them.

Larry is the instigator for Beaver getting in trouble in "Beaver's Bad Day." Beaver goes over to a forbidden construction site AND he wears his good clothes. Two wrongs don't make a right, especially on *Leave it to Beaver*. He rips his good pants on a nail and there is no hiding his misdeeds when he comes home. Then he lies about what happened. Ward tells Beaver he is going to be punished and asks Beaver to suggest what his own punishment should be. Beaver takes this opportunity and says his punishment should be no stewed figs for dessert. He doesn't like stewed figs, Ward says. He then gives Beaver a more appropriate punishment, spending the afternoon in his room and taking a nap. That's not much of a punishment. Ward sure learned how to discipline better as the seasons progressed.

If children like Beaver always have someone to blame for the trouble in which they find themselves, in "Beaver's Ring," this person would be Judy Hensler. She's the one who told Beaver the ring he brought to school was not his. But his other friends believe him when he says his umbrella aunt gave it to him, but not Judy. He proves her wrong by sticking the ring on his finger. Unfortunately for Beaver, the ring fit on, but it won't fit off. It's stuck and a visit to the school nurse doesn't help. Eventually, the ring has to be cut off his finger. Yes, he's punished. But he doesn't have to stay in his room like other times. For this infraction, Beaver is forced to write a letter to Aunt Martha, apologizing for ruining the ring. He reads the letter to Ward and his sincerity and sorrow is evident. Ward then crumbles up the letter. Just writing the letter was punishment enough and he could tell that Beaver was very sorry. That's some real good fathering right there.

Did you ever get the feeling that when someone, like a parent, would tell you something was no good for you, that it was really a fun thing to do? That's how Beaver in "The Pipe," explains his experimenting with smoking. Fred Rutherford sent Ward a pipe as a souvenir from Germany. Only Fred Rutherford could cause tumult in the Cleaver house all the way from Europe. When it is discovered by Ward that the pipe had been smoked, he immediately blames Wally. However, Wally is adamant. He did not smoke the pipe. This confuses Ward. He punishes Wally by making him stay in his room, all weekend if necessary or, as he tells June, until he admits what he had done. After Wally is punished, Beaver admits it was he who had smoked the pipe. Ward tells Beaver he will be punished, but no punishment is determined by the end of the episode. A minor punishment for Beaver is his telling Wally he was sorry for getting him in trouble. This is something Beaver chose to do himself. At least Ward later apologizes to Wally for not believing him when he said he had not smoked the pipe.

With Larry out of the picture after the season four episode, "Beaver's Big Contest," Beaver had to find a new friend to get him into trouble… Gilbert easily became the lead instigator going forward. In "The School Picture," Gilbert encourages Beaver to make a funny face when the photographer shoots their school picture. He does so by saying they'll both make funny faces. You guessed it, Gilbert reneges and only Beaver makes a face. Beaver's punishment is being grounded to his room every day after school and all weekend. This is one of the harsher punishments, which demonstrates the punishments were never too harsh.

How often does a parent get to dish out discipline to their own child and other kids too? That's what happens in "Long Distance Call." When left alone at home, Gilbert comes up with the idea of making some crank phone calls. Then he, Alan and Beaver decide to call Don Drysdale at Dodger Stadium in Los Angeles. The phone call cost over $9.00 and their punishment was pulling weeds at the Cleaver house for an hour every day after school. In addition to that, Gilbert's father grounded him from phone use for an entire month. I wonder if anything additional happened to Alan, but the episode ends without us finding out.

When the cat's away, what happens? Yes, the mice will play. This is seen in action, at least in a minor way, in "Uncle Billy's Visit." Beaver and Alan make plans to go to the movies. They see Gilbert outside the movie theater, and he talks Beaver into opening the side door when he scratches on it. Beaver does and immediately gets caught. Since his parents are out of town, his Uncle Billy must come down to the theater and get him. Beaver tells Gilbert that his Uncle Billy likes him and won't let the theater manager do anything bad to him. Boy, was Beaver in for a surprise. When the theater manager suggests banning Beaver from the theater for two weeks, Uncle Billy tells him, "Two weeks? I wouldn't do that…I'd make it two months." Back home, Uncle Billy tells Beaver that he took him as some sort of a pushover. Beaver begins to say something and Uncle Billy interrupts him, "Don't Uncle Billy me. Don't give me any more of your lame excuses. Young man, you go up to your room." One positive thing for Beaver is that Uncle Billy doesn't tell Ward and June about his movie theater mishap.

Television got Beaver in trouble earlier in the series and it does so again in season six. This time it was because of procrastination. Beaver has a book report to do on *The Three Musketeers*. But instead of using his time wisely and getting to work on reading the book, he puts it off until it's too late to get the entire book read. Instead, at Gilbert's insistence, he watches *The Three Musketeers* movie on television. However, this was a comedic version of the movie starring Don Ameche and the Ritz Brothers. Beaver writes up the report and immediately, Mrs. Rayburn knows what has done. His punishment is having to write two extra book reports for class. That's a lot of writing that could have been avoided if he'd only done his work right the first time.

Both Beaver and Wally

In "Voodoo Magic," Beaver (and Wally) get in trouble, not for putting a voodoo curse on Eddie Haskell, but for Wally taking Beaver to see the movie *Voodoo Curse*. They told them to go to the Valencia to see *Pinocchio* instead. They disobeyed and then they lied, just like Pinocchio. At one point, Beaver even looks at his own nose, checking to see if it was growing. Their punishment was going up to their room after supper for the rest of the night and all day on Sunday.

Another example of both boys getting into trouble is seen in "The Boat Builders." It was an inadequate feat of engineering and construction that helped them get into trouble in this episode. It was a nice effort by Wally, Tooey and Chester to create a real Eskimo boat, but as they find out in Miller's Pond, an effort doomed to fail. The first problem they find is that none of the boys will fit in the boat. It is left up to Beaver to take it out for a test sail. This act alone is enough to get the boys in trouble. However, after Beaver falls into the pond, he and Wally sneak into the house with enough subterfuge for a late 1950s Cold War thriller. It was these actions that really got the boys in trouble. Listen to Ward's words: "Well, fooling around with that boat was a very dangerous thing to do, Wally. And both of you trying to cover up what you'd done afterwards was inexcusable. So, you're going to have to be punished." Their punishment was that they must stay around the house for the rest of the weekend and no television or movies for two weeks. Not a bad punishment for dishonesty, almost drowning Beaver, and almost burning down the house.

The punishment received in "Larry Hides Out" is quite docile for the crime of hiding a fugitive in their bathtub. Larry runs away from home and Beaver hides him. He feeds him and they only get caught when Ward and Mrs. Mondello see Larry's suitcase being pulled up on a rope outside a window. The only punishment the boys receive, basically for lying about Larry, is they have to pull weeds in their yard on Sunday and then on Monday after school.

Beaver and Larry

In a punishment experience that seems a bit lopsided, Larry receives a harsher punishment than Beaver. In "Beaver Plays Hooky," Beaver once again gets reeled in by Larry to do something wrong. They play hooky and are caught because they wind up on television during a grocery store promotional event. Beaver is made to go see Miss Landers and explain to her what he did. When June says she feels that is being too tough on Beaver, Ward explains, "June, he broke one of the rules of the school. Sooner or later, he's got to learn that when you do that, you have to face the people who make the rules." It's difficult listening to Miss Lander's lecture and admitting what he had done, but at least Beaver didn't get walloped like Larry.

Similar to Larry in "Found Money," Beaver gets punished twice in the "Beaver's Prize" episode. His first punishment is having to stay home all day on Saturday. He is punished for getting into Ward's desk when he was told to stay away from his desk. Beaver left the top off the ink and Ward spills it over some papers. The next day, Larry comes over and again, encourages Beaver to do something he was told not to do. This time, he gets Beaver to go to the movies with him at the Mayfield Theater. Beaver wins a prize, a bicycle, and of course, Ward finds out and Beaver is punished. His punishment is no movies for two weeks. I think we can all agree, this was an appropriate punishment.

The angriest we probably ever see Ward, and with this anger, the harshest punishment doled out by Ward, happens in "Ward's Baseball." He buys a stand for his prized autograph baseball his uncle gave him when he was young. It was autographed by many stars including Babe Ruth. Larry, once again, convinces Beaver to throw the ball with him in the front yard. Larry throws the ball over Beaver's head, and it rolls into the street and is crushed by a passing truck. They try to fix the problem by forging the signatures on a new baseball, but it doesn't fool Mr. Rutherford who points out with laughter, the forged names. Beaver is yelled at and punished by having to go to his room for the rest of the day and eat supper in his room. The entire next week he is also to have no company, be confined to his room and watch no television.

When Beaver gets in trouble in "Beaver Won't Eat," Eddie is there to help Beaver out of his jam. No, really, he does help Beaver. When Beaver is told he cannot go to the football game because he won't eat Brussels sprouts, he thinks that's the end of his chances to go to the game. But Eddie tells him, his parents will make a deal with him. Sure enough, the day of the game arrives, and Ward strikes a deal with Beaver. The next time he is served Brussels sprouts, Beaver has to promise to eat them. He reluctantly agrees to the deal. All is good. Beaver gets to go to the game. But first, a formal meal at a nice restaurant. When the entrée arrives, bad news… Brussels sprouts. With a helpful slap on the back from Wally, Beaver swallows a Brussels sprout and finds out they're not so bad and he eats them. The game was enjoyed by all.

Wally

No young boy wants to be kissed by a girl. This was no different with Beaver Cleaver. When he finds out he is the only boy invited to Linda Dennison's party in "Party Invitation." Wally tells Beaver they want him there for kissing games. Beaver decides he won't go to the party, but Ward and June make him attend. There's one last ditch thing Wally can do; he calls Linda Dennison and imitates Ward, telling Linda that Beaver is too sick to attend any parties. Wally is proud of himself and his great imitation of his father, then hangs up the phone and turns around and there is Ward. When asked how long he'd been there, Ward says, "Long enough." Wally is sent to his room for the rest of the day. Beaver receives his punishment too, he gets dropped off at the party. Eventually, Wally shares with June that Beaver would be the only boy there. After she explains that to Ward, he apologies to Wally for punishing him.

Wally talks about a possible punishment in "Eddie's Girl." After he finds out June made a date with him to go to a dance with Caroline (pronounced Carolyn) Cunningham, Wally is furious because Caroline is Eddie's girl. Tony Dow gives some of his best acting in this episode. Wally stands on the stairs, and yells, "I won't go, even if I have to spend the rest of my life in my crummy old room!" As he says, "crummy old room" he points above his head to really make the point hit home. This is a brilliant scene thanks to Tony Dow and director Norman Tokar.

Wally experienced punishment from someone other than his parents in "Wally's Track Meet." His track coach warns the guys about goofing off. When he leaves the locker room, Eddie and Lumpy begin throwing wet towels. When Wally gets hit with a towel, he throws it back, but it hits the coach who had just walked back into the locker room. Even though Wally was one of the team's best chances to win the track meet, he was kicked off the team for a week. That's the way things were back in the days of *Leave it to Beaver*, you broke a rule, you were punished, no matter what.

Once, for being dishonest and sneaky in "Lumpy's Car Trouble," Wally endures a punishment with absolutely no teeth. In this episode, Lumpy drives Wally up to Bellport for a track meet in Ward's car because his own won't run. Lumpy suggests he drive it since Wally has no license. Fred had picked up Ward for work, so his car is available. They just need Ward's permission. It is granted, but with the caveat, they only drive straight to Bellport and straight back, no speeding and take Highway 7 there and back. Well, they don't come straight back on Highway 7 and encounter some car trouble too (Lumpy's fault). They fix the car at a service station. A co-worker of Ward's saw the boys pushing Ward's car along the Camelback Cutoff. Ward inquires with them about what happened, and Wally comes clean. His punishment, Ward says, "It'll be a long time until you have use of the car again." Not much of a punishment when you consider Wally had no license.

Eddie

Never give a teenager a credit card. That's especially true if your teenager is Eddie Haskell. In "The Credit Card," Eddie buys Wally a car battery with his father's credit card when his battery fails while they are coming back from a football game in Lynbrook, where they were scouting their future opponent. When Ward finds out about this, he's wary of the deal. Wally paid Eddie for the cost of the battery. Eddie was then to give that money to his father. But figuring the bill wouldn't come in the mail for a couple weeks, Eddie doesn't pay his father immediately. He then buys a wild looking vest with the cash. Eddie gets himself into more trouble and more debt and he finally gets punished for his irresponsibility. His father punished him appropriately. He had his use of the credit card taken away, as well as his car, both for a month.

Lumpy

In "The Merchant Marine," Lumpy gets punished, having his car keys taken away from him after he knocks over the next-door neighbor's gate. When offered a job to help park cars in "The Parking Attendants," Lumpy has to decline because he had his license suspended. His dad had "pull" with the judge and after Lumpy received his last ticket, his dad asked the judge to suspend his license.

Larry Mondello

In the episode "Larry Hides Out," Larry runs away to Beaver's house after telling Beaver he was going to run away to Mexico. He hides in his bathtub and his mom is frantic, not knowing where he went. After being found at the Cleaver's house, she gives him an ear full and doles out a punishment, no TV or movies for a month. Earlier in the episode he received another punishment, this one for looking at his sister's diary because she had repeatedly told him to not look at his sister's diary. For that act of disobedience, he was sent to his room.

Larry gets punished in "Found Money" two times. First, he gets punished for using too much credit at the drug store. His punishment for that is no allowances for two weeks. Next, he gets punished for stealing his mom's emergency money she keeps in her sewing basket. This punishment is not too bad when one looks at what he did. He stole money from his mom and all he must do is pull weeds, even it is for the rest of his life, like Beaver thinks it might be.

Over at http://leaveittobeaverbooks.com, there are more punishments to investigate. While there, don't forget to sign up for the chance to win free *Leave it to Beaver* prizes.

56

SCHOOL

Throughout the seasons of *Leave it to Beaver*, many episodes have scenes that take place in school or in which school is mentioned. This chapter will look at teachers, coaches, principals, school subjects, school activities and miscellaneous school stuff. Let's start with the teachers.

Beaver's Teachers / Coaches / Others

Miss Canfield – Beaver's second grade teacher at Grant Avenue Grammar School (season one)
Mr. Thompson – A teacher Beaver bumps into in the school cafeteria (season one)
Miss Landers – Beaver's teacher in third, fourth and fifth grades (season one)
Mrs. Rayburn – Principal of Grant Avenue Grammar School (season one)
Mr. Willett – Assistant principal at Grant Avenue Grammar school and teacher, subs for Miss Landers. He is also a music teacher (season one)
Mr. Harris – Janitor at Grant Avenue Grammar School (season one)
Miss Thompson – The school nurse that tries to help Beaver get his ring off his finger (season one)
Dr. Hendrix – The school physician at Grant Avenue Grammar School (season one)
Coach Grover – Gym teacher at Grant Avenue Grammar School (season two)
Mr. Crawford – Bus driver (season three)
Mr. Proudy – Teacher or administrator at Grant Avenue Grammar School (season three)
Mr. Blair – English teacher at Grant Avenue Grammar School (season five)
Miss Lawrence – Drama teacher at Grant Avenue Grammar School (season five)
Mr. Colins – English teacher at Grant Avenue Grammar School (season five)
Mr. Watson – Social Science teacher at Grant Avenue Grammar School (season six)
Mr. Ingersoll – Coach of 8th grade football team at Grant Avenue Grammar School (season six)
Mr. Thompson – English teacher at Grant Avenue Grammar School (season six) History teacher also.

Wally's Teachers / Coaches / Others

Mr. Wilkerson – A new teacher for Wally at Grant Avenue Grammar School (season one)
Mr. Bloomgarten – Assistant principal and one of Wally's teachers at Grant Avenue Grammar School (season one)
Mr. Briggs – Algebra teacher at Mayfield High (season two)
Miss Wade – Girls' Field Hockey Coach at Mayfield High (season two)
Mr. Haines – Gym teacher at Mayfield High (season two)
Miss Wakeland – Mayfield High drama teacher (season two)
Mr. Driscoll – Wally's science teacher at Mayfield High and part time umpire (season two)
Mr. Hatfield – An algebra teacher at Mayfield High (season two)
Mr. Nelson – Wally's science teacher at Mayfield High (season two)
Mr. Hayes – English teacher at Mayfield High (season two)
Mr. Haller – Principal of Mayfield High (season two and later)
Mr. Wilson – English teacher at Mayfield High (season three)
Mr. Griffin – Biology teacher at Mayfield High (season three)
Mr. Cartwright – English teacher at Mayfield High (season three)

Mr. Gannon – History teacher at Mayfield High (season three)
Mr. Hyatt – Teacher at Mayfield High, Wally's homeroom teacher (season three)
Coach Driscoll – Swim coach at Mayfield High / could also be the science teacher (season four)
Mr. Bromley – Science teacher (season four) and math teacher (season five) at Mayfield High.
Mr. Foster - English teacher at Mayfield High (season four)
Mr. West - English teacher at Mayfield High (season four)
Mrs. Thompson - English teacher at Mayfield High (season four)
Mr. Al – A coach at Mayfield High (season four)
Mrs. Mulligan -Social Sciences teacher at Mayfield High (season five)
Coach Henderson – Track coach at Mayfield High (season five)
Mr. Farmer – Principal at Mayfield High (season five)
Ed Barton – Vice-Principal at Mayfield High, a friend of Ward's (season five)
Mr. Thomas – Wally's homeroom teacher at Mayfield High (season five)
Mr. Barnes – Teacher at Mayfield High (season six)
Mrs. Borton – Study Hall teacher at Mayfield High (season six)
Mrs. Whitney – Teacher at Mayfield High (season six)

School Activities at Grant Avenue Grammar School

The second-grade class is participating in a fire prevention pageant. Miss Canfield would like Beaver to play Smokey Bear in the pageant.

Grant Avenue School Holiday Festival 8:30 p.m.in the school auditorium. There will be refreshments, entertainment, and carols.

The school keeps money in school bank accounts for the students. On certain days, like one featured in the "Bank Account" episode, students are allowed to make deposits and withdrawals.

The school has an eighth-grade dance and June is on the dance committee ("My Brother's Girl").

There are tryouts for the school orchestra, and they have a band concert on a Thursday night at 7 p.m.

The school has a drive to raise money and students are supposed to bring 20¢ but Beaver has no idea what type of drive.

There is a school program where students will recite poetry (Beaver is to read his poem) and there will be dancing and more.

The students say the pledge of the allegiance soon after school begins, probably each day, but only shown once. They recite it in "Ward's Problem" at 8:10 a.m.

A Father and Student picnic is held. Box lunches must be brought, and the picnic will feature apple bobbing, and there will be games and a three-legged race and an egg race.

Grant Avenue School Festival, with performances by the first through fifth grade classes. Beaver has the lead in the play. He's playing a yellow canary.

Beaver's class raises money by selling cookies from the Acme Biscuit Company. Beaver and Larry are in charge of the money. He and Larry are co-chairs of their class cookie committee.

Beaver's class has a baby beauty contest at the suggestion of Angela Valentine, a contest she wins.

Beaver's class went on a field trip with Miss Landers to a Chinese restaurant.

Parent Teacher meetings are on the first Tuesday of the month.

Field trip to sing to Mother's Club Tea at Mrs. Harrison's house. Beaver sees his mom not wearing the blouse he bought her.

Beaver's class holds a Pet Fair

A class assembly in which Mrs. Rayburn tells all the boys and girls that no one is to go steady.

Cake sale for which June is to make a coconut cake

School has I.Q. tests and Beaver does quite well.

Dramatic Club tryouts and Dramatic Club production of *The Little Dutch Boy.*

Miss Landers' class is to have a school picture after it had been cancelled the first time because four students had measles and the second time because three guys had black eyes.

Junior Fire Chief Prevention project

School pageant where Beaver plays a bunny, and all kids have parts as animals.

A Father/Son football awards banquet is held in the school gym

A newspaper man speaks at a school assembly and inspires Beaver to enter the newspaper business.

Beaver's graduation

Class clothing drive

School Activities at Mayfield High School

The freshman girls have a school dance and Gloria Cusick wants Wally to go with her.

School pictures are being taken at Mayfield High and all boys are to wear ties, or they will automatically receive a D in cooperation on their report cards per Mr. Haines.

School graduation for which Wally must go help set up chairs.

Wally is chairman of the Blind Date Committee for an upcoming school dance.

Big Brother program

Wally and Eddie attend cheerleader tryouts in case some girls cry when they don't make the squad.

Class elections and Wally is nominated by Eddie Haskell to run for sophomore class president.

School picnic for which boys had to pick the name of a girl from a drawing and go with them

Pep Rally for upcoming track meet, but Wally does not attend because he doesn't feel so peppy.

Open house at Mayfield High, June goes with Wally.

Junior Class Spring Dance

School dance which has guys from Mayfield High forced to ask girls from Riverside High, an idea put forth by social science teacher Miss Mulligan.

The Lettermans have a jamboree at Mayfield High

A high school prom held at the country club

School fashion show

Graduation practice

Misc. School Stuff

Beaver had an arithmetic test and got eight wrong, making him have the best grade among those who failed the test ("The Shave").

Wally's locker combination is 10 Left 30 Right 11 Left ("Wally's Pug Nose").

Gloria Cusick's locker combination is 25 Left 15 Right 15 Left ("Wally's Pug Nose").

Wally takes Spanish class as a sophomore ("Teacher Comes to Dinner").

Beaver is on the chalk committee for his class ("Teacher Comes to Dinner").

At Mayfield High, they put up grades on the wall for student to see their scores. Wally calls this a "goon list" ("Teacher's Daughter").

The school nurse gave Beaver a gold star for having the cleanest ears in class ("Beaver, the Model").

In season five, Beaver has three different teachers instead of just one ("Beaver's English Test").

The school team is the Mayfield Bulldogs ("Three Boys and a Burro") and the Mayfield Crusaders ("The Younger Brother").

Portion of or full school song: We're the fighting sons of Mayfield. Onward Mayfield High. We will always honor Mayfield. Mayfield do or die. ("Lumpy's Car Trouble")

Other high schools mentioned include Buchannan High ("Wally and Dudley"), Union High ("Mother's Helper"), Grover Cleveland High, William Howard Taft High, James Monroe High ("Lumpy's Scholarship") Fallbrook ("Beaver's Prep School")

Colleges mentioned are Muhlenberg College ("The Perfect Father"), State University or College, MIT, Stanford, Yale and Ridgewood College ("Lumpy's Scholarship").

Six grammar schools feed into Mayfield High ("Beaver's Graduation").

Beaver has a perfect attendance record ("Beaver's Graduation").

57

ILLNESSES, SICKNESS, INJURIES

The mentions of illness, being sick, or injuries written about in this chapter include all of the following a) times when a character currently finds themselves in the situation b) past references to the character in such a situation c) times when the character may be, but is not necessarily, sick or injured and d) sick or injured situations that are untrue i.e. Beaver hurting his ankle ("Wally's Girl Trouble") or Eddie being sick in bed ("Voodoo Magic").

The illnesses Beaver endured over the years, whether during the run of the series or beforehand include the following: measles ("Beaver's Old Friend"), chicken pox ("Beaver's Pigeons" / "Beaver's Autobiography"), scarlatina / scarlet fever ("Beaver's I.Q."), tonsilitis ("Beaver's Tonsils"), poison oak ("A Night in the Woods"), poison ivy ("Beaver's First Date") seasick ("Summer in Alaska"), and he got sick from smoking ("The Pipe").

Okay, if you think about all the times Beaver is mentioned as being sick or feeling sick or the times, he says he might or will get sick, it's almost amazing that in the show he is only shown as being sick four times. These are seen when he gets sick after smoking a pipe, when he gets an upset stomach, and when he gets tonsillitis and chicken pox.

A closer look at the times Beaver could be or might be sick include three different categories and those are him saying he feels sick or doesn't feel good, those times he's saying he is sick, but he knows he's not really sick, and those times someone says he looks sick or is acting sick. The first category is seen when Beaver says he doesn't feel well while working on his poem with Ward ("Beaver's Poem"). There are a few other episodes in which this also happens. Beaver says he feels sick and says everyone in the house is against him and that he won't eat any more ("Beaver's Freckles"), he says he feels sick like the time his turtle died ("Miss Landers' Fiancé"), feels sicker than ever ("Beaver's Accordion"), and feels sick ("Beaver Takes a Ride").

The times he says he is sick but isn't include "Brotherly, Love" when he tells his dad he doesn't feel good when Gus comes calling on him for their fishing date. The most obvious example is in "The New Doctor" where he just wants the attention that Wally received the previous day when he really was sick. Eddie spouts his famous line in this episode, "Man, you better look sicker than that when the doctor gets here." In "Lumpy Rutherford," Beaver fibs about being sick for a good reason, because the Rutherfords come over after he and Wally had just caused Fred Rutherford to fall and hurt himself on the barrel hoops they put in his driveway. Other such episodes are "Beaver's Football Award," after he sees his teammates wearing suits and he is wearing more casual attire, and "Beaver, the Sheepdog," when he says he has an upset stomach when June wonders if he is okay when she sees him holding his stomach but is just holding inside his jacket, the glop he just bought for his hair.

In the third category, Mrs. Rayburn is the first to believe he looks sick. She takes him to the nurse's office because he looks "positively green" in "Beaver's Crush." Ward thinks Beaver is sick when he doesn't eat his ice cream after dinner ("The State vs. Beaver"). June thinks Beaver's sick in "Beaver Says Good-bye" and feels his forehead and looks at his tongue. When asked to get his kite and bring it downstairs, Beaver looks sick to June. She asks Wally if he's sick and he says, "not yet" ("Kite Day"). Richard tells Beaver he doesn't look so good when they find Beaver's doll buggy and tell him they're taking it ("Beaver's Doll Buggy"). In "Substitute Father," June asks Wally to check in on Beaver because she thought he looked like he was coming down with something at supper. In "Nobody Loves Me," June suggests Beaver is catching a cold to give her an excuse to pay attention to him when he thinks he's repulsive and no one loves him.

We cannot forget all the times Beaver says he will get sick. In "Beaver's Dance" he contemplates getting sick, so he doesn't have to go to the Mayfield Cotillion. He says he'd get sick if he'd have to play a girl in front of everyone in "Wally's Play." In "Beaver Won't Eat," he says he will get sick if forced to eat Brussels sprouts. He makes the threat of getting sick in "The Dramatic Club" if he has to kiss a girl in *The Little Dutch Boy* performance at school. The final time he says he'll get sick is in "Beaver, the Bunny," if he must tell the story about going through town in his bunny outfit. The word "might," is used a few times. The first of these is in "Music Lesson" where he says he might get sick in the car on the way to the band concert. He says he might get pneumonia if he leaves his window open ("Pet Fair") and Ward says he might get pneumonia after being out in the cold and perspiring ("Beaver, the Athlete"). Aunt Martha says he "might" get curvature of the spine if he keeps slouching.

Trips to the dentist are either mentioned or seen in a few episodes including "The Party Invitation," when he uses going to the dentist to get some teeth put back in as an excuse to keep from walking home with Linda Dennison. He visits the dentist twice in "The Tooth," thoroughly embarrassing Ward in front of Fred Rutherford during one visit. In "Beaver's Report Card," he gets to leave school early to go to the dentist, but this visit is unseen. Another unseen visit is found in "Mother's Helper."

Times when Beaver is hurt or injured include getting punched in the eye ("The Black Eye"), sticking himself with a nail file ("Cleaning Up Beaver"), getting his ring stuck on his finger ("Beaver's Ring"), getting his head stuck in a fence ("The Price of Fame"), getting into a fight and scraped up ("Beaver and Gilbert"), getting beat up by Clyde Appleby ("Beaver and Ivanhoe") and getting stung by a bee after picking it up ("The Silent Treatment").

Unlike Beaver, who in 20% of all episodes, has a reference to him being sick, having an illness, being hurt or feeling sick or thinking he will get sick, Wally is a bit different, as those things only occur with him in 7 % of all episodes. Throughout the series, Wally is sick in "The New Doctor," "Beaver Plays Hooky," "Wally's Dream Girl," and "Wally's Chauffeur."

Wally is mentioned as having been sick in several episodes including "The Visiting Aunts" (measles), "Wally's Track Meet" (getting sick behind the stands), "A Night in the Woods" (poison oak five times) and "All-Night Party" (he once had food poisoning).

There are a number of times when Wally felt like he was going to get sick, or someone says he looked sick. When he finishes talking to Penny Jamison on the phone, Beaver says he looks sick ("Wally's Girl Trouble"). There's the time June thinks he may be sick after getting caught in the rain on a camping trip ("Lonesome Beaver"). Wally thinks he might get sick playing a girl in a play ("Wally's Play"). Beaver wonders if he didn't like June's carrots when he looks sick after eating them ("Wally's Glamour Girl"). He says he thought about getting sick to get out of his expensive dinner date ("Wally's Dinner Date"). He thinks he may catch pneumonia ("Sore Loser"), and June thinks he has girl trouble ("Teacher's Daughter"), while Ward thinks it's just an upset stomach.

As for injuries or times Wally is hurt, that seems to be just one time shown in the series in "The Shave," when he cuts himself while using Ward's razor.

Beaver's friend Larry is sick in as many episodes as Beaver but appeared in 167 less episodes. One might say, Larry was a sickly child. The episodes in which we see him being sick or hear about him being sick and missing school or unable to play are "Lonesome Beaver" (swollen glands), "Beaver's Guest" (diarrhea"), "Beaver and Poncho" when he tells Miss Landers he was sick when the assignment was given, after smoking in "The Pipe," having a swollen throat in "Beaver's Hero," and just sick in "Beaver's Paper." Larry is concerned about hopping in "School Play" because during the previous month, he had an operation to remove his appendix. Then, in "Beaver Makes a Loan," Beaver thinks Larry may be walking around with amnesia because he forgets to go to his house to pay him back the money he borrowed the previous day at school.

As for Eddie, his illnesses are sometimes humorous as in "Voodoo Magic" when he fakes being sick, and after learning he's had a curse placed on him by Beaver, he becomes psychosomatically ill. It's also humorous in "Beaver's Fear," when he's the one who gets sick on the roller coaster after teasing Beaver mercilessly about his being afraid of the roller coaster. In "Eddie's Girl," he pretends being sick so he can convince Wally he's doing him a favor by taking his girl to the dance. When not appearing in the "Beaver's House Guest" episode, Eddie is mentioned by Wally as having the mumps. He gets psychosomatically sick once again in "Summer in Alaska," just thinking about sea sickness and cutting open fish. Oh, that Eddie!

Ward and June suffer a little bit too. Well, June not so much. Wally thinks she's sick when he comes home and finds her lying down on the couch in the middle of the day ("Beaver's Monkey") and Beaver lies about her having pneumonia ("Last Day of School"), but her feet do hurt in one episode because her shoes are too tight ("Beaver Takes a Bath"), and she actually hurts her finger when she closes it shut in the refrigerator door ("The Haircut"). She plays off that "real life" injury mighty well and continued on with the scene.

For Ward, his illnesses or injuries are mostly fabrications courtesy of Beaver. His young son says he has "symptoms" ("Beaver Gets Spelled"), has allergies ("Beaver and Poncho"), and Beaver tells the train conductor Ward is in the hospital after falling out of an airplane ("The Train Trip"). Ward does get a headache from helping Beaver with his math homework ("Beaver's Report Card"), and he does get hurt when their pet alligator saws at his finger ("Captain Jack").

Ward's good buddy Fred Rutherford is injured in three different episodes. He falls down and is hurt when Beaver and Wally place barrel hoops in his driveway ("Lumpy Rutherford"), gets bit by a squirrel ("Wally's Test") and may have broken this toe ("Beaver Finds a Wallet").

Some of Beaver's other friends speak of being sick or get sick. Whitey Whitney speaks of or is car sick in three different episodes ("School Bus" / "Beaver Becomes a Hero" / "Wally, the Lifeguard"). Whitey also gets a stomachache after eating too many desserts ("Don Juan Beaver") and he mentions that he got hives the previous summer to Mary Margaret Matthews ("Beaver Sees America"). Other friends or classmates who are sick include Elephant Ears with the measles ("Party Invitation"), Charles Fredericks who gets sick at school ("Ward's Problem"), Harry Henderson had a virus ("Beaver's Tonsils"), Angela Valentine once got sick in the back of the school bus ("Beaver's Frogs"), Gilbert had his tonsils taken out ("Beaver's Frogs") and he had the mumps ("Beaver's Electric Trains"), Harry Henderson had his appendix removed ("Beaver's Doll Buggy"), and Donna was given a trauma when forced to give back the locket Beaver had given her ("More Blessed to Give").

But what about the animals? Remember when Stanley the monkey got pneumonia after being stuck out in the rain all night ("Beaver's Monkey")? Beaver's fictional parrot ("Pet Fair") was going to call up Miss Landers and tell her he was too sick to go to school for the pet fair (Wally was going to imitate his voice). Beaver and Wally think Nick, their horse was sick when he laid down in the garage, but Gus tells them he's just fine and that he wanted to rest ("A Horse Named Nick"). Beaver's pigeons get sick while he's in bed with tonsilitis. They get lice from Larry's pigeons. They eventually die, but it wasn't from lice ("Beaver's Pigeons").

Wow! That's a lot of sickness or references to being sick. As you read, most of the time, the mentions were just thinking some character was sick or a feeling one was going to be sick if the character had to do something they disliked as in kiss a girl in front of an audience for Beaver or be chauffeured by a girl to a dance at the country club for Wally.

You can read more about illnesses and injuries over at http://leaveittotbeaverbooks.com.

58

JUNE CLEAVER FASHION

June was a fashionable woman. Viewers don't get to see it often, but she had a flair for fashion. She wore fur stoles, white gloves, and charming hats. She didn't dress to the nines too often, but she does dress up well. In "Beaver's Tree," Beaver and Wally tell her she looks almost as ritzy as when Uncle Henry died. That was a high compliment. In this chapter about her fashion sense, the discussion will center around two opposite looks, her wearing pants, typically when gardening, and her moments of elegance, which on occasion include white gloves, hats and fur. You will even get to look at her various hairstyles over the years.

Pants

There are certain chores that are made for dresses (at least in *Leave it to Beaver*) like vacuuming, dusting, and cooking. But when it comes to going outside the house to cut flowers ("Dance Contest"), work in the garden ("The Paper Route"), trim grass ("Wally's Girl Trouble") or paint trash cans ("Wally's Job"), pants are more appropriate for those types of jobs. Then, there is the time when June wears pants in the cabin up at Shadow Lake ("Happy Weekend"). One never knows when there may be a dirty job to do while staying in a cabin.

It is interesting to note that June is never seen wearing pants after they move to the new house in season three. It's possible the producers thought of the new house as being too upscale to be the home of a woman who wore pants. Better yet, it could be that the writers never needed her gardening to advance a plot as seen in "The Paper Route." Viewers will probably never know the real reason why, but of course, you'll have some people say *Leave it to Beaver* was just a TV show and it doesn't matter why she didn't wear pants after season two. Yes, that is moderately correct, but then again, there are just some things fans of a TV show like to speculate about. For some it may be the location of Mayfield and for others, it may be why June never wore pants again after the "Happy Weekend" episode.

Elegance

If there was one thing June Cleaver was, it was elegant. She had a beauty and a sophisticated charm that surrounded her wherever she went. This is most evident when she would dress up for a night out with Ward or when she attended a wedding or another social function. Even when she was only meeting with a school principal like Mr. Haller or Mrs. Rayburn, or with a teacher, June brought a touch of class into every room into which she walked.

This elegance is first seen in the dress she wears to attend a wedding with the Wilsons in "Child Care." In the words of Beaver, she looks "spensive." The unique, almost pillbox hat, and white gloves, are a very nice touch. I'm sure she looked better than the bride. One of June's more elegant moments was her wearing a fur stole, possibly mink, when away with Ward on a business trip ("Beaver Takes a Bath"). June wears the same dress, minus the fur, when visiting the Rutherfords in the" Beaver's Tree" episode. In "Community Chest," June is immaculately dressed for a school open house with Wally, nice hat, brown or tan gloves and a stunning light-colored business suit like dress. She wears a fur stole again in "No Time for Babysitters," and again in the next episode, "Wally's Car," when they went to go eat with the Algers.

June wore hats in many different episodes. Most often these were pillbox hats, or hats that a guy like me, with no fashion taste at all, may say are similar to pillbox hats. Ward never demeans June's appearance when she gets dressed up to go out. He may wonder on occasion why she's wearing a certain item, and one time, he does say something rather unkind to her. In the season two episode, "The Shave," she rushes him upstairs to put on his blue suit, but before he heads upstairs, she asks him what he thinks about her hat. She asks if he likes it. He softly pats her left cheek and says, "No." Then adds, "Maybe the Mitchells will like it."

Barbara Billingsley stated in her *Archive of American Television* interview that her clothes weren't that expensive. A lot of them, she said, were bought at J.C. Penny. Others were bought at wholesalers where the studio had a connection. The most expensive items were probably the sweaters, she said. Barbara never mentions the few times she wore furs, but it's probably safe to say they were the most expensive item on the show she wore. As for shoes, she wore flats in the beginning of the series and as the boys grew, they put her in heels, so she'd be taller than them. She jokingly said as that section of the interview ended, "I'm lucky they didn't have me stand on an apple box." And on what she called her biggest contribution on how the episodes were filmed, she insisted that the skirts not be too short or too long. But just "there" as she made a motion with her hand.

Hairstyles

Just like the boys grew and changed in appearance over the various seasons of *Leave it to Beaver*, June changed her style and especially her hair over the six seasons. She started off with short hair and it grew over the years and in quite a few episodes, she mentions going to the hair salon or beauty shop. She went to the salon in the "Beaver's Frogs" episode and received a compliment from Beaver that was not very complimentary. When asked if Beaver liked her hair and the new way she had it done at the beauty parlor, he says, "Yeah, it makes you look older." June responds by saying, "That beauty parlor lost me."

Below are June's different hair styles from the first episode of each *Leave it to Beaver* season.

59

59

LOVE

If you're in your 60s or 70s, it is doubtful you heard the phrase "I love you" from your parents very often. You experienced the real *Leave it to Beaver* era, and the lack of outward affection that Wally and Beaver experienced on the show. During that time period and earlier, parents, especially fathers, weren't touchy feely kind of people who were able to express their feelings. Beaver wrote in his "Most Interesting Character" essay the way a father expressed love to his children during the *Leave it to Beaver* era. "He works hard and takes care of us…he brings me ice cream when I'm sick …. When I tell him things or ask him things, he listens to me." What Beaver wrote in that essay …. is love. One of the co-writers of this episode was the producer and co-creator Joe Connelly. Producer and brainchild behind the *New Leave it to Beaver*, Brian Levant, wrote a eulogy that was not read at Joe Connelly's funeral, but included words similar to Beaver's essay, especially the part about working hard. Brian Levant's touching words aimed to let Joe Connelly's children know that the way their father said "I love you" was done through the scenes he would write for the episodes that wound up on the small screen. It was one of the ways he showed his children he cared for them. It was hard to say, I love you in what Wally would often call, "the olden days." One thing for sure, love on *Leave it to Beaver* was shown to the boys, if not always said.

In this chapter, we'll look closer at the various times Ward, June or one of the boys said they loved something or someone or speak about love in an abstract manner. But to see love in action, just re-watch every episode and look for those touching moments that are always there but are sometimes hard to find. However, one of those moments which is very easy to see is in the last few moments of the "Bank Account" episode. The love for Ward is easily seen, but Beaver also says it in words after Ward apologizes for jumping to conclusions about the boys spending their money. Beaver responds to the apology by saying, "That's okay dad, we still love you."

Ward

The times Ward says "I love you" is minimal. In fact, I don't believe there's one time he says the phrase. But he does tell the boys that he knows they love Captain Jack, right before telling them they can't keep him ("Captain Jack"). He does the same thing, assures Beaver that he is loved, before telling Beaver he can't keep the car he wins in a raffle ("Beaver's Big Contest"). Ward also tells Beaver he's loved in "Beaver's Secret Life." However, in this episode, he doesn't take anything away from Beaver after telling him he's loved. When June is worried that Wally thinks he's in love and might get hurt ("Wally's Dream Girl"), Ward gives June some commonsense advice when he tells her, "You know, after all, love just... Well, it just isn't something you can run and put a band-aid on."

June

In a couple episodes, June does say she loves someone, but as "I love you" was not something said directly to people too often of that generation, her saying she loved someone was indirect. Examples are seen when she tells ward that she loves Aunt Martha very much ("Beaver's Short Pants") and when she tells Beaver that his father is a very fine man and that she loves him very much ("Beaver's House Guest"). When Wally tells June that they are giving in to Beaver by letting him go to the football game, June has another take on the matter. She tells Wally that they love each of them very much. Because they love them, they like to give them second chances. However, in this episode it just seems like a guilty conscience is more so the reason she says to give Beaver another chance.

June talks a few times about love. In trying to explain away Beaver's actions when he took Poncho to school, she tells Ward how a dog's love is different than that of a parent ("Beaver and Poncho"). She says a dog is different than a parent, "When a dog loves you, it doesn't ask a lot of questions and make a lot of rules, it just... loves you." In another episode, she again talks to Ward about love saying, "The only guide a little fella has is the love and approval of his parents ...now if he thinks he's lost that, it's worse than a beating." ("The Haircut"). She said this to explain why Beaver didn't just go to Ward saying he'd lost his haircut money. He had given him one last chance to prove he could be responsible, and he lost the money. In an honest discussion about love, she tells Beaver that she told him she liked the blouse he gave her because of kindness and the love she has for him ("June's Birthday").

Others

Talk of love isn't only limited to members of the Cleaver family. Two times Beaver's friend Whitey Whitney speaks of love. The first is when Beaver admits to him that Violet Rutherford kissed him at Friend's Lake and shows him the magazine with his and Violet's picture on it. Whitey then pontificates on love saying that anyone that kisses someone is in love with them ("Beaver and Violet"). Whitey is also the friend who makes things worse for Beaver when he's lovesick about Miss Landers ("Miss Landers' Fiancé"). He calls him on the phone and tells Beaver that he saw in the newspaper that she's getting married.

The other characters who talk about or mention love are Mary Ellen Rogers ("New Doctor") who tells Eddie to give Wally all her love when she finds out he is ill and at home in bed. Eddie then says she made a face like she was going to be sick. Mrs. Mondello also speaks about love, her love for Larry. That sounds surprising, doesn't it? Well, the reason and way she says it is after he runs away and she tells him, "How could you do this to your mother who loves you?" ("Larry Hides Out") The final time love is mentioned by a friend occurs when Eddie tells Beaver he loves him ("The Silent Treatment"). Wait!. Eddie loves Beaver? "Well, sure, I love you 'ol buddy. You're alright Charlie. Besides, you're the only one small enough to get underneath the dash and hook up all the wires."

Wally

Wally talks about love on a few occasions. He admits to Beaver he had a case of puppy love with Miss Hildebrand who lived next door to them when they stayed up at the lake. He doesn't think he'll ever get over her ("Beaver's Crush"). He describes to Beaver what love must be like when he shares the feelings he has for Mary Ellen Rogers ("Her Idol"). "I don't like Mary Ellen Rogers, but I feel kinda bad when I see her talking to some of the other guys in school. I guess that bad feeling is what makes people get married." Wally also has a deep conversation about girls and love and wonders later to June how his dad could know so much about love and stuff ("Tennis, Anyone?").

When asked by Beaver if he is in love with Jill Bartlett, after he admits she's not so bad and that he had a good time with her, Wally tells Beaver he's not in love ("Blind Date Committee"). In season six, Beaver tells Ward and June that Wally is in love with the girl who works at the box office of the Madison Theater ("Box Office Attraction").

Beaver

Beaver's experiences love during the series. For him, it's never actual love, but bouts of puppy love, or crushes. The first example is with his second-grade teacher Miss Canfield ("Beaver's Crush"). The second girl, this time, really a girl, is Linda Dennison ("Her Idol"). He doesn't realize he has feelings for her until he sees her up in the tree with Larry Mondello. Wait! He's looking at the bird eggs with her. That's supposed be him up there with Linda. He also has momentary bouts of affection with Violet Rutherford ("Beaver and Violet") and Penny Woods ("Farewell to Penny"). His next experience with puppy love is with another teacher, Miss Landers ("Miss Landers' Fiancé"). Love later finds Beaver via a transfer student named Mary Tyler. They seem like they'll really become an item until she sees Wally, that's when Beaver becomes yesterday's news ("Brother Vs. Brother"). While there are other girls he goes out with ("The Late Edition") ("Beaver's First Date"), and a couple that he becomes infatuated with ("Don Juan Beaver") ("Beaver Sees America"), the only girl he really shows a strong attraction toward is Donna Yeager ("More Blessed to Give"). Gilbert asks him if he is in love with Donna. If he is in love, Gilbert says he thinks there's more to it than just standing around and looking at her as she walks by him after school. Beaver eventually gives her an expensive locket he wins at a carnival. That causes some trouble with her father. He would've been better off just taking the Mickey Mantle ashtray the carnival barker offered him.

Beaver also speaks about love and that is seen in the above-mentioned time when he buys June an ugly blouse, she says she will wear it to a meeting, but winds up wearing something decent instead of the "ghastly" gift he gave her ("June's Present"). He also tells Wally that he doesn't think he is loved by their parents any longer ("Nobody Loves Me"). Puberty sometimes does that to a guy. Ward and June correct his faulty thinking when late in the episode, they make a real fuss about him. Beaver is the 'ole Beaver once again by the time the closing credits roll.

And how can we finish a section about Beaver and love without mentioning his love for a thing, instead of a person? Of course, you remember when Beaver dug up a tree at his old house, a tree given to him for his birthday ("Beaver's Tree). His digging it up without permission of the new homeowner causes some trouble, but all is well in the end and Wally tells him he's pretty lucky to have parents who understand his having a crush on a tree.

There's always more that can be said about love and if you would like to read more about love and *Leave it to Beaver*, please visit http://leaveittobeaverbooks.com.

60

HISTORY AND CIVICS

Wally Cleaver spent most of his time on *Leave it to Beaver* in high school and he endured the typical high school class schedule. English, algebra, and history were among his many classes. Because history was one of his classes, he talks about historical events in various episodes. Sometimes he talks about history in relation to everyday life and does the same with government and civics too, probably another class he took at Mayfield High. Wally is not the only character to speak about such things as world history, civics, United States government and politics.

This chapter will look at many mentions of any of the above topics as they were spoken about throughout the run of *Leave it to Beaver* on CBS and then ABC. The topics will be divided into three categories: World History, World Politics/Government and United States Politics/Government. The lists below are more illustrative than exhaustive.

World History

Not sure where Wally may have heard about the story of Ann Boleyn, maybe in eighth grade history class, but he shares this bit of English history with Beaver in the "Haunted House" episode. He does so because Beaver talks about ghosts and the spooky house he and Larry passed on the way home. Wally tells Beaver that Boleyn had her head chopped off and now haunts the Tower of London.

In "Eddie's Double-Cross," Ward suggests Wally tell Eddie about overhearing Caroline (pronounced Carolyn) Schuster making fun of Eddie. He does, and Eddie gets furious with Wally and accuses him of wanting to steal Caroline from him. Ward explains to June about a couple historical figures who told the truth and what happened to them. He speaks of Socrates who told the truth and was poisoned. He then mentions Demosthenes who went looking for the truth and wound-up living in a barrel.

Beaver speaks of learning about King Henry VIII in history class. He says how neat of a king he was because he would chop off the heads of his wives ("In the Soup"). His second wife Anne Boleyn was mentioned by Wally early in the season one episode "Haunted House."

World Politics / Government / Historical Figures

In "The Price of Fame," June has purchased some frozen Chinese dinners. Since Wally and Beaver do not like Chinese food, Ward suggests they just leave them in the freezer in case Chiang Kai-shek ever decides to drop by. He was the Republic of China (Taiwan) president. Other world leaders (past and present) who are mentioned include General Charles De Gaulle ("Wally and Alma"), Napoleon ("Beaver's I.Q."), Nikita Khrushchev ("Eddie Spends the Night").

In "The Younger Brother," Eddie makes a reference to communism when he says, "What is this, East Berlin?" In the episode, "Water, Anyone?" Tooey's mother is very offended that Beaver has the entrepreneurial spirit and chops to sell water to kids in the neighborhood after the water is shut off. She calls Ward Cleaver and demonstrates her ignorance about economics, political systems, and the free market. She complains that Beaver is taking advantage of his playmates and ends with saying, "… it's things like this that lead to juvenile delinquency and communism." Ward assures her that he doesn't believe democracy is in danger. I think he meant republic, but she probably got his point.

United States Politics / Government / Historical Figures

One of the funniest lines ever recited in *Leave it to Beaver* accompanies the only time the Pledge of Allegiance is recited in the show. It occurs in "Ward's Problem," which is Miss Landers' debut. Tattletale Judy Hensler sees that Beaver was looking outside during the pledge and promptly tells on him, "Miss Landers, when we were pledging allegiance to the flag, Beaver was looking out the window…and I don't think that's very patriotic." Beaver explains he was looking at the flag outside, problem solved. This is mentioned here as it is an American tradition, the beginning of what was taught as civics in our schools at younger ages, but in most places no longer is taught. The pledge is mentioned one other time in "Beaver the Athlete," when Beaver says Larry got a C in citizenship for chewing gum during the pledge.

When Wally and his friends are working on a project in "The Boat Builders," Ward goes to check out the damage being done to his garage. Wally explains they are building a real-life Eskimo canoe. Ward then speaks about one of America's great inventors, "Don't be discouraged fellows. This is how Robert Fulton started." Chester thinks Ward is giving them "the business," but Wally says he's not and that he just thinks they're goofy but doesn't want to come right out and say it. Another great American inventor mentioned is Thomas Edison in "Beaver's Electric Trains."

President Eisenhower is mentioned by Wally in "The Garage Painters." It's a rainy day and there's nothing to do so Wally decides to write the president of the United States a letter. If he sends him a letter back, Wally figures he can make some money and sell his autograph. Smart thinking by Wally. He asks Ward if the letter would be sure to get to him if he sent it Air Mail, Ward suggests instead, to just mark it "personal."

Wars in which Americans have fought are referenced several times. In "Beaver's Hero," Beaver's class is taught by substitute teacher Mr. Willett who discusses World War II and the War of 1812. In that same episode Wally tells Beaver that there were two world wars. Beaver and Jackie Waters play "Korea" in "Beaver's Old Buddy." Jackie comments that "Korea was a popular war when you lived at your other house." The Cold War is mentioned in a few episodes in season six. Ward mentions listening from upstairs to Wally's party makes him feel like a U2 plane in "The Party Spoiler." Then, a few episodes later, in "Beaver's Good Deed," Wally explains when listening to his transistor radio, that they play world news after every ten records. He says that's how Lumpy found out about Cuba. This is likely a reference to the Cuban Missile Crisis that took place about two months before this episode aired.

How the U.S. Government and money works is mentioned in "Wally, the Lifeguard" when Wally tells Beaver that withholding taxes will be taken out of his paycheck to help run the government. How the U.S. government irresponsibly handles money is referenced by Ward in the episode, "Ward's Millions." Ward asks June about an $8.69 check she wrote. She tells him she couldn't balance the checkbook, so she wrote an $8.69 check and ripped it up. He says, "They could use you in Washington." Richard Rickover tells Beaver in "Beaver's Frogs," that he'll have to get a social security card if he gets a job. Beaver doesn't know what that is, and Richard explains that social security is when the government pays you money when you get too old to work, just to do nothing. When Beaver asks how old, Richard replies, "Real old…thirty or thirty-five I guess."

The philosophical ideas of America are mentioned by Wally when he says Ward and

Beaver are upstairs acting like Patrick Henry, "Give me liberty or give me death" in "Beaver's Football Award." Wally also tells Beaver in "Beaver's Newspaper, "This is a free country." That sentiment is repeated in "Junior Fire Chief," when Wally tells Beaver after he cites someone for having faulty wiring that it's a free country and if a guy wants to get electrocuted, he can get electrocuted. Finally, in "Eddie, the Businessman," Eddie Haskell says, "This is America, land of opportunity," a sentiment actor Ken Osmond lived out in real life.

There are many episodes not written about in this chapter in which some government, political, or historical reference is made. Some of them can be found at the website http://leaveittobeaverbooks.com.

61

HOLIDAYS AND BIRTHDAYS

Holidays

We all enjoy a good holiday, don't we? I'm sure the producers of *Leave it to Beaver* did too. Unfortunately, we do not have in the *Leave it to Beaver* canon, any episodes that strictly focus on a specific holiday. There are mentions of holidays and allusions to holidays, but no specific holiday themed episodes.

Christmas is by far, the most popular holiday among the characters in *Leave it to Beaver*. It is mentioned or alluded to twenty-four times over the run of the series. In two of these episodes, Christmas is only an allusion as the word "Christmas" is not used. In "The Haircut," Beaver plays an angel in a school pageant and this episode is regarded by many *Leave it to Beaver* fans as the closest thing to a Christmas episode. In the play, Beaver is seen in his stocking cap to hide the horrible haircut he and Wally gave him, and we see him singing *Hark, The Herald Angels Sing*.

The only other episode in which Christmas is alluded to, but not mentioned directly was "The Train Trip." What does Christmas have to do with a train trip home to Mayfield from Aunt Martha's home in Riverside? Not so much until George Haskell tells Ward what happened on the train trip. To sum up the episode, Wally and Beaver ask Aunt Martha if they could buy their own train tickets for the trip home. She agrees. They then promptly spend too much money on hot dogs and junk food, leaving them with only enough money to buy a ticket for Bellport. The conductor finds out about this, and after some storytelling, the boys admit their bad deed and agree to send the conductor the money for the full ticket price to Mayfield. George Haskell hears this and tells Ward later that night. This is where the Christmas allusion comes from.

If not for George Haskell informing Ward about the hilarious situation his children were in earlier in the day, Ward would not have asked the children about that situation at bedtime. He does so and both Wally and Beaver are shocked at how he might know what happened since he wasn't there to witness it. Beaver tells Wally after Ward leaves their room, "You know Wally, maybe it's the same way Santa Claus finds out about stuff." Wally replies, "Santa Claus? Beaver, don't you know......?" Before he tells Beaver there is no Santa Claus, he stops himself. Voila, a Christmas allusion.

Other references to Christmas in the series are minor but direct. These fall into a couple different categories, one being just things about Christmas or things that are like Christmas. The other category would be things that happen "at" Christmas or "on" Christmas. Not much of a distinction, but there is one. Let's start of by looking at that first category.

In "Wally's Girl Trouble," Miss Higgins at the gift store says she'll wrap up Beaver's box, just like it was Christmas. In another episode, "Beaver Becomes a Hero," Beaver sings "Jingle Bells" and Wally wonders why he is singing that when it is nowhere near Christmas. In "Beaver's Accordion," Beaver hides the accordion he received through the mail in the upstairs closet. The logic for hiding it in the upstairs hall closet is because their parents don't use it accept to store umbrellas and old Christmas ornaments. Then, we see a possible tonsillectomy in "Beaver's Tonsils" cause Beaver some fear until Ward explains what happened to him when he had tonsils taken out. Not only was he able to eat ice cream but he also received a lot of gifts. Beaver said, having his tonsils taken out will be just like Christmas.

The other category of Christmas mentions consist of characters talking about gifts they might receive or give at Christmas or about something that happens on or around Christmastime. For example, in the pilot episode, "It's a Small World," Wally talks about why the boys didn't get bicycles the previous Christmas. Other Christmas gifts spoken of by characters include soap and umbrellas that are sent to the boys by an unidentified aunt and Aunt Martha in "Beaver's Short Pants," and Aunt Martha is mentioned again in "Beaver's Ring," as someone who gives umbrellas at Christmas. Ward jokes with June in "Beaver's Poem," that if he got her a dishwasher, what would he get her for Christmas. He also jokes with her in "Beaver Makes a Loan" to not have the windows washed until after Christmas. Beaver talks about his dad not working on Christmas or Thanksgiving in "Most Interesting Character." In "Beaver's Tree," Beaver talks about his tree and being able to hang lights on it if it were a Christmas time. The "Pet Fair" episode has a non-recurring character named Mr. Allen, the pet shop owner, speak about Christmas Eve. In "Beaver and Andy," Beaver talks about the brandy his Uncle Billy sent his dad as a gift. He tells Andy that his dad pours it over cake at Christmas. June mentions Christmas to Beaver in "Mother's Day Composition." She explains to Beaver that during one Christmas season when she was young, she worked in the book section of a department store. Wally talks about seeing Mr. Compton the previous Christmas and not receiving a gift in "Beaver, the Model." Chopper, Beaver's friend from Camp König spends the night in "Beaver's House Guest," and says he gets twice the gifts at Christmas because of his divorced parents. Two characters speak about Christmas in "Beaver's Birthday." Gilbert talks about having to put his Christmas money in the bank and Beaver wonders if he might get a model car at Christmas. In "Beaver's Electric Trains," Ward tells June about the time when his uncle from the city gave him a pogo stick for Christmas.

Other mentions include Larry saying he only sees his married brother at Christmas in "Wally's Girl Trouble." The boys think they can unload their stinky perfume at Christmas in "The Perfume Salesmen." In "Beaver's Old Friend," when June sees the boys' room clean she wonders why since it isn't Christmas time. Ward tells June that brothers go from being best of friends to, later in life, just exchanging Christmas cards with one another in "Beaver's Doll Buggy."

Christmas is mentioned once in the pilot episode, three times in season one, seven times in season two, six times in season three, five times in season four, two times in season five and none in the final season.

Other holidays mentioned are Arbor Day in "Beaver Gets 'Spelled," Mother's Day in "Mother's Day Composition" and "Wally's Test," and Thanksgiving in "Beaver's Poster" and in "Most Interesting Character."

Birthdays

Birthdays are usually a time for joy. But that isn't exactly the case for Theodore "Beaver" Cleaver. Some of the feelings he's experienced on birthdays as seen in the show include fear, anger, disappointment, even more disappointment, guilt, anxiety, and embarrassment, and not necessarily in that order.

The first birthday experience for Beaver that we see on the series is in "Party Invitation," which featured the young and talented Patty Turner as Linda Dennison. This is the episode in which Beaver is afraid, and it isn't an irrational fear either. He's scared to death that HE WILL BE KISSED BY A GIRL! After all, it's an all-girl party. Every single boy he's called from his class says he is not attending. It's just going to be Beaver and the girls. But as in every *Leave it to*

Beaver episode, everything turns out just fine in the end. He finds her father's den and a lot of old west memorabilia and guns, a pure delight for a boy Beaver's age.

Beaver typically would enjoy a birthday, especially those of his brother Wally. But on Wally's fourteenth birthday, he has plans that would exclude Beaver. No party, just hamburgers with Eddie at the drugstore and then movies with Eddie and hopefully, some girls. Beaver is to get no fun out of Wally's birthday and even after planning to buy him a nice camera for his birthday. Of course, Larry talks him out of buying Wally the camera and instead, convinces Beaver to buy himself a bow and arrow, a "punk" bow and arrow set, at that. He buys Wally a juvenile paddle ball toy for his birthday instead. Wally says he likes it, but it really is just a hunk of junk. Beaver feels guilty for giving Wally such a hunk of junk and he might also be mad because the bow and arrow set broke on the way home. Wally forgives him and understands why Beaver did what he did.

An embarrassing birthday moment for Beaver, as if being the only boy at an all-girl party wasn't bad enough, is when his old friend David Manning in "Forgotten Party," invites him to his birthday party. Forgetfulness and a rush to get Beaver to David's house on Saturday in time for the party has June buying a gift for Beaver to give David. She buys a gift suitable for a toddler, not one Beaver could give to a fellow third grader. To not be embarrassed at the party, Beaver makes a sacrificial act and gives his old friend David his new camera. He explains to Ward that it wasn't just because he was embarrassed, that he gave him his new camera, but because David had told all his new friends that Beaver was his pal, and he didn't want to let David down. Beaver is a swell guy.

Disappointment reigns in "June's Birthday." Beaver and Wally argue about what type of present to buy their mother and wind up each buying one with half of the money Ward gave them for a gift. Fans of the show, know Beaver buys June a "ghastly" blouse, her words, not mine. She tells Beaver she'll wear it to a mother's meeting and to her surprise, Beaver's class is there to perform some songs and he catches her not wearing it. Disappointed is probably an understatement. Beaver was devastated that his mother lied about wearing the blouse. She finally does "square" things with Beaver and explains tact to him. A lesson well learned, although, a bit painful for the Beave.

In "Beaver's Birthday," the little boy is grown up so much that he's now too old for parties. However, this does cause some anxiety for Beaver. He's searched for hidden birthday presents and can't find any. He asks Wally if he thinks he'll get any presents at all. If only he hadn't sworn off birthday parties… but his parents don't forget and neither do his other relatives. He comes away with a good amount of loot, a whopping $32.00 if you include the ten bucks that Uncle Billy eventually kicks in with a couple days later. This episode is a bit more complex than what is explained here but check it out on a streaming service or the DVD set and enjoy.

Check out http://leaveittotbeaverbooks.com to find out more about holidays and birthdays.

62

GROWING UP

There are three different ways to look at the subject of growing up in the various episodes of *Leave it to Beaver*. The first and most often thought of way one speaks about growing up is what a child wants to be when they grow up. Another way to look at the subject is a child insisting they're grown or growing up and now they can do something they want like buy their own suit ("Wally's Suit") or that they don't need something like a babysitter ("No Time for Babysitters"). Finally, Wally and Beaver have ideas of what they think being a grown up is all about, like growing hair on your chest ("The Pipe") and getting smarter ("Wally's Glamour Girl").

Below, let's look at these three areas in detail. This chapter won't include every single mention that could be included in these categories, but you will read a great wealth of information on all three.

Being a grown up

While there aren't many episodes in which the boys talk about what being an adult involves, it is interesting to hear their thoughts on the subject when they do express them. Here are some examples: A person gets coordination when they get old. Beaver assumes it is similar to how a guy gets hair on his chest when he's an adult ("The Pipe"). Beaver thinks it's creepy how things work when you grow up that you get married and have a family ("Beaver's I.Q."). When a person grows up, they should get smarter ("Wally's Glamour Girl"). Beaver always thought growing up was the best thing that could ever happen to a guy but doesn't really think so after his Jackie Waters experience ("Beaver's Old Buddy"). Wally tells Beaver that growing up is rough on a guy and explains about a mid-life crisis when a guy can act like a kid again ("Beaver's Doll Buggy"). Wally tells his mother acting like an adult feels creepy. He also says that he doesn't know how adults can act the way they do without laughing ("Substitute Father"). When a guy turns fifteen years old, he knows everything about cars, or so Wally believes ("Wally's Car"). Beaver thinks grownups must drive four door cars ("Wally's Chauffeur"). Finally, being grown up is a big responsibility ("Wally's License"). While some of these are not so true, the last sentiment is a definite fact.

When I grow up

Beaver Cleaver always had dreams of what he wanted to be when he grew up. He had wanted to be a banker, but changed his mind about that, and decided to be a policeman instead ("The Lost Watch"). Ten episodes later, Beaver says he always wanted to be a policeman, but after seeing a woman give an officer a hard time, he tells Larry that he no longer wants to be one ("The Grass is Always Greener"). In other episodes, Beaver says he'll probably be a janitor when he gets out of college ("The Price of Fame"), a sheriff ("Beaver's I.Q."), a writer ("Beaver's Secret Life") a newspaper man ("The Late Edition"), and a big leaguer ("The Spot Removers").Wally tells Beaver he thought he wanted to be a lawyer ("The Cookie Fund").Then, in the final season of the show, his friend Mike says he should be a private eye since he's so sneaky ("Tell it to Ella"). Ward asks him if he wants to be president, but Beaver says he doesn't even want to be a monitor at school ("Beaver's Autobiography"). Finally, Mr. Langley suggests Beaver will probably be a space scientist, even though Beaver says he might be a forward for the Lakers ("Beaver the Caddy").

Wally has some preferred professions for when he grows up. Among them are a tree surgeon ("Wally's Election"), a soldier in the army ("Larry's Club"), an Igloo Ice Cream salesmen with a truck ("Wally, the Businessmen"), an electrical engineer ("Beaver Becomes a Hero"), and an engineer ("Beaver's Big Contest").

I am grown up

When it comes to being grown up, it's understandable why Wally is the one that usually says he's getting too old for being treated like a child or that he's now old enough to be able to do something or handle more responsibility. After all, he's the older brother and he's always the one getting closer to an age threshold for which more responsibility is given. Beaver also has his "getting older" moments too. Let's look at Beaver first.

Wally says that Beaver must be growing up because he never used to care what he looked like ("Beaver's Freckles"). Beaver says he's old enough to take Chuckie shopping for shoes since he's a hall monitor at school and knows how to yell at kids ("Chuckie's New Shoes"). Beaver says he's too old to have a babysitter ("No Time for Babysitters"). Beaver thinks he's too old for parties ("Beaver's Birthday"). Beaver complains about having his parents go with him every time he wants to buy something, another sign he thinks he's growing up. This time his insistence causes him some trouble ("Beaver's Ice Skates"). Beaver doesn't want his mom to call up the mother of a girl for him because it will make him look like a baby ("Beaver's First Date"). Beaver no longer calls aftershave smelly stuff ("Double Date"). Now, that final example is a sure sign he is growing up.

When it comes to Wally growing up, let's look at what new responsibilities he wants or gains because of his newfound age or maturity. He wants to shave ("The Shave"). He wants to buy his own suit ("Wally's New Suit"). He want's privacy ("Wally's Pug Nose"). Wally wants to go on a weekend getaway with friends without parental supervision ("Weekend Invitation"). Wally is old enough to get his drivers' license ("Wally's License"). Finally, June says he's old enough to go on a dinner date ("Wally's Dinner Date").

Wally thinks he's grown too old for certain things and among these are carrying a lunchbox to school ("Cleaning Up Beaver"), going with his father to buy a suit ("Wally's Suit"), having a birthday party ("Wally's Present"), going to a grocery store and getting free samples ("Beaver's Monkey"), and having his father drive him to a dance with his date ("Wally's Chauffeur").

Finally, Wally tells Beaver, about whether Ward told him he couldn't join the Barons. "I'm growing up and he wants me to make my own decisions," he said. He continued, "He's training me for life, so I can handle my own stuff" ("One of the Boys"). This sentiment from Wally is exactly what a father should do for a boy and is what growing up should be all about.

Growing up is a good thing. Unfortunately for *Leave it to Beaver* fans, it also meant the eventual end of the series.

There is a lot of information that can be gleaned from the episodes on growing up, most of which will, over time, be included at http://leaveittobeaverbooks.com. While you're there, don't forget to sign up for the chance to win free *Leave it to Beaver* prizes.

63

WARD'S JOB

There are two things *Leave it to Beaver* fans discuss with a lot of fervor, the location of Mayfield and Ward Cleaver's occupation. While there are many absolutes in life, they don't always exist in situation comedies, especially those which aired in the 1950s and early 1960s.

A lot of information can be gathered about Ward's job just from watching episodes of the show. Unfortunately, a lot of the information is contradictory. One episode will include information that makes it seem as if Ward is a stockbroker ("Lumpy's Car Trouble"), and another episode makes Ward sound as if he is in accounting ("Ward's Baseball"), and yet another, provides tidbits that sound like he has a marketing job ("The Boat Builders"). Let's look at a lot of those details more in depth right now.

The Home Office

The Mayfield office where Ward and Fred Rutherford work is a branch office of a big company as Fred calls it ("Tire Trouble") or a substantial company as Ward calls it ("Mistaken Identity"). The home office is mentioned as being in in New York City in most episodes in which it is spoken of by Ward or Fred. However, early in the series, Ward describes his being in business with Fred Rutherford, implying they run their own business ("Lumpy Rutherford").

When speaking of the Thompson deal in "The Black Eye," Fred Rutherford refers to company executives as the "New York Brass." Fred refers to the executives again as the "brass" or the "big brass" in "Tenting Tonight" and tells Ward they received a wire from New York and says the big boys in New York want the Farmington report on their desk. Ward speaks to the home office in New York all morning ("The Last Day of School"). Ward speaks of having a very busy day at work, and lots of phone calls to New York ("The Dramatic Club"). Another reference to the home office seems to give a clue about the location of Mayfield at least in the episode, "Lumpy's Car Trouble." Ward tells Wally a secret about big business and that's never send a letter when you can accomplish the same thing by making a 1000-mile trip.

The home office references which omit New York begin in the third season ("Beaver's Prize") when Ward tells June he's expecting a report from the home office to be sent to him. Fred speaks of the home office when he wonders if anyone there ever reads the reports he and Ward send them ("Tire Trouble"). Fred also talks about the home office when he stops over at the Cleavers to see if Ward wanted him to go over the Miller audits ("Ward's Baseball"). Ward and June both refer to the home office in "The Hypnotist" when Ward says he's expecting a call from them while working at home on a Saturday and June asks him how the survey they are doing for the home office is going.

The home office is sometimes the reason why Ward is unable to spend time with the boys. This is seen in the above mentioned "Lumpy's Car Trouble." In this episode, the "boys" come from the home office for a Saturday meeting and because of that meeting, Ward is unable to see Wally participate in a track meet at Bellport. The next time the home office is mentioned, Ward was scheduled to take Beaver and his friends camping. But Tom Clifton from the home office schedules a weekend meeting ("A Night in the Woods") and Ward must miss the weekend outing.

Co-workers

Ward works with several people in the Mayfield office. Chief among them is Fred Rutherford. Willis "Corny" Cornelius is a co-worker Ward drops off at home in "Part-Time Genius." Whether Corny is a co-worker or just a friend who lives in the neighborhood who he drives to and from work is debatable because in "The Broken Window" episode, Corny is a man showing the Cleavers lots outside of town for them to purchase for a new house. In that episode, he has the same name and seems to have a dumb child. In "Part-Time Genius," his children seem to be some of the smartest in Mayfield, but in "The Broken Window," he speaks of one getting stuck in a cat door. Another person who may be a co-worker, or a contractor working for Ward's employer is Collins. He's a man who Ward gives an earful to because of the slipshod work he is either doing or is allowing to happen ("Beaver and Poncho"). Mr. Compton could also be added to this group of possible workers as he is the firm's lawyer, although he is not employed directly by the company ("Beaver, the Model"). The final "possible" co-worker is Mr. Byington, a man Ward takes to lunch along with his staff ("Un-Togetherness"), but it is unclear if he works at the office or if he may be a client.

There are other workers who are absolutely working at the same company as Ward. They include his secretary Grace ("New Doctor" and "Beaver Plays Hooky"), Charlie Bennett ("Beaver's Ring"), Janice, the good-looking secretary or steno pool worker ("Wally's New Suit"), Charlie Hennessy whose son had a tryout with the Detroit Lions ("School Play"), Mr. Peck whose son bought a jalopy to fix up years ago and it still sits in his garage ("Wally's Car"), Harvey Stone who has a son who is about Beaver's age and doesn't think anyone loves him and is going through that awkward age for a boy ("Nobody Loves Me"), Norm March who has a brother-in-law who buys Beaver, Gilbert and Richard's burro ("Three Boys and a Burro"), Tom Clifton, a worker from the home office but on occasion comes to Mayfield to meet with Ward and others ("A Night in the Woods") and Mr. Miller who had to fly to the coast and gave Ward two tickets for a big baseball game ("The Poor Loser").

Unidentified workers in the office include "the girls around the water cooler" which Fred Rutherford spends his time worrying what they may be saying about him ("Beaver and Kenneth"). The only two women named in the office are Janice and Grace, but this reference infers there may be others. Ward mentions that there are multiple guys in the office who work under Fred ("Wally, the Lifeguard").

What we know for certain is that we do not know how many people work in the Mayfield office at any one time. However, over the six seasons, Grace, Charlie Bennett, Janice, Charlie Hennessy, Mr. Peck, Harvey Stone, Norm March, and Mr. Miller work with Ward and Fred at some point in the series. Other possible or probable co-workers include Willis "Corny" Cornelius, Mr. Byington and Mr. Collins, while Mr. Compton is a lawyer with his own firm who has the office Ward and Fred work at as one of his clients.

Good vs. Bad Days

"We never know what kind of a mood you're gonna come home in." – June Cleaver

Every job has its ups and downs but let's look season by season at how the workdays are described by Ward and see if the longer he works there, if things get better or worse. Starting in season one in eight episodes which mention what type of day Ward had, it was hard, bad, or terrible in six of those episodes or 75% bad and 25% good, and in one of those episodes, he says the entire week was bad. In season two his day at the office is mentioned four times and his good and bad days were split evenly so it was 50% good and 50% bad. In season three, the type of day Ward had at the office is mentioned or alluded to three times and they are all negative. Season four finds three episodes in which Ward's Day at work is mentioned and twice they were bad or hard days. The final tally is 67% bad days and 33% good days. In season five, Ward has two bad days at work and one good day or 67% bad days and 33% good. Finally, in season six, there are no workdays mentioned with such specificity that we can determine if his days were good or bad.

There you have it… many more bad days than good ones, but then again, that may be why it's called work. And remember, he did work with Fred Rutherford. To add up the stats, of all workdays mentioned as being good or bad, they were 75% bad and 25% good.

Occupation

So, what was this job where Ward had many more bad days than good days? There is no way to know for certain. It's just like the location of Mayfield. One can piece clues from one episode and another episode, but since the shows were written by over forty different script writers and because there was no series bible as there is today on every TV show, there is no continuity as to the location of Mayfield and Ward's occupation. And you know what…. that is just fine as that was just TV back in the 1950s and early 1960s. Nevertheless, it's still interesting to look at the details we can glean from the various episodes. So, what are some of the clues that point to Ward's occupation?

The company makes deals as is seen with the Thompson deal ("The Black Eye"), the company does a lot of business with the local newspaper ("The Paper Route"), Ward looks at some property for the office ("The Bank Account"), they have sales meetings at the office with a good sized sales force ("Cleaning Up Beaver"), Ward and Fred write reports for the home office ("Tenting Tonight" and "Beaver's Ring"), they conduct marketing surveys ("Borrowed Boat"), they conduct audits ("Ward's Baseball"), Ward mentions having three or four millionaire clients in the office ("Kite Day), Ward travels to St. Louis for a few days on business ("Substitute Father").

In "Lumpy's Car Trouble," there is a certificate on Ward's office wall from "The Stock Exchange." A lot of people will argue about how this proves Ward was a stockbroker or worked in a stock brokerage firm. Maybe so, at least in THAT episode. Again, over forty writers worked on the show and there was no series bible where every fact about the episode was listed for prospective writers to use for the sake of continuity. From the above details about Ward's job, he could've worked in an accounting firm, worked in an advertising firm, a marketing firm, or a sales office. There's just no telling for certain what his occupation was. But if it makes a person feel better to discuss his occupation and say he absolutely did this or that thing for a living, let that person do so.

After Work

Ward usually comes home around 5 p.m. after he gets off work. There are many episodes where we see him come home earlier or later, but like most men who worked in an office in the late 1950s, the workday ended at 5 p.m. and since Mayfield was not very large, he arrives home soon after leaving the job. When he arrives home, he sometimes brings in the afternoon newspaper and greets his wife. He often gives June a kiss, but not always. Of course, his home arrival routine was examined by our network of researchers, wait, I mean, examined by me. Specifically, the research involves, kissing, briefcases and bringing the afternoon newspaper inside.

A kiss hello is typically normal as seen in classic TV sitcoms like *The Dick Van Dyke Show* where Rob often kissed Laura when he came home from a hard day of work dealing with Mel Cooley. This affection was also seen on *The Donna Reed Show* when Alex would come home and kiss Donna and on *Father Knows Best* when Jim came home from a difficult day at the insurance agency and kissed Margaret. In *Leave it to Beaver,* Ward kisses June 61% of the time when he comes home from work. Of those kisses, 91% of them were Ward kissing June on the lips and 9% were kisses on the check. The kisses on the cheek mostly occurred in season five.

As a hard-working businessman, Ward carried a briefcase to and from work, well, sometimes. Unlike Dudley McMillan, who also carried a briefcase ("Wally and Dudley"), it was okay for a father to carry one, but a "kid oughta not to" as Larry so eloquently once explained briefcase carrying ("Beaver and Gilbert"). In fact, of the over 120 episodes in which Ward is seen coming home from work, Ward brings home a briefcase in only 55% of the episodes and in 12% of those episodes he is shown arriving home multiple times with or without a briefcase. While he didn't often need to take home his briefcase, in "Eddie's Double-Cross," Ward says, "If you leave the office without your briefcase, everybody thinks you're doggin' it."

As it was in most 1950s households, the daily newspaper was a big part of an after-work routine for the Cleavers. Ward and June would often sit in the living room and read it. Ward would read it more often than June and occasionally, the boys would read the sports, comics or if Beaver needed a current event, he'd read the front section or the local news. How the paper entered the house was part of Ward's afternoon coming home from work routine. In the over 120 episodes in which he entered the house after work, Ward brought the newspaper in with him in 13% of the episodes. Of those episodes, 75% of them were in seasons four, five and six. Don't let this miniscule amount of times Ward brought the paper in with him after work fool you. They read the newspaper quite a bit. Over the six seasons, the newspaper was read in the Cleaver household by either Ward, June, Wally or Beaver in 48% of all episodes. Oh yeah, and that one-time Uncle Billy read it ("Uncle Billy's Visit").

For even more information on Ward's job, check out http://leaveittobeaverbooks.com.

64

WORRY

Fans on occasion say June worries too much about her children, especially Beaver. In "Price of Fame," June worries about Beaver still being gone when she finds out Larry has been home for quite a while. She's worried about the boys running away with the circus in "A Horse Named Nick." June also worried about leaving the boys alone in "Beaver Takes a Bath." Okay, that was justified.

She worries, but it may surprise you to find out that all Cleavers worry, but she does worry more than the others. Throughout the series, June expresses worry in fifty different episodes. That means she worries in 21% of all *Leave it to Beaver* episodes. But it's not like it's unnecessary worry, every time. Of course, what I'm about to write is very subjective. I personally feel that seventeen of the times she worried (or 34%), that she had a legitimate reason to worry. That may say more about me than it does about her.

Some of those worries I deem to be legitimate deserve a closer look. The first time June expresses a legitimate worry is when she looks into the boys' room late at night and their beds are empty. This occurs in "Beaver's Crush," when they have gone to sneak into the school and remove a toy from Miss Canfield's desk which might scare her. That's a legitimate worry.

One of her borderline legitimate worries is when Beaver is later than Wally when they are coming home from school during a heavy rain in "Beaver and Poncho." A similar borderline incident is in "Lonesome Beaver," when Wally goes off to camp with the Boy Scouts. Knowing he'll be with Eddie Haskell in the woods for a couple days and nights, may be a good reason to worry.

The last legitimate worry June has in season one is when Ward tells her that Aunt Martha left the boys at the train station by themselves, allowing them to buy their own tickets. What could go wrong? I can only imagine all the scenes of "wrong" that went through June's head.

Sometimes, when a mother worries, they do not just have a legitimate worry, but something actually goes wrong. This happens in "Beaver Takes a Bath." Here, June is worried about leaving the boys alone for the weekend while she is with Ward on a business trip. If she hadn't gone on the trip, it is very doubtful Beaver would have allowed the bathtub to overflow. Also, if she had been there, Beaver would not have been fed a hamburger that had fallen on the floor.

Other times she was worried about Beaver and had a right to be worried include him going to the lake with Larry in "Borrowed Boat," her worrying that Beaver may be a thief in "Beaver and Kenneth," and Beaver getting into a fight with Sonny Cartwright in "Beaver's Fortune." But that last one might be considered borderline legitimate by some or way out of bounds for worry, at least back in Beaver's time. You know one thing is for sure, Ward wasn't worried about Beaver fighting Sonny Cartwright, especially after those boxing lessons he gave Beaver back in "The Black Eye" episode.

Of all the time June spent worrying, over twenty of those were for what one might call unnecessary or illegitimate reasons. For example, eleven times, she worried about Beaver being late. Many other times her worries were about girls Wally, and to a lesser extent, Beaver, were involved with. There are times when a mother should worry about the girl her son is dating, but sometimes she worried about simple things like finding a phone number in Wally's pocket in "Wally and Alma." However, June had a very good reason to worry about Frances Hobbs and the lies she told her girlfriends at the drug store about Wally in the "School Sweater" episode.

As Beaver got older, June's worries turned away from him and toward Wally. As just mentioned, a few of those had to do with the girls he liked. In "Teacher's Daughter," Beaver tells

Wally that not only is June worried, but the whole family is worried about his involvement with her. There doesn't seem to be any real reason to be concerned except for the fact that she seems to be a secret that he's kept from them. But otherwise, she's a very nice girl. A couple other times June maybe went a bit overboard with worry about Wally and a girl were in "Mother's Helper" and "Wally's Dream Girl." In each of these episodes Wally is doing what June calls "mooncapping" or "lollydolling" (see slang dictionary on page 147). This kind of behavior is very worrisome to June.

There are other times June worries about Wally's girls, and she has a good reason. The "School Sweater" episode is the first of these in which her concern and worry is justified. One of the more serious times is in "Going Steady," in which Wally and Evelyn Boothby are going out and have a dinner date at Evelyn's sisters' apartment. This might give Wally ideas about being married. Oh yeah, he gets ideas about being married… he comes back home and says that marriage stuff is for the birds. Even when June has a legitimate worry about Wally and a girl, it's often all for naught.

Where did June's worries gravitate toward when the girls Wally liked were out of the picture? Mostly, they centered on driving and his friends. In "Borrowed Boat," June worries about he and Tooey fixing a motor scooter and driving it. She again worries about him driving in "Wally and Dudley." Here, she's concerned about him riding in Lumpy's old wreck. As any parent would have, she has some worries about Lumpy driving Wally up to a track meet in Ward's car in "Lumpy's Car Trouble," especially when he is late coming home. One of her biggest worries concerning driving is shown in "Wally's License," when he turns the legal age to drive and wants to get his license.

June worries about Wally getting wrong ideas from Eddie in "Eddie's Double Cross" (going steady) and "Bachelor at Large" (moving out of the house). She has a legit concern about Wally going unsupervised to a lake house with a new friend she doesn't know in "Weekend Invitation." Then, in "One of the Boys," when the Barons recruit Wally and Eddie for their social club, she's concerned they may be the wrong crowd. Ward is too, but leaves the decision to join up to Wally.

If only June knew she was a star in a situation comedy and that every struggle and problem would be solved in thirty minutes or less, she probably wouldn't have worried nearly as much.

She wasn't the only Cleaver to worry. Beaver worried the second most of all the Cleavers and then came Ward, and Wally brought up the rear. When it comes to Beaver's worries, they were sometimes big ones. He was worried about being kicked out of school in "Beaver Gets 'Spelled." In "Voodoo Magic," he was worried about Eddie being cursed by the voodoo doll he made. Lumpy has Beaver very worried in "The Lost Watch." In this episode, Lumpy threatens Beaver with the police. Eddie gets Beaver worried that the police will take away his father in "Beaver's Library Book." Beaver also demonstrates that parents can cause a child to worry when he's concerned about Wally in "Wally Goes Steady." In "Beaver's Report Card," he says what many people think today, "I'm just worried about getting through tomorrow." His worries were typically very reasonable for a child.

To round out this chapter, a couple of Ward and Wally's worries are in order. Ward is worried about a job the boys take in "Cat Out of the Bag." His worry is justified when the boys let Puff-Puff, the cat they are taking care of, get loose and he runs away, only to be found in a tree later that evening. Ward is very concerned, or worried, that Beaver is not taking his schooling serious enough in "Beaver's I.Q." Finally, Ward is quite worried when Wally confides to him about being involved in a "triangle" which involves an older woman in "Tennis, Anyone?"

For Wally, his worries are few and far between, but when they come, they usually involve school or a girl. In "Wally's Test," his teacher calls him at home. Wally says, "Anytime a teacher calls you up at night, you've got something to worry about." He worries about school again in

"Teacher's Daughter" because Eddie has convinced him that if he breaks Julie Foster's heart, his teacher, Mr. Foster, will give him a bad grade.

We are all human and because of that, we worry. As I mentioned at the beginning of this chapter, some fans say June worried too much. What that demonstrates is a mother who cares. Can you imagine having a mother who never or rarely worries? That would be awful. But like June, we can let our worries get a little out of control sometimes. It happened to June. It happens to me. It probably happens to you too.

65

WANTS

There's something a lot of parents tell us, and that is to know the difference between a need and a want. There are a lot of things that we want, but how many of those wants are actually things we need? The percentage is likely to be very low. While not an exhaustive list, below you will find a number of different things that the characters on *Leave it to Beaver* want. As you read the items listed, see if you can identify which of them are also needs. You'll also notice in this list that not everything a character wants is a physical thing. Sometimes a want is a desire to go someplace or have someone come over and spend the night or something else that is more abstract like world peace… well, that last one is never stated in the series, but it's nice to think about. These wants are focused on Wally and Beaver. Sure, Ward and June want things too, like a hunting jacket for Ward ("The Bank Account") and a dishwasher for June ("Beaver's Poem"), but we'll focus on the boys in this chapter.

Beaver and Wally

There are quite a few times when Wally and Beaver want things, and in the first two seasons, it's often the same thing. We find this in multiple episodes and sometimes it's an actual physical item and at other times it is to go someplace. They both want baseball related items in "Water, Anyone?" and "The Bank Account." In the former, they want baseball uniforms, and, in the latter, they want baseball gloves. While "The Paper Route" episode has them asking Ward for their own bicycle, probably so they can ride to baseball games.

In "The Pipe," Wally and Beaver say they want something a bit odd, or at lcast June thinks it's strange. They want an egg in a milk bottle. To that end, they are softening an egg by soaking it in vinegar. But why would they want an egg in a milk bottle wonders June. Beaver has the perfect answer for a child… "Because nobody else has one."

There are a couple other times we see the boys both wanting the same thing. In "The Visiting Aunts," June welcomes Aunt Martha and her friend Mrs. Hathaway. They stay for lunch and that messes up the plans of Beaver and Wally. They had both wanted to go to a carnival with the guys (Lumpy, Chester and Tooey). Those plans are derailed temporarily. Instead of going with the guys in the afternoon, the entire Cleaver family visits the carnival in the evening. They even eat Doggie Burgers at the Chuckwagon restaurant.

In "Happy Weekend," the boys plans are ruined once again, this time by Ward. Both Beaver and Wally want to see *Jungle Fever* at the Olympic Theater. It's the last weekend the movie will be showing in Mayfield, and they don't want to miss it. Ward won't budge. The entire family is going to Shadow Lake, a four-hour trip away from Mayfield to have a happy weekend, whether the boys like it or not. They do watch some of *Jungle Fever* through a pair of binoculars while away in the mountains. They see it on a drive-in movie theater screen. The boys eventually have a good time at the lake and mountains, despite their plans going awry.

The episode "Next Door Indians" sees Wally and Beaver wanting different things, but with money that will come from a single source. For that matter, Tooey and Eddie also have access to this newfound source of wealth. They find garnets on the vacant lot across from the Cleaver house. They all believe they will be rich. Wally wants to buy a sporting goods store and an amusement park. Beaver wants to get a gold tooth. Tooey wants to buy the biggest automobile in the world with red leather upholstery. Eddie wants to buy a great big house and get his dad to quit his job. Wow! That Eddie is so nice. He then says he'll put his dad on an allowance.

Beaver and Wally get the opportunity to want things from their father for the same reason in "New Doctor." Wally gets sick first, then Beaver gets sick the next day. Ward ends up wondering if Beaver got Wally's illness or if he just got the idea to be sick from Wally. It's the latter. But before that, each boy has a list of wants for him that he fulfills. For Wally, his list includes bicycle tape and a pint of chocolate chip ice cream. The next day, Beaver's list includes turtle food and a pint of chocolate chip ice cream.

Beaver

When a child wants something like the coolest toy for Christmas and instead gets a package of underwear, that's a big disappointment. Beaver experiences a similar disappointment in "Beaver's Short Pants." Aunt Martha, who is in town watching over the boys and Ward while June is helping her sister Peggy with a new baby, is the one who provides the disappointment. She takes Beaver down to the clothing store after lunch. Beaver thinks he might be getting the black leather jacket with the eagle on the back which he's wanted for quite a while. He soon finds out that isn't exactly what she has in mind. Instead of a black leather jacket, he gets some black short pants and matching jacket, along with a very proper bowtie. Beaver's disappointment turns to terror a couple days later when he is made to wear the short pants to school. Ward saves the day in the end, but not before Beaver gets into a fight at school.

While Beaver did not get the black leather jacket he wanted, there are a couple clothing items he wanted that he did that he did get. In "Beaver's Sweater," as he and Larry are walking downtown, they see a genuine Eskimo sweater in a shop window. Beaver and Larry both want one. After some discussion with his parents, June takes Beaver to get the sweater. Beaver wanted this sweater so much that he uses his own money to purchase it. Soon after arriving to school wearing his new genuine Eskimo sweater, he sees Judy Hensler walking the hall wearing the same sweater. Larry informs Beaver that he bought a girls' sweater… Beaver then mentions the worst part… "and with my own money too."

Beaver's next wearable want is a jacket just like the one his friend Richard Rickover owns. He gets the jacket soon after he expresses this want to his parents. It doesn't turn out to be a girls' jacket, so Beaver is safe there, but when Richard loses his jacket, he gets Beaver to help him out of a tough jam. Every afternoon, he throws the jacket out the window and lets Richard take it home so his mom doesn't know he lost his jacket. Richard then brings it back to Beaver the following morning and Beaver pulls it up by a rope to his room. You guessed it, they get caught and Richard eventually finds his lost jacket.

The final clothing want to mention is Beaver's desire for a new suit. This is actually a want and a need. Beaver's growing and he needs a new suit. But he wants a new suit for only one reason, a girl. He's about to go on his first date in a dancing school sponsored event. He helps June with the dishes so he could ask her for a new suit, and she agrees he could use a new suit. The suit works out well, but the date…. It was going fine until Betsy left Beaver to dance with Billy McKinzie, but that was Beaver's own fault for not asking any other girls if they would dance with him.

A few times, Beaver's wants trend toward the more violent side, not really violent, but weaponry. This first occurs in "Wally's Present" when Larry shows him a bow and arrow set at the store. Beaver's there to get a camera for Wally, but Larry convinces him that Wally doesn't deserve the camera since he didn't invite Beaver to hang out with him for his birthday. This turns into a mini disaster after Larry breaks the bow and arrow set on the way home. In "Beaver's Pigeons," Beaver is mentioned as wanting a tomahawk that was used in Custer's Last Stand which cost $1.98. Sounds like a gyp to me and it's not made clear in the episode whether or not he ever did get such a tomahawk. Fast forward to "Beaver Finds a Wallet" and Beaver makes a list of many things he's going to get if no one claims the wallet from the police. Among the items is a sword. We see with the above-mentioned items, that Beaver Cleaver is a typical boy.

Animals are also among the various things Beaver wants throughout the series. In two specific episodes, animals are the focus of the plot. In "Beaver's Pigeons," he never interacts with his birds. Beaver comes down with the chicken pox at the beginning of the episode and the pigeons are brought home by Ward, and Wally must take care of them. An interesting note about this episode is that in the January 10, 1959 issue of the San Mateo Times, the Bob Foster TV column mentions that actor Jerry Mathers has come down with the chicken pox and the writers of *LITB* had to revise the script to accommodate him. This coincides with the time the "Beaver's Pigeons" episode would have been filmed.[99] The rest of the episode contains good news and bad news. Beaver gets over the chicken pox and his pigeons die. At least it wasn't the other way around. In the episode "Three Boys and a Burro," Beaver wants to go in thirds on a burro they see for sale. Gilbert, Richard and Beaver will each chip in to own their very own burro. This is another one of those wants of Beavers that does not go the way he had hoped. Pepe the burro destroys everything in his path. He is eventually sold to the brother-in-law of Ward's co-worker. In another episode an animal Beaver wants is not a part of the plot but mentioned as a want. In "Wally's Big Date," Beaver says he wants 15 cents so he can have half interest in Gilbert's garter snake.

Some miscellaneous things Beaver wants from time to time, that aren't relevant to the plots of the episodes in which they are mentioned include colored pencils in "A Horse Named Nick," flashlight batteries in "Wally, the Lifeguard," Gilbert's German war helmet in "Beaver's Rat," and a surfboard in two different episodes, "One of the Boys" and "The Late Edition."

Outside of the surfboards Beaver wants, there are some other pricey items he wants his dad to either give him, or in a couple cases, he tries to earn money to buy them himself. Beaver wants an outboard motor in "The School Picture." It won't even cost money, just 350 books of trading stamps. That's a lot more than the one book of trading stamps it will take to get a basketball he also wants. Two episodes later, in "Beaver's Frogs," Beaver wants a $25.00 canoe. Like most of the things Beaver wants, he doesn't get the canoe. In "Beaver's Birthday," Beaver wants a toy car with a gasoline engine. It costs nearly $10.00, and he buys it with the birthday money Uncle Billy sends him. Although he's allowed to get what he wants with his money, he should've told his parents first. Other high-priced items wanted by Beaver include professional racing ice skates in "Beaver's Ice Skates," and in "Beaver's Typewriter," he wants, you guessed it, a typewriter. But he has a good reason for wanting a typewriter, it's to do his schoolwork.

Some final wants to look at for Beaver include things he'd like to do. He wants Ward to play catch with him in "The Book Report," wants Gilbert to spend the night in "Wally Stays at Lumpy's," wants to ride his bike to school with Larry and Whitey in "Beaver's Bike," (Don't let him Ward!), and wants to keep the car he wins in the raffle in "Beaver's Big Contest."

A final compound want from Beaver is his wanting three different things for his new

---

[99] Foster, Bob. "Bob Foster." *San Mateo Times*. January 10, 1959.

football team. He wants a football helmet, a sweatshirt with numbers on it and football pants. Through the kindness of his father, Beaver gets all the things he wants for his team and more. He also gets Eddie Haskell as an assistant coach and his team gets clobbered. But that's what he gets for playing football in baseball season.

Wally

There are very few things that Wally wants that are small. There is the time he wants a fishing reel in "The Train Trip" and new football shoes in "Beaver's House Guest," and he wants to purchase Eddie's father's rowing machine in "Beaver and Ivanhoe." He also makes an outlandish request when he says he wants a monkey in "Beaver Takes a Bath" and a parrot in "Baby Picture" that he could keep in the bird cage he got out of MacGregor's trash.

The things that Wally mostly wants are things to do or places to go. For example, he wants to go to Bellport Military Academy after Johnny Franklin comes over in "Boarding School." Wally wants Eddie Haskell to spend the night in "Beaver's House Guest" and Eddie talks him into wanting to buy his own suit, by himself, in "Wally's Suit." As for going places, in the "Beaver and Violet" episode, he talks about wanting to go to Hawaii if he wins a contest he's entering. In "The Cookie Fund," Wally wants to go on a trip with his science teacher and other classmates to Mexico. Then, later in the series, in "Mistaken Identity," Wally wants to take a cross-country bus trip, similar to the one Beaver takes in "Beaver Sees America."

What growing boy does not want his own car? That's probably Wally's biggest want, a car. This is seen in two episodes, "Wally's Car," (before he has a license), and "Wally Buys a Car." But before he gets his own car, he wants to borrow his dad's new car to take a date to a dance. He's given permission but pushing Lumpy's heap breaks the headlight and causes some body damage in "Wally's Car Accident."

Of all the wants above, there's possibly one need, and that's a new suit for Beaver. Oh, Yes, turtle food was necessary too. But that's what makes life great, getting things you want, but don't absolutely need. As you probably noticed in the lists, there are many things the boys wanted that were never had by the boys. That's another part of life.

There's more that can be said about wants the boys have, and you'll find it at http://leaveittobeaverbooks.com. While you're there, sign up for website updates and to be eligible for free *Leave it to Beaver* prizes.

66

TRAVEL, TRIPS AND VACATIONS

A family vacation is always nice, except for the problems that may arise. Look at any of the Vacation movies from *National Lampoon* if you want some examples of what could go wrong. In *Leave it to Beaver,* the Cleaver's most often take weekend trips. The ones that take real vacations are the Rutherfords. They're the family on the show who really likes to travel.

Let's look closer at the travel that is undertaken by characters on the show. Some of the trips the Cleavers take result in very entertaining times for them, and very entertaining times for the viewers. After all, if they had not gone out of town in "Beaver Takes a Bath," I seriously doubt that tub would have run over. It just wouldn't have happened if June was at home.

By far, the biggest trips on the show were the vacations taken by Fred and Geraldine Rutherford. These were taken in season one when Fred's wife had not yet become Gwendolyn, (more on that in another chapter). The first we hear about such trips is in the episode which introduces Lumpy, appropriately called, "Lumpy Rutherford." When the Rutherfords come over to play cards after Fred was waylaid in the driveway with barrel hoops, he talks about their vacation to Peru and Ecuador. As Ward mentions, he's talked about that trip the last six times they've played cards together. Mentioned in this episode is also a trip they took to Mexico on some previous vacation. Fred and Geraldine are on vacation later in season one when they visit Germany and send Ward and his family a souvenir pipe, called a meerschaum pipe ("The Pipe"). They also take a vacation to London. Ward tells June about a postcard he sent the office of Buckingham Palace ("Wally, the Lifeguard). So, for Fred, that's four vacations, South America, Mexico, Germany and London.

We'll get to the Cleavers, but let's see who else traveled to far off places in *Leave it to Beaver*. Believe it or not, those haughty Hansons traveled to Hawaii the year prior to their appearance in the "Wally and Alma" episode. In "Substitute Father," Richard Rickover says his dad traveled to Canada the previous year. Not sure if that was for work but could have been since he said it in relation to Beaver saying his dad went to St. Louis for work.

Uncle Billy is the Cleaver family member who has traveled the most outside of America. He mentions in "Uncle Billy's Visit," that he has some gifts for the boys from his last trip to the Far East. In this same episode, he gives June a gift he picked up in Paris. In the "Uncle Billy" episode, he speaks of taking Ward when he was young, down to Mexico to go sail fishing. He also says he has traveled all the way to Alaska.

Ward has traveled quite a bit on his own. When Ward's travel is referenced, it seems to imply that he did it alone or he's quite specific about that fact as in "Train Trip," when he mentions he traveled to Chicago when he was Wally's age. He also travels to St. Louis for work in "Substitute Father and is mentioned as having traveled to Seattle in "Eddie, the Businessman." The only travel June seems to have done without Ward is flying on an airplane to visit her sister Peggy in "Beaver's Short Pants," she mentions traveling to New Mexico with Aunt Martha ("Kite Day") and she went to New York when she was young and had lots of fun ("Beaver's Big Contest"). In this episode, June may give her best line in the entire series. Wally says, "Gee, a guy never thinks of his mother having a good time. She seems quite exasperated when she replies, "I wasn't born a mother." That line is priceless!

Ward and June traveled many times, although most of those getaways were only regional weekend trips. The one time they seem to have taken a real vacation was, at least according to the timeline of the show, the summer before the first season aired. This time span is determined by Wally saying to June in "Beaver's Sweater" (S2. E31) that she and Ward went out of their way "a couple summers ago" to look at the Grand Canyon. For a moment, viewers watching the "Pet Fair" will think this loving couple took one of their first vacations to San Francisco in 1939. But after Ward says something to her about remembering that trip, she tells him, "We were never in San Francisco."

Ward and June go out of town a few times without the boys. In "Beaver Takes a Bath," they travel to Freeport for a work conference being held by Ward's job. We also see them go out of town with their friends, the Haneys ("Wally's Car Accident"). The Haneys will be doing the driving which allows Wally to borrow the car on Friday night. The Millers also invite the Cleavers on a weekend getaway. This one to a lake house and the timing is perfect because Uncle Billy is in town to watch over the boys (Uncle Billy's Visit"). The other time Ward and June go by themselves out of town it's to see Wally compete in a football game against Lynwood ("Borrowed Boat").

The boys travel on their own when they visit Aunt Martha in the episode "Train Trip." Talk about trouble, they find it in this episode. Then there's the time Wally accompanies Beaver to Crystal Falls to see his friend Billy Peyton in "The Bus Ride." Unfortunately, Beaver only makes it halfway to Crystal Falls with Wally. He winds up heading back to Mayfield on the wrong bus after a stopover halfway to their destination. In "Beaver the Magician," Beaver goes for the weekend to visit Aunt Martha. However, that trip is cut short when he has to come back early to prove to Bengie he isn't a rock. Beaver also takes a trip by himself in the aptly named episode, "Beaver Sees America." Gilbert goes along, but no one in Beaver's family travels with him. This is just for teenagers and it's a great way to get Beaver away from that really advanced girl Mary Margaret Matthews

For more information on travel, trips, or vacations seen on *Leave it to Beaver* please visit http://leaveittobeaverbooks.com.

67

VISITORS TO THE CLEAVER HOUSE

The Cleaver house is a place of refuge and a place of peace. It's the type of home I would've wanted to visit when I was a kid. As the product of a broken home, then another and another, the Cleaver house was a pure paradise to me. Sure, there were some arguments occasionally, some raised voices when the boys misbehaved, but it was ideal that there were no rowdy neighbors and the backyard in their second home was spacious and very nice. Who wouldn't want to visit their home?

Wally and Beaver's friends were around their house quite often. We rarely see Wally or Beaver at any of their friends' homes. Of course, that's most likely due to the fact the show was called *Leave it to Beaver* and featured the Cleaver family. The homes of Larry, Eddie and Lumpy are seen a few times, even Richard's home is seen ("Three Boys and a Burro") and Gilbert's house is seen in that episode and a couple others, Beaver visits Whitey's home once ("Lonesome Beaver").

It is understood that Wally and Beaver's friends visited their home, but there were many other people who also visited, friends that were only seen in one or two episodes, friends of Ward and June, city workers, other service people, babysitters, maids, the list of people is monumental, and I hope you enjoy it. The list includes named individuals, and a few of the unnamed individuals who visited. Some of these visitors are not seen, as they wait out in a vehicle for one of the boys.

Season 1 (in order)

Fred Rutherford, Lt. Gus the fireman (in car waiting), Chester Anderson, Mr. Anderson (in car waiting), Aunt Martha, George Haskell, Miss Canfield, Charles Fredericks, Gwendolyn Rutherford, Herb and Janet Wilson, Helen Wilson, Mr. Norton, Mrs. Bennett, Mary Ellen Rogers, Mr. Rogers (in car waiting), Dr. Richardson, Dr. Bradley, Whitey, Judy, Mrs. Mondello, Mr. Mondello (in car waiting), taxicab driver,

Season 2 (in order)

Chuey Varela, Carlotta Varela, Enrique Varela, milk man, Aunt Martha, Mrs. Claudia Hathaway, Charlie the bug man, Mrs. Bellamy, Bengie Bellamy, Dr. Bradley, Miss Cooper, Gus the fireman, board of health official, rendering man, Mary Ellen Rogers, Mrs. Rogers (in car waiting), Mr. Rogers (in car waiting), Mr. Johnson (real estate man)

Season 3 (in order)

Mrs. Mondello, Judy Hensler, Mrs. Bellamy, Bengie Bellamy, Fred Rutherford, Mrs. Mondello, Larry Mondello's sister (in car waiting), Andy Hadlock, Mr. and Mrs. Hanson, police officer Sgt. Peterson, Harold Hathaway (The Duke), Mr. Hanson (from the nursery, unseen)

Season 4 (in order)

Bread man, milk man (both unseen), Mrs. Murdock, Chuckie Murdock, Mr. Franklin from the Worldwide Academy of Music, Uncle Billy Cleaver, Mr. & Mrs. Waters, Jackie Waters, Dr. Kirby, Margie Manners, Mrs. Manners, Lt. Barnes, Officer Medford, Fred Rutherford, Mr. Bellamy, cab driver

Season 5 (in order)

Tom and Judy Henderson, Evelyn Boothby, Ray and Don (Wally's friends), Mr. Garvey, Georgia Baston, Fred Rutherford, Mary Tyler, Mr. Hill

Season 6 (in order)

Paper girl, Mr. Tyler (dry cleaning man), Mr. Jeff (a tramp), Fred Rutherford

When looking at the above list, season by season, it is interesting to see the number of visitors to the Cleaver house drop as the seasons progress. This may have been just because the boys were getting older and more of the episodes featured action outside or away from the home. Whatever may be the case, it was always fun to see visitors to the Cleaver house. As fans of the *Leave it to Beaver* TV show, the Cleaver house is someplace any fan would want to spend a good amount of time, just hanging out with Wally or Beaver and enjoying some good talk with Ward and June around the dinner table, these are all things that could make any childhood memorable.

Visit http://leaveittobeaverbooks.com for more information on visitors to the Cleaver house.

68

WARD'S CHORES

We know that June Cleaver had a lot of chores to do. There is an entire chapter dedicated to her chores within the pages of this book. So, it's only fair that while the number of chores Ward does is not nearly as much as June's, he should have his own chapter. His are usually done on Saturday, instead of every day of the week like June. Still, after working hard all week at whatever occupation he had, it must be tiring for June to put him to work on the weekends.

One of the first tasks Ward must do is fix cords. In "New Neighbors," Ward fixes the toaster cord, by replacing it with a new one because as he tells Beaver, "Your mother always pulls it out by the cord instead of by the plug. In "The Perfume Salesmen," Ward is in the living room fixing the cord on the lamp when the boys come home from not selling any perfume. They go upstairs and Ward looks to June and pleads with her, "Dear, please don't pull them out by the cord." The cord problems continue in "The Price of Fame." After working on the doorbell and getting that fixed, Ward then walks over to a lamp and asks her if it's the one that needs the cord fixed. Since there are no more cords that need fixed after they move to their new house in season three, it's obvious June learned to no longer pull small appliances and lamps out by the cord.

Not all of Ward's chores are solitary. He also enlists the boys to help sometimes. This happens in "Beaver's Old Friend," when the Cleaver men are cleaning out the garage. In this episode, they are supposed to be throwing away junk, but Beaver rescues an old stuffed teddy bear from the trash and Ward rescues his old shot put. He also has Wally and Beaver help with the yard, most often they do it on their own, but in "Bachelor at Large," Wally is raking the front yard while Beaver and Ward trim hedges on the side of the house. In "Eddie, the Businessman," Ward warns Beaver that with Wally working weekends, that Beaver will have to help him with the lawn and garden. Other times when Ward works, or has plans to work in the yard alone, include the time in "My Brother's Girl" when he wants to clip the hedges but finds someone had been cutting tar paper with the clippers, the opening scene in "Beaver and Chuey" when he is raking the backyard, and the Saturday when he plays an extra nine holes in the "Wally's Car" episode so he wouldn't feel obliged to work in the yard if he arrived home too early. Another chore in which the boys help is painting the garage. One time, Ward must leave in the middle of the job and the boys ask if they could finish for him. Obviously, this episode is titled, "The Garage Painters."

Ward has many chores that take place outside the house that do not involve mowing the yard or trimming hedges. These include barely stepping outside the house in "The Price of Fame" and fixing the doorbell to going to the garage to polish the car in "Beaver and Chuey." Other outside the house chores include painting the patio table in "Beaver's Newspaper," painting the patio furniture with Wally in "Beaver's Accordion," painting the lawn chairs and the picnic table in "The Silent Treatment," with help from Beaver, cleaning screens in "Most Interesting Character," which Beaver does not think is very interesting and Ward paints screens in "Wally's Dinner Date." Ward brings in logs for the fireplace in "Beaver, the Magician," he fixes a burned-out lamp on the front porch in "Beaver's Dance," and one night, in "Beaver's Autobiography," Ward takes the trash out.

June is not usually very demanding of her husband, but there are a couple times that June has multiple tasks for Ward to perform. In "Beaver's Team," June's "to do" list for Ward include fixing the kitchen window, which is sticking, changing the burned-out lightbulb in the basement, getting rid of the funny looking bugs on the roses, fixing the vacuum cleaner and buying some wax to wax the kitchen floor. It's not certain if she only wants him to buy the wax so she can wax the floor or for him to do that too. The other episode where June gives him a rather long list, although shorter than the previous one, is in "The Parking Attendants." After she has him fix the towel rack in the kitchen, she says she needs an extra broom holder in the closet, the boys' dresser has a stuck drawer, the doorstop is lose in the bathroom, and the sliding door won't open.

In "Weekend Invitation," June has Ward wax the kitchen floor. That may be the biggest task she asks him to complete. The rest of the episodes which mention a chore or task are smaller and less time consuming and include, filling the lighters with lighter fluid in "Baby Picture," fixing a heating vent in "The Boat Builders," fixing a teapot in "Beaver Says Good-Bye," fixing a kitchen cabinet in "June's Birthday," draining the bottom of the water heater in "Larry's Club," and fixing a stopped up sink in "Beaver's Doll Buggy."

I don't know about you, but just compiling this list has me tired and in need of a nap. If you'd like to see more about Ward's chores, visit http://leaveittobeaverbooks.com.

69

WEATHER

No matter where you believe Mayfield is located, you'll have to admit the weather in Mayfield is generally warm, as the coolest it typically gets is "jacket weather." There's not much rain and winter simply doesn't seem to exist. Sounds like southern California to me. As Jerry Mathers has said on numerous occasions, "Mayfield is a state of mind and anywhere you want it to be." The producers also went to great lengths to not to show Mayfield as in any particular state, but let's get back to the weather.

I think the following sums up the weather in Mayfield the best:

> This week there was no weather, so the newspaper doesn't have any. Next week, the paper will have weather, if there is any.
>
> - The Maple Drive News

Although, Mayfield weather is typically the same in every episode as is mentioned so elegantly above by Beaver in his newspaper, there are quite a few times in which there is what one would call "weather." This is most often seen in the form of rain and usually that rain is a good soaky shower or a thunderstorm. A closer look at the weather in such episodes is definitely in order.

The following episodes are the ones in which rain is seen falling or spoken of as currently falling in Mayfield:

"The Clubhouse" – Ward looks outside the kitchen window and sees a heavy rain falling. He laments that the weatherman was wrong again. Good to know that's not only a modern-day occurrence. The newspaper had said it was going to be fair and warmer, but they missed that forecast by a lot. The boys are bored until Beaver looks out the window and sees Tooey and Eddie running across the lawn. Wally remarks, "That crazy Tooey is wearing rubbers!"

"Beaver and Poncho" – At the beginning of this episode, June and Ward are watching out the living room window waiting for the boys to come home. They are late because of the afternoon storm. Ward sees Wally jump right into a puddle. Beaver arrives a few moments later because he stopped at Larry's after watching a man take a car out of the mud. He's wearing Larry's raincoat and he has his jacket rolled up, holding it under his arm. Obviously, at least to Ward, he's hiding something. He sure is hiding something.

"Tenting Tonight" – Ward feels bad after having to work on the Saturday of a promised camping trip and letting the boys down on what was supposed to be a fun weekend. He works all day Saturday, even coming home late, but when he arrives home, he finds the boys are camping in the back yard. They are excited about camping out, even if it is only about fifty feet from the back door. The one thing they had not counted on was rain, but it pours down on them. It floods their tent and in the middle of the night, they go inside to take cover and go back to the tent when it stops raining. Few things could be so fun for a child.

"The Garage Painters" – The TV is busted or as Wally says, "The tube goofed out." And it's raining. What are the boys to do all weekend with no TV inside and rain outside? Well, Ward has an idea… read a book. When Beaver hears that suggestion, he wonders why his dad is punishing them. Rain doesn't play a giant role in this episode, but it is the impetus to get the boys reading *Tom Sawyer* which then inspires them to paint the garage doors.

"School Sweater" – This is a favorite episode of many. It's got rain, a girl, and great lines. After a Thursday night basketball game in which Wally scores two points in three minutes before fouling out, he gives his school letterman sweater to a girl who tells him she's cold. The next day, it begins raining in the morning and it continues until at least the afternoon. Ward and June suggest he wear his sweater to school. He can't because he doesn't have it. He's told to bring his sweater home. That's his plan when he sees Frances Hobbs at school. But when he asks to have it back, she tells him that it's still raining, and he wouldn't want her to get "all soaky" on the way home. She promises to bring it to school the next day. Eddie then reminds Wally that the next day is Saturday.

"Beaver's Monkey" – When Beaver brings home a new pet rat, June objects. Ward tells him he must get rid of it. He tells Beaver that if it was a normal pet, something like a cat or dog, he could maybe keep it. At the grocery store, the next day, Beaver sees an ad for a free monkey. He tells Larry that a monkey is a normal pet. He arranges to get the monkey, complete with its own cage. The monkey named Stanley is allowed to stay at the Cleaver house. Unfortunately, he escapes while Beaver is at school and that night it storms, and the temps are cool and Stanley is out in the elements. He eventually is found and because of the rain is shivering and very sick. No worries though, he ends up nursed back to health and in a new home, the Mayfield Zoo.

Rain plays a role of some sort in the plots of all the above-mentioned episodes. The role it plays ranges from causing the boys to think about things to do ("The Clubhouse"), being the cause for them to read a book ("The Garage Painters") to being the reason for Stanley the Monkey's illness and his resulting care given to him ("Beaver's Monkey"). But even the threat of rain could play a role, and does play a role in several episodes, and here are a few of those below:

"Beaver Gets 'Spelled" – When Beaver hides in the tree near the end of the episode, he reasons that it may rain so he should come down and get his raincoat.

"Beaver's Short Pants" – When Ward helps Beaver change out of the short pants in the garage, he notices Aunt Martha gave him an umbrella. He tells Beaver, it looks a little like rain and says he should take the umbrella.

"Lumpy Rutherford" – Beaver tells Wally that he hopes it rains because he thinks Lumpy won't bully them if it rains.

"Beaver's Graduation" – Eddie visits Wally and Ward opens the door. He tells Ward that he rolled up his car windows because it looked like rain. Afterward, June tells him the weatherman says no rain for five days.

While not essential to the plots, there are a couple additional episodes in which it rains. In "Lonesome Beaver," June bothers Ward at the country club while he's playing golf and tells Ward it looks like rain up north where Wally is camping with the Boy Scouts. Wally comes home drenched because it did rain. Another time is in "The Paper Route." Midway through the episode, Wally comes home after delivering papers in a storm. He comes home to get another list of customers because the one he had was wet and the names ran together. Ward then takes him out in the car to finish his deliveries.

There is other weather in Mayfield, but it is seldom spoken of by the characters. That weather is the temperature, both hot and cold. There are only a few mentions of this phenomena in Mayfield. By far, the biggest, is in "Water, Anyone?" The heat in this episode is the background to the entire plot. Other mentions of temperatures are in the cool and cold range but are only secondary to the plots of both "Borrowed Boat" in which Ward and June are seen wearing heavy coats and "Uncle Billy's Visit" where Wally speaks about there being no reason to freeze while driving around town.

There are other times that weather is mentioned, but not necessarily seen. One of those times is mentioned above when Beaver wishes it would rain in "Lumpy Rutherford." But other such times include "Kite Day" when Beaver wants it to rain, so he tries to find out who in town might be able to do an Indian rain dance. In "Happy Weekend," Beaver asks if he can bring comics on their trip to Shadow Lake in case it does rain. Allusions to rain include Beaver saying the slippers Fred Rutherford sent them last year smell when it rains and when June cleans out the downstairs closet, she finds many galoshes and a couple raincoats that don't belong to them.

How do you close out a chapter that basically consists of rain on a happy note? Well, you can go to the "Beaver and Chuey" episode and quote the words of Enrique Varela. In his somewhat broken English, he says, "It is good weather we are …obtaining." Yes, that was a very nice day in Mayfield.

To find out even more about the weather in Mayfield, you can always go on over to the http://leaveittobeaverbooks.com website to learn more. Don't forget to sign up for updates so you'll be eligible for free *Leave it to Beaver* prizes that will be given away after every 100th sale of *The World Famous Beaverpedia*.

70

LOST EPISODES

One of the more interesting things revealed in many episodes of *Leave it to Beaver* are those times or memories shared about something that happened in the past that were never shown in an episode. Typically, the memories that are recalled seem to have happened months or a year or two earlier. I call these, "The Lost Episodes." Sometimes they are just minor mentions of something that would be no greater than a scene in an episode, like the time Beaver found one of June's old flowery hats and insisted on wearing it while walking to church with Wally ("Wally's Haircomb"). However, sometimes, these memories could be turned into an entire new episode of *Leave it to Beaver*. I guess you call that fan fiction. Once, Wally mentions that Beaver, a year earlier, had played a dwarf in the school play in first grade ("The Haircut"). I can see an entire new script written about that, couldn't you? Another time, Ward speaks of the time when an English Bulldog moved in down the street and Beaver hid under the bed because he was so scared of it ("New Neighbors"). This memory would make a good script too. Maybe turning some of the following memories into scripts could be something I tackle later, but until then, we can simply take our time and enjoy the memories of the characters written about here. Maybe your June, or your Ward, can pour you a cup of coffee and then sit down in the living room with you on the sofa and you can both enjoy these memories, just a thought. Or if you must, like me, just enjoy them alone. Word of warning, the memories listed below only scratch the surface, there are many more not recorded in this chapter.

Mary Ellen Rogers Lost Episodes

There are three memories that could be part of episodes we've never seen that include Wally's girl interest Mary Ellen Rogers. The first of these is found in "Her Idol" from season two. When talking about girls, Beaver mentions to Wally that he walked Mary Ellen Rogers home from school. Wally shrugs it off and then Beaver says, "You used to throw rocks at her." It would be interesting to see how a scene like that might play out, but it's difficult to picture Wally acting so immature. No, I am not condoning violence against women, and neither were the writers of the episode.

The second of these Mary Ellen memories is found in the season five episode, "Brother vs. Brother." This is when Beaver brings home a new girl from school and they play Monopoly up in his room. Her name is Mary Tyler and Beaver really likes her. Her affection switches from Beaver to Wally when he walks into the room. Wally later talks to June about Beaver going flaky over a girl. She reminds him that when he was Beaver's age, he used to hang by his toes from the tree outside their house, waiting for Mary Ellen Rogers to walk by. "Hmm, forgot about that," he says.

A final memory of Mary Ellen Rogers, this one, a memory from Wally, was about one time when they were in the malt shop. This comes from the season six episode, "Beaver, the Sheepdog." He tells Beaver that she began crying and right into her hot fudge sundae. In explaining why it happened, Wally says he was just looking at her. She told him it was the kind of look that said she was too fat to be eating sweets.

The Angela Valentine Lost Episodes

While there are many references of Angela Valentine throughout the series, here are a couple that could make good scenes in episodes that were never filmed. In "Beaver's Accordion,"

June finds a Campfire Girl t-shirt and she reminds Ward that Beaver wore the shirt home from Angela's birthday party when he was about seven years old. Someone had pushed him into the Valentine's fishpond. Mrs. Valentine sent him home in that t-shirt and a pair of pedal pushers. The second memory that could be an entire "lost episode" is related by Beaver to Wally in "Eddie Quits School." He says he told the guys he was going to kiss Angela Valentine. He got so scared that he pretended to be sick for two days. He figured she might croak in that time, or something else might happen.

The Beaver Lost Episodes

There are plenty of these to choose from, but I narrowed it down to just five episodes. The first is a memory Beaver has of a field trip he recollects in "Teacher Comes to Dinner." The field trip involves food and Miss Landers too. At the breakfast table Beaver and Wally are comparing teachers and Beaver says Miss Landers is better than Wally's teacher and tells about the field trip she took the class on to a Chinese Restaurant. Whether they had a meal or not, we don't know, bet you one thing for sure, the students at least received one fortune cookie each as a souvenir.

Here's a memory from Beaver I would have liked to have seen filmed. This memory he shares in "Wally's Test," shows what a kind person Eddie Haskell could be, when he wanted to be one. Beaver said a bunch of big guys in the eighth grade were throwing apples at he and Larry. When Eddie saw this happening, he stopped the kids and even forced one of them, Clyde Bonnefield to eat an entire rotten apple. It is unknown whether this is the older brother of Claude Bonnefield who Beaver beats out for lead in the class play in third grade.

In "Beaver's Monkey," Beaver shares two memories, sort of a bonus episode you could call it. The first memory could also be in the chapter on continuity since he mentions when he had his tonsils taken out and he not wanting to be around a bunch of strange people. For die hard *LITB* fans, you may recall that in the next season of the show, season four, is when Beaver has tonsillitis. That's a pretty good trick to pull when one has no tonsils. The second memory Beaver has in this episode, is one of he and Ward previously going to the zoo and Ward reminds him of the big, steam heated monkey house. He is trying to assure Beaver it's the place Stanley belongs and a place he'll be happy. I would've enjoyed seeing father and son enjoying a day at the zoo in an early episode of *Leave it to Beaver*.

When Wally tells Beaver he's concerned about the guys giving him the business about dating Mr. Foster's daughter in the episode aptly named, "Teacher's Daughter." Beaver then tells him of a time he remembers from the second grade when guys gave him the business. This will sound very familiar to *Leave it to Beaver* fans…. Beaver says the business, the guys were giving him, was saying he drank gutter water. He tells Wally, "… they said it so much, my stomach started feeling like I did drink gutter water." So, he had a lot in common with Violet Rutherford. Their classmates believed they both shared a love for gutter water.

A final Beaver lost episode to mention, which would have been fun to see filmed, is spoken of in "Substitute Father," when Wally goes to school to see Miss Landers about the bad word Beaver said in the hallway. When Wally first enters the room, Miss Landers thinks the two brothers are trying to pull a fast one on her. That's when Beaver says that's not what is happening and tells her how Wally is good at explaining how he shouldn't do things. He then relates a time in Sunday School the previous year when he was horsing around. He said Wally told him he shouldn't behave the way he was because he was in God's house and people would think he came from a family where nobody had respect for anything. Beaver told Miss Landers that he never did it again. It would've been great to see an episode in which there was a scene inside their church.

Wally's Lost Episodes

There are some memories of Wally's that would've made good episodes. To begin with, there was the time the Cleavers were at the lake and next door to them lived a beautiful woman named Miss Hildebrand. One summer at the lake Wally would row her across the lake to get her mail. Wally said he had a big crush on her. In fact, he says, he doesn't know if he'll ever really get over her. Beaver mentions that she's the woman who eventually married the man who smoked the pipe. Wally confirmed that was her. Wally told Beaver the memory in "Beaver's Crush," because of the way Beaver felt for Miss Canfield. This is something the two brothers share in common.

The "friendship pact" made between Wally and Beaver in season one may have been the first in the show, but not the last. Wally has a memory of a pact he once made with Lumpy and Eddie. This pact was that the three friends would get tattoos. Wally shares this with Beaver in the "Sweatshirt Monsters" episode. Beaver and his friends made a pact to wear their scary monster sweatshirts to school and he was the only one to do so, meaning he was the only one to get in trouble. Wally goes on to tell Beaver that he, Lumpy and Eddie went to watch the tattoo artist downtown through the window and after Lumpy fainted, they gave up on the idea.

A final Wally lost episode which should have been a real episode was when he, as a young boy, was scared to walk past the wooden Indian that stood outside the cigar store downtown. He tells this story to Beaver in "Beaver, the Magician," when Beaver asks Wally if he ever believed something goofy. Wally finishes his story by telling Beaver he thought it was a real Indian and he was only pretending to be made from wood so when little kids passed him, he could scalp them.

The Other House Episodes

You are probably one of those *Leave it to Beaver* fans who believe the Cleavers only lived in two houses with the boys, the house at 485 Mapleton or Maple Drive (depending on the episode) and 211 Pine Avenue or Street (depending on the episode.) According to Beaver and two of his memories, that's incorrect. The following two memories show there was another house. While neither memory would make much of an episode, just one scene in a different house, their first house, would be neat to see, or a scene of them moving into the Mapleton home.

In "Beaver's Old Friend," the boys help Ward clean out the garage. In the midst of the cleaning, Beaver finds his old friend Billy. He's an old smelly teddy bear. Beaver has fond memories of him. When Wally sees Beaver has saved Billy from the garbage man, he wonders what is so special about Billy. Beaver tells him, "Well, you remember at the **other** house... when I had the measles, and they wouldn't let you or any of the other guys in... 'cause they might get 'em?" Beaver goes on to say that Billy, given to him by Aunt Martha, was just a bear, but he believed he was a real person. The key word is "other" as in a house, other than the one in which they currently live, a house before Mapleton or Maple Drive.

The other memory of Beaver's that demonstrates they lived elsewhere before Mapleton is mentioned in "The Grass is Always Greener." Beaver asks Wally if he'd stay around and hang out with Pete and Chris, the sons of the garbage man who are coming by to spend the afternoon. Wally talks about how there is nothing to do around their house and how he's going to hang out with Tooey and Chester. Beaver agrees with him about not having anything to do around the house and says, "Yeah, there used to be a lot of stuff to do when we first moved in." I'd love to see the non-existent episode where they first move into the Mapleton house. That would be interesting.

There's so much more to read about memories that could make a good scene or an entire episode. To read more about the "lost episodes," please visit http://leaveittobeaverbooks.com.

71

CONTINUITY

Here it is, possibly the chapter you've been waiting for while reading through this entire book. It's either this one on continuity or the next one on the location of Mayfield … wait… don't go there yet. You are about to witness in this chapter many of the problems that a series bible[100] would have fixed had one existed for *Leave it to Beaver*. Unfortunately for those people who absolutely hate inconsistencies, there was no series bible, no blueprint about how the entire series and how every character interacted with one another, including every detail about each family, so no writer (of the forty plus that worked on the show over its six years) would ever add an extra brother or accidentally change a name, or give a character a memory of a pet that we, the dedicated fans of *Leave it to Beaver*, know in our heart of hearts, never existed.

On the other hand, it's fortunate that there was no series bible, at least for those who don't mind the inconsistencies found within the 234 episodes, and believe me, after months of research, they appear in almost every single episode. After all, it's the inconsistencies which give people something to talk about in those many *Leave it to Beaver* Facebook groups. The two Facebook groups in which I am most active are Bryon Nelson's "Leave it to Beaver Fan Club" and Randall Greenlee's "Leave it to Beaver Show." If there had been a series bible, many of the posts in those groups would not need to be written, because sometimes inconsistencies make for the best discussion. I think Bryon and Randall would agree.

This chapter will examine a fraction of the inconsistencies that are found within *Leave it to Beaver* episodes. You won't find anything earth shattering, but you will see some things you'll find very interesting and fun. The chapter will cover the inconsistencies by topic. Sit back, relax, and enjoy!

Animals

In "Pet Fair," we get a little insight into how responsible or irresponsible Beaver is when it comes to animals. Ward tells him he doesn't have a pet because he couldn't take care of his rabbit, I think we can assume he's talking about Henry/Henrietta. He scolds him for not being able to take care of his pigeons. We know that was not Beaver's fault, but the writers, Dale and Katherine Eunson seem not to have known. How does something like that happen? I can imagine when they were charged with writing this episode, they may have asked Bob Mosher and Joe Connelly, "Did Beaver ever have any pets?" And the reply was ... "Yeah, a rabbit and some pigeons." And off Dale and Katherine went typing up the episode, only knowing that Beaver did not have either of those pets any longer. So, they wrote what they wrote. That's just a possibility of how this inconsistency may have occurred.

With the "Beaver's Pigeons" episode referenced above, one can look at that script and see what we'd call an inconsistency. Wally says he hopes Beaver owning pigeons doesn't end up like the hamsters. Wally complains how he had to take care of them all the time and when they died, he was blamed. Now, there's another "lost episode" for you, a memory of something we've never seen or heard spoken about on the show before this mention in "Beaver's Pigeons."

---

[100] A series bible … maintains consistency as a show progresses over multiple seasons. It is something given to new writers on a show in order to provide them with an idea about where the characters are and it provides them with details about the world in which they live, in this case, it would have been for Mayfield USA.

We know what happened to the alligator in "Captain Jack," but what about the dog they were gifted with by their parents which appears in the final scene. Not an equal substitute for an alligator, but it seems he lasted just as long as the alligator, one episode. The funny thing is that Ward doesn't mention the dog when he mentions in "Pet Fair" the pets Beaver had in the past that he didn't take care of properly.

In "Beaver's Monkey," when Stanley escapes and gets stuck out in the rain, the next day when he's examined by a veterinarian, he tells the Cleavers that he's a macaque monkey and that it is at home in the tropics, not in a climate like Mayfield. Beaver later wonders how much it would cost to send a monkey to South America. Stanley would certainly be one lonely macaque monkey in South America as they are native to Asia, North Africa and Gibraltar.

When the Cleavers trap a rabbit that's been munching on flowers in June's Garden in "Beaver and Henry," they keep it in their garage. They name the rabbit Henry, but June says it would be more appropriate to name it Henrietta because SHE is pregnant. After the babies are born, Larry and Beaver are in the garage looking at them. Beaver tells Larry his dad says in a couple days they will open their eyes, but when Beaver picks one up, it has its eyes open.

Outside the Cleaver home, there is also a lack of continuity when it comes to animals. One has to look no further than their next-door neighbors, the Donaldsons. In "New Neighbors," Eddie remarks that they are creepy because they don't have any kids, no fishing poles and no dogs or cats, just a canary. But later in the season, Mr. Donaldson gets the boys to help take care of his prized and prize-winning cat, Puff, Puff, but never mentions a canary. He acts towards and speaks of the cat as if they've had it a lot longer than the eight months it's been in Mayfield time since they moved in with no dogs and cats. Not only that, but Mr. Donaldson is also now played by actor Ray Kellogg, replacing Charles H. Gray as the original Mr. Donaldson. In "Forgotten Party," late in season two, the Donaldson's now have a dog, and then in "Beaver's Old Buddy," the second Mr. Donaldson has become Mr. Waters, the father of Beaver's old buddy Jackie. It's all so confusing!

Around the Cleaver House (and another house or two)

In "Wally's Girl Trouble," Wally talks to Penny Jamison on the phone at the bottom of the stairs where Ward is practicing his putting. Wally has a sly smile on his face as he asks, "Dad, would you mind closing the door on your way out?" It's a closed swinging door through which Ward exits, it closes on its own.

The boys build a go-cart in "The State vs. Beaver," and part of their building it requires them taking the engine off the power mower. They own a power mower to cut their lawn. However, in "The Paper Route," June complains about Ward helping the boys out too much like he did when he rented a power mower to cut their lawn for them.

Inside the kitchen in "Beaver's Newspaper," June takes a coffee pot off the stove to serve Ward a new cup of hot coffee. Close ups then show both Ward and then June, their faces are shown when they say lines, the coffee pot June is holding and the cup she is pouring the coffee into are not shown. On her close up, viewers know she is pouring coffee from a pot, but when the close up goes to Ward, the coffee pot is back on the stove, and she hasn't moved.

The Cleavers move to a new house after the end of season two. They now live at 211 Pine. Wally seems to have forgotten that because when he takes the wet towels to put them in the dryer in "Beaver Takes a Bath." He takes the towels to the basement. That's where the washer and dryer are at their Mapleton Drive house. In this new house, they have a laundry room and the first time it is mentioned is in "The Spot Removers," later in the same season as "Beaver Takes a Bath."

For friends of Beaver and Wally, there are some inconsistencies too. Beaver says in "Found Money," that a rat got loose in Whitey's house. But in the next episode, "Most Interesting Character," the class must write an essay of the same name. Whitey says he knows no interesting characters because he lives in an apartment. The fact that there is a lack of continuity here is nothing new, but the idea that there are no interesting characters in an apartment complex probably surprises many of us.

Eddie Haskell spends the night at the Cleaver house in you guessed it, "Eddie Spends the Night." Wally must go retrieve Eddie after he gets mad and goes home to an empty house. Wally knocks on the door and waits for Eddie inside while he pretends to go upstairs and tell his father he's going back to the Cleavers. Fast forward to "Summer in Alaska," and we see Wally again at Eddie's house, and the front door and the interior are entirely different.

Locations or Places

In "Water, Anyone?" Beaver is speaking to Ward in the kitchen as he squeezes lemons, turning his water into lemonade, so he can charge more. Ward tells Beaver he is taking advantage of his friends by charging them for water. Beaver asks if Mr. Michaelson is his father's friend. He says yes, they went to school together. But wait, Ward is from Shaker Heights in six different episodes filmed seasons later. In season two, he is again born and raised in Mayfield in the "Most Interesting Character" episode.

June is from East St. Louis. This is discovered in "Kite Day," an episode from season four. But in season one, she is from Mayfield. In "Beaver and Poncho," she mentions that Mrs. Rayburn used to be one of her teachers and she still gets nervous around her. However, in "Beaver Gets 'Spelled," that doesn't seem to bother her one bit when she gladly meets with Mrs. Rayburn.

Wally does Beaver a big favor in "Borrowed Boat." In fact, by the time the episode is over, Wally has done him two big favors. The first is getting the coach to allow Beaver to ride on the bus with the team to their away game, and even to be able to sit on the bench and eat with the team. Beaver turns him down to go with Larry to Friend's Lake. The second favor happens when Beaver is at the police department accused of stealing a boat. Wally goes down to get him because Ward and June are out shopping. The big inconsistency here is that Friend's Lake is within walking distance of both the Mondello house and the Cleaver house. But in season one, Friend's Lake is fifty miles north of Mayfield in "Lonesome Beaver," when Wally and the scouts go camping there. Then, in "Wally, the Lifeguard," Wally takes the bus to the lake.

In "Child Care," when Puddin' Wilson locks herself in the Cleaver bathroom, the boys enlist the help of a neighbor boy Bengie Bellamy. He says he's been watching them try to get Puddin' out of the bathroom. He's been watching for a while. It seems like he was either outside somewhere or nearby in his house, watching from there. Whichever it is, he's close by. If you look to season three, it is stated that Bengie lives across the street from the Cleavers in "Larry's Club." When the Cleaver's moved, the Bellamys either moved with them, or the Cleavers stayed in their same neighborhood which is not what it seems like when the Cleavers talk about their move in "Beaver's Tree."

Ward Cleaver provides a double whammy of inconsistency in "Beaver's Accordion." Early in the episode, Ward tells June when he was about Wally's age, a girl told him he looked like the actor Melvyn Douglas. A few scenes later, Ward arrives home, June says she's glad to see him. He says, "And why not? I'm the only man on Maple Drive with eyes like Melvyn Douglas." There are two things wrong with that statement, the obvious one is that Ward and June moved away from Maple or Mapleton Drive over a year and a half earlier. The other is that the girl he mentioned earlier to June, said he looked like Melvyn Douglas, not that he had eyes like Melvyn Douglas.

The scenes of downtown Mayfield, anytime the boys are shown walking its streets, is obviously not a very big city. However, in "Wally's Car Accident," "The Grass is Always Greener," and "Beaver, the Caddy." There is stock footage that shows a huge downtown area in these episodes, portraying Mayfield as being a large city with tall buildings and busy traffic. In fact, that stock footage is of traffic in downtown Albuquerque, New Mexico with traffic on Central Avenue (Route 66).

School

Miss Canfield tells Beaver in "Beaver's Crush," that she's been teaching second grade for six months, but just six episodes earlier she was a brand-new teacher. She admits that if she had opened the drawer with a spring snake in it back when she started teaching, she may have been scared.

In "Party Invitation," a close examination of the chalk board shows that the same writing and assignments are on it as in the previous episode. The same thing happens in "Beaver and Poncho" where the information on the chalk board is the same as in the previous two episodes.

Wally regularly walks to Mayfield High School, so do Lumpy and Eddie. They aren't shown walking in season two, but a bus is never mentioned or shown, and Wally does make mention of him walking or running to or from school. So, when Larry says that his grandmother lives over by the high school in "Beaver's Guest," and exclaims, "That's six miles!" That sure is a long way for Wally to walk to school each day, and back. He's living the life of Ward Cleaver when he was a child, walking such a long distance to school. This would only apply to season two.

Ward may be wondering what to do in "Ward's Problem," but there's a much bigger problem than whether he takes Wally fishing or Beaver to his Father and Student picnic. There's a big problem in Beaver's classroom. On the day Miss Landers announces the picnic, she does so in such a manner that it stops time. The clock in the classroom in over five minutes of film time does not move one minute.

In "Mother's Helper," Wally is seen by Beaver walking hand in hand with the girl helping June keep house. She goes to Union High School and Wally attends Mayfield. But on this afternoon, they are walking together after school. Either Mayfield has two high schools, or we can chalk this up to an oversight on the part of the writers.

In "Wally's Practical Joke," when Wally is not home around the time Beaver arrives home, June asks Beaver if Wally had practice. With Wally's graduation happening in the next episode, it is highly unlikely, there would be any athletic practice of any type that late in the school year.

In the final episode of the entire series, "Family Scrapbook," after both boys have graduated timewise in the context of the series, June wonders if the boys enjoyed looking at the scrapbook filled with family photos. Ward says he doesn't know, but then remarks that it took them away from their homework for a few minutes.

People

Fred Rutherford says he has two sons in "The Black Eye," and both of them were offered football scholarships. Maybe one of those is Lumpy and he is foretelling the future. Needless to say, the family dynamics change in the Rutherford house as the seasons progress. Another inconsistent Rutherford moment is found in "The Tooth." In this episode Fred sees Ward at the dentist office and says his daughter Violet may need braces. However, in "The Black Eye," Fred is fretting because he thinks Beaver's going to punch his daughter and exclaims she has had a lot of expensive orthodontist work done.

In "Brotherly Love," Ward talks about his brother and uses the following language, "I remember my brother and I …." This is him talking about his brother, his one brother, his only brother. If he had more than one, he would've said, older brother, or younger brother. He does do this in "Beaver Becomes a Hero," when he says his older brother used to take him fishing. Just an oversight, but maybe his parents did later adopt an almost grown boy because they wanted a third son. Another note for continuity interests, in "Boarding School," Ward mentions his "younger brother."

When the boys are continually late getting home from school in "Lumpy Rutherford," Ward confronts them about their struggle to get home on time. They tell him there is this big kid Lumpy who has been picking on them. He's a bully and won't let them walk home the way they want to walk. This is Ward's co-workers' son and Ward knows nothing about Lumpy Rutherford. That's because Fred refers to him as Clarence. Still seems kind of strange that even Fred has no idea the kids call him Lumpy.

Larry's family has some serious changes too. In "Cleaning Up Beaver," Larry says he now sleeps back in a room with his older brother and says his brother got lonely sleeping on his own. However, back in the episode, "Wally's Girl Trouble," Larry mentions how his brother got married, and he also mentions this in "Wally's Present."

In "Beaver's Bad Day," Eddie picks on Beaver and even says he can beat up Wally. On Sunday, as Wally and Beaver walk home from church, Wally asks Beaver if Eddie hangs out a lot at the new house construction site. Beaver says he does, and they go over there for Wally to confront Eddie. The interesting part here is that Wally asks if Eddie hangs out there and just a couple episodes prior to this one, "Tenting Tonight," Eddie seems to be a regular Sunday School attendee along with Wally and Beaver.

When Eddie tries to convince Wally to ask out Myra in "Wally's Orchid," he tells him she and her boyfriend Roger Clark just had a big fight and broke up. Eddie suggests he should take advantage of the timing before they get back together. He says that's the way his dad buys houses cheap. So, in this episode Mary Ellen is Myra and Eddie's Father, the mechanic, is in real estate.

Richard Rickover in "Mother's Day Composition," tells an untruth, is exaggerating, or simply repeating something he was told by his cousin when he says his cousin was in the army with Sal Mineo. After much research, there is no indication that Sal Mineo was ever in any of America's armed forces.

When Beaver and his friends call Dodger pitcher Don Drysdale in "Long Distance Call," and later find out it cost almost $10.00, the boys are on edge. Gilbert looks out the window and says Beaver's parents are coming home. He and Alan run out of there to the safety of their homes. A look out the window shows a car pulling into the driveway, but it's the typical stock footage used in multiple episodes of Ward coming home from work. There is no second person in the car, just Ward and you can clearly see it. Again, just something the producers never thought anyone would notice, and something that makes it fun for some fans to examine.

A final look at the lack of continuity in some of the episodes which feature "people" inconsistencies should be the season five episode, "Beaver, the Babysitter." Here, Beaver is asked to babysit for the Murdock family. Wally says Chuckie is five years old and he was supposed to babysit for the Murdocks but asks Beaver to do it for him. Beaver acts as if he doesn't know who Chuckie is even though he took him downtown to buy shoes a few episodes earlier.

Miscellaneous Inconsistencies

In "Wally, the Businessman," Wally begins selling Igloo ice cream bars from a cart he pedals down the street. He sells three different types of Igloo bars, chocolate, vanilla and pistachio. Moving onward to "Chuckie's New Shoes," Beaver and Chuckie, as they are walking to the shoe store, come upon an Igloo ice cream truck and right on the side is a sign which reads, "2 Tasty Flavors."

A prop gets misplaced in "Beaver's Accordion." This episode begins with June cleaning out some trash from the upstairs closet. After bringing it downstairs, Ward throws in a letter from the Accordion company and a starfish is seen in the box. She's throwing away the starfish that prior to this episode, was in the boys' room on their shelf. Don't worry… it's back on the shelf in their room in future episodes.

"Beaver's Prep School" is the episode in which Aunt Martha offers to pay for Beaver to go to Fallbrook, a prestigious New England school. Although Beaver hasn't made up his mind, Wally begins moving around furniture in their room. When Beaver sees he's moved the desk, Wally tells him he just wanted to see how it would be with so much extra room after Beaver goes off to school next fall. I guess Wally forgot that he was going away to college.

While "Family Scrapbook" is known as being the first episode in TV history to be produced as a series finale (although somewhere in my research I read that is debated by some TV historians), it is now also known as one that has a bit of a continuity problem. When June points out Beaver's sixth grade class picture, they speak about Miss Landers and how Beaver had a crush on her. June even tells Beaver that he talked them into inviting her over for dinner. But, as you'll remember when Miss Landers thanks Beaver at school for the invite to dinner in "Teacher Comes for Dinner," he is surprised and knew nothing about the invite but pretends he does know.

There's one reason in "School Sweater," that Wally doesn't want to go up to Frances and ask for his sweater back. He tells Eddie that he doesn't know her that well. But in "Wally's Election," she tells Wally that he's known her since grammar school when he approaches her, introduces himself and ask her to vote for him for sophomore class president.

Penny Woods is leaving Mayfield and Grant Avenue Grammar School. In "Farewell to Penny," there's a going away party for her at school and the invitation says the party starts at 3:30 p.m. The party is held in the classroom and is attended by her classmates, including Beaver, who she laments is coming. The little inconsistency here isn't that she and Beaver begin liking one another, but that the party seems to be in full swing when the scene in the classroom opens and the clock shows it's 3:25 p.m. and a moment later, Whitey admits he's eaten three pieces of cake already.

There are so many more moments on *Leave it to Beaver* that would fit into this chapter on continuity. What you've read here just scratches the surface of the inconsistencies and as stated earlier, the show wouldn't be nearly as enjoyable if every episode was perfectly in tune with every other episode. Some of the charm of *Leave it to Beaver* is the number of different writers that created its episodes over the years. They brought memories and experiences from their own childhoods and inserted them into these 234 different and quite entertaining morality plays.

If you want to read some more about continuity, please visit http://leaveittobeaverbooks.com. While there, don't forget to sign up for free *Leave it to Beaver* gifts that will be given away after every 100th sale of *The World Famous Beaverpedia.*

72

(IN THIS EPISODE) MAYFIELD IS LOCATED IN …

I've said this before about *LITB* fans, that there are two kinds. This is especially true when it comes to the location of Mayfield. There are those who believe Jerry Mathers and his statement that Mayfield is located anywhere in the United States. Then, there are those *Leave it to Beaver* fans who insist Mayfield is in … (name the state).

To those of us in the first category, let us pretend we are being forced to believe Mayfield is located in a particular state. That way, we can all read this chapter in the same way, looking at the clues viewers decipher in various episodes that show Mayfield is likely located in a certain state or where Mayfield is likely not located. Here we go, the moment you've all been waiting for… well, half of you.

This chapter begins with a season-by-season list of clues you can take to make a hypothesis, if you would like, on the location of Mayfield. Afterward, will be a rundown on the most probable state locations based on the clues mentioned. This will be followed by the conclusion that this writer, agrees with Jerry Mathers and that Mayfield is a state of mind, and not located in any one of the United States.

Season One

There are prices posted on a travel agency sign to go to the following locations: Chicago $12.50; Miami $58.50; Mexico City $98.95; Toronto $52.00 ("Beaver Gets 'Spelled). The Donaldsons move to Mayfield from Binghamton, a city in New York state ("New Neighbors). Also in this same episode, Eddie talks about 200 shootings by jealous husbands in "California alone." Ward says the boys may be taking the door off their closet to make a surfboard again ("Brotherly Love"). An ice cream man says their advertising department is located in New York ("The Clubhouse"). Aunt Martha tells Ward she hopes he's still considering an eastern college for the boys ("Beaver's Short Pants"). The Donaldsons leave for the beach in the evening. This would mean it probably isn't more than a few hours away.

Season Two

In a letter sent home with Beaver about his bad behavior, the heading of the letter has the Cleaver address as 485 Mapleton Mayfield, State ("Her Idol"). A box sent by Fred Rutherford from Germany to Ward is addressed to "485 Mapleton, Mayfield, USA" ("The Pipe"). The mountains and Shadow Lake are only about a three-hour drive away from Mayfield ("Happy Weekend"). Wally receives a gift from his Uncle Tom in Florida ("Wally's Present"). Ward says they are twenty miles from the ocean ("The Boat Builders"). When Beaver finds the box from Conutra Products mailed to Wally, the box in which they sent his nose flattener, he picks it up and looks at it with his thumb covering up the state ("Wally's Pug Nose"). When the dentist office calls his house, Beaver says the Cleavers moved to Alaska ("The Tooth").

Season Three

The boyhood home of Bob Mosher, co-creator, writer, and producer of *Leave it to Beaver*, was located on Lake Avenue in Auburn New York. In one episode Beaver walks in the mud on Lake Avenue ("Beaver and Andy"). Ward tells June he told Beaver a story about castles. He then wonders what parents in castles tell their kids about to get their attention. June says, "probably stories about Levittown" This is a hamlet or small community on Long Island or a town in Pennsylvania. Lumpy plays in the school band for the governor in Madison ("Wally and Alma"). June is having Camellia bushes delivered and they do not grow well in every state ("Beaver Finds a Wallet").

Season Four

Ward talks about cold weather coming in a few weeks ("Wally, the Lifeguard"). This episode aired on October 22, 1960. Ward shares a childhood memory of Shaker Heights ("Beaver's Accordion"). Wally says all the oil is down in Texas ("Ward's Millions"). Richard says his dad told him some of the McMahon family croaked and the rest moved to California ("Mistaken Identity"). When June asks Beaver if Ginny Townsend just moved from Indianapolis, Beaver says, "I think one of those states." Eddie says she is from Indianapolis. Ward shares a childhood memory of Shaker Heights. All of these happen in the same episode ("Wally's Dream Girl"). Ward mentions he was the best kite maker in Shaker Heights ("Kite Day"). In the same episode, June mentions she was once in New Mexico with Aunt Martha. Finally, Wally mentions a go-cart Eddie was going to turn into an ice boat and to sail it on the river when it froze over ("Beaver's Doll Buggy").

Season Five

Ward explains to Wally how he needs a license and insurance whether he wants to drive a car around the block or drive it to California ("Wally's Car"). Bootsy the cat has an owner who lives on Lake Avenue ("Beaver's Cat Problem"). This is the name of the street on which co-creator and producer of *Leave it to Beaver* Bob Mosher lived on in Auburn New York during his summers growing up. There are multiple pennants in the malt shop where high school kids hang out and they have the names Bixby, Ogden and Carlton on them ("Wally's Big Date"). When Beaver looks up a phone number, he looks in a very huge phone book, indicating Mayfield is near a large city ("Beaver's First Date"). The establishing shot for the carnival in Bellport is the Fun Zone at the Los Angeles County Fair ("Beaver's Fear"). Richard says his grandmother lives in California ("Beaver's Laundry"). When Lumpy is paid ten cents per mile to take members of the track team to Bellport. Beaver jokes that Lumpy will probably go to Bellport by way of California ("Lumpy's Car Trouble"). The mountains are only thirty to fifty miles away when the boys are taken camping by Wally ("A Night in the Woods").

Season Six

The boys make a long-distance call to Los Angeles ("Long Distance Call"). The vehicle code book Wally reads from is the California Vehicle Code Summary book ("Wally's License"). Ward says Fred will talk about the seventeen-pound muskie fish he caught in Minnesota ("Eddie, the Businessman"). Eddie says he may go to Arizona or Texas on spring break ("The Mustache"). Wally talks about the Big Dipper roller coaster and at the time, there was one in Ohio, but also one or two in California ("Beaver's Fear"). Gilbert tells Beaver his aunt in Pittsburgh would like it if he said hi to him when on TV ("Beaver on TV"). Marlene's parents live in California and June wishes they lived in someplace like Ohio ("Box Office Attraction"). New England is a few hours east of Mayfield ("Beaver's Prep School"). A co-worker of Ward's must fly to the coast ("The Poor Loser"). Eddie mentions there's a point in California named after Charles Dana (although it's really named after author Richard Henry Dana Jr.) and Eddie goes to a large dock for an interview with a fishing boat captain ("Summer in Alaska"). Uncle Billy is flying in from California for Beaver's graduation ("Beaver's Graduation"). Ward mentions being the Shaker Heights swinger ("All-Night Party").

So…Where is Mayfield located?

Mayfield is not located in any state, but it is a state of mind. I know for some of you, the "location absolutists" among us, are probably fuming at that statement. If you are, then you're fuming at Jerry Mathers and other actors from the show who say the city of Mayfield can be anywhere a fan of the show wants it to be as it is just a state of mind. But for those who still want to debate the matter, you will find below some reasons why people might believe Mayfield is located in either Ohio, Oregon, Washington, Michigan, Wisconsin or Pennsylvania.

Where Mayfield is located

Ohio

For location absolutists, this is typically their state. If I were a location absolutist, this would be the state I would choose. There are many little clues viewers can decipher from the words written in the scripts, here are some of them: Shaker Heights is found in Ohio. Ward is mentioned as being from Shaker Heights in six different episodes in the later seasons. That is a whopping 2.5% of all episodes. Not definite proof *Leave it to Beaver* takes place in Ohio, but it's something. There is even a village named Mayfield thirteen miles ENE of Cleveland, Ohio.

Also, Larry Mondello's Dad is always on business trips to Cincinnati, and Larry's brother lives there. Then there's the "Voodoo Magic" episode in which an Ohio State pennant hangs on Eddie Haskell's bedroom wall. In another episode, a girl named Allison moves to Beaver's school and says she is from Hamilton, a city about thirty miles north of Cincinnati. There is also the Giant Dipper roller-coaster in Chippewa Lake, Ohio. In the episode about Lumpy's football scholarship to "State," his friend asks for tickets if they go to Rose Bowl. Even up to the 1980s, the Rose Bowl featured the winners of the Big Ten and Pac-10 Conferences, and Ohio State was and still is in the Big Ten.

Oregon or Washington

In "Summer in Alaska," Eddie goes to a dock to interview for a summer job on a fishing boat in Alaska. There is a boat in the water, so it only makes sense that this is on the coast. The fishing boat will be sailing to Alaska, so Mayfield could be on the west coast.

Michigan

Crystal Falls is a town in Michigan's Upper Peninsula. It is a town of about 1600 people.

Wisconsin

In "Wally and Alma," Wally tells Alma when he brings Lumpy over to her house, that he played in the school band for the Governor in Madison. In "Her Idol," a close-up view of a prop letter from Mrs. Rayburn mentions a home run hit by the Milwaukee Braves in the World Series. There are a couple episodes in which the Green Bay Packers are mentioned. The "W" pennant above Beaver's bed is similar to the Wisconsin Badgers logo. Finally, Beaver tells Don Drysdale that he had a Warren Spahn baseball glove and he played for the Milwaukee Braves (1946-64).

Pennsylvania

In the episode, Perfect Father, Ward says he use to play Muhlenberg in basketball –Muhlenberg College is located in Allentown, Pennsylvania. This is a current Division III NCAA college. Ward could have played at any of the colleges in their division, many which are located in Pennsylvania. Also, co-creator, producer and writer, Bob Mosher went to small school in the same area of Pennsylvania.

Finally, the clue almost everyone has missed

In the episode, "Train Trip," Mayfield is located about an hour from the ocean or the Gulf of Mexico.
Don't believe me, then just do some research on starfish. They live in sea water, not fresh water. So, in this episode, the Cleavers definitely live about an hour from either the Atlantic Ocean, the Pacific Ocean or the Gulf of Mexico. The reason? Because Beaver found a starfish as he was walking on the beach during their visit to Aunt Martha and starfish are marine animals that live in saltwater. The starfish is seen in their bedroom on their shelf for a few seasons, even though it is thrown away in "Beaver's Accordion." But like a cat buried in the Stephen King version of a pet cemetery, the starfish comes back to life and goes back on the shelf in their room for many more episodes.

So, there you go… possibly no closer to the answer many of you have been looking for all these years.

73

EPISODES

Introduction: You will notice small snapshots about each episode in this section in contrast to a full treatment. Doing otherwise would have limited space for the other information included in the episode summaries. Also, you'll see "notable lines" from each episode, at least one, and sometimes up to three. If they are part of a conversation, there will be no space between each listed speaker. If there is a space between the notable lines, that indicates a new conversation.

Pilot Episode: It's a Small World
Apr 23, 1957
Director: Jerry Hopper
Writers: Joe Connelly & Bob Mosher

Snapshot: Frankie Bennett tells Beaver he can win a bicycle by entering the Franklin Milk bottle-cap contest. However, no such contest exists, but the big oaf at the local Franklin Milk office believes there is such a contest and gives Wally and Beaver their prize, a brand-new bike, after he has his secretary go to the store to buy one.

The Players

Jerry Mathers…Theodore 'Beaver' Cleaver
Paul Sullivan…Wally Cleaver
Barbara Billingsley…June Cleaver
Max Showalter…Ward Cleaver (as Casey Adams)
Richard Deacon…Mr. Baxter
Diane Brewster…Miss Simms
Joseph Kearns…Fred Crowley

Russell Thorson…Man With Milk Bottles
Leonard Bremen…Milk Bar Proprietor
Harry Shearer…Frankie Bennett
Tommy Randall…Frankie's Friend
Tim Graham…Doc
Virginia Carroll…Nurse
Joel Aldrich…Self - Host

Notable line(s)

Ward Cleaver: Mr. Baxter, I know you work for a milk company, but there are indications of a much stronger beverage here.

Ward Cleaver: Oh, come now, Mr. Baxter. You make it sound like those two boys stuck a gun in your stomach and said, 'Your money or your bicycle.'

June Cleaver: Bottle caps?

Beaver: Wally, why does dad want us to change our shirts?
Wally: I guess he just likes to pick on us.

S1 E1 - Beaver Gets 'Spelled'
Oct 4, 1957
Director: Norman Tokar
Writers: Joe Connelly & Bob Mosher

Snapshot: Beaver is convinced he's going to be kicked out of school. Wally does his best to help his little brother. His efforts aren't successful, and June Cleaver is called to the principal's office to sort everything out.

The Players

Miss Canfield…Diane Brewster
Doris Packer…Mrs. Cornelia Rayburn
Burt Mustin…Gus the Fireman
Stanley Fafara…Whitey Whitney
Jeri Weil…Judy Hensler
Gary Allen…First Man

Stephen Paylow…Boy #2
Ralph Sanford…Fats Flannaghan
Alan Reynolds…Second Man
Rory O'Connor…Beaver (double)
(uncredited)

Notable line(s)

Beaver: One of the big kids from the third grade said they just might "suspender" me.

Wally (typing): I have whipped him. His father has whipped him. He is very sorry. We are very sorry.

♦   ♦   ♦   ♦   ♦   ♦

S1 E2 - Captain Jack
Oct 11, 1957
Director: Norman Tokar
Writers: Joe Connelly & Bob Mosher

Snapshot: Not everything a child orders out of a magazine is life size. Beaver and Wally find this out when they order an alligator. They raise it at home until their father finds out about it. Then, it's off to the local gator farm.

The Players

Edgar Buchanan…Captain Jack
Connie Gilchrist…Minerva
Irving Bacon…Postal Clerk

Penny Carpenter…Girl to see 'Captain Jack'
Rory O'Connor…Beaver (double)
(uncredited)

Notable line(s)

Beaver: Maybe if you put him in water, he swells up.
Wally: Who ever heard of a dehydrated alligator?

Captain Jack: He won't bite your arm off… he'll saw it off.

S1 E3 - The Black Eye
Oct 18, 1957
Director: Norman Tokar
Writers: Joe Connelly & Bob Mosher (teleplay), Hendrik Vollaerts (story)

Snapshot: Beaver comes home from school with a black eye. There's nothing abnormal about a schoolyard fight according to Ward. What he does find abnormal is Beaver's running away after getting punched. Little does he know; it was a girl who hit Beaver.

The Players

Richard Deacon…Fred Rutherford
Burt Mustin…Gus the Fireman
Wendy Winkelman…Violet Rutherford
Jeri Weil…Judy Hensler
Philip Grayson…First Boy
Julie Bennett…Waitress

Lonnie Thomas…Second Boy
Tommy Berwald…Third Boy
Richard Smiley…Fourth Boy
Rory O'Connor…Beaver (double)
(uncredited)

Notable line(s)

Wally: What did the sign say?"
Beaver: Violet Rutherford drinks gutter water.

Beaver: Don't get 'gressive with me, Violet Rutherford.

♦   ♦   ♦   ♦   ♦   ♦

S1 E4 - The Hair Cut
Oct 25, 1957
Director: Norman Tokar
Writers: Joe Connelly & Bob Mosher (teleplay), Hendrik Vollaerts (story)

Snapshot: After losing his lunch money multiple times, Beaver is given a final chance to prove he can be responsible with money. He's given money for a haircut and loses it. Instead of admitting what happened, Beaver gives himself a haircut with some help from his brother Wally.

The Players:

Benny Baker…Barber
Gil Frye…Mr. Tyne (as Gilbert Frye)

Rory O'Connor…Beaver (double)
(uncredited)

Notable line(s)

Barber: Anyone can lose money.
Beaver: Yeah, but not as good as I can.

Beaver: Are you finished?
Wally: I don't know, but I think I better stop.

S1 E5 - New Neighbors
Nov 1, 1957
Director: Norman Tokar
Writers: Joe Connelly & Bob Mosher

Snapshot: Here, Eddie Haskell makes his first appearance, and right away, he gives Beaver "the business." After seeing the new neighbor give Beaver a kiss, Eddie lets Beaver know that could mean death if her husband finds out. That's his biggest dose of "the business" he ever gives.

The Players:

Phyllis Coates…Betty Donaldson
Charles H. Gray…Harry Donaldson
Ken Osmond…Eddie Haskell
Yolanda White…Julie

John Philip Dayton…Panelist (uncredited)
Rory O'Connor…Beaver (double)
(uncredited)

Notable line(s)

Beaver: After I 'splained to him, he said I could kiss his wife any time I wanted.

Eddie: Gee, Mrs. Cleaver, that's a nice dress.
June: I know, Eddie. I know.

♦   ♦   ♦   ♦   ♦   ♦

S1 E6 - Brotherly Love
Nov 8, 1957
Director: Norman Tokar
Writers: Joe Connelly & Bob Mosher (teleplay), Norman Tokar (story)

Snapshot: June forces the boys to sign a "friendship pact" after one of their latest fights. Ward warns her pacts like that don't work and gives the example of his sister hitting him in the head soon after he and his sister signed such a friendship pact.

The Players:

Burt Mustin…Gus the Fireman
Buddy Joe Hooker…Chester Anderson (as Buddy Hart)
Herb Vigran…Stanley the Barber
Rory O'Connor…Beaver (double) (uncredited)

Notable line(s)

June: Oh, Ward, I've just failed as a parent!

June: And, Ward, you have my promise, I'll never listen to another Arab again.

S1 E7 - Water Anyone?
Nov 15, 1957
Director: Norman Tokar
Writers: Clifford Goldsmith, Joe Connelly & Bob Mosher (uncredited)

Snapshot: Wally and his friends decide to start a baseball team and buy uniforms. The parents employ each boy to do yard work in order to earn money. Beaver wants someone to give him a job too, but instead, creates his own, selling water.

The Players:

Francis De Sales…Mr. Anderson
Katherine Warren…Mrs. Brown
Buddy Joe Hooker…Chester Anderson
Tiger Fafara…Tooey Brown
Eddie Marr…Water Dept. Worker

Norman Alden…Water Dept. Worker
John Philip Dayton… Boy (uncredited)
Rory O'Connor…Beaver
(double)(uncredited)

Notable line(s)

Beaver: Is Mr. Michaelsen your friend?
Ward: The grocer? Oh, sure, we went to school together.
Beaver: Well, he's got a whole store full of food. Why doens't he give it to you for free?
Ward: Uh, well, Mr. Michaelsen is a businessman.
Beaver: So am I dad.

◆   ◆   ◆   ◆   ◆   ◆

S1 E8 - Beaver's Crush
Nov 22, 1957
Director: Norman Tokar
Writers: Joe Connelly & Bob Mosher (teleplay), Phil Leslie (story)

Snapshot: A lot of school kids wind up having a crush on a teacher. Beaver Cleaver is no exception to the rule. His classmates make fun of him for being a teacher's pet and he tries to prove them wrong by placing a spring-loaded toy snake in her desk drawer. Will she, or won't she open her drawer and be scared? That's what Beaver worries about after his dastardly deed.

The Players

Diane Brewster…Miss Canfield
Doris Packer…Mrs. Cornelia Rayburn
Jeri Weil…Judy Hensler
Stanley Fafara…Whitey Whitney

Robert 'Rusty' Stevens…Larry Mondello
William Fawcett…Mr. Johnson
Rory O'Connor…Beaver (double)
(uncredited)

Notable line(s)

Beaver (to Miss Canfield): I asked my mom this morning when I could marry you.

S1 E9 - The Clubhouse
Nov 29, 1957
Director: Norman Tokar
Writers: Joe Connelly & Bob Mosher (teleplay), Lydia Nathan (story)

Snapshot: Wally and his friends decide to build a clubhouse across the street. Eddie tells Beaver he can join at the special price of $3.00. Beaver capitalizes on capitalism to come up with the money to join the club and be one of the fellas.

The Players

Tiger Fafara...Tooey Brown
James Gleason...Pete
Gary Hart...Harold-Boy in Club
Raymond Hatton...Charlie the Fireman
Ken Osmond...Eddie Haskell

Johnny Silver...Man on Bridge
Charles Wagenheim...Painter
Allen Windsor...Ice Cream Man
Rory O'Connor...Beaver (double)
(uncredited)

Notable line(s)

Eddie Haskell: Don't put any mayonnaise on mine, Mrs. Cleaver. My mom says I'm allergic to it.

Ward: Anyway, if we gave them everything they wanted, they'd be bored and we'd be broke.

◆   ◆   ◆   ◆   ◆   ◆

S1 E10 - Wally's Girl Trouble
Dec 6, 1957
Director: Norman Tokar
Writers: Joe Connelly & Bob Mosher, Ben Gershman & Mel Diamond

Snapshot: Penny, the new girl at dancing school has a face like a flounder according to Beaver. But Wally acts as if he is in love. It's sad when a girl comes between two brothers.

The Players

Cindy Carol...Penny Jamison
Barbara Dodd...Librarian
Louise Lewis...Miss Higgins
Erik Nielsen...First Boy in Library
Paul Engle...Second Boy in Library

Stephen Hammer...Third Boy in Library
Robert 'Rusty' Stevens...Larry Mondello
Rory O'Connor...Beaver (double)
(uncredited)

Notable line(s)

Larry: My big brother started looking at girls like that, and the next thing I knew, he went out and got married.
Beaver: He got married to a girl?
Larry: Sure, that's all there is.

S1 E11 - Beaver's Short Pants
Dec 13, 1957
Director: Norman Tokar
Writers: Joe Connelly & Bob Mosher

Snapshot: A few episodes after this one, June makes quite a deal out of Beaver watching scary movies. However, Beaver experiences a real-life horror when Aunt Martha comes to visit.

The Players

Madge Kennedy…Aunt Martha Bronson
William Schallert…Mr. Bloomgarden
Eric Snowden…Clothier
Jeri Weil…Judy Hensler

Robert 'Rusty' Stevens…Larry Mondello
Rory O'Connor…Beaver (double)
(uncredited)

Notable line(s)

June: Aunt Martha's never been married. She doesn't know anything about babies and things.
Ward: Someone must have explained a few things to her somewhere along the line.

◆　◆　◆　◆　◆　◆

S1 E12 - The Perfume Salesmen
Dec 27, 1957
Director: Norman Tokar
Writers: Joe Connelly & Bob Mosher, Mel Diamond & Ben Gershman

Snapshot: Selling perfume door-to-door is not as easy as Wally and Beaver think it will be. However, when Ward gets involved, the sales seem too good to be true. The boys won't look a gift horse in the mouth when a free film projector is the reward for selling the entire box of perfume.

The Players

Anne Dore…Mrs. Wentworth
Helen Jay….Perfume Customer
Rory O'Connor…Beaver (double) (uncredited)

Notable line(s)

June: Now aren't you a little curious?
Ward: Not unduly.
June: It's an enormous box. It might be a machine gun or a bomb or something.
Ward: Well, if it is, we'll hear about it soon enough.

Wally: I don't know. Women are funny. Maybe they like to smell like old catcher's mitts.

S1 E13 - Voodoo Magic
Jan 3, 1958
Director: Norman Tokar
Writers: Bill Manhoff, Joe Connelly & Bob Mosher (supervisors)

Snapshot: The black magic of a voodoo practitioner is not what one excepts to find in Mayfield. But with scary movies, comes scary things. Eddie Haskell gets Beaver and Wally in trouble and Beaver gets revenge by making a voodoo doll for Eddie.

The Players
Doris Packer…Mrs. Cornelia Rayburn
Ann Doran…Agnes Haskell

Karl Swenson…George Haskell
Ken Osmond…Eddie Haskell

Notable line(s)

Beaver: Wally, what if Eddie dies? Will they give me the electric chair?
Wally: Sure. They got a little seat they put on for kids . . . just like they got in the barbershop.

Beaver: Nobody likes you, Eddie, not even Wally, and he's your best friend

Beaver: I don't like you very much, but I'd feel kind of bad if you died.

♦   ♦   ♦   ♦   ♦   ♦

S1 E14 - Part-Time Genius
Jan 10, 1958
Director: Norman Tokar
Writers: Joe Connelly & Bob Mosher (teleplay) Hendrik Vollaerts (story)

Snapshot: After Beaver takes an I.Q. test at school, Mrs. Rayburn notifies the Cleavers they have a genius living under their roof. Ward uses this new info to brag to his braggart co-worker Corny Cornelius who swore he had the smartest kids in school, but that's no longer true.

The Players
Diane Brewster…Miss Canfield
Doris Packer…Mrs. Cornelia Rayburn
John Hoyt …Doctor Compton
Charles Davis…Willis 'Corny' Cornelius
Dian Van Patten…Donna Sims (uncredited)

Jeri Weil…Judy Hensler
Stanley Fafara…Whitey Whitney
Robert 'Rusty' Stevens…Larry Mondello
Bobby Mittelstaedt…Charles Fredericks

Notable line(s)

June: Ward, we all can't be "A" students. Maybe the boys are more like me.
Ward: Oh, of course they're not.

S1 E15 - Party Invitation
Jan 17, 1958
Director: Norman Tokar
Writer(s) Joe Connelly & Bob Mosher (supervisors) Mel Diamond & Ben Gershman

Snapshot: Beaver is the only boy invited to a birthday party. He must get out of this disaster, but how? Enter Wally. He calls Linda and imitates Ward, telling her Beaver is sick and won't be able to attend… and Ward hears every single word.

The Players

Claudia Bryar…Mrs. Dennison

Lyle Talbot…Mr. Dennison

Jeri Weil…Judy Hensler

Stanley Fafara…Whitey Whitney

Robert 'Rusty' Stevens…Larry Mondello

Patty Turner…Linda Dennison

Dorothy Best…1st Girl at Party

Betty Lynn Budzak…2nd Girl at Party

Notable line(s)

Wally: They made us come out and play kissing games.
Beaver: With the girls?
Wally: Sure, that's what you kiss in kissing games.

Wally: Did you have to kiss all the girls?
Beaver: No, but I won a doll.
Wally: A doll? Well, what did you do with it?
Beaver: I gave it to a fat lady who was waiting for a bus.

♦   ♦   ♦   ♦   ♦   ♦

S1 E16 - Lumpy Rutherford
Jan 24, 1958
Director: Norman Tokar
Writers: Joe Connelly & Bob Mosher

Snapshot: Ward is full of great ideas and when the boys want to get back at a local bully named Lumpy, they take Ward's idea bout barrel hoops, and the results don't go exactly as planned.

The Players

Helen Parrish…Geraldine Rutherford

Richard Deacon…Fred Rutherford

Frank Bank…Clarence Rutherford

Notable line(s)

Fred Rutherford: They enticed me out of the house and when I ran out, I stumbled all over these barrel hoops.
June: Barrel hoops?
Ward: Barrel hoops?
Fred Rutherford: Barrel hoops.

S1 E17 - The Paper Route
Jan 31, 1958
Director: Norman Tokar
Writers: Joe Connelly & Bob Mosher, Fran van Hartesveldt

Snapshot: "Let me tell you a little story…" Ward says this phrase time and again. In this episode, it's about getting a job, which the boys do at the local newspaper. Situations arise in which Ward and June feel compelled to help, but there is such a thing as helping too much.

The Players
Jackie Kelk… Mr. Merkel
Alan Reynolds…Newspaper Delivery Man
Gil Frye…Newspaper Customer

Yvonne White…Newspaper Customer
Lyn Osborn…Newspaper Customer #2

Notable line(s)

Beaver: You know, workin' isn't as much fun as I thought it would be. I wonder why older people do it so much.
Wally: They have to. If they had fun like kids, people would say they were silly

Ward: It seems to me that even a man with your limited perspicacity should be able to see that's the only thing fair to do.
Old Man Merkel: Are you trying to insult me Jack?

♦   ♦   ♦   ♦   ♦   ♦

S1 E18 - Child Care
Feb 7, 1958
Director: Norman Tokar
Writers: Joe Connelly & Bob Mosher

Snapshot: Pete, the fireman to the rescue. The boys call him when a little girl they are babysitting locks herself in the bathroom and all attempts to retrieve her fail.

The Players
Will Wright…Pete at Firehouse #7
Shirley Mitchell…Janet Wilson
Ray Montgomery…Herb Wilson

Gabrielle des Enfants…Helen 'Puddin'
Wilson
Joey Scott…Bengie Bellamy

Notable line(s)

Beaver: Weddings are too sissy. When I get married, I'm not going to have a wedding.
Wally: Nah, Beave. Weddings aren't bad. You get to throw things at people and everything.

Beaver: You know Wally, when I get married and raise a family, I'm not gonna have any kids.

S1 E19 - The Bank Account
Feb 14, 1958
Director: Norman Tokar
Writer(s) Joe Connelly & Bob Mosher (supervisors), Phil Leslie

Snapshot: Wally and Beaver take money from their school bank account to buy a hunting jacket for Ward. However, he believes they've squandered it on unnecessary baseball gloves. When a delivery is made to their house, he sits the boys down and opens the package to see if it should be sent back to the sporting goods store. Ward is visibly touched by the boys' kindness.

The Players
Doris Packer...Mrs. Cornelia Rayburn
Eric Snowden...Salesman at Abernathy Potts

Notable line(s)

Wally: These aren't ducks, they're decoys.
Beaver: They sure look like ducks. What are they for?
Wally: Well, when you're hunting ducks, you put these out in the water, and then the real ducks come down and you shoot 'em.
Beaver: But why do they come down? These are only made of wood.
Wally: Yeah, but they don't know that until they get there. Then it's too late.
Beaver: It must be tough being a duck.

◆　　◆　　◆　　◆　　◆　　◆

S1 E20 - Lonesome Beaver
Feb 28, 1958
Director: Norman Tokar
Writer(s) Joe Connelly & Bob Mosher

Snapshot: Beaver usually hangs out with his brother Wally, but Wally is growing up and now he's joined a scouting troop. He'll be away at camp, going on hikes, having scout meetings and now, what is Beaver to do?

The Players
Burt Mustin...Gus the Fireman
Ken Osmond...Eddie Haskell
Tiger Fafara...Tooey Brown

Buddy Joe Hooker...Chester Anderson
John Hart...Troop #21 Scoutmaster Norton
Lillian O'Malley...Woman on sidewalk

Notable line(s)

June: I was just looking up north towards Friend's Lake. Ward, it looks like rain up that way.
Ward: June, you didn't get me out of a sand trap to give me a weather report, did you?

S1 E21 - Cleaning Up Beaver
Mar 7, 1958
Director: Norman Tokar
Writers: Joe Connelly & Bob Mosher (supervisors), Bill Manhoff

Snapshot: Beaver is a slob, but he's not as dirty as Larry Mondello. Nevertheless, he can't stand being around his super clean brother. But when he moves into the guest room, yowling cats, a dark closet, and more, scare him back into his room, with Wally there to protect him.

The Players

Ken Osmond…Eddie Haskell   Robert 'Rusty' Stevens…Larry Mondello

Notable line(s)

June: You smell quite nice too.
Eddie: Oh, that's my aftershave lotion.
June: Why Eddie, do you shave?
Eddie: No, but I like to smell like I do.

♦   ♦   ♦   ♦   ♦   ♦

S1 E22 - The Perfect Father
Mar 14, 1958
Director: Norman Tokar
Writers: Joe Connelly & Bob Mosher (teleplay) Fran van Hartesveldt (story)

Snapshot: Sometimes Ward likes to know where the boys are, so maybe they should just play basketball in their own driveway instead of going to the Dennison's house. That works out well until Eddie Haskell points out that Ward has put up a backboard that is not regulation height.

The Players

Lyle Talbot…Chuck Dennison   Buddy Joe Hooker…Chester Anderson
Ken Osmond…Eddie Haskell   Richard Smiley…Willie Dennison
Tiger Fafara…Tooey Brown

Notable line(s)

Beaver: Gee, Dad, that ain't trash. That's a lot of valuable junk.

June: Yes. And I must remember not to put mayonnaise on Eddie's. He's informed me he's allergic to it.

June (after seeing Eddie push Beaver): Ooh. just for that, I'm gonna put mayonnaise on his sandwich.

S1 E23 - Beaver and Poncho
Mar 21, 1958
Director: Norman Tokar
Writers: Joe Connelly & Bob Mosher

Snapshot: Sneaking things into the house is normal, but Beaver can't fool Ward. Ward knows he has snuck something inside when he sees Beaver's bundled jacket. Soon, Beaver shares his guest, a small dog. The trouble is that home isn't the only place Beaver sneaks this small dog.

The Players

Diane Brewster…Miss Canfield
Doris Packer…Mrs. Cornelia Rayburn
Maudie Prickett…Mrs. Bennett
Robert 'Rusty' Stevens…Larry Mondello

Stanley Fafara…Whitey Whitney
Jeri Weil…Judy Hensler
Patty Turner…Linda Dennison
Joanna Lee…Classified ad lady

Notable line(s)

Wally: I think he's what they call a Mexican Hairless.
Beaver: He's hairless all right, But I don't know if he's Mexican.

Ward: I had to cancel a business conference in order to go over to school and find out my son has no respect for the truth.

♦   ♦   ♦   ♦   ♦   ♦

S1 E24 - The State Versus Beaver
Mar 26, 1958
Director: Norman Tokar
Writers: Joe Connelly & Bob Mosher

Snapshot: Wally and Beaver make a go-cart with Ward's help and Larry convinces Beaver to take it for a drive around the block. When a policeman gives Beaver a ticket for driving without a license, Beaver finds himself in traffic court. It's a good thing the judge *spunges* his record.

The Players

Robert 'Rusty' Stevens…Larry Mondello (as Rusty Stevens)
Frank Wilcox…District Court Judge
William Kendis…Charlie - Police Officer

Notable line(s)

Wally: Boy, it's sure going to be great, Dad helping us…
Beaver: I sure hope so.

S1 E25 - The Broken Window
Apr 2, 1958
Director: James Neilson
Writers: Joe Connelly & Bob Mosher

Snapshot: Don't play ball near the house is a routine parental refrain. When that rule is ignored, shattered glass often happens. And a cover up usually ensues, like is the case here.

The Players

Charles Davis…Willis Cornelius
Rusty Stevens…Larry Mondello
Tiger Fafara…Tooey Brown
Ken Osmond…Eddie Haskell

Buddy Joe Hooker…Chester Anderson
Ralph Sanford…Fats Flannaghan
William Hunt…Grocer

Notable line(s)

Beaver: I still think we ought to pack our stuff and run away
Wally: No, we can't do that now. It's almost our bedtime.

Eddie: You know something, you guys have got a real goofy father.
Wally: You cut that out Eddie, or you really will be getting it across the puss.

♦   ♦   ♦   ♦   ♦   ♦

S1 E26 - Train Trip
Apr 9, 1958
Director: Norman Tokar
Writers: Joe Connelly & Bob Mosher

Snapshot: Left by Aunt Martha to buy their return train tickets on their own, the boys run out of money buying junk food. Only able to afford tickets to Bellport, on board the train, they spin a tall tale to the conductor on why they didn't buy tickets to Mayfield.

The Players

Madge Kennedy…Aunt Martha Bronson
Joseph Crehan…Train Conductor
Karl Swenson…George Haskell
Eddie Marr…Ticket Salesman
Mary Foran…Lady in Train Station
Ricky Allen…Boy in Train Station

Alan Reynolds…Man in Train Station
Don Ames…Train Station Commuter
Duke Fishman…Train Station Commuter
Bess Flowers…Train Station Commuter
Herschel Graham…Passenger

Notable line(s)

Aunt Martha: I see, you boys are so grown up you don't want a fussy old aunt putting you on the train.
Wally: We don't mind you being fussy…. I mean, we can do things by ourselves.

Wally (when asked by June about the trip): Uh, you know how train trips are... you get on at one station, you get off at another. And in between, you look out at cows and stuff.

S1 E27 - My Brother's Girl
Apr 16, 1958
Director: Norman Tokar
Writers: Joe Connelly & Bob Mosher (teleplay), Bill Manhoff (story)

Snapshot: Mary Ellen Rogers may be a nice girl, but she's not adverse to using a little boy to get what she wants from his big brother, like a date for the school dance.

The Players
Ken Osmond...Eddie Haskell   Pamela Baird...Mary Ellen Rogers
Jan Gillum...Kathleen   Raymond Karr...Boy
Linda Lowell...Frances   Buddy Joe Hooker...Chester Anderson

Notable line(s)

June: We had a little sock problem.
Ward: Sock?
June: Beaver wasn't wearing any and Wally had on a pair of yours.
Ward: Oh. (pause) Now, how could Wally wear ...
June: (looks back at Ward) ...folded the toe back.

♦   ♦   ♦   ♦   ♦   ♦

S1 E28 - Next Door Indians
Apr 23, 1958
Director: Norman Tokar
Writers: Joe Connelly & Bob Mosher, (suggested by a story by) Robert Paul Smith

Snapshot: Beaver tells Eddie, Tooey and Chester that there was an Indian fight right across from their house where the vacant lot is located. But when Wally's friends try to confirm this statement by digging for Indian artifacts, they find precious jewels instead, or so they think.

The Players
Ken Osmond...Eddie Haskell

Tiger Fafara...Tooey Brown
Buddy Joe Hooker...Chester Anderson (as Buddy Hart)
Burt Mustin...Gus the Fireman

Notable line(s)

June: Beaver, if the boys asked you to keep a secret, I don't think anyone should try to get it out of you.
Beaver: But gee, mom. It doesn't seem like a real secret, unless somebody wants to know what it is.

S1 E29 - Tenting Tonight
Apr 30, 1958
Director: Norman Tokar
Writers: Joe Connelly & Bob Mosher (teleplay), Fred Shevin (story)

Snapshot: Wally and Beaver pitch a tent in the backyard after their father cancels a promised camping trip. A heavy rain ruins their night, but Ward leaves the back door unlocked in case they need to come inside, which they eventually do, after getting just a little bit soaked.

The Players

Richard Deacon…Fred Rutherford
Buddy Joe Hooker…Chester Anderson (as Buddy Hart)
Ken Osmond…Eddie Haskell
Tiger Fafara…Tooey Brown
Frank Bank…Clarence Rutherford

Notable line(s)

Ward: I should think you boys would want to be outside today, out in the fresh air where you could breathe."

Wally: "Gee Dad, we can breathe all week. We only get to go to the movies on Saturday.

◆   ◆   ◆   ◆   ◆   ◆

S1 E30 - Music Lesson
May 7, 1958
Director: Norman Tokar
Writers: Joe Connelly & Bob Mosher (teleplay), John Patrick (story)

Snapshot: Beaver wants to make his father proud by doing some sort of extracurricular activity. He decides to join the school band but gets cut during tryouts. Not wanting to disappoint, Beaver keeps the news to himself, but continues his "I'm a member of the band," charade.

The Players

Wendell Holmes…Mr. T.J. Willet   Jeri Weil…Judy Hensler
Stanley Fafara…Whitey Whitney   Douglas Wade…Thomas

Notable line(s)

Mr. Willet: Well Beaver, can't you go any further?
Beaver: I could, but it wouldn't be America.

Beaver: But dad was so proud of you for gettin' on the baseball team. I wanted him to have somethin' to be proud of me for.

S1 E31 - New Doctor
May 14, 1958
Director: Norman Tokar
Writers: Joe Connelly & Bob Mosher

Snapshot: During a house call from the new doctor, Beaver learns about the story, *The Boy Who Cried Wolf.* He then admits to his parents that he wasn't really sick but wanted the attention they had given Wally when he was sick and stayed home from school the previous day.

The Players

Ken Osmond…Eddie Haskell   Jeri Weil…Judy Hensler
Tiger Fafara…Tooey Brown   Stuart Wade…Dr. Bradley
Stanley Fafara…Whitey Whitney

Notable line(s)

Eddie (to Beaver): Boy, you better look sicker than that when the doctor gets here.

Beaver: Maybe when she takes your temperature, you can hold back, so it won't show.

Beaver: (looking at magic set pamphlet) Hey, here's a picture of a guy sawing a girl in half. Can you do that with it? (The magic set)
Tooey: Not for $2.30

♦   ♦   ♦   ♦   ♦   ♦

S1 E32 - Beaver's Old Friend
May 21, 1958
Director: Norman Tokar
Writers: Joe Connelly & Bob Mosher, Dick Conway & Roland MacLane

Snapshot: While cleaning the garage, Ward finds his old shot put and Beaver finds his old teddy bear. Both are thrown in the trash, and then rescued, but Beaver has a much better reason for his rescue than Ward does.

The Players

Stanley Fafara…Whitey Whitney   David Halper…Friend #2
Dennis Holmes…Friend #1   Jess Kirkpatrick…Garbage Man

Notable line(s)

Beaver: What's a roadster?
Wally: Well, I think it's something people used to ride around in in the olden days.
Ward: Yeah, that's uh... that's right. It replaced the covered wagon.

S1 E33 - Wally's Job
May 28, 1958
Director: Norman Tokar
Writers: Joe Connelly & Bob Mosher

Snapshot: Eddie Haskell does it again. He causes trouble in the Cleaver house. This time he causes Wally to go back on a handshake deal made with Ward for painting the trash cans. Beaver is then given the job and that causes friction between the brothers.

The Players
Ken Osmond…Eddie Haskell

Notable line(s)

Beaver (about Ward): Why would a grown up like him wanna go to a fire?
Wally: I don't know. I guess maybe he wanted to see if fires have changed any since he was a kid.

♦   ♦   ♦   ♦   ♦   ♦

S1 E34 - Beaver's Bad Day
Jun 4, 1958
Director: Norman Tokar
Writers: Joe Connelly & Bob Mosher (supervisors), John Whedon

Snapshot: Truth is valued by the Cleaver family and when Beaver lies about tearing his pants, he is punished. He also hears Ward lie to Fred Rutherford and wonders if he'll be punished too. June speaks with Beaver about God, who sees all things, and Beaver wonders if God saw his father lie. She later has Ward make things right with Fred. Great lessons learned all around.

The Players
Ken Osmond…Eddie Haskell
Robert 'Rusty' Stevens… Larry Mondello (as Rusty Stevens)

Notable line(s)

Larry: Look, how can you get dirty just seesawin'?
Beaver: I can get dirty doin' anything.

Eddie: Yeah, but if you go around squealin' on guys, nobody's gonna like you.
Larry: Is that why nobody likes you Eddie?
Eddie: Shut up, fat boy!

S1 E35 - Boarding School
Jun 11, 1958
Director: Norman Tokar
Writers: Joe Connelly & Bob Mosher, Dick Conway & Roland MacLane

Snapshot: When Beaver asks his father why he doesn't like Wally anymore, you know something is seriously wrong in the Cleaver house. That happens in this episode and Eddie's big mouth is absolutely part of the problem.

The Players
Ken Osmond…Eddie Haskell
Barry Curtis…Johnny Franklin

Notable line(s)

Beaver: I wonder how a snake makes a hole in the top of himself so he can climb out.
Wally: Well, I don't know. I guess you have to be a snake to know that.

♦　　♦　　♦　　♦　　♦　　♦

S1 E36 - Beaver and Henry
Jun 18, 1958
Director: Norman Tokar
Writers: Joe Connelly & Bob Mosher

Snapshot: Beaver almost puts the life of a baby rabbit in danger, but not on purpose. He then goes to Gus, the fireman to see what can be done. With a couple helpful hints from Gus, Beaver saves the baby bunny from being abandoned by its mother.

The Players
Burt Mustin…Gus the Fireman
Robert 'Rusty' Stevens…Larry Mondello (as Rusty Stevens)

Notable line(s)

Wally: I bet every guy doesn't have a father that can think like a gopher.

Beaver: And in a couple days, their eyes will open (the baby rabbits)
Larry: Boy, I bet they'll be surprised when they see where they are.

S1 E37 - Beaver Runs Away
Jun 25, 1958
Director: Norman Tokar
Writers: Joe Connelly & Bob Mosher

Snapshot: Larry Mondello is Beaver's friend, but he sure gets Beaver in a lot of trouble. This time, Larry convinces Beaver they can use Ward's electric drill. When they do, Larry drills holes in the garage wall and Ward blames Beaver. Thinking this is unfair, Beaver runs away from home and only returns when Ward finds out he is at Larry's eating supper.

The Players

Madge Blake…Mrs. Margaret Mondello   Robert 'Rusty' Stevens…Larry Mondello

Notable line(s)

June: You know your father will be perfectly fair.
Beaver: I know, that's what I'm a scared of

Ward: Beaver, you know what Larry was doing was wrong. You could've stopped him.
Beaver: Well, gee dad, I have enough trouble keeping myself good. without keeping all the other kids good.

♦   ♦   ♦   ♦   ♦   ♦

S1 E38 - Beaver's Guest
Jul 2, 1958
Director: Norman Tokar
Writers: Joe Connelly & Bob Mosher

Snapshot: Wally thinks Beaver's idea of Larry Mondello spending the night is terrible. Larry gets punched in the stomach by Beaver and he later gets sick, but all ends up well.

The Players

Madge Blake…Mrs. Margaret Mondello   Frank Sully…Cab Driver
Robert 'Rusty' Stevens…Larry Mondello

Notable line(s)

Ward: Well, why do you want to go home?
Larry: 'Cause Beaver hit me in the stomach, right where I almost had my operation.

Larry: He hit me Mrs. Cleaver. He hit me right where I almost had my operation.
Beaver: I hit you cause you wrecked my fort.

Wally: I cranked the grill up so the hamburgers wouldn't burn again .
Ward: Oh fine.
Wally: Some of them are starting to curl up.
Ward: Uh, so am I.

S1 E39 - Cat Out of the Bag
Jul 16, 1958
Director: Norman Tokar
Writers: Joe Connelly & Bob Mosher (teleplay) Dick Conway and Roland MacLane (story)

Snapshot: Not sure if Beaver and Wally are up to the task, Ward does not stop the boys from taking a job caring for the neighbor's cat over the weekend. Eddie Haskell makes an appearance in this episode and while he doesn't cause the trouble Beaver experiences, his dog does.

The Players
Ken Osmond…Eddie Haskell
Ray Kellogg…Mr. Donaldson

Notable line(s)

Ward: Well, Wally, uh, don't you have anything to say?
Wally (after coming to dinner table late): Uh, yeah, my soup's cold.

Ward: Now, look, fellas. Did something happen I should know about?
Beaver: No dad, nothing happened that you should know about. Nothing at all.

Ward (mad): Tomorrow you'd better be ready with some very snappy answers. Come on, let's go to bed (to June)
Wally: I think we'd better take Puff Puff upstairs and then get to sleep.
Beaver: You can get to sleep if you want to, but I'm gonna spend the rest of the night thinking up snappy answers for dad.

S2 E1- Beaver's Poem
Oct 2, 1958
Director: Norman Tokar
Writers: Joe Connelly & Bob Mosher, Dick Conway & Roland MacLane

Snapshot: Parents should not do their children's homework for them. Ward makes this innocent mistake when Beaver procrastinates writing a poem for school. A surprise to everyone is that the poem, as corny as it sounds, wins a prize.

The Players
Doris Packer…Mrs. Cornelia Rayburn
Robert 'Rusty' Stevens…Larry Mondello (as Rusty Stevens)

Notable line(s)

Ward: I want to talk to you about something, Sit down. (Ward pats Beaver's bed)
Beaver: (on floor): I am sitting down
Ward: Well, get up and sit down.

♦   ♦   ♦   ♦   ♦   ♦

S2 E2 - Eddie's Girl
Oct 9, 1958
Director: Norman Tokar
Writers: Joe Connelly & Bob Mosher

Snapshot: Caroline Cunningham's mother calls June, asking if Wally could accompany her daughter to a dance. June accepts the invite, not knowing that this will be a big problem. Wally's not having any part of it because Caroline Cunningham, as Wally loudly yells, is "Eddie's Girl!"

The Players
Ken Osmond…Eddie Haskell   Aline Towne…Mrs. Cunningham
Karen Green…Caroline Cunningham

Notable line(s)

June: Oh, you have a girl, Eddie?
Eddie: Oh yeah, she goes away to boarding school. My father says that's a good indication that her family has money.

Ward: I don't think I'd like it if my best friend stole my girl.
June: Oh, Ward. Wally had nothing to do with it. I made the date.
Ward: I'd like it even less if my best friend's mother stole my girl.

Wally: Just 'cause I'm a kid, you could have asked me before you practically get me engaged.

S2 E3 - Ward's Problem
Oct 16, 1958
Director: Norman Tokar
Writers: Joe Connelly & Bob Mosher (teleplay), Ed James (story)

Snapshot: Ward must decide between taking Wally fishing or Beaver to a school picnic. Both events fall on the same day, and this causes Beaver a lot of trauma, especially since if Beaver does not attend, he'll be the only student who does not go.

The Players

Sue Randall…Miss Alice Landers	Jeri Weil…Judy Hensler
Robert 'Rusty' Stevens…Larry Mondello	Bobby Mittelstaedt…Charles Fredericks
Stanley Fafara…Whitey Whitney	Patty Turner…Linda Dennison

Notable line(s)

Judy: Miss Landers, when we were pledging allegiance to the flag, Beaver was looking out the window.
Miss Landers: Thank you
Judy: And I don't think that's very patriotic.

Wally: Sometimes grownups tell you stuff just to keep you quiet.

◆　◆　◆　◆　◆　◆

S2 E4 - Beaver and Chuey
Oct 23, 1958
Director: Norman Tokar
Writers: Joe Connelly & Bob Mosher (supervisors) George Tibbles

Snapshot: Beaver and his new friend Chuey perfectly demonstrate the power of friendship. They prove it is stronger than language. In this episode, Eddie Haskell also proves something, and that's his ability to give someone "the business" in more than one language and in the process, he almost causes an international incident.

The Players
Ken Osmond…Eddie Haskell
Alan Roberts…Chuey Varela (as Alan Roberts Costello)
Maria Andre…Carmela Varela (as Mary Andre)
Abel Franco…Enrico Varela

Notable line(s)

Wally: You know Dad, sometimes it must be tough having kids.
Ward: You know Wally, that's the nicest thing you've said to me in a long time.

S2 E5 - The Lost Watch
Oct 30, 1958
Director: Norman Tokar
Writers: Joe Connelly & Bob Mosher (supervisors) Richard Baer

Snapshot: Bullying is something Lumpy does very well. He demonstrates this when he threatens Beaver with the police and accuses him of stealing his watch. That's not exactly what happens here as it was Lumpy who lost the watch, not Beaver.

The Players

Richard Deacon…Fred Rutherford
Robert 'Rusty' Stevens….Larry Mondello
Frank Bank…Clarence Rutherford

Buddy Joe Hooker…Chester Anderson
Tiger Fafara…Tooey Brown
Jonathan Hole…Bank Teller

Notable line(s)

Bank teller: If you hold on to this (bond) for ten years, it'll be worth $25.00
Beaver: I don't need $25.00 in ten years; I need $15.00 now

♦   ♦   ♦   ♦   ♦   ♦

S2 E6 - Her Idol
Nov 6, 1958
Director: Norman Tokar
Writers: Joe Connelly & Bob Mosher (teleplay) Dick Conway & Roland MacLane (teleplay)

Snapshot: The adorable Linda Dennison is sitting in a tree. Beaver climbs up to join her. The rumors and accusations start soon afterward. Beaver's friends tease him about her being his girl and they tell him to prove them wrong. He can do so, they say, by calling her a name.

The Players

Robert 'Rusty' Stevens…Larry Mondello
Patty Turner…Linda Dennison
Sue Randall…Miss Alice Landers

Stanley Fafara…Whitey Whitney
Jeri Weil…Judy Hensler
Susan Marshall…Third Grade Girl

Notable line(s)

June: Did you get to the bottom of it?
Ward: Yeah, more or less. He sat in a tree with Linda Dennison. Then he called her an ape, and then he punched Larry Mondello in the stomach.
June: Now, why would he do all that?
Ward: I guess our boy's growing up dear.

Beaver: You walked her (Mary Ellen Rogers) home from school on Thursday.
Wally: Well, so, I walked her.
Beaver: You used to throw rocks at her.
Wally: Well, I used to do a lot of things when I was a kid.

S2 E7 - Beaver's Ring
Nov 13, 1958
Director: Norman Tokar
Writers: Joe Connelly & Bob Mosher (teleplay) Ed James (story)

Snapshot: Beaver receives a family heirloom from his Aunt Martha. It's a 14k gold ring and he is told by his parents to not *take* the ring to school. Wait, he's told not to WEAR it to school. That's the loophole Beaver uses to take it to school and that's when the real problem begins.

The Players

Robert 'Rusty' Stevens…Larry Mondello
Stanley Fafara…Whitey Whitney
Jeri Weil…Judy Hensler

Sue Randall…Miss Alice Landers
Anne Loos…Nurse Thompson

Notable line(s)

Wally: Well, gee, didn't Aunt Martha send me anything?
June: Well, Wally, Aunt Martha is Beaver's Godmother.
Wally: Gee, yeah. Uncle Frank is my Godfather, and all he ever did was promise to send me to Europe when I'm out of college. But heck, who wants to go to Europe when you're an old man?

♦   ♦   ♦   ♦   ♦   ♦

S2 E8 - The Shave
Nov 20, 1958
Director: Norman Tokar
Writer(s) Joe Connelly & Bob Mosher, Bob Ross

Snapshot: Wally makes a wonderful play in the football game for Mayfield High. Chester, Tooey and Beaver congratulate him, but Eddie downplays his effort and gets the guys to pay attention to him, by saying he's now shaving. Wally tries his hand at shaving, and it doesn't make Ward very happy.

The Players

Ken Osmond…Eddie Haskell
Tiger Fafara…Tooey Brown
Howard McNear…Andy the Barber

Frank Bank…Clarence Rutherford
Charles Cirillo…Barber
Buddy Joe Hooker…Chester Anderson

Notable line(s)

Andy the Barber: A man likes to look right, over the weekend.

Beaver: You want I should hold your nose?
Wally: No, I can hold my own nose… Ow!

S2 E9 - The Pipe
Nov 27, 1958
Director: Norman Tokar
Writers: Joe Connelly & Bob Mosher (teleplay) Fran van Hartesveldt (story)

Snapshot: Leave it to Fred Rutherford to cause trouble for Ward and his family while he is on vacation in Europe. He sends a pipe to Ward and who displays it on a shelf in the living room. When Beaver shows it to Larry one afternoon, his friend suggests they smoke it. With friends like that… you know the saying.

The Players
Robert 'Rusty' Stevens…Larry Mondello

Notable line(s)

Ward: Only Fred Rutherford could cause this much trouble all the way from Germany.

Beaver (after hearing Ward tell the story of Pandora): She must be like Judy Hensler… she causes most of the trouble in my class.

◆   ◆   ◆   ◆   ◆   ◆

S2 E10 - Wally's New Suit
Dec 4, 1958
Director: Norman Tokar
Writers: Joe Connelly & Bob Mosher (supervisors) Richard Baer

Snapshot: If Eddie Haskell is involved, something is going to go wrong. He convinces Wally that he should be old enough to buy his own new suit. Ward tells Wally if he doesn't want his help … and Wally jumps at that opportunity and Ward is none too pleased.

The Players
Tiger Fafara…Tooey Brown   Ken Osmond…Eddie Haskell (uncredited)
John Hoyt…Clothier

Notable line(s)

Wally: It (the suit) didn't look so bright in the store.
Ward: They never do.

Eddie: You picked it out all by yourself.... your parents didn't have anything to do with it?
Ward: Honest.

Ward: Beaver, Wally doesn't have to do everything Eddie and Tooey do. If they jumped off a roof, you wouldn't expect him to, would you?
Beaver: Well, how high a roof, dad?

S2 E11 - School Play
Dec 11, 1958
Director: Norman Tokar
Writers: Joe Connelly & Bob Mosher

Snapshot: To Ward, a canary doesn't seem like the lead role in a school play. Beaver, however, seems very pleased with his part. Ward tries to encourage Beaver the night of the play but does an awful job. So much so, that Beaver no longer wants to perform.

The Players

Sue Randall…Miss Alice Landers
Dorothy Adams…Miss Wakeland
Stanley Fafara…Whitey Whitney
Jeri Weil…Judy Hensler
Robert 'Rusty' Stevens…Larry Mondello

Linda Beardon…Girl
Ralph Brooks…Audience Member
(uncredited)
Ray Pourchot…Audience Member
(uncredited)

Notable line(s)

Larry (to his dad): Gee, Dad, I couldn't help it. I couldn't find the hole in the curtain.
Larry's Dad: (laughs)

Beaver: Hey Wally, the worms don't look any fatter than yesterday.
Wally: Well, it probably takes a worm a long time to put on weight.

♦   ♦   ♦   ♦   ♦   ♦

S2 E12 - The Visiting Aunts
Dec 18, 1958
Director: Norman Tokar
Writers: Joe Connelly & Bob Mosher (teleplay) Bob Ross (story)

Snapshot: Aunt Martha drops by for a surprise visit with her friend Mrs. Hathaway. She loves to see how the boys are doing. Typically, they wouldn't be upset about this visit. But on a day when they plan on having fun at the carnival, the boys demonstrate some very passive aggressive behavior.

The Players

Madge Kennedy…Aunt Martha Bronson
Irene Tedrow…Mrs. Claudia Hathaway
Tiger Fafara…Tooey Brown

Frank Bank…Clarence Rutherford
Buddy Joe Hooker…Chester Anderson

Notable line(s)

June: Now, boys, your Aunt Martha hasn't seen you for almost a year. She wants to see how much you've grown.
Beaver: Can't she just look at our marks in the wall, and we can go to the carnival?

S2 E13 - Happy Weekend
Dec 25, 1958
Director: Norman Tokar
Writers: Joe Connelly & Bob Mosher

Snapshot: The boys are forced to go to Shadow Lake. They think they'd be happier to stay in Mayfield so they can watch *Jungle Fever* and read comic books. But fishing, exploring the woods, and finding a nearby town, gives them plenty of fun on their weekend away from home.

The Players
Harry Tyler…Boat Rental Man (as Harry O. Tyler)

Notable line(s)

Ward (raising his voice): Right now, we're all going up to Shadow Lake, and we're going to have a wonderful time. Okay?
Wally: Well, okay, if we have to.

Ward: (singing): Nita, Juanita, ask thy soul if we should part.
Beaver: Gee, dad, why would you sing goofy songs like that?
Ward: Well, I don't know Beaver. I guess to keep the mountain lions away.

♦   ♦   ♦   ♦   ♦   ♦

S2 E14 - Wally's Present
Jan 1, 1959
Director: Norman Tokar
Writers: Joe Connelly & Bob Mosher (teleplay) Keith Fowler (teleplay)

Snapshot: Revenge doesn't always taste better when served with birthday cake. Beaver is mad for Wally not inviting him for his birthday activities. With Larry's help, Beaver decides to take the money he saved for Wally's gift and use it on himself instead.

The Players
Robert 'Rusty' Stevens…Larry Mondello   Arthur Space…Mr. Judson
Ken Osmond…Eddie Haskell

Notable line(s)

Larry: Hey, Beave, it's only $6.50. Why don't we buy it?
Beaver: Have you got some money, Larry?
Larry: No. But you've got $6.98.

Eddie: Hello, Mr. and Mrs. Cleaver. It's nice of you to have me. I brought Wally a present. My father bought it in the city. He says you can't get anything good around here.

S2 E15 - The Grass Is Always Greener
Jan 8, 1959
Director: Norman Tokar
Writers: Joe Connelly & Bob Mosher (teleplay) John Whedon

Snapshot: Beaver doesn't know any poor people. He wonders what life is like for a poor person. When Henry the garbage man comes to pick up the trash, Beaver inquiries about his torn sweater, where he lives, and about his family. Henry invites him over to his home to play with his kids and Ward lets him go with him in the garbage truck. June returns home and is not too happy.

The Players

Billy Chapin…Pete Fletcher
Robert 'Rusty' Stevens…Larry Mondello
Don Lyon…Chris Fletcher

Jess Kirkpatrick…Henry Fletcher
Helen Jay…Woman
Eddie Marr…Traffic Policeman

Notable line(s)

Beaver: Dances? With Girls? Says Beaver.
Wally: Well, sure Beave, That's all there is to dance with.

◆   ◆   ◆   ◆   ◆   ◆

S2 E16 - The Boat Builders
Jan 15, 1959
Director: Norman Tokar
Writers: Joe Connelly & Bob Mosher

Snapshot: Wally and his friends decide to make a boat and sail it in Miller's Pond, before taking it to the ocean. Beaver tags along to watch but is recruited to be the test boat captain since he's the only one who will fit in the boat. It doesn't end well and neither does their cover up.

The Players

Tiger Fafara…Tooey Brown
Buddy Joe Hooker…Chester Anderson (as Buddy Hart)

Notable line(s)
Tooey: Why'd you do a crazy thing like tipping our boat over?
Beaver: Well, I didn't do anything. I just s-sat there. The boat did all the tipping over.

Chester: Beaver, you kind of smell like a swamp.
Beaver: I feel like one too.

Ward: But afterwards, why couldn't you have at least come to me and just simply said, "Dad, I did a very foolish thing and Beaver fell out of the boat." Well, you'd have been in a lot less trouble than you're in now, if you had.
Beaver: I wish we had known that then.

S2 E17 - Beaver Plays Hooky
Jan 22, 1959
Director: Norman Tokar
Writers: Joe Connelly & Bob Mosher (teleplay) Dick Conway & Roland MacLane (teleplay)

Snapshot: There should be one rule kids obey when playing hooky… that rule is "Don't go on television while playing hooky." Larry and Beaver ignore that rule and TV host Marshal Moran, in between corny jokes, corners them on their jumping the old corral fence.

The Players

Richard Lane…Marshal Moran
Robert 'Rusty' Stevens…Larry Mondello
Sue Randall…Miss Alice Landers
John Hart…Construction Worker

Robert Mitchell…Husband at Supermarket
Berniece Janssen…Wife at Supermarket

Notable line(s)

Larry: Hey Beaver, maybe we can go to one of the supermarkets. Sometimes they give away free food samples.
Beaver: Yeah, but one time, they gave way soap chips.
Larry: We'll just have to take a chance.

Marshal Moran: Looks to me like you two mavericks just kinda jumped the old corral fence.

♦   ♦   ♦   ♦   ♦   ♦

S2 E18 - The Garage Painters
Jan 29, 1959
Director: Norman Tokar
Writers: Joe Connelly & Bob Mosher

Snapshot: Beaver wonders why their father is punishing them by suggesting they read a book while the TV is broken and it's raining outside. Ward says reading isn't a punishment and can be fun. He gives them *Tom Sawyer* to read. Once, the boys start reading it, they can't stop.

The Players

Robert 'Rusty' Stevens…Larry Mondello
Frank Bank…Clarence Rutherford

Sara Anderson…Mrs. Bellamy
Joey Scott…Bengie Bellamy

Notable line(s)

Beaver: Wally, look at my ear and see if there's any paint in it
Wally: Yeah, there's still a little in there.
Beaver: Hey Wally, I can't get it out. What if the school nurse looks and sees it's green?
Wally: Ah, leave it there. Maybe she'll think it's some sort of disease and send you home.

Beaver: Bengie, what did you do that for?
Bengie: I wanted to see what I would look like if I was green.

S2 E19 - Wally's Pug Nose
Feb 5, 1959
Director: Norman Tokar
Writers: Joe Connelly & Bob Mosher (supervisors) George Tibbles

Snapshot: What there seems to be here, is a failure to communicate. Soon after meeting, Gloria Cusick tells Wally he has a pug nose. She doesn't say it in a repulsive manner, but Wally sure hears it in such a way. That sets into motion a lot of insecurity for Wally.

The Players
Cheryl Holdridge...Gloria Cusick   Frank Bank...Clarence Rutherford
Tiger Fafara...Tooey Brown   Ralph Brooks...Mailman

Notable line(s)

Ward: You know, when I was your age, I went through an experience very much like this.
Wally: About your nose.
Ward: No, my ears. Some kid called me Elephant Ears, and I got to thinking I was a regular Dumbo. Well, they didn't sell ear flatteners in those days, so I started putting adhesive tape right here, to keep the ears flat.
Beaver: How come it didn't work, dad?

♦   ♦   ♦   ♦   ♦   ♦

S2 E20 - Beaver's Pigeons
Feb 12, 1959
Director: David Butler
Writers: Joe Connelly & Bob Mosher

Snapshot: Beaver, along with Whitey and Larry start a pigeon club. Before he has a chance to buy his pigeons, Beaver comes down with the chicken pox and must be isolated. Wally, despite his history of taking care of Beaver's hamster (it died), is now in charge of Beaver's pigeons.

The Players
Robert 'Rusty' Stevens...Larry Mondello
Stanley Fafara...Whitey Whitney

Notable line(s)

Beaver: Gee, the last time I slept alone, I thought I saw a ghost. Do you think I'll see one tonight?
Wally: Course not, you think a ghost would come in there and get the chicken pox?
Beaver: Yeah, anyway, where would he scratch himself?

Wally: A cat ate 'em.
Beaver: Gee, Wally, did he eat 'em all up?
Wally: No, he just ate enough so they're no good anymore.

S2 E21 - The Tooth
Feb 19, 1959
Director David Butler
Writers: Joe Connelly & Bob Mosher (teleplay) Bob Ross (teleplay)

Snapshot: There's always a little bit of fear when visiting the dentist. For Beaver, that fear is amped up when Lumpy gives him "the business" about the dentist drilling bigger holes so he can charge more money. Beaver believes the Lump and it winds up embarrassing Ward.

The Players

Richard Deacon…Fred Rutherford

Frank Wilcox…Dr. Frederick W. Harrison, DDS

Robert 'Rusty' Stevens   Larry Mondello

Veronica Cartwright…Violet Rutherford

Frank Bank…Clarence Rutherford

Alice Backes…Nurse

Notable line(s)

Ward: I'm sure Beaver's very happy to be getting this over with, isn't he Wally?
Wally: Gee, I don't know Dad, he sure doesn't look very happy.

Wally: Don't worry Beave. Dad'll be proud of you someday again.
Beaver: When, Wally?
Wally: Oh, I don't know. Maybe like sometime when you save someone from drowning. Then he'll probably stop thinking you're chicken

◆　◆　◆　◆　◆　◆

S2 E22 - Beaver Gets Adopted
Feb 26, 1959
Director: Norman Tokar
Writers: Joe Connelly & Bob Mosher

Snapshot: Sometimes accidents happen, and that's what how Beaver breaks Wally's new trophy from the city field day events. Wally thinks he broke it on purpose and Ward agrees. With Beaver upset and telling his father he is being unfair, Ward says if Beaver can find better parents, then he's free to do so and that's exactly what Beaver attempts to do.

The Players

Lurene Tuttle…Mrs. Brady

Lee Torrance…Miss Walker

Robert 'Rusty' Stevens…Larry Mondello

Notable line(s)

Beaver: Where are you goin' Wally?
Wally: Oh, uh, just over to Chester's.
Beaver: In your Sunday School suit?
Wally: Well, Uh, Yeah, A guy doesn't want to be a slob, all the time.
Beaver: You usually do.

S2 E23 - The Haunted House
Mar 5, 1959
Director: Norman Tokar
Writers: Joe Connelly & Bob Mosher (supervisors), George Tibbles

Snapshot: Walking a dog is good pay for a young boy like Beaver, but not if it means walking the dog of a witch. Beaver is convinced Mrs. Cooper is a witch because she lives in what all the kids think is a haunted house.

The Players
Lillian Bronson…Miss Cooper
Robert 'Rusty' Stevens…Larry Mondello

Notable line(s)

Beaver: I'm gonna be real nice to her dog, in case, once upon a time it was a little boy.

Ward: There isn't any diplomatic way to tell a woman she looks like a witch.

♦   ♦   ♦   ♦   ♦   ♦

S2 E24 - The Bus Ride
Mar 12, 1959
Director: Norman Tokar
Writers: Joe Connelly & Bob Mosher

Snapshot: Beaver's friend Billy invites him to visit his farm. Ward can't drive Beaver there and Wally agrees to accompany Beaver on a bus ride to Crystal Falls. Ward finds Wally back at home safe and sound late that afternoon and thanks him for doing a fine job. That's when Wally tells him the truth about how things went, including Beaver getting on the wrong bus.

The Players
Yvonne White…Bus Passenger   Eddie Marr…Bus Passenger
Douglas Evans…Bus Passenger   Frank Sully…Cab Driver
Bill Idelson…Newstand Worker

Notable line(s)

June (unaware Ward is listening): I want you to take those orange peels off the table in the living room. Now if your father comes home and sees them, he's gonna be in a terrible mood all through supper.

June: Hello. I was down in the basement. I didn't know you were here.
Ward: Oh, yes. The monster has returned to his cave.

S2 E25 - Beaver and Gilbert
Mar 19, 1959
Director: Norman Tokar
Writers: Joe Connelly & Bob Mosher (teleplay) George Tibbles (teleplay)

Snapshot: There's a new kid in school. His name is Gilbert. He is weird. He also tells some whoppers like his brother plays for the St. Louis Cardinals. Almost everything he tells Beaver turns out to be a lie. After a scuffle with Gilbert in the Cleaver front yard, Gilbert's dad talks with Ward and Ward learns a bit about Gilbert and why he acts the way he does.

The Players
Robert 'Rusty' Stevens…Larry Mondello   Stanley Fafara…Whitey Whitney
Carleton G. Young…John Gates   Stephen Talbot…Gilbert Gates

Notable line(s)

Beaver: And Gilbert was almost to the North Pole once!
Ward: The North Pole?
Beaver: Yeah, with an expedition. And he can talk Eskimo,

Beaver: Yeah, Mom, I just beat up Gilbert, and now Dad's going to beat up his father.

◆   ◆   ◆   ◆   ◆   ◆

S2 E26 - Price of Fame
Mar 26, 1959
Director: Norman Tokar
Writers: Joe Connelly & Bob Mosher (teleplay) Dick Conway & Roland MacLane (story)

Snapshot: What does conspicuous mean? Well, getting a ride home from school at night on a fire engine is conspicuous. Also, having your head stuck in a wrought iron fence in the city park is conspicuous. Beaver has a way of being conspicuous, but his parents love him anyway.

The Players
Robert 'Rusty' Stevens…Larry Mondello
Jeri Weil…Judy Hensler
Bill Erwin…Man

Notable line(s)

Beaver: Gee, I didn't know aunts got married.
Larry: Well, sure, where do you think you get uncles?

Ward: Let's just get him out of the fence first June, and then you can all sit around and tell me how wrong I was.
S2 E27 - A Horse Named Nick

Apr 2, 1959
Director: Norman Tokar
Writers: Joe Connelly & Bob Mosher (teleplay) Hugh Beaumont (story)

Snapshot: Working at a carnival as a child is one of life's simple joys. Getting paid for such work is a huge bonus. The boys just don't know how huge and tall that bonus will be and that it has a name… his name is Nick.

The Players
Burt Mustin…Gus the Fireman   Bill Baldwin…Board of Health Officer
Michael Ross…Rendering Man

Notable line(s)

Man from health department: I'm sorry madame, I can't touch them unless they're dead (about horse in the Cleaver garage).

Beaver: Hey, Wally, do you think dad's mad for us not selling the horse to the rendering man?
Wally: Well, I don't know. He said to get rid of him, and we've still got him.
Beaver: Yeah. If we'd have sold him to that man, well, I would have never used glue again for the rest of my life. Every time I would have licked a stamp, I would have thought of Nicholas.

♦   ♦   ♦   ♦   ♦   ♦

S2 E28 - Beaver's Hero
Apr 9, 1959
Director: Norman Tokar
Writers: Joe Connelly & Bob Mosher

Snapshot: Beaver knows his father was in World War II. He doesn't know that all his dad did in the war was help build bases and barracks on islands in the South Pacific and install basketball backboards. He tells the kids in class he was so much more than a builder. Thanks to Ward, he doesn't get caught in this exaggeration.

The Players
Wendell Holmes…Mr. T.J. Willet   Stephen Talbot…Gilbert Bates
Jeri Weil…Judy Hensler   Bobby Mittelstaedt…Charles Fredericks
Stanley Fafara…Whitey Whitney

Notable line(s)

Ward: Never trouble trouble until trouble troubles you
June: And you were once a philosophy major?

S2 E29 - Beaver Says Good-bye
Apr 16, 1959
Director: Norman Tokar
Writers: Joe Connelly & Bob Mosher, George Tibbles

Snapshot: The Cleavers are moving to a new house. Beaver is excited about the move and tells his friends. At school, they throw him a surprise going away party and he receives a lot of gifts. Not long after, he finds out that the house they were going to buy was sold to another family. Now, Beaver has all those gifts under false pretenses, what will he do?

The Players

Sue Randall…Miss Alice Landers   Jeri Weil…Judy Hensler
Robert 'Rusty' Stevens…Larry Mondello   Bobby Mittelstaedt…Charles Fredericks
Stanley Fafara…Whitey Whitney   Rodney Bell…Mr. Church

Notable line(s)

Wally: Well, maybe he'll come over once a year or something. And you'll be gettin' bigger, and he'll be gettin' bigger, and pretty soon you'll see a big fat man, and it'll be Larry.

♦   ♦   ♦   ♦   ♦   ♦

S2 E30 - Beaver's Newspaper
Apr 23, 1959
Director: Norman Tokar
Writers: Joe Connelly & Bob Mosher, Elon Packard

Snapshot: Wally is full of regret for allowing Beaver to have his old broken typewriter after Beaver gets it fixed. Beaver and Larry start their own local newspaper, The Maple Drive News. When Larry gets sick and can no longer help, the paper becomes too burdensome for one young boy, and it ceases operation.

The Players

Burt Mustin…Gus the Fireman
Robert 'Rusty' Stevens…Larry Mondello (as Rusty Stevens)

Notable line(s)

Wally: I'm first-string shortstop. Look at the hole it would leave in the infield if I'm not there.

Beaver: Hey, Wally, look at the neat globe. We could put it up in our room.
Wally: Nah, that one's out of date. They've rearranged the whole world a couple times since then.
Beaver: Gee, why would they want to rearrange the world?
Wally: Well, I don't know. Maybe they do it, so you have to buy new globes.

S2 E31- Beaver's Sweater
Apr 30, 1959
Director: Norman Tokar
Writers: Joe Connelly & Bob Mosher (supervisors) Dale and Katherine Eunson

Snapshot: Instead of having his dad buy him his heart's desire, an Eskimo sweater, Beaver uses his own money on the purchase. Beaver beams with pride when he wears it to school the following day, until he sees Judy Hensler wearing the same exact sweater.

The Players
Robert 'Rusty' Stevens…Larry Mondello
Jeri Weil…Judy Hensler

Notable line(s)

Wally: Who knows besides you that it's a girl's sweater?
Beaver: Just you and Larry Mondello
Wally: You think he's going to tell?
Beaver: He took a scout's honor on it.
Wally: Yeah, but he's not a scout.
Beaver: I know, that's what's bothering me.

♦ ♦ ♦ ♦ ♦ ♦

S2 E32 - Friendship
May 7, 1959
Director: Norman Tokar
Writers: Joe Connelly & Bob Mosher (teleplay) Theodore & Mathilde Ferro (story)

Snapshot: After Beaver has a big fight with his best friend Larry Mondello, Ward talks to Beaver about real friendship, a Damon and Pythias type of friendship, a sacrificial two-way type of friendship. Beaver and Larry give it a try, but in doing so, Larry takes advantage of Beaver.

The Players
Sue Randall…Miss Alice Landers
Robert 'Rusty' Stevens…Larry Mondello

Jeri Weil…Judy Hensler
Stanley Fafara…Whitey Whitney

Notable line(s)

Beaver: If I ever see that Larry again, I'm going to tie him to a tree, and then I'll get an Indian hatchet, and scalp all his hair off, and then I'll shoot arrows into his great big stomach!
Wally: Aw, cut it out Beaver. People don't do stuff like that anymore.

Beaver: And if Larry fell out of a window, I could catch him as he comes down. And if Larry fell on top of me, I'd be dead all-right.
S2 E33 - Dance Contest

May 14, 1959
Director: Norman Tokar
Writers: Joe Connelly & Bob Mosher

Snapshot: Wally has just been invited to a dance by Mary Ellen Rogers, the girl his friends say is the "most." His friends are impressed with his pull, but Wally later finds out she's entered him into a dance contest. She tells him, she can tell he's a good dancer … by the way he walks, but he has no idea how to do the "cha-cha."

The Players

Robert 'Rusty' Stevens…Larry Mondello   Frank Bank…Clarence Rutherford
Pamela Baird…Mary Ellen Rogers   Buddy Joe Hooker…Chester Anderson
Tiger Fafara…Tooey Brown

Notable line(s)

June: Tooey, Where are you boys going?
Tooey: We're all going to watch Wally talk to Mary Ellen Rogers, Mrs. Cleaver.

Mary Ellen Rogers: I just know you're a smooth dancer, by the way you walk.

June: We weren't waiting up. We were just sitting here in case you wanted to come in and tell us about the dance.

Larry: Gee, Wally, what's the matter? Me and Beaver were just doing the choo-choo.

♦   ♦   ♦   ♦   ♦   ♦

S2 E34 - Wally's Haircomb
May 21, 1959
Director: Norman Tokar
Writers: Joe Connelly & Bob Mosher (teleplay) George Tibbles (story)

Snapshot: A young teen's first way to express himself and his individuality is styling his hair the way he wants. Unfortunately for Ward and June, Wally's desired hair style is truly embarrassing, and they don't know how to make Wally come to his senses.

The Players

Frank Bank…Clarence Rutherford   Howard Wendell…Mr. Haller
Richard Deacon…Fred Rutherford

Notable line(s)

Fred Rutherford: We sent him (Lumpy) to school this morning a fine strapping boy…. and tonight, he came home looking like a rather ugly girl.

S2 E35 - The Cookie Fund
May 28, 1959
Director: Norman Tokar
Writers: Joe Connelly & Bob Mosher

Snapshot: It's a big responsibility being cookie chairmen for the third-grade class. Beaver and Larry find this out when their cookie money account is $3.00 short after being scammed by Roger, an older student at Grant Avenue Grammar School.

The Players

Danny Richards Jr.….Roger Delacy

Sue Randall…Miss Alice Landers

Jeri Weil…Judy Hensler

John Eldredge…Mr. Preston

Robert 'Rusty' Stevens…Larry Mondello

Notable line(s)

Ward: … a boy who's lost three pairs of socks on the way home from school... is hardly the banker of tomorrow.

Roger: Look, if you guys go around spreadin' lies like that about me, I got a gang, and they're gonna fix you real good.

♦   ♦   ♦   ♦   ♦   ♦

S2 E36 - Forgotten Party
Jun 4, 1959
Director: Norman Tokar
Writers: Joe Connelly & Bob Mosher

Snapshot: In a rush to get Beaver ready for a birthday party he forgot, June runs to the store to get a gift. She comes home with a "baby" toy, according to Beaver. He tells her he can't give it to his friend. Beaver comes up with a very surprising solution to the problem.

The Players

Robert 'Rusty' Stevens…Larry Mondello

John Collier…David Manning

Mary Lawrence…Alice Manning

Bill Baldwin…Mr. Johnson

Notable line(s)

Beaver: Hey, Wally, what's going on?
Wally: I think if you're smart, you'll just keep your mouth shut.

S2 E37 - Beaver the Athlete
Jun 11, 1959
Director: Norman Tokar
Writers: Joe Connelly & Bob Mosher (teleplay) George Tibbles (story)

Snapshot: Beaver is not very talented in his physical education class. He receives a bad grade, and it really bothers Ward. It was all due to his inability to tumble, but Beaver is not very good at baseball either and makes a joke out of the class. His classmates think he's funny at first, but that feeling doesn't last long.

The Players
Robert 'Rusty' Stevens…Larry Mondello   Robert Carson…Coach Grover
Jeri Weil…Judy Hensler   LeiLani Sorenson…Girl in left field
Stanley Fafara…Whitey Whitney

Notable line(s)

Ward: What's this D in physical education?
June: Oh Ward, he did so well in everything else. Now, why'd you have to bring that up?
Ward: I don't know. It just sort of hit me.
June: Well, didn't the A's and B's hit you?
Ward: Not like the D.

◆   ◆   ◆   ◆   ◆   ◆

S2 E38 - Found Money
Jun 18, 1959
Director: Norman Tokar
Writers: Joe Connelly & Bob Mosher (supervisors) Dale & Katherine Eunson

Snapshot: Some things are too good to be true. Nevertheless, Beaver always believes Larry when he says something ridiculous, like an airplane pilot flying upside down and dropping coins in Larry's yard. In fact, they find so much money, they struggle to spend it all at the carnival.

The Players
Robert 'Rusty' Stevens…Larry Mondello   Madge Blake…Mrs. Margaret Mondello
Tiger Fafara…Tooey Brown   Eddie Marr…Carnival Barker

Notable line(s)

Beaver: Well, this wasn't any dump rat. It was a trained rat.

Beaver: Yeah, Larry. My father says I can go with you. You sure you're treatin' me?
Larry: Sure, Beaver. What do you think I am, an Indian asker or somethin'?

Mrs. Mondello: Larry, you're giving me a headache.
Larry: Every time I wanna do somethin' good, you get a headache.

S2 E39 - Most Interesting Character
Jun 25, 1959
Director: Norman Tokar
Writers: Joe Connelly & Bob Mosher, Theodore & Mathilde Ferro

Snapshot: The class essay is to write on the most interesting character the students know. Wally convinces Beaver that their father would like Beaver to write about him. Beaver chooses to do so but it's difficult for him to find anything interesting to write about Ward.

The Players
Sue Randall…Miss Alice Landers
Robert 'Rusty' Stevens…Larry Mondello
Jeri Weil…Judy Hensler
Stanley Fafara…Whitey Whitney

Notable line(s)

Judy Hensler: An interesting character is someone who goes around doing interesting things, and that's what makes him an interesting character.

Ward: They want us to take a pickup truck as part of the down payment. Well, here's your chance, dear. You always wanted a car of your own.
June: Uh-uh. Can you imagine me going to the P.T.A. meetings in a pickup truck?

Ward: Well, boys, we sold the house.

♦   ♦   ♦   ♦   ♦   ♦

S3 E1 - Blind Date Committee
Oct 3, 1959
Director: Norman Tokar
Writers: Joe Connelly & Bob Mosher, Dale & Katherine Eunson

Snapshot: Each new year in high school brings more responsibility. Wally discovers this when he's made chairman of the blind date committee for a school dance. The responsibility aspect really hits home when he's left going with the only girl who can't find a date.

The Players:

Rusty Stevens…Larry Mondello   Tommy Ivo…Duke Hathaway
Ken Osmond…Eddie Haskell   Beverly Washburn…Jill Bartlett

Notable line(s)

Beaver: Yesterday Angela Valentine ate library paste.

Wally: There's an awful lot of girls that still give me the creeps.
Ward: Just hang on to that feeling as long as you can, son.

Wally (on phone with Chester): Nah, she can't be that bad. No, I haven't seen her. She was taking a bath, but her mother says she's okay. What do you mean her mother's prejudiced? Look, are you gonna take her or not? Okay, okay.

♦   ♦   ♦   ♦   ♦   ♦

S3 E2 - Beaver Takes a Bath
Oct 10, 1959
Director: Norman Tokar
Writers: Joe Connelly & Bob Mosher

Snapshot: In one of the rare episodes where the boys are left home alone, trouble happens when Wally drops a hamburger patty on the floor. Well, not really. He gives that one to Beaver. The real trouble happens when Wally calls him down to eat and Beaver leaves the bathtub running and it floods the bathroom, and even worse, it begins leaking through kitchen ceiling.

The Players:

Robert 'Rusty' Stevens…Larry Mondello
Madge Blake…Mrs. Margaret Mondello

Notable line(s)

Wally: That's beaver's and that's mine

Wally: I guess it's better if we both keep quiet.
Beaver: It always has been.

S3 E3 - School Bus
Oct 17, 1959
Director: Norman Tokar
Writers: Joe Connelly & Bob Mosher

Snapshot: Ward believes walking to school is one of life's simple joys, but Beaver's school now offers a school bus to their neighborhood. No more walking to school. This bus riding privilege is soon taken away from Beaver for behavior not in keeping with fourth grade expectations. How will he ever get back on the bus?

The Players
Robert 'Rusty' Stevens…Larry Mondello
Sue Randall…Miss Alice Landers
Jeri Weil…Judy Hensler

Stanley Fafara…Whitey Whitney
James Parnell…Mr. Crawford
Bobby Mittelstaedt…Charles Fredericks

Notable line(s)

Judy: Where do you think you're going, Beaver, to Europe?

Judy: Beaver, your new home is just lovely.
Beaver: Since when did you begin to like stuff?

S3 E4 - Beaver's Prize
Oct 24, 1959
Director: Norman Tokar
Writers: Joe Connelly & Bob Mosher

Snapshot: When a child is grounded and are told to not leave the yard, they should do that, even if their parents are not around to enforce the punishment. Beaver doesn't heed this advice and goes with his friend Larry to watch a movie. He gets caught and eventually gets punished twice in one weekend when one punishment was more than enough.

The Players
Robert 'Rusty' Stevens…Larry Mondello
Madge Blake…Mrs. Margaret Mondello

Ken Osmond…Eddie Haskell
Peter Leeds…Theater Manager

Notable line(s)

Wally: Why is Larry asking you if he can ride his bicycle?
Beaver: I guess cause he's a goofy kid.

June: Dear, just because you didn't get pears, you don't have to take it out on the boys.

S3 E5 - Baby Picture
Oct 31, 1959
Director: Norman Tokar
Writers: Joe Connelly & Bob Mosher

Snapshot: Baby pictures can be embarrassing… but nude baby pictures are traumatizing. Beaver is traumatized when he finds out his mom chose such a picture of him for the class contest. Ward comes up with a great solution and does some editing, well, quite a bit of editing.

The Players

Robert 'Rusty' Stevens…Larry Mondello   Stanley Fafara…Whitey Whitney
Sue Randall…Miss Alice Landers   Bobby Mittelstaedt…Charles Fredericks
Jeri Weil…Judy Hensler

Notable line(s)

Judy: I have a baby picture that was taken in color. My mother was gonna send it to Hollywood, but she loved me too much to let me go. To Hollywood!

Beaver: My mother and father don't allow me to be in contests.
Miss Landers: Really, Beaver? Why not?
Beaver: Uh, well, it's against their religion.

Judy: I'll bet you were a real homely-looking baby.

◆   ◆   ◆   ◆   ◆   ◆

S3 E6 - Beaver Takes a Walk
Nov 7, 1959
Director: Norman Tokar
Writers: Joe Connelly & Bob Mosher (teleplay) Theodore & Mathilde Ferro (story)

Snapshot: Gambling in grade school becomes a problem when Beaver makes a bet with Whitey. He bets his baseball glove that he'll walk ten miles in one day, just like his dad said he did when he was a young boy. Unknown to Beaver, Ward was exaggerating about his childhood exploits.

The Players

Robert 'Rusty' Stevens…Larry Mondello   Stanley Fafara…Whitey Whitney

Notable line(s)

Ward: You know, walking's one of the greatest sports in the world. I guess when I was a boy, I must've walked twenty miles a day.

Ward: I think it's a very nice tribute for a boy to want to be like his father.
June: I suppose so, as long as he doesn't overdo it.

S3 E7 - Borrowed Boat
Nov 14, 1959
Director: Norman Tokar
Writers: Joe Connelly & Bob Mosher

Snapshot: Being hauled down to the police station on suspicion of theft is a harrowing experience for Beaver and Larry. They learn in this episode that sometimes they don't meet "friends" at Friend's Lake.

The Players

Robert 'Rusty' Stevens…Larry Mondello
Madge Blake…Mrs. Margaret Mondello
Frank Gerstle…Police Sergeant

Tommy Cole…Red Bennett
Tom Masters…Fred Thornton
Martin Smith…Police Officer #1

Notable line(s)

Beaver: I wish when you went to the hospital to get Wally, they had given you Larry Mondello instead.

Ward (to Wally): Telephone call for you, it's the police department.

◆   ◆   ◆   ◆   ◆   ◆

S3 E8 - Beaver's Tree
Nov 21, 1959
Director: Norman Tokar
Writers: Joe Connelly & Bob Mosher (teleplay) Dick Conway & Roland MacLane (story)

Snapshot: Miss Landers has the children read a poem about trees. Their lackluster performance causes her to show them how it should be read, filled with emotion. Her reading inspires Beaver to go back to his old house and take his tree, which the family left behind when they moved.

The Players

Robert 'Rusty' Stevens…Larry Mondello
Sue Randall…Miss Alice Landers

Jeri Weil…Judy Hensler
Stanley Fafara…Whitey Whitney

Notable line(s)

Beaver: You mean it works for a million dollars, but it doesn't work for trees.

Wally: You know, Beav, you're pretty lucky.
Beaver: I am, Wally?
Wally: Having parents that understand that you've got...well, like, a crush on a tree.

S3 E9 - Teacher Comes to Dinner
Nov 28, 1959
Director: Norman Tokar
Writers: Joe Connelly & Bob Mosher (story) Dale & Katherine Eunson (teleplay)

Snapshot: June invites Miss Landers to dinner. Larry takes this opportunity to charge Whitey and Gilbert a quarter each for a good spot to watch their teacher eat. He says, she might even smoke. They jump at the chance to watch her at the Cleaver house.

The Players

Robert 'Rusty' Stevens...Larry Mondello   Stanley Fafara...Whitey Whitney
Sue Randall...Miss Alice Landers   Stephen Talbot...Gilbert Bates
Jeri Weil...Judy Hensler   Bobby Mittelstaedt...Charles Fredericks

Notable line(s)

Larry: Should I really sing Monday, or should I still just make my mouth go?

Beaver: You can't invite somebody to dinner without letting them eat.

June: Here, dear, have an olive. I understand they have a calming influence.

Beaver: I'd like to present my brother Wally. He's a sophomore in high school, and he took a bath.

◆   ◆   ◆   ◆   ◆   ◆

S3 E10 - Beaver's Fortune
Dec 5, 1959
Director: Norman Tokar
Writers: Joe Connelly & Bob Mosher (story) Theodore & Mathilde Ferro (teleplay)

Snapshot: Beaver pays a penny to see how much he weighs. On the back of his weight ticket is his fortune. Beaver is to have a lucky day. But is he lucky enough to beat up Sonny Cartwright when Larry tells Sonny he will be happy to fight him in the park?

The Players

Robert 'Rusty' Stevens...Larry Mondello   Bobby Mittelstaedt...Charles Fredericks
Stanley Fafara...Whitey Whitney   Callen John Thomas Jr....Sonny Cartwright

Notable line(s)

Beaver: You don't have enough stuff to use up a hundred labels.
Larry: Well, the rest I can stick on telephone poles and write my name on them.
Beaver: What's the good of that?
Larry: How many guys do you know with their name stuck on telephone poles?

Beaver: Gee, Larry, I don't know anybody that weighs 114 pounds.

S3 E11 - Beaver Makes a Loan
Dec 12, 1959
Director: David Butler
Writers: Joe Connelly & Bob Mosher

Snapshot: Never loan a friend money. Beaver finds this bit of wisdom to be true when he loans Larry money for a school notebook. Larry turns out to be a real rat, but that's nothing new.

The Players

Robert 'Rusty' Stevens…Larry Mondello   Stanley Fafara…Whitey Whitney
Madge Blake…Mrs. Margaret Mondello   Stephen Talbot…Gilbert Bates

Notable line(s)

Larry: Last night he (his dad) caught me eating a piece of pie in bed.

Ward: Beaver? Beaver, you come down here!
June: Now, dear, don't get him crying.
Ward: Dear, I'm just gonna talk to him like a father.
June: That's what I mean.

♦   ♦   ♦   ♦   ♦

S3 E12 - Beaver the Magician
Dec 19, 1959
Director: David Butler
Writers: Joe Connelly & Bob Mosher, George Tibbles

Snapshot: Bengie, a local neighbor boy is tricked by Larry into thinking Beaver has been turned into a rock. Not seeing him turned back into Beaver leaves Bengie quite frightened.

The Players

Robert 'Rusty' Stevens…Larry Mondello   Eddie Marr…Uncle Artie
Madge Kennedy…Aunt Martha Bronson   Joey Scott…Bengie Bellamy
Ann Doran…Mrs. Bellamy

Notable line(s)

Beaver: What's this new big trick?
Larry: I haven't thought of it yet, but we should be able to fool a kid who talks to ants.

Wally: Did Aunt Martha flip her lid?
June: Wally, you get right out of here!
Wally: Sure, Mom. Sure. I was just trying to help.

S3 E13 - June's Birthday
Dec 26, 1959
Director: David Butler
Writers: Joe Connelly & Bob Mosher (teleplay) Dale & Katherine Eunson (story)

Snapshot: "Ghastly!" That is what June thinks about the birthday present Beaver gives her. Of course, she doesn't tell this to her youngest son. She tells him she likes it and that she'll wear it to her mother's meeting. Beaver finds out that is nothing but a lie and his heart breaks.

The Players

Robert 'Rusty' Stevens…Larry Mondello
Sue Randall…Miss Alice Landers
Madge Blake…Mrs. Margaret Mondello
Jeri Weil…Judy Hensler

Stanley Fafara…Whitey Whitney
Claire Carleton…Saleslady
Jean Vander Pyl…Woman's Club Member

Notable line(s)

Wally: Boy, Beaver, there's nothing worse in the world than having a little dumb brother!

Beaver: Gee, Mrs. Mondello, if it was your birthday, what would you like?
Mrs. Mondello: Well, I'd just like Larry to be a good boy.

June: Ward, who would sell a child a ghastly thing like this?
Ward: Some tool of big business, no doubt.

Beaver: Are you gonna wear my blouse tonight?
June: Well, no, Beaver. I think I should save it for special occasions.

♦   ♦   ♦   ♦   ♦   ♦

S3 E14 - Tire Trouble
Jan 2, 1960
Director: Norman Tokar
Writers: Joe Connelly & Bob Mosher (teleplay) Jon Zimmer (story)

Snapshot: Eddie Haskell gives the boys an idea and of course, it's a sneaky idea. After flattening their father's car tire with a nail, the boys take off the tire and roll it to a service station to be patched. Like always, Ward finds out, this time, thanks to some help from Eddie.

The Players

Ken Osmond…Eddie Haskell

Richard Deacon…Fred Rutherford

Notable line(s)

Beaver (about chinchillas): You mean they gotta be dead?
Wally: Sure, you're not going to make $10,000 by just petting them.

June (to Ward): All I know is everything was peaceful and quiet around here until you got home.

S3 E15 - Larry Hides Out
Jan 9, 1960
Director: David Butler
Writers: Joe Connelly & Bob Mosher

Snapshot: This is the only episode when viewers get to see Larry's sister's bedroom. And boy, Mrs. Mondello is not happy. After being punished, Larry tells Beaver he's running away to Mexico, but doesn't make it any further than the Cleaver's house, and their bathtub.

The Players
Robert 'Rusty' Stevens…Larry Mondello
Madge Blake…Mrs. Margaret Mondello

Notable line(s)

Beaver: Hey Larry, what's this?
Larry: My sister's always putting this junk on her hair so it shouldn't be crummy.
Beaver: What's this Larry?
Larry: That's perfume to make her smell good and these are beauty creams that she's always smearing on her face.
Beaver: Boy, it sure is a lot of trouble being a girl.
Larry: It is when you look like my sister.

◆   ◆   ◆   ◆   ◆   ◆

S3 E16 - Pet Fair
Jan 16, 1960
Director: David Butler
Writers: Joe Connelly & Bob Mosher, Dale & Katherine Eunson

Snapshot: Beaver's class is having a pet day. All of his classmates have pets and Beaver is feeling left out because he has no pet. Miss Landers asks Beaver what type of pet he will bring, and he tells a fib and says he owns a parrot. Where is he ever going to get a parrot?

The Players
Robert 'Rusty' Stevens…Larry Mondello
Sue Randall…Miss Alice Landers
Jeri Weil…Judy Hensler
Stanley Fafara…Whitey Whitney

Tim Graham…Mr. Allen
Patty Turner…Alice
Darcy Hinton…Kathleen

Notable line(s)

Wally: Parents are no good. Parents are no good.

Beaver: I have a very nice pet. My parents have made me the proud possessor of a... parrot.

S3 E17 - Wally's Test
Jan 23, 1960
Director: Norman Tokar
Writers: Joe Connelly & Bob Mosher

Snapshot: Cheaters never win and Eddie and Lumpy find this out the hard way. They make plans to cheat, but their history teacher Mr. Gannon ruins their plans. Thinking it was Wally, they send an anonymous letter to Mr. Gannon telling on their friend.

The Players

Ken Osmond…Eddie Haskell   Frank Albertson…Mr. Gannon
Frank Bank…Clarence Rutherford   Cindy Carol…Nita Norton

Notable line(s)

Mr. Gannon (to Lumpy): Oh, that's right. We've fought through World War I before, didn't we?

Wally: Hey, Beaver, what are you doing?
Beaver: I'm death-raying guys from Mars … Ah-ah-ah-ah-ah-ah!

♦   ♦   ♦   ♦   ♦   ♦

S3 E18 - Beaver's Library Book
Jan 30, 1960
Director: Norman Tokar
Writers: Joe Connelly & Bob Mosher

Snapshot: Ward in jail? What? No, say it ain't so! Well, that's what Eddie says could happen. He tells Beaver the "library police" may come around looking for Ward after Beaver loses a library book he checked out with Ward's library card. Boy, that Eddie Haskell is a rat.

The Players

Robert 'Rusty' Stevens…Larry Mondello   Theodore Newton…Mr. Davenport
Ken Osmond   Eddie Haskell   Claudia Bryar…Librarian

Notable line(s)

Beaver: Didn't fathers ever do anything bad when they were in school?
Larry: If they did, they keep it quiet.

Beaver: I'm not reading it for fun lady, I'm reading it for a book report

S3 E19 - Wally's Election
Feb 6, 1960
Director: Norman Tokar
Writers: Joe Connelly & Bob Mosher

Snapshot: Wally is not happy about Eddie nominating him for sophomore class president. But with a little encouragement from Ward, Wally really gets into the political groove, and his classmates dislike this new Wally Cleaver.

The Players

Ken Osmond...Eddie Haskell

Richard Deacon...Fred Rutherford

Frank Bank...Clarence Rutherford

Tiger Fafara...Tooey Brown

Buddy Joe Hooker...Chester Anderson

Ross Elliott...Mr. Hyatt

Ann Barnes...Frances Hobbs

Cindy Carol...Alma Hanson

Dennis Kerlee...Tall Sophomore

Notable line(s)

Wally: A guy can't just sit back, he's gotta be... aggressive.
Eddie: You're gonna be aggressive, this I've got to see.

June: If you hadn't urged him last year, he never would've made the track team.
Ward: Yes, but you don't have to warp your entire personality to run the 100-yard dash.

♦   ♦   ♦   ♦   ♦   ♦

S3 E20 - Beaver and Andy
Feb 13, 1960
Director: David Butler
Writers: Joe Connelly & Bob Mosher

Snapshot: An episode where communication is the key, and missing, Beaver becomes friends with Andy, an alcoholic Ward hires to paint their house. If only Beaver knew about his problem, he never would have given Andy the Brandy that helped him fall off the wagon.

The Players
Wendell Holmes...Andy Hadlock

Notable line(s)

Beaver: What kind of trouble do you think Andy has?
Wally: If must be pretty neat if they don't want him to do it around us.

Wally: All Whiskey smells awful.
Beaver: Then why do people drink it?
Wally: Well, it's like when grownups have a party. They drink it to have a good time.
Beaver: Gee, if it's a party, don't they have a good time anyway?
Wally: Well, grownups have a harder time having a good time than kids do.

S3 E21- Beaver's Dance
Feb 20, 1960
Director: Bretaigne Windust
Writers: Joe Connelly & Bob Mosher

Snapshot: The Mayfield Cotillion is not Beaver's idea of fun and Larry doesn't like it either. After the first dance they decide to never go back. They skip the next dance and wind up meeting a girl with a horse and go back home covered in horsehair.

The Players

Robert 'Rusty' Stevens…Larry Mondello   Karen Sue Trent…Cowgirl
Madge Blake…Mrs. Margaret Mondello   Katherine Warren…Mrs. Prescott

Notable line(s)

Beaver: I took my bath and cleaned my ears, but I'm not putting the suit on.
June: Beaver, are you defying me?
Beaver: Uhn uh, I'm just not putting on the suit.

June: Beaver, look at you, you're covered with hair.
Beaver: Gee, mom, maybe some of the girls were shedding.

◆　◆　◆　◆　◆　◆

S3 E22 - Larry's Club
Feb 27, 1960
Director: David Butler
Writers: Joe Connelly & Bob Mosher

Snapshot: The "Bloody Five" and "The Fiends" are gangs in Mayfield and nowhere near as dangerous as the real-life Bloods and Crips. Nevertheless, whether they are called gangs or clubs, the exclusivity of such groups bothers Mrs. Mondello when her son is excluded, and this causes Larry to start the Fiends and he lures Beaver to join, even though it is a fictitious club.

The Players

Robert 'Rusty' Stevens…Larry Mondello   Gary Allen…Boy in Club
Madge Blake…Mrs. Margaret Mondello   Neil Seflinger…Boy in Club
Stanley Fafara…Whitey Whitney   Bobby Beakman…Boy in Club

Notable line(s)

Wally: Maybe he (Beaver) went across the street again to watch little Bengie eat snails.

Beaver: I, Theodore Cleaver, promise to be a loyal member of the Bloody Five, and only go around with other Bloody Five guys as long as I live. And not to squeal.

Beaver: Tomorrow, I'll just say "Hi, Larry," and he'll say "Hi, Beaver," and then we'll go start doing something, and we'll forget all about hating each other.

S3 E23 - School Sweater
Mar 5, 1960
Director: Norman Tokar
Writers: Joe Connelly & Bob Mosher

Snapshot: Wally is in the clutches of a devious teenage vixen, or so that's what Ward and June think after seeing her at the drug store soda fountain wearing Wally's school sweater.

The Players
Ken Osmond…Eddie Haskell   Cindy Carol…Helen (uncredited)
Ann Barnes…Frances Hobbs

Notable line(s)

Wally: Look Beaver, when your parents give you something that is worth $19.00, it's never really yours.

Frances: Wally, the rain certainly makes your hair curly, doesn't it?

Frances: Well, I guess I'd better be getting home. He might phone me. And the poor dear's just terribly jealous.

June: Well, who is she, and what's she doing to our baby?

Wally: Thank you. Oh, and another thing, Frances, just watch what you're saying around in drugstores about me, huh?

♦   ♦   ♦   ♦   ♦   ♦

S3 E24 - The Hypnotist
Mar 12, 1960
Director: David Butler
Writers: Joe Connelly & Bob Mosher (teleplay) Dale & Katherine Eunson (story)

Snapshot: In yet another movie come to life for Beaver, with Eddie as the antagonist, this episode has Beaver hypnotizing Wally's best friend. However, Eddie is not really hypnotized, he's simply giving Beaver "the business."

The Players
Robert 'Rusty' Stevens…Larry Mondello   Ken Osmond…Eddie Haskell

Notable line(s)

June: I'm awfully busy getting supper. Look, you go hypnotize your brother or your father.

Eddie: Uh, Mr. Cleaver, I'm not one for carrying tales, but I believe your younger son is outside annoying the cat from across the street.

S3 E25 - Wally and Alma
Mar 19, 1960
Director: Hugh Beaumont
Writers: Joe Connelly & Bob Mosher

Snapshot: Wally learns that mothers of girls who like him can be meddlesome and troublesome. Alma Hanson's mother is the ultimate example. She not only exemplifies those traits; she is also a high-class snob. With Ward's help, Wally eventually pawns Alma off onto one of his classmates.

The Players

Ken Osmond…Eddie Haskell

Barry Curtis…Harry Myers

Frank Bank…Clarence Rutherford

Jean Vander Pyl…Mrs. Hanson

Cindy Carol…Alma Hanson

Rodney Bell…Mr. Alfred Hanson

Notable line(s)

Ward: I hardly approve on him going steady with one girl and I certainly don't approve of him going steady with her mother.

Mrs. Hanson: Mrs. Cleaver, I hope we didn't keep you away from your dishes.
June: Not at all, they are used to being alone.

♦   ♦   ♦   ♦   ♦   ♦

S3 E26 - Beaver's Bike
Mar 26, 1960
Director: Hugh Beaumont
Writers: Joe Connelly & Bob Mosher

Snapshot: Larry talks with everyone and just because he talks with someone doesn't mean he knows them. Unfortunately, Beaver didn't realize this when he let a boy Larry speaks with downtown, ride his bicycle. After all, he thought, he was a friend of Larry's. But nooooooo….and moments later, the bicycle and the boy disappear.

The Players

Robert 'Rusty' Stevens…Larry Mondello

Paul Bryar…Sgt. Peterson

Stanley Fafara…Whitey Whitney

Paul Engle…Bicycle Thief

Notable line(s)

Ward: What did you do after you found out it was gone?
Beaver: I wished I was dead.
June: You wished you were dead?'
Beaver: Yeah, I wished it for about 15 minutes, but nothing happened so I came home.

S3 E27 - Wally's Orchid
Apr 2, 1960
Director: Norman Abbott
Writers: Joe Connelly & Bob Mosher, Bob Ross

Snapshot: Myra is a girl Wally is afraid to ask to the sophomore dance. Eventually, he does ask and she happily agrees to go with him. She's a popular girl and expects an orchid, the most expensive type of corsage that is sold at the florist. Wally finds out a difficult lesson after escorting her to the dance, that some girls are just out of his league, and should stay there.

The Players
Robert 'Rusty' Stevens…Larry Mondello   Pamela Beaird…Myra Barker
Ken Osmond…Eddie Haskell   Dee Carroll…Florist
Doris Packer…Mrs. Cornelia Rayburn   Sandra Lytle…Judy

Notable line(s)

Ward: You're going to take a young lady?
Wally: A couple's gotta be a young lady and a fella.

Beaver: I think I'm gonna hang around Mrs. Rayburn and talk to her.
Larry: Gee, no kid ever talked to a principal on purpose.

♦   ♦   ♦   ♦   ♦   ♦

S3 E28 - Ward's Baseball
Apr 9, 1960
Director: Earl Bellamy
Writers: Joe Connelly & Bob Mosher

Snapshot: Ward comes home and shows off his autographed baseball to June. This is his prized possession, but that doesn't stop Beaver from playing catch with it, after some convincing from his friend Larry.

The Players
Robert 'Rusty' Stevens…Larry Mondello   Richard Deacon…Fred Rutherford

Notable line(s)

June: KiKi Cuyler... sounds like a fan dancer.

June: I was just thinking how sad it is to have an empty place at the table. Beaver always said such cute things at dinner.
Wally: Yeah, it used to be real neat when he was around.
Ward: Shall we not try to dramatize the incident any more than we have to?

S3 E29 - Beaver's Monkey
Apr 16, 1960
Director: Norman Abbott
Writers: Joe Connelly & Bob Mosher (supervisors) George Tibbles

Snapshot: After being told he can only have a real pet, unlike the field mouse he recently brought home, Beaver jumps at the chance to own a pet monkey … and for free too. His name is Stanley and he's the most adorable monkey ever seen inside a home in Mayfield.

The Players

Robert 'Rusty' Stevens…Larry Mondello   Mary Alan Hokanson…Luncheon Guest
Norman Leavitt…Veterinarian   Bess Flowers…Luncheon Guest
Dee Carroll…Luncheon Guest   (uncredited)

Notable line(s)

Ward: Just imagine the appeal a monkey has for a child. Didn't you want one when you were a little girl?
June: Well, I may have been peculiar, but I didn't.

Wally: So long, Stanley.

♦   ♦   ♦   ♦   ♦   ♦

S3 E30 - Beaver Finds a Wallet
Apr 23, 1960
Director: David Butler
Writers: Joe Connelly & Bob Mosher (teleplay) Theodore & Mathilde Ferro (story)

Snapshot: Beaver finds a wallet lying in the gutter in downtown Mayfield. He does the right thing and turns it into the police. After ten days, the wallet and the money inside is all his if no one claims it. It's all a matter of time, hmmm, will he be rich, or will someone claim the wallet?

The Players

Robert 'Rusty' Stevens…Larry Mondello   Valerie Allen…Miss Tomkins
Ken Osmond…Eddie Haskell   Edith Terry Preuss…Secretary
Jess Kirkpatrick…Police Sergeant

Notable line(s)

Beaver: We have to find out who it belongs to because that's what we're supposed to do

Ward: If they started arresting people for selfishness, half the world would be in jail.

Eddie: Look kid, your pop said you had to put an ad in the paper. He didn't say you had to draw a map.

S3 E31 - Mother's Day Composition
Apr 30, 1960
Director: Norman Abbott
Writers: Joe Connelly & Bob Mosher, Bob Ross

Snapshot: Beaver finds it difficult to write fifty words about his mother before she was married. He tries writing his Mother's Day composition with facts she has told him about her life, but he finds the life of an actress being interviewed on television much more interesting.

The Players

Robert 'Rusty' Stevens…Larry Mondello
Stanley Fafara…Whitey Whitney
Jeri Weil…Judy Hensler
Doris Packer…Mrs. Cornelia Rayburn

Richard Correll…Richard Rickover
Bill Baldwin…Frank
Dee Arlen…Laura

Notable line(s)

June: Dear, can you imagine what's going to happen when the other children go home and tell their parents that I was a chorus girl who danced in beer joints?
Ward: Yeah. I'm afraid this kills your chances for Mother of the Year.

♦   ♦   ♦   ♦   ♦   ♦

S3 E32 - Beaver and Violet
May 7, 1960
Director: David Butler
Writers: Joe Connelly & Bob Mosher

Snapshot: If there's one thing Fred Rutherford will always do, it is something that causes trouble for Ward or for one of his family members. In this case, the trouble comes to Beaver when he has Violet kiss him on the cheek for a photo during a picnic outing.

The Players

Richard Deacon…Fred Rutherford
Stanley Fafara…Whitey Whitney
Richard Correll…Richard Rickover

Veronica Cartwright…Violet Rutherford
Majel Barrett…Gwen Rutherford

Notable line(s)

Fred: Wally, it's too bad we didn't bring along another little girl to sit on your lap.

Violet: They want you
Wally: Who wants us?
Violet: My mommy and daddy and your mommy and daddy
Wally: Hey look, don't be so cute, huh Violet.
Violet: I can't help it, that's what I call them.

S3 E33 - The Spot Removers
May 14, 1960
Director: Norman Tokar
Writers: Joe Connelly & Bob Mosher, Bob Ross

Snapshot: It is unlikely that Eddie Haskell will do something nice for Beaver. In this episode, that's exactly what happens when Eddie convinces Wally to not wear his jacket to a party they attend. Since Beaver ruined that jacket and Eddie knew about it, this was pure kindness on Eddie's part, a new side to Eddie that is rarely seen.

The Players
Ken Osmond…Eddie Haskell
Richard Correll…Richard Rickover

Notable line(s)

Richard: Hey beaver, you got a horse?
Beaver: Naah
Richard: Then how come you got horseshoes?
Beaver: For good luck
Richard: Well, heck, if you had good luck, you'd have a horse.

Beaver: Gee Eddie, where'd you come from?
Eddie: (looks afar) I came from outer space on a ray of light.

◆　◆　◆　◆　◆　◆

S3 E34 - Beaver, the Model
May 21, 1960
Director: Norman Tokar
Writers: Joe Connelly & Bob Mosher

Snapshot: If you are told something is a gyp, then it's a gyp. But when Eddie Haskell is right there to tell you it's not, who are you going to listen to if you're Beaver Cleaver, him or your father? Yes, he listens to Eddie and boy, is Beaver ever in trouble this time!

The Players
Ken Osmond…Eddie Haskell   Aline Towne…Mr. Compton's Secretary
Bartlett Robinson…George Compton

Notable line(s)

Beaver: Yeah. I guess even if Frankenstein had a mother, she'd say he was good looking, too.

Ward: You know, a parent can tell a child something's wrong until he's blue in the face, but when someone else tells him, then it really makes an impression.

S3 E35 - Wally, the Businessman
May 28, 1960
Director: Norman Tokar
Writers: Joe Connelly & Bob Mosher

Snapshot: When Ward was a child, he followed his big brother around everywhere. Beaver does the same with Wally, pestering him as he sells Igloo ice cream bars. This causes some anger between the two brothers and an unlikely solution to a problem bothering Wally.

The Players

Ken Osmond…Eddie Haskell   Dana Dillaway…Peggy
Tiger Fafara…Tooey Brown   Ann Jillian…Little Girl (as Anne Nauseda)
Cheryl Holdridge…Gloria Cusick   Buddy Joe Hooker…Chester Anderson
Rory Stevens…Little Boy

Notable line(s)

Ward: If I knew why teenagers act the way they do, I could write a book and make a fortune.

June: Wally looked worried, Ward.
Ward: Well, sure. He's an American businessman. It's obligatory to look worried.

♦   ♦   ♦   ♦   ♦   ♦

S3 E36 - Beaver and Ivanhoe
Jun 4, 1960
Director: David Butler
Writers: Joe Connelly & Bob Mosher

Snapshot: Beaver finds out that defending womanhood and the community is not all it's cracked up to be after he reads the book *Ivanhoe* by Sir Walter Scott.

The Players

Sue Randall…Miss Alice Landers   James Parnell…Mr. Crawford
Jeri Weil…Judy Hensler   Bobby Beakman…Harold
Stanley Fafara…Whitey Whitney   Karen Sue Trent…Penny Woods
Stephen Wootton…Clyde Appleby   Neil Seflinger…Boy
Stephen Talbot…Gilbert Bates

Notable line(s)

Ward: I hope I'm wrong dear, but I'm afraid Sir Walter Scott and I gave our son a bum steer.

Beaver: I guess this Ivanhoe stuff just doesn't work anymore.
Ward: Well, Beav, the virtues are still good, but the violence isn't.

S3 E37 - Wally's Play
Jun 11, 1960
Director: David Butler
Writers: Joe Connelly & Bob Mosher (teleplay) George Tibbles (story)

Snapshot: Wally is invited to join The Crusaders, a club at school. He's delighted to be part of the club until he finds out he must play the part of a dance hall girl in a play put on by The Crusaders. Now he has to figure out how to trade parts with someone else in the play, enter the pigeon, Eddie Haskell, stage right.

The Players
Ken Osmond...Eddie Haskell
Stephen Talbot...Gilbert Bates
Tommy Ivo...Duke Hathaway

Notable line(s)

Wally: Look Beaver, I'm telling ya, if you say anything to anybody about this, I'm gonna fix ya good.
Beaver: Don't worry Wally, I'd be too ashamed to tell anybody I had a brother who was going to be a girl.

Ward: Well Duke, is Mayfield going to have another good basketball team next year?
Duke: Oh, I don't think so Mr. Cleaver... I'm graduating.

♦　♦　♦　♦　♦　♦

S3 E38 - The Last Day of School
Jun 18, 1960
Director: Norman Abbott
Writers: Joe Connelly & Bob Mosher

Snapshot: When Beaver informs his mom that he needs a gift for Miss Landers, she gets right to work and calls the department store to place an order for some lovely handkerchiefs. Unfortunately, the gift she orders and an order she places for herself get mixed up and Beaver is left in an embarrassing predicament.

The Players
Sue Randall...Miss Alice Landers
Stanley Fafara...Whitey Whitney
Jeri Weil...Judy Hensler
Stephen Talbot...Gilbert Bates
Richard Correll...Richard Rickover

Notable line(s)

Miss Landers: Why, Beaver, are you sticking your tongue out at Judy?
Beaver: No, Miss Landers. I was just giving it some air.

S3 E39 - Beaver's Team
Jun 25, 1960
Director: David Butler
Writers: Joe Connelly & Bob Mosher (teleplay) Edward J. O'Connor (story)

Snapshot: Beaver thinks Penny is a goofy girl and it's this episode where that thought probably originates. He shares a secret play that his football team will use to beat Richard and his team. She lets the secret out of the bag, causing Beaver to experience a crushing loss.

The Players
Ken Osmond…Eddie Haskell
Stanley Fafara…Whitey Whitney
Stephen Talbot…Gilbert Bates
Richard Correll…Richard Rickover
Karen Sue Trent…Penny Woods
Bobby Beakman…Harry (as Bobby Beekman)
Neil Seflinger…Football Player (uncredited)

Notable line(s)

Eddie: Hey kid what are you doing? Playing football or looking for Indians?

Beaver: That's what I get for playing football in baseball season.

S4 E1 - Beaver Won't Eat
Oct 1, 1960
Director: Norman Abbott
Writers: Joe Connelly & Bob Mosher (supervisors) Bob Ross

Snapshot: Refusal to eat food is rude, and typically met with parental disdain. That happens here when Beaver refuses to eat his Brussels sprouts. Eddie sees him sitting at the table alone and tells him his parents will crack. Just wait… they'll make a deal. This time, Eddie is correct.

The Players

Ken Osmond…Eddie Haskell   Bea Silvern…Waitress
Hal Smith…Restaurant Manager   Leoda Richards…Restaurant Patron
Netta Packer…Restaurant Customer

Notable line(s)

Eddie: Hey Beaver...Hold the fort kid... they're crackin'

Ward: Dear, don't you think you're sort of making a mountain out of a Brussels sprout?
June: No, Ward, I don't!

◆   ◆   ◆   ◆   ◆   ◆

S4 E2 - Beaver's House Guest
Oct 8, 1960
Director: Norman Abbott
Writers: Joe Connelly & Bob Mosher (supervisors) Arthur Kober

Snapshot: Beaver met a boy named Chopper at summer camp. Chopper is what some may call very much advanced for his age. The sad part is that this growing up early was not his choosing, but because of circumstances he's been dealt by his parents. When he spends the night, Beaver comes up with some nutty ideas that he soon finds out are exactly that… nutty.

The Players

Barry Gordon…Chopper Cooper
Clark Howat…Uncle Dave

Notable line(s)

Wally: Hey, how come they call him Chopper anyway?
Beaver: Because his first name's Dryden.
Wally: Oh. No wonder they call him Chopper.

Ward: Chopper, do you have any brothers?
Chopper: No, not real ones. But I do have three half-brothers and one half-sister, and I used to have two stepbrothers before Pop's second divorce.

S4 E3- Beaver Becomes a Hero
Oct 15, 1960
Director: Gene Reynolds
Writers: Joe Connelly & Bob Mosher (teleplay) Frank Gabrielson (story)

Snapshot: Don't let the title of this episode fool you, Beaver does not become a hero, not really. But momentarily, his classmates turn him into one and the story of his fictitious heroic acts are printed in the local paper, catching his parents totally off guard.

The Players

Sue Randall…Miss Alice Landers   Jeri Weil…Judy Hensler
Stanley Fafara…Whitey Whitney   Larry Thor…Willard Watson
Richard Correll… Richard Rickover   Neil Seflinger…Student

Notable line(s)

Beaver: ♪ Jingle bells, jingle bells ♪ - ♪ Jingle all the way ♪
Wally: What are you singing that for? It's not even anywhere near Christmas.

Beaver: Maybe an Indian lost it.
Wally: Who ever heard of an Indian with a plastic canoe?

Judy: Don't forget the spelling test, Miss Landers.
Miss Landers: Thank you, Judy.

Judy: I think we should call up the newspaper and have them print on the front page that Theodore Cleaver's a big liar.

♦   ♦   ♦   ♦   ♦   ♦

S4 E4 - Wally, the Lifeguard
Oct 22, 1960
Director: Andrew McCullough
Writers: Joe Connelly & Bob Mosher, George Tibbles

Snapshot: The government makes a lot of laws that stink. Wally finds this out when he's told he cannot be a lifeguard at Friend's Lake because the law now says he must be 18 years old. Instead, he becomes a candy butcher, something his younger brother finds rather embarrassing.

The Players

Ken Osmond…Eddie Haskell   Pamela Beaird…Mary Ellen Rogers
Stephen Talbot…Gilbert Bates   Dick Gering…Lifeguard
Stanley Fafara…Whitey Whitney   Cindy Carol…Alma Hanson
John Hiestand…Mr. Burton

Notable line(s)

Alma: You look cute in your hot dog suit Wally.

S4 E5 - Beaver's Freckles
Oct 29, 1960
Director: Norman Abbott
Writers: Joe Connelly & Bob Mosher (teleplay) William Cowley (story)

Snapshot: Lumpy Rutherford has a knack for causing trouble for Beaver. He scares him, he threatens him and here, he embarrasses Beaver by making fun of his freckles. That sends Beaver on the biggest mission of his childhood, finding a way to rid his face of those tiny red and brown dots.

The Players

Robert 'Rusty' Stevens…Larry Mondello	Stanley Fafara…Whitey Whitney
Frank Bank…Clarence Rutherford	Stephen Wootton…Clyde Appleby

Notable line(s)

Beaver: Boy, those creepy Bronsons.

Wally: Gee, he must be growing up. He used to didn't care whether he was funny-looking or not.

♦   ♦   ♦   ♦   ♦   ♦

S4 E6 - Beaver's Big Contest
Nov 5, 1960
Director: Gene Reynolds
Writers: Joe Connelly & Bob Mosher (teleplay) Arthur Kober (story)

Snapshot: For every booklet of raffle tickets sold by Beaver, he gets one ticket for free. He has total faith that he will win one of the big prizes, either a trip to Hawaii or a brand-new sports car. He wins the sports car, but that's just the beginning of the story and for Beaver, it has an unhappy ending.

The Players

Ken Osmond…Eddie Haskell	Mark Allen…Policeman
Burt Mustin…Gus the Fireman	Lenore Kingston…Lady at Mailbox
Robert 'Rusty' Stevens…Larry Mondello	

Notable line(s)

Wally: Gee, a guy never thinks of his mother having a good time.
June: Wally, I wasn't born a mother

Eddie: Listen, squirt. Parents can do anything they want, and they got laws to have you put away if you squawk. You better just keep driving this box, kid, because that's all you're going to get.

S4 E7 - Miss Landers' Fiancé
Nov 12, 1960
Director: Norman Abbott
Writers: Joe Connelly & Bob Mosher

Snapshot: Beaver is lovesick when he finds out that Miss Landers will soon become Mrs. Brittingham. He can't imagine that she is doing this to him, and she must explain that teachers can fall in love and have a family, just like everyone else.

The Players

Sue Randall…Miss Alice Landers   Jack Powers…Tom Brittingham
Stanley Fafara…Whitey Whitney

Notable line(s)

Whitey: We always get tomorrows' paper tonight. My pop says he'd rather read tomorrows' stuff tonight instead of waiting until tomorrow.

Tom Brittingham: Well, I guess Alice knows what you little fellas like, huh, Teddy?

◆ ◆ ◆ ◆ ◆ ◆

S4 E8 - Eddie's Double-Cross
Nov 19, 1960
Director: Norman Abbott
Writers: Joe Connelly & Bob Mosher

Snapshot: Eddie Haskell is more about giving people "the business" than having "the business" given to him. But Caroline Schuster is the one who doles out "the business" in this episode. She thinks Eddie is a creep and is using him to stay occupied on the weekends while her boyfriend is grounded. When Wally informs him of the situation, Eddie is not very happy.

The Players

Ken Osmond…Eddie Haskell   Audrey Caire…Waitress (as Audrey Clark)
Cindy Carol…Alma Hanson   Howard Wright…Mr. Newton
Reba Waters…Caroline Shuster   Leslie Towner…Caroline's Friend

Notable line(s)

Eddie: What kind of phony tax deduction is dad gonna take on this junk
Wally: Maybe you'd like to give us an appraisal on it Eddie.

Wally: Well, uh, can I talk to you dad, in the den?
Ward: What's the matter with in here?
Wally: Well, um, there's no one else in the den.
June: Wally, if you want to talk to your father alone, you don't have to be so subtle.

S4 E9 - Beaver's I.Q.
Nov 26, 1960
Director: Norman Abbott
Writers: Joe Connelly & Bob Mosher (supervisors) Theodore & Mathilde Ferro

Snapshot: An upcoming I.Q. test at school has Beaver worried. Will he please his father and be as smart as Wally with a good future ahead of him or not? He stays up late studying the night before the test, but it's doubtful they're going to ask what the longest river of Africa is on an I.Q. test, but he still informs Mrs. Rayburn, afterward, that it is the Nile at 4150 miles in length.

The Players

Stanley Fafara…Whitey Whitney   Burt Mustin…Gus the Fireman
Karen Sue Trent…Penny Woods   Keith Taylor…Harry Harrison
Doris Packer…Mrs. Cornelia Rayburn

Notable line(s)

Penny: It was easy. I did the whole test with just half my brain.
Whitey: I hope it wasn't the dumb half.

♦   ♦   ♦   ♦   ♦   ♦

S4 E10 - Wally's Glamour Girl
Dec 3, 1960
Director: Norman Abbott
Writers: Joe Connelly & Bob Mosher

Snapshot: When Wally was away at camp, he corresponded with Kitty Bannerman. He told her some tall tales about his life because she was such a glamorous girl. Later, he finds out she also was not telling the truth. When Wally picks her up for a dance, he must admit he doesn't really have a car and that starts the series of admissions from each of them.

The Players
Ken Osmond… Eddie Haskell
Bernadette Withers…Kitty Bannerman

Notable line(s)

June: Beaver, you're storing food in your cheek there like a squirrel.
Beaver: Sure, Mom. By doing it this way, I get more mileage out of one mouthful.

Eddie: I'm the manager of the high school basketball team, the Mayfield Crusaders, and the coach often consults me when he needs someone to lean on.

Eddie: Look, like I told you before, Sam, we got to stick together or we're gonna lose this Cold War with the adults.

S4 E11- Chuckie's New Shoes
Dec 10, 1960
Director: Norman Abbott
Writers: Joe Connelly & Bob Mosher

Snapshot: It's hard to imagine how bad a trip to the shoe store could go, but it happens when Beaver takes the neighbor boy Chuckie to get a pair downtown. Beaver loses Chuckie or Chuckie loses Beaver. Oh man, with all that crying… who knows what really happened?

The Players

Ken Osmond…Eddie Haskell
Rory Stevens…Chuckie Murdock
Marjorie Reynolds…Mrs. Murdock

Jess Kirkpatrick…Shoe Salesman
Vince Williams…Man in Shoe Store

Notable line(s)

Ward: I never thought that a boy who's a junior in high school could cause a mess like this.
Wally: Gee, Dad, neither did I

Eddie: Oh, I was just about to ring Mr. Cleaver. It's a lovely day out.
Ward: No, it is not.

Eddie: I got a feeling they don't like me.
Wally: Aw, Let's face it Eddie, they've never liked ya.
Eddie: Yeah, but they're usually polite about it.

♦   ♦   ♦   ♦   ♦   ♦

S4 E12 - Beaver and Kenneth
Dec 17, 1960
Director: Norman Abbott
Writers: Joe Connelly & Bob Mosher

Snapshot: Beaver is a thief. That's what June thinks when she finds recently stolen items from school lockers in Beaver's room. When the truth is revealed, she and Ward find out it was Beaver's so-called friend who had stolen them and gave them to Beaver to win his friendship.

The Players

Sue Randall…Miss Alice Landers
Gil Rogers…Kenneth Purcell

William Bakewell…Mr. Purcell
Jean Vander Pyl…Mrs. Thompson

Notable line(s)

June: And Beaver, if you do something bad, you're going to hurt Him.
Beaver: I wouldn't want to do anything to hurt God. He's got enough trouble with the Russians.

Wally: It's kinda funny the way Beaver always believes crazy stuff.

S4 E13- Beaver's Accordion
Dec 24, 1960
Director: Gene Reynolds
Writers: Joe Connelly & Bob Mosher

Snapshot: Companies will do anything to "getcha." Free trials are just one avenue they pursue. Beaver sends away for a free trial of an accordion, thanks to Eddie Haskell's urging. He has a few days to return the accordion but does not have enough money for postage. The most interesting thing about this episode is that it includes one of the biggest goofs in the series. Watch and see if you can identify it!

The Players:

Ken Osmond…Eddie Haskell
John Hoyt…Mr. Franklin

Stanley Fafara…Whitey Whitney
Rankin Mansfield…Express-agency Clerk

Notable line(s)

Wally: Look, I want to take a shower first. I don't want to go over there smelling like paint.
Eddie: Well, look, Sam, it never slowed down Rembrandt.

◆　◆　◆　◆　◆　◆

S4 E14 - Uncle Billy
Dec 31, 1960
Director: Norman Abbott
Writers: Joe Connelly & Bob Mosher

Snapshot: Uncle Billy makes his first appearance in the show when he visits Mayfield. He says a lot, but his actions leave a lot to be desired. Beaver learns the meaning of disappointment in this episode.

The Players

Edgar Buchanan…Uncle Billy Cleaver
Henry Hunter…Sports Store Clerk

Nancy Reynolds…Gloria

Notable line(s)

June: What do you mean by messing around?
Wally: Well, I don't know, you just go someplace and wait for something to happen.

Uncle Billy: Say, can I help you do the dishes, June?
June: Do you really want to, Billy?
Uncle Billy: No, of course not. It's always polite to offer, isn't it, boys?

S4 E15 - Teacher's Daughter
Jan 7, 1961
Director: Norman Abbott
Writers: Joe Connelly & Bob Moshor (teleplay) Alan Lipscott (story)

Snapshot: Eddie Haskell convinces Wally that his new home room teacher will give him a bad grade if he breaks his daughter's heart. After their breakup, Wally is worried, but Mr. Foster tells him he'll get the grade he deserves, nothing more and nothing less.

The Players
Ken Osmond…Eddie Haskell
Cheryl Holdridge…Julie Foster

Frank Bank…Clarence Rutherford
Ross Elliott…Mr. Foster

Notable line(s)

Beaver: How do you like that? He's putting on clean underwear just to play touch football.

Wally: Oh, well, her name is Julie Foster, and she goes to my school, and could I have another hunk of butter?

Lumpy: Daddy Dear, don't flunk my sweetie pie, give him a nice big Asey Waysey.

◆   ◆   ◆   ◆   ◆   ◆

S4 E16 - Ward's Millions
Jan 14, 1961
Director: Hugh Beaumont
Writers: Joe Connelly & Bob Mosher (teleplay) Theodore & Mathilde Ferro (story)

Snapshot: Beaver loves his father so much that he hates to see him worry. When Beaver sees a book that is guaranteed to make the reader a millionaire, he buys it for his father because he has recently been worrying about money. Unfortunately, Ward tells Beaver later, making money is not as easy as just reading a book.

The Players
Stanley Fafara…Whitey Whitney

Notable line(s)

Wally: If you could be a millionaire just by reading a book, the whole world would be crawling with millionaires.

June: Well, I couldn't get the checkbook to balance, so I wrote a check for $8.69 and then tore it up.
Ward: You know, dear, they could use you in Washington.

S4 E17 - Beaver's Secret Life
Jan 21, 1961
Director: Norman Abbott
Writers: Wilton Schiller, Joe Connelly & Bob Mosher

Snapshot: The best way for Beaver to be a writer, the career he has chosen for himself, is keeping a diary according to Ward. Beaver begins putting down entries in his diary and since they are boring, he then makes things up that are more exciting. However, Ward and June don't know that when they venture into its pages.

The Players

Sue Randall…Miss Alice Landers
Richard Correll…Richard Rickover
Stephen Talbot…Gilbert Bates

Karen Sue Trent…Penny Woods
Keith Taylor…Harry

Notable line(s)

Ward: Wally, Beaver's diary is a very personal thing. We wouldn't think of looking in it.
Wally: Okay, but if he runs off and becomes a beatnik, ya can't say I didn't tell ya.

June: We're his parents, we owe it to him to be sneaky every once in a while

♦   ♦   ♦   ♦   ♦   ♦

S4 E18 - Wally's Track Meet
Jan 28, 1961
Director: Norman Abbott
Writers: Joe Connelly & Bob Mosher

Snapshot: When a coach warns players, or in this case, track team members, not to goof off, they better listen. But Eddie and Lumpy never listen to any authority figures. This time, they get Wally caught up in their shenanigans and he must pay for it. He's off the team for a week.

The Players

Ken Osmond…Eddie Haskell
Frank Bank…Clarence Rutherford
Richard Deacon…Fred Rutherford
John Close…Coach Henderson

Harold Daye…Track Team Member
Tom Jackman…Track Team Member
Richard Correll…Richard Rickover

Notable line(s)

Ward: Come on, let's face it Dear. Our boy just isn't a little angel.
June: Why of course he is. You ought to see how sweet he looks when he's asleep.

Lumpy: Oh, you doll, you – (While combing hair while looking at reflection in his front door)

Beaver: When I went over there, I figured I could make an impression on his brain. But when he looked in the glass and called himself a doll, I figured it was kinda hopeless.

S4 E19 - Beaver's Old Buddy
Feb 4, 1961
Director: Norman Abbott
Writers: Joe Connelly & Bob Mosher, Dick Conway & Roland MacLane

Snapshot: Sometimes the saying "you can't go home," is quite true. This episode demonstrates a similar fact about old friends showing up after a couple years and things just aren't the same. Jackie Waters returns to see Beaver after moving away and all the fun things they used to do, just aren't fun any longer.

The Players

Gary Hunley…Jackie Waters   Shirley Anthony…Mrs. Waters
Ray Kellogg…Mr. Waters

Notable line(s)

Mrs. Waters: We'll be by tomorrow around noon to pick you up.
Jackie: Noon? By the time we have breakfast and go to Sunday school, there won't be time to mess around.

Beaver: I try to imagine me being a man, but I just can't figure myself walking around in a big overcoat and having kids being scared of me and all that stuff.

♦   ♦   ♦   ♦   ♦   ♦

S4 E20 - Beaver's Tonsils
Feb 11, 1961
Director: Norman Abbott
Writers: Theodore & Mathilde Ferro, Joe Connelly & Bob Mosher

Snapshot: Beaver's sore throat turns into something more serious. The doctor tells him his tonsils may need to come out. After first fearing the operation, Ward says everything will be just fine, telling him of his experience as a child and all the good things that happened due to the operation. Beaver then finds out he won't need an operation and is very disappointed.

The Players

Ken Osmond…Eddie Haskell   Keith Taylor…Harry
Richard Correll…Richard Rickover   John Gallaudet…Dr. Kirby
Karen Sue Trent…Penny Woods   Jimmy Carter…Herman
Burt Mustin…Gus the Fireman

Notable line(s)

Richard (looking at Beaver's throat): If you ask me, it's all gotta come out.
Beaver: Boy!
Richard: Yeah, well, I better be going now Beave. I promised my mom I'd stay just long enough to cheer you up.

S4 E21- The Big Fish Count
Feb 18, 1961
Director: Norman Abbott
Writers: Joe Connelly & Bob Mosher, Dick Conway & Roland MacLane

Snapshot: Small businesses run lots of contests to drum up business. Mr. Parker decides to run a fish counting contest. The winner will receive a small Collie puppy. Mr. Parker also makes a bad decision in this episode, to hire Eddie Haskell as an after-school employee.

The Players

Ken Osmond…Eddie Haskell	Karen Sue Trent…Penny Woods
Frank Bank…Clarence Rutherford	Carol Wakefield…Cathy Maddox
Stephen Talbot…Gilbert Bates	Jennie Lynn…Sally Ann Maddox
Jess Kirkpatrick…Mr. Parker	

Notable line(s)

Wally: Gee, I guess they practically didn't have anything when you were a kid, huh?
June: No, just people.

Eddie: I've heard of very few men who've become millionaires running the 220.

Mr. Parker: Edward Haskell…You're fired!

♦ ♦ ♦ ♦ ♦ ♦

S4 E22 - Beaver's Poster
Feb 25, 1961
Director: Norman Abbott
Writers: Joe Connelly & Bob Mosher (teleplay) Ellis Marcus (story)

Snapshot: Miss Canfield has the class make various items for a project on Colonial America. Beaver volunteers to make a poster and he expects his expert artist father to help him make it. He declines and Beaver's finished product looks like a kindergartener spilled paint on a posterboard.

The Players

Sue Randall…Miss Alice Landers	Patty Turner…Linda Dennison
Stephen Talbot…Gilbert Bates	LeiLani Sorensen…Phyllis
Karen Sue Trent…Penny Woods	Betty Lynn Budzak…Student
Keith Taylor…Harry	Jimmy Carter… Herman (uncredited)

Notable line(s)

Miss Landers: I don't think that was very funny Gilbert.
Gilbert: Well, Gee, everybody laughed.

S4 E23 - Mother's Helper
Mar 4, 1961
Director: Norman Abbott
Writers: Joe Connelly & Bob Mosher, Dick Conway & Roland MacLane

Snapshot: Wally gets a crush on the new cleaning girl who has been employed to help June around the house after school. His crush is so bad, that he is neglecting his homework and his athletic responsibilities at school.

The Players
Candy Moore…Margie Manners
Mary Carroll…Mrs. Manners

Notable line(s)

Beaver: Can you make gingerbread
Margie: I'm afraid not
Beaver: I didn't think so. I figured you were too skinny to make gingerbread.

Wally: What do you want now? I've got homework to do,
Beaver: Is that how you do high school homework, staring off into the air with a goofy look on your face?

♦   ♦   ♦   ♦   ♦   ♦

S4 E24 - The Dramatic Club
Mar 11, 1961
Director: Dann Cahn
Writers: Joe Connelly & Bob Mosher

Snapshot: When Beaver joins the dramatic club at school, he earns the lead role in *The Little Dutch Boy*. It's not until he starts running lines with Ward and Wally that he finds out he must kiss the leading actress. He doesn't want to do it but agrees to IF Ward and June don't watch.

The Players
Sue Randall…Miss Alice Landers
Stephen Talbot…Gilbert Harris
Karen Sue Trent…Penny Woods
Keith Taylor…Harry

Richard Correll…Richard Rickover
Katherine Warren…Mrs. Prescott
Betty Lynn Budzak….Victoria Bennett

Notable line(s)

Harry: Did you practice being a cow in the play last night?
Richard: Yeah, I sure did. I was up in my room mooing all over the place. Then my dad came up and told me to cut it out and do my homework.
Harry: Yeah?
Richard: Yeah, and then I told him it was my homework. Boy, I really had him then.

S4 E25 - Wally and Dudley
Mar 18, 1961
Director: Hugh Beaumont
Writers: Joe Connelly & Bob Mosher (supervisors) George Tibbles

Snapshot: Ruth McMillen is June's best friend from childhood. She has just moved to Mayfield and her son Dudley will now attend Mayfield High with Wally. Unfortunately, he'll also attend there with Lumpy and Eddie who begin to give him the business on his first day.

The Players

Ken Osmond…Eddie Haskell   Marta Kristen…Christine Staples
Jimmy Hawkins…Dudley McMillan   Pamela Beaird…Mary Ellen Rogers
Frank Bank…Clarence Rutherford   Eddie Pagett…Danny (as Ed Pagett)

Notable line(s)

Eddie: Boy, your mother sure got her nerve sticking you with this Dudley creep.

Dudley: Well, I went out for football, but I got my finger stepped on in the first scrimmage, so my mother made me quit.

Wally: But you just invited him to that party so you can get everybody to laugh at him.
Eddie: Well, what's wrong with a few laughs?

♦   ♦   ♦   ♦   ♦   ♦

S4 E26 - Eddie Spends the Night
Mar 25, 1961
Director: Norman Abbott
Writers: Joe Connelly & Bob Mosher, Dick Conway & Roland MacLane

Snapshot: An argument between Eddie and Wally is not a rare thing, but when Eddie is spending the night at the Cleavers and the argument happens, Eddie leaves and goes home. Wally and Ward go after him when Ward learns from his father, that Eddie is home alone while his parents are out of town and Eddie is scared of staying on his own.

The Players

Ken Osmond…Eddie Haskell   John Alvin…Frank Haskell

Notable line(s)

Eddie: Wally and Beaver were mean to me.

Eddie: A guy tries to do the right thing and you guys get all shook up
Wally: We were just going by the creepy way that you usually act.
Beaver: Yeah, even the bad guys on television don't do anything nice unless they're gonna croak or something.

S4 E27 - Beaver's Report Card
Apr 1, 1961
Director: Norman Abbott
Writers: Joe Connelly & Bob Mosher (teleplay) Theodore & Mathildo Ferro (story)

Snapshot: Math is one of Beaver's worst subjects, so he's quite surprised when the grade on his report card is much better than expected. Maybe all his hard efforts are paying off, or maybe Eddie Haskell had something to do with his improved grade.

The Players
Sue Randall…Miss Alice Landers   Stephen Talbot…Gilbert Bates
Ken Osmond…Eddie Haskell   Frank Bank…Clarence Rutherford

Notable line(s)

Lumpy: What are you staring at me for Gilbert?
Gilbert: Well, my mother keeps telling me not to grow up like you and I just wanted to see what she meant.

Wally: If you ever pull another trick like this again, I'm gonna murder you.
Eddie: Okay, okay, but you're gonna have to stand in line cause your pop's gonna murder me first.

♦   ♦   ♦   ♦   ♦   ♦

S4 E28 - Mistaken Identity
Apr 8, 1961
Director: Norman Abbott
Writers: Joe Connelly & Bob Mosher

Snapshot: With a friend like Richard Rickover, why would Beaver need an enemy? When caught breaking windows by a police officer, Richard gives the officer Beaver's name and address. This turns out to be embarrassing for Ward. When the officer sees Beaver isn't the boy he caught, it turns out embarrassing for the officer.

The Players
Stephen Talbot…Gilbert Bates   Alan Hewitt…Lieutenant Barnes
Richard Correll…Richard Rickover   Marvin Bryan…Officer Medford

Notable line(s)

June: Ward, dear, do you think all parents have this much trouble?
Ward: Oh, just the parents with children

S4 E29 - Wally's Dream Girl
Apr 15, 1961
Director: Norman Abbott
Writers: Joe Connelly & Bob Mosher (supervisors) Dale & Katherine Eunson

Snapshot: It's always best to approach a dream girl instead of keeping her in your dreams. That's what Wally finds out about Ginny Townsend, a transfer student from Indianapolis. June's interference with his love life, inviting her on a family picnic, is in this case, very much appreciated by Wally.

The Players
Ken Osmond...Eddie Haskell   Linda Bennett...Ginny Townsend

Notable line(s)

Wally: There goes just about the most beautiful girl I've ever seen in my whole life.
Eddie: Okay, okay, so she's beautiful. So, she's a dream walking. So, there she goes, and here you stand with your mouth hanging open.

Wally: I just like to look at her like some people like to look at Mona Lisa or something.
Eddie (after a long pause): You better have a serious talk with your counselor:

♦   ♦   ♦   ♦   ♦   ♦

S4 E30 - The School Picture
Apr 22, 1961
Director: Norman Abbott
Writers: Joe Connelly & Bob Mosher (story) Dick Conway & Roland MacLane (teleplay)

Snapshot: Gilbert convinces Beaver to make an ugly face when the photographer takes their class photo for the yearbook. This may be the worst thing Beaver and Gilbert ever do, but Gilbert doesn't do it, leaving Beaver the bad guy, the one who ruins the entire school yearbook.

The Players
Sue Randall...Miss Alice Landers   Lenore Kingston...Mrs. Bruce
Stephen Talbot...Gilbert Bates   Gage Clarke...Mr. Baxter (as Gage Clark)
Karen Sue Trent...Penny Woods   Keith Taylor...Harry
Doris Packer...Mrs. Cornelia Rayburn   LeiLani Sorensen...Classmate (uncredited)

Notable line(s)

Beaver: Boy, this is the first time I ever felt like Sunday on Thursday.

June: Well now Wally, we can't turn all of our problems over to the school. Your father feels that the parents should be responsible for the discipline of the children.

S4 E31 - Beaver's Rat
Apr 29, 1961
Director: Hugh Beaumont
Writers: Joe Connelly & Bob Mosher

Snapshot: Beaver, never the gypper and always the gypped. He gets taken advantage of by everyone with whom he makes a trade. He says the kids like him because of that. He finally gets the better of a deal when selling a rat to Violet Rutherford. You can imagine, Fred Rutherford is not very happy with the transaction.

The Players
Frank Bank…Clarence Rutherford   Veronica Cartwright…Violet Rutherford
Richard Deacon…Fred Rutherford

Notable line(s)

Violet: But Daddy, he's the sweetest rat I ever knew.

Fred Rutherford: Well, when has your father ever made you look silly?
Violet: Gee, daddy, lots of times.

♦   ♦   ♦   ♦   ♦   ♦

S4 E32 - In the Soup
May 6, 1961
Director: Norman Abbott
Writers: Joe Connelly & Bob Mosher (supervisors) Dick Conway & Roland MacLane

Snapshot: We know curiosity kills the cat, but steam from the bowl on a billboard kills Wally's chance at having a successful party with his friends. Instead of being at his house for the party, they're down the street watching firemen rescue a dumb kid from a bowl of soup on a billboard. It's Beaver, and he just had to see if that steam meant there was soup inside the bowl.

The Players
Ken Osmond…Eddie Haskell   Lenore Kingston…Mrs. Whitney
Frank Bank…Clarence Rutherford   Jack Mann…Fireman
Stanley Fafara…Whitey Whitney   Jimmie Lee Gaines…Little Boy
Harry Holcombe…Frank Whitney

Notable line(s)

Whitey: I must have lost. I didn't hear a splash.

Mr. Whitney: This wasn't one of your ideas, was it Whitey?
Whitey: Gee dad, why would I tell a kid to climb in a bowl of soup?

June: Oh no, it couldn't be…. he's over at Whitey's.

S4 E33 - Community Chest
May 13, 1961
Director: Norman Abbott
Writers: Joe Connelly & Bob Mosher, Raphael Blau

Snapshot: It's nice to see Beaver so conscious of his community. He volunteers to collect money for their local Community Chest organization. Losing the money was not part of his plans. After losing the money, he must go back to find out how much each person gave, and his father will replace it. This does not make Ward very well thought of by some in the community.

The Players

Stephen Talbot...Gilbert Bates
Dorothy Neumann...Older Woman Neighbor
Lee Meriwether...Young Woman Neighbor

Claudia Bryar...Mrs. Harris
Bruno VeSota...Angry Neighbor

Notable line(s)

Wally: A guy likes his mother to look good. He just doesn't want her looking so good that people notice her.

Gilbert: Excuse me lady, this dumb kid lost the money you gave him yesterday.

◆ ◆ ◆ ◆ ◆ ◆

S4 E34
Junior Fire Chief
May 20, 1961
Director: Norman Abbott
Writers: Joe Connelly & Bob Mosher, Dick Conway & Roland MacLane

Snapshot: Fire Prevention Week teaches Beaver a lot more than how to prevent fires. He learns how to best relate to people if he wants them to learn a lesson. Thank goodness he has a good friend like Gus, the fireman, to teach him some real-life lessons.

The Players

Sue Randall...Miss Alice Landers
Burt Mustin...Gus the Fireman
Stephen Talbot...Gilbert Bates
Richard Correll...Richard Rickover

Karen Sue Trent...Penny Woods
Keith Taylor...Harry
Stanley Fafara...Whitey Whitney

Notable line(s)

June: Well, my goodness Wally, You're home almost an hour early.
Wally: Well, I'm on the junior dance committee and we had a meeting.
June: Oh, did you accomplish anything?
Wally: Sure, I got out of my last two classes.

S4 E35 - Beaver's Frogs
May 27, 1961
Director: Norman Abbott
Writers: Joe Connelly & Bob Mosher (supervisors) Lou Breslow

Snapshot: Beaver wants to buy a used canoe and he finds out from Richard that there's a man who buys frogs and it's an easy way to make money. But when Beaver finds out the man croaks the frogs for research purposes, he's not so sure he wants to sell them.

The Players
Richard Correll…Richard Rickover   Rory Stevens…Chuckie Murdock
Stephen Talbot…Gilbert Bates

Notable line(s)

June: I guess it is kind of hard to imagine your parents were ever human

Beaver: Boy, you know Wally, I sure wish I was an Indian.
Wally: Why an Indian?
Beaver: Because all Indian kids got canoes for free just on account, they were Indians.

♦   ♦   ♦   ♦   ♦   ♦

S4 E36 - Beaver Goes in Business
Jun 3, 1961
Director: Norman Abbott
Writers: Joe Connelly & Bob Mosher, Dick Conway & Roland MacLane

Snapshot: Summer vacation is almost here, and Beaver needs some extra money. He decides to go into the lawn cutting business, just like his father did when he was Beaver's age. Gilbert turns out to be a bad partner and gives up when there is trouble. Beaver, however, is a paragon of persistence and it eventually pays off.

The Players
Ken Osmond…Eddie Haskell
Stephen Talbot…Gilbert Bates
Amzie Strickland…Woman Who Pays Beaver $5 to Mow Her Lawn
James Nolan… Man #1
William Stevens…Man who got his lawn mowed

Notable line(s)

Gilbert: Yeah, we asked a whole mess of people, but they all said no.
Wally: All of them?
Beaver: Yeah, some of them just said it louder than others.

Wally: If you carry around a bunch of cash today, that's just a sign that you're poor.

S4 E37 - Kite Day
Jun 10, 1961
Director: Norman Abbott
Writers: Joe Connelly & Bob Mosher (teleplay) Dale & Katherine Eunson (story)

Snapshot: Let the glue set! Ward should have screamed that after making a kite with Beaver for the local kite day event. Proud of the kite, Beaver shows it to Gilbert who immediately convinces him to give it a try. One crash later and poof, no more handmade kite.

The Players

Stanley Fafara…Whitey Whitney
Richard Correll…Richard Rickover
Stephen Talbot…Gilbert Bates

Jason Robards Sr.…Mr. Henderson
Keith Taylor…Harry

Notable line(s)

Gilbert: You know they're not giving prizes for the kite that's glued together the best.

Beaver: Hey Wally, Are there any Indians in Mayfield?
Wally: Why, do you want one of them to scalp you before dad gets home?

♦   ♦   ♦   ♦   ♦   ♦

S4 E38 - Beaver's Doll Buggy
Jun 17, 1961
Director: Anton Leader
Writers: Joe Connelly & Bob Mosher, Dick Conway & Roland MacLane

Snapshot: Pushing a doll buggy down the street could get a guy pulverized. Beaver takes his chances and takes the doll buggy home from Penny's house so he can use the wheels for his coaster car. Possible embarrassment gets the best of him when he sees Richard and Gilbert and he pushes the buggy down an incline and in the bushes. They find it and take it home instead.

The Players

Stephen Talbot…Gilbert Bates
Richard Correll…Richard Rickover
Ken Osmond…Eddie Haskell
Karen Sue Trent…Penny Woods

Jean Vander Pyl…Mrs. Woods
Jennie Lynn…Patty Ann Maddox
Mike Mahoney…Man in the Street

Notable line(s)

Beaver: Too bad a guy can't stay a kid all his life.

Mrs. Woods: Very nice boy, he's cute too, don't you think so?
Penny Woods: Yeah, but it's kinda hard to think of him as cute, cause up till now, I've been thinking of him as a little rat.

Wally: Man, Beaver pushing a doll buggy down the street. A thing like this could put a curse on the whole family.

S4 E39 - Substitute Father
Jun 24, 1961
Director: David Butler
Writers: Joe Connelly & Bob Mosher

Snapshot: Wally becomes the man of the house when Ward is sent on a business trip to St. Louis. He takes the job very seriously, but Beaver makes the job more difficult than it needs to be. Beaver is told to bring a parent to meet with Miss Landers after he's caught saying a bad word in school. Wally proves he really is a good substitute father in how he handles the situation.

The Players

Sue Randall…Miss Alice Landers
Ken Osmond… Eddie Haskell
Richard Correll…Richard Rickover
Stephen Talbot…Gilbert Bates
Stanley Fafara…Whitey Whitney
Fred Sherman…Taxi Driver
Jennie Lynn…School Girl (uncredited)

Rickie Sorensen…Arthur (uncredited)

Notable line(s)

Wally: Mom, do you have my phone number at the high school?
June: Well, I think so. Why?
Wally: Well, in case you fall down the stairs and break your leg or something, you can call me.

Beaver: You know what you are, Arthur? You're a big, dumb...

Eddie: I believe I'll go home and change, Mrs. Cleaver. A person has to be very careful when he's wearing a $42 sport coat.

Wally: Well, I just feel creepy in a grammar school. That's all. Somebody might see me and think I'm a stupid kid that got left back four or five years or something.

Rickie Sorensen (1946-1994) (bio added here as he was never given credit on the episode and his bio is not in the actor biography section)

Some of Rickie's earliest roles were those on the TV shows *My Friend Flicka, Perry Mason, The Frank Sinatra Show* and *Death Valley Days*. His early movies included *Man of a Thousand Faces, The Hard Man* with Lorne Greene, and he played Tarzan's adopted son in the film, *Tarzan's Fight for Life*. According to IMDB, Rickie's last two roles were in *Airport '77* and *The Cat from Outer Space*. To Leave it to Beaver fans, he will always be known as Arthur, the bully who tripped Beaver in the hallway in "The Substitute Father" episode. Although uncredited in that role, he did have a speaking part, and in this book, we now give Rickie the credit he deserves for that role. Rickie died at the young age of 47 from Esophageal cancer. Like his sister LeiLani, Rickie was a graduate of Cal State Long Beach. On the campus, he has an alumnae brick installed by the 49er statue in his honor.

S5 E1 - Wally Goes Steady
Sep 30, 1961
Director: Norman Abbott
Writers: Joe Connelly & Bob Mosher (teleplay) Dick Conway & Roland MacLane (story)

Snapshot: June and Ward are worried when they find out Wally is going steady with Evelyn Boothby. It's not so much his going steady as it is his hanging out with Evelyn's sister and her husband… HUSBAND? Wally is hanging out with a married couple? This can't be good.

The Players

Mary Mitchel…Evelyn Boothby

Gloria Gilbert…Judy Henderson

Ryan O'Neal…Tom Henderson

Pat McCaffrie…Bill Boothby

Frederick DeWilde…Jack Bennett

Notable line(s)

Bill Boothby: Well, I just thought I'd introduce myself. With kids the way they are these days, you and I might just find ourselves in the back of a church, listening to wedding bells.

Ward: June, nowadays a parent can't even say hello to his child without putting him on the defensive.

Wally: Uh, do you think Maris or Mantle will hit sixty home runs this year?
Judy: I really haven't given it much thought, Wally.

◆   ◆   ◆   ◆   ◆   ◆

S5 E2 - No Time for Babysitters
Oct 7, 1961
Director: David Butler
Writers: Joe Connelly & Bob Mosher (supervisors) Dick Conway & Roland MacLane

Snapshot: Beaver tells Gilbert and Richard he won't have a babysitter when his parents go out. As far as he knew, that was true, but his parents eventually decide to hire a babysitter. His friends try to prove he's lying, but the babysitter helps Beaver out of his jam. When Gilbert and Richard come over to find a babysitter, she hides in the kitchen, and then outside in the backyard.

The Players

Barbara Parkins…Judy Walker

Richard Correll…Richard Rickover

Stephen Talbot…Gilbert Bates

Notable line(s)

Beaver: Having a babysitter like you almost makes me wish I was a baby.

S5 E3 - Wally's Car
Oct 14, 1961
Director: David Butler
Writers: Joe Connelly & Bob Mosher (supervisors) Dick Conway & Roland MacLane

Snapshot: When Wally buys his first car, he brings the property values down for the entire neighborhood. Ward tells Wally to get rid of it and Wally winds up selling it piece by piece and still has money left over to have the shell hauled away and make a profit.

The Players

Ken Osmond…Eddie Haskell	George Spicer…Ray
Frank Bank…Clarence Rutherford	Dick Foster…Don
Ralph Sanford…Mr. Garvey	Audrey Swanson…Mrs. Ashby

Notable line(s)

Wally: Oh, hi Eddie, hey, maybe you can help me. I'm going to sell the car and I thought I'd advertise it in the newspaper.

Eddie: Yeah, where ya gonna put it...the obituary column?

Mr. Garvey: "All the parts are there," he says. It looks like a fish that had been boned.

♦   ♦   ♦   ♦   ♦   ♦

S5 E4 - Beaver's Birthday
Oct 21, 1961
Director: Hugh Beaumont
Writers: Dick Conway & Roland MacLane (teleplay) Bob Ross (story)

Snapshot: Forced may be too harsh of a word, but Beaver is strongly persuaded to put his birthday money in the bank. The next day he gets $10.00 in the mail from Uncle Billy. Gilbert convinces him to keep it a secret and spend it. The sneakiness is what causes Beaver trouble.

The Players

Stephen Talbot…Gilbert Bates	William Newell…The Postal Clerk

Notable line(s)

Postal clerk: Well Mr. Theodore Cleaver, do you have any identification?
Beaver: Identification?
Postal clerk: Something with your name on it.
Beaver: Oh, just my underwear. My mom sewed it on when I went to camp.
Postal clerk: Yes, I mean, do you have anything a little handier?

June: Ward, isn't Beaver too old to tell us lies?
Ward: Uh, no. dear. But he's too old to think he can get away with it.

Gilbert: Boy Beaver, I just can't figure you out. Sometimes you don't act like a kid at all.

S5. E5   Beaver's Cat Problem
Nov 4, 1961
Director: David Butler
Writers: Joe Connelly & Bob Mosher

Snapshot: Never feed a stray cat unless you want it to come back to your house. Beaver learns this lesson too late. He feeds Bootsy who, he finds out later, belongs to Mrs. Prentiss. The whole ordeal does earn Beaver some easy money from Mrs. Prentiss.

The Players

Stephen Talbot…Gilbert Bates   Grace Wallis Huddle…Mrs. Prentiss

Notable line(s)

Wally: Hey, what did Mom say when you brought him up here?
Beaver: She didn't say a word.
Wally: You sneaked him up, huh?
Beaver: Well, sure.

Ward: If the cat shows up here, I'll have him phone home.
June: You did have a hard day at the office today, didn't you?

◆   ◆   ◆   ◆   ◆   ◆

S5 E6 - Wally's Weekend Job
Nov 11, 1961
Director: Norman Abbott
Writers: Joe Connelly & Bob Mosher (supervisors) Dick Conway & Roland MacLane

Snapshot: Wally gets a weekend job as a soda jerk and the girls love watching him on the job. Wally's so-called friends Lumpy and Eddie are jealous of the attention he is receiving, and Eddie figures out a way to fix him. But as usual with Eddie, he's the one who gets fixed in the end.

The Players

Ken Osmond…Eddie Haskell   Pamela Baird…Mary Ellen Rogers
Frank Bank…Clarence Rutherford   Tim Graham…Mr. Gibson
Cheryl Holdridge…Julie Foster   Bill Baldwin…Mr. Rogers
Richard Correll…Richard Rickover   Donna Conn…Jan
Stephen Talbot…Gilbert Bates   Rita Norma Somers…Ann

Notable line(s)

Beaver: When do you start being a jerk down at the soda fountain?

Jan: Oh Wally, you make the yummiest malts ever.
Julie: You haven't even tasted it yet.

Eddie (after having Wally name all sandwiches): No, that doesn't hit me.
Wally: It may in a minute.

S5 E7 - Beaver Takes a Drive
Nov 18, 1961
Director: Charles F. Haas
Writers: Joe Connelly & Bob Mosher (supervisors) Dick Conway & Richard MacLane

Snapshot: Playing in a 3500-pound hunk of steel is not a good thing for two boys to do, but Gilbert and Beaver do it anyway. Ward's car winds up in the street, blocking traffic and Wally saves the day, but a very obtuse officer gives Wally a ticket for driving without a license.

The Players

Stephen Talbot…Gilbert Bates
Frank Bank…Clarence Rutherford
Maurice Manson…Judge Morton
Gail Bonney…The Woman Clerk
Stephen Courtleigh…The Father
Brad Morrow…The Boy
Dick Foster… Barry

Stuffy Singer…Steve
Bill Hale…The Officer
George Hickman…1st Man
Bob Golden…2nd Man
Lillian O'Malley…The Woman
Bobby Barber…Man in Juvenile Court

Notable line(s)

Gilbert: My sister's all the time pinching me.
Beaver: Your sister? Gee, she always looks so nice sitting in Sunday School.
Gilbert: She just does that to fool people.

Gilbert: You ought to hear him. "Cub Scouts, playground, music lessons, library, over to Richard's, over to Beaver's. What do I look like I'm running around here, a bus service?"

Beaver: Boy Gilbert, what am I going to do now?
Gilbert: I don't know. But I know what I'm going to do. I'm going home.

◆　　◆　　◆　　◆　　◆　　◆

S5 E8 - Wally's Big Date
Nov 25, 1961
Director: David Butler
Writers: Joe Connelly & Bob Mosher (supervisors) Bob Ross (teleplay)

Snapshot: Eddie gets a laugh when he trades his date, a super tall girl, for Wally's date. But it's Wally who gets the last laugh when his date wears her hair down and uses flats instead of heels.

The Players
Ken Osmond…Eddie Haskell
Frank Bank…Clarence Rutherford

Laraine Stephens…Gail Preston
Judee Morton…Marjorie Muller

Notable line(s)

Wally: Wow, she's a giant.

S5 E9 - Beaver's Ice Skates
Dec 2, 1961
Director: Hugh Beaumont
Writers: Joe Connelly & Bob Mosher (supervisors) Joseph Hoffman

Snapshot: Beaver thinks he's big enough to buy ice skates on his own. He would be, if not for a dishonest salesman down at the cut rate sporting goods store. Wally and Ward both try to help Beaver get his money back. Wally is unsuccessful, but Ward does get Beaver's money returned.

The Players

Richard Correll...Richard Rickover   Stanley Clements....Shoe Salesman
Stanley Fafara...Whitey Whitney   Allan Ray...Bert

Notable line(s)

Ward (after giving Beaver $6.00): You just wait and see what happens. I know how these things build up.
June: So do I. I remember the time that you bought the five iron to get a little exercise at the golf range. Next, I knew, you bought a bag full of woods and irons and we joined the country club.

♦   ♦   ♦   ♦   ♦   ♦

S5 E10 - Weekend Invitation
Dec 9, 1961
Director: David Butler
Writers: Joe Connelly & Bob Mosher, Dick Conway & Roland MacLane

Snapshot: A new friend named Scott invites Wally and others to a weekend at his parent's lake house. The only problem for Wally, is when he finds out there won't be any parental supervision. He keeps this fact from his parents for a little while, but before he can share it, they find out on their own.

The Players

Frank Bank...Clarence Rutherford   David Kent...Scott
Richard Deacon...Fred Rutherford

Notable line(s)

Beaver: Gee, it's not enough that you tell the truth anymore. It looks like you gotta tell it at the right time, or you still get clobbered.

S5 E11 - Beaver's English Test
Dec 16, 1961
Director: Norman Abbott
Writers: Joe Connelly & Bob Mosher (supervisors) Dick Conway & Rich MacLane

Snapshot: It's not really being dishonest if you know all the answers to an English test beforehand, if you learn of them by accident, is it? That's the dilemma Beaver and Gilbert must deal with in this episode.

The Players
Stephen Talbot   Gilbert Harrison
Wendell Holmes   Mr. Blair

Notable line(s)

Gilbert: 96... if Wally hadn't been so stupid, we would've got a hundred.

Gilbert: Why, it's about the best thing to happen at our house since my sister started noticing boys.

♦   ♦   ♦   ♦   ♦   ♦

S5 E12 - Wally's Chauffeur
Dec 23, 1961
Director: Hugh Beaumont
Writers: Joe Connelly & Bob Mosher (supervisors) Dick Conway & Roland MacLane

Snapshot: I'm sure Wally was all for women's rights, but not when it comes to being driven by a girl to a dance at the country club. The worst thing about this night is that she's coordinated with their friends to meet out front... oh boy!

The Players
Frank Bank...Clarence Rutherford   Eddie Pagett...1st Boy (as Ed Pagett)
Mary Mitchel...Evelyn Boothby   Brad Morrow...2nd Boy
James Seay...Mr. Boothby   George Spicer...3rd Boy
Mark Allen...Policeman

Notable line(s)

Beaver: It sounds like one of those things he's liable to blow his top about.
Wally: Why would he do that?
Beaver: I don't know. I guess 'cause it sounds like it'd be too much fun.

Ward: You're going to take this dinner jacket downstairs. You're going to drive to the dance with that girl and you're going to have a good time. Do you understand?

S5 E13 - Beaver's First Date
Dec 30, 1961
Director: David Butler
Writers: Joe Connelly & Bob Mosher (teleplay) Joseph Hoffman (story)

Snapshot: Beaver finally finds a girl that he likes. Basically, it's just because she's new. He meets Betsy at dancing school, and he asks her to an upcoming dance sponsored by the school. By the end of the dance, he's hanging out with Richard and Whitey and demonstrating some new sounds he's created instead of dancing with Betsy. That's how Beaver's first date turns out.

The Players

Frank Bank…Clarence Rutherford
Richard Correll…Richard Rickover
Cheryl Holdridge…Julie Foster
Pam Smith…Betsy Patterson

Stanley Fafara…Whitey Whitney
Donna Conn…Lumpy's Date
Estelle Etterre…Mrs. Thompson
Kent Bodin…Billy McKenzie (uncredited)

Notable line(s)

Wally: You don't have to bribe girls to go to dances and parties and stuff, they got a natural instinct for standing around looking stupid.

June: Ward, do you think Beaver's having a good time (at the dance)?
Ward: No.

♦   ♦   ♦   ♦   ♦   ♦

S5 E14 - Ward's Golf Clubs
Jan 6, 1962
Director: David Butler
Writers: Joe Connelly & Bob Mosher (supervisors) Bob Ross

Snapshot: Gilbert takes golf balls to Beaver's house and the two get a driver from Ward's bag to hit them in the back yard. Beaver swings the club and the head of the driver flies, while the ball stays put. Beaver comes up with a great plan to replace the club on his own. Too bad, the club was already broken and now, Ward knows that some funny business has happened.

The Players

Stephen Talbot…Gilbert Bates
Henry Hunter…Mr. Briggs

Notable line(s)

Gilbert: Listen Beaver, if you're a girl and you don't think somebody wants to steal you, you might as well be dead.

Gilbert: I'm your best friend, I don't want to be around when your father's killing you.

Beaver: Boy, when you grow up, your toys sure cost a lot of money don't they?

S5 E15 - Farewell to Penny
Jan 13, 1962
Director: David Butler
Writers: Dick Conway & Roland MacLane, Joe Connelly (uncredited) Bob Mosher (uncredited)

Snapshot: Penny hates Beaver and Beaver hates Penny. Well, until she finds out she's moving out of town and won't see Beaver any longer. Beaver feels the same way when he finds out she's leaving. Their mutual attraction grows stronger after her farewell party, but then dissipates altogether when Beaver finds out she will remain at school when she moves in with her grandma.

The Players
Karen Sue Trent…Penny Woods
Stanley Fafara…Whitey Whitney

Wendell Holmes…Mr. Blair
Jean Vander Pyl…Mrs. Woods

Notable line(s)

Beaver: If her face was on television, parents wouldn't let little kids watch it.

Ward: Wally, you're being a big help this morning.
Wally: I guess by that, you mean I'm not, huh?
Ward: That's just what I mean.

Ward (about Beaver): Well dear, he's dealing with the opposite sex now. We can expect a certain amount of inconsistent idiotic behavior.

◆   ◆   ◆   ◆   ◆   ◆

S5 E16 - Beaver, the Bunny
Jan 20, 1962
Director   Anton Leader
Writers: Joe Connelly & Bob Mosher (supervisors) Dick Conway & Roland MacLane

Snapshot: Beaver has the part of a bunny rabbit in the school play. Lumpy gives him a ride, but when he gets a flat tire, Beaver must make his way to school on his own, in his bunny costume. This may be almost as traumatizing as a nude baby photo, or maybe not.

The Players
Frank Bank…Clarence Rutherford
Richard Correll…Richard Rickover
Stanley Fafara…Whitey Whitney
Karen Sue Trent…Penny Woods
Alice Backes…Miss Lawrence
John Damler…Sergeant
Sid Kane…1st Man

Jean Cook…1st Woman
John McKee…Policeman
Jimmy Carter…Herman
Wally Wood…Boy
LeiLani Sorensen…Phyllis
Stephen Talbot…Gilbert Bates (uncredited)

Notable line(s): Beaver: I didn't volunteer to be a crummy bunny. I wanted to be a zebra or a snake or something…

S5 E17 - Beaver's Electric Trains
Jan 27, 1962
Director: Hugh Beaumont
Writers: Joe Connelly & Bob Mosher (supervisors) Dick Conway & Roland MacLane

Snapshot: Beaver's too old to play with electric trains. He hasn't played with his in a few years. June decides to give them away to Johnny Battson. There's a problem, after getting them out, Beaver decides he wants to keep them. But when Georgia Battson comes by to pick them up, Wally gives them to her. Beaver and Gilbert are furious whey the find out what Wally did.

The Players

Stephen Talbot…Gilbert Bates   Toby Michaels…Georgia Battson

Notable line(s)

Wally: Yeah, but a guy your age isn't supposed to have fun playing with kids' stuff.
Gilbert: I think it's okay Wally, as long as you don't go around telling everybody.

Beaver: Wally, you mean you gave my train away to a girl, just because she was pretty?
Wally: No, I didn't give them to her just because she was pretty.
Gilbert: What'd she do Wally? Knock you down and take them away from you?

♦   ♦   ♦   ♦   ♦   ♦

S5 E18 - Beaver's Long Night
Feb 3, 1962
Director: Hugh Beaumont
Writers: Joe Connelly & Bob Mosher (supervisors) Dick Conway & Roland MacLane

Snapshot: On a night when Gilbert spends the night, Beaver calls the police to report a suspicious vehicle parked outside their house. The police arrive and take away the two men, Wally's friends Lumpy and Bill Scott, who were there to take Wally to a masquerade party. When Ward comes home, he receives a nasty call from Fred Rutherford who is quite upset.

The Players

Stephen Talbot…Gilbert   Richard Deacon…Fred Rutherford
Frank Bank…Lumpy   David Kent…Bill Scott

Notable line(s)

Gilbert: What are you going to say? "Wally, we just had the police throw your two friends in jail"?

S5 E19 - Beaver's Jacket
Feb 10, 1962
Director: David Butler
Writer(s) Joe Connelly & Bob Mosher (supervisors) Bob Ross

Snapshot: Richard Rickover has a new leather jacket. Beaver buys one too. When Richard loses his jacket, he enlists Beaver in his plan to keep his mother from finding out he lost it. Beaver agrees to help, but like usual, he shouldn't have.

The Players
Richard Correll…Richard

Notable line(s)

June: Well, you're just going to have to be punished for this Beaver.
Beaver: But Why mom? I didn't do anything wrong. And I got my jacket cleaned for nothing.

♦   ♦   ♦   ♦   ♦   ♦

S5 E20 - Nobody Loves Me
Feb 17, 1962
Director: David Butler
Writers: Joe Connelly & Bob Mosher (supervisors) Dale & Katherine Eunson (teleplay)

Snapshot: Every boy reaches an awkward age. Some kids take it better than others. Richard describes this age to Beaver, and he instantly becomes sclf-conscious. Beaver begins to feel he is no longer loved. It's a good thing he has parents that can fix any problem, especially this one.

The Players
Sue Randall…Miss Alice Landers   Burt Mustin…Gus
Richard Correll…Richard

Notable line(s)

Richard: Look at all the books telling what's wrong with kids.
Beaver: Yeah. Boy, I never knew we were so creepy before.

Ward (in den): Well, June, isn't this the time of day you should be slaving over a hot stove?
June: I am... Waiting for the TV dinners to thaw out.

June: Beaver, would you mind terribly if I kissed you?
Beaver: Oh, no, Mom, go ahead if it will make you feel better.

Richard: Nope, I just can't go home until I see a New Jersey license plate.
Beaver: Says who?
Richard: Me.

S5 E21 - Beaver's Fear
Feb 24, 1962
Director: David Butler
Writers: Joe Connelly & Bob Mosher (supervisors) Dick Conway & Roland MacLane

Snapshot: Beaver gets to hang out with the big guys, something he's always been excited about doing. But they're going to an amusement park with a roller coaster that Beaver is quite frightened to ride. Gus, the fireman gives Beaver some good advice and it helps tremendously.

The Players

Ken Osmond…Eddie   Frank Bank…Lumpy
Richard Correll…Richard   Burt Mustin…Gus
Stanley Fafara…Whitey   David Kent…Bill Scott

Notable line(s)

Beaver: Gus and the net. Gus and the net. Gus and the net.

Wally: Well, Beav, how'd you like it?
Beaver: Boy, it was neat, Wally. Even neater than I thought it'd be.

♦ ♦ ♦ ♦ ♦ ♦

S5 E22 - Three Boys and a Burro
Mar 3, 1962
Director: David Butler
Writers: Joe Connelly & Bob Mosher (supervisors) Dick Conway & Roland MacLane

Snapshot: Beaver promises his parents if he can buy a burro with his friends, that the burro will stay at Gilbert and Richard's houses, not at his house. Ward okays the purchase, but soon comes to regret giving permission.

The Players

Stephen Talbot…Gilbert   Jane Dulo… Mrs. Rickover
Richard Correll…Richard   Claudia Bryar…Mrs. Bates

Notable line(s)

Ward: Oh, well, if your wife is hysterical, I guess there's not much we can do about it.

Richard (to Beaver): Well, you're always saying what a neat father you got.
Gilbert: Yeah, and here's your chance to prove it.

S5 E23 - Eddie Quits School
Mar 10, 1962
Director: Jeffrey Hayden
Writers: Joe Connelly & Bob Mosher (supervisors) Dick Conway & Roland MacLane

Snapshot: Wally is all the time saving the day, usually for his brother Theodore. In this episode, he saves the day for Eddie, who, after quitting school, is lonely and feeling like a failure at his new job. Wally convinces the principal to talk to Eddie at the service station where Eddie works and the next day, he's back in school.

The Players

Ken Osmond…Eddie
Frank Bank…Lumpy
David Kent…Bill

Frank Wilcox…Mr. Farmer
Bert Remsen…Mr. Thompson

Notable line(s)

Eddie: Tomorrow morning I'm starting to work at Thompson's Garage. And get this…I'm going to haul down a fat eighty bucks a week.

Eddie: When the credit manager checked me out and found I was making a fat eighty bucks a week, the whole joint flipped. The clerks were tripping all over each other trying to be first to wait on me.

♦   ♦   ♦   ♦   ♦   ♦

S5 E24 - Wally Stays at Lumpy's
Mar 17, 1962
Director: David Butler
Writers: Joe Connelly & Bob Mosher (supervisors) Dick Conway & Roland MacLane

Snapshot: "I think we got 'em." That's what Gilbert says about Beaver's parents when they're talking with Wally on the phone about his spending the night at Lumpy's house. Yes, because of a technicality, Wally was able to spend the night at Lumpy's and Gilbert was able to spend the night with Beaver, when neither had permission to do so.

The Players

Stephen Talbot…Gilbert
Frank Bank…Lumpy

Richard Deacon…Fred Rutherford

Notable line(s)

June: Ward, Wally's best friend is Eddie Haskell and yours is Fred Rutherford. What's wrong with this family?

Lumpy: At least my party was different.
Wally: Yeah, I think your father had a real good time.

S5 E25 - Beaver's Laundry
Mar 24, 1962
Director: David Butler
Writers: Joe Connelly & Bob Mosher (supervisors) Joseph Hoffman

Snapshot: Eddie is not used to helping mop a kitchen floor, but that is what he does when Wally ropes him in to help clean the mess Richard and Beaver make in the kitchen after they try washing Richard's laundry but fail miserably.

The Players
Richard Correll…Richard   Ken Osmond…Eddie

Notable line(s)

Beaver: Listen, if you can't tell a phone from a washing machine, you shouldn't even be walking around.

♦   ♦   ♦   ♦   ♦   ♦

S5 E26 - Lumpy's Car Trouble
Mar 31, 1962
Director: David Butler
Writers: Dick Conway & Roland MacLane, Joe Connelly & Bob Mosher

Snapshot: Lumpy has car trouble, but Wally gets in trouble. When Lumpy drives the Cleaver's car to the track meet, Wally doesn't stop him from breaking the rules he had been given and faces the consequences.

The Players
Ken Osmond…Eddie Haskell   Richard Deacon…Fred Rutherford
Frank Bank…Lumpy   Pat McCaffrie…Bill Boothby

Notable line(s)

Fred Rutherford: You needn't worry about Clarence, Ward. When it comes to brains, he's got a head on him like the rock of Gibraltar.

Beaver: Eddie, did anyone ever tell you you're the best-looking guy in high school?
Eddie: No, they didn't.
Beaver: I didn't think so.

S5 E27 - Beaver the Babysitter
Apr 7, 1962
Director: David Butler
Writers: Joe Connelly & Bob Mosher (supervisors) Joseph Hoffman

Snapshot: Beaver agrees to do Wally a favor and babysit Chuckie Murdock. Unknown to both Wally and Beaver, the babysitting job is not for Chuckie, but for his older sister Pat.

The Players

Ken Osmond…Eddie   Marjorie Reynolds…Mrs. Murdock
Stephen Talbot…Gilbert   Stephen Courtleigh…Mr. Murdock
Rory Stevens…Chuckie   Jennie Lynn…Pat

Notable line(s)

Wally: If Chuckie threw himself on the floor and started chewing the rug or something, Beaver could call mom and you guys could get over there before he could eat enough of it to make him sick.

Wally: Look, Beaver, she's probably just got a crush on you.
Beaver: Why would any girl have a crush on me? I'm kind of a mess.
Wally: Sure, you are, but you're not enough of a mess to scare her away.

◆   ◆   ◆   ◆   ◆   ◆

S5 E28 - The Younger Brother
Apr 14, 1962
Director: David Butler
Writers: Joe Connelly & Bob Mosher (supervisors) Dick Conway & Robert MacLane

Snapshot: Not everything is genetic when it comes to brothers. That is especially true in the Cleaver family when it comes to basketball skills. Wally is a great. Beaver is not. Beaver is ashamed to tell his dad he's been cut from the team after the first tryout, so Beaver carries on a charade of still being part of the team for as long as he can.

The Players

Richard Correll…Richard   Richard Deacon…Fred Rutherford
Ken Osmond…Eddie Haskell   Russ Conway…Mr. Doyle

Notable line(s)

Ward: Well, Beaver, I think you'd really enjoy basketball.
Beaver: Well, I guess I could make myself enjoy it if you want me to, Dad.

Richard: Do basketball players get paid big bonuses like baseball players do?
Mr. Doyle: Well, I wouldn't know about that, but they do quite well.
Richard: Oh. Well, my father just wanted to know.

S5 E29 - Beaver's Typewriter
Apr 21, 1962
Director: David Butler
Writers: Joe Connelly & Bob Mosher (supervisors) Dick Conway & Roland MacLane

Snapshot: Beaver should know better than to accept help from Eddie Haskell, because although he can show kindness on occasion, it really is hard for a leopard to change its spots. He doesn't get Beaver in a lot of trouble here, but he does get him to be sneaky, and that's never good.

The Players

Stephen Talbot…Gilbert   Ed Prentiss… Mr. Bailey
Ken Osmond…Eddie

Notable line(s)

Eddie: What are you so amazed about?
Beaver: Well, you can actually do something. I thought you were only good for being a wise guy.

Gilbert: Boy, Beave, do you think we'll grow up to be as smart as Eddie.
Beaver: I asked my brother that one time. He said if I did, he'd croak me.

◆   ◆   ◆   ◆   ◆   ◆

S5 E30 - The Merchant Marine
Apr 28, 1962
Director: David Butler
Writers: Joe Connelly & Bob Mosher (supervisors) Dick Conway & Roland MacLane

Snapshot: When Lumpy gets his car keys taken away by his father, Lumpy decides to leave home and join the Merchant Marines. But he's too scared to get the mail from the Merchant Marines sent to his home and asks Wally to receive it instead. Thinking their son is going to leave home and run off to sea has Ward and June quite concerned.

The Players

Frank Bank…Lumpy
Richard Deacon…Fred Rutherford

Notable line(s)

Wally: Lump, sit down a minute.
Lumpy: Don't talk like that, you sound just like my father.

June: Well, of course, but can't you be firm without getting angry?
Ward: Well, I haven't found a way yet.

S5 E31 - Brother vs. Brother
May 5, 1962
Director: David Butler
Writers: Joe Connelly & Bob Mosher (supervisors) Bob Ross

Snapshot: Mary Tyler is quite a looker, and she catches Beaver's eye right away when she's introduced as a new student. Beaver takes her home after school and they play a game of Monopoly in his room, and then she sees Wally. She instantly likes him more than Beaver. What a little young homewrecker!

The Players

Stephen Talbot…Gilbert
Richard Correll…Richard

Mimi Gibson…Mary Tyler
Hardie Albright…Mr. Collins

Notable line(s)

June (speaking of school): I never did. I always went out with the boys in my own class.
Wally: Gee, mom, can you remember that far back?

♦   ♦   ♦   ♦   ♦   ♦

S5 E32 - The Yard Birds
May 12, 1962
Director: David Butler
Writers: Joe Connelly & Bob Mosher (supervisors) Dick Conway & Roland MacLane

Snapshot: In charge of getting the yard cleaned of trash and brush and calling Mr. Peck to pick it all up, Wally and Beaver get right to work, but eventually get distracted. They wind up playing a little too much and then call Mr. Peck a little too late for a pickup. That's when Eddie and Lumpy come to the rescue, well, that's not exactly what happens.

The Players

Richard Correll…Richard
Ken Osmond…Eddie Haskell

Frank Bank…Lumpy
Bartlett Robinson…Mr. Hill

Notable line(s)

Wally: Tomorrow? Sure, Eddie, I can make it. We'll pick up Mary Ellen and Cathy. Yeah, Cathy'll go. I spent half an hour convincing her that you were really not a creep.

Beaver: Aw, gee, Dad, that seems like a gyp. All Richard has to do around his house is clean up his room and carry out the trash.
Ward: Thanks for reminding me, Beaver. You can go upstairs right now and pick up your room.

Beaver: Boy, Wally, I didn't know playing catch could be so much fun.
Wally: Yeah, and you know why it's so much fun? Because we got work to do, that's why.

S5 E33 - Tennis, Anyone?
May 19, 1962
Director: Hugh Beaumont
Writers: Joe Connelly & Bob Mosher (supervisors) Dick Conway & Roland MacLane

Snapshot: Wally has found himself in a love triangle at the tennis court. If only Eddie Haskell had shown up at the tennis court for their match. Instead, Carole meets Wally, plays tennis with him, and does her best to make her boyfriend, the tennis instructor, jealous.

The Players

Cynthia Chenault…Carole Martin   Frank Bank…Lumpy
Ken Osmond…Eddie Haskell   James Drake…Don Kirk
Stephen Talbot…Gilbert

Notable line(s)

Eddie: Look chum, when you're flying with the nightingales, you don't mingle with the bats.

Wally: It's about girls.
Ward: I see
Wally: Yeah, dad, I'm in a triangle.
Ward: (shocked) A triangle?

♦   ♦   ♦   ♦   ♦   ♦

S5 E34 - One of the Boys
May 26, 1962
Director: Jeffrey Hayden
Writers: Joe Connelly & Bob Mosher, Gwen Bagni

Snapshot: Wally and Eddie have been invited to join the Barons, a social club populated by fellow Mayfield High students. They're supposed to be the coolest, at least that's what Eddie thinks. Ward and June don't want him to join, but this is a test to Wally's intelligence, and he passes it with flying colors.

The Players

Ken Osmond…Eddie Haskell   Reuben Singer…Ted (as Robert Singer)
Frank Bank…Lumpy   Martin Dean…Rick
Stephanie Hill…Bessie

Notable line(s)

June: Hello Beaver, did you have a nice day?
Beaver: No, I went to school.

S5 E35 - Sweatshirt Monsters
Jun 2, 1962
Director: David Butler
Writers: Joe Connelly & Bob Mosher (supervisors) Dick Conway & Roland MacLane

Snapshot: Once again, Beaver has the opportunity to do the right thing instead of going along with the crowd. He and his friends each buy a monster t-shirt and they all agree to wear them to school the next day. The parents of each forbid them to wear the sweatshirt, even Ward and June forbid it, but Beaver finds a way to sneak to school while wearing it anyway.

The Players

Richard Correll…Richard	Hardie Albright…Mr. Collins
Stanley Fafara…Whitey	Jane Dulo…Mrs. Rickover
Doris Packer…Mrs. Rayburn	Mark Murray…Alan Boothby

Notable line(s)

June: Do other people's children get into trouble like this too?
Ward: Aw, cheer up June. They didn't put that long bench outside the principal's office just for us.

♦   ♦   ♦   ♦   ♦   ♦

S5 E36 - A Night in the Woods
Jun 9, 1962
Director: David Butler
Writers: Joe Connelly & Bob Mosher (supervisors) Dick Conway & Roland MacLane

Snapshot: After complimenting Wally on the way he drinks milk; Wally knows Beaver is up to something. He then asks Wally in front of his parents if he'll take he and his friends camping. He agrees to do so, but this upsets Eddie who comes up with a plan to get Wally back in time for a date they have scheduled for Saturday night.

The Players

Ken Osmond…Eddie Haskell	John Hart…Forest Ranger
Stephen Talbot…Gilbert	Stanley Fafara…Whitey
Frank Bank…Lumpy	Mark Murray…Alan Boothby

Notable line(s)

Eddie (after falling onto a ledge): You aren't going to leave me alone, are you?
Wally: Okay, we'll leave Whitey here.
Eddie: Not that Whitey, he'll throw rocks at me.

Eddie (alone on ledge, Gilbert above): Talk to me, will you Gilbert?
Gilbert: What'll I say?
Eddie: Say Anything
Gilbert: All-right... you're a dumb stupid creep and a big wise guy.

S5 E37 - Long Distance Call
Jun 16, 1962
Director: Norman Abbott
Writers: Joe Connelly & Bob Mosher (supervisors) Dick Conway & Roland MacLane

Snapshot: Every kid has played on the phone and made crank phone calls, well, at least before caller ID existed. Beaver wouldn't have got into trouble if that had been all he had done. But nooooooo, he Gilbert and Alan had to call Los Angeles and speak with Don Drysdale. That call cost almost ten dollars, which was a fortune in 1962.

The Players
Stephen Talbot…Gilbert   Kevin Jones…1st Boy
Mark Murray…Alan Boothby   Johnny Eimen…2nd Boy
Dennis Olivieri…Kenny (as Dennis Joel)   Don Drysdale…Don Drysdale
Ray Montgomery…Kenny's Father

Notable line(s)

Gilbert: Mr. Drysdale, this is Gilbert, and Beaver and Alan are with me, and we called you because you're our favorite baseball player.
Don Drysdale: Well, thanks, boys. Where are you calling from? Well, gee, that's quite a distance to be calling from, isn't it?

Beaver: Hey, you guys, what am I gonna do when my dad sees that $9.35 on the telephone bill?
Gilbert: Tell him Wally's got a girl in Los Angeles.

♦   ♦   ♦   ♦   ♦   ♦

S5 E38 - Stocks and Bonds
Jun 23, 1962
Director: Norman Abbott
Writers: Allan Manings (teleplay) Joe Connelly & Bob Mosher (story)

Snapshot: There's nothing better than real life lessons. Ward teaches his boys about money when he provides them $100 to invest in the stock market. Which stock they choose is up to them, but Ward does make a strong suggestion they should buy a utility stock even though Eddie says they should buy a space age type of stock like Jet Electro. Maybe Eddie was right.

The Players
Ken Osmond…Eddie Haskell

Notable line(s)

Beaver: You know, Wally, you may not know stocks and bonds, but you sure know parents.

Eddie: You see, you guys stick wih me, you'll be wearing diamonds.

Ward: When your sons think you're smarter than their friends, you know you've really got it made.

S5 E39 - Un-Togetherness
Jun 30, 1962
Director: Norman Abbott
Writers: Joe Connelly & Bob Mosher (supervisors) Dick Conway & Roland MacLane

Snapshot: Beaver is very excited for the upcoming family trip to the lake. But Wally tells the family he can't go because of his summer job. That's really a ruse because his reason is Lori Ann, a girl who works at the library. Wally finds out she's going away for the summer, and he'll be staying behind all alone, foregoing the family vacation. But before the episode ends with the Cleavers leaving town, Eddie lets Ward know what happened with Lori Ann and Ward heads back home to get Wally. Ward assures Wally, "The family's one place where you're always wanted. Don't you ever forget it."

The Players
Ken Osmond…Eddie
Brenda Scott…Lori Ann

Notable line(s)

Beaver: Well, sure, but the school might close for some reason, like they might have an epidemic or something. *(Author note: This line will always have a new meaning to us now)*

Ward: Ah, two whole weeks with nothing to do but lay around fishing, swimming. What a life.
June: While I'm cooking the meals, doing the dishes, making the beds, cleaning the cabin. Yeah, what a life. Don't worry, honey. I love every minute of it.

Beaver: Hey, Wally, I'll bet I know what's wrong with you.
Wally: Yeah?
Beaver: It's that new girl that works over at the library. Yeah, you've been acting real funny ever since you met her. That's what's eating you.
Wally: Who are you all of the sudden? Dear Abby?

S6 E1 - Wally's Dinner Date
Sep 27, 1962
Director: Norman Abbott
Writers: Joe Connelly & Bob Mosher (story) Dale & Katherine Eunson (teleplay)

Snapshot: Wally decides to take Julie Foster on a dinner date. He lets her choose the restaurant and it turns out to be the swankiest joint in town. The cheapest meal is $6.25 and that's a lot of money for 1962. On top of the expensive price, Wally forgets his wallet.

The Players

Cheryl Holdridge…Julie Foster

Ken Osmond…Eddie Haskell

Than Wyenn…The Waiter

Ralph Brooks…Waiter (uncredited)

Notable line(s)

Beaver: I have to have a current event for school, for social science.
Ward: (looking at newspaper) Ah, let's see, ah yeah, how about this one The Indians have predicted a long and severe winter.
Beaver: Dad, you gave that one to me when I was in first grade.
Ward: Oh, well, the Indians always do predict a long and severe winter.

♦   ♦   ♦   ♦   ♦   ♦

S6 E2 - Beaver's Football Award
Oct 4, 1962
Director: David Butler
Writers: Joe Connelly & Bob Mosher, Dick Conway & Roland MacLane

Snapshot: Beaver is scheduled to receive an award for being the most inspiring player on his football team, but he refuses to wear a jacket and tie because the other guys are going casual. If only Beaver could win an award for refusing the group think of his friends, especially that of Terry, the teams' quarterback.

The Players

Richard Correll… Richard

Stephen Talbot…Gilbert

Kim Charney…Terry

Bobby Barber…Father at Award Dinner

Ralph Brooks…Father at Award Dinner

George Bruggeman…Father at Award Dinner

Rex Hill…Ronald

Don Dillaway…Mr. Rickover

Allan Ray…Mr. Bates

Dick Cherney…Father at Award Dinner

George DeNormand …Father at Award Dinner

John Roy…Father at Award Dinner

Notable line(s)

Ward: June, Do I always have to be the one to see that they do what they are told?
June: I guess so.

S6 E3 - Wally's License
Oct 11, 1962
Director: Norman Abbott
Writers: Joe Connelly & Bob Mosher, Bob Ross

Snapshot: It's Wally's 17th birthday and it's the day he is now of legal age to drive. He wants to get his license, but June wants him to wait even longer. But Ward promised, and Wally begins his driver's education class and by the end of the episode, he's got a license and June still isn't ready for him to drive.

The Players
Ken Osmond…Eddie Haskell   Russ Bender…Mr. Barnsdall
Beverly Lunsford…Shirley Fletcher   Larry J. Blake…The Instructor

Notable line(s)

Ward: How long have you been driving Eddie?
Eddie: In three weeks, it will be two months.
Ward: I never realized you were such an old hand.

Wally: Well, you'd think I was taking a test to be an astronaut or something.
Beaver: Good luck Wally, and I'll say some driving prayers for you.

June: Oh, but Wally, you just got your license... it's it isn't even cold yet.

♦   ♦   ♦   ♦   ♦   ♦

S6 E4 - The Late Edition
Oct 18, 1962
Director: Norman Abbott
Writers: Joe Connelly & Bob Mosher, Dick Conway & Roland MacLane

Snapshot: Beaver has found his life's ambition. He wants to work in the newspaper business. His first step, taking over the local paper route. There's an opening and he wants it, but a boy at school gets to the office before him and is hired first. That's when Beaver begins scheming on how to take the job away from him.

The Players
Richard Correll…Richard
Chrystine Jordan…The Paper Boy (as Chrystie Jordan)

Notable line(s)

Richard: The paper boy's a girl!

Beaver: Yes, mom, I'm out here... But I wish I was in some nice, safe place, like the moon.

S6 E5 - Double Date
Oct 25, 1962
Director: David Butler
Writer: Joe Connelly & Bob Mosher, Dick Conway & Roland MacLane

Snapshot: Wally's surprised Beaver agrees to go on a double date with him. The only way Wally's date Carolyn can go is if her younger sister goes too. That's where Beaver enters the picture. However, Carolyn's sister gets cold feet. Beaver acts disappointed but is relieved.

The Players
Vicky Albright…Carolyn (as Vicki Albright)
Diane Mountford…Susan

Notable line(s)

Wally: Hey, I'm sorry about the mix-up.
Beaver: That's okay, Wally. But next time you cook something like this up, get me a girl who knows the score, huh?

♦   ♦   ♦   ♦   ♦   ♦

S6 E6 - Eddie, the Businessman
Nov 1, 1962
Director: Hugh Beaumont
Writers: Joe Connelly & Bob Mosher (story) Dick Conway & Roland MacLane (teleplay)

Snapshot: Ward helps Wally and Eddie get a job at the Mayfield Dairy. Ward is weary about helping Eddie. After all, it's his own good name that could get besmirched by wisecracking Eddie Haskell. When the dock foreman recruits Eddie to unknowingly help him steal dairy products, the trouble begins, but thank goodness Wally is there to help Eddie out of this jam.

The Players
Ken Osmond…Eddie Haskell   Don Haggerty…Ted Worden
Howard Caine…Foreman   John Baer…Assistant

Notable line(s)

Beaver: You know what you are Eddie, you're a hypocrite.
Eddie: I am not and where'd you learn a word like that?
Beaver: In school, and it means a deceitful person who's underhanded. And if that doesn't fit you, I don't know what does.
Eddie: I Tell you; the school system is ruining the youth of the nation. They ought to teach you a little respect for your elders, kid.

Eddie: This is America, land of opportunity.

Eddie: Yeah, well, would you tell your father for me, that I'm a big stupid dope.
Wally: Don't worry about it Eddie. I think he's kind of suspected it for years.

S6 E7 - Tell It to Ella
Nov 8, 1962
Director: David Butler
Writers: Joe Connolly & Bob Mosher, Dick Conway & Roland MacLane

Snapshot: When Beaver is forbidden from going out on school nights, he wants to prove his parents are being unfair. Eddie tells Beaver about the local newspaper which has an advice columnist who is quite friendly toward children with problems. That may be true on some occasions, but she's not friendly towards Beaver's problem.

The Players
Ken Osmond…Eddie Haskell   Tim Matheson…Michael
Robert Eyer…Kevin

Notable line(s)

Wally: Mom and dad don't make up these rules just to be making them up. They're doing it for your own good.
Beaver: For my own good? What are you doing Wally, practicing to be a father or something.

Eddie: (after Beaver tells him he's punished and not allowed out at night): Hey, that's rough. If that ever happened to me, eight or nine girls would kill themselves.

♦   ♦   ♦   ♦   ♦   ♦

S6 E8 - Bachelor at Large
Nov 15, 1962
Director: Hugh Beaumont
Writers: Joe Connelly & Bob Mosher, Dick Conway & Roland MacLane

Snapshot: Eddie Haskell, still in high school, moves out after a big fight with his father. He moves to a rooming house on the poor side of town. He plays it cool, telling Wally and Lumpy he's having the time of his life. Wally finds out that nothing could be further from the truth.

The Players
Lurene Tuttle…Mrs. Evans   Frank Bank…Clarence
Ken Osmond…Eddie Haskell

Notable line(s)

Eddie: Yeah, I should've made the move (moving out of the house) ten years ago.
Wally: Eddie, ten years ago you weren't old enough to put your underwear on right side out.

Beaver: The only time your father will start bawling is when you move back home.

Lumpy: About a half an hour ago, I'm sitting in my room watching Captain Kangaroo, and my pop walks in and lowers the boom on me.
Wally: Well, maybe your pop doesn't want you watching Captain Kangaroo.

S6 E9 - Beaver Joins a Record Club
Nov 22, 1962
Director: David Butler
Writers: Joe Connelly & Bob Mosher, Dick Conway & Roland MacLane

Snapshot: Beaver is given more responsibility with money than he can handle when he's allowed to join a record club. But at least he's got some groovy tunes blaring in the background as he sinks deeper in debt each week.

The Players

Stephen Talbot…Gilbert   Robert E. Dugan…Mr. Tyler
George Cisar…The Postman

Notable line(s)

Beaver: Don't bother me Wally, I'm sailing.

Beaver: I never knew a guy could get in this much trouble, just liking music.

♦   ♦   ♦   ♦   ♦   ♦

S6 E10 - Wally's Car Accident
Nov 29, 1962
Director: Hugh Beaumont
Writers: Joe Connelly & Bob Mosher, Dick Conway & Roland MacLane (teleplay)

Snapshot: Wally is blessed with the use of Ward's brand-new car for his prom date Shirley at the country club Friday night. But he gives in to Eddie's pressure to help Lumpy with a jump-start and in the process, breaks the headlight on the borrowed car. He gets it fixed without Ward noticing a single flaw, but in typical father fashion, Ward magically finds out what happened.

The Players

Ken Osmond…Eddie Haskell   Beverly Lunsford…Shirley Fletcher
Frank Bank…Lumpy   Will J. White…Al

Notable line(s)

Beaver: You know, Wally, sometimes you're almost as dumb as I am.

Beaver: Does a guy have to look like Tony Curtis just to watch television?

Lumpy (on telephone with Ward): Look, Wally, there's something I got to know before your dad gets home. Are you going to tell him about busting the headlight on his car or not? Well, are you or aren't you? Come on, tell me. Uh... I think you're crazy if you do after we went and spent our own dough to get it fixed. But if you think you have to tell him, just don't mention my name, okay, Wally?

S6 E11 - Beaver, the Sheep Dog
Dec 6, 1962
Director: David Butler
Writers: Joe Connelly & Bob Mosher, Dick Conway & Roland MacLane

Snapshot: There's nothing worse than a girl making fun of a boy's looks, especially if he is a young teenager. When Shirley makes fun of Beaver for looking like a sheep dog, he remedies the situation by taking drastic and rather comedic measures.

The Players

Ken Osmond…Eddie Haskell
Ed Prentiss…Mr. Bailey
Billy E. Hughes…Chuck (as Billy Hughes)
Hank Stanton…Fred

Gretchen Voeth…Shirley
Pamela Duncan…The Woman Clerk
Leslie LaTourette…The 1st Girl
Tina Brady… The 2nd Girl

Notable line(s)

Eddie: Did papa send you to your room without your supper because you spilled your Pablum?

Eddie: What's the matter with his hair? That's the way they're wearing it this year down at the dog pound.

♦   ♦   ♦   ♦   ♦   ♦

S6 E12
Beaver, the Hero
Dec 13, 1962
Director: David Butler
Writers: Joe Connelly & Bob Mosher, Dick Conway & Roland MacLane

Snapshot: Beaver becomes a hero on the football team when he catches the game winning touchdown. He takes the act in stride, but his humility soon turns into pride, and before the next game, he takes a big fall.

The Players
Ken Osmond…Eddie
Stephen Talbot…Gilbert
Stanley Fafara…Whitey
Wendy Ferdin…Charlene

Carol Faylen…Donna
Leslie LaTourette…Patsy
Kim Charney…Terry
Michael Agate…Denny

Notable line(s)

Wally: But, gee, dad, you've been lecturing the Beaver for thirteen years now, and he's still pretty stupid.

Beaver: What right have you got to start analyzing me? You got a license or something, Where's your couch?

S6 E13 - Beaver's Autobiography
Dec 20, 1962
Director: David Butler
Writers: Joe Connelly & Bob Mosher, Joseph Hoffman

Snapshot: A lesson is to be learned when Beaver butters up a girl he thinks is a goon just so she can help him with his autobiography class assignment. The lesson is to never trust a girl to do your homework for you, and a greater lesson is to just do it yourself.

The Players

Annette Gorman…Betsy   Terry Burnham…Virginia
Stephen Talbot…Gilbert   Frances Mercer…Mrs. Carter
Harlan Warde…Mr. Thompson

Notable line(s)

Gilbert: Every once in a while, my pop likes to do my homework because he wants to see what kind of marks the teacher will give him. Last week he wanted to come over and holler at Mr. Walker for flunking him in arithmetic.

Beaver: Girls always have more words than they can use. That's why they're all the time yakking so much.

◆   ◆   ◆   ◆   ◆   ◆

S6 E14 - The Party Spoiler
Dec 27, 1962
Director: Norman Abbott
Writers: Joe Connelly & Bob Mosher, Dick Conway & Roland MacLane

Snapshot: When Wally decides to host a party, Beaver is left out of the planning. He's not invited and he's not happy about it. That's when his good and devious friend Gilbert gives Beaver the great idea of pranking Wally and his guests with many childish gags.

The Players

Ken Osmond…Eddie   Cheryl Miller…Helen
Frank Bank…Lumpy   Reuben Singer…The Boy (as Robert
Stephen Talbot…Gilbert   Singer)
Vicky Albright…Carolyn

Notable line(s)

Beaver (talking about fake candy): Boy, wait till those big guys bite into these soapy centers.
Gilbert: Yeah, I hope it's Eddie Haskell. Then when he starts foaming at the mouth, maybe they'll call the dog catcher.

S6 E15 - The Mustache
Jan 3, 1963
Director: Hugh Beaumont
Writers: Joe Connelly & Bob Mosher, Dick Conway & Roland MacLane

Snapshot: Have you ever done something to change your appearance that you thought made you look better, but didn't? Wally has such an experience when he grows a mustache over a short school vacation. The result? Riotous laughter and a quick shave after his first day back at school.

The Players
Ken Osmond...Eddie Haskell
Frank Bank...Lumpy
Cheryl Holdridge...Julie Foster
Robert Koff...Wayne Gregory

Clark Howat... Mr. Barnes
Brenda Fraley...1st Girl
Karen Lawrence...2nd Girl

Notable line(s)

Beaver: (chuckles at Wally looking at the early stages of his mustache in the mirror)
Wally: Hey, what are you laughing at?
Beaver: I was just thinking. That's like looking for a wheat field in Death Valley.

(Wally comes in and runs upstairs after school)
June: Well, what brought that on?
Beaver: Maybe he's being chased by a gang who saw his mustache and thinks he's Hitler

♦   ♦   ♦   ♦   ♦   ♦

S6 E16 - Wally Buys a Car
Jan 10, 1963
Director: David Butler
Writers: Joe Connelly & Bob Mosher (story) Wilton Schiller (teleplay)

Snapshot: A touching episode of a father helping a son buy his first car. A truly fine coming of age episode about Wally Cleaver.

The Players
Ken Osmond...Eddie Haskell
Jess Kirkpatrick...Mr. Nelson
Ed Peck...The Salesman

Robert Hyatt...Frank (as Bobby Hyatt)
Kathleen O'Malley...The Woman

Notable line(s)

Wally: Boy, Dad, how do you know so much about buying a car?
Ward: Well, Wally, you know they did have cars when I was a boy.
Wally: Used cars?

S6 E17 - The Parking Attendants
Jan 17, 1963
Director: Earl Bellamy
Writers: Joe Connelly & Bob Mosher, Dick Conway & Roland MacLane

Snapshot: Is too much responsibility being given Wally and Eddie when they are hired to park cars for the big Langley wedding? When Eddie parks Mr. Rutherford's car in a no parking zone, we find out it was obviously too much responsibility for Eddie Haskell.

The Players

Ken Osmond… Eddie   Dick Simmons…Mr. Langley
Frank Bank…Lumpy   Margaret Stewart…Mrs. Rutherford
Richard Deacon…Fred Rutherford   Kim Hamilton…The Maid

Notable line(s)

Eddie (to Beaver): What are you reading? Look, look, Mary. John has the ball. The ball is round. Throw the ball to Mary, John.

Eddie (to Wally): How many times have I ever let you down?
Beaver: A couple of hundred times.
Eddie: You stay out of this, boy creep.

◆   ◆   ◆   ◆   ◆   ◆

S6 E18 - More Blessed to Give
Jan 24, 1963
Director: Hugh Beaumont
Writers: Joe Connelly & Bob Mosher, Dick Conway & Roland MacLane

Snapshot: Beaver learns a lot about life and boy / girl relationships when he gives an expensive locket to the beautiful Donna Yeager, a girl he may be in love with.

The Players

Ken Osmond… Eddie Haskell   Buddy Lewis…The Pitchman
Stephen Talbot…Gilbert   Ben Bryant…The Assistant
Paul Langton…Bob Yeager   George Cisar…The Postman
Chrystine Jordan…Donna Yeager   Bobby Barber…Carnival barker (uncredited)
Ann Staunton…Mildred Yeager

Notable line(s)

Wally: What about the girls' parents? Why, they see the present, they'll go through the roof.
Beaver: You think so?
Wally: Well sure, a kid like you isn't supposed to go running around like Frank Sinatra.

Mr. Yeager: Do you understand?
Donna: Oh, yes, Daddy, but a thing like this could absolutely give me a trauma.

S6 E19 - Beaver's Good Deed
Jan 31, 1963
Director: David Butler
Writers: Joe Connelly & Bob Mosher, Dick Conway & Roland MacLane

Snapshot: Ward admonishes Beaver to be more kind and when he comes face to face with a tramp knocking at the door, Beaver shows kindness. He makes his new friend Mr. Jeff a sandwich and when asked, he permits him to also take a bath. The one thing he did not tell Jeff he could do, was to take one of Ward's suits.

The Players
Stephen Talbot…Gilbert
Frank Ferguson…Jeff

Notable line(s)

Mr. Jeff (stranger at door): Good morning gentlemen.
Gilbert: Golly, a bum.

◆   ◆   ◆   ◆   ◆   ◆

S6 E20 - The Credit Card
Feb 7, 1963
Director: David Butler
Writers: Joe Connelly & Bob Mosher, Dick Conway & Roland MacLane

Snapshot: Eddie has a new credit card, and he uses it to buy Wally a new battery when his old one clunks out on the way home from Lynbrook. Wally pays him cash for the battery when they arrive home, but Eddie never pays it to his father and now Eddie must play fast and loose with the credit card to pay off the current month's bill.

The Players
Ken Osmond…Eddie Haskell   Anne Barton…Agnes Haskell
Frank Bank…Lumpy   Harp McGuire…The Attendant
George Petrie…George Haskell

Notable line(s)

Eddie: The other night, we drove down to the beach, and it (Lumpy's radiator) started spouting, people thought Moby Dick had washed ashore.

Beaver: How come a big oil company trusts a creep like you?
Eddie: Pull, Charlie. Pull. Knowing the right people.

Beaver: Wally, Dad wants to see you right away, but I wouldn't be in a hurry about coming in.

Eddie: Pretty swanky, huh? They say it brings out the Peter Lawford in me. (Speaking of a vest)

S6 E21 - Beaver, the Caddy
Feb 14, 1963
Director: Earl Bellamy
Writers: Joe Connelly & Bob Mosher, Dick Conway & Roland MacLane

Snapshot: Beaver could be charged with accessory to fraud if he doesn't find a way to fix things after Mr. Langley uses Beaver and his caddying experience as a way to win a $500 bet.

The Players

Dick Simmons…Mr. Langley

Ralph Montgomery…The Caddy Master

Stephen Talbot…Gilbert

Dorothy Abbott…The Secretary

John Gallaudet…Arthur Howard

Notable line(s)

Gilbert: I sure hope they have something for breakfast that agrees with them.
Beaver: How come?
Gilbert: Well, 'cause there's nothing like indigestion to cut down on the size of your tips.

Mr. Langley: Beaver, look, you keep score for us. You look like you might be an A math student. Probably planning to be a space scientist, huh?
Beaver: Yes, sir. Or play for the Los Angeles Lakers.

◆　◆　◆　◆　◆　◆

S6 E22
Beaver on TV
Feb 21, 1963
Director: David Butler
Writers: Joe Connelly & Bob Mosher, Dick Conway & Roland MacLane

Snapshot: Gilbert suggests Beaver may be residing in the *Twilight Zone* when he participates as a panelist on the TV show *Teen Age Forum*, and none of his friends see him on the show. It takes a bit of sleuthing on the part of Ward to find out what really happened.

The Players

Stephen Talbot…Gilbert

Kevin Jones…The 1st Boy

Richard Deacon…Fred Rutherford

Brad Berwick…The 2nd Boy

Doris Packer…Mrs. Rayburn

Carol Faylen…The 1st Girl

Jack Smith…The Director

Patty Ann Gerrity…The 2nd Girl

Johnny Jacobs…Mr. Thornton

Barbara Hunter…Janet Lynch

Marian Collier…The Girl In The TV Station

Larry Adare…Phillip Jones

Notable line(s)

Wally (speaking of Teen Age Forum): It's kind of a stupid *Meet the Press*.

S6 E23 - Box Office Attraction
Feb 28, 1963
Director: David Butler
Writers: Joe Connelly & Bob Mosher, Dick Conway & Roland MacLane

Snapshot: A great example of how a teenager can fall for a pretty face and then realize he's been fooled. Wally thinks Marlene is the bomb, but after a few moments of their first and only date, he finds out she's a fraud and a floozy. Mary Ellen Rogers is a better match for him.

The Players
Stephen Talbot…Gilbert   Dennis Richards…Gus
Ken Osmond…Eddie Haskell   A.G. Vitanza…Hank
Diane Sayer…Marlene Holmes

Notable line(s)

June: Why doesn't she live with her mother and father?
Ward: Well, I think Wally said her parents live in California.... What's wrong with that?
June: Nothing. Just wish it was Ohio or someplace like that.

Gilbert: You know what she is?
Beaver: What?
Gilbert: She's what they call a woman of the world.
Beaver: Yeah, and my brother's in love with her.

◆　　◆　　◆　　◆　　◆　　◆

S6 E24 - Lumpy's Scholarship
Mar 7, 1963
Director: Hugh Beaumont
Writers: Joe Connelly & Bob Mosher, Dick Conway & Roland MacLane

Snapshot: Wally throws a party for Lumpy after he receives a scholarship to State, and it becomes a somber event for Lumpy when his dad calls to tell him (while he's at the party) that he lost the scholarship because he had flunked a class. Ward speaks with a friend at State and asks if there's a way Lumpy can still attend. He never even tells Fred about his good deed.

The Players
Frank Bank…Lumpy   Nino Candido… Buzz
Ken Osmond…Eddie Haskell   Dennis Pepper…Denny
Richard Deacon…Fred Rutherford   Terry Burnham …Beaver's Date
Ahna Capri…Cinda Dunsworth   (uncredited)
Dana Dillaway…Sally

Notable line(s)

June: Aren't you ever going to tell Fred what you did?
Ward: No, he'd never believe someone could do something that nice for someone like him.

S6 E25 - The Silent Treatment
Mar 14, 1963
Director: David Butler
Writers: Joe Connelly & Bob Mosher, Theodore & Mathilde Ferro

Snapshot: When Beaver feels disrespected by June, he gives her the silent treatment and pays a lot of attention to Ward. When Ward finally notices this behavior, and before he can force Beaver to stop, a bee swoops in and saves the day with a sting on Beaver's finger.

The Players
Ken Osmond...Eddie Haskell

Notable line(s)

Beaver: Yeah, Eddie, I guess when you're on a date, you need all the help you can get.
Eddie: Look, Junior, who let you out of your sand box?

Wally: What are you trying to be, a junior Eddie Haskell or something?

Beaver: Tomorrow for history, we have Robert E. Lee. What was his father's name?
June: Beaver, I wouldn't have any idea.
Ward: Henry "Light Horse" Harry Lee
Beaver: Boy, you sure know your history dad. But mom knows a lot about other things

◆   ◆   ◆   ◆   ◆   ◆

S6 E26 - Uncle Billy's Visit
Mar 21, 1963
Director: David Butler
Writers: Joe Connelly & Bob Mosher, Dick Conway & Roland MacLane

Snapshot: Ward and June are heading out of town for the weekend and Uncle Billy is passing through, just in time so he can supervise the boys. June is weary, but Uncle Billy turns out to be a substitute parent who can lecture Beaver just as well as Ward can.

The Players
Stephen Talbot...Gilbert   Martin Dean...The Usher
Kevin Jones...Alan   Edgar Buchanan...Uncle Billy
William Woodson   Mr. Gaines

Notable line(s)

Beaver: I bet I'm the only kid in school who has an uncle who ever lived with the Indians.
Wally: Well, I think Billy just lived in a hotel that had some Indians living in it.
Beaver: That's still living with the Indians. What are you trying to do, wreck a neat story?

Alan: It must be good (the movie), even the ads got blood in them.

S6 E27 - Beaver's Prep School
Mar 28, 1963
Director: Hugh Beaumont
Writers: Joe Connelly & Bob Mosher, Dick Conway & Roland MacLane

Snapshot: When given the opportunity to attend Fallbrook, a prep school in New England that has been attended by many in the Bronson family, or attending good old Mayfield High, Beaver has a difficult choice to make. What will be the swaying factors in his ultimate decision?

The Players

Madge Kennedy...Aunt Martha
Doris Packer...Mrs. Rayburn
Stanley Fafara...Whitey
Kim Charney...Terry

Patty Ann Gerrity...1st Girl
Carol Faylen...2nd Girl
Larry Adare...Alan
Henry Hunter...Mr. Thomas

Notable line(s)

Beaver: I just wanted to talk to you and thank you for wanting to send me to Fairfield.
Aunt Martha: Fallbrook.
Beaver: Uh, Fallbrook.

◆   ◆   ◆   ◆   ◆   ◆

S6 E28 - Wally and the Fraternity
Apr 4, 1963
Director: David Butler
Writers: Joe Connelly & Bob Mosher, Dick Conway & Roland MacLane

Snapshot: Both Eddie and Wally have decided to attend State, Ward's alma mater. The big decision to make is which fraternity to join. Wally and Eddie get some bum advice from a disgruntled former member of Alpha Kappa. This is yet another episode in which Eddie must have his mess cleaned up by Mr. Cleaver.

The Players

Ken Osmond...Eddie Haskell
Don Voyne...Ted

Randy Herron... Barry
Jeff Malloy...Chuck Bradford

Notable line(s)

June: That's where your father got me.
Wally: Yeah, that's right. You and dad met at State.

Eddie: If I did something like this to my father, he'd clobber me.
Ward: Don't think I didn't consider it Eddie.

S6 E29 - Eddie's Sweater
Apr 11, 1963
Director: Earl Bellamy
Writers: Joe Connelly & Bob Mosher (teleplay) Kenneth A. Enochs (story)

Snapshot: Whenever there is secrecy between a guy and his girlfriend, there is going to possibly be trouble, and definitely jealousy, whether it's warranted or not. The secrecy in this case is Eddie's girlfriend making him a sweater and Wally modeling for her, and Julie Foster not knowing about it.

The Players

Ken Osmond…Eddie Haskell
Frank Bank…Lumpy

Cheryl Holdridge…Julie Foster
Ahna Capri…Cindy Andrews

Notable line(s)

Ward: You know, I was under the impression that Wally's main interest was Julie Foster.
Beaver: I think he's getting some new impressions, Dad.

Beaver: I know all about love and romance. I saw two whole Gidget pictures.

Lumpy: Well, if it isn't the Elvis Presley of Mayfield High School.

Eddie: I'm going right home and write that Wally a real nasty letter.

♦   ♦   ♦   ♦   ♦   ♦

S6 E30 - The Book Report
Apr 18, 1963
Director   Hugh Beaumont
Writers: Joe Connelly & Bob Mosher, Dick Conway & Roland MacLane

Snapshot: It doesn't take Beaver long after he begins reading his book report to the class to figure out he's done something wrong. He has written his book report without reading the book. Instead, he watched the musical comedy movie version of *The Three Musketeers*. Mrs. Rayburn is not pleased.

The Players

Stephen Talbot…Gilbert
Doris Packer…Mrs. Rayburn

Carol Faylen…Janet
Fletcher Allen…The Man

Notable line(s)

Beaver: Man, what a dumb book.
Wally: Dumb book? *The Three Musketeers* is a great book.

Wally: I've lived in the same room with Beaver for almost thirteen years now. You know, like in those prison pictures, a guy always knows more about his cellmate than the warden does.

S6 E31 - The Poor Loser
Apr 25, 1963
Director: David Butler
Writers: Joe Connelly & Bob Mosher, Dick Conway & Roland MacLane

Snapshot: Beaver, when given a choice to go to a major league baseball game, declines the opportunity. But once his plans with Gilbert fall through, he mopes around until Wally tells him he can use the one extra ticket Ward had been given. That's mighty big of Wally, but really, he can't believe Beaver takes him up on his offer.

The Players

Stephen Talbot…Gilbert   Vince Williams…Radio Announcer (voice)

Notable line(s)

Gilbert: She even got violin lessons and I didn't.
Beaver: I thought you hated the violin.
Gilbert: They didn't even give me a chance to tell them that I hate the violin.

June: Wally's been studying child psychology. Maybe he's doing a little homework on Beaver.

♦   ♦   ♦   ♦   ♦   ♦

S6 E32 - Don Juan Beaver
May 2, 1963
Director: Hugh Beaumont
Writers: Joe Connelly & Bob Mosher (teleplay) David Levinson (story)

Snapshot: Beaver is Don Juan? He's got two girls on the string in this episode. There's the very kind, cute and authentic Peggy and then there is the pushy and snobbish southern belle, Melinda. This new girl with a southern accent may be attractive, but Beaver made a date with Peggy and should've kept it. Instead, he winds up home alone with no date at all.

The Players

Stephen Talbot…Gilbert   Veronica Cartwright…Peggy MacIntosh
Ken Osmond…Eddie Haskell   Charla Doherty…Melinda Neilson
Stanley Fafara…Whitey

Notable line(s)

Gilbert: The way I feel about girls, they're nothing to get shook up about. They're just something that happens, like shaving or getting cavities.

Eddie: What's the matter with you Junior, did you get drummed out of the Mouseketeers?
Beaver: I got girl trouble.
Eddie: Girl trouble, you? Now I've heard everything.

S6 E33 - Summer in Alaska
May 9, 1963
Director: David Butler
Writers: Joe Connelly & Bob Mosher, Dick Conway & Roland MacLane

Snapshot: Eddie has summer plans, and they include being a big man on a small fishing boat in the rugged Alaskan waters. That is, until he meets with the boat's captain and finds out his summer job won't be as glorious as he thinks it will be.

The Players

Ken Osmond...Eddie Haskell
Frank Bank...Lumpy
George Petrie...George Haskell

Anne Barton...Agnes Haskell
Harry Harvey...Captain Drake

Notable line(s)

Agnes Haskell: It's such a rough life and Edward's so sensitive.
George Haskell: Sensitive? He's about as sensitive as an armadillo.

Captain Drake: You friends of the owner too?
Lumpy: Oh, no. sir. We're not friends of anybody.
Wally: No, we just came down to.... well, to be with him.
Captain Drake: Oh, now, isn't that nice? Couldn't his nurse maid make it?

Eddie: But what do you do about sea sickness?
Captain Drake: Don't worry, you'll do it.

◆   ◆   ◆   ◆   ◆   ◆

S6 E34 - Beaver's Graduation
May 16, 1963
Director: Hugh Beaumont
Writers: Joe Connelly & Bob Mosher, Dick Conway & Roland MacLane

Snapshot: Sneaking through the principal's office is not a good thing to do. Beaver suffers the consequences of doing so when he doesn't find his graduation certificate with all the others in Mrs. Rayburn's office. He's not going to graduate. Poor Beaver. He shouldn't have goofed off the last week of school. But there's an entirely good reason he didn't find his certificate.

The Players

Stephen Talbot...Gilbert
Ken Osmond...Eddie

Doris Packer...Mrs. Rayburn
Dorothy Abbott...Miss Walker

Notable line(s)

Ward: Well, I guess the only thing for you to do is go in and see Mrs. Rayburn tomorrow and tell her what you found out. Maybe there's some explanation for all this.
Wally: Yeah. Maybe it wasn't your goofing around. Maybe it's just 'cause you're stupid.

S6 E35 - Wally's Practical Joke
May 23, 1963
Director: David Butler
Writers: Joe Connelly & Bob Mosher

Snapshot: One practical joke deserves another. That's what Eddie and Wally believe after becoming victims of Lumpy's practical jokes. Boy, they sure get even with him, and then some.

The Players

Ken Osmond…Eddie   Richard Deacon…Fred Rutherford
Frank Bank…Lumpy   Kathleen O'Malley…Mrs. Halloran

Notable line(s)

Ward: I remember when I was in high school, one of the fellas had one of those Austin cars. About ten of us got together and carried it up the school steps and put it right ---
June: Ward....
Ward: Oh, I keep forgetting I'm not to have had any fun when I was a kid.

Eddie: Listen, every night before supper, he (Lumpy) goes down to the malt shop for a sundae. He's not supporting that blubber on skim milk, you know.

♦   ♦   ♦   ♦   ♦   ♦

S6 E36 - The All-Night Party
May 30, 1963
Director: David Butler
Writers: Joe Connelly & Bob Mosher, Dick Conway & Roland MacLane

Snapshot: Wally is graduating high school and wants to attend an all-night graduation party at the country club. He receives permission but must talk his date's parents into allowing her to go with him. Mr. Gregory gives his permission because they believe Wally to be a nice safe boy. But he comes to regret giving his permission when he sees his daughter the morning after.

The Players

Ken Osmond…Eddie   Frank Sully…The Drunk
Frank Bank…Lumpy   Mary Benoit…The 1st Woman
Marjorie Reynolds…Mrs. Gregory   Carole Wells… Kathy
Patricia Morrow…The 1st Girl   Herbert Rudley…Mr. Gregory
Judy Short…Sue (as Judie Short)

Notable line(s)

Wally: I'm going over to talk to Kathy's Father.
Lumpy: Wow. There goes the bravest guy in the whole world.
Eddie: Either that, or the stupidest.

S6 E37 - Beaver Sees America
Jun 6, 1963
Director: Hugh Beaumont
Writers: Joe Connelly & Bob Mosher (teleplay) Dale & Katherine Eunson (teleplay)

Snapshot: Wally warns Ward that Beaver has gone back on his desire to go on a summer trip across America because of a girl named Mary Margaret Matthews. He says that this girl is not like the girls he knew when he was Beaver's age. In fact, he even warns Beaver about her by telling him that he's playing in the Pony league and she's batting in the World Series.

The Players

Ken Osmond…Eddie   Stanley Fafara…Whitey Whitney
Stephen Talbot…Gilbert   Lori Martin…Mary Margaret

Notable line(s)

Wally: Boy Beaver, you sure picked a heck of a time in your life to start panting over women.
Beaver: I didn't pick it. It just happened.
Wally: Yeah. Come to think of it. The whole mess snuck up on me the same way.

Wally: Uh... Uh, Dad, I don't want to tell you how to run your family or anything, but if I were you, I'd make sure Beaver gets on that bus.

S6 E38 - The Clothing Drive
Jun 13, 1963
Director: Charles F. Haas
Writers: Joe Connelly & Bob Mosher, Allan Manings

Snapshot: There's a "good citizen" award on the line and whoever gives the best donations for the class clothing drive will win it. Beaver's got this award won after he donates three of Ward's good suits. Unfortunately, Ward must take those suits back as they weren't Beaver's to give. They were put out to be picked up by the dry cleaner, not for Beaver to take to school.

The Players

Doris Packer…Mrs. Rayburn
Ed Prentiss…Mr. Bailey
Tim Matheson…Michael
John Yount…Chuck

Notable line(s)

Mike: I wonder if the President's little kid has to wear his sister's old clothes.
Beaver: Nah, I think when you live in the White House, you just wear stuff once, and then you throw it away.

S6 E39 - Family Scrapbook
Jun 20, 1963
Director: Hugh Beaumont
Writers: Joe Connelly & Bob Mosher

Snapshot: June finds a scrapbook filled with memories of the boys and the family spends the episode reminiscing over old times. This is a sad episode for *Leave it to Beaver* fans as this marks the end what many consider the best family situation comedy in TV history.

The Players:
Ken Osmond…Eddie (archive footage)
Sue Randall…Miss Landers (archive footage)
Madge Blake…Mrs. Mondello (archive footage)
Pamela Beaird…Mary Ellen Rogers (archive footage) (as Pamela Beaird)
Robert 'Rusty' Stevens…Larry Mondello (archive footage)

Notable line(s)

Beaver: Hey, Mom, how come when I was a little kid, you guys started calling me Beaver?
June: Well, that started because Wally couldn't pronounce Theodore.
Beaver: But why Beaver?
Ward: Well, "Theodore" came out as "Tweedor," and we thought Beaver was a little better.
Wally: Gee, I'm sorry, Beav. I didn't know what I was saying.

♦   ♦   ♦   ♦   ♦   ♦

A very attractive Barbara Billingsley with a new hair style in season four.

Entrance to the Los Angeles County Fair ("Beaver's Fear") 1962

Check out that font. Jerry Mathers has mentioned this was a possible inspiration for the TV show's title.

Actor Paul Sullivan, the original Wally (and Beaver) In the mid-1980s

Co-creator, writer and co-producer Bob Mosher lived here on Lake Avenue in Auburn, NY during the summers of his youth.

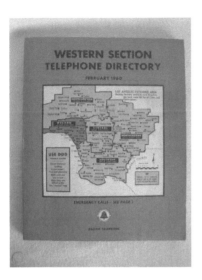

This is the phone book used by Beaver to look up Betsy Patterson's number in "Beaver's First Date."

(below) Cindy Carol (Sydes), Tony Dow and Hugh Beaumont on the set, while he directs "Wally and Alma." Hugh was lauded as being a very good director by many he worked with.

One of the rare times, the entire family heads to church together (See Chapter 48).

(Below) Actor Jackie Kelk (Old Man Merkel) in 1951 while working on The Aldrich Family radio show. The show also featured Norman Tokar as Henry Aldrich for a few years.

74

LEAVE IT TO BEAVER ACTOR ENCYCLOPEDIA

REGULARS OR SEMI REGULARS

Billingsley, Barbara (1915-2010) 235 episodes (June Cleaver)

A week after turning twenty-two, Barbara made her way to Broadway. She arrived in New York City just before the end of 1937 with a stage show she had worked with in Los Angeles titled *The Straw Hat*. The show ran on Broadway from December 30, 1937 to January 1, 1938, a total of four performances.[101] While the play focused on a female lead (Sylvia Leigh) in a New Hampshire summer stock theater who desired more than anything to be discovered by Hollywood, Barbara did not have that immediate desire and stayed in New York after the play closed. She earned her living in New York as a fashion model. She also toured in the play *Accidentally Yours* with Billie Burke, who is best known for her role as the Good Witch of the North in *The Wizard of Oz*.

Signing her first movie contract in 1945 (MGM), Barbara, now married to restaurateur Glenn Billingsley, moved west to Hollywood. For years, she worked in "B" movies, often in uncredited roles. She eventually made her way to bigger films, yet the roles were still small. Two of those films were *Three Guys Named Mike* starring Jane Wyman and *The Bad and the Beautiful* starring Kirk Douglas, Lana Turner and Dick Powell.

In 1957 Barbara landed her dream role. "I used to lie in bed at night and say, 'Now what would I like to do? I want my children to be proud of it. I want my children to be able to look at it.' I used to dream about a show like *Beaver*. Don't figure that dreams don't come true, because they do."[102] One day she was filming on the set of *Leave it to Beaver* and had an epiphany, "This is the show I always wanted to do." She also says in that interview with Karen Herman, that Hugh Beaumont had different feelings. He wanted to do the show and then move on which was in stark contrast to Barbara. Eventually, during the show's run, Hugh Beaumont, she admits, came to greatly appreciate *Leave it to Beaver* for the high-quality family show it was.[103]

After *Leave it to Beaver*, Barbara stayed out of the limelight for many years, except for two appearances on the crime drama, *The F.B.I.* Her preference was to stay at home in Malibu or travel the world with her husband William Mortensen. But in 1980, she came back to the screen, thanks to the producers of *Airplane*, a parody of those 1970s airline disaster movies. In that film, she portrayed a woman who translated jive for a flight attendant who couldn't understand two men in need of help.

Three years later she starred in, *Still the Beaver*, the *Leave it to Beaver* TV movie, and a year after that, she starred in *The New Leave it to Beaver*. Barbara wasn't finished with TV after the second incarnation of *Leave it to Beaver* ended. She later had TV roles in *Parker Lewis Can't Lose*, *Empty Nest* and *Murphy Brown*. Her last role was in the 2003 TV movie *Secret Santa*.

In the years after the original *Leave it to Beaver* series, Barbara Billingsley became close friends with her two television sons from the show and also with Ken Osmond (Eddie Haskell) and Frank Bank (Lumpy). Tony Dow and his family seem to have been the closest with Barbara as they ate dinners together once a month for many years. She loved them all and many times reunited with the four actors for TV interviews, *Leave it to Beaver* retrospectives and other public appearances.

Barbara died at her Santa Monica home in 2010 after a long illness at the age of 94.

---

[101] Hischak, Thomas S. *Broadway Plays and Musicals* (Jefferson, NC: McFarland and Co. Inc., 2009), 441.
[102] Interview with Barbara Billingsley by Karen Herman.
[103] Ibid.

Mathers, Jerry (b. June 2, 1948) 235 episodes (Theodore "Beaver" Cleaver)

Jerry Mathers was the consummate child actor. He had a knack from the very beginning for remembering his lines. Directors and producers were amazed at his ability. Jerry wasn't pushed into acting by his mother like so many child actors of the 1950s and 1960s were. It all began quite naturally while shopping for clothes at Desmond's, a big Los Angeles department store in the San Fernando Valley.

While shopping for clothes, Jerry's mother was approached by a woman who said he looked just like a boy in the family featured in their store catalog. The woman asked if she would allow Jerry to model clothes for them. Mrs. Mathers wasn't quite sure about this offer, but when told it came with cash considerations and free clothes, she assured the woman Jerry could do that modeling job. The rest is history. After many times walking down a runway with a stunning model holding his hand, Jerry grew accustomed to working in front of live audiences. This came in very handy while working on TV with their live studio audiences.[104]

Not soon after the modeling job, Jerry made his way to the NBC show *Four Star Revue,* a variety show which featured a rotation of four hosts. These hosts included Jimmy Durante, Danny Thomas, Jack Carson and Ed Wynn. The show later changed its name to *All-Star Revue* when it began featuring additional hosts. It was on this TV show where Jerry Mathers' stock as an actor rose to great heights, a very impressive feat seeing that it was his first TV appearance ever... and he was only two years old.[105]

On the *Four Star Revue*, Jerry's first TV acting job, he walked through a set of swinging doors and into a saloon wearing a diaper, a ten-gallon hat and a holster with two six guns. Cowboys were fighting, throwing chairs everywhere. The scene was total chaos. It was live TV and Jerry was calm as could be and a cowboy picked him up and placed him on the bar. Ed Wynn, played the bartender, placed PET Milk on the bar and Jerry recited his first televised line ever as he slams his little hands down on the bar, "I'm the toughest hombre in these parts, and you'd better have my brand!"

After his calm portrayal of this little cowboy, chairs flying all around him, Jerry became popular with directors of early TV shows like *The Ray Bolger Show* and *December Bride*, among many others. His popularity was due in part because there were very few child actors in Los Angeles at the time, and fewer still who could recite lines and not be frightened in front of a live audience. His intelligence helped with the first, his experience as a model helped with the second. Jerry's work piqued the interest of *Lux Video Theater*, the television version of the very famous and long-lasting *Lux Radio Theater* which had starred host Cecile B. DeMille. While filming *Lux Video Theater*, Jerry was seen by Alfred Hitchcock who was present on the set to promote his latest film, *To Catch a Thief.* [106]

Alfred Hitchcock saw Jerry's performance and was immediately impressed with the maturity and acting abilities of the young Mr. Mathers. He offered Jerry a role in his next film, *The Trouble with Harry*, an experiment by Hitchcock in making a film without a star lead and featuring

---

[104] Interview with Jerry Mathers by Gary Rutowski, 2006.

[105] In the Archives of American Television interview conducted on June 20, 2006, Jerry mentions his first job in television as an advertisement for Pet Milk on the Colgate Comedy Hour but adds "or some variety show." Further research has shown that Pet Milk sponsored the Four Star Revue on NBC in 1950 and on that series, Ed Wynn was a host and did a commercial for Pet Milk. Most likely, this is the one featuring Jerry Mathers as a little cowboy.

[106] In the same interview, Jerry states Alfred Hitchcock was "promoting his latest film." Hitchcock's latest film at that time was *It Takes a Thief* and he next made *The Trouble with Harry* in which he cast Jerry Mathers in his biggest role up to that time.

more subtle humor.[107] Two years later, Jerry was cast as the lead in *Leave it to Beaver*. It all began with a modeling job when he was two years old. That job prepared him for live TV which was a springboard to his role in an Alfred Hitchcock movie, eventually leading Jerry to his new agent Glen Shaw, who encouraged he try out for the role of The Beaver.

The show for which Jerry Mathers is most famous, ran six seasons. The first season, aired on CBS but due to ratings which weren't as high as CBS execs had hoped for, was cancelled. The situation comedy was then picked up by ABC where it aired in numerous nights and time slots until 1963. Due to its popularity today, many fans believe *Leave it to Beaver* was a huge hit during its original run, but it never did crack the top thirty shows from 1957-1963.

After the show left the air in 1963, Jerry never lost the acting bug. Immediately after high school he had roles on *Batman*, *Lassie*, and *My Three Sons*, but his career went on hiatus while in the Air National Guard and in college at the University of California at Berkley[108] where he graduated with a degree in philosophy. He later went on to work in banking and real estate before getting back into acting in a stage play with his television brother Tony Dow in *Boing, Boing* which ran for eight weeks. He later had a successful run on the dinner theater circuit for seventeen continuous months in the comedy *So Long, Stanley*.

After their success in *So Long, Stanley*; Jerry and Tony knew there was an audience for them, and it didn't take long for others in Hollywood to figure that out. Director and writer Brian Levant was driven down to San Diego by Richard Correll to watch Jerry and Tony in *So Long, Stanley*. That moment put into motion a movie idea that had been in Levant's mind for quite a few years.[109] In 1983, *Still the Beaver*, a movie of the week, was produced and was met with great response. It was spun off into its own television series. The show was called *Still the Beaver*, airing on the Disney Channel for one year. Cancelled after its debut season, the show moved to Superstation TBS for the following three seasons. Renamed *The New Leave it to Beaver*, Jerry starred in all 101 episodes and many of the cast of the original series joined him. Exceptions included Hugh Beaumont who had died in 1982 of a heart attack, Stanley Fafara (the original Whitey Whitney), and Stephen Talbot (Gilbert Bates).

Since the end of *The New Leave it to Beaver*, Jerry Mathers has gained even more fame around the world for his role as Beaver Cleaver. In 1980 the original show was shown in over twenty countries and translated into fifteen different languages.[110] A quarter of a century later, the show was televised in 127 countries and Jerry's words had been translated or subtitled in over ninety languages.[111] As Jerry has often said, "I can go anywhere in the world, and people know me."[112] Smiling in the interview in which he shared these stats, Jerry speaks positively about the role he cherishes and made him a household name with worldwide fame and that is commendable.

If you've ever wondered which episode was his favorite, he admitted to Stu Shostak in a 2008 interview that "Wally, the Lifeguard," was his favorite. He and Wally would spend their off time during the filming at Friend's Lake (later known as Jaws Lake at the Universal backlot) and fish for blue gill. Jerry caught more fish than Wally the day they went fishing and caught the biggest fish ever to come out of that lake.[113] That's a good memory.

Over the years, in snail mail or social media messages, I've always addressed Jerry as Mr.

---

[107] "Trouble with Harry", IMDB.com

[108] Mathers, Jerry. *And Jerry Mathers as "The Beaver."* (New York: Berkley Boulevard, 1998), 137, 147.

[109] Author interview with Brian Levant, November 2022.

[110] Reilly, Pattie. "Leave It to Beaver: Tony Dow and Jerry Mathers Find a New Channel for Their Talent—Dinner Theater,"*People*, May 05,1980.

[111] Jerry Mathers, interviewed by Gary Rutkowski. Further research to confirm these stats have not borne fruit, but there is evidence of syndication rights being sold to Japan, Australia, Canada and England.

[112] Robertson, Campbell. "And Jerry Mathers as... Tracy Turnblad's Father?" *New York Times*, June 5, 2007.

[113] Stu's Show interview with Jerry Mathers, November 8, 2008.

Mathers. That's the way Alfred Hitchcock addressed him, and I always felt, if that was good enough for Hitch, it was good enough for me. In November 2022, I was finally able to address him as such in person at the Gallatin, TN ComicCon event. I can truly say it was a treat to meet a celebrity as down to earth and nice as Mr. Jerry Mathers was, on that cold Tennessee afternoon.

Beaumont, Hugh (1909 or 1910 -1982) 234 episodes (Ward Cleaver)

Hugh Beaumont is a parental hero to many people. His portrayal of an idyllic father on *Leave it to Beaver* was, and still is, much loved because of the unyielding patience he demonstrated with his children and their repeated problems. Okay, maybe not so much patience when doing homework with Beaver, but otherwise, Ward Cleaver was a very patient man.

In real life, he was a very patient man too and quite caring, a centerpiece of his Christianity. Hugh Beaumont, as many may not know, was a Methodist lay minister and earned a Masters of Theology degree from USC in 1946. He remained a Methodist and dedicated to church work throughout his life, even being invited to preach in churches a few times a year while appearing on *Leave it to Beaver.* When he preached, he asked the local minister to not introduce him and said there would be no autographs after his sermon. He told TV critic Hal Humphrey in 1961, "When I go to church to preach a sermon, I go as a preacher, not an actor." [114] Speaking of acting, Beaumont also played the role of a clergyman on TV and in the movies ten different times; the most prominent was on *The Lone Ranger* episode, "Godless Men," from the show's third season. He even wrote a short story for the *Saturday Evening Post* in 1951 titled, "Reverend Telford's Failure."[115]

Hugh married actress Kathryn (Hohn) Adams in 1941. The two knew each other from the "Gateway to Hollywood" contest they had entered. This is how Beaumont got his big break. According to Jerry Mathers, because the congregation where he worked as a minister could barely afford to pay him, he needed extra funds to supplement his income and he found this extra income through work on the big screen.[116] "Sometimes my work as an actor presents a conflict with my ideals as a clergyman. I don't believe in the old saying that the end justifies the means, and no money that I can earn as an actor can accomplish so much good that I would feel justified in violating my ideals to earn it… If the question ever arises in a serious way, of course I would have to give up my acting."[117]

The above quote could be seen in action in one of his more popular roles, that of detective Michael Shayne. Beginning in 1940 actor Lloyd Nolan brought this hardboiled detective from radio and turned him into a popular character on the big screen via seven films for 20th Century Fox. In his film portrayal and in the original Shayne books, Michael Shayne was not averse to physical violence to get his way with a bad guy. But in the Michael Shayne films featuring Hugh Beaumont, beginning in 1946, according to various IMDB reviews, Beaumont's Michael Shayne is more easy going, pleasant and likes to crack jokes, somewhat similar to Dick Powell's portrayal on radio of Detective Richard Diamond sans the singing. But true to all 1940s "B" detective movies, Beaumont does inflict harm via his fists on movie antagonists when he must.

A role much better suited for his personality, one that would fit his Christian religion, wound up being the father Ward Cleaver in *Leave it to Beaver*. This does not mean to say he immediately loved the role, as situation comedy was looked down upon by many serious actors at the time. But he did, according to Barbara Billingsley, come to admire the role of Ward Cleaver

---

[114] Humphrey, Hal. "Meet Beaver's Father." *Los Angeles Mirror.* April 8, 1961.
[115] "Hugh Beaumont" IMDB.com.
[116] Jerry Mathers, interviewed by MeTV Monitor, January 28, 2014, *MeTVnetwork.com.*
[117] Hugh Beaumont Obituary *Associated Press*, May 16, 1982.

over time.[118] Playing Ward also helped typecast Hugh as well as all *Leave it to Beaver* actors for a period of time after the series ended. This is never enjoyable for actors who want to branch out to a broader range of acting after a successful series.

After *Leave it to Beaver*, Hugh Beaumont acted in bit roles, many in dramas such as *The Virginian, Marcus Welby M.D., Mannix, Medical Center* and *Wagon Train*. In 1972 he suffered a stroke, from which doctors thought he might not recover. However, Hugh surprised the pessimistic docs and returned to live an active life as a Christmas tree farmer in Minnesota and he still did a little work in local theater.

Hugh Beaumont suffered a heart attack in 1982 while visiting his son Hunter, a professor living in Germany. He passed away one year before the reunion movie *Still the Beaver* was filmed. It would have been a tremendous blessing if Ward Cleaver could have been part of that movie and the subsequent series.

Dow, Tony (1945-2022) 234 episodes (Wally Cleaver)

A very talented athlete, Tony Dow was much more interested in sports, specifically swimming and diving, when he was a child, than he was in acting. He had won a junior Olympic championship and was a Western States champion diver. Tony was such a good swimmer that in one swim meet where he came in first place, his closest competitor was future Olympic gold medal winner Roy Allen Saari.[119] His athletic abilities came to him by way of his mother, Muriel Montrose. She was a stuntwoman in early cowboy movies. She had mastered jumping from a horse onto a moving stagecoach and then back to her horse. Very few people could do that in early Hollywood and because of that, she was a stunt double for both actors and actresses. She was also a stand in for silent screen star Clara Bow and was a Mack Sennett Bathing Beauty. Instead of pushing her son Tony into acting like many "stage" mothers were known for, Tony's mother encouraged him to swim and dive.[120] [121]

Because of his swimming and diving expertise, Tony got a break on the small screen. A lifeguard and aspiring actor named Bill Bryant, at the Hollywood Athletic Club where Tony practiced his swimming, encouraged him to go with him to an audition.[122] He was going to interview for a pilot named *Johnny Wildlife*. Bryant was up for the part of a father and Tony would audition for his son. Tony agreed, and earned the part, but his friend came away from the audition empty handed.[123] The *Johnny Wildlife* series did not go into production. If it had, the show would've been one of the more groundbreaking programs on the air. Its main character was a single parent, the storylines were environmentally friendly, and it would've been filmed in color.

It wasn't long before Tony did contract a little of the acting bug and secured other auditions, one of those being for *Leave it to Beaver*. In an interview with Eric Greenburg for his "Just My Show" podcast, Tony explained that the executive producer for *Johnny Wildlife*, Harry Ackerman, was also the executive producer for *Leave it to Beaver* and encouraged Tony to go for the audition.[124] Not yet titled *Leave it to Beaver*, this audition was for an older brother on a situation comedy called *Wally and Beaver*.

---

[118] Barbara Billingsley interviewed by Karen Herman.

[119] Stu's Show interview with Tony Dow, December 3, 2008

[120] Clifford Terry, "Tony Dow: Living with Depressive Illness," *Baltimore Sun*, August 1, 1993. http://articles.baltimoresun.com/1993-08-01/features/1993213175_1_depression-tony-dow-sweet-simplicity.

[121] Stu's Show interview, December 3, 2008

[122] Tony Dow, interviewed by Eric Greenburg.

[123] According to IMDB.com, actor Bill Bryant went onto a long Hollywood career with over 200 acting credits.

[124] Tony Dow interviewed by Eric Greenburg.

Many of the other actors had already been cast. However, the part of Wally, which had been played by actor Paul Sullivan in the pilot episode, "It's a Small World," was being re-cast because between filming the pilot and selling the pilot, Sullivan had grown 3 ½ inches. No longer looking like a big brother but like basketball player. He met with the producers and when they saw him, Sullivan said, "That was the end of that."[125] Without regard to height, Tony Dow was a much better fit to be Beaver's big brother. There was chemistry between the two, and Tony, despite having no acting credits, came off as a much better actor, although his modesty often made him downplay his ability.[126]

Tony Dow was the perfect big brother. Everyone in America seemed to wish he was theirs. He became more popular as the seasons progressed, having more story lines feature him and raising his star power among American teenage girls. His fan mail ranged from 1000-2500 letters a week. After *Leave it to Beaver*, he appeared on *Mr. Novak*, *Dr. Kildare* and *My Three Sons* and acted regularly in the soap opera, *Never Too Young*. He then took a hiatus from acting after entering the National Guard in 1965.

In the 1970s, Tony continued to act, but also started a successful small construction firm. Toward the end of the decade, Tony asked his television brother Jerry Mathers to join him in a production of the play, *Boing, Boing*, which had an eight-week run in Kansas City, Missouri. The production sold out in days. After that success, both he and Jerry starred in a production of the comedy *So Long, Stanley*. This production lasted eighteen months as it toured the country to sold out audiences. An interesting note about the successful play *So Long, Stanley* is that in the "Beaver's Monkey" episode of *Leave it to Beaver*, Wally leaves his room to go to school and says goodbye to the monkey sitting in his cage, Wally's exact words were, "So long, Stanley."[127]

In 1983, the *Beaver* cast reunited for the TV movie, *Still the Beaver* and its success brought on an effort to revive their TV series which had ended over twenty years earlier. The new show was titled, *Still the Beaver,* during its first year on the Disney Channel, but when it moved to TBS, it was renamed, *The New Leave it to Beaver*. There were 101 episodes of the show, and Tony directed five of its episodes in 1988 and 1989. Tony sharpened his directing skills and was in much demand in the early 1990s working on such shows as *Get a Life*, *Harry and the Hendersons*, *Swamp Thing*, *Coach* and *Babylon Five*.

By 2003, Tony had begun taking his lifelong passion of sculpting more seriously and relied less and less on Hollywood for accolades and his self-esteem. Knowing for years, Hollywood was becoming more of a young kids' game, being run by young executives and producers, it became a game he no longer wanted to play. He first noticed this while on an audition and a twenty-eight-year-old executive asked, "Have you ever done comedy before?" That's when Tony thought to himself, "Hmmm, maybe it is time for me to retire. Maybe it is time to take the art seriously."[128]

Specifically, his art is semi-abstract burl wood and bronze sculptures. Tony found the burl wood for his sculptures in the woods of Topanga Canyon. His art has found admiration throughout the world. In 2008, one of his pieces was featured in an exhibit in the famed Louvre Art Museum in Paris, France. You can learn more about his sculptures at https://tonydowsculpture.com/.

---

[125] Seymour, Gene. "How 2 in 'Beaver' Pilot Crashed and Lived." Philadelphia Daily News. November 18, 1988.

[126] On the December 3, 2008 Stu's Show interview with wife Lauren present, Tony said his acting was very subpar early on in the series, but the host and Tony's wife gently rebuked his self-assessment. Fans would agree with both Lauren and Stu.

[127] While Tony was being interviewed by Stu Shostak, *Leave it to Beaver* superfan and operator of the first ever *Leave it to Beaver* website, Mark Smeby, emailed Stu with this tidbit.

[128] John Rogers, "Beav's Brother Tony Dow Now an Abstract Artist," *The Big Story*, September 22, 2012.

In the last decade of his life, he continued to love acting and directing, but did so on a more intimate level, doing so for smaller stage audiences. In 2009 he toured with Judy Norton in the production of *Love Letters*, a Pulitzer Prize winning play which made its successful tour in various cities. It was so popular, that some areas had Judy and Tony back in 2010 for repeat performances and in 2012 Tony toured with the play with actress Joyce DeWitt.

The world was saddened to hear of the passing of Tony Dow on July 27, 2022. Tony Dow, husband, father, friend, director, artist and actor is dearly missed . . . every single day by family, friends, and fans alike.

Osmond, Ken (1943-2020) 96 episodes (Eddie Haskell)

Ken Osmond didn't have a typical childhood, but maybe it was more typical in the Hollywood area than some people might think. Instead of going outside to play ball with the fellas after school, Ken and his brother Dayton were regularly ushered to auditions for commercials, TV shows and films by their mother. "It was what it was," Ken mentioned when interviewed by Stu Shostak. He also told Stu that after school he had lessons of all sorts he had to attend. He had lessons in drama, diction, dialects, equestrian riding, martial arts and more. When asked if enjoyed it, Ken said, "I didn't know any different. it was just part of life. It wasn't good or bad, it was just, 'Doesn't everybody do this?'"[129] While some childhood actors harbor bitterness toward their early career or toward those responsible for that career, like a parent, Ken has stated he has no bitterness at all because he enjoyed acting.[130]

In a 2006 interview, Ken told Bill O'Reilly, "Eddie has been good to me for almost fifty years now, has opened doors, and I've got to go places, and see things, and meet people, it's just unimaginable."[131] Ken has, over the years, imparted the same sort of accolades for *Leave it to Beaver* as the rest of the cast has done, "I am so proud to have been part of that show."[132]

But there was life before *Leave it to Beaver* for Ken Osmond. His acting career began in 1952, five years before becoming Eddie. His first role was in *Plymouth Adventure* (starring Spencer Tracy) as one of the kids crossing the Atlantic in the Mayflower. His brother Dayton was also a fellow shipmate in the film. He had a few more uncredited film roles before focusing on TV shows. In 1957 alone, he appeared in five television shows before his debut in *Leave it to Beaver* in November of that year. During the filming of *Leave it to Beaver*, Ken also appeared in one episode of each of the following shows, *Lassie*, *Wagon Train* and *Maverick*.

Like most actors from *Leave it to Beaver*, due to its popular success in syndication, Ken was typecast. For him, casting directors saw him only as Eddie Haskell, the smug, annoying teen who was quick with insincere flattery. He did obtain a few roles post-*LITB* in shows like *Lassie*, *The Munsters* and *Petticoat Junction*, but Ken turned his pursuits elsewhere. His first venture was as owner of a helicopter service with his brother which only lasted until a helicopter crash in 1966[133] Four years later, he entered the LAPD. He only passed the weight requirements by drinking shakes and eating bananas for days before his physical.[134]

Ken worked as a motorcycle officer for the LAPD. One evening he chased after a stolen taxi and eventually wound-up in a foot chase with the thief. He followed him down an alley,

[129] Stu's Show interview with Ken Osmond, March 5, 2008.
[130] Goudas, John N. "From Eddie Haskell to the LAPD," *Chicago Tribune*, November 12, 1992. http://articles.chicagotribune.com/1992-11-12/features/9204120704_1_beaver-motorcycle-cop-top-cops.
[131] Ken Osmond, interviewed by Bill O'Reilly, 2006.
[132] Ken Osmond, interviewed by Jamie Colby, 2007.
[133] *People*, Where Are They Now?, March 04.1985, 97.
[134] Jerry Mathers interviewed by Gary Rutkowski.

assuming he had kept running, but the suspect had stopped in the alley and pointed the gun and shot three times at the former child actor. After being shot, the thief walked toward him methodically and was about to put a final deadly bullet into Ken until his partner Henry Lane, jumped the thief and scuffled with him. Both Ken and the thief were transported to the hospital in the same ambulance.[135]

After retiring from the LAPD, Ken returned to acting in the 1983 TV movie, *Still the Beaver*. He acted on the subsequent TV series, *The New Leave it to Beaver*, in 100 episodes, which was four more appearances than he made in the original series. Ken's sons, Christian and Eric, appeared with him in the new series.

Over all the years since the original show aired, Ken Osmond has grown fonder of the show. In one of his later interviews, he was asked if he ever watched episodes of *Leave it to Beaver*. "When they're on, sure, they're good shows." And asked if he ever sees scenes in which he'd change something, Ken answered, "I watch them as a viewer, not a participant. They're more enjoyable that way." [136]

Fellow cast member Barbara Billingsley said of Ken Osmond, "That man was so good in that role…He is a very nice man." She spoke of how well he acted because in real life, he was not the annoying pest he portrayed in the series. He basically was the only actor who had to be a totally different person than in real life. Billingsley also spoke of a time she accepted a dinner invite from Ken and his wife during the filming of *The New Leave it to Beaver*, "We sat down to have dinner and that awful Eddie Haskell, sitting at the end of the table said grace. Now that doesn't sound like Eddie, but nice man, nice family."[137] The kindness of Barbara Billingsley was not lost on Ken. At a reunion of *Leave it to Beaver* castmates for the release of the series on DVD, he mentioned in answer to a question about the Cleaver matriarch, who was too ill at the time to attend the release party, "My favorite person in the world is Barbara Billingsley."[138]

Jerry Mathers has expressed the same feelings about Ken and his acting ability, "Probably the best actor on the show…the reason I find Ken Osmond to be such a wonderful actor is the juxtaposition between Ken Osmond and Eddie Haskell." Mathers went on to describe Osmond's duties as a police officer for eighteen years on the LAPD, his getting shot while chasing a car thief and his dedication to the job. "That's nothing that Eddie Haskell would ever do, but that's the kind of person Ken Osmond is. I think he's the best actor on the show because he's so different [than his character]."[139]

Stevens, Robert "Rusty" (b. 1948) 68 episodes (Larry Mondello)

Playing one of the most popular characters on *Leave it to Beaver* during its first three seasons, and two episodes in season four, Rusty Stevens seemed destined for a long Hollywood career. After a few acting credits, one when he was only three years old for the TV show *Racket Squad* (a show Hugh Beaumont later narrated), Rusty Stevens went on an audition for *Leave it to Beaver* and earned the part of Larry Mondello.

Rusty Stevens was a very good actor and played the part of a best friend perfectly. His character was also a very annoying student during class time, whether for Miss Canfield or Miss Landers, and wound up in the principal's office quite often. He could even play a bully when the

---

[135] Goudas, "From Eddie Haskell to the LAPD."

[136] Ken Osmond, interviewed by LA TV Examiner, December 2013, Hollywood, CA.

[137] Barbara Billingsley interviewed by Karen Herman.

[138] Buckman, Adam. "Leave It to Beaver: Where Are They Now?," Xfinity.comcast.net, July 14, 2010, http://xfinity.comcast.net/blogs/tv/2010/07/14/leave-it-to-beaver-where-are-they-now/.

[139] Jerry Mathers interviewed by Gary Rutkowski.

occasion arose. In the episode "Beaver's Ring," after Miss Landers leaves the room, Larry gets on top of a desk to reach the classroom clock and moves the hands forward so they could get out of class earlier. He steps down from the desk and says, "If anyone squeals on me, I'll punch them right in the nose." In that episode, no one was really scared of him, because even with that threat, he still wound up in the principal's office.

Larry was seen quite often in *Leave it to Beaver*. In season one, Rusty made thirteen appearances. That was one third of the episodes that season. In the second season, Rusty appeared in two-thirds of the thirty-nine episodes. In season three he appeared in twenty-five episodes. In season four, Rusty only appeared in the fifth and sixth episodes. His biggest hiatus from the show before leaving entirely in 1960 was when he didn't appear in the last eight episodes in season three and the first four episodes on season four. His final episode was "Beaver's Big Contest" (S4 EP6).

Rusty didn't outgrow his role. His voice didn't begin squeaking. He didn't grow a beard at twelve years old. As any good reporter or journalist will do, they thoroughly research a subject and report both sides of a story and so far, the story of Rusty leaving the show has been a bit one-sided, as Rusty has never told it in his own words. Although this story seems to be much more important to some members of *Leave it to Beaver* related Facebook groups than it is to Robert "Rusty" Stevens, I still feel obliged to tell it here. In late December 2022, I had the chance to speak to Rusty and he took time away from watching his beloved Philadelphia Eagles to speak with me. First, let's look at what others have said about Rusty's departure from *Leave it to Beaver*. Be forewarned, these accounts portray Rusty's mom as a difficult stage mother, but there is no confirmation any of what has been said, actually happened. As this is a story about Rusty, he will be given the last word, so Barbara Billingsley and the others will go first.

Barbara Billingsley said on her Archives of American TV interview, "We all loved Rusty so much. He was so good in that role. But unfortunately, they had to let him go because of his mother. She'd be up in the producers' office and make demands and everything, so they finally let him go."[140] Other actors from the show support this account like Rich Correll, Ken Osmond and Frank Bank who give similar accounts to Barbara Billingsley's.[141]

One person who gave a different story was Los Angeles Mirror News TV Critic Hal Humphrey, a man who had been on set many times, interviewed many of the actors, knew the producers, ate dinner with Jerry Mathers' father Norman Mathers, was syndicated in almost 100 newspapers and was considered by Time Magazine as one of the more influential TV critics in the early 1960s.[142] He wrote the following in his column on the TV and radio industry: "*Leave it to Beaver* fans won't see Rusty Stevens in the role of Larry Mondello, Beaver's pudgy buddy, next season. Rusty's parents asked for his release from the series. It was a case of incompatibility among the parents of the three boys on the show."[143] We can only assume, he meant the parents of Tony, Jerry and Rusty. The timing of this article is very interesting because it appeared in the newspaper at the end of the filming of season three. However, Larry still appeared in two episodes in season four.

When I spoke to Rusty (he goes by Bob, as Rusty was a name given to him by his agent when he was young), I told him the story from Hal Humphrey and the story he also knew from Barbara Billingsley. As far as the Hal Humphrey column, Bob shared his opinion, "I don't know where that comes from…There was no animosity because my parents hardly knew them (the parents of Tony and Jerry). I had somebody come with me, a lot of times, it wasn't my parents.

---

[140] Barbara Billingsley interviewed Karen Herman.
[141] Stu's Show interview with Frank Bank and Ken Osmond, May 28, 2008.
[142] "The Press: Measuring the Giant." Time Magazine, November 9, 1959. https://content.time.com/time/subscriber/article/0,33009,811390,00.html
[143] Humphrey, Hal. *Los Angeles Mirror News*. May 14, 1960.

They had somebody come with me to the set." He went on to say that his mom did become friends with Adele Weil, the mother of Jeri Weil (Judy Hensler). Speaking specifically about Barbara Billingsley, he lauded her as being a very nice woman, but had no idea why she said what she did. He simply wasn't aware of any tension between his mom and the producers or with the mothers of Tony or Jerry. He did mention that the producers at one point did want him to sign a contract and it was something he didn't do. He opined that it is possible the producers did not like the way his agent or parents handled things, like his not singing a contract. The contract, he said, would have limited him from being able to do outside work and also to have a somewhat normal life, doing the things kids his age normally did, like play baseball, something he must have done quite a bit, as a fan once wrote him saying his swing when at the plate in "Beaver the Athlete" was very good, and it was a very good swing.

As for other cast members, Bob (Rusty) said although he is asked quite often if he and Jerry were close friends, he admitted he felt closer to Tony Dow, even having a chance to talk with Tony about meeting up for dinner, before his cancer returned. Bob said he didn't really do much with Jerry, but he and Tony would often throw the football around on the lot. Tony was the age of his older brother and was like an older brother to him. He also echoed the sentiments of Stu Shostak, when he said that Tony Dow and the character of Wally were exactly the same person. Other than playing around on the set with a football or a baseball, he also remembered in the mornings he and Tony going to the commissary and ordering the same thing, buttered rye toast and orange juice. Bob (Rusty) commented, "When you think back to stuff like this, it seems like it was for a couple years we did that, but it may have been just five or six times." Of all the fond memories Robert "Rusty" Stevens had of his time on *Leave it to Beaver*, those moments hanging out with Tony at various times, were some of the fondest.

Continuing with his career for three more years after *Beaver,* Robert "Rusty" Stevens made appearances on some popular early 60s TV shows, including, *My Three Sons*, *National Velvet*, *Perry Mason*, *Wagon Train* and *The Rifleman*, in which he played a bully and beat up Lucas McCain's son Mark. After that role, Rusty did not show up on the small screen again until his part in the *Leave it to Beaver* reunion movie, *Still the Beaver* in 1983. The most interesting part he had soon after his departure from *Leave it to Beaver* was that of Alexander "Sandy" Cleaver on *The Jim Backus Show.* Yes, for one thirty-minute show, Larry Mondello became a Cleaver.

The New Leave it to Beaver could've been a revival of Bob's acting career, but he only appeared twice in season four. After *The New Leave it to Beaver* left the air in 1989, Robert "Rusty" Stevens did not act again. His character Larry Mondello is a favorite among *Leave it to Beaver* fans. He is part of a treasured past so many people love, gains new fans every day, and is popular all around the world, due in part to international syndication. I think we can all agree that *Leave it to Beaver* would not be as endearing to us if Robert "Rusty" Stevens, had not been such an integral part of the show as he was during the first three seasons. There's just something we love about a boy eating an apple who often convinces Beaver to do something mischievous. Here's a big "thank you" to Bob for all his hard work on the show.

Fafara, Stanley (1949-2003) 57 episodes (Whitey Whitney)

Only the actors who portrayed the Cleaver family, Eddie Haskell and Larry Mondello appeared in more *Leave it to Beaver* episodes than did Stanley Fafara. He acted in fifty-seven episodes and mentioned in many others. These mentions occurred as a telephone call from Whitey, or he was mentioned as someone Beaver would play with outside. His most memorable episode was "In the Soup," from season four. In this episode, Whitey and Beaver are walking to Whitey's house where Beaver is to spend the night. On their way over, they pass a billboard with a lady holding a steaming cup of soup. Whitey makes a bet with Beaver that there's soup in the cup. Beaver says there isn't and at Whitey's taunting, Beaver climbs up and gets stuck in the cup.

Before *Leave it to Beaver*, Fafara acted in a few commercials and had only previously appeared once on the small screen in a role on *Casey Jones* and once on the big screen, his debut, in the much-respected 20th Century Fox release, *Good Morning, Miss Dove*. This is a film which had many future *Leave it to Beaver* actors in uncredited roles. He had a few other appearances during the run of *Beaver*, but none afterward. One of those other appearances was for the pilot, *Where There's Smokey*, which starred Gale Gordon and Soupy Sales. Actor Johnny Eimen also appeared in this pilot. Fafara and Eimen were friends since the age of six and in high school, played in a garage band together named *The Shades*, later changing their name to *The Odd Assortment*. The band practiced at Stan's house in the valley. [144]

Fafara, who was the younger brother of another recurring cast member, Luke "Tiger" Fafara (Tooey Brown), after leaving the show, attended North Hollywood High School. He was urged by his parents to attend a Christian school and he rebuffed their advice, years later admitting, "I think one of my downfalls was not listening to my parents."[145] While at North Hollywood High, he fell in with a popular crowd and enjoyed more than the occasional party. The fast life caught up with Stan (as he preferred to be called) when he befriended the guys in the 60s rock band Paul Revere and the Raiders. He became involved in drugs in the mid-1960s, finally becoming clean and sober in 1995, after many failed attempts at sobriety.

In 1998, through an email correspondence with Tim Schmitt, the founder of leaveittobeaver.org, Fafara spoke about a book he was writing about his life and said it was a story about a man who seemed to throw his life away only to eventually find the "loving powerful hand of God," the one thing he, himself had been searching for all along.[146] Stan admits in one email, "That is what happened to me. I just took the long way home." He also, in a later email, talks about the brutal honesty the book would contain. Unfortunately, the 100 pages he had finished in 1998 have never surfaced for his fans to read.

Stan Fafara died in 2003 after complications from surgery on an intestine constricted by a hernia. Seven friends surrounded him in his hospital room as he passed, one commented on the moment, "We were all holding hands. He was a good man who had the ability to see beyond people's sordid pasts and see the good in everyone. He will be missed."[147]

Talbot, Stephen (b. 1947) 56 episodes (Gilbert Bates)

Both Richard Correll (Richard Rickover) and Stephen Talbot (Gilbert Bates) came from acting families. They were both raised around Hollywood people. For Correll, his neighbors included Humphrey Bogart and Judy Garland. Stephen Talbot also lived among Hollywood talent. He mentioned in a 2022 interview with Jeff Tamarkin that *Route 66* star Martin Milner lived a couple blocks away from him. He also says that the actor who voiced Tony the Tiger lived close by too. In fact, he and his friends would visit and ask for him to do the voice. The actor would protest a little and then give in to the pressure from the young boys, "They're Greeaeaaaaatttt!" You can tell by who their neighbors were, that while Stephen and Rich both grew up around Hollywood people, one lived in Studio City and the other in Beverly Hills.

Talbot's father was the very well-respected and prolific character actor Lyle Talbot. He

---

[144] Author interview with John Eimen. November 2022.

[145] Stanley Fafara, emailed to Tim Schmitt, August 10, 1998.

[146] Ibid.

[147] Hallman Jr., Tom. "Stanley Fafara Obituary," LITB.com, September 26, 2003 http://www.litb.com/obit.htm.

appeared in about 350 TV shows and films over his fifty plus years in Hollywood. He was also a very talented stage actor, working on Broadway and in touring summer stock shows all across America. During one of these stock show stops, his young son Stephen asked his parents if he could act too. While his father continued touring, Stephen and his mother stayed in Chicago, and he filmed an industrial short. When they returned to California, his parents found Stephen an agent.[148] The rest, as they say, is history.

Talbot's first year acting on television was a busy one, working in nine different shows, among them were *Lawman, Sugarfoot, Men into Space, Lassie*, and his debut on *Leave it to Beaver*. His favorite roles were ones in any TV show that he was a fan of and watched regularly.[149] His initial role on *Leave it to Beaver* turned into an almost sixty episode stay over five seasons. Any fan of *Leave it to Beaver* will find out while watching the many episodes in which Talbot appears, that the producers gave him some the best lines in the show. You've probably read some of those lines in the episode summaries found in this book. Talbot remained with the show until it ceased production in late May of 1963. During the run of *Leave it to Beaver*, Stephen also had the opportunity to act on his favorite TV show, *The Twilight Zone*. He appeared in two episodes.

Stephen Talbot appeared in fifty-six episodes of *Leave it to Beaver*. The producers wanted to put him under contract to make him an almost weekly player, but that never happened. When Stephen's parents first agreed to him becoming an actor, they had only one requirement, that he stay in a regular school, not a studio school, and signing a contract and becoming a regular on *LITB* would have necessitated leaving his regular school.

While on the set, he still had to attend school for three hours a day, doing schoolwork he had received from his teachers where he attended. Stephen recalls a couple different teachers on the set, one of them was quite strict. Also, the room in which they did their work was just a room constructed on the sound stage. The way he describes it, the room sounded more like a police station interrogation room, than a real classroom, no chalkboard, no globes, or posters. The kids just sat a table and did their work. The students did their schoolwork while wearing the clothes they wore for their parts and in full make up, which was orangish in color. He turned in his homework to his teacher back at his home school with orange marks on it sometimes. He had to explain to his teacher it was his makeup, a minor embarrassment for a pre-teen boy.

He was usually packed a sack lunch by his mom. But when he and Jerry were older, they would sometimes go to the studio commissary to eat. Then, on occasion, they were in for a real treat when Tony Dow's stand in, Patrick Curtis, would take he and Jerry, with their mother's permission, to eat at Bob's Big Boy in Burbank. The best part wasn't so much eating away from the studio but getting to ride in Patrick's Corvette.

Stephen continued acting for one year after the end of *Leave it to Beaver*. But after filming an episode of *The Lucy Show*, which caused him to miss a football practice, and after a talk from his coach / English teacher, he decided to quit acting. Acting was not going to interfere with his playing time on the football team. After high school, Stephen attended Wesleyan University in Connecticut, became involved with concert promotion, anti-war protests, politics and worked on his English major.[150] After college, he worked at TV station KQED in San Francisco and later became a producer for *Frontline* on PBS. His first documentary for *Frontline*, was his most

---

[148] Tamarkin, Jeff. "Whatever Happened to Stephen Talbot, 'Leave It to Beaver's Gilbert? We Asked Him!'" *Best Classic Bands*. May 11, 2022. https://bestclassicbands.com/stephen-talbot-beaver-interview-5-11-22/
[149] Author interview with Stephen Talbot November 3, 2022
[150] Tamarkin, Jeff.

memorable, "The Best Campaign Money Can Buy," about the Bush vs. Clinton campaign. He also has fond memories of creating *Sound Tracks: Music Without Borders*. Some of the segments in this documentary are simply amazing. Talbot has traveled the world filming documentaries and has won numerous awards for his work. He is one of the world's best documentarians and continues his work today. His latest, *The Movement and the Madman* is due out in the spring of 2023.

Stephen, for quite a few years, put away his child acting past while establishing himself as a journalist. He has now re-engaged with co-stars and fans over the past couple of years. He's even active on the *Leave it to Beaver* Fan Club Facebook group. Go sign up, speak about one of his episodes, and he might even chime in with a comment.

Many of us would agree that actor Stephen Talbot has brought a lot of joy to fans of *Leave it to Beaver*. In fact, he's still bringing that joy to *LITB* fans, each and every time fans watch the show when it airs on television in reruns, or when it is watched on a streaming service or on DVD. During the final few seasons of *Leave it to Beaver*, one of the best things to look forward to is anytime Gilbert makes an appearance. And about his time on the show and acting as a child, Steve had this to say, "I don't have any bad stories. I had a very enjoyable time, and I did it because I wanted to do it, cause it was fun." It definitely shows.

Bank, Frank (1942-2013) 50 episodes (Lumpy Rutherford)

If you like Frank Bank's portrayal of Lumpy Rutherford, you will enjoy it much more after listening to him being interviewed by TV historian Stu Shostak. He's interviewed Bank on three occasions, and all can be found in the Stu's Show archives (stusshow.com). It is astonishing to know that "Dumpy Lumpy" and Beaver had become friends along with becoming financial advisor/client. Frank tells some wonderful stories to Stu, and also does so in his book, *Call Me Lumpy*: *My Leave it to Beaver Days and Other Wild Hollywood Life*.

One could say Frank Bank started off his Hollywood career with a splash. His first role, at age seven, was in the Broderick Crawford film, *Cargo to Capetown* (1950). Here is how his role is listed in IMDB, "Frank Bank: He got washed overboard in the first scene (uncredited)." From that humble beginning, no one could have suspected that Frank would one day stay in front of the public on the small screen, continuously, for over sixty-five years, as he has done through *Leave it to Beaver* reruns.

Following his debut role, which was almost over before the movie began, Frank appeared in three more TV shows before his audition for *Leave it to Beaver*. The most prominent of those was in *Father Knows Best*. Even after he earned the role of Lumpy Rutherford and while *Leave it to Beaver* was in production, Frank worked on the TV Movie *Life of Archie*, playing the title role opposite *Leave it to Beaver*'s Cheryl Holdridge who played Julie Foster, one of Wally's love interests. The TV movie was basically the pilot for a new *Life of Archie* TV series which never materialized, due in part to the sponsor seeing more Lumpy Rutherford in his performance than Archie Andrews. With that typecasting in place, Frank called it a career.

There is no denying the importance of Lumpy Rutherford to the show. He is one of the most loved characters, even though he was a bumbling oaf at times and really mean to Beaver on occasion, especially in "Beaver's Freckles." Fans will recognize the character of Lumpy Rutherford becoming more essential in storylines as Beaver Cleaver grew older and the focus of the show turned towards Wally. Here is a breakdown of how many episodes featured Frank Bank over the run of *Leave it to Beaver*; Season one (2); season two (8); season three (3); season four (8); season five (18); and season six (11).

After *Leave it to Beaver*, with the *Archie* series off the radar, Frank Bank focused his future on business and investing. While other characters on the set of *Leave it to Beaver* read comic books during breaks in filming, he claims to have read the Wall Street Journal.[151] As Ken Osmond noted in the introduction of Frank's sometimes tawdry autobiography, "Frank has some working brain cells. They just don't show when you first meet him."[152] Before branching out into his own career in business, he and his brother worked in their parent's thriving meat market.[153]

Frank went on to make a living as a licensed financial advisor who dealt mostly in tax-free municipal bonds. He did venture back onto the small screen when the entire gang filmed *Still the Beaver* in 1983 and he co-starred in *The New Leave it to Beaver* from 1984-1989. He often talked fondly of his time on *Leave it to Beaver* in interviews and at cast reunions up until his death in 2013, one day after his 71st birthday.

Correll, Richard (b. 1948) 32 episodes (Richard Rickover)

One of the most successful actors who appeared on *Leave it to Beaver* is Rich Correll. His acting success is only one minor aspect of his life that makes it so interesting. Hollywood was pumping through his veins when he was born in 1948. At the time, his father Charles, was a radio actor on *Amos 'n' Andy*, which first aired in Chicago on WMAQ in 1928 and later moved its production to Hollywood in 1937.

Rich Correll was raised in Beverly Hills around Hollywood royalty like Judy Garland and Humphrey Bogart. At one family party, Correll even asked guest Walt Disney to go down to the basement to check out a project he had been working on and Disney obliged, even complimenting him on his hard work and being an industrious young man.

Having a lifelong interest in monsters, he, and Jerry Mathers, while working on the Universal set when filming *Leave it to Beaver*, had ample opportunity to visit the prop department and put on monster heads and generally, just be goofy kids having fun on a movie set. Rich related in a Stu Shostak interview in 2021 about how he was good friends with Ricky Connelly, the son of *Leave it to Beaver* co-creator Joe Connelly. The elder Connelly had the opportunity to pick both boys' brains about their love of monsters and a possible future TV idea. A few years later, *The Munsters* became a reality, but Rich Correll and his friend were disappointed in the final product as Herman and the others weren't what the two called, "real" monsters. Rich has always had a love for what might scare someone. He has amassed the world's most extensive, privately-owned collection of authentic sci-fi, fantasy, and horror movie memorabilia. His collection is displayed at the *Icons of Darkness* exhibit at the Hollywood & Highland Mall. This is a must see visit if you live in Southern California or are planning a visit.

Something scarier than any of the props he has collected from *Nightmare on Elm Street,* or any other horror movie, is what happened in real life early on Saturday morning, August 9, 1969. In his car, Rich was about to turn right onto Benedict Canyon Road around 3:30 a.m. when he heard, and then saw, a car driven by a "man with long hair, what looked like another man in the passenger seat, and a couple of young women in the back. Their windows were down, music was blaring, and they were carrying on so loudly I thought they must be drunk college kids. They were no more than ten feet in front of me."[154] That was Tex Watson and the other members of the Manson family who had just killed actress Sharon Tate, but he didn't know exactly who they were until the news reports about their arrests. He mentioned in his 2022 Stu's Show interview that

[151] Charles, Nick. "Forever Lumpy," *People*, May 04, 1998.
[152] Woo, Elaine. "Frank Bank Dies at 71; Played 'Lumpy' on 'Leave It to Beaver'," *Los Angeles Times*, April 15, 2013.
[153] Charles, "Forever Lumpy."
[154] Beauchamp, Cari. "How the News of Sharon Tate's Death at the Hands of the Manson Family Spread Through Hollywood." *Town & Country Magazine*. August 9, 2021.

when at the stop sign at Benedict Canyon, that the driver of the car, Tex Watson, had stared at him for a few moments. That had to be very frightening, after finding out who it was.

Rich began acting at the age of eight years old with a role on *The Bob Cummings Show*. Over his career as a child actor (under age eighteen), which lasted from 1958 to 1964 and a total of thirteen roles, he had the distinction of playing characters named Richard or Richie four different times; they include *The Danny Thomas Show*, *The Adventures of Ozzie and Harriet*, *LITB* and *Hazel*. Some of the other shows in which he appeared include *National Velvet, Bonanza* and *Lassie*. He later reprised his role of Beaver's friend Richard Rickover on the *Still the Beaver* TV movie in 1983 and on *The New Leave it to Beaver* TV show in a few episodes in 1985.

While there was much more that Rich did behind the scenes in TV before any of the work that is officially listed on his IMDB profile, the earliest credit seen on it, is his role as a technical advisor on the film *I Wanna Hold Your Hand* (1978), a comedy directed by Bob Zemeckis and produced by Steven Spielberg about the Beatles coming to America in 1964. He mentioned on *The Jason Hennessey Podcast* about his work with Nick Vanoff, who ran Yonge Street Productions. Vanoff, he said, had produced *The Hollywood Palace*, *Hee Haw* and *The Sonny & Cher Hour*. Rich gained a lot of experience working for Vanoff in post-production work, in addition to what he had already learned earlier working while preserving films of the Harold Lloyd library.

Rich then moved in 1976 or 1977 to 20ᵗʰ Century Fox Television to work on the show *That's Hollywood* where he worked as an archivist and put together clips for shows. He then scored a position around 1979 as a music coordinator at Paramount for producer Gary Marshall. Six months later, after doing some dubbing work for Marshall, this led to an associate producer position on *Laverne and Shirley*, then *Happy Days* and also work as a line producer. He later worked as an associate producer on *Police Squad,* and around the same time, also wrote some episodes of *Happy Days*. In 1985, he moved to Lorimar, where he began producing *Valerie* with Miller Boyette Productions. About one year after the show had been on the air, Correll was offered a chance to direct some episodes of *Valerie*.[155]

Once Rich Correll began directing, he never looked back. He started with *Valerie* and soon became a fixture in situation comedies. He went on to work on many other Miller/Boyette productions, including *Perfect Strangers*, *Going Places*, *The Family Man*, *Family Matters*, *Step by Step* and then found himself the king of Disney sitcoms, especially after co-creating and directing *Hannah Montana*, and then moving on to direct *The Suite Life of Zack & Cody* and many other shows on the Disney Channel. After his first directing job in 1987, Rich went on to direct a total of 719 individual television episodes. The final series he directed was *Fuller House* on Netflix, a spinoff of his work with the original series *Full House* (ABC), which he directed and produced.

Weil, Jeri (b.1948) 31 episodes (Judy Hensler)

Jeri Weil made her acting debut in the big screen gangster thriller *Because of You*, starring Loretta Young and Jeff Chandler. Her next role was also uncredited, but the stars in the movie were bigger and brighter, as in the male lead of John Wayne and his leading lady Donna Reed. The TV shows she appeared on before *Leave it to Beaver* were *Lux Video Theater* and *I Led Three Lives*, a popular anti-Communist TV show.

In 1957, Jeri beat out many other little girls for the role of Judy Hensler. She had a knack for getting under the skin of Beaver Cleaver. She also ruffled the feathers of the other boys at Grant Avenue School. Larry and Whitey also couldn't stand her smug attitude and tattletale ways. In real life, she was a very nice person, demonstrating that she, like Ken Osmond could play a part very different than her real-life persona.

[155] Interview with Jason Hennessey on The Jason Hennessey Podcast March 2, 2022

A staple on the show from its beginning, Jeri left after the third episode of season four. She never acted on the small or big screen again. She left the show about the same time as Rusty Stevens (Larry Mondello), but for entirely different reasons. Jeri simply grew into the role of a lifetime, that of a beautiful young woman.

While her professional acting career ended, she never ceased being a creative woman. She is a writer, a gardener, an artist and an "old hippy" at heart.[156] Her semi-autobiographical books, a set of three, are stories that are conveyed through the different cars she has owned over the years; a 1961 MG Roadster, a 1973 Super Beetle Convertible and a 2001 Audi Avant.[157] Jeri is full of life and energy and is accessible through her Facebook page. Go add her as a friend on Facebook and see if she doesn't return the favor. She still lives in sunny Southern California and over the years, has sold real estate in the Studio City area of Los Angeles.

Deacon, Richard (1921-1984) 23 episodes (Fred Rutherford)

The role of Fred Rutherford is one of only two parents of any significance on *Leave it to Beaver* outside of Ward and June Cleaver, the other being Larry's mom, Mrs. Mondello. While Richard Deacon only appeared in twenty-three episodes, he, like quite a few *Beaver* characters, is referred to in many others.

During season four, he only appeared in two episodes of *Leave it to Beaver*. But during this same time period, Deacon stayed quite busy with other work, appearing in twenty-five television shows in addition to his *LITB* work. Some of those TV shows included *The Untouchables*, *Bonanza*, *The Rifleman*, *My Three Sons*, *Perry Mason*, *The Jack Benny Program*, *The Donna Reed Show* and *Mister Ed*. One can only imagine that if Deacon had not been such a successful actor, he may have had even more appearances on *Leave it to Beaver*.

Before his role as Fred Rutherford came to an end, Richard Deacon had a larger recurring role on prime time, that of Mel Cooley on *The Dick Van Dyke Show*. It's hard to imagine an actor having two recurring roles on television shows at the same time, especially during an era when there were only three networks, but that's exactly what happened to the man who played an irritating oaf in Mayfield and a bumbling example of nepotism in New York as the producer of the Alan Brady Show.

The TV shows he worked on after *Leave it to Beaver* are simply too long to list. Suffice it to say, he played on the best the 1960s and 70s had to offer. He also appeared in the Broadway production of *Hello Dolly*, playing the part of Horace Vandergelder. Over his career, he appeared in 180 TV shows and films.

Whether in film, TV, Broadway or in the kitchen, Richard Deacon remained busy. Fans may not know he was a gourmet chef and even hosted a Canadian TV program on microwave cooking in the 1970s. He also wrote a cookbook about the subject.[158] So at the Rutherford house, it probably wasn't his wife Gwen doing all the cooking. The family sometimes had to wait for him to return from the "old salt mine" before they could eat.

Fafara, Luke "Tiger" (b.1945) 18 episodes (Tooey Brown)

The actor who played one of Wally Cleaver's best friends grew up around Hollywood, spending most of his youth in Studio City. Tiger Fafara was one of many children whose acting desire was prodded along by a very enthusiastic mother. At a young age, both Tiger and his

---

[156] Weil, Jeri. "Jeri Weil," LITB.com, accessed September 17, 2014, http://www.litb.com/jeriweil.htm.
[157] Ibid.
[158] "Richard Deacon," IMDB.com

younger brother Stanley, who portrayed Whitey Whitney on *Leave it to Beaver*, were chauffeured by their mother to auditions all over Hollywood for commercials and TV shows in the early 1950s.

Tiger was quite active in the years before his *Leave it to Beaver* audition and subsequent role as Tooey Brown. He had acted in sixteen TV shows and two movies from 1953 to 1957. He also had numerous commercials under his belt. A few of his acting credits included, *I Led 3 Lives*, *My Friend Flicka*, and *Lassie*.

In early 1957, their mother took both boys to an open casting call for *Leave it to Beaver*. After their auditions, Tiger secured the role of Wally's friend Tooey while his younger brother was offered the part of Whitey Whitney. Tiger acted in eighteen episodes of the show through the first three seasons. He appeared in eight episodes in season one, eight episodes in season two, and only "Wally's Election" and "Wally, the Businessman," in season three. After *Leave it to Beaver*, Tiger acted in only one other show, *My Three Sons*, before taking a twenty- year absence from the small screen. He later returned in *Still the Beaver*, a 1983 TV reunion movie and he appeared in two episodes of *The New Leave it to Beaver* series.

Tiger made a great contribution to the early seasons of *Leave it to Beaver*. He's known to an entire generation as Tooey Brown. He may be better known to groove metal and nu metal fans as the father of the talented Dez Fafara, lead singer DevilDriver and former lead singer of Coal Chamber.

Packer, Doris (1904-1979) 17 episodes (Principal Cornelia Rayburn)

Appearing in seventeen different episodes of *Leave it to Beaver*, Packer had her biggest influence in the first and sixth seasons of the show. Born in Menominee, Michigan, it didn't take long for her family to move to warmer climates after her birth. She spent her formative years in Los Angles where she caught the acting bug during high school, participating in many school productions. She later attended UCLA and after college, moved to New York City to study acting.[159]

While in New York City, during the 1930s, Packer performed in numerous Broadway plays. She later married stage director Roland G. Edwards. When not performing in Broadway shows, Packer also performed on radio. Among the shows she was heard in were *The Aldrich Family* and *Mr. & Mrs. North*.[160]

During World War II, Packer enlisted in the Women Army Corps. She entered the army as a private and mustered out as a Sergeant. After the war, she continued living in New York City until the early 1950s when she moved to Glendale, CA, possibly in 1952 or early 1953.

While Doris Packer may be best known, at least to *Leave it to Beaver* fans, as the very proper, authority figure Principal Cornelia Rayburn, she also had very successful runs on other TV Shows during the 1950s and 1960s. She appeared in nine episodes of the *George Burns and Gracie Allen Show* as Mrs. Sohmers, along with seven other characters in earlier episodes. She played Clarice Osborn in *The Many Loves of Dobie Gillis* from 1960 to 1963. She played this role while simultaneously appearing in *Leave it to Beaver*.

Other TV shows in which she had multiple or recurring roles were *The Jack Benny Program*, *The Bob Cummings Show*, *It's a Great Life*, *The Beverly Hillbillies* and *The New Dick Van Dyke Show*. Doris Packer's last appearance came in the 1975 film *Shampoo* as Rozalind.

---

[159] "Doris Packer," *IMDB.com*.
[160] Ibid.

Hooker, Buddy Joe (b.1942) 15 episodes (Chester Anderson)

Although some fans still insist that the actor who portrayed Chester Anderson was the son of the Lone Ranger actor, John Hart. This is not true. When appearing on *Leave it to Beaver*, Buddy Joe Hooker (son of stuntman Hugh Hooker), used the stage name of Buddy Hart.

His acting on *Leave it to Beaver* began in 1957. During his time on the show, he also appeared in the *Schlitz Playhouse* and in the film, *Outlaw's Son*. His work in television after *Leave it to Beaver* was sparse. He appeared on one episode of *My Three Sons* in 1961, a *Twilight Zone* episode in 1962, an episode of *The Donna Reed Show* in 1963. His final TV appearance before turning his career towards stunts was in 1965 on *Wagon Train*. He is best known for being a prolific and record-breaking Hollywood stuntman, beginning work in the late 1960s and he's still working today. In fact, he has a job as a stunt coordinator for the upcoming Francis Ford Coppola film *Megalopolis* which is currently in pre-production (as of December 2022).

Hooker's Chester Anderson was not a major character in any *Leave it to Beaver* episodes, but Hooker played the part well. He was one of the first friends of Wally we get to meet. He first appeared in the sixth episode of season one in, "Brotherly Love."

Mustin, Burt (1884-1977) 14 episodes (Gus the Fireman)

One of Beaver Cleaver's best friends on the show was not a classmate or next-door neighbor, but a fireman named Gus who worked alone at auxiliary fire station #7. There must not have been mandatory retirement laws in Mayfield since the actor who portrayed Gus was seventy-three years old when *Leave it to Beaver* debuted. It's interesting to note that actor Burt Mustin did not even begin professional acting until he was sixty-seven years old. Not that he didn't act before Hollywood, he certainly did.

Burt was a performer from the age of six when a drunk man heard him singing on his way home from kindergarten and took him into a saloon to sing. He stayed there all afternoon and evening and arrived home after dark. His pockets were full of money, but his parents didn't care. He still received a stern punishment. In 1889, you can imagine what that punishment was, a big 'ole whippin' from his dad. Burt was a singer, dancer and actor his entire life, but instead of hitting the road on the vaudeville circuit, he stayed put in Pittsburgh, working first as an engineer and then selling cars until 1941.[161]

In his first Hollywood role, Mustin played a marshal in *The Last Outpost* which starred Ronald Reagan and featured Hugh Beaumont. After that appearance, Burt Mustin was in great demand. He landed numerous roles in TV shows before *Leave it to Beaver*, these included, *The Adventures of Kit Carson*, *The Abbott and Costello Show*, *Schlitz Playhouse*, *The Loretta Young Show*, *Mayor of the Town*, *The Great Gildersleeve*, *Dragnet*, *Father Knows Best*, *Our Miss Brooks* and *The Lone Ranger*. The above are just some of the over thirty TV shows in which he appeared in before *Leave it to Beaver*. By the time he became Beaver's friend, Burt Mustin was a very seasoned professional actor.[162] After *Leave it to Beaver*, Burt Mustin worked almost up to the day he died. His last TV role was on the show *Phyllis* in 1976 at the age of ninety-two.

A testimonial on how he lived and prospered so long, Burt once told a friend the following when he was at the ripe old age of eighty: "Don't drink, don't smoke, married to one girl for fifty-four years and never fooled around, watch my diet and exercise."[163] Sounds like a winning

[161] Smith, Cecil. "For Burt Mustin, Life Begins at 87," *Toledo Blade*, June 5, 1971.
[162] "Burt Mustin" IMDB.com.
[163] Smith, "For Burt Mustin, Life Begins at 87."

combination for everyone, doesn't it? Fireman Gus was a wealth of wisdom and now we know he lived out that wisdom himself.

Trent, Karen Sue (b. 1948) Multiple episodes (Penny Woods)

The first thing that needs to be mentioned is IMDB lists her death as occurring in Florida in February 2022. Whether or not the actress Karen Sue Trent is alive or not is up for debate, but the woman named Karen Sue Trent who died in Florida in February 2022, as listed in IMDB and never corrected, as has been asked numerous times to do so, was NOT the actress named Karen Sue Trent. As the first piece of research done for this book, I called the deceased Karen Sue Trent's brother in West Virginia and he confirmed they were indeed, two different people. Common sense would allow fans who read the obituary for Karen Sue Trent to know they were not the same person.

In her short career as a child actor, she only appeared in six different TV shows after her Hollywood debut at age six in the film *Garden of Eden*, portraying a child, who along with her mother, get lost and find shelter at a nudist colony. Her TV appearances on *Matinee Theater*, *Death Valley Days*, *Shirley Temple's Storybook*, *Wagon Train* and *The Rifleman*, were much more traditional roles. Years ago, the woman who ran a *Rifleman* fan website phoned and interviewed Karen (just a few questions), but as she told me, Karen wasn't too pleased about being contacted and so one would suspect, she enjoys her privacy since she quit acting.

Blake, Madge (1899-1969) 12 episodes (Mrs. Margaret Mondello)

Along with her husband, during WW II, she worked in Utah on making the detonator for the atomic bomb. Her work required her to have top secret credentials. After her government work had ended in 1949, she enrolled in acting classes in order to fulfill her dream of becoming a regular working actress in Hollywood.[164] The proof of a fulfilled dream is a resume with over 100 TV shows and movies listed on it. Among them, are some of America's most cherished like *Leave it to Beaver*, *The Real McCoys*, *Batman*, *Brigadoon*, *Ain't Misbehavin'*, *Lassie*, and *I Love Lucy*. She also appeared in two Connelly and Mosher projects before *Leave it to Beaver*, those were *The Ray Milland Show* and the film, *The Private War of Major Benson*.

Mittelstaedt, Robert (b.1947) 8 episodes (Charles Fredericks)

Born and raised in Tujunga, California, Robert Mittelstaedt was the son of a Lutheran pastor. A parishioner in the church where his father pastored was an actress, something not unheard of in Southern California. She had provided her agent's name to Robert's father and living on a meager minister's salary, he thought getting his son into acting could help the family budget. Robert's salary went into the total family budget, but he, himself, took away much more money from his work than he would have made delivering papers or mowing lawns on the weekends.

It wasn't long after obtaining an agent that his father began taking Robert on auditions for commercials, films and TV shows. "I probably did twenty-five casting interviews for every job I landed," said the former actor in a recent interview. Robert went on to recount the most fun part of the interview process, "My dad would take me to the Brown Derby for chicken pot pie after the interviews. It was cool leaving school early to drive the hour or two to Hollywood, which is what it took pre-freeways."[165]

---

[164] "Madge Blake" IMDB.com
[165] Robert Mittelstaedt, emailed to author, September 12, 2014.

Before landing his first big part in the pilot episode for the Broderick Crawford vehicle, *Highway Patrol*, Robert had parts in numerous TV commercials, including one for Lava Soap. He was on the set for three days for the *Highway Patrol* pilot, earning himself a whopping $104.00. That was a huge sum back in 1955, about $907 in today's money. Robert still has the check today.

The auditions for *Leave it to Beaver* were tedious and lasted a long time, longer than for any other role he auditioned for at that time. The casting, he says, "went on for six months and it came down to me and Jerry Mathers. He got the role of course, and I was given a small part in 6-10 episodes."[166]

About the same time as *Leave it to Beaver* began, Robert continued going on other auditions, acting in a few commercials, landing a movie role in *The Music Box Kid* and getting a back-up role for a character in the traveling production of *Annie Get Your Gun*. Eventually, the calls for parts in *Leave it to Beaver* stopped coming and at age sixteen, when he would've had to join the Screen Actors' Guild and pay dues higher than what he was earning, Robert made the decision not to join.

After his stint on *Leave it to Beaver*, Robert never acted again. But he has no bitterness about the show or a lack of an acting career. He looks back at his time as an actor with good memories. "The best part was hanging around the set" (even though he did get in trouble once for being late to the director's call when he and Jerry were playing in Jerry's trailer). He added that the best part of all was, "Going to the studio dining room and eating next to the stars." He also preferred his work in commercials and on *Leave it to Beaver* to the hard work his friends did delivering newspapers.

His time on *Leave it to Beaver* was also a great way to get in touch with old friends. Sometimes they would give him a call at his office at 2:00 p.m. and say, "I just saw you on *Leave it to Beaver*." He may have never said so out loud, but often wondered, "What were they doing watching TV at 1:30 in the afternoon?" His child and stepchildren have seen him in the show, and he can't wait until he can show his granddaughter who at eighteen months, is still a little too young to appreciate his acting chops on *Beaver*.

With acting no longer on his radar, Robert turned to education. He attended Claremont Men's College where he graduated magna cum laude and then attended the University of Virginia Law School, graduating in 1973. Before law school, Robert took time to join the Peace Corps and dreamed of spending his time in Nigeria, but war prevented that dream from coming true. Instead, he was sent to the middle of the Pacific Ocean to an atoll named Pulap in Micronesia. The island was home to fifty men in loincloth, fifty women in skirts, topless, and 100, for the most part, naked children. They had no electricity, no modern conveniences, but as Robert tells it, "They were the happiest, healthiest, most together people I'd ever known."[167]

His next stop in the United States was law school, a place where he sported a Fu Manchu mustache, hair down to the middle of his back and he was known as someone who never wore sandals or shoes. Former FBI Director Robert Mueller said at a UVA Law School speech years later, that Robert looked like a slacker who could care less about grades, but the man who would help hunt for Osama Bin Laden and become one of Robert's best friends, admitted Robert received some of the best grades in the class.[168]

His time in law school and his forty years as an anti-trust lawyer (in 2008 he was given the

---

[166] Ibid.

[167] Ibid.

[168] Mueller III, Robert S. "Presentation of the Thomas Jefferson Foundation Medal in Law" (lecture, University of Virginia School of Law, Charlottesville, VA, April 12, 2013).

"Attorney of the Year Award for Litigation")[169] have proven that his first appearance on *Leave it to Beaver*, as the smartest kid in the school ("Part-Time Genius") was true to life.

Carol, Cindy a.k.a. Cindy Sydes (b. 1944) 7 episodes (Multiple characters)

Cindy Carol appeared in seven episodes, playing four different characters, Alma Hanson, Penny Jamison, Helen, and Nita Norton. After her stint on *Leave it to Beaver* ended in 1960, she later found success on *The New Loretta Young Show* in the role of Binkie Massey (26 episodes) and later played Susan in the soap opera *Never Too Young* (20 episodes). Tony Dow also appeared in a recurring role on *Never Too Young*.

Beaird, Pamela (b. 1945) 6 episodes (Mary Ellen Rogers / Myra Barker)

There is so much to be said about Pamela Beaird, the actress who played Mary Ellen Rogers on the *Leave it to Beaver* TV show. She was a fine actress, and even a better person. A good wife, mom, sister, cousin, daughter and a very dedicated follower of Christ. She was also the third woman to ever break the sound barrier. More on that in a moment.

Born at St. Nicholas hospital, a few blocks from the Alamo in San Antonio, Pamela only lived a few years in Texas before her dad moved the family to what was in the late 1940s and early 1950s, the land of opportunity for anyone in the building industry. "Daddy was a builder," she said in an August 2022 interview.[170] Her father had a couple cousins already in southern California who were builders and he found work immediately, building churches, schools, and luxury homes. The Beaird family landed in Culver City, CA in 1949 or 1950.

Her sister, seven years older than Pamela, took singing lessons in the Los Angeles area from the performer Johnny Ukulele. Seeing her sister sing and play, Pamela wanted to do it too. Always a girl who loved to sing, she would often gather with her cousins Deanna and Joyce at her house to sing and harmonize. They formed a trio which was later named the Holly-Tones and sang at churches and at banquets. She took singing lessons from Al Brickman around 1954 or 1955 and in a recital he held at the Troupers Club on LaBrea, Pamela sang, "A Good Man is Hard to Find," accompanied by her ukulele. In the back of the auditorium stood Hazel McMillan, one of Hollywood's best child agents. Her, daughter played Harriet Conklin on *Our Miss Brooks*. As Pamela tells the story of their meeting, McMillan introduced herself backstage and asked Pamela if she would like to work in television and motion pictures. Remembering the warning from her father that she would meet some strange people in Hollywood who would promise and offer her things, Pamela politely said, "No thank you." After meeting her parents, Pamela signed to become a client of Hazel McMillan.[171]

About that time, Pamela entered a nationwide talent contest for singers (Talent Round Up Day) put together by Walt Disney. Competing against singers from all around the United States, Pamela won the contest. She was presented the award by Walt Disney and was given a special appearance on an episode of *The Mickey Mouse Club*. She was featured on the "Talent Round-Up Day" episode on November 2, 1956. A month later she appeared on the "Fun with Music Day: Land-of-Me-Oh-My" episode.

---

[169] "Robert A. Mittelstaedt," *JonesDay.com*, accessed September 9, 2014, http://www.jonesday.com/ramittelstaedt/.
[170] Author interview with Pamela Beaird Hensley, August 2022.
[171] Ibid.

Her singing talent was featured along with her cousins Joyce and Deanna on the *Dixieland Small-Fry* TV series which featured band leader Bill Hollingsworth and his orchestra made up of high school and junior high musicians. She is credited by herself in a Christmas episode but with her cousins on two subsequent episodes. Her performances on *Dixieland Small-Fry* occurred from 1957-1960, well after her first TV and film appearances (according to IMDB). Her first role was in a short called *The Dark Wave* with Nancy Davis. Pamela played a girl afflicted with epilepsy. The profits went to the forerunner of the National Epilepsy Foundation. She then worked on a feature film, *Good Morning, Miss Dove*. The year before her debut on *Leave it to Beaver*, she had guest appearances on *Father Knows Best*, *Schlitz Playhouse*, *The Adventures of Jim Bowie*, *The Guns of Fort Petticoat*, *Telephone Time*, *Ford Television Theater* and *Circus Boy*.

When asked about auditions, Pamela spoke of how competitive they were. But added that the competitors sometimes became her friends, like in the case of Cheryl Holdridge (Julie Foster) and Cindy Carol (Alma Hanson). She and her family noticed the different types of parents who would accompany their children to auditions, and she said it was about an equal amount of overbearing stage mothers and parents who were more like her dad with a happy-go-lucky approach of you win some, you lose some. She related a story of the time she missed out on a part with actor Dan Duryea. She told her father, "Dad, I didn't get it. They gave it to another girl." He replied, "Well, you can't get them all. Don't you want some of your friends to get some roles?" She said she thanked God she had a daddy who could make it real reasonable (being a child actor).

There was one situation that almost ended her short career, and it was due to a vindictive casting director who will remain unnamed. She had sent a script to Pamela's agent because by this time, Pamela had gained script approval. She and her parents read the script and afterward, Pamela looked at her father and said, "I can't do this." Her father agreed. Ever since Pamela had accepted Jesus as her Lord and Savior at the Culver West Baptist Church a few years earlier, they prayed about the scripts she would accept and they either had to bring honor to God, or at the least, not disgrace Him. This script was the opposite of that latter category. When the casting director was informed of Pamela's decision, the casting director was enraged and told her agent she would black ball Pamela. Her father, always the bearer of as much, or more wisdom than Ward Cleaver, told her, "Remember one thing, she's not in total control. The Lord is in total control of your life."

It wasn't too long after this incident that her classmates at Covina High School nominated her for Miss Covina. One of the final events before announcing the winner in the competition was making a speech. She noticed that the casting director who threatened to black ball her, was one of the judges. When all was over, Pamela was announced the winner. She then had to shake the hands of each judge. Her nemesis said, "I voted for you." Pamela let out a laugh and the casting director gave her a smile, all was good. Her father was correct, and her career was just fine. Plus, she became Miss Covina.

In 1958 *Leave it to Beaver* fans became familiar with Pamela's character Mary Ellen Rogers. This character appears in only five episodes, and these are in seasons one, two, four and five. However, she's mentioned numerous other times when Wally says he's taking her to the movies or going to her house to play records or going to walk by her house with Eddie. Her character winds up marrying Wally as is seen on *The New Leave it to Beaver*, and in it, her character is played by Janice Kent. The Wally/Mary Ellen romance doesn't rate as high on the charts as Kelly and Zack on *Saved by the Bell*, Luke and Laura on *General Hospital*, or that of Shawn Spencer and Jules on *Psych*, but they had chemistry on screen, especially on the "Dance Contest" episode, and it was nice to see continuity in the new series with the couple being married.

Pamela had seen at least one episode of *Leave it to Beaver* before auditioning for the part of Mary Ellen Rogers. She does not remember the audition but remembers being excited about the opportunity to be on the show. When asked about acting on *Leave it to Beaver*, and the atmosphere she encountered on the set, she said, "I never heard anyone swear. I can't remember seeing people smoking. On other sets they would smoke right in your face as they were preparing you for your scene and lighting you."[172] Unlike *Leave it to Beaver*, she also shared her one terrible experience on a set, and that was at MGM where she said a director, "who will remain unnamed," asked her opinion about something and she politely answered him. He then began cursing at her and yelling. The star of the show, a woman, came over and stood next to Pamela and the director shut up and slithered away.[173]

There's so much more to be said about Pamela. In 1969-1970, she toured the United States, singing with Joy Eilers. Then, from March 1, 1970-1971, the two of them toured overseas in dozens of countries, with an itinerary of engagements set before they left the States. Other engagements were picked up along the way, as they were heard, and received more invitations. They typically performed two shows a night, as they did during their stay in Romania, while it was a Communist country. She even had a Maître 'd at the hotel they were singing at in Bucharest, pull a gun on her while she was eating lunch. It was only for a moment, and hidden under a towel, complete with evil grin on his face, something akin to a scene in a James Bond film. During that three-week engagement, her and Joy could not talk in their room without their conversations being recorded by the Securitate, the Romanian secret police. She was advised by an official at the U.S. Embassy to speak on the patio and have the radio turned up very loud. The two were also approached by an African man one night with a plea to help him get out of the country. They did help, and he later wrote them a thank you letter when they were back in California and he was safe in Africa.[174]

Oh my, I'm running out of room, and I still never got to her being the third woman ever to break the sound barrier, which happened during a trip to NASA in Texas. Pamela has an entire book of stories to tell, and many have to do with meeting and marrying her husband singer/songwriter Bob Hensley, and their time in ministry in Hollywood, and time spent singing gospel music across the United States and planting churches.

Turner, Patty (b. 1949) 6 episodes (Linda Dennison / Alice)

Originally from Winnipeg Manitoba, Patty Turner's family relocated to the United States after her father read a book which said the healthiest place to live in North America was a town in Southern California. One day while vacationing at a lake near their new home, Patty's mother was chatting up a fellow vacationer and was told that her daughters were very cute and that they should have an agent. She told Patty's mom about getting her children into acting.

Back home, her mother inquired about an agent and Patty was soon signed. She first filmed commercials and then was in the movie *The Ten Commandments*. Although she had no lines in the film, she was signed as a principal, not as an extra. When interviewed, she mentioned that she was on set for two weeks and every day began the same, in the makeup department, where she stood on a table and the makeup artists would put make up on their arms, on their legs and face, to darken

---

[172] Author interview with Pamela Beaird Hensley, August 2022.

[173] Author interview with Pamela Beaird Hensley in August 2022.

[174] Ibid.

their skin a little bit. In the film, she was on the mountain with Moses. About Cecil B. DeMille, she mentions, "I never saw him, but I did hear his voice."

About *Leave it to Beaver*, the big difference she noticed about that set and the set of her only previous TV or film work was that it was a lot more peaceful than her time at the Paramount studio filming *The Ten Commandments*. At the Republic lot, there were no animals and a lot less people. While filming *Beaver*, she was in Miss Lander's classroom and the studio school classroom as well. Her regular teacher would give her mother the assignments she would miss while working and she'd have to sit in the studio school room for three hours a day. While some of the older kids would mess around and cut up, she concentrated on her studies, but she does remember Ken Osmond teasing her because of her shyness, "You're so quiet," he would say, and then remark to others, "Look, she's so quiet."[175] I could picture Eddie Haskell doing that.

Being a very athletic girl, Patty enjoyed what little downtime they had on the Republic set during filming. She mentioned they played either wiffle ball or kickball, and not having a field in which to play, they just played behind the soundstage. Her favorite episode in which she appeared was "Her Idol," where she and Beaver become a bit of an item when they both sit in a tree and admire some bird eggs. They never were an item, never boyfriend / girlfriend, but Beaver's friends thought they were, and they teased him mercilessly until he called her a smelly old ape. A couple other *LITB* notes, she played Alice in the "Pet Fair" episode, not Linda Dennison. Her favorite episode outside of her own, is "Wally's New Suit." Her other *LITB* episodes were "Party Invitation," "Beaver and Poncho," "Ward's Problem," and "Beaver's Poster."

Post *LITB*, Patty mentioned she was painfully shy and not very interested in acting. She did a few commercials after *Leave it to Beaver*, but nothing else. Instead, she concentrated on school and athletics. She also has something in common with Pamela Beaird who played Mary Ellen Rogers, both were winners of local beauty contests. Patty was Miss Arcadia in 1966, while Pamela was Miss Covina in 1962. Patty was also an award-winning springboard diver and won some competitions as a teenager. Never again spending time in Hollywood as an actress, she did spend some time in Hollywood as the mother of an aspiring actress. Her daughter, when she was fifteen, began taking acting lessons and even filmed a commercial or two. The Turner family is very talented. In addition to Patty, both of her sisters, Michelle and Debbie have had their time on the small and big screens. Her sister Debbie was Marta von Trapp in *The Sound of Music*.

Kennedy, Madge (1891-1987) 5 episodes (Aunt Martha)

Unlike a lot of actors with guest appearances on *Leave it to Beaver*, the woman lovingly known (at least by her niece June Cleaver) as Aunt Martha, had a long career (fifty-nine years) but did not wind up with hundreds of small roles. Instead, her total output was much less, but filled with good to very good roles, not uncredited walk on roles so many character actors must take to put food on the table. Here's just a few of her movies and TV shows: *Lust for Life* starring Kirk Douglas, *Houseboat* starring Cary Grant, *They Shoot Horses, Don't They?* starring Jane Fonda, and *Alfred Hitchcock Presents*. Maybe her obtaining good roles had something to do with her years of success on Broadway, which began in 1912.

---

[175] Interview with Author, August 2022

Brewster, Diane (1931-1991) 5 episodes (Miss Canfield / Miss Simms)

   Diane Brewster first appeared in the *Leave it to Beaver* television pilot tilted "It's a Small World," in the role of Miss Simms, a secretary. She was one talented woman who had a busy career before *Leave it to Beaver* was on her radar, beginning TV work when she was twenty-four years old. During and after *Leave it to Beaver*, Diane Brewster also had roles on many westerns such as *Cheyenne*, *Wagon Train*, *Death Valley Days* and *Maverick*. She was one of the original cast who filmed the *Still the Beaver* movie in 1983 and she also appeared in four episodes of *The New Leave it to Beaver*. It is hard to believe Diane Brewster only appeared in four episodes of Leave it to Beaver. She passed away of heart failure in Studio City, CA in 1991.

Randall, Sue (1935-1984) 29 episodes (Miss Alice Landers)

   Other than her work on the Spencer Tracy and Katherine Hepburn movie, *Desk Set*, Sue Randall spent her entire career on the small screen. Not soon after she began work on TV, she landed the role of Diane Emerson Soames on the daytime soap *Valiant Lady* which ran daily on CBS for over 1000 episodes. Sue Randall appeared in over 500 of them. While she worked in her recurring role as Beaver's teacher Miss Landers, she was also seen on many different shows, including multiple roles on *Have Gun – Will Travel*, *The Roaring '20's*, *77 Sunset Strip*, *Hennesey*, *Michael Shayne*, *Sea Hunt*, and *Gunsmoke*. Popular shows she appeared on after *Beaver* included *My Favorite Martian*, *The Fugitive*, *Bonanza* and *Death Valley Days*. A heavy smoker, Sue Randall was diagnosed with cancer, and died from the disease in 1984, a couple weeks after her 49th birthday.

OTHER ACTORS

A

Abbott, Dorothy (1920-1968) "Beaver, the Caddy" (The Secretary)

Dorothy Abbott, pre-Hollywood, spent some time as a Las Vegas showgirl. Her first few movie parts were real to life as she played showgirls in uncredited roles in *The Razor's Edge*, *Road to Rio* and *Words and Music* between 1946-1948. She began working in credited roles around 1953 when she began a six-episode run playing Joe Friday's girlfriend on *Dragnet*. Abbott later had uncredited roles in *Jailhouse Rock* and *That Touch of Mink*. In addition to her two roles on *Leave it to Beaver* (she also played Miss Walker in "Beaver's Graduation"), she was in twenty-five episodes of *The Adventures of Ozzie and Harriet*.

Adams, Dorothy (1900-1988) "School Play" (Miss Wakeland)

She was given the task of teaching Beaver how to float like a canary. A veteran of TV from its earliest days, if anyone could make Beaver float it would be Dorothy Adams. She began working in TV in 1950 with a part on *The Silver Theater* hosted by Conrad Nagel. Before 1953, Adams had worked on ten different television programs, including *I Married Joan* and *The Adventures of Kit Carson*. She had bit parts in *The Ten Commandments* and *An Affair to Remember*. She later lectured on theater arts at UCLA.

Adare, Larry (1947?) "Beaver on TV" (Phillip Jones)

With an acting career that lasted only for a couple years in childhood (1961-1963), Adare is best known for his two roles on *Leave it to Beaver*, "Beaver on TV" and "Beaver's Prep School."

Agate, Michael (1947?) "Beaver, the Hero" (Denny)

His character Denny is one of the guys who builds Beaver up into a conceited athlete with his compliments after Beaver catches a winning touchdown. This was Agate's biggest role of his three television appearances.

Albertson, Frank (1909-1964) "Wally's Test" (Mr. Gannon)

One of at least two actors who guested on *Leave it to Beaver* and were also in the film *It's a Wonderful Life*, the other being Jimmy Hawkins (Dudley). He began working as an actor in films in 1923 with a minor role in *The Covered Wagon.* He appeared in 200 film and TV roles over forty-one years. His longest recurring role was as Mr. Cooper in *Bringing Up Buddy* in 1961. He also performed with Tony Dow in an episode of *Mr. Novak*.

Albright, Hardie (1903-1975) "Brother vs. Brother" (Mr. Collins).

Albright's appearances on *Leave it to Beaver* came late in his acting career. He began acting in Vaudeville and moved on to Broadway before his first film role in 1931. He acted until the late 1940s in film. He then retired and became an acting instructor at UCLA. He also authored many books on acting and returned to the trade on the small screen in the early 1960s. He and his daughter Vicky Albright are one of at least two father / child tandems to act in *Leave it to Beaver,* the most famous of which is Lyle Talbot and Stephen Talbot.

Albright, Vicky (1945 –) "Double Date" (Carolyn)

The daughter of fellow *Leave it to Beaver* actor Hardie Albright, Vicky appeared in two episodes of the series, both times as a date for Wally. Her acting career was short, leaving the screen after her 1966 appearance in *The Trouble with Angels.* A couple years after her roles in *Leave it to Beaver*, she appeared on *Mr. Novak* with Tony Dow and David Kent, who played Bill Scott on *Beaver* in a few episodes.

Alden, Norman (1924 - 2012) "Water Anyone" (Water Dept. Worker)

During his first year acting in TV, Norman Alden played a bit role on the seventh episode of *Leave it to Beaver*, "Water Anyone?" He plays a water department worker who tells Beaver that the water will be shut off for the afternoon. After *Leave it to Beaver*, Alden went on to become a prolific character actor. Internet Movie Database mentions he acted or did voice over work in 2,500 movies, TV shows and commercials.

Allen, Fletcher (1922-2004) "The Book Report" (The Man)

Not appearing on a screen, small or big, until he was thirty-six years old, Allen did find himself in some large films, even if his roles were small. He had parts in *Psycho*, *A Gathering of Eagles* and Arthur Hailey's *Airport.* He also appeared in *The Jack Benny Program, Bonanza* and *Adam-12.* He had twenty-two film and TV roles over twenty years in Hollywood, most of them small like his role as "The Man" in his one *Leave it to Beaver* appearance.

Allen, Gary (b. 1942) "Beaver Gets 'Spelled'" (First Man); "Larry's Club" (Boy in Club)

Gary Allen's best-known works were small parts in *Annie Hall*, *Mommie Dearest* and *The Hudsucker Proxy*. He worked continually from 1975 through 1986 in many TV shows and films although he began his career on *The Jack Benny Program* in 1956. He worked sparingly in the 1950s and 1960s.

Allen, Mark (1920-2003) "Beaver's Big Contest" (Policeman)

Mark Allen appeared in two episodes of *Leave it to Beaver* and in each, he portrayed a policeman. His second episode was "Wally's Chauffeur." He began his acting career in television in 1952. He had over sixty acting credits and had recurring roles in *Dark Shadows* in seven episodes and *The Travels of Jaimie McPheeters* in nineteen episodes.

Allen, Ricky (b. 1945?) "The Train Trip" (Boy in station)

As with many *Leave it to Beaver* actors, Ricky Allen also made an appearance on *Lassie*. He made one appearance on *Leave it to Beaver* as "Boy in station" on the episode "The Train Trip." His biggest acting success came as Sudsy Pfeiffer on *My Three Sons* from 1961-1963. In 1967 and 1969 he made his final two television appearances; these were on *My Three Sons* as the characters "Hoby" and "Larry" respectively.

Allen, Valerie (1936-2013) "Beaver Finds a Wallet" (Miss Thompkins)

This is the woman who did not send Beaver a gift for finding her wallet. Maybe it was karma that she languished in roles in "B" movies like *I Married a Monster from Outer Space*. Of course, that's a joke. Her father was a booking agent who suggested to comedian Fred Sullivan to change his name to Fred Allen.

Alvin, John (1917-2009) "Eddie Spends the Night" (Frank Haskell)

Playing one of the Haskell Fathers, Alvin had only one appearance in *Leave it to Beaver*. Before playing Mr. Haskell, he played in many "B" movies and had dozens of roles on television in the 1950s. He had almost 200 acting credits by the time he retired in 1994 when he last appeared on the big screen with a role in *Milk Money* starring Ed Harris and Melanie Griffith.

Ames, Don (1921-1995) "The Train Trip" (Train Station Commuter)

A prolific Hollywood extra, Ames finished his career with over 130 different acting roles. Patrons, customers, and party goers comprised many of his roles. Other than *Leave it to Beaver*, he appeared in many TV's great shows such as *The Rockford Files*, *Charlie's Angels*, *Rhoda*, *Bonanza* and *The Big Valley* with twenty-five appearances on that show, mostly playing townsmen, but also the occasional bartender, hotel guest or barfly.

Anderson, Sara (1920-1998) "The Garage Painters" (Mrs. Bellamy)

After *Leave it to Beaver,* Anderson only had a few more roles before leaving acting. One of those was on *The Real McCoys* and her final role was in the Joan Crawford film *I Saw What You Did*.

Andre, Maria (1921-2011) "Beaver and Chuey" (Carmela Varela)

Born Mary Isabella Pugliano, this actress plays the wife of a diplomat from South America in her lone *Leave it to Beaver* appearance. Her roles over a twelve-year career were sparse, but she did have bit parts in *The Unsinkable Molly Brown* and Arthur Hailey's *Airport.*

Anthony, Shirley (1928 - ?) "Beaver's Old Buddy" (Mrs. Waters)

With *Leave it to Beaver* being her first acting role on either the small or big screen, Anthony went on to do a lot in Hollywood. She finished her career with over fifty acting credits and appeared in *The Lucy Show, Here's Lucy, The Towering Inferno, The Rockford Files, The Blues Brothers, Seems Like Old Times, The Scarecrow and Mrs. King* (recurring role), and had a recurring role in four *Rockford Files* TV movies from 1994 to 1999.

Arlen, Dee (1930 -?) "Mother's Day Composition" (Laura)

With only three acting roles, this one on *Beaver* as the actress being interviewed on a TV show, was possibly the highlight of her short career. She was married to actor and Broadway performer Gill Stratton.

B

Backes, Alice (1923-2007) "The Tooth" (Nurse)

A grand woman, full of class, she had a storied career, appearing in radio, television and in film. With over 100 screen roles, she had appearances in every genre of TV show from *Ben Casey* to *Barney Miller* to *Knight Rider* and *Mr. Belvedere*. Backes appeared in two episodes of *Leave it to Beaver,* the other was "Beaver, the Bunny."

Bacon, Irving (1893 - 1965) "Captain Jack" (Postal clerk)

Irving Bacon is one of the most prolific character actors who appeared in *Leave it to Beaver.* He debuted in a silent short in 1915 and his final screen appearance was on The Dick Van Dyke Show in 1965. But 538 of his 540 credits were filmed between 1923-1960. That averages over fourteen films or TV shows each year. Amazingly, he only played one part on *Leave it to Beaver* in all those many roles. He played the postal clerk who handed Wally and Beaver their pet alligator in a very small box on the episode "Captain Jack."

Baer, John (1923-2006) "Eddie, the Businessman" (Assistant)

Was the star of his own TV show, *Terry and the Pirates* in 1952-1953, a radio show that was brought to the small screen. He had over seventy acting credits and was a regular on TV throughout the 1950s and 1960s in shows such as *My Little Margie, Mr. & Mrs. North, Fury, Wagon Train, Dr. Kildare* and *The Green Hornet.*

Baker, Benny (1907-1994) "The Haircut" (Barber)

On the fourth episode of *Leave it to Beaver*, "The Haircut," Beaver tries convincing a barber to cut his hair even though he "losted" his money, Benny Baker was this barber. This was his only *Leave it to Beaver* appearance out of his 133 acting credits. He began his career in vaudeville in the 1920s and eventually wound up working in film from the 1930s through the 1940s. Beginning in 1952, Benny Baker had regular work in television, his livelihood, with an occasional foray onto the big screen as he did in *Boy, Did I Get a Wrong Number* with Bob Hope and *Paint Your Wagon* starring Lee Marvin and Clint Eastwood.

Bakewell, William (1908-1993) "Beaver and Kenneth" (Mr. Purcell)

He's not well thought of from his role of Kenneth's father on *Leave it to Beaver*, but he must be given respect for the prolific nature of his career in Hollywood. He had almost 200 credits and roles in two big Hollywood films, *All Quiet on the Western Front* and *Gone with the Wind*. For television, it would be easier to name all the shows during the Golden Age in which he did not appear, than those in which he did appear.

Baldwin, Bill (1913-1982) "A Horse Named Nick" (Board of Health Officer)

With over 170 acting credits, he had four appearances on *Leave it to Beaver* and three appearances in the Sylvester Stallone *Rocky* franchise. In between those, he appeared in the best of 60s and 70s TV including parts in *Dragnet, Perry Mason*, *Emergency!, Mannix* and *The Streets of San Francisco*. Many times, his parts were those of a radio announcer or a reporter. His appearances in *Rocky* were as a boxing announcer.

Barber, Bobby (1894-1976) "More Blessed to Give" (Carnival barker)

An actor with over 250 acting credits, Barber spent a lot of time in bit parts for Abbot & Costello, in both their movies and their TV show. He appeared in three *Leave it to Beaver* episodes, the two other episodes are "Beaver Takes a Drive" and "Beaver's Football Award."

Barnes, Ann (1945-2005) "School Sweater" (Frances Hobbs)

A very talented child actress. She starred in the TV show *Blondie* as Cookie Bumstead and appeared in two *Leave it to Beaver* episodes, the other was "Wally's Election." She later worked with Paul Peterson's group *A Minor Consideration*.

Barrett, Majel (1932-2008) "Beaver and Violet" (Gwen Rutherford)

Best known for her roles as Nurse Chapel on the original *Star Trek* and the voice of computers on *Star Trek* and its subsequent re-boots, she did appear on one episode of *Leave it to Beaver*. She was married to Gene Roddenberry, the creator of *Star Trek*.

Barton, Anne (1924-2000) "The Credit Card" (Agnes Haskell)

Appearing in two episodes in the final season of *Leave it to Beaver*, she has one of the best lines about her son Eddie, "But it's such a rough life, and Edward's so sensitive" in "Summer in Alaska." Soon after *Leave it to Beaver*, Barton had multiple guest appearances on *Perry Mason* and *Gunsmoke*.

Beakman, Bobby (1949-1998) "Larry's Club" (Boy in Club)

The short career for Beakman includes three appearances in *Leave it to Beaver*. He acted from the age of seven to fifteen. His last TV appearance was as Jimmy Bryce on *Voyage to the Bottom of the Sea* in 1964.

Beardon, Linda (1948 -) "School Play" (Girl)

Born in Los Angeles, Linda Beardon appeared in only one episode of *Leave it to Beaver*, her only acting role.

Bell, Rodney (1915-1968) "Wally and Alma" (Mr. Alfred Hanson)

In his role as Mr. Hanson, Bell didn't say much. This was the case with many of his roles over his time in television before an untimely death at age fifty-two. Years before his *LITB* appearance, he played a reporter in *The Winning Team* about Hall of Fame baseball pitcher Grover Cleveland Alexander, starring Ronald Reagan.

Bender, Russ (1910-1969) "Wally's License" (Mr. Barnsdall)

He helps teach Wally how to drive as one of Mayfield's finest driving instructors. With over 100 roles, Bender was a fine character actor who appeared in many "B" movies and on TV, including repeat appearances on *Perry Mason*, *77 Sunset Strip*, *Rawhide*, *Gunsmoke* and Bonanza.

Bennett, Julie (b. 1929) "The Black Eye" (Waitress)

Well known for her work in animated shorts and features such as *Spider Man*, *Yogi Bear* and *The Bugs Bunny & Tweety Show*, Julie made her only appearance on *Leave it to Beaver* as a waitress in "The Black Eye." She was also a co-writer on Woody Allen's debut film *What's Up Tiger Lilly?*

Bennett, Linda (b. 1946) "Wally's Dream Girl" (Ginny Townsend)

Her final TV role was that of a dream girl. Prior to *Leave it to Beaver*, her biggest role was as Penny Walker in *Creature with the Atom Brain*. Linda gained more popularity for her voice than her acting skills. She released numerous LPs and was a regular on *The Merv Griffin Show* from 1966-1970.

Benoit, Mary (1911-2002) "The All-Night Party" (The 1st Woman)

Her first part in Hollywood was an uncredited role in the Ginger Rogers film, *Kitty Foyle* (1940). She continued in uncredited roles until playing three minor roles in *The Ten Commandments* (1956). Those uncredited roles continued afterward until her part as "The First Woman" in *LITB*. Some of her final roles included parts in *Batman, Mod Squad* and *Love, American Style*.

Berwald, Tommy (b. 1945) "The Black Eye" (Third boy)

The career of Tommy Berwald began and ended with his playing the third boy in "The Black Eye."

Berwick, Brad (1947? -) "Beaver on TV" (The 2nd Boy)

After *Leave it to Beaver*, Brad Berwick did not act again on television or in film. His career began in 1961 with a supporting role on the Robert Young vehicle, *Window on Main Street* where he played Arny Logan.

Best, Dorothy (b. 1948) "Party Invitation" (First girl at the party)

Now a producer, Dorothy Best made her acting debut on *Leave it to Beaver* in "Party Invitation," as the First Girl at the Party. She married James Best (Roscoe P. Coltrane from *The Dukes of Hazzard*) since 1986.

Blake, Larry J. (1914-1982) "Wally's License" (The Instructor)

Blake was sixty-eight years old when he died and had over 250 film and TV roles. He packed a lot of acting into his forty-two years on the small and big screens. These include two amazing and underrated baseball movies, one starring Ronald Reagan (*The Winning Team*) and one starring a cat (*Rhubarb*). TV shows in which he had recurring roles include *The Pride of the Family*, *Yancy Derringer* and *Saints and Sinners*.

Bodin, Kent (b. 1948?) "Beaver's First Date" (Billy McKenzie)

This is the boy Beaver's first date, Betsy, dances with at the dance sponsored by their dancing school. This was his first and last acting role according to IMDB.

Bonney, Gail (1901-1984) "Beaver Takes a Drive" (The Woman Clerk)

There's busy and then there's monumentally busy. Gail Bonney, in the year she appeared in *Leave it to Beaver*, also appeared in nine other TV shows during that twelve-month period. Among those shows were *Maverick*, *The Untouchables*, *Pete and Gladys*, *Whispering Smith*, and *Hawaiian Eye*. One can easily understand how she accumulated over 200 credits in her thirty-one years of acting in Hollywood.

Brady, Tina (b. 1947) "Beaver, the Sheepdog" (The 2nd Girl)

Beginning and ending after one episode of *Leave it to Beaver*, Tina Brady left acting for other pursuits after her debut as "The 2nd Girl."

Bremen, Leonard (1915 - 1986) "It's a Small World/Pilot" (Milk Bar Proprietor)

Appearing in uncredited roles, Leonard Bremen had parts in many big movies of the mid-1940s such as *Dark Passage* starring Humphrey Bogart, *Deep Valley* with Ida Lupino, and *Buck Privates Come Home* with Abbott & Costello. He finished his career with bit parts in comedies like *The Beverly Hillbillies* and *The Brady Bunch*.

Bronson, Lillian (1902-1995) "The Haunted House" (Miss Cooper)

In her lone *LITB* episode, Ms. Bronson plays a kind elderly woman, but Beaver has been convinced she's a witch. A woman playing a witch is not groundbreaking, but her role as the first woman judge on *Perry Mason*, certainly was groundbreaking. It's unfortunate the producers couldn't have given her more roles on *Leave it to Beaver*, after all, she was a Bronson.

Brooks, Ralph (1904-1991) "School Play" (Audience Member)

This actor, who played many uncredited extra parts over his years in Hollywood, appeared in four *Leave it to Bever* episodes. The others were "Wally's Pug Nose," "Wally's Dinner Date," and "Beaver's Football Award." Before he began to work in television, he had already appeared in over 330 films, most of them "B" movies.

Bruggeman, George (1904-1967) "Beaver's Football Award" (Father at Award Dinner)

This actor was another superstar extra who found his way to the *Leave it to Beaver* set. With more than 300 total film and TV credits, Bruggeman was a Hollywood fixture. He was also a stuntman, playing the cowardly lion in the *The Wizard of Oz* when he runs down a hallway and jumps through a glass window.

Bryan, Marvin (1927-2002) "Mistaken Identity" (Officer Medford)

Had a recurring role in *Yancy Derringer* (1958) and left acting after his role on *Leave it to Beaver*. He then went into writing and producing. He later entered advertising and was vice-president of Campbell-Ewald advertising agency in 1977, eventually becoming a writer of books on typography and graphic design.

Bryant, Ben (1941-2000) "More Blessed to Give" (The Assistant)

Bryant acted for just a few years. His most interesting role was in an episode of *Alfred Hitchcock Presents* where he played the "Fat Boy." His final role came in 1963 in *The Jack Benny Program*.

Bryar, Claudia (1918-2011) 4 episodes

In addition to *Leave it to Beaver* where she worked on four episodes, "Party Invitation," "Beaver's Library Book," "Community Chest," and Three Boys and a Burrow," there were four other TV shows in which Claudia Bryar played multiple roles. These shows were *The F.B.I.*, *Wagon Train*, *Bonanza* and *Barnaby Jones*. She also had small roles in movies such as *Psycho II* and *Bad Company* with Jeff Bridges. Claudia even had an uncredited role as a beauty operator in the film *Giant*.

Bryar, Paul (1910-1985) "Beaver's Bike" (Sgt. Peterson)

Married to actress Claudia Bryar, the two are possibly the only husband and wife to have roles on *Leave it to Beaver*. Almost similar, was when Norman Tokar directed his wife Phyllis Coates in a *LITB* episode. Paul Bryar was another extra extraordinaire with almost 400 film and TV credits, his wife had over 120.

Buchanan, Edgar (1903-1979) 3 episodes (Captain Jack / Uncle Billy)

Better known to *Leave it to Beaver* fans for his portrayal of Uncle Billy, Edgar Buchanan was first seen on the show in the episode titled, "Captain Jack." His two other appearances were in "Uncle Billy," and "Uncle Billy's Visit." His first big role on TV was as Sheriff Red Connors on *Hopalong Cassidy*. He made forty appearances on *Hopalong*. Buchanan is best known for his role on *Petticoat Junction* as Uncle Joe Carson, a character he also portrayed on *Green Acres* and *The Beverly Hillbillies*. Before acting, Buchanan was a dentist for many years in Eugene, Oregon. He met his wife Mildred while attending dental school and the two were married for fifty years. Edgar Buchanan passed away in 1979 from a stroke, ten days before their 51st anniversary.

Budzak, Betty Lynn (b. 1947) 3 episodes

Betty Lynn Budzak appeared on three episodes of *Leave it to Beaver*. In her final appearance, "The Dramatic Club," she played opposite Beaver in a school play where the two have to kiss. Her other *LITB* appearances were in the season one episode, "Party Invitation," and "Beaver's Poster in season four. Her only other appearance in Hollywood was in the film, *Summer and Smoke*.

Burnham, Terry (1949-2013) "Lumpy's Scholarship" (Beaver's Date)

Some *Leave it to Beaver* fans may know about actress Terry Burnham, not from her two roles on *Leave it to Beaver*, but from her role on *The Twilight Zone*. She played a young girl named Markie in the episode "Nightmare as a Child." There's too much to write about her in this section, but I would advise you to enter her name in the search box at IMDB.com.

C

Caine, Howard (1926-1993) "Eddie, the Businessman" (Foreman)

Best known for his role as Major Hochstetter on *Hogan's Heroes*, Howard Caine, was a very busy actor in the early 1960s. He made appearances during those years on shows like *Gunsmoke*, *The Untouchables*, *My Three Sons*, *The Twilight Zone*, *Ben Casey*, *The Lucy Show* and *Rawhide*. An interesting note about his final role in the mini-series *War and Remembrance* is that he played Lord Maxwell Beaverbrook. If that name sounds familiar, it was a nickname Eddie Haskell called Dudley McMillen in the "Wally and Dudley" episode.

Caire, Audrey (1927-2007) "Eddie's Double-Cross" (Waitress)

Audrey Caire is remembered by *LITB* fans as the waitress to whom Wally gives a very small tip when paying for Carolyn Schuster and Alma Hanson's bill at the malt shop. But to her fans, she may be better known as having one of the leading roles in the film *They Saved Hitler's Brain*.

Candido, Nino (1943-2008) "Lumpy's Scholarship" (Buzz)

Leave it to Beaver was Candido's first acting role. He continued to act sporadically up until 1976. Soon after, he went to the other side of the camera and worked as a prop master for over 30 years on many productions including *The A-Team*, *Bull Durham*, *The Bernie Mac Show*, and *My Name is Earl*.

Capri, Ahna (1944-2010) "Lumpy's Scholarship" (Cinda Dunsworth)

Appearing in two episodes of *Leave it to Beaver* in 1963, Ahna Capri was a very experienced actress by the time she became impressed by Lumpy's athletic prowess. She had already had a recurring role in *Room for One More*. She's also had parts on *Father Knows Best*, *77 Sunset Strip*, *Cheyenne* and *Sugarfoot*.

Carpenter, Penny (b. 1945) "Captain Jack" (Girl to see Captain Jack)

The pinnacle of Penny Carpenter's Hollywood career was her role as a girl to see Captain Jack in the episode "Captain Jack." Before *Leave it to Beaver*, she did have uncredited roles in *The Harder They Fall* starring Humphrey Bogart and *Gun For a Coward* starring Fred MacMurray, but nothing after *Leave it to Beaver*.

Carroll, Dee (1925-1980) "Wally's Orchid" (Florist)

Also appearing in "Beaver's Monkey," as a guest at the Cleavers, Dee Carroll had minor roles in over 100 films and TV shows throughout her career. Her best-known role was as housekeeper Adele Winston Hamilton on the daytime soap opera *Days of Our Lives*.

Carroll, Mary (1908-1989) "Mother's Helper" (Mrs. Manners)

Known for her role as the maid who could make great gingerbread and having a good-looking daughter. Carroll, around the same time as her role in *Leave it to Beaver* also had parts in few episodes of *Mister Ed*, *Rawhide* and *Petticoat Junction* and finished her career in 1970 with a role as a middle aged woman in *Beyond the Valley of the Dolls*.

Carroll, Virginia (1913-2009) "It's a Small World" (Nurse)

After co-starring in numerous "B" westerns, Virginia Carroll tried her hand at television beginning in the 1950s. She had bit parts on such shows as *The Adventures of Superman*, *Fireside Theater* and *The Adventures of Kit Carson* before her appearance on the *Leave it to Beaver* pilot, "It's a Small World" in 1957. Virginia Carroll appeared most often on *The Roy Rogers Show* (5 episodes) and *Dragnet* (4 episodes).

Carleton, Claire (1913-1979) "June's Birthday" (Saleslady)

If you ever wondered who would have the gall to sell Beaver such an ugly bouse for his mother, here she is. Carleton worked in over 180 films and TV shows in minor roles. She also worked on Broadway from 1932-1950. Some TV shows in which she played multiple roles include *Wagon Train*, *Alfred Hitchcock Presents*, *The Munsters*, and *M Squad*. She also had a recurring role as Alice Purdy on *Cimmaron City*.

Carson, Robert (1909-1979) "Beaver, the Athlete" (Coach Grover)

The coach who gave Beaver a bad grade in P.E. was the real-life uncle of Kit Carson, the chief of staff to the most popular talk radio host in history, Rush Limbaugh. Kit Carson was also a producer of *The Rush Limbaugh Show*. Carson's TV and movie career spanned forty years and 215 roles. His first was as Scott in *Dick Tracy's G-Men* (1939) and his final role was as a minister in *Hawaii Five-O* (1979). He had multiple roles in a few TV shows including *The Lucy Show*, *Here's Lucy*, *Perry Mason*, *The Lone Ranger* and a few others.

Carter, Jimmy (b. 1947 or 1948) "Beaver's Tonsils" (Herman)

In addition to the above episode, Carter also appeared in "Beaver's Poster" and "Beaver, the Bunny." After the Larry Mondello character left the series, there were a number of boys who made one or two appearances to fill space in the classroom scenes who were also given minor lines. Carter's career was short and also included appearances in *The Lucy Show*, *Route 66* and *Bonanza*.

Cartwright, Veronica (b. 1949) 4 episodes (Violet Rutherford / Peggy McIntosh)

Cartwright played the sugary sweet character of Violet Rutherford perfectly. This is especially seen in the episode "Beaver and Violet," possibly the best episode in season three. Other than that episode, she also appeared in "The Tooth" and "Beaver's Rat." Her final episode was in "Don Juan Beaver," where she played the character Peggy McIntosh.

Moving past *Beaver*, if there were two words to describe the career of Veronica Cartwright so far, they would be "quality" and "prolific." The number of good roles she has had over the years in both TV and film is nothing less than stellar. The quality began early with TV appearances on *Alfred Hitchcock Presents, Route 66, The Twilight Zone, Leave it to Beaver* and *Daniel Boone*. Not to be outdone, films came knocking on her door, and her film resume soon became just as impressive. In the 1960s, these included *The Children's Hour*, *The Birds*, and *Spencer's Mountain*. She admits that after her role on *Daniel Boone*, her career was in limbo, as she was at an age between child and adult roles. That problem remedied itself a couple years later acting again regularly by 1968.

While her roles in the 1970s were sporadic, she did score two of the biggest parts in her career up to that point with roles in the remake of *The Invasion of the Body Snatchers* in 1978 and the following year she played Lambert in *Alien*. The 1980s saw her reprising the role of Violet Rutherford in *The New Leave it to Beaver*, as well as acting in two outstanding films, *The Right Stuff* and *The Witches of Eastwick*. She had recurring roles in *L.A. Law* and *The X-Files* in the 1990s, and during this decade, she also appeared on *Chicago Hope*, and *Will & Grace*.

When it comes the 2000s to today, it seems like she's only become more active than ever… On television she's worked on *Six Feet Under*, *Bosch, Criminal Minds*, *The Good Doctor* and many other shows. In film, she made a second *Invasion of the Body Snatchers* remake, *The Invasion*, and in 2023, she will be seen in a couple episodes of *Gotham Knights*, playing the role of Eunice. That show is tentatively scheduled to be shown on the CW Network.

Chapin, Billy (1943-2016) "The Grass is Always Greener" (Pete Fletcher)

A child actor who became popular after his role in *Night of the Hunter* (1955) with Robert Mitchum and Shelly Winters. As a child actor, Chapin stayed busy, having most of his film and TV credits during a seven-year period in the 1950s. He left acting after his final appearance on *Fury* in 1959. He was one part of a trio of Chapin child stars. His sister Lauren Chapin starred in *Father Knows Best* and brother Michael also acted.

Charney, Kim (b. 1945) "Beaver's Football Award" (Terry)

A quarterback on *Leave it to Beaver*, the real Kim Charney left acting a few years after appearing as the teammate who would throw a winning touchdown to Beaver to become a successful surgeon. He left an acting career that was successful in its own right. He had fifty TV and film credits by the time he retired from Hollywood. He also appeared in "Beaver, the Hero" and "Beaver's Prep School."

Chenault, Cynthia (b. 1937) (Carole Martin)

A few years prior to *Beaver*, Chenault had a recurring role in *The Tom Ewell Show* as Carol Potter. She left acting in 1964 and later worked as a writer with *ABC Weekend Specials*, *Heathcliff: The Movie* and as a producer on *CBS Schoolbreak Special*.

Cherney, Dick (1914-2017) "Beaver's Football Award" (Father at Award Dinner)

Born Isaac Cherniavskyin in Kryvyi Ukraine, his family emigrated to the United States when he was very young. His first acting role was as an uncredited office worker in the James Cagney film, *Ceiling Zero*. Over a forty-year career, Cherney acted in almost 300 TV shows and films. He retired from acting when he was sixty-three years old but lived almost another forty years. He had multiple roles on *Perry Mason*, *Gunsmoke*, *Kojak*, *The Doris Day Show* and *Get Smart* among others.

Cirillo, Charles (1908-1999) "The Shave" (Barber)

For *LITB* fans he is the barber watching on as Wally receives a shave at the barber shop. He had multiple roles in *Soldier of Fortune*, *Tales of Wells Fargo*, *Mister Ed*, *I Spy* and *Murder, She Wrote*.

Cisar, George (1912-1979) "Beaver Joins a Record Club" (The Postman)

With almost 150 TV and film roles on his resume, sometimes there will be a film among those credits with a unique name. His was *Attack of the Giant Leeches*. As for *Leave it to Beaver*, he was typecast as a postman, bringing new records to the Cleaver house in one episode and delivering a locket in "More Blessed to Give."

Clarke, Gage (1900-1964) "The School Picture" (Mr. Baxter)

Clarke plays the school photographer in an episode of *Leave it to Beaver*. A few years after *LITB*, he had a recurring role as Mr. Botkin in *Gunsmoke*.

Clements, Stanley (1926-1981) "Beaver's Ice Skates" Shoe Salesman

Best known for replacing actor Leo Gorcey in the *Bowery Boy* series of films, playing the character Stanislaus 'Duke' Coveleskie. He and his wife in 1964 were the first couple to adopt a child from behind the Iron Curtain.

Close, John (1921-1963) "Beaver, the Athlete" Coach Henderson

In only thirteen years as an actor in Hollywood, Close played in over 150 TV shows and films. He appeared in some very early TV shows beginning in 1951 with *The Bigelow Theater* and *Front Page Detective*. In this same year, he had parts in the films *Jim Thorpe, All American*, *The Day the Earth Stood Still* and *Halls of Montezuma*.

Coates, Phyllis (b. 1927) "New Neighbors" (Betty Donaldson)

You've heard of stars being discovered at the corner of Hollywood and Vine, here is one example. Phyllis Coates was discovered by comedian Ken Murray in a restaurant on that famous corner after her move from Wichita Falls, Texas. She worked in his Vaudeville show and the rest is history. In

1957 she played the role of Betty Donaldson in the episode "New Neighbors." At the time, she was married to director Norman Tokar. She is best known for her role as Lois Lane in *The Adventures of Superman.*

Cole, Tommy (b. 1941) "The Borrowed Boat" (Red Bennett)

Cole had a recurring role in his first series *Annette,* starring Annette Funicello in 1958. He then went on to play in *Leave it to Beaver* and *My Three Sons*. After ending his career of looking good in front of the camera in 1966, he later went behind the scenes to help others look good, working as a makeup artist in Hollywood for almost forty years. He worked on *Mary Hartman, Mary Hartman, Evening Shade* and many others.

Collier, John (b. 1944) "Forgotten Party" David Manning

Collier's acting career lasted from 1958-1961, ending with a role on *Dennis the Menace*. The year prior to his part on *Leave it to Beaver*, his sister Dorothy had a role as a birthday party guest at Linda Dennison's house.

Collier, Marian (1931-2021) "Beaver on TV" The Girl in The TV Station

Had many small roles in a variety of TV shows in the 1960s and 1970s. In addition to *Leave it to Beaver*, she also appeared in *The Dick Van Dyke Show, Bachelor Father, Perry Mason, Mr. Novak, Emergency!,* and *Welcome Back Kotter*. In the late 1980s, she began a string of appearances in the *Lethal Weapon* franchise, playing a different character in three *Lethal Weapon* movies.

Conn, Donna (b. 1945) "Wally's Weekend Job" (Jan)

Had an acting career that spanned the duration of two *Leave it to Beaver* episodes in season five. The other episode was "Beaver's First Date" where she plays Lumpy Rutherford's date at a dance.

Conway, Russ (1913-2009) "The Younger Brother" (Mr. Doyle)

An actor best known for his work in *Whatever Happened to Baby Jane?* Conway had a busy career with over 250 acting credits, appearing in some of the best TV shows of the 1950s including *Rawhide, Navy Log, The George Burns and Gracie Allen Show, Sergeant Preston of the Yukon* and *The Lone Ranger*. In the 1970s, he had roles in such classic crime dramas as *Barnaby Jones, Cannon* and *Mannix*.

Cook, Jean "Beaver, the Bunny" (First Woman)

Not much is known about this actress. Among her five acting credits, she also appeared in *My Three Sons* and *The Donna Reed Show*. She does have the distinction of being credited as "First Woman" in 40% of all her roles.

Corby, Ellen (1911-1999) "Lonesome Beaver" (Pedestrian)

From 1933 to 1947 she had uncredited roles in many films before playing Aunt Trina in the 1948 film *I Remember Mama*. However, she is best known for her role as Grandma on *The Walton's*. She was a pedestrian in "Lonesome Beaver," the only episode of *Leave it to Beaver* in which she appeared.

Courtleigh, Stephen (1913-1967) "Beaver, the Babysitter" (Mr. Murdock)

He also played one of the divers in "Beaver Takes a Drive." Noted as playing Abraham Lincoln in both *The Philco Television Playhouse* (1950) and in the TV movie *Abe Lincoln in Illinois* (1945). He later played General Robert E. Lee in the TV movie *Soldier of Peace* (1953).

Crehan, Joseph (1883 - 1966) "Train Trip" (Train Conductor)

Appearing in his first film in 1916, Crehan eventually worked in almost 400 films and television shows. He played the role of the train conductor on the "Train Trip" episode. He had moderate success in the early 60s with regular work on *The Untouchables* and *The Andy Griffith Show*.

Curtis, Barry (b. 1943) "Boarding School" (Johnny Franklin); "Wally and Alma" (Harry Myers)

Before appearing on *Leave it to Beaver* episodes "Boarding School," and "Wally and Alma," Barry Curtis had a starring role in *The Adventures of Champion* as Ricky North. He retired from his acting career after his final appearance in *Leave it to Beaver*.

D

Damler, John (1919-1984) "Beaver, the Bunny" (Sergeant)

Attesting to his great acting abilities, Damler was used regularly in many TV shows throughout his career, including *The Lone Ranger*, *Death Valley Days*, *The Life and Legend of Wyatt Earp* and *Stagecoach West*.

Davis, Charles (1925-2009) "Part-Time Genius" and "The Broken Window" (Corny Cornelius)

Playing many bit parts in film and on TV in the 1950s, Charles Davis found regular work in the late 1950s and early 60s in shows such as *Perry Mason*, *Alfred Hitchcock Presents* and *The Wild Wild West*. He closed out his career in the mid-1980s with small roles on shows like *Remington Steele, L.A. Law, Dynasty* and *Falcon Crest*.

Daye, Harold (b. 1943) "Wally's Track Meet" Track Team Member

Also appeared in *Wagon Train* and *Death Valley Days*, but his appearance in *Leave it to Beaver* was his final acting role in a career that spanned six years and five film and TV roles.

Dayton, John Philip (b. 1947) "Water, Anyone?" (Boy)

While his acting career was sporadic with only eighteen roles over forty-three years, Dayton was Hollywood through and through. He is best known with his close working relationship with Katherine Hepburn, working on some of her final films. He was an actor, writer, producer and director over his long career in Hollywood.

Dean, Martin (b. 1938) "One of the Boys" (Rick)

Played in two episodes of *Leave it to Beaver*, the other being "Uncle Billy's Visit" in which he plays the usher who catches Beaver sneaking Gilbert into the movie theater. Had a recurring role in

Dick Tracy in his first TV acting job. Also had multiple roles in *Dragnet* and *The Gertrude Berg Show*.

DeNormand, George "Beaver's Football Award" (Father at Award Dinner)

He may be one of the most colorful characters to ever appear in a *Leave it to Beaver* episode. He was a very well-respected man in Hollywood. After leaving the military, he became a professional boxer. He then went on to become a stuntman and appeared in numerous films, often as a double for a fight scene or in a barroom brawl. He appeared in over 650 films and TV shows over his career, 200 as a stuntman and 450 as an actor. He had multiple appearances in various roles of the greatest of 1960s TV. You name the show, he was in it.

De Sales, Francis (1912-1988) "Water Anyone?" (Mr. Anderson)

De Sales was best known for his role on the series *Mr. & Mrs. North* as Lt. Weingand. He found regular work after *Leave it to Beaver* on *The Adventures of Ozzie and Harriet* and in a recurring role as Sheriff Maddox on *Two Faces West*.

DeWilde, Frederick (1914-1980) "Wally Goes Steady" (Jack Bennett)

With only a few acting credits, DeWilde did manage to score roles in two of the best comedies in the 1960s, *Bachelor Father* and *Leave it to Beaver*.

des Enfants, Gabrielle (b. 1953) "Child Care" (Helen "Puddin'" Wilson)

A cute child actor, Gabrielle guest starred on "Child Care" in season one of *Leave it to Beaver*. She also appeared in three other television shows, *Tales of Wells Fargo*, *Wagon Train* and *McHale's Navy*.

Dillaway, Dana (b. 1950) "Wally, the Businessman" (Peggy)

At four years old, her career began in the film *Giant*. Most of her future work in Hollywood occurred through 1963. An additional two parts came in 1971 on *My Three Sons*. A film released in 1978 titled *Legend of the Northwest*, in which she co-starred, was filmed much earlier.

Dillaway, Don (1903-1982) "Beaver's Football Award" (Mr. Rickover)

Career began on Broadway, performing there from 1925 to 1937. Acted in many "B" films in the 1930s and 40s. Early TV roles included parts on *Dangerous Assignment*, *The Racket Squad* and *Mr. District Attorney*.

Dodd, Barbara (b. 1930) "Wally's Girl Trouble" (Librarian)

When Wally in "Wally's Girl Trouble" goes to the library for Penny Jamison, he asks the librarian, played by Barbara Dodd where he could find *Rebecca of Sunnybrook Farm*. This was Barbara's only appearance on *Leave it to Beaver* and she later went behind the scenes in Hollywood to work as a casting director while still accepting occasional TV roles. Her last was as Ellen on *Modern Family* in 2012.

Doherty, Charla (1946-1988) "Don Juan Beaver" (Melinda Neilson)

Early acting jobs were on popular sitcoms of the early 1960s, *The Donna Reed Show*, *Leave it to Beaver* and *Mr. Ed.* Later appeared on *My Three Sons* and *Gidget*. Best known for her work on *Days of Our Lives* from 1965-1966. Father won second place in the "I Can't Stand Jack Benny" contest associated with his radio program.

Doran, Ann (1911-2000) "Voodoo Magic" (Agnes Haskell); "Beaver the Magician" (Mrs. Bellamy)

Ann Doran was a prolific actor. Some accounts have her working in over 1500 movies and television shows. However, IMDB only lists her with 366 acting credits. First film was Douglas Fairbanks' silent *Robin Hood*.

Dore, Anne (b. 1930) "The Perfume Salesman" (Mrs. Wentworth)

Her most regular work in the 1950s was on *The Red Skelton Hour* and *Space Patrol*. Her last Hollywood role was as a female giant in *Land of the Giants* (1968).

Drake, James (1932-1976) "Tennis, Anyone?" (Don Kirk)

Acted in Hollywod only in his 20s and 30s, beginning with an uncredited role in *Malta Story* starring Alec Guinness. His last role was as an uncredited security guard on *Star Trek* in 1969. In between, he had minor parts in many shows including *F Troop*, *Burke's Law* and *Gunsmoke*.

Drysdale, Don (1936-1993) "Long Distance Call" (Don Drysdale)

Played himself in one-third of all his acting credits. He appeared on *Leave it to Beaver* as himself when the boys call him at Dodger Stadium, and he also appeared in the *Donna Reed Show* four times and on *The Brady Bunch* once.

Dugan, Robert E. (1927-1993) "Beaver Joins a Record Club" (Mr. Tyler)

Not much is known about Robert Dugan. He had appearances on three shows in his short career which spanned ten years. His first two appearances occurred in 1961-1962 with his *Beaver* appearance and a role on *Wagon Train*. Then, after nine years away from the screen, he appeared twice in *Ironside* in 1971.

Dulo, Jane (1917-1994) "Sweatshirt Monsters" (Mrs. Rickover)

Comedy character actress with almost 100 acting credits. She appeared in some of the most iconic sitcoms of the 1950s, 60s, 70s, and 80s. These included *The Life of Riley*, *Leave it to Beaver*, *The Andy Griffith Show*, *The Dick Van Dyke Show*, *The Odd Couple*, *Welcome Back, Kotter*, *The Wonder Years* and *Gimme a Break* where her character was married to fellow *Leave it to Beaver* alum, actor John Hoyt.

Duncan, Pamela (1924-2004) "Beaver, the Sheep Dog" (The Woman Clerk)

Began her career in 1950 with an appearance on *Colgate Theatre*. Many of her early TV appearances were on crime shows such as *Front Page Detective*, *The Files of Jeffrey Jones*, *Gang*

Busters and *Craig Kennedy, Criminologist.* Her career culminated with over 100 acting credits. Among her credits is the Roger Corman cult classic *Attack of the Crab Monsters* (1957).

E

Eimen, Johnny (b. 1949) "Long Distance Call" (2nd Boy)

While he had only a very small extra roles in *Leave it to Beaver*, one mentioned on IMDB.com and another, "Beaver Gets 'Spelled," which is missing from that website. Eimen is best known for his recurring role on *McKeever and the Colonel* where he played a cadet named Monk. He also made appearances on *Bachelor Father*, *Petticoat Junction*, *The Untouchables* and *The Twilight Zone.* He lived in Japan for many years, teaching English and translating manga to English for a large Japanese publisher. He also became a flight attendant, only retiring in 2021. Late in his teen years, he turned his interest from acting to singing and later, sang in supper clubs in Beverly Hills and Los Angeles. He also sang at small clubs in Osaka while living in Japan. Was a member of a garage band, *The Shades*, later renamed *The Odd Assortment,* while in high school. The drummer was his friend Stan Fafara who portrayed Whitey Whitney on *Leave it to Beaver.*

Eldredge, John (1904-1961) "The Cookie Fund" (Mr. Preston)

In only twenty-seven years in Hollywood, Eldredge had over 225 acting credits. His career dates back to 1934 when he had his first role in *The Man with Two Faces* starring Edward G. Robinson and Mary Astor. He had a recurring role as Harry Archer on the 1950s sitcom *Meet Corliss Archer.*

Elliott, Ross (1917-1999) "Teacher's Daughter (Mr. Foster)

Best known to *LITB* fans as Mr. Foster, Julie's father, Ross had 266 acting credits in Hollywood besides his two appearances on *Leave it to Beaver*. In many shows, he appeared in multiple episodes playing different roles, among them were *The Mod Squad, Barnaby Jones, The Felony Squad, Laramie, Sea Hunt* among others. He also had recurring roles in *The Jack Benny Program, The Virginian, Sam Benedict* and *General Hospital.*

Engle, Paul (b. 1948) "Wally's Girl Trouble" (Second boy in library); "Beaver's Bike" (Bicycle thief)

Regular work in Hollywood was no stranger to Paul Engle. His career spanned from 1955-1962 and during that time he amassed forty acting credits, most of those in television. His last TV show was *Hazel* in 1962.

Etterre, Estelle (1899-1996) "Beaver's First Date" (Mrs. Thompson)

Most of her career was spent in uncredited film roles. She performed in everything from *Life Begins for Andy Hardy* to *The Manchurian Candidate.* The only time she did receive credit was in her few TV roles which also included *The Lucy Show* and *The George Burns and Gracie Allen Show.*

Erwin, Bill (1914-2010) "The Price of Fame" (Man)

All *LITB* fans are grateful to this man for getting Beaver unstuck from the park fence. But as evidenced by his 250 film and TV roles, working as a parks department employee was not a very big part of his acting portfolio. He had sixty-four acting credits in film and TV even before he appeared in *Leave it to Beaver*. Early in his career he appeared in *The Stu Erwin Show* (no relation), and in later years, he appeared in *The West Wing*, *Monk*, *The King of Queens* and his final role came in *My Name is Earl*.

Evans, Douglas (1904-1968) "The Bus Ride" (Bus Passenger)

With over 160 credits in Hollywood, one of his interesting roles for *Leave it to Beaver* fans should be his appearance on *Amos 'n' Andy* which was created by Richard Rickover's real-life father and written by *LITB* creators/producers Bob Mosher and Joe Connelly. He also appeared in the 1951 film *Leave it to the Marines*.

Eyer, Robert (1948-2005) "Tell it to Ella" (Kevin)

Had minor parts in many TV shows from the mid-1950s to his last role in *LITB* in 1962. His older brother Richard had a career spanning sixteen years and over fifty credits.

F

Faylen Carol (b. 1948) "Beaver the Hero" (Donna)

Best known for her work on *The Bing Crosby Show* where she played one of Bing's daughters (1964-1965). In addition to her work with Bing Crosby, she had four appearances on *Leave it to Beaver* in "Beaver on TV," "Beaver's Prep School," and "The Book Report" along with "Beaver the Hero." In an interview with actor Stephen Talbot (Gilbert), when asked about any crushes he had on fellow actresses, he mentioned that he and Carol dated soon after the end of *Leave it to Beaver*. Nothing serious of course, as he was only about fourteen or fifteen at the time.[176] He also mentioned that Carol's father, like his, was also an actor. A role featuring Carol Faylen's father, that most everyone has probably seen, was his role as the cab driver Ernie in the film *It's a Wonderful Life*. He also played Herbert T. Gillis in *The Many Loves of Dobie Gillis*.

Fawcett, William (1894-1974) "Beaver's Crush" (Mr. Johnson)

In "Beaver's Crush," Fawcett plays the character of Mr. Johnson in one of his almost 400 television and film roles. Before acting, Fawcett was a professor at Michigan State University teaching theater arts. He played in numerous television productions in which he appeared in six or seven episodes, such as *The Cisco Kid*, *Wagon Train*, *Gunsmoke*, *Bonanza* among many others. Had a recurring role as Clayton in *Duffy's Tavern*.

Ferdin, Wendy (b. 1950) "Beaver, the Hero" (Charlene)

Other than *Leave it to Beaver*, Ferdin acted in *One Man's Way*, the story of Norman Vincent Peale.

Ferguson, Frank (1906-1978) "Beaver's Good Deed" (Jeff)

With well over 300 acting credits in only thirty-five years, Frank Ferguson was one of the most prolific actors to appear on *Leave it to Beaver*. He was also the only actor on the show to be seen taking a bath. The show progressed from season one being unable to show a toilet to season six

---

[176] Author interview with Stephen Talbot November 3, 2002.

when they could show a grown man taking a bath. Fans of *The Andy Griffith Show* may remember Ferguson from his roles as Mr. Foley or Sam Lindsey. He appeared in *Andy Griffith* five times and twice each as the beforementioned characters.

Fishman, Duke (1906-1977) "Train Trip" (Train Station Commuter)

Had multiple roles on two 1950s television shows which took place in the Yukon Territory. They were *Sergeant Preston of the Yukon* and *Klondike*. For over forty years, he spent his summers as a lifeguard on the beach of Avalon California. His career ended with over 150 credits, ending in the 1970s with uncredited appearances on *Starsky and Hutch*, *The Rockford Files* and *Quincy M.E.*

Franco, Abel (1922-2000) "Beaver and Chuey" (Enrico Varela)

With over his thirty-five years in Hollywood, some of his notable performances include playing Ricky Ricardo's cousin in "The Ricardos Visit Cuba" episode of *I Love Lucy*, a Mexican bandit in *Blazing Saddles* and his role of Papa Sanchez in *The Three Amigos*.

Flowers, Bess (1898-1984) 2 episodes (Luncheon Guest / Train Station Commuter)

In *Leave it to Beaver*, Bess Flowers made two uncredited appearances, the first in "Train Trip" and the second in "Beaver's Monkey." The Internet Movie Database has her listed officially as acting in 847 TV shows and movies, most of those as uncredited townspeople, lunch guests, diners, or department store customers.

Foran, Mary (1919-1981) "Train Trip" (Lady hitting her little boy in train station)

With small roles in popular sitcoms in the 1960s, Mary Foran stayed busy in Hollywood helping people smile. The shows she appeared on are icons of American comedy, shows such as *Gilligan's Island*, *The Lucy Show*, *Mr. Ed*, *That Girl*, *The Monkees*, *I Dream of Jeannie* and *Bewitched*.

Foster, Dick (b. 1945) "Wally's Car" (Don)

Foster's career was short but did appear in two episodes of *Leave it to Beaver* and *The Donna Reed Show*. He also had an uncredited role as a farm boy in the Rosalind Russell and Natalie Wood film *Gypsy*.

Fraley, Brenda (b. 1941) "The Mustache" (1st Girl)

Her only roles in Hollywood were this one on *Leave it to Beaver* and in a series titled *Follow the Sun* which followed the adventures of magazine writers based in Hawaii.

Frye, Gil (1918-2000) "The Paper Route" (Newspaper customer); "The Hair Cut" (Barber shop customer)

From 1942 to 1950, Gil Frye worked on numerous "B" movies in small roles. At the onset of the television era, he worked continuously through 1965, making his last appearance almost twenty years later on *Vega$* as a medical examiner. The television series in which he found the most work was *Perry Mason*.

G

Gaines, Jimmie Lee (b 1955) "In the Soup" (Little Boy)

Between the ages of five and ten, Jimmie Lee accumulated twenty acting credits and appeared on some of the most popular sitcoms of the 1960s including *The Donna Reed Show*, *The Beverly Hillbillies*, *The Lucy Show*, and *My Three Sons*. His Leave it To Beaver appearance was his first acting role and he was also the youngest actor to appear in *Leave it to Beaver* and was in the most expensive episode of the series.

Gallaudet, John (1903-1983) "Beaver's Tonsils" (Dr. Kirby)

He appeared in two *Leave it to Beaver* episodes. The other was as Art Howard in "Beaver, the Caddy." He had over 200 acting credits and among them were recurring roles as a judge on *Perry Mason*, Bob Anderson on *My Three Sons*, Lt. Dan Harmon on *Johnny Midnight,* and there were quite a few others.

Gering, Dick (1935-2003) "Wally, the Lifeguard" (Lifeguard)

Had a recurring role of Johnny Green in the TV show *Margie*. Also appeared in *Father Knows Best*, *The Many Loves of Dobie Gillis* and had his final role in *Wide Country* in 1962.

Gerrity, Patty Ann (1948-1991) "Beaver on TV" (2nd Girl)

Gerrity had many credits beyond her two roles on *Leave it to Beaver* where she played the 2nd girl in "Beaver on TV" and the 1st girl in "Beaver's Prep School." She also appeared on *The Lucy Show*, *Lassie* and *My Three Sons*. Her career ended in 1966 with an appearance in the film *The Trouble with Angles* starring Haley Mills.

Gerstle, Frank (1915-1970) "Borrowed Boat" (Police Sergeant)

Played many doctors and policemen throughout his career. Although Gerstle died young at fifty-four, he amassed over 200 acting credits, including multiple roles on *Lassie*, *Perry Mason*, *The Jack Benny Program* and a recurring role on *The Life and Legend of Wyatt Earp*. Later in his career, he became a successful voice actor, working on *The Arabian Knights* which was part of the *Banana Splits Adventure Hour*.

Gibson, Mimi (b. 1948) "Brother vs. Brother" (Mary Tyler)

Mimi was one of the most productive child actors during the 1950s. According to IMDB, she appeared in over 100 TV shows and thirty-five films, although they only provide seventy-two acting credits. Having had her earnings as a child actor spent by others, she found out at age eighteen that her money was gone and soon left work in Hollywood. She has worked with Paul Petersen's organization A Minor Consideration as an advocate for child performers.

Gilbert, Gloria (b. 1946) "Wally Goes Steady" (Judy Henderson)

Her only acting role was her appearance in *Leave it to Beaver* as Evelyn Boothby's sister.

Gilchrist, Connie (1901-1985) "Captain Jack" (Maid)

Playing a maid in the first ever filmed *Leave it to Beaver* episode, "Captain Jack," she refuses to clean the boy's bathroom if they're going to keep an alligator in there. She eventually gets fired for drinking Ward's brandy. Her longest running role was as Purity Pinker on the series, *The Adventures of Long John Silver*.

Gillum, Jan (b. 1945) "My Brother's Girl" (Jan Gillum)

In "My Brother's Girl," Jan Gillum plays Kathleen who is sitting at a lunchroom table with Mary Ellen Rogers. She also played twelve-year-old Yolanda in the movie *Somebody Up There Likes Me* starring Paul Newman.

Gleason, James (1882-1959) "The Clubhouse" (Pete)

By two years, James Gleason was the oldest actor to appear on the first season of *Leave it to Beaver*. Burt Mustin (Gus the Fireman) was two years his junior. The role he played on his only *Leave it to Beaver* episode, "The Clubhouse," was that of Pete, a dishonest tramp who talks Beaver into donating him his hard-earned money. In an odd circumstance, Gleason's last role ever was in the film, *The Last Hurrah*.

Golden, Bob (1926-1979) "Beaver Takes a Drive" (2nd Man)

When he appeared in *Leave it to Beaver*, he had only just begun his acting career at the age of thirty-five. He went on to appear in over fifty other TV shows and movies. His last appearance was an uncredited role in the film *Every Which Way but Loose* with Clint Eastwood. His heyday was in the 1970s when he appeared in *The Brady Bunch*, *The Mod Squad*, *Barnaby Jones*, *Kojak*, *Police Story*, *Hawaii Five-O* and *Quincy M.E.*

Gordon, Barry (b. 1948) (Chopper Cooper)

Leave it to Beaver fans know Barry Gordon as the lovable and unfortunate Chopper Cooper. After *LITB*, he journeyed far in Hollywood and life in general. He had a top ten Billboard hit in 1955 called "Nuttin' for Christmas," he became president of the Screen Actors Guild and ran for congress twice. He became a successful voice artist with some notable performances being the Nesquick Bunny in TV ads and as Donatello in *The Teenage Mutant Ninja Turtles*. He also voiced characters in over a score of animated TV shows.

Gorman, Annette (b. 1947) "Beaver's First Date" (Betsy)

Other than breaking Beaver's heart by leaving him to dance with Billy McKenzie, Gorman also played a few other parts in 1960s TV. These included Amanda Jean Faversham on *The Many Loves of Dobie Gillis*, Pauline on *Mister Ed* and Addie Slaughter on the Disney production *Texas John Slaughter*.

Graham, Herschel (1904-1964) "Train Trip" (Passenger)

Graham did not start acting regularly until he was thirty years old when he played a waiter in *A Night at the Ritz*. From there, he went on to act in 330 more TV shows and films over his twenty-nine-year career. Many of his parts were exactly like the one he had in *LITB*, an uncredited train passenger.

Graham, Tim (1904 - 1979) "It's a Small World" (Doc)

Born in Kansas, Tim Graham moved to Hollywood and began his career late in life, in his late 40s. He had bit parts and uncredited roles in the late 1940s and the 1950s before playing "Doc" on the *Leave it to Beaver* pilot, these included two times playing uncredited roles in *Francis the Talking Mule* films. He may be the only actor to ever appear in a film with a talking mule and a TV show with a talking beaver.

Gray, Charles H. (1921-2008) "New Neighbors" (Mr. Donaldson)

As Beaver's neighbor Mr. Donaldson, Charles Gray terrified Beaver in the episode, "New Neighbors." This was his only appearance on *Leave it to Beaver*. He is best known for his work on the western *Rawhide*, where he appeared on thirty episodes as cowboy Clay Forrester.

Grayson, Phillip (b. 1945) "The Black Eye" (First boy)

Appearing In only one *Leave it to Beaver* episode, "The Black Eye," Philip Grayson acted in an additional five television shows between 1957-1961. Finally retiring from the screen after a 1971 episode of *Hawaii Five-O*.

Green, Karen (b. 1945 or 1946) "Eddie's Girl" (Caroline Cunningham)

Green acted as a child from 1952 until 1967. She appeared in shows such as *Captain Midnight*, *Fury*, *Father Knows Best*, and *My Three Sons*. She also had a recurring role on *The Eve Arden Show*. Later in life, she returned to the screen in *The Wayne & Shuster Superspecial* (1984) and in the series *Savannah* (1996).

H

Haggerty, Don (1914-1988) "Eddie, the Businessman" (Ted Worden)

Had a recurring role as Sheriff Elder in *State Trooper* (1956-1957). He played multiple roles in *Bonanza*, *Death Valley Days*, *Rawhide*, *Cheyenne* and many others among his 200+ acting credits.

Hale, Bill (1922-2011) "Beaver Takes a Drive" (The Officer)

This is the actor who portrayed the unreasonable police officer who gave Wally a ticket for simply driving the car into the driveway from the street where it had rolled when accidentally taken out of gear. Hale was a talented stuntman and actor and had a twenty-four-year career in Hollywood. Three of his uncredited roles in the 1950s were in the blockbuster films *Giant* with James Dean, *Jailhouse Rock* with Elvis and *3:10 to Yuma* with Glenn Ford.

Halper, David (1947-2005) "Beaver's Old Friend" (Friend #2)

In "Beaver's Old Friend," David Halper played one of the friends who were going out looking for pop bottles. Before heading out, they stop at Beaver's house and tease him because he's holding an old teddy bear Beaver has rescued from the trash. Halper's last known part was as Tommy Platt in a 1961 episode of *Bat Masterson*.

Hamilton, Kim (1932-2013) "The Parking Attendants" (The Maid)

Maybe best known for being married to Werner Klemperer (Col. Klink in "Hogan's Heroes"), Hamilton was a successful actress. The peak of her career in the 1970s and 80s saw her on TV in shows like *Here's Lucy*, *Adam-12*, *Good Times*, Vega$ and *Simon & Simon*. She also appeared in many films, including *The Leech Woman*, *To Kill a Mockingbird*, *Kotch*, and *Body and Soul*.

Hammer, Stephen (b. 1944?) "Wally's Girl Trouble" (Third boy in library)

Had a few roles in the late 50s and early 60s, his last being Roger on *The Donna Reed Show* in 1962.

Hart, Gary (b. 1945-1947) "The Clubhouse" (Harold – Boy in Club)

Going by the credits he has on IMDB, he was in the above episode of *Leave it to Beaver*, but his scene must have been left on the cutting room floor. If his other credits are accurate, his short career included appearances on *Perry Mason* and he played one of the Beaver club members in *The Jack Benny Program* in his first acting gig. He is not the only actor on *Leave it to Beaver* to play a "beaver" on *The Jack Benny Program*. Frank Bank (Lumpy) was president of The Beavers in the *Jack Benny Program* on radio.

Hart, John (1917-2009) 3 episodes (Scoutmaster)

Appeared in three episodes of *Leave it to Beaver*. His first two episodes were, "Lonesome Beaver," in which he played the scoutmaster and "Beaver Plays Hooky," as a construction worker. His later role was as the forest ranger in "A Night in the Woods." Hart is probably best known for his work as the Lone Ranger, replacing Clayton Moore in 1952 after a salary dispute.

Harvey, Harry (1901-1985) "Summer in Alaska" (Captain Drake)

Harry Harvey is probably the only actor on *Leave it to Beaver* to be born in what was then called "Indian Territory," the present-day state of Oklahoma. His entertainment career began in music when he played with "Gus Hill's Honey Boy Minstrels" in 1918. His work in music led to parts on Broadway and he later moved on to Hollywood, beginning his career there in 1934. His career was filled with small character parts, but on occasion, among his almost 500 acting credits, he did have recurring roles such as his role of Sheriff Blodgett on *The Roy Rogers Show* and as Mayor George Dixon on *Man Without a Gun*.

Hatton, Raymond (1887-1971) "The Clubhouse" (Charlie the Fireman)

It's almost unreal to think about an actor entering the movie business in 1909, but that's what Pete the Fireman from *Leave it to Beaver* did. He was only in one episode of *Leave it to Beaver*, "The Clubhouse." Hatton appeared in approximately 300 silent films and "B" movies from 1909-1950 before turning to the new medium of television. His last appearance was in the film, *In Cold Blood* in which he played an elderly hitchhiker.

Hawkins, Jimmy (b. 1941) "Wally and Dudley" (Dudley McMillan)

A microscopic part of Jimmy Hawkins' career was his portrayal of Dudley McMillan on *Leave it to Beaver*. However, the story of his Hollywood life could take up the entirety of a book, all by itself. Following his brother into acting, Jimmy's mother took him on his first interview to MGM when he was two and a half years old. He got a part on Spencer Tracy's film, *The Seventh Cross*. During a break in filming, the assistant director walked over to Jimmy's mother to tell her MGM was filming a Lana Turner movie on the next stage and said they were having a difficult time finding a young boy to play her son and said that Jimmy would be perfect. Jimmy's first two roles were back-to-back, beginning work on *Marriage is a Private Affair*, playing Lana Turner's son as soon as his work on the Spencer Tracy film ended.

A couple years later, Jimmy played the role of Jimmy Stewart's son Tommy in the film, *It's a Wonderful Life*. One of his most cherished roles, he has done much charity work related to the film. This work has involved going into Attica prison in New York to show the film to prisoners and having a Q&A discussion afterward, making sure it was played in all ninet-four state prisons in New York on the film's 75th anniversary, or working with the *It's a Wonderful Life* Museum in Seneca Falls. Jimmy Hawkins, since his earliest days in Hollywood, has always been a very charitable person, many times doing charitable events for the archdiocese of Los Angles with his horse Pixie from the show *Annie Oakley*.[177]

Jimmy's connection to producers and writers Joe Connelly and Bob Mosher began before his work on their production, *Leave it to Beaver* and his later work on their show, *Ichabod and Me*. He first appeared on their situation comedy *Bringing Up Buddy* as the character Fennimore Cooper. After working with Jimmy, Connelly and Mosher wanted to continue their relationship and wrote an episode of *Leave it to Beaver* specifically with him in mind. This was for the role of Dudley on the "Wally and Dudley" episode. They filmed that episode when his schedule was clear, and he fit the role perfectly. He mentioned in a 2022 interview that his role as Dudley wasn't the only time he played an unpopular guy. He also did so in the shows *Margie* and *Petticoat Junction*. In quite a few of his roles, he was either "the dreamboat who anchored in the harbor of love on the show for the girl," or a guy like Dudley, who's out of step with the popular set.

When working on *Leave it to Beaver*, Jimmy was familiar with Ken Osmond since he had worked on an episode of *Annie Oakley* with him a few years earlier. Jimmy said it was fun doing *Leave it to Beaver*, but he was the stranger on the set and was just there to do his magic. The actors were all very professional and he admitted it was an honor to have the producers write a part for him based on his previous work they had admired. He was also very complimentary about Hugh Beaumont, who directed the episode. "Hugh did a real good job. No strain. Nothing difficult. If I said, 'Can we try that again?' he said, 'Oh yeah sure.' He was very nice, very obliging. He set up his shots very well."[178]

A few other interesting notes about Jimmy include a meeting he had with Sherwood Schwartz a few years after Gilligan's Island had been on the air. Schwartz told Jimmy he had tried buying him out of his contract with another studio so he could play Gilligan. Jimmy also filmed a pilot for the *Andy Hardy* TV show which was picked up by NBC, but never aired because of their insistence it air in a timeslot to which the producers objected. That show was to co-star Pamela Beaird (Mary Ellen Rogers). He also was a friend of actor Buck Taylor from Gunsmoke fame, who

---

[177] Interview with author in August 2022.
[178] Ibid.

he knew from his time on *The Adventures of Ozzie and Harriet*. He confessed that Buck tried to teach him how to bounce on the trampoline using the gymnastic moves that Buck could perform. Jimmy said he was no good at the trampoline but said, "I could jump a horse through a ring of fire,"[179] something he did twice a day when he went out on tour with his horse Pixie at county fairs and other events.

Jimmy has been a recognizable name in Hollywood since the 1940s and still is today. In addition to being an actor, he's also worked behind the scenes as a producer, and is the author of multiple books. Until reading this bio, many *Leave it to Beaver* fans only knew Jimmy as the squarish or nerdish character of Dudley, but now you know him for so much more.

Herron, Randy (1942-1986) "Wally and the Fraternity" (Barry)

The only role in Herron's acting career was this one on *Leave it to Beaver*.

Hewitt, Alan (1915-1986) "Mistaken Identity" (Lieutenant Barnes)

After working on Broadway from the 1930s to the early 1950s, Hewitt then turned to Hollywood to begin his career on the small and big screen. He is best known for his recurring role as Detective Brennan on *My Favorite Martian*. Over his career, he worked on over 100 TV shows and films.

Hickman, George (1906-1984) "Beaver Takes a Drive" (1st Man)

George Hickman had a rough and tumble life and that led to much work in westerns and multiple roles on *Rawhide* in the early 1960s. He began his career in Hollywood in 1925 and it ended in 1983, one year before his death. It is very likely that IMDB has a list of only some of the roles in which he appeared over the length of his career. The total amount is probably much higher than only fifty-two TV shows and films.

Hiestand, John (1907-1987) "Wally, the Lifeguard" (Mr. Burton)

We could all tell the way he barked candy when demonstrating to Wally how to do it, that John Hiestand had a great voice. His voice earned him a lot of work in Hollywood as an announcer or narrator in many TV shows and films. In fact, his last role was that of an announcer in *It's an Adventure, Charlie Brown*. He had success in animation with his voicing of the Weisenheimer character in the cartoon short *The Funny Company* in 1963, a cartoon that appeared on *Bozo's Circus* in Boston and probably in other markets too. Other shows in which he had either a recurring role or multiple roles included *Room for One More*, *Bachelor Father*, and *The Waltons*.

Hill, Rex (b. 1947 or 1948) "Beaver's Football Award" (Ronald)

After a few minor roles on TV, his final appearance on the screen was his moment in *Leave it to Beaver* in the hallway talking about the football awards banquet.

Hill, Stephanie (n/a) "One of the Boys" (Bessie)

She played a more advanced girl on *Leave it to Beaver* than Wally was used to dealing with. Her career only spanned from 1961-1967. She appeared twice on *The Adventures of Ozzie and Harriet* and twice on *Alfred Hitchcock Presents*.

---

[179] Interview with author in August 2022.

Hinton, Darcy (b.1951) "Pet Fair" (Alice)

As a child actor, Darcy Hinton only appeared in four television shows, *Sky King*, *Death Valley Days*, *Leave it to Beaver* and *Johnny Staccato*. After a fifteen-year hiatus, she then appeared twice on *Hawaii Five-O*. On *Leave it to Beaver,* in "Pet Fair," she is credited as playing Alice, but Miss Landers addresses actress Patty Turner as Alice in this episode.

Hokanson, Mary Alan (1916-1994) "Beaver's Monkey" (Luncheon Guest)

With over 100 credits to her name, she has only about ten percent of the number of acting roles as a fellow actress in the episode "Beaver's Monkey." Keep an eye out for that other actress in the following pages. Still, Hokanson was quite busy, and among her many credits are appearances in films with great titles like, *The Killer That Stalked New York*, *Strangers on a Train,* and *The Mob*. On TV, she appeared in *Public Defender*, *State Trooper* and *The D.A.'s Man*. She also had work on some very popular shows including *I Love Lucy*, *Alfred Hitchcock Presents*, *Maude*, and *Death Valley Days*.

Holcombe, Harry (1906-1987) "In the Soup" (Frank Whitney)

In the late 1970s, the actor who played Whitey's father, who some say looked more like a grandfather at the time, portrayed a grandpa in a series of Countrytime Lemonade TV commercials. In the 1960s, he had parts on some of the best television shows including *The Donna Reed Show*, *77 Sunset Strip*, *Surfside 6*, *The Andy Griffith Show*, *Perry Mason*, *Bewitched*, *Death Valley Days* and *Days of Our Lives*. He had one recurring role in *My Mother, the Car.* Holcombe also appeared in many films, among the best were *Birdman of Alcatraz*, *The Manchurian Candidate*, *King Kong vs. Godzilla*, *The Unsinkable Molly Brown* and *The Graduate*.

Holdridge, Cheryl (1944-2009) 8 episodes (Julie Foster / Gloria Cusick)

After taking dance lessons as a young child, she performed professionally in a New York City ballet production of *The Nutcracker.* Soon after arriving in Hollywood, Cheryl became a Mouseketeer, a job she held from 1956-1958. In addition to *Leave it to Beaver*, she also had roles on other popular 1960s sitcoms. Just a sample include *Bachelor Father*, *Dennis the Menace*, *The Donna Reed Show*, *The Dick Van Dyke Show*, and *My Three Sons*. In the 1980s, she reprised her role as Julie Foster on *The New Leave it to Beaver*.

Hole, Jonathan (1904-1998) "The Lost Watch" (Bank Teller)

An entertainer who began in Vaudeville, worked on the stage, moved to radio, and then to TV and film. He had over 200 acting credits and many TV shows in which he had multiple parts. Some of those shows included *Green Acres*, *Petticoat Junction*, *The Lucy Show*, *The Virginian*, *Perry Mason*, *Burke's Law*, *Dennis the Menace* and he had a recurring role on *The Andy Griffith Show*, playing Orville Monroe in season one.

Holmes, Dennis (b. 1950) "Beaver's Old Friend" (Friend #1)

In "Beaver's Old Friend," Dennis Holmes is the friend who leads a couple other boys in making fun of Beaver for playing with dolls. In this case, the doll was a Teddy Bear Beaver had rescued from the garbage can. Holmes continued acting until 1964 and is best known for his role as Mike Williams in *Laramie*.

Holmes, Wendell (1914-1962) 5 episodes (Multiple characters)

One of the few character actors on *Leave it to Beaver* who had a long career, but found his most regular work with the Beav. He appeared in a total of five episodes. He died in Paris France of a heart attack not long after finishing his last episode on *Leave it to Beaver*. He appeared in "Music Lesson," "Beaver's Hero," "Beaver and Andy," "Beaver's English Test," and "Farewell to Penny."

Howat, Clark (1918-2009) "Beaver's House Guest" (Uncle Dave)

Howat had two roles on *Leave it to Beaver*, his other role was as Mr. Barnes in "The Mustache." He appeared in over 160 TV shows and films during his career. He had multiple roles on Perry Mason, and also appeared on the reboot *The New Perry Mason* in 1973. He had recurring roles in *The Adventures of Dr. Fu Manchu*, *Harbor Command*, and in *Dragnet*, he played a police captain multiple times. Two of the characters he played in *Dragnet* appeared three times during the series and two of the characters appeared twice.

Hoyt, John (1905-1991) 3 episodes

A very talented actor, John Hoyt had parts in some very good movies such as *Blackboard Jungle* and *Spartacus*. He also has a distinction among character actors, at least of all those in season one of *Leave it to Beaver*, of playing multiple roles (at least two) on most of the television shows on which he worked. In *Leave it to Beaver*, Hoyt's roles were Dr. Compton in "Part-Time Genius," the clothier in "Wally's New Suit," and Mr. Franklin from the accordion company in "Beaver's Accordion." He had a resurgence in his career in the 1980s when he was tapped to play Grandpa Stanley Kanisky for seventy-eight episodes on *Gimme a Break*.

Huddle, Grace Wallis (1908-1980) "Beaver's Cat Problem" (Mrs. Prentiss)

Fans watching this episode of *Leave it to Beaver* can tell the actress who portrayed Mrs. Prentiss was not a novice. IMDB lists this appearance as her only acting credit. Who decides at age fifty to become an actress, goes to a casting call, gets hired, does her part and then quits acting? Most likely, no one. There's a possibility that she was a stage actress, but research has not brought any evidence to prove that assumption.

Hughes, Billy E. (1948-2005) "Beaver, the Sheep Dog" (Chuck)

His career spanned only a few years, with most of his roles occurring between 1961 – 1964. These included appearances on quite a few shows that only lasted one season. One of these was *Arrest and Trial* a show with a premise much like *Law & Order* but thirty years earlier than the Dave Wolf production. The others were *Our Man Higgins, Wide Country* and *The New Breed*. He also had parts in some very successful westerns including *Gunsmoke, Wagon Train* and *The Rifleman*. He died in Alma, Arkansas in 2005.

Hunley, Gary (b. 1948) "Beaver's Old Buddy" (Jackie Waters)

From 1954-1962, Gary Hunley acted in twenty-six TV shows and films. He had a short recurring role in *Sky King* as Mickey and played two different roles on *Wagon Train*. He played in a handful of films, the most memorable of them were *The Big Operator* starring Mickey Rooney, Mel Torme and Jim Backus and *The Legend of Tom Dooley* starring Michael Landon.

Hunt, William (??-??) "The Broken Window" (Grocer)

Hunt played a grocer in "The Broken Window," his only *Leave it to Beaver* episode. After *Leave it to Beaver*, he had a few roles in the 1960s and from 1964 to 1976 was absent from the small screen before returning to CBS for one shot roles in *One Day at a Time* and *All in the Family* in 1977.

Hunter, Henry (1907-1985) "Uncle Billy" (Sports Store Clerk)

Beginning his career in Hollywood in 1936, when he played "Doc" in the film *Nobody's Fool*, Henry Hunter continued to work regularly in films until 1939. After that, probably along with a stint in WW II, he returned to Hollywood with a role playing a doctor in the series *Navy Log*. Talk about typecasting, he also played doctors in *The Millionaire* (1955), *Medic* (1956), *Lux Video Theater* (1956-57), *General Electric Theater* (1957), *Whirlybirds* (1958), *Alcoa Theater* (1958), *Rescue 8* (1959), *Tales of Wells Fargo* (1959), *Playhouse 90* (1959), *State Trooper* (1959), *Wagon Train* (1960), *Laramie* (1960) and *The Ann Southern Show* (1960). Oh, there's more… Maybe that time off between 1939 and 1955 was used to go to medical school. Over the rest of his career, he played a doctor in eleven more television shows. He even had a recurring role as a doctor in *Hazel*. In *Leave it to Beaver*, he had three roles, the others were as Mr. Briggs in "Ward's Golf Clubs," and Mr. Thomas in "Beaver's Prep School."

Hunter, Barbara (b. 1948) "Beaver on TV" (Janet Lynch)

In her limited career, Barbara Hunter played parts in some of the 60s best shows, including *Lassie*, *Family Affair*, *Leave it to Beaver* and *Mister Ed*. She left acting in 1969 and in 1976 is shown on IMDB with having her first producer credit on *The Price is Right*. Those credits continued on *The Price is Right* through 1983.

Hyatt, Robert (1939-2007) "Wally Buys a Car" (Frank)

Early in his career, Hyatt appeared in films with some big names like Lucille Ball in *The Fuller Brush Girl*, Rosalind Russell in *Roughly Speaking* and William Holden in *The Dark Past*. He even performed in one film, *Caught*, in which Barbara Billingsley had a bit part. He had roles in three different films with actor Edmund Gwenn, *Miracle on 34th Street*, *Les Misérables*, and *Of Human Bondage*. He also appeared in the normal fare of television programs for child actors in the 1950s and 1960s like *Leave it to Beaver*, *Bachelor Father*, *Dennis the Menace*, and *Father Knows Best* and he had a recurring role in *The Pride of the Family* as Junior Morrison. He ventured into producing, writing and directing after his final acting role in *Combat!* in 1963.

I

Idelson, Bill (1919-2007) "The Bus Ride" (Newsstand Worker)

For *Dick Van Dyke Show* fans, Idelson is best known for his recurring role as Sally Roger's boyfriend. He played Herman Glimscher in four episodes on the show and later reprised his role in the TV Movie *The Dick Van Dyke Show Revisited* (2004). Idelson also had plenty of writing credits which began in 1961 with an episode of *The Twilight Zone*. As his writing continued in the 1960s, his credits included episodes of *The Dick Van Dyke Show*, *The Flintstones*, almost twenty episodes of *The Andy Griffith Show* between 1964-1967, over twenty episodes of *Gomer Pyle U.S.M.C.*, *The Odd Couple* and he finished off his writing career with two episodes of *Punky Brewster*. He was married to Seemah Wilder for fifty-six years, until his death in 2007.

Ivo, Tommy (b. 1936) "Blind Date Committee" (Duke Hathaway)

The next Shirley Temple? Well, that's how much execs at Republic thought of Ivo's tap dancing and singing skills at the age of three. That Shirley Temple prophecy didn't materialize, but it didn't stop him from having a fine career as a child actor. Before his role on *Leave it to Beaver*, Ivo acted in *Dragstrip Girl* in 1957. This was art imitating Tommy Ivo's life. He had become a drag racer a few years earlier and was known on the drag racing circuit as *TV Tommy Ivo*. He was sure to draw a crowd at every race. On *Leave it to Beaver*, if he looked older than Wally and the rest of Mayfield High students when he appeared in "Blind Date Committee" and "Wally's Play," it's because he was twenty-four years old at the time of his first *LITB* episode. Tommy never regretted walking away from his acting career and concentrating on racing. One of the main reasons his career in Hollywood ended was because insurance (in case he could not complete a film or TV project due to his racing) was either unavailable to him or cost prohibitive, making it more difficult to obtain work.

J

Jackman, Tom (b. 1946) "Wally's Track Meet" (Track Team Member)

A child actor for only one role, or rather, a teen actor, Jackman portrayed a track team member in an episode of *Leave it to Beaver* in 1961. He then did not act in any films or TV until 1978 when he reappeared in Hollywood in Disney's *The Cat from Outer Space*. Over the next two years, he acted in an independent film, another Disney film, *The Apple Dumpling Gang Rides Again*, and an episode of both *Starsky and Hutch*, and *B.J. and the Bear*. He then took another break from acting that lasted eight years until an appearance in the TV series *Starman*, followed by an appearance in *Hunter*, the next year. Again, another break from Hollywood occurred until 2020 when he portrayed presidential candidate Joe Biden in the short film *If I Were President* which featured poet rapper Prince Ea.

Jacobs, Johnny (1916-1982) "Beaver on TV" (Mr. Thornton)

Best known for his voice work, he was the announcer for multiple TV shows including *I Love Lucy* and *Full Circle*. He also appeared in various TV shows portraying an announcer, TV host, or news report and a few of those shows were *Ripcord*, *The Munsters* and *My Favorite Martian*.

Janssen, Berniece (1910-1985) "Beaver Plays Hooky" (Wife at Supermarket)

Miss Nebraska of 1928, Berniece Janssen became a Ziegfeld girl in New York City after leaving her native Nebraska. Later, moving to Los Angeles, she became an extra in TV and film during the 1950s and 1960s. Her son David Janssen is best known for his role in *The Fugitive*.

Jay, Helen (1925-1989) "The Perfume Salesmen" (Perfume customer)

After playing many uncredited and bit roles in "B" movies, including a few sci-fi films such as *The Space Children* and *Space Master X-7,* Jay Helen made it to the set of *Leave it to Beaver* in "The Perfume Salesmen," and "The Grass is Always Greener." Her regular work in Hollywood ended in 1965 with an appearance in the film *Looking for Love* starring Connie Francis.

Jillian, Ann (b. 1950) "Wally, the Businessman" (Little Girl)
In *Leave it to Beaver*, Ann Jillian played a child purchasing an Igloo bar from Wally as he made his rounds on his bike powered ice cream cart. After a career as a child actor, she successfully moved into voice work in the 1970s with *Sealab 2020*, *The New Scooby-Doo Movies*, and *Captain Caveman and the Teen Angels.* In the 1980s, Jillian began the decade with roles on *The Love Boat* and finished the decade with a self-titled TV series, *Ann Jillian*, playing the role of Ann McNeil. In between, she was the star of *It's a Living* on ABC. Even more important than her success as an actress, Jillian is a successful cancer survivor. Winning that battle was portrayed in *The Ann Jillian Story* TV movie in 1988.

Jones, Kevin (b. 1947 or 1948) "Long Distance Call" (1st Boy)

Jones appeared in three different episodes of *Leave it to Beaver*. The other episodes were "Beaver on TV" and "Uncle Billy's Visit." In his short career, he also acted in *The Twilight Zone*, *The Many Loves of Dobie Gillis*, *The Ann Southern Show* and *Death Valley Days* and in a few other programs.

Jordan, Chrystine (b. 1950) "The Late Edition" (Donna Yeager)

Appearing in two episodes of *Leave it to Beaver*, the other being, "More Blessed to Give," Chrystine had a short, but memorable career on the small screen. From 1962 to 1967, she appeared in two episodes of *Leave it to Beaver*, four episodes of *My Three Sons*, an episode of *Bob Hope Presents the Chrysler Theatre*, and one episode of *Perry Mason*. In addition to television, her first role ever was playing the title character of Ruth (as a child) in the movie *The Story of Ruth*. If not for a friend of her mother who was taking her child to an agent's office and asked the Jordan's to accompany them, Chrystine may have never become an actress. During the visit, the agent asked to sign her to a contact and some commercials soon followed and now, she's a part of *Leave it to Beaver* history as the girl who almost had a "trauma" because her father in "More Blessed to Give" made her return the gold locket Beaver gave her as a gift. Fast forward to 2011 and Chrystine appeared on an episode of *Paula's Best Dishes* with Paula Deen. I think we can assume Chrystine is an amazing cook.

K

Kane, Sid (1911-1987) "Beaver, the Bunny" (1st Man)

In the 1950s, Kane acted in *The Great Gildersleeve* TV series and *The Jack Benny Program* TV series. Kane also had a role in Elvis' movie *Jailhouse Rock*. He played a waiter on *The Lucy Show* and a Maitre d' on *The Adventures of Ozzie and Harriet*. His last role was as a wedding guest on *Moonlighting* in 1986.

Karr, Raymond (b. 1946) "My Brother's Girl" (Boy)

Karr only appeared in two television shows in his career. He appeared in "My Brother's Girl" credited as "boy." His only other TV show appearance was in *The Real McCoys*, a year after Beaver.

Kearns, Joseph (1907-1962) "It's a Small World" (Mr. Crowley)

Playing the role of Mr. Crowley in the pilot episode "It's a Small World," Kearns did not appear in any other *Leave it to Beaver* episodes. He worked on many 1950s television shows including *The Burns and Allen Show*, *The Jack Benny Program* and *Gunsmoke*, but is best known for his work as Mr. Wilson on *Dennis the Menace*. He was also a well know Old Time Radio actor, best known for his work on *Sherlock Holmes*. He also appeared along with Barbara Billingsley on the short-lived TV series, *Professional Father* in 1955. Joseph Kearns died of a cerebral hemorrhage in Los Angeles on February 17, 1962.

Kelk, Jackie (1923-2002) "The Paper Route" (Old Man Merkel)

Who could forget Old Man Merkel? He was the boy's boss in the episode, "The Paper Route." Jackie Kelk had moderate success on TV. However, he was a great radio actor and for years, portrayed Henry Aldrich's best friend Homer Brown on *The Aldrich Family*. After *Leave it to Beaver*, his last two TV appearances were on *Bachelor Father* and *The Donna Reed Show*.

Kellogg, Ray (1919-1981) "Cat Out of the Bag" (Mr. Donaldson); "Beaver's Old Buddy" (Mr. Waters)

Best known for two shows on which he worked quite regularly, *The Life and Legend of Wyatt Earp* and *The Red Skelton Comedy Hour*, Ray Kellogg also appeared on two *Leave it to Beaver* episodes. He played Mr. Donaldson in "Cat Out of the Bag," the last episode in season one where he replaced Charles H. Gray who originally played Mr. Donaldson earlier in the season. He later played Mr. Waters in "Beaver's Old Buddy."

Kendis, William (1916-1980) "The State Versus Beaver" (Charlie - Police Officer)

How could anyone give a traffic ticket to sweet, little, adorable Beaver Cleaver? It was easy for William Kendis in his role as police officer Charlie in the episode "The State vs. Beaver." Kendis broke into television with a bang, making his debut on the crime drama *Dragnet* in 1956. He worked steadily until 1961 with appearances in *The Twilight Zone*, *The Rifleman*, *Perry Mason* and many other shows.

Kent, David (b. 1944 or 1945) "Weekend Invitation" (Scott)

His first appearance on *Leave it to Beaver* had him playing the part of Scott which later morphed into Bill Scott in his three subsequent appearances in "Beaver's Long Night," "Beaver's Fear," and "Eddie Quits School." Most of his acting credits occurred between 1960-1964. His final two credits were in 1969 and 1978 and both were films starring Lee Majors, *The Ballad of Andy Crocker* and *The Norseman*.

Kerlee, Dennis (b. 1945) "Wally's Election" (Tall Sophomore)

Short career spanning four years and five roles. Best known for multiple roles on *Bachelor Father*.

Kingston, Lenore (1913-1993) "In the Soup" (Mrs. Whitney)

Appeared in two episodes of *Leave it to Beaver* and given credit for being in a third. The episodes were "Beaver's Big Contest" (credit only), "The School Picture" (Mrs. Bruce) and "In the Soup" (Mrs. Whitney). She had roles in some of the more popular comedies of the 1960s including *Petticoat Junction*, *The Beverly Hillbillies* and *My Three Sons*.

Kirkpatrick, Jess(e) (1897-1976) 6 episodes (Multiple characters)

He appeared in "Beaver's Old Friend" (Garbage Man), "The Grass is Always Greener" (Henry Fletcher), "Beaver Finds a Wallet" (Police Sergeant), "Chuckie's New Shoes" (Salesman), "The Big Fish Count" (Mr. Parker), and "Wally Buys a Car" (Mr. Nelson). If only Jess Kirkpatrick had been in a *Leave it to Beaver* episode in season five, he would've been on the show at least once in every season. His final television appearance, out of his total of 169, was on *Mayberry R.F.D.* in 1969.

Koff, Robert (b. 1943) "The Mustache" Wayne Gregory

Like many *Leave it to Beaver* actors, Koff also appeared on *Perry Mason*. However, that was his only other acting credit in a career that spanned months during 1963.

Kristen, Marta (b. 1945) "Wally and Dudley" Christine Staples

The Hungarian born Marta Kristen played her part on *Leave it to Beaver* quite well, which shows she was a talented actress since it was only her second role. After *Beaver*, Kristen went on to play parts in *Alfred Hitchcock Presents*, *Dr. Kildare*, *Mr. Novak* and *My Three Sons* before earning a co-starring role on *Lost in Space*, playing Judy Robinson. She has acted in many quality TV shows, even into the 1980s, including *Remington Steele*, *Fame*, *Trapper John M.D.*, *Scarecrow and Mrs. King* and *Murphy Brown*. She played a reporter in the movie remake of *Lost in Space* (1998).

L

Lane, Richard (1899-1982) "Beaver Plays Hooky" (Marshal Moran)

Richard Lane had almost 200 acting credits and of them, only three were TV roles. One of those was on the show *Crossroads*, the others are two, Mosher / Connelly creations, *Leave it to Beaver* and *The Munsters*. In television, he also appeared on the premiere of KTLA, the first TV station west of the Mississippi in 1947.

Langton, Paul (1913-1980) "More Blessed to Give" (Bob Yeager)

His resume proves that Paul Langton was a fine actor from the moment he was seen on the big screen in *We've Never Been Licked*, a WW II film which featured a young Robert Mitchum. His first five films were all WW II themed and of them, the most popular was *Thirty Seconds Over Tokyo* starring Spencer Tracy and Van Johnson. One year after his role on *LITB*, he was hired to play the character of Leslie Harrington in *Peyton Place*. He appeared in over 200 episodes of *Peyton Place* and became a household name. He acted only a few more years after *Peyton Place*, his last role coming on *Emergency!* in 1972.

LaTourette, Leslie (b. 1949) "Beaver, the Sheep Dog" (1ˢᵗ Girl)

Her acting career lasted the two episodes in which she appeared with Jerry Mathers. Leslie also appeared on "Beaver, the Hero" as one of the many who told Beaver how amazing he was for catching a touchdown.

Lawrence, Karen (b. 1945) "The Mustache" (2nd Girl)

Had a very short career which spanned three TV shows and two years. She also appeared on an episode of *My Three Sons* and the daytime soap *Paradise Bay*.

Lawrence, Mary (1918-1991) "Forgotten Party" (Alice Manning)

Before her appearance as David Manning's mother on *Leave it to Beaver*, Mary Lawrence was a well-respected actress with notable recurring roles on both *Casey Jones* and *The Bob Cummings Show*. Outside of acting, she authored two books on art, and founded a philanthropic group in Los Angeles called "The Colleagues."

Leavitt, Norman (1913-2005) "Beaver's Monkey" (Veterinarian)

Leavitt's first screen credit was the opportunity of a lifetime for a guy from Lansing Michigan. He played a small part as a cowboy in the gay and lusty musical romance from MGM, *The Harvey Girls*. The film starred Judy Garland and also included Ray Bolger, Angela Lansbury and Cyd Charisse. He went on to have roles in much bigger films such as *The Ten Commandments*, *Harvey* and *Friendly Persuasion*. In television, he had recurring roles in *Trackdown* and *Mayberry R.F.D.* and multiple appearances on *The Andy Griffith Show*.

Lee, Joanna (1931-2003) "Beaver and Poncho" (Classified Ads Clerk)

From 1956 to 1961, Joanna Lee was an aspiring actress. Beginning in 1961, she tried her hand at the other side of the TV camera and became a writer. She concentrated her efforts on animated fare when she began, writing shows for *Top Cat*, *The Jetsons*, *Mr. Magoo* and *The Flintstones* in the first half of the 1960s. She later wrote for sitcoms and dramas, winning a Primetime Emmy for her writing on *The Waltons*.

Leeds, Peter (1917-1996) "Beaver's Prize" (Theater Manager)

A popular character actor with over 250 acting credits, he also appeared with Bob Hope on numerous USO tours. He performed in many of the best 1960s TV shows but continued working into the 1970s and 1980s with appearances on *The Jeffersons*, *Hawaii Five-O*, *Chico and the Man*, *Riptide* and *Silver Spoons*. He also did voice work for animated shows like *Honk Kong Phooey*, *The Dukes*, and *The New Yogi Bear Show*.

Lewis, Buddy (1916-1986) "More Blessed to Give" (The Pitchman)

Didn't start acting in Hollywood until his early 40s. It didn't take long until he became an in-demand actor which led him to having multiple roles on shows like *The Dick Powell Theater, The Joey Bishop Show, Burke's Law, The Red Skelton Hour* and *Here's Lucy.*

Lewis, Louise (1914-1996) "Wally's Girl Trouble (Miss Higgins)

A very talented character actor who had her best success in the early 1970s drama *Medical Center*, Louise Lewis (Fitch) made only one appearance on the original *Leave it to Beaver* series. Lewis also holds the distinction of being only one of three actors from season one to appear in *The New Leave it to Beaver* who did not have a recurring role in the original Beaver series, the others being William Schallert and Lyle Talbot.

Loos, Anne (1915-1986) "Beaver's Ring" (Nurse Thompson)

Her first big screen appearance was in *Hitler's Children*, an expose about the Hitler Youth. She had many other "B" movies in the 1940s before moving into the new medium of TV. One of those movies was the film, *Leave it to Blondie*, which is rumored to be the inspiration for the name *Leave it to Beaver*. She had a regular role on *Mr. Novak* as Mrs. Danfield and a semi-regular role on *Days of Our Lives* in 1966.

Lowell, Linda (b. 1945) "My Brother's Girl" (Frances).

In *There's No Business Like Show Business*, Linda Lowell played eight-year-old Katy (the adult Katy was played by Mitzi Gaynor). Working in the same film as Ethel Merman and Marylin Monroe must have been exciting for Lowell and especially for her parents. The future was bright as this was only her third role in Hollywood. Four years later, she made her final small screen appearance in *Leave it to Beaver*.

Lunsford, Beverly (1945-2019) "Wally's License" (Shirley Fletcher)

She appeared in two episodes of *Leave it to Beaver*, once as his nemesis in driving school, and the other is "Wally's Car Accident" in which she goes to the prom with him. IMDB has her listed as playing the same character in each. Guess he no longer found her an annoyance. During her short career, she also appeared in *The World of Mr. Sweeny, National Velvet, My Three Sons* (her final acting credit) and a few other shows.

Lyon, Don (b. 1949) "The Grass is Always Greener" (Chris Fletcher)

Other than this episode of *Leave it to Beaver*, his only other acting credit was for the teen exploitation film *Party Crashers* in 1958.

Lynn, Jennie (b. 1952) "The Big Fish Count" (Sally Ann Maddox)

She appeared in four different episodes of *Leave it to Beaver*, in addition to the above episode, they were "Beaver's Doll Buggy," "Substitute Father," and "Beaver, the Babysitter." Her life as an innocent child actor took a big turn in a different direction after appearing on an episode of *My Three Sons*. After that appearance, she took a five-year break from Hollywood and then made a couple movies that were probably filmed in the valley, and in one, she played a character named "Sin."

Lytle, Sandra (b. 1945) "Wally's Orchid" (Judy)

Born in Los Angeles, the career of Sandra Lytle was very short, one could say momentary. After Eddie Haskell asks to speak with her character away from her friend Myra, she walks away with Eddie and is never seen again … ever.

M

Mahoney, Mike (1918-1988) "Beaver's Doll Buggy" (Man in the Street)

Working hard to make it into Hollywood, then getting a scene filmed and it winds up on the cutting room floor, happens a lot. But for it to happen and be listed as your first film credit, has got to be frustrating. This happened to Mike Mahoney when he thought he was going to appear in *The Babe Ruth Story*. But all was made up for when the following year he appeared in (albeit in uncredited roles) *I Was a Male War Bride* starring Cary Grant and *Twelve O'Clock High* starring Gregory Peck. Mahoney went on to amass over 100 acting credits over his next twenty-nine years in Hollywood. Most of his roles were in films, but he did round out his career with a few TV roles including parts in *Room 222*, *Ironside* and *Alias Smith and Jones*.

Malloy, Jeff (1934-1984) "Wally and the Fraternity" (Chuck Bradford)

Of his eleven acting credits, only his *Leave it to Beaver* appearance and one on *McHale's Navy* were in situation comedies. He later pursued a career in dance and ended up dancing in the Ginger Rogers Revue and later, he danced with Connie Stevens and Ann Miller. He retired from dancing in 1981 and moved to Las Vegas where he narrated shows at a few Vegas hotels, did some work in commercials and wrote for movie magazines. His obituary lists his name as Jackie Wess "Jeff" Parker.

Mann, Jack (1920-1993) "In the Soup" (Fireman)

In 1958, he appeared in the film *No Time for Sergeants* starring Andy Griffith. In 1960, he appeared in *The Andy Griffith Show* episode, "Andy the Matchmaker." His biggest claim to fame, may be rescuing Beaver from the steaming bowl of soup.

Mansfield, Rankin (1895-1969) "Beaver's Accordion" (Express-agency Clerk)

Mr. Mansfield began his career in Hollywood much later in life than most actors. His first role came when he was fifty-four years old. However, he was there to appear in one of the earliest television shows when he appeared in the late 1940s courtroom drama, *Your Witness* (1949). He later had roles in the films *To Hell and Back*, starring Audie Murphy, *A Summer Place*, starring Sandra Dee, and *The Manchurian Candidate*. He also had parts in numerous westerns including *The Cisco Kid*, *Sugarfoot* and *Cheyenne*.

Manson, Maurice (1913-2002) "Beaver Takes a Drive" (Judge Morton)

During the 1950s, Manson had roles on many television shows which did not run more than one or two seasons, many of which have been forgotten by the public. Among such shows were *Wire Service*, *The Adventures of McGraw*, *Official Detective*, *The Court of Last Resort*, *How to Marry a Millionaire*, *Cool and Lam* (pilot) and *Frontier Doctor*. However, once the 1960s arrived, so did his appearances in many of that decade's most popular TV shows. This included roles in *The Real McCoys*, *The Donna Reed Show*, *The Adventures of Ozzie and Harriet*, *77 Sunset Strip*, *Bachelor Father*, *Hazel*, *Perry Mason* and *My Three Sons*.

Marr, Eddie (1900-1987) 6 episodes (Multiple characters)

Marr was probably most famous for asking Jack Benny, on his February 8, 1948 radio program the question, "Your money or your life?" That is one of the most famous questions asked in any entertainment medium. His most regular TV work occurred on *Lux Video Theater*, *Leave it to Beaver* and *The Bob Hope Show* (his last appearance on TV, April 1971).

Marshall, Susan (b. 1947) "Her Idol" (Third Grade Girl)

After her performance in the movie *Burlesque in Hawaii* as a five-year-old, she graduated to something more age appropriate when appearing on *Leave it to Beaver* as an extra in Miss Landers' classroom. This was her final acting job in her short career.

Martin, Lori (1947-2010) "Beaver Sees America" (Mary Margaret)

She became famous for her role in the TV show *National Velvet*. She was chosen for the role over almost 1000 other young girls. This led to a film role in *Cape Fear* starring Gregory Peck and Robert Mitchum. After *Leave it to Beaver*, she continued to act a few more years, finding parts in *Please, Don't Eat the Daisies*, *Family Affair*, *My Three Sons* and her final role was as Sally Reid in *Days of Our Lives* in 1974. Actor Rich Correll has spoken about the massive crush he had on her during his interviews with TV historian and broadcaster Stu Shostak.

Masters, Tom (b. 1944 or 1945) "Borrowed Boat" (Fred Thornton)

Although he had a short career in Hollywood, Masters worked on some very good TV programs. These shows include *Dragnet*, *Zane Grey Theater* and *My Three Sons*. His *My Three Sons* appearances came after a four-year hiatus from acting. Just an assumption, but this could have been him returning to act after high school.

Matheson, Tim (b. 1947) "Tell it to Ella" (Michael)

A man who has worn many different Hollywood hats, that's Tim Matheson. He began his career as a child actor, working on Robert Young's series *Window on Main Street* in 1961. His next role was on *Leave it to Beaver* where he admits he was a bit star-struck meeting Jerry Mathers. He's never stopped acting; he currently portrays Dr. Vernon Mullins on the Netflix series *Virgin River*. Matheson began directing regularly in 1994 with the movie *Breach of Conduct*. His most recent directorial work was on four episodes of *Virgin River*. He put on the producer hat beginning in 1988 with *Just in Time* and produced eleven episodes of *Cold Case* in 2004-2005. Tim Matheson has done it all in Hollywood and viewers everywhere have been the benefactors of his talent.

McCaffrie, Pat (1919-1992) "Wally Goes Steady" (Bill Boothby)

A regular on *Bachelor Father*, he played Chuck Forrest in fourteen episodes. He also had a recurring role on *Outlaws*, playing Dr. Edgar Harris. He played multiple roles on *The Adventures of Ozzie and Harriet* and on *The Munsters* too. On *Leave it to Beaver*, he also had a role in the episode, "Lumpy's Car Trouble."

McGuire, Harp (1921-1966) "The Credit Card" (The Attendant)

Worked in Australia on radio in the mid-1950s, typically on Australian adaptations of American radio shows. He moved into films when he appeared as Mannix in *Captain Thunderbolt*. This movie and his next two were filmed in Australia. He then moved back to his native America and became a regular in Hollywood. He worked continually in TV and movies from 1960 to 1963, appearing in nineteen more roles in only three years. However, his appearance on *Leave it to Beaver* was his final role and he died three years later of coronary artery disease at the young age of forty-four.

McKee, John (1916-2013) "Beaver, the Bunny" (Policeman)

With over 160 acting credits on a resume, one can assume there would be some quality films among them. That's the case with John McKee. Some of the great films he had the opportunity to work on include *Twelve O'Clock High*, *The Gunfighter*, *The Wrong Man*, *The Spirit of St. Louis*, *Pork Chop Hill*, *Elmer Gantry*, *Cape Fear*, *Rio Lobo* and *MacArthur*. Like most other adult actors in *Leave it to Beaver* with at least 100 acting credits, he too played in multiple episodes of *Perry Mason*. Other TV shows in which he appeared include *Bourbon Street Beat*, *Laramie*, *Wagon Train*, *Lancer*, *McMillan and Wife* and *Quincy M.E.*

McNear, Howard (1905-1969) "The Shave" (Andy the Barber)

He began his career in Vaudeville, added radio to his repertoire, working on the original radio broadcast of *Gunsmoke*, worked in many films and had a recurring role on *The George Burns and Gracie Allen Show*. After he gave a shave to Wally on *Leave it to Beaver* in 1958, he appeared in many more shows, before landing his role as a barber named Floyd on *The Andy Griffith Show*. He spent six years on that program, acting in eighty episodes. He did this, despite suffering a massive stroke during his third season on the show. He did come back afterward, but his scenes then had him usually sitting outside his barber shop on a bench. Howard McNear passed away in 1969, two years after the end of *The Andy Griffith Show*.

Mercer, Frances (1915-2000) "Beaver's Autobiography (Mrs. Carter)

As a teenager, Frances Mercer worked as a model for John Robert Powers' modeling agency in New York. From there, she acted on stage and in radio. Had a recurring role as Nurse Ann Talbot on *Dr. Hudson's Secret Journal*, a syndicated medical drama. One of her last roles was in *Leave it to Beaver*. After retiring from the acting profession, she held down various jobs which included a bank teller, medical assistant and antiques dealer.

Meriwether, Lee (b. 1935) "Community Chest" (Young Woman Neighbor)

After acting for over ten years in Hollywood, her big break occurred with two different roles in 1966. At about the same time, she played Catwoman in the *Batman: The Movie* and its subsequent series and she also portrayed Dr. Ann MacGregor for the entire thirty episode run of *Time Tunnel*, beginning in 1966. Her two other biggest TV roles were playing Betty Jones in the crime drama *Barnaby Jones* and her role of Lilly Munster in *The Munsters Today*. Meriwether has remained active in Hollywood almost up to the present day, her last credit being the 2019 film, *Love and Debt*.

Michaels, Toby (b. 1940) "Beaver's Electric Trains" (Georgia Battson)

A majority of her career occurred between 1959 and 1963. The daughter of a costume designer on *Batman* and several previous productions, Toby was around Hollywood even before she began acting on the small and big screen. She acted in multiple episodes of *The Adventures of Ozzie and Harriet* and after taking a nine-year hiatus from Hollywood, came back in 1972 and filmed one final role on *Bonanza* in 1972.

Miller, Cheryl (b. 1943) "The Party Spoiler" (Helen)

Starting off like many other young actresses, she made the rounds of the popular sitcoms and dramas of the late 1950s and early 1960s with appearances in *Bachelor Father*, *Perry Mason*, *Leave it to Beaver* and *My Three Sons*. Her career lasted until 1980 and was most popular for her role as Paula Tracy in the drama *Daktari* which ran from 1966-1969.

Mitchel, Mary (b. 1940) "Wally Goes Steady" (Evelyn Boothby)

She appeared in two episodes of *Leave it to Beaver*, the other being "Wally's Chauffeur." Acting while a student at UCLA, she acquired an agent and soon after, began work in the early 1960s on television. Her role as Evelyn Boothby was her first in TV. Her career in front of the camera continued until 1967. She remained active in film and TV behind the scenes, working in various capacities through the 2000s, including as a script supervisor on the films *Dracula*, *8 Heads in a Duffel Bag*, *Scary Movie 4* and *The Mask of Zorro*.

Mitchell, Robert (n/a) "Beaver Plays Hooky" (Husband at Supermarket)

Other than this episode of *Leave it to Beaver*, Mitchell acted in one other production, a movie in 1956, titled *Full of Life*. These credits make up the sum of his acting career.

Mitchell, Shirley (1919-2013) "Child Care" (Janet Wilson)

It's debatable whether Shirley Mitchell was best known for her work on radio or television. On radio, she worked on *Suspense*; *Fibber McGee & Molly*; *The Great Gildersleeve* as Leila Ransom (her best-known part); *Amos 'n' Andy* and *My Favorite Husband*. On *My Favorite Husband*, she struck up a friendship with Lucille Ball. She later guest starred on *I Love Lucy* as Marion Strong. She acted in a plethora of good TV comedies, but none of her TV roles lasted as long as her role as that Southern Belle Leila on *The Great Gildersleeve*. At age eighty-six, Mitchell lent her voice to a *Desperate Housewives* video game. Her second husband was Jay Livingston, the man who wrote the lyrics to "This is It," the theme song for *The Bugs Bunny Show* series.

Montgomery, Ralph (1911-1980) "Beaver, the Caddy" (The Caddy Master)

From *Henry Aldrich Plays Cupid* to *Helter Skelter*, the films in which actor Ralph Montgomery worked were quite varied. In his long career he appeared in about 250 different films and TV shows. His TV show appearances included *I Love Lucy*, *I Led 3 Lives* and *The Adventures of Ozzie and Harriet* in the 1950s. The following decade they included *The Addams Family*, and *Bonanza*. In the 1970s he worked on *The Brady Bunch*, *McCloud* and his final role came in *Salvage I* which starred Andy Griffith.

Montgomery, Ray (1922-1998) "Child Care" (Herb Wilson); "Long Distance Call" (Kenny's Father)

Life imitates art sometimes and Ray Montgomery is an example of it. He broke into films after signing with Warner Brothers in 1941, just before America entered World War II. His first few films included *Action in the North Atlantic*, *Air Force*, *Captains of the Clouds* and *You're in the Army Now*. In 1943, Montgomery himself entered the armed services, taking a three-year break from Hollywood. Upon his return from the armed forces, he began his career over, playing small roles on TV through his final appearance on NBC's *Hunter* in 1990.

Moore, Candy (b. 1947) "Mother's Helper" (Margie Manners)

Best known for her role as Lucille Ball's daughter, Chris Carmichael, in *The Lucy Show*, she also played multiple roles on *The Donna Reed Show*. Except for a couple movie roles in the early 1980s, her career in Hollywood ended in 1966. There are some differing accounts about whether she is the same actress who appeared in *Lunch Wagon* in 1981. Reports by some sources say she is also the model who appeared on the Candy-O album cover from The Cars release in 1979. While still circulating in some places on the internet, a reference to this bit of trivia was removed from her IMDB profile page during the summer of 2022. In November 2022, The Cars drummer David Robinson confirmed that she was not the model for their album cover.[180]

Morrow, Brad (1942-1997) "Beaver Takes a Drive" (The Boy)

Morrow worked on two episodes of *Leave it to Beaver*, the other being "Wally's Chauffeur." Way before his work on the small screen, his acting career began on Broadway when he was only two years old. He was later signed by MGM and worked in many of their films including *Annie Get Your Gun*, *The Wild North*, *Cause for Alarm!*, *The Skipper Surprised His Wife* and *The Girl in White*. He went on to play Louie on *The Adventures of Spin and Marty* and had a couple roles on *Buffalo Bill Jr.*, *Adventures of Wild Bill Hickok*, and *The Lone Ranger*. After *Leave it to Beaver,* he only had a few more credits including *Rawhide*, *Wagon Train* and *Son of Flubber*. After Hollywood, he entered the world of business management and eventually became president of CII Premium Finance in Burbank.

Morrow, Patricia (b. 1944) "The All-Night Party" (The 1st Girl)

For fans of Cold War TV shows and movies, some may instantly recognize Patricia Morrow from her IMDB profile picture. She played Connie, the daughter of Herbert Philbrick in *I Led 3 Lives*. After her appearance in *Leave it to Beaver*, she found much success with the role of Rita Harrington in *Peyton Place*, portraying her in 378 episodes. She later reprised that role in two *Peyton Place* movies, one in 1972 and the other in 1985.

Morton, Judee (b. 1940) "Wally's Big Date" (Marjorie Muller)

After going on a date with Eddie Haskell in her second acting role, her career in Hollywood could only go up from there. After *Leave it to Beaver*, Judee Morton acted in *Lassie*, *My Three Sons*, *The Twilight Zone*, *Perry Mason*, *Bonanza*, *Petticoat Junction*, *The Fugitive*, and on multiple roles in *The F.B.I.*, her final role before her acting credits became more sporadic and she spent time raising

---

[180] Author interview with David Robinson in November 2022.

her family. She returned to more active acting in 1999 with a recurring role on *General Hospital*. Her last role was in the "Brave Heart" episode of *House*.

Mountford, Diane (b. 1947) "Double Date" (Susan)

Had a very active career in Hollywood between 1958 and 1971. Not long after beginning work in Hollywood, she obtained a recurring role on *Assignment: Underwater* as the daughter of actor Bill Williams. She also appeared in the 1960s situation comedies, *My Three Sons* and *Family Affair*. Her final appearance was on a comedy titled, *The Smith Family*, starring Henry Fonda and Ron Howard.

Murray, Mark (b. 1947 or 1948) "Sweatshirt Monsters" (Alan Boothby)

Murray appeared in three episodes of *Leave it to Beaver*, the other episodes were, *A Night in the Woods* and *Long Distance Call*. His career as a child actor was short, but he did appear in eight shows and every one of them was a popular series in the 60s. Here is the entire list: *Beaver, Dennis the Menace, Dr. Kildare, My Three Sons, Perry Mason, The Alfred Hitchcock Hour, Lassie* and *Gunsmoke*. Mr. Murray seems to have had a very good agent or he had very discerning taste and turned down many roles.

N

Neumann, Dorothy (1914-1994) "Community Chest" (Older Woman Neighbor)

Before her acting career in Hollywood, Neumann was a graduate of Carnegie Tech and the Yale Drama School. She also wrote a children's book titled *Come Meet the Clowns*, which was published in 1941. Her long-acting career which began in 1944 and lasted until 1991. She is one of only a few actors to have roles on both *Adam-12* and *The New Adam-12*. She had multiple roles on quite a few shows, including *The Red Skelton Hour, Gunsmoke, Bonanza* and *Dr. Kildare*. She also had a recurring role on the situation comedy *Hank*.

Newell, William (1894-1967) "Beaver's Birthday (The Postal Clerk)

When looking at the prolific careers of many actors, the question that arises naturally, how did he work in twenty movies in this year or that year? That's what could be asked about Billy Newell's output in the 1930s and the 1940s. After twenty-two years in films, his first TV appearance was on *My Little Margie* in 1952. He appeared on *The Ray Milland Show*, a series produced and created by Connelly and Mosher. That show also used the same house on the Republic Studios back lot as was used the first two seasons of *Leave it to Beaver*. After appearing on *Leave it to Beaver*, he only had a few more acting jobs and those included parts on *The Andy Griffith Show, The Beverly Hillbillies* and *Gomer Pyle U.S.M.C.*, his final role in 1965.

Newton, Theodore (1904-1963) "Beaver's Library Book" (Mr. Davenport)

Was prolific on the stage, performing in two long lasting Broadway plays that each had two-year runs. These were *Dead End* and *The Man Who Came to Dinner*. In Hollywood, he played second leads for Warner Brothers and later played in many "B" movies for Monogram and RKO. He began his television work with *Studio One* and *Suspense* in 1949. The following year he appeared in *Robert Montgomery Presents, Lights Out, Believe it or Not, Sure as Fate*, and another episode of

Suspense. He continued his work in television until the year he died of cancer in 1963, appearing in many popular programs of the 1950s and 1960s.

 Nielsen, Erik (b. 1945) "Wally's Girl Trouble" (First boy in library)

The year 1957 was a good one for Erik Nielsen. In addition to his work on *Leave it to Beaver*, he had two appearances on *The Loretta Young Show*, one on *Dragnet* and had a bit part in the movie *Slander* which starred Van Johnson and Ann Blyth. But after 1958, he no longer worked in Hollywood.

Nolan, James (1915-1985) "Beaver Goes in Business" (Man #1)

Nolan worked on the small and big screen in six different decades. He amassed over 150 acting credits. His specialty was playing policemen or detectives and other such figures. He closed out his career in the early 1980s with parts on *Quincy M.E.*, *The Waltons* and *Father Murphy*.

O

O'Connor, Rory (b. 1945 to 1948?) 13 episodes (Beaver double)

While there were many stand in actors on *Leave it to Beaver*, the only one mentioned in the IMDB credits of any shows was Rory O'Connor. He had some extra roles in other TV shows and movies in the 1960s, the biggest being a "teenager" in *Bye Bye Birdie*. It's behind the scenes in Hollywood where he achieved his success. Rory has had fourteen Emmy nominations and received six Emmy's for technical achievements, crane camera operation, sound design, and sound mixing.

O'Malley, Kathleen (1924-2019) "Wally Buys a Car" (The Woman)

Has the distinction of working in Hollywood during seven different decades, but not consecutively. Her first acting job was in a silent film in the 1920s on which her father was working. She then skipped the 1930s and began full-time work as an actress in the 1940s. In the year she made her *Leave it to Beaver* debut, she also appeared in *The Alfred Hitchcock Hour*, *General Hospital*, *Perry Mason*, *Bonanza*, and *Hazel*. That's more quality TV shows than some actors of the time appeared in during their entire careers. O'Malley also appeared in "Wally's Practical Joke." She later had multiple roles on *Wagon Train* and *The Waltons*. The most popular movie in which she had a part was *Black Sheep*, starring David Spade and Chris Farley.

O'Malley, Lillian (1892-1976) "Beaver Takes a Drive" (Woman)

An uncredited role in *The Plough and the Stars*, starring Barbara Stanwyck and directed by John Ford was Lillian O'Malley's first job in Hollywood. After that beginning, she had a bright future but only worked sporadically until 1960 when regular work came her way on shows like *The Rebel*, *The Twilight Zone* and *Alfred Hitchcock Presents*. Her last role came in 1962 on *Alfred Hitchcock Presents* at the age of seventy. She is credited with playing Mrs. Whitney in "Lonesome Beaver," but instead, she plays a random woman in a scene where Beaver is playing outside.

O'Neal, Ryan (b. 1941) "Wally Goes Steady" (Tom Henderson)

During his first couple years in the business, O'Neal had parts in *The Many Loves of Dobie Gillis*, *The Untouchables*, *Bachelor Father* and *Leave it to Beaver*. His most regular work of his career came while in *Peyton Place* from 1964-1969 when he appeared in over 500 episodes, playing the part of Rodney Harrington. He was in two of the 1970s most remembered films, *Love Story* and *Paper Moon*. In the latter, he appeared with his daughter Tatum O'Neal in her first movie role.

Oliveri, Dennis (1947-2006) "Long Distance Call" (Kenny)

Began his career on the stage in a touring rendition of the play *Auntie Mame*. A year later in Hollywood, his first small screen credit was a recurring role in *The Betty Hutton Show*. He worked regularly, mostly in TV, until 1976. In 1969, he had a regular role on Aaron Spelling's *The New People* on ABC.

Osborn, Lyn (1926-1958) "The Paper Route" (Newspaper Customer #2)

Popularity came early to Lyn Osborn through his work as Cadet Happy on the radio and television series *Space Patrol* on the ABC network. He wound up his career with three films which were released after his untimely death in 1958 following brain surgery.

P

Packer, Netta (1895-1962) "Beaver Won't Eat" (Restaurant Customer)

Began working in films in the late 1930s but may be best known as the nosy woman who gives June Cleaver a piece of her mind when June tries getting Beaver to eat his Brussels sprouts at a restaurant. She also has the distinction of being involved with two *Leave it to Beaver* misconceptions. The first is her being in a scene along with a dark-haired woman many *LITB* fans claim is actress Sue Randall (Miss Landers), a well-established actress with a non-speaking extra role and looking like she has gained twenty pounds for the part. That's misconception #1. The second is that Netta Packer is actress Doris Packer's sister. Doris played Mrs. Rayburn. Although this is a possibility, there is no evidence that would support the claim.

Pagett, Eddie (1944) "Wally and Dudley" (Danny)

Although he had a short career in acting, he did make it into two episodes of *Leave it to Beaver*. The other episode in which he appeared was "Wally's Chauffeur."

Parkins, Barbara (b. 1942) "No Time for Babysitters" (Judy Walker)

She appeared in *Leave it to Beaver* during her first year in Hollywood. Watching her in *LITB*, one just knew she was destined for much more. A few years later, she starred in two of the 1960s most notable productions, *Peyton Place* beginning in 1964 and *Valley of the Dolls* in 1967, which co-starred Patty Duke and Sharon Tate. She would later be the maid of honor at the wedding of Sharon Tate and Roman Polanski in 1968.

Parnell, James (1923-1961) "School Bus" (Mr. Crawford)

His career spanned over 100 films and TV shows and twelve short years. The length of his career may be long by some standards, but he died in the prime of his acting career at the young age of thirty-eight. He played in two episodes of *Leave it to Beaver* and in each, Beaver hits somebody. The other episode was "Beaver and Ivanhoe." Parnell made appearances in many 1950s TV westerns: *The Lone Ranger*, *The Cisco Kid*, *The Adventures of Wild Bill Hickok*, *Maverick*, *Broken Arrow*, *Trackdown*, *Have Gun – Will Travel*, *The Texan*, *Black Saddle*, *The Zane Grey Theater*, *The Life and Legend of Wyatt Earp*, *Man Without a Gun*, *Johnny Ringo* and *The Rifleman*. Add in the other nine westerns he was in during the 1960s and you get a grand total of twenty-three TV westerns in which he acted. Well-respected in Hollywood, it is shame he was gone before appearing in another 100 TV shows and films.

Parrish, Helen (1923-1959) "Lumpy Rutherford" (Geraldine Rutherford)

Beginning her acting career at the age of five, Helen Parrish was the daughter of a stage actress and sometime film actress Laura Parrish. Her first film starred Babe Ruth, with her playing his daughter. Parrish later worked in several films with Deanna Durbin including *Mad About Music*, *Three Smart Girls Grow Up* and *First Love*. She had over sixty acting credits to her name at the time of her untimely death due to cancer.

Paylow, Stephen (1949-2011) "Beaver Gets 'Spelled'" (Boy)

The Internet Movie Database is not the be all and end all of Hollywood research, one time *Leave it to Beaver* actor Stephen Paylow proves this to be true. He wound up his career with forty-five acting credits,[181] but IMDB only lists five. His first film was *The Silver Chalice* with Paul Newman, and it was this film which helped birth Paylow's lifelong love for history and ancient civilizations. He appeared on *Rawhide*, *Gunsmoke* and many other shows in the 1950s. He left Hollywood but not before working in the dietary department of the Motion Picture Hospital as a teen. For the rest of his life, Paylow worked in the food industry either in restaurants or in the dietary departments of various institutions.

Peck, Ed (1917-1992) "Wally Buys a Car" (The Salesman)

He often played police officers or military officers during his career. In fact, one of his first roles on television was as Major Dell Conway in the show *Major Dell Conway of the Flying Tigers*. Then, in the 1970s and 1980s, he had recurring roles in which he played police officers, they were *The Super* (1972), *Benson* (1981-1982), and *Happy Days* (1975-1983).

Pepper, Dennis (b. 1944) "Lumpy's Scholarship" (Denny)

An actor who dabbled in Hollywood with half of his acting credits on shows in which his mother Barbara Pepper worked. These included *The Adventures of Ozzie and Harriet*, *Petticoat Junction*, *Green Acres* and *The Jack Benny Program*. In his early 20s, Dennis aimed his pursuits away from

---

[181] Williams, Natalia. "*Child star and longtime Santa Cruz resident Stephen C. Paylow dies.*" June 9, 2011. The Mercury News. https://www.mercurynews.com/2011/06/09/child-star-and-longtime-santa-cruz-resident-stephen-c-paylow-dies/.

the small screen. His mother Barbara continued to act until her death in 1969 and is best known for playing Doris Ziffel on both *Green Acres* and Petticoat Junction.

Petrie, George (1912-1997) "The Credit Card" (George Haskell)

He appeared in two episodes of *Leave it to Beaver*, the other was "Summer in Alaska." With nearly 150 acting credits, beginning with a couple films in the 1940s, Petrie was a non-stop actor from the 1950s up until a year before his death 1997. It looks like his most lean years in Hollywood were from 1958 to 1960, with no acting roles listed in IMDB. However, the 1960s was his most prolific decade. He began with appearances on *Rawhide* and *Bachelor Father* and wound up the decade with multiple roles on *The Jackie Gleason Show.* The 1980s and 1990s were good to George Petrie. He remained quite busy during his 70s and 80s. In addition to reprising his role as George Haskell in *The New Leave it to Beaver*, he had parts in *Dynasty*, *Quincy M.E.*, *Knight Rider*, *The Facts of Life*, *Who's the Boss?*, *Dallas*, *L.A. Law* and he had a recurring role on *Mad About You* which he began when he was eighty-two years old. He also graced the big screen in two iconic movies of the 1980s, *Baby Boom* and *Planes, Trains and Automobiles.*

Pourchot, Ray (1924-2010) "School Play" (Audience Member)

His first work in Hollywood came in the form of being an extra in productions that needed football players. At the time he was an end with the USC Trojans. After college, he began to work full-time in film and TV as an extra and later as a stand-in for other actors. While he did a lot of work in television, he was in many notable films, including *Around the World in 80 Days*, *Raintree County*, *All the President's Men*, *The China Syndrome*, *Heaven Can Wait* and *American Gigolo*.

Powers, Jack (n/a) "Miss Landers' Fiancé" (Tom Brittingham)

After breaking Beaver's heart by asking Miss Landers to marry him, becoming her fiancé, Powers appeared in only a few other TV shows. His final appearance occurred in 1964 in an episode of *12 O'Clock High*.

Prentiss, Ed (1908-1992) "Beaver's Typewriter" (Mr. Bailey)

Began his career in radio and acted on many of that medium's top soap operas and also acted in *Captain Midnight.* He transferred that success into one of TV's earliest soap operas, appearing in eleven episodes of *Guiding Light* from 1953 to 1955. He had many roles on the typical 1960s TV shows on which many *Leave it to Beaver* actors played including *Perry Mason*, *Hazel*, *Bonanza*, *77 Sunset Strip* and *Dr. Kildare.* But he also was unique in his appearances on *21 Beacon Street*, *Grand Jury*, *Dan Raven*, *Judd for the Defense* and *Morning Star*. In the 1980s he began voice work on Warner Bros. cartoons voicing various characters and narrating. In addition to "Beaver's Typewriter," he also appeared as Beaver's teacher in "Beaver, the Sheep Dog," and "The Clothing Drive."

Preuss, Edith Terry (n/a) "Beaver Finds a Wallet" (Secretary)

Her career, according to IMDB, lists her with two roles in her career. She is credited with playing Marie in *Hollywood Mystery* in 1934 and as a secretary in *Leave it to Beaver* in 1960.

Prickett, Maudie (1914-1976) "Beaver and Poncho" (Mrs. Bennett)

Maudie Prickett was a very successful character actor with over 150 acting credits. She had multiple or recurring roles on numerous television shows. Some of the better-known shows were *The Red Skelton Hour, The Jack Benny Program* (Miss Gordon), *Hazel* (Rosie), *Bewitched* and *The Andy Griffith Show*.

R

Randall, Tommy (b. 1943?) "It's a Small World" (Frankie Bennett's Friend)

Other than the LITB pilot, his only other role was on *The Ford Television Theater* in 1956.

Ray, Allan (1909-1998) "Beaver's Ice Skates" (Bert)

He appeared in two episodes of *Leave it to Beaver*, the other was as Gilbert's father in "Beaver's Football Award." He worked on nearly 100 TV shows and films during his forty-year career. Most of his work was done on television. He appeared in multiple episodes of both *I Love Lucy* and *The Lucy Show*. He also had repeat appearances in *Sky King* and *The Whistler*.

Remsen, Bert (1925-1999) "Eddie Quits School" (Mr. Thompson)

A man with a face like Bert Remsen cannot be forgotten. Almost everyone that has turned on a television has seen him in some TV show they enjoyed, no matter what genre is their favorite. He has been seen in shows as varied as *Rawhide* to *One Step Beyond* and from *Route 66* to *Voyage to the Bottom of the Sea* and from *Wonder Woman* to *Melrose Place*. He also appeared in numerous movies such as *Pork Chop Hill, Fastbreak, Inside Moves, The Sting II, Code of Silence, Peacemaker* and *The Player*.

Reynolds, Alan (1908-1976) 3 episodes (Multiple roles)

Reynolds appeared in three episodes of *Leave it to Beaver*. They were "Beaver Gets 'Spelled," "The Paper Route," and "Train Trip." As for his other work, simply name every television series in the 1950s and you will see Alan Reynolds in the cast of many of them. Included on his resume are some of the biggest shows of the decade including: *The Adventures of Superman, Lassie, Alfred Hitchcock Presents, Dragnet, Studio 57, The Loretta Young Show, Wanted Dead or Alive, Wagon Train, The Adventures of Ozzie & Harriet, Maverick, Rawhide* and *Bonanza*.

Reynolds, Marjorie (1917-1997) "Chuckie's New Shoes" (Mrs. Murdock)

Appearing on three episodes of *Leave it to Beaver*, Marjorie Reynolds played Mrs. Murdock in "Chuckie's New Shoes," and in "Beaver, the Babysitter." She also played Mrs. Gregory in "All-Night Party." She accumulated nearly 100 acting credits during her career before retiring from acting in 1978. She is best known for playing Peg, the wife of actor William Bendix, in *The Life of Riley* from 1953-1958.

Reynolds, Nancy (n/a) "Uncle Billy" (Gloria)

Acted in a few shows as a child and an appearance in *The Candidate* starring Robert Redford, in 1972.

Richards Jr., Danny (b. 1942) "The Cookie Fund" (Roger Delacy)

His acting career lasted from 1949 when he appeared in two episodes of *Oboler Comedy Theater* to his 1962 role as Danny on *Pete and Gladys.* In between, he appeared on *I Married Joan, My Little Margie, Bachelor Father* and many others. Also had a recurring role of Franklin Sanders in this sitcom *Willy* (1954-1955).

Richards, Dennis (n/a) "Box Office Attraction" (Gus)

He took Wally's girl away from him and that was a good thing. Wally was much classier than Marlene. Richards had a very short career in Hollywood, only appearing in four TV shows and one movie, *The Young and the Brave* in 1963, a film about the Korean War, starring Rory Calhoun and William Bendix.

Richards, Leoda (1907-1998) "Beaver Won't Eat" (Restaurant Patron)

In *Leave it to Beaver*, she plays a restaurant patron who thinks June shouldn't force Beaver to eat Brussels sprouts. Rarely saying no to an extra role, she was a bit player and extra who performed in almost 300 TV shows and films. She played a restaurant patron in many shows, among them were *Death of a Scoundrel, I Love Lucy, Route 66, My Three Sons, The Lucy Show, Hellfighters, Family Affair, The Partridge Family, Kojak, Starsky and Hutch, Good Times* and *The Blues Brothers* and many more. The show she appeared on most was *Bewitched* and she may be the only actor who appeared on *Leave it to Beaver* and *The Monkees*.

Robards Sr., Jason (1892-1963) "Kite Day" (Mr. Henderson)

A famed American stage actor and trained at the American Academy of Dramatic Art. His first work in Hollywood was as a leading man. He then evolved into a character actor. His final role came in *The Adventures of Ozzie and Harriet* in 1963, the year he suffered a fatal heart attack. His son is actor Jason Robards and his grandson is actor Sam Robards.

Roberts, Alan (1948-2008) "Beaver and Chuey" (Chuey Varela)

A child actor with a career that lasted about eight years. With his dark complexion, he was cast in quite a few roles as a Hispanic boy or as an Indian boy. In his *Leave it to Beaver* appearance, viewers could see his character was very friendly. He was also that way in real life as an adult, helping as many people as possible who were in need. He retired from acting after his final role in an episode of *Rawhide* and later became a truck driver. Other than his family, his other loves were playing guitar and riding his motorcycle.

Robinson, Bartlett (1912-1986) "Beaver, the Model" (George Compton)

Robinson began his career on the stage in New York and also had roles on many radio shows before turning to the small screen in Hollywood. He appeared in many TV shows in the 1960s, and among them was probably the most popular TV episode in *Twilight Zone* history, "To Serve Man." He acted into the 1980s when he appeared on *Lou Grant* in his final role. His acting genes have passed down through his family to his great-grandson Noah Munck who is best known for his work on ABC sitcom *The Goldbergs.*

Rogers, Gil (b. 1949) "Beaver and Kenneth" (Kenneth Purcell)

Gil put his short-lived acting career aside for a guitar. That turned out to be a wise choice as about a year after his last acting job, a role on *My Three Sons*, he began working with singer Johnny Mathis and toured with him as a guitarist for almost fifty years. He also sang with Johnny and acted as his production and stage manager.

Ross, Michael (1911-1993) "A Horse Named Nick" (Rendering Man)

Had the distinction of acting on *The Red Skelton Hour* TV program during three different decades. Talk about longevity of an actor and a TV show, this is the ultimate example. After his role on *Leave it to Beaver*, he went on to have multiple roles in some of the 1960s most popular comedies including *Petticoat Junction*, *The Munsters* and *The Beverly Hillbillies*. He worked steadily on the small screen until his final acting credit on *Little House on the Prairie* in 1975.

Roy, John (1898-1975) "Beaver's Football Award" (Father at Award Dinner)

One of the most prolific extras and bit players in Hollywood during the 1950s and 1960s, John Roy amassed almost 300 credits in TV and films. His TV appearances were quite diverse, appearing in *Leave it to Beaver* to *Batman* and from *The Andy Griffith Show* to *Mission Impossible*. However, his mainstay was movies. Look at this partial, but impressive list: *Yankee Doodle Dandy*, *Miracle on 34th Street*, *Creature with the Atom Brain*, *Jailhouse Rock*, *North by Northwest*, *The Great Imposter*, *Cat Ballou* and *Funny Girl*.

Rudley, Herbert (1910-2006) "All-Night Party" (Mr. Gregory)

Beginning his career on Broadway, he first appeared in a show in 1928. After moving to Hollywood in the 1940s, he scored some good roles in films such as *Rhapsody in Blue*, *The Seventh Cross* and *Joan of Arc*. In TV, he had quite a few recurring roles. These were seen in *Michael Shayne*, *The Californians*, *The Bob Cummings Show*, *Mona McCluskey*, *The Mothers-In-Law* and *Dallas* (1981)

S

Sanford, Ralph (1899-1963) "Beaver Gets 'Spelled'" (Fats Flannaghan)

Sanford played bit roles in scores of movies in the 1930s and 1940s, many uncredited. He was a regular on *The Life and Legend of Wyatt Earp* as Mayor Jim Kelley and also played four other roles on the same series. He also enjoyed regular work on *General Electric Theater*. He also appeared on *LITB* in "Broken Window" and "Wally's Car."

Sayer, Diane (1938-2001) "Box Office Attraction" (Marlene Holmes)

Sayer was an in-demand actress as she was active her entire career from 1962 to 1971. But her heyday was in 1963 and 1964 when she had seventeen film and TV credits, including roles in *The Twilight Zone*, *The Adventures of Ozzie and Harriet*, *Dirty Dingus Magee* and *Support Your Local Gunfighter*.

Schallert, William (b. 1922) "Beaver's Short Pants" (Mr. Bloomgarden)

If you wonder how William Schallert could have over 350 acting credits, maybe it's because as of 2014, at the age of 92, he was still acting. His last role was as an elevator operator in the CBS comedy *2 Broke Girls* in the episode "And the Not Broke Parents." His most popular role was as Martin Lane on the *The Patty Duke Show*. Schallert is one of only three actors without regular recurring roles on *Leave it to Beaver*'s first season who also appeared on *The New Leave it to Beaver* (the others were Louise Lewis and Lyle Talbot).

Scott, Brenda (b. 1943) "Untogether-ness" (Lori Ann)

Was quite active after beginning her Hollywood career with a couple of appearances on Robert Young's *Window on Main Street*. Her career never gave up steam until she divorced and remarried in 1979, obviously dedicating more time to her family and only acting in one role in the 1980s, one in the 1990s and one in the early 2000's. Some of the more popular TV shows in which she appeared were *Dragnet*, *Dr. Kildare*, *The Fugitive*, *Hawaii Five-O*, *Here Come the Brides*, *Mannix*, *Quincy M.E.* and *Simon & Simon*.

Scott, Joey (b. 1953) "Child Care" (Bengie Bellamy)

He played on a total of three *Leave it to Beaver* episodes, the others were "The Garage Painters" and "Beaver the Magician." He also appeared in *National Velvet* (all fifty-eight episodes), *Bonanza*, *My Three Sons*, *The Andy Griffith Show*, *Dr. Kildare* and *The Munsters*. In an interview with Stu Stoshak, Rich Correll mentioned that Joey Scott still works in the industry, doing some work, possibly on a few Disney comedies in the 2000s or 2010s.

Seay, James (1914-1992) "Wally Goes Steady" (Mr. Boothby)

A familiar face in many sci-fi films, these included *The Day the Earth Stood Still*, *When Worlds Collide*, *The War of the Worlds*, *Killers from Space* and *The Amazing Colossal Man*. On TV, he had many recurring roles including *Fury*, *The Life and Legend of Wyatt Earp* and *Lassie*. His career ended with over 200 acting credits.

Seflinger, Neil (b. 1950) "Larry's Club" (Harold)

This young actor should've been given a chance to have a recurring role. In his four *Leave it to Beaver* episodes, he was credited as Harold, boy, football player, and student. These episodes were "Larry's Club," "Beaver and Ivanhoe," "Beaver's Team," and "Beaver Becomes a Hero." He had talent. But he soon left acting behind as a ten-year-old. Later in life, he owned an insurance agency in southern California.

Shearer, Harry (b. 1943) "It's a Small World" (Frankie Bennett)

The man known for the film *This is Spinal Tap*, voicing twenty-one characters on *The Simpsons* and who honed his comedy chops on *Saturday Night Live*, appeared in the pilot episode of *Leave it to Beaver* titled "It's a Small World." While he didn't play Eddie Haskell, he did play the role that would later become Eddie. His character's name in the pilot was Frankie Bennett. Two years before landing a part on the *Leave it to Beaver* pilot, Harry Shearer appeared on *The Jack Benny Program* as a member of a club named "The Beavers." In an interview with Bob Costas in 1998,

Shearer admitted he may be one of the few people in America who had never seen an episode of *Leave it to Beaver*. That's almost sacrilegious.

Sherman, Fred (1905-1969) "Substitute Father" (Taxi Driver)

Fred Sherman began his career in vaudeville, eventually landing in Hollywood to begin a career on the big screen. His parts were often small, but plentiful. He added television to his repertoire in the early 1950s and stayed busy until suffering a stroke in 1962, after filming an episode of *The Andy Griffith Show*. There were many TV shows that trusted this dependable actor to come through with a good performance. This was demonstrated by them hiring him for multiple roles. These shows included *My Little Margie*, *Schlitz Playhouse*, *The Roy Rogers Show*, *Sergeant Preston of the Yukon*, *The Lineup*, *The Life and Legend of Wyatt Earp*, *Lawman* and *Wagon Train*.

Short, Judy (n/a) "All-Night Party" (Sue)

A short career, her acting credits include *Telephone Time*, *Circus Boy*, *The Loretta Young Show*, *Official Detective*, and *The Joey Bishop Show*. She left acting in 1963.

Showalter, Max (1917-2000) "It's a Small World" (Ward Cleaver)

Unknown to many fans, an actor other than Hugh Beaumont first played the role of Ward Cleaver. This portrayal only occurred in the pilot episode. Fans who have seen the pilot are thankful that Hugh Beaumont took over the role. Showalter was a very accomplished actor and had in his lifetime, over 100 acting credits, his last coming as Grandpa Fred in the film *Sixteen Candles*. He also worked in films with beautiful women such as Marilyn Monroe (*Niagara* and *Bus Stop*), Hedy Lamarr (*The Female Animal*) and Bo Derek (*10*). He was also a talented composer and pianist.

Silvern, Bea (1926-2013) "Beaver Won't Eat" (Waitress)

She tries to substitute Beaver's brussels sprouts for another vegetable, but June isn't having any of that. From that waitress role in the beginning of her career, she had three more roles in the 1960s, leaving acting until a return in 1973 with a role on *The New Dick Van Dyke Show*. From there, she worked continuously through the early 1990s. Her longest recurring role was in *The Secrets of Midland Heights,* a show produced by Lorimar in an effort to replicate the success of *Dallas*. Unfortunately, that formula didn't work in this series.

Simmons, Dick (1913-2003) "The Parking Attendants" (Mr. Langley)

Hailing from Minnesota, Dick Simmons probably fit in very well starring in *Sergeant Preston of the Yukon*, a show about the frigid Yukon Territory and its mounted police in the 1890s. This is the show he was best known for, but whatever show he appeared in, knew they had a quality actor on their set. He appeared in two episodes of *Leave it to Beaver*, the other being "Beaver, the Caddy," in which he plays a very unsavory fellow. His last acting credits came in the early 1970s and include an episode of *The Brady Bunch* and the film *The Resurrection of Zachary Wheeler*, a sci-fi drama that must be remade sometime in the future.

Singer, Reuben (1926-1983) "One of the Boys" (Ted)

Rueben Singer appeared in two episodes of *Leave it to Beaver*, the other was "The Party Spoiler." His career only spanned sixteen roles and ended in the early 1980s with an episode of *Cagney*

Lacey and three movies, *Foolin' Around*, *Author! Author!* and *The Soldier*.

Singer, Stuffy (b. 1941) "Beaver Takes a Drive" (Steve)

Although his child acting days were quite impressive, work on *My Three Sons, Blondie, The Patty Duke Show, The Adventures of Ozzie and Harriet* among others, Stuffy Singer decided to leave it all behind to play sports. He could've chosen any sport; he was talented at baseball, tennis, and football, but he decided to become the best in the sport of handball. He went for his goal to be the best and in 1996, was inducted into the Southern California Handball Hall of Fame after a career of winning many four wall singles and doubles championships. He has worked as a tax consultant and in 2004 was the San Fernando Valley financial services representative of the year.

Silver, Johnny (1918-2003) "The Clubhouse" (Man on Bridge)

Appearing on *The Jack Benny Program* in the episode, "Jack Takes the Beavers to the Fair," Silver is the second actor from *Leave it to Beaver* to appear in this Jack Benny episode, Harry Shearer was the other. Silver played multiple roles on many popular TV shows of the 1960s and 1970s including *Make Room for Daddy, The Joey Bishop Show, The Dick Van Dyke Show, Mannix, Ironside* and *The Odd Couple*. He also had two small roles in the Mel Brooks' films *History of the World Part I* and *Spaceballs*.

Smiley, Richard (b. 1946) "The Perfect Father" (Willie Dennison)

The boy whose father was the bane of Ward Cleaver's existence, at least for part of one episode, appeared only in two episodes from season one, the other was "The Black Eye." He did not act on television again following these two appearances.

Smith, Hal (1916-1994) "Beaver Won't Eat" (Restaurant Manager)

Hal Smith played Otis Campbell, the beloved town drunk of Mayberry, on *The Andy Griffith Show*. Most people will recognize him as that character. However, his claim to fame is as a voice actor. He had a voice credit in 1957 for the animated short *The Bongo Punch*, but beginning in 1959, he began to regularly lend his voice to animated characters. He didn't leave acting in front of the camera until the early 1980s when his last major appearances were on *Little House on the Prairie* and *Fantasy Island*. An interesting character he played on *The Brady Bunch* was that of the "Kartoon King," a very appropriate role for Hal Smith.

Smith, Jack (1913-2006) "Beaver on TV" (The Director)

His first acting credit was as a reporter on the original *King Kong* movie in 1933. His acting career was sporadic and mostly centered around roles as an announcer or some sort of TV station employee. He was best known as a tenor and in 1928, when he was only fifteen years old, he began signing lead in a trio at L.A.'s Ambassador Hotel's Cocoanut Grove, replacing the Bing Crosby's trio, *The Rhythm Boys*. His final acting role was as an announcer in *Cannonball Run II* in 1984.

Smith, Martin (1927-1994) "Borrowed Boat" (Police Officer #1)

His career lasted six years and sixteen acting credits. He only appeared in two situation comedies, *Beaver* and *The Donna Reed Show*. However, in both of these shows, he played an authority figure as a policeman in *Beaver* and a park ranger in *The Donna Reed Show*.

Smith, Pam (b. 1947 or 1948) "Beaver's First Date" (Betsy Patterson)

Other than her role on *Leave it to Beaver* in 1961, Pam Smith also filmed the movie *Misty* and an episode of *The Rifleman* that same year. The following year, she appeared in an episode of *Bonanza* and took eight years off from working in Hollywood, possibly to attend high school and college. She then came back in 1970, in one final appearance, with an uncredited role in the Jerry Lewis film *Which Way to the Front?*

Snowden, Eric (1888-1979) "Beaver's Short Pants" (Clothier)

This Eric Snowden, born in England, (not the American) was a distinguished old time radio actor. On radio he was heard in *Escape*, *The Jack Benny Program*, *Yours Truly Johnny Dollar* and many more. He made his way in the 1950s onto the small and large screen where he worked regularly throughout the decade. His last appearance was on the Twilightzonesque series *One Step Beyond* in 1959. He appeared on two episodes of *Leave it to Beaver*, the second was in *The Bank Account*.

Somers, Rita Norma (1945 or 1946) "Wally's Weekend Job" (Ann)

Like most girls in the early 1960s, Ann, had a thing for Wally Cleaver. That's why she's at the soda fountain watching him while he works his weekend job. After this episode, Rita Norma Somers seems to have left work in Hollywood. This is her only acting credit.

Sorensen, LeiLani (b. 1949) 5 episodes (Multiple characters)

LeiLani began dancing at a very young age. Her mother used to attend exercise classes at Compton College in the early 1950s. While she did that, she dropped LeiLani and her brother off at the dance studio for lessons while she exercised. Doreen Taylor, the instructor, taught the Sorensen kids adagio dancing. LeiLani also took lessons at the Norton Studio of Music and Dancing and at Cosmo Morgan in Hollywood, among a few other places and she performed locally in the Lynwood and South Gate areas of Southern California in talent festivals.

On how she was discovered, LeiLani spoke about Chef Milani, a celebrity Chef, who had his own TV show on a local L.A. station, KCOP – channel 13. He would sometimes do live remotes at grocery stores like *Roth's Market* on Sepulveda or go out to supermarkets like *Thrifty Market* or *Market Basket* for grand openings or grand re-openings and provide entertainment or hold his children's talent hunt show.[182] Renown children's agent Lola Moore discovered LeiLani.at one such event. Not long after, she began work in commercials and moved onto television and film.

Before *Leave it to Beaver*, Leilani worked on the popular TV shows *West Point*, *The Danny Thomas Show* and *Perry Mason*. She also filmed an episode of *Father Knows Best*, about six months after her first filming of an *LITB* episode in early May of 1959, "Beaver, the Athlete." This is just one of the episodes of *Leave it to Beaver* for which she is not credited on IMDB. The actual number in which she may have appeared, according to LeiLani, could be upwards seven or eight.[183] She was also in "Big Fish Count," but not credited.

An interesting thing to note about her post-*Leave it to Beaver* life, is that she graduated

---

[182] "Chef Milani to Conduct Talent Show at Market Basket in Culver Center." *Evening Vanguard Newspaper*, August 12, 1955.
[183] Interview with author in August 2022.

from Lynwood High School, which was the name of a rival school to Mayfield High for many of the seasons of *Leave it to Beaver*. She attended Cal-Lutheran University in the San Fernando Valley after high school. For a while, Jerry Mathers attended college with her, even as a fellow student in her History of Drama class, before he moved on to the UC-Berkely, and she moved on to Cal-State Long Beach. LeiLani's twenty-seven-year career after receiving a Speech Communication degree was as Vice President - Real Estate Development and Special Assets Officer for Bank of America. Then, fourteen years as a realtor with Coldwell Banker.

Space, Arthur (1908-1983) "Wally's Present" (Mr. Judson)

In forty years, Arthur Space worked on almost 300 different films and TV shows. In high demand for his skills and professionalism, he often worked on multiple episodes and in different roles for the shows he was hired. Examples of this include his various roles in *The Gene Autry Show*, *Whirlybirds*, *Death Valley Days*, *Colt .45*, *Wagon Train*, *Perry Mason* and *Lou Grant*. His most notable TV work was found on two shows *National Velvet* (as Herbert Brown) and *Lassie* (as Doc Brown). Some notable movies include *Andy Hardy's Double Life*, *Thirty Seconds Over Tokyo*, *Leave it to Blondie*, *The Spirit of St. Louis* and *Herbie Rides Again*.

Spicer, George (b. 1944 or 1945) "Wally's Car" (3rd Boy)

Appearing in two episodes of *Leave it to Beaver*, George Spicer was also in the "Wally's Chauffeur" episode. The only other series in which he appeared twice was *Going My Way* which starred Gene Kelly and Dick York. His career was at its end by 1979, the year he appeared momentarily as the 4th technician in *The Billion Dollar Threat*.

Stanton, Hank (b. 1950) "Beaver, the Sheep Dog" (Fred)

With a career that ran from 1961 to 1964, Stanton made multiple appearances on *My Three Sons* as well as his work on *Leave it to Beaver*, *Lawman* and the film *One Man's Way*, the life story of Norman Vincent Peale.

Staunton, Ann (1920-1994) "More Blessed to Give" (Mildred Yeager)

Had a career as a professional ice skater before moving to Hollywood to try her hand in films. Before focusing on television, she appeared in some well received films like *Call Northside 777* starring Jimmy Stewart, *The Snows of Kilimanjaro* starring Gregory Peck and *Band of Angels* starring Clark Gable. In TV, she worked on many popular shows including *One Step Beyond*, *Johnny Staccato*, *Alfred Hitchcock Presents*, *Wagon Train*, and *Perry Mason*. She retired from acting in 1971 after her role in the forgettable film, *The Beautiful People*.

Stephens, Laraine (b. 1941) "Wally's Tall Date" (Gail Preston)

A great way to start a career, guest starring in an episode of *Leave it to Beaver* and unintentionally giving Eddie Haskell "the business." Stephens did that in her *LITB* appearance. From this humble beginning, she went on to a twenty-year career and almost sixty acting credits. Just a few years after dating Wally Cleaver, she had a recurring role in *O.K. Crackerby!* (1965-1966). She ended the 1960s with another recurring role in a longer lasting series, *Bracken's World*. The 1970s saw her with another recurring role in the series *Matt Helm,* and saw her featured in *Rich Man, Poor Man – Book II*, *Police Story*, and *Hawaii Five-O*. The early 80s saw her career wind down, but it did so with some notable roles. She reprised her *Dallas Cowboys Cheerleaders* role as Suzanne Mitchell in *Dallas Cowboys Cheerleaders II*, she also appeared on *The Love Boat*, *T.J. Hooker* and *Fantasy Island*. She was married for almost forty years to producer and TV executive David Gerber.

Stevens, Rory (b. 1954) 4 episodes (Boy / Chuckie Murdock)

His first acting role was as an unidentified boy in the *Leave it to Beaver* episode "Wally, the Businessman." He then appeared in three more episodes over two years as the character Chuckie Murdock. These episodes were "Chuckie's New Shoes," "Beaver's Frogs," and "Beaver, the Babysitter." More interesting than his roles on *Beaver* and the other fine sitcoms in the 1960s in which he appeared, and even more interesting than his role in Alfred Hitchcock's *The Birds*, is the story of his early life. He grew up poor, sometimes finding it hard to eat as his parents often had no money for food. He had to eat out of the trash or find food growing on trees near where he lived. His parents physically abused him and pushed him into acting, taking his earnings to support themselves and their four children. Rory survived this abusive upbringing, becoming a successful real estate professional in southern California. Congratulations to Rory for being a survivor.

Stevens, William (n/a) "Beaver Goes in Business" (Man who had his lawn mowed)

His Hollywood career seems to have had a false start in 1945, when he appeared in a low budget Republic picture and a Republic serial and then nothing else until 1955. But once he got started again in 1955, he worked constantly until 1978 when he retired from film and TV work. His notable TV appearances, besides *Leave it to Beaver* include *The Outer Limits*, *Daniel Boone*, *Ben Casey*, *Daktari* and *Adam-12* where he had a recurring role as Officer Jerry Walters in twelve episodes in 1968-1969, but then with a five-year layoff from the series, returns in 1974 in two episodes as Officer Lou Walters.

Stewart, Margaret (n/a) "The Parking Attendants" (Mrs. Rutherford)

Did Fred Rutherford put off Margaret Stewart so much that she quit acting? That's always possible, especially with the way he treated his wife in this 1963 episode of *Leave it to Beaver*. Nevertheless, this was the final TV role in her short career. Other notable shows she worked, beginning in 1952, were *The Big Story*, *The Lone Ranger*, and *Sergeant Preston of the Yukon*.

Strickland, Amzie (1919-2006) "Beaver Goes in Business" (Woman Who Pays Beaver $5 to Mow Her Lawn)

The woman with the longest credit ever on any episode of *Leave it to Beaver* is also one of the hardest working women in Hollywood history. She worked during eight different decades in Hollywood as an extra and bit player in films and TV. Along with this she appeared in many advertisements and voiced characters in over 3000 radio shows. The minimum number of roles she performed in each year between 1937 -1971 was four, except for 1946 and 1951 when she only worked on three productions. From 1952 until her retirement in 2001, she had work in multiple shows each year except for only a few occasions. Hard work was her middle name. She has the distinction of working on the original *Twilight Zone* and the 1980s remake. She also had roles on both *Dragnet* and *Dragnet 1967*. In film, she played a nurse in Shirley Temple's *Little Princess* and had minor parts in *Dark Victory*, *Mr. Lucky* and *Holiday Inn*.

Sullivan, Paul (b. 1944) "It's a Small World" (Wally Cleaver)

Unless you've purchased the DVD for season one, you have probably never seen Paul Sullivan in a *Leave it to Beaver* episode. This is the original actor who portrayed Wally Cleaver in the pilot episode, "It's a Small World," later replaced by Tony Dow. This was his second TV role. He first appeared in the series *Official Detective*. He later had bit roles on *Bachelor Father*, *The Donna Reed Show*, *Father Knows Best* and *The Adventures of Ozzie and Harriet*. He ended his Hollywood career in 1962 as an uncredited teen in the film, *Don't Knock the Twist*. At eighteen, he left acting and later went to college to study music. In the early 1980s, he started his own software company and had no regrets about not continuing with *Leave it to Beaver*. "No, not at all. Tony was terrific in the role…It all works out for the best. I'm a happy man," said Sullivan in a 1988 interview.[184]

Sully, Frank (1908-1975) "Beaver's Guest" (Cab Driver)

Best known for playing cab drivers in bit parts, doing so sixteen times throughout his career. Frank Sully was almost as popular playing bartenders, especially in westerns. On *The Virginian*, his only long recurring role, he played Danny the Bartender. He played this role from 1963-1967. Frank Sully also had the occasional small part in popular movies in the 1940s such as *The Grapes of Wrath* (Noah Joad), *Some Like it Hot*, *Yankee Doodle Dandy* and *The Talk of the Town*. He appeared in three episodes of *Leave it to Beaver*. He played a cab driver in "Beaver's Guest," a cab driver once again in "The Bus Ride," and a drunk man in "The All-Night Party."

Swanson, Audrey (n/a.) "Wally's Car" (Mrs. Ashby)

In her thirty-five film and TV credits, Audrey Swanson portrayed a nurse in eight different shows. The best known are *Wagon Train* and *The Alfred Hitchcock Hour*. Some other notable shows in which she appeared were *The Virginian, The Bob Cummings Show* and *The Munsters*, her final appearance on the small screen.

Swensen, Karl (1908-1978) "Voodoo Magic" (George Haskell) "Train Trip" (George Haskell)

One of the most difficult parts to play on *Leave it to Beaver* had to be the father of the annoying Eddie Haskell. Not really. In life, Ken Osmond who played Eddie was a very nice person. You may be surprised to know Karl Swensen is best remembered for playing Lars Hanson, the lumber mill owner in Little House on the Prairie. Michael Landon had remembered Swensen from his days playing multiple roles on *Bonanza*. Talk about typecasting, in six different shows or films, Swenson played characters whose first name was Lars. His recurring role on *Little House on the Prairie* lasted until 1978 when he died of a heart attack. His character in Little House was also written to have passed away.

T

Talbot, Lyle (1902-1996) "Party Invitation" (Mr. Dennison); "The Perfect Father," (Mr. Dennison)

The one thing to know about Lyle Talbot is that he loved acting. It was his life. Even more important was his ability to be a loving, caring and dedicated husband and father despite his

---

[184] Seymour, Gene. "How 2 in 'Beaver' Pilot Crashed and Lived." Philadelphia Daily News. November 18, 1988.

tremendously busy work schedule. His career began right after high school when he ran off with the circus. He worked as a magician and later in tent shows around the Midwest, eventually starting his own theater company in Memphis, *The Talbot Players*. His father and stepmother were also members of the company. He was popular in the Midwest and made his way with a touring company to Dallas, TX in the middle of the Great Depression where he performed in his final play before starting a career in Hollywood. After the play had ended, the stage manager ran off with the receipts from the play. The theater company was stranded in Dallas. Soon after, Lyle received a telegram from an agent in Hollywood.

He made his way to California, and it wasn't long until he was a contract player for Warner Brothers. In the 1930s he had small roles in some early Warner Brothers films, and in the 1940s, the quite dashing Talbot was the leading man in quite a few "B" movies, many of them westerns. He was the first Warner Brothers contract actor to join the Screen Actors Guild and because of that, he never worked for Warner Brothers again. In the 1950s, his career was re-born as a character actor on television. He did have some roles in film, but most of his work was on TV.

His love of working in Hollywood wasn't lost on his son Stephen, who followed him into acting. He played the character of Gilbert on *Leave it to Beaver*. When speaking of the fond memories he had of growing up in Hollywood, Stephen mentioned in a 2022 interview that his dad often took he and his brother with him to the sets he worked on, especially when he had roles on TV shows that he and his brother enjoyed. One distinct memory Stephen mentioned was when his father worked on *The Adventures of Rin Tin Tin*. "My brother and I wanted to meet the dog."[185] Lyle Talbot continued to act well into the 1980s with appearances on *Who's the Boss*, *Newhart* and *The New Leave it to Beaver*.

Taylor, Keith (1950-2019) 8 episodes (Harry)

His first role as a child actor was as Harry on *Leave it to Beaver*. His appearance on the show occurred after the departure of Rusty Stevens and while many believe he was a replacement for the character of Larry, no one actor could replace Larry. Actor Stephen Talbot said in a 2022 interview that it took three characters to take Larry's place, Gilbert, Richard and Whitey.[186] Leaving Beaver after only eight episodes, Taylor went on to play Tubby, a regular on *McKeever and the Colonel*. Throughout the 1960s, he had roles in numerous shows like *My Three Sons*, *My Favorite Martian* and *Star Trek*. Taylor worked in the 1970s in *Here's Lucy*, *All in the Family* and *Maude*.

After leaving acting, Taylor entered the field of banking, where he eventually became a vice-president at Bank of America. He later founded his own financial services company, and he owned the Hatchet Hall Restaurant in Culver City. He married his beautiful of thirty-eight years Christine and had one daughter, Diane, born in 1986. He was a long-time resident of Van Nuys and a leading member of the community. He served the Boy Scouts for almost twenty years and was decorated with their Silver Beaver Award for Service.

How and why he became an actor is quite impressive. His mother Sylvia was bedridden with Multiple Sclerosis and at the age of ten, he took it upon himself to take various buses to get to Hollywood and he eventually found himself an agent, Mary O'Grady. That's a type of Hollywood discovery story one doesn't hear very often.

---

[185] Stephen Talbot interview with the author in November 2022.
[186] Ibid.

Tedrow, Irene (1907-1995) "The Visiting Aunts" (Mrs. Claudia Hathaway)

Irene was formally trained in drama at Carnegie Tech in Pittsburgh, Pennsylvania. She graduated with a Bachelor of Arts degree in 1929. She had worked on the stage, even before attending school and continued afterward, before heading to Hollywood in 1937. In addition to film work, she also appeared on many radio shows. Her most well-known radio role being that of Corliss Archer's mother, Janet in the series *Meet Corliss Archer* (1943-1952). What *LITB* fans will find interesting is that while she played Aunt Martha's friend Mrs. Hathaway in one episode of *Leave it to Beaver*, she played Aunt Martha on two episodes of *The New Leave it to Beaver*. Her TV appearances over the decades ranged from comedies like *The Jack Benny Program*, *Three's Company*, and *It's Gary Shandling's Show* to dramas and thrillers *Passport to Danger*, *The Twilight Zone*, *Perry Mason* and *The Six Million Dollar Man*. The final of her over 200 roles came in 1989 with her appearance in the TV movie *A Deadly Silence*.

Thomas Jr., Callen John (b. 1947) "Beaver's Fortune" (Sonny Cartwright)

Speaking of "fortune" Callen John Thomas Jr. had the good fortune to appear in three of the most popular situation comedies of the late 1950s. His career spanned only two years and three television shows, but those shows were *Leave it to Beaver*, *Bachelor Father*, and *The Adventures of Ozzie and Harriet*.

Thomas, Lonnie (b. 1947) "The Black Eye" (Second Boy)

At the age of one, Lonnie Thomas got his first taste of Hollywood when he appeared in the short film *Parlor, Bedroom and Wrath* which was produced by the famed *Three Stooges* producer Jules White. He went on from there to roles in films that starred Shirley Temple, Walter Brennan, Fred MacMurray and Joan Crawford, all of this by the age of five. Just six years later, Lonnie Thomas would see his last Hollywood role as Jimmy in *The Adventures of Wild Bill Hickok*.

Thor, Larry (1916-1976) "Beaver Becomes a Hero" (Willard Watson)

A radio and newscaster, Thor first appeared on radio shows in his native Canada. He came to America and worked as a radio announcer and newscaster as well as on radio dramas *The Green Hornet*, *Rocky Jordan,* and *Suspense*. He gained familiarity with his role in *Broadway is My Beat*. He later began his work on the big and small screen. Some of his first appearance in films and on TV included work as baseball announcers (*The Pride of St. Louis*, *The Kid from Left Field*, the *Climax!* episode, "Fear Strikes Out," and he played an umpire in *The Danny Thomas Show*). One of the most popular films in which he appeared was 1957's cult classic *The Amazing Colossal Man*. He had a recurring role on *Mr. Novak* (1963-1965) and one of his last credits was voicing the character of Tock the Watchdog in the Chuck Jones directed full length animated film, *The Phantom Tollbooth*.

Thorson, Russell (1906-1982) "It's a Small World" (Man with milk bottles)

In the *Leave it to Beaver* pilot, Russell Thorson appeared as the "man with milk bottles." He was very busy about the time he filmed this pilot episode. He also appeared in three "B" movies and seven other television shows during 1957. In the 1970s, he appeared in some of the best crime dramas on television including *Cannon*, *The Streets of San Francisco*, *Barnaby Jones* and *The*

Rockford Files. Russell began his career in radio and played characters on *One Man's Family*, *Adventures by Morse* and many other shows.

Towne, Aline (1919-1996) "Eddie's Girl" (Mrs. Cunningham)

Aline Towne appeared in two *Leave it to Beaver* episodes. They were "Eddie's Girl" and "Beaver the Caddy." Early in her career she appeared in some memorable films, *White Heat*, *I Can Get it for you Wholesale*, *A Woman of Distinction*, *Homecoming* and the Republic serial in twelve chapters, *Zombies of the Stratosphere*. She appeared in almost 100 TV shows and films during her career. Near the end of her career and afterwards, she did what she loved most, travel. Before her death in 1996, she visited many different countries on five of the world's seven continents.

Towner, Leslie (1945-2020) "Eddie's double Cross" (Caroline's Friend)

This beautiful woman had a short career in Hollywood. She also acted in *The Man from U.N.C.L.E.*, *Gidget* and in the film *The Singing Nun*.

Torrance, Lee (n/a) "Beaver Gets Adopted" (Miss Walker)

Her career lasted two years, 1958-1959. During this time, she appeared on *Leave it to Beaver*, *Perry Mason* and in a mini-series titled *The Veil.*

Tuttle, Lurene (1907-1986) "Beaver Gets Adopted" (Mrs. Brady)

A star of radio shows and a very much-admired actress on the small and big screen, *LITB* fans got to know Lurene Tuttle from her two roles on *Leave it to Beaver,* "Beaver Gets Adopted" and "Bachelor at Large." Long before these appearances, Tuttle made a name for herself on many different radio shows, during that medium's golden age. Radio audiences knew her well from her roles on *The Great Gildersleeve*, as Marjorie and on *Sam Spade* as Spade's secretary Effie. In the late 1930s, Tuttle was influential in starting the first union to represent radio actors, giving them more money and more respect, especially for supporting actors and extras.[187] In addition to her hundreds of appearances on radio shows, Tuttle was also a prolific actor on the small screen in addition to roles on the big screen. These credits totaled nearly 300 by the time of her retirement in … wait, she never did retire, but worked up to the time of her passing in 1986. She had recurring roles on television in *Life with Father* (1953-1955), *Father of the Bride* (1961-1962) and *Julia* (1968-1970). In her last decade of acting, she had parts in Charlie's Angels, *The Dukes of Hazzard*, *Trapper John M.D.*, *Fantasy Island*, *Murder She Wrote* and *Crazy Like a Fox*. Lurene Tuttle was always hard working, always talented and she is to be commended as one of entertainment's great performers.

Tyler, Harry (1888-1961) "Happy Weekend" (Boat Rental Man)

What can be said about a man with 400 film and TV roles on his resume? Well, we can probably assume he worked hard and worked on sets that finished production as quickly as possible, especially during his "B" movie days early in his career. His career in Hollywood

---

[187] "AFRA's First Lady: The Career of Lurene Tuttle." http://www.radiospirits.com/email/lurene_tuttle_080913.asp

began in 1929 and he was quite prolific throughout his career, but most of all in the 1930s when he had parts in 100 different films. His output didn't slack off much in the 1940s and then he began in TV during the 1950s. Tyler had scores of credits in TV's most popular shows, but only two minor recurring roles in *Mayor of the Town* (1954) and *Black Saddle* (1959). But there were a few programs in which he played multiple parts and those include *Alfred Hitchcock Presents*, *Perry Mason*, *Cheyenne* and *The Roy Rogers Show*.

V

Vander Pyl, Jean (1919-1999) 5 episodes (Multiple roles)

Ms. Vander Pyl appeared in five episodes of *Leave it to Beaver*. They were "June's Birthday," "Wally and Alma," "Beaver and Kenneth," "Beaver's Doll Buggy," and "Farewell to Penny." You probably know her better as the voice of Wilma Flintstone or any of the hundreds of other characters she voiced during her long career as a voice actress. Although she most often worked voicing animated characters, she did appear in some situation comedies other than *Leave it to Beaver*. Those included *The Donna Reed Show*, *Please, Don't Eat the Daisies* and *Petticoat Junction*.

Van Patten, Dian (b. 1951) "Part-Time Genius" (Donna Sims)

Worked as a child actor beginning in 1953 with a part on *Commander Comet* as a toddler. A couple roles later and she was on *Leave it to Beaver* and added appearances on *The Rifleman*, *The Andy Griffith Show*, *Dennis the Menace*, and *The Beverly Hillbillies* to her resume in the 1960s. After a long break, she had a bit part on Bette Midler's *The Rose*. Her roles since that time have been many short videos, and those began in the early 1990s. But, occasionally, she makes it back to the small screen like her appearances on *24* from 2007-2010 and on *Ghost Whisperer* in 2009. Dian is now an ordained minister and living in a rural suburb of Los Angeles with her six goats and a dog.

VeSota, Bruno (1922-1976) "Community Chest" (Angry Neighbor)

Bruno was an actor and director, working both trades in the realms of radio, the stage movies and television. VeSota had a flair for cultish Sci-Fi films in the late 1950s and early 1960s. He appeared in front of the camera in *Attack of the Giant Leeches*, *Wasp Woman*, and *War of the Satellites* while he was behind the camera as a director for *The Brain Eaters* and *Invasion of the Star Creatures*. In television, his roles tended to trend toward the more traditional fare of *Peter Gunn*, *The Untouchables*, *The Wild Wild West*, *My Mother the Car*, *Bonanza*, *Hogan's Heroes* and *Kojak*, his final small or big screen role, in 1974.

Vigran, Herb (1910-1986) "Brotherly Love" (Stanley the Barber)

You may not know the name Herb Vigran, but you'd know him if you saw him. He was one of the most recognizable faces on the small screen in the 1950s and 1960s. He appeared regularly in multiple roles on *The Jack Benny Program*, *Dragnet*, *The Lucy Show*, *The Adventures of Superman* and *Four Star Playhouse*. Vigran was also a supporting actor on many radio shows during the 1940s and early 1950s. He died of cancer in 1986 and was active in Hollywood until that time.

Vitanza, A.G. (1917-2004) "Box Office Attraction" (Hank)

Early in his career, he found *Sea Hunt*, to be the first television show where he had multiple roles over a two-year period (1959-1960). Similarly, he also had multiple appearances on shows like *The Untouchables* and *The Red Skelton Hour*, while he snared a recurring role as the character Ramon on *The Flying Nun* (1967-1970).

Voeth, Gretchen (b. 1951) "Beaver, the Sheep Dog" (Shirley)

Had two roles in Hollywood. Her first was an uncredited part with Ernie Kovacs in *Wake Me When It's Over*. The other as the girl who told Beaver he looked like a sheep dog.

Voyne, Don (1937-2020) "Wally and the Fraternity" (Ted)

His Hollywood career lasted from 1961 to 1965 with small roles on the TV shows *Leave it to Beaver*, *Michael Shayne*, *It's a Man's World* and *My Three Sons*. He also had bit parts or uncredited roles in a few movies, including *A Gathering of Eagles*, *Honeymoon Hotel* and *For Those Who Think Young*.

W

Wade, Douglas (b. 1949) "Music Lesson" (Thomas)

After his one appearance in *Leave it to Beaver*, Douglas Wade is listed in the Internet Movie Database as having played the part of a bartender in *The Return of Superfly* in 1990. It would be very interesting to fill in the missing years between 1958 and 1990. Look for future info on the *Leave it to Beaver* books website, if any becomes available.

Wade, Stuart (1928??- ??) "New Doctor" (Dr. Bradley)

Making his film debut in a short documentary about disc jockey Martin Block in 1948, Stuart Wade played himself along with his orchestra leader Freddy Martin. Wade was a very talented singer, the best employed by orchestra leader Freddy Martin. He also had roles in Broadway musicals before concentrating on film and TV. His career lasted in Hollywood from 1954 to 1964. In addition to a few TV roles, he also had prominent roles in horror flicks such as *Monster from the Ocean Floor* and *Teenage Monster*.

Wagenheim, Charles (1896-1979) "The Clubhouse" (Painter)

Debuting in 1929's *The Trial of Mary Dugan*, Charles Wagenheim's career lasted for fifty years. He died in 1979, still a very much in demand character actor, murdered by a burglar he surprised upon his return home from grocery shopping. His longest recurring role of his career came in *Gunsmoke* where he played Halligan from 1966 to 1975 in twenty-eight episodes. Wagenheim was very active during the last decade of his life, with parts in thirty-two different TV shows or movies. Among those were appearances in *The Six Million Dollar Man*, *Kojak*, *Baretta*, *All in the Family* and the movie *Missouri Breaks*.

Wakefield, Carol (n/a) "The Big Fish Count" (Cathy Maddox)

Her only two acting roles were this one for *LITB* and in a horror/thriller film, *The Couch*, about a serial killer who warns the police each time he is about to kill, and after he kills, goes to his regularly scheduled therapist appointment.

Warde, Harlan (1917-1980) "Beaver's Autobiography" (Mr. Thompson)

An actor with a wealth of experience in Hollywood, he acted in more than 200 TV shows and movies. He was even hired by a neurology professor at USC to simulate neurological disorders for medical student instructional videos. During his career, he had a few recurring roles on TV, these included such parts on *Code 3*, *87th Precinct*, *The Rifleman*, *Lassie* and *The Virginian*. His final role was as Evan Grange on a 1979 episode of *The Rockford Files*.

Warren, Katherine (1905-1965) "Mrs. Brown" (Water Anyone?); "Beaver's Dance" (Mrs. Prescott); "The Dramatic Club" (Mrs. Prescott)

In the early 1950s, Warren garnered good roles in films such as *The Caine Mutiny*, *The Glenn Miller Story*, *The Steel Trap* and *This Woman is Dangerous*. Her first ever role was historic. She was in the cast of *Blind Alley*, a live televised ninety-minute movie for WNBT in New York City. WNBT was one of the first two commercially licensed television stations in the USA. WNBT later became WNBC. *Blind Alley* was one of the first commercially made TV movies ever.

Waters, Reba (b. 1947) "Eddie's Double-Cross" (Caroline Shuster)

Whether it's the *Los Angeles Times*' entertainment section, or IMDB, someone has the credits and possibly, the age of actress Reba Waters incorrect. The *Times*, in an article dated April 13, 1958, writes that she is an eleven-year-old actress. If that were true, when her role as Caroline Schuster was filmed, she would have only been thirteen years old. I hope all *LITB* fans can agree, that girl who double-crossed Eddie was no thirteen-year-old. The *Times* article also stated that Reba Waters had "about 35 other shows" (TV credits) at the time of its writing. However, IMDB only had fourteen listed for her up to the time the article was written. Some may say, "whatever," and your point is well taken. As for her career, according to IMDB, she had a total of twenty-five film and TV credits. These include *My Friend Flicka*, *Lassie*, *Father Knows Best* and a recurring role as Francesca on *Peck's Bad Girl*.

Washburn, Beverly (b. 1943) "Blind Date Committee" (Jill Bartlett)

Beverly Washburn was a veteran actor, with over forty roles on her resume before going on a date with Wally Cleaver in "The Blind Date Committee." One role had her playing an orphan girl named Susie on *The Ray Milland Show*. This was a situation comedy created, produced and oftentimes, written by Bob Mosher and Joe Connelly, the creators of *Leave it to Beaver*. In the episode, "The Christmas Story," (proving that Mosher and Connelly did know there was such thing as Christmas episodes despite there never being one on *LITB)* the Washburn character is at the home belonging to the main characters, Ray and Peggy McNulty. This home in which she experiences a traditional Christmas, is the same exact home, the exterior at least, that Mosher and Connelly use for the Cleaver home just a couple years later during the production of *Leave it to Beaver* in its first two seasons. This is the type of trivia us *LITB* fanatics crave. Although she has appeared in scores of TV shows and films, most people probably know Washburn for her appearance in the original *Star Trek* series in which she played Lieutenant Arlene Galway. No matter what show or movie she appears in, Beverly brings a flash of brightness to the final product on the screen, whether that screen is a small one inside a home, or a big screen inside a theater, or in front of a couple hundred cars outside at a drive-in. She's just that talented of an actress.

Wells, Carole (b.1942) "All-Night Party" (Kathy)

Leave it to Beaver was one of Carole's first appearances after she co-starred on *National Velvet* for two seasons. A tidbit very few might know is that each co-star of *National Velvet* appeared on *Leave it to Beaver* at some point during its run. This includes Lori Martin, Arthur Space, Ann Doran and Joey Scott. In fact, Doran and Scott were mother and son on two different *LITB episodes*. Rich Correll, who appeared on four episodes of *National Velvet*, would be another *National Velvet* actor to appear on *Leave it to Beaver*. Carol also had a recurring role as Lucy Hanks on *Pistols n' Petticoats* (1966-1967). She worked regularly in TV and movies until 1978 and then took a hiatus, coming back in 1989 for an episode of *1ˢᵗ and Ten* and then in 2019, she appeared in the ABC comedy *Single Parents*. In addition to acting, Carole Wells is an author, world traveler, humanitarian and coloratura soprano.

Wendell, Howard (1908-1975) "Wally's Haircomb" (Mr. Haller)

The character he plays in the "Wally's Haircomb" episode, offers June a lot of good advice about teenage boys. Unfortunately, he was only in this one episode of *Leave it to Beaver*. But when would he have ever had the time to be in more *LITB* episodes? Howard Wendell was a very busy actor. He acted in ten TV shows or movies in the year he portrayed Wally's principal Mr. Haller. While he appeared in many different TV shows, in some of them, he played in multiple episodes, making his workload even heavier than it looks at first glance. Among those shows in which he had multiple roles are *Public Defender, You are There, Dragnet, The George Burns and Gracie Allen Show, The Life and Legend of Wyatt Earp, Bonanza, Hazel, The Dick Van Dyke Show, The Adventures of Ozzie and Harriet,* and *Laredo*. This man was one busy actor. He retired from acting in 1971.

White, Will J. (1925-1992) "Wally's Car Accident" (Al)

Was a well-known figure skater before attending the American Academy of Dramatic Arts in New York City. His resume of over 100 acting credits points to him making the right decision to pursue acting over ice skating. Will was a successful character actor and appeared in the top shows on television during his career. A partial list includes *The Loretta Young Show, Sergeant Preston of the Yukon, Wagon Train, Death Valley Days, One Step Beyond, The Twilight Zone, Maverick, Lassie, Gunsmoke, Bonanza, The Six Million Dollar Man,* and *Quincy M.E.*, his final role in 1979.

White, Yolanda (b. 1951?) "New Neighbors" (Julie)

Not much is known about actress Yolanda White. Her first screen appearance was in the film *All Mine to Give* which was written by Dale Eunson who also wrote twelve episodes of *Leave it to Beaver*, albeit not "New Neighbors." It is possible Yolanda White was a family friend or a niece of Dale Eunson. When more info is found out, it will be included at http://leaveittobeaverbooks.com.

White, Yvonne (b. 1927?) "The Paper Route" (Newspaper Customer); "The Bus Ride" (Bus Passenger)

Most of Yvonne White's career was spent on the small screen, with a few exceptions being her minor roles in *The Best Things in Life Are Free*, *Bye Bye Birdie* and *Sex and the Single Girl*. That final film also included roles for three other *Leave it to Beaver* alumnae; Burt Mustin, William Fawcett and Max Showalter.

Wilcox, Frank (1907-1974) 3 episodes (Multiple roles)

A prolific character actor with over 300 acting credits, Frank Wilcox had a connection with Hugh Beaumont years before appearing on *Leave it to Beaver*. In 1952, Wilcox was cast in two episodes of *Racket Squad* in which Hugh Beaumont was the narrator. Before making acting his career choice, Wilcox worked in a lemon grove and ran his own tire repair store. But acting turned out well for Frank Wilcox. Many honors have been bestowed upon him. Los Angles declared January 11, 1964 as "Frank Wilcox Day," and also named him Honorary Fire Chief. Also, during the 1960s, Granada Hills, CA named him "honorary mayor." The final and maybe best honor to be bestowed upon Frank Wilcox was his hometown of DeSoto, Missouri honoring him on March 13, 2013 with their own "Frank Wilcox Day," and the First Annual Frank Wilcox Film Festival. Wilcox was nothing less than a character actor legend.

Williams, Vince (n/a) "Chuckie's New Shoes" (Man in Shoe Store)

Appearing in two episodes of *Leave it to Beaver*, he also worked on the episode, "The Sore Loser," but he wasn't seen, only heard, as his role was that of an announcer. In many of the roles during his career he played a new reporter or a newscaster. He appeared in the original *Dragnet*, *Dragnet 1967*, *Whirlybirds*, multiple episodes of *The Alfred Hitchcock Hour*, *McHale's Navy*, and *Ironside*, his last acting credit, in which he played a newscaster.

Windsor, Allen (b. 1922? - ??) "The Clubhouse" (Ice Cream Man)

In 1952 Allen Windsor debuted on the big screen with a small part in *Scorched Fury*. After this film, Windsor remained dormant in Hollywood until his role on *Leave it to Beaver*. He finished his career in *The Purple Gang* starring Robert Blake in 1959, a very underrated "B" movie about a tough 1920s gang in Detroit, Michigan.

Winkleman, Wendy (b. 1948) "The Black Eye" (Violet Rutherford)

Wendy was one of the few experienced child actors on *Leave it to Beaver*'s first season who did not have a recurring role. She had about the same experience as both Jerry Mathers and Ken Osmond and had more experience than Tony Dow, Jeri Weil, Stanley Fafara and Rusty Stevens. Even with that experience, she did not come back to play Violet Rutherford in Violet's next appearances in the series. Wendy went on to do more TV, but her career ended by 1966. Her brother Michael played Luke McCoy on the ABC series *The Real McCoys*.

Withers, Bernadette (1946-2019) "Wally's Glamour Girl" (Kitty Bannerman)

Best known for her recurring role on *Bachelor Father* as Ginger, Bernadette Withers was on the situation comedy from 1957 to 1962. While she was working on *Bachelor Father*, she appeared in other shows like *Leave it to Beaver*, *The Eve Arden Show*, *Father Knows Best*, *Tales of Wells Fargo*, *Peck's Bad Girl*, *Wagon Train*, *Shirley Temple's Storybook*, and *The Real McCoy's*. Bernadette continued to work in Hollywood for a few years after *Bachelor Father* ended. Her last few credits include roles on *My Three Sons*, *Going My Way*, *The Adventures of Ozzie and Harriet*, *Karen*, *The Trouble with Angels (a movie with Rosalind Russell)*, and *The Beverly Hillbillies*. For *Leave it to Beaver* fans who may be interested, Bernadette was known for her red hair and freckles.

Wood, Wally (1941-2020) "Beaver, the Bunny" (Boy)

He appeared in one film (*The Bus is Coming*) and one TV show (*Target-The Corruptors!*) besides his appearance in *Leave it to Beaver*.

Woodson, William (1917-2017) "Uncle Billy's Visit" (Mr. Gaines)

William Woodson was the narrator for ABC Radio's *This is Your FBI* which aired from 1945 to 1953. He also worked on other radio programs and continued his narrator role when he turned his talents to television. Some of those many television shows were *Lights Out*, *Dick Tracy*, *The Americans*, *McHale's Navy*, *Jericho*, *The Invaders*, *Get Smart* and *The Odd Couple*. When not narrating, he found success with a recurring role in *This Man Dawson*, where he played Sgt. Ed Blankey for thirty-one episodes. He also had multiple roles on *Perry Mason* and in 1977, he turned his attention to voice work on animated shows such as *Superfriends*, *Plastic Man*, *Spiderman* and he did work for various other cartoons.

Wootton, Stephen (1945-2014) "Beaver and Ivanhoe" (Clyde Appleby)

A decade in Hollywood and working continuously proves one is a successful actor. This was the story of Stephen Wootton. He appeared on two episodes of *Leave it to Beaver*, the second being "Beaver's Freckles." Some of the popular shows he appeared in were *My Little Margie*, *Death Valley Days*, *I Love Lucy*, *My Friend Flicka*, *The Adventures of Superman*, and the *Real McCoys*. He had multiple roles on *Cavalcade of America*, *Playhouse 90*, *The Jack Benny Program*, and he had a recurring role on *This is Alice*. Two years before the debut of *Leave it to Beaver*, Wootton appeared in the film *The Private War of Major Benson* which was based on a story by Mosher and Connelly, was directed by Jerry Hooper who directed the *LITB* pilot *It's a Small World* and included four other actors who also worked on *LITB* – Madge Blake, Anne Barton, Mary Alan Hokason, and Jess Kirkpatrick.

Wright, Howard (1896-1990) "Eddie's Double-Cross" (Mr. Newton)

An army officer in WW I, a talented songwriter, a Vaudeville performer and radio actor, Howard Wright had lived a full life, even before he set his sights on Hollywood in the early 1950s. Early on, he found himself playing multiple parts on *Space Patrol*, and later, did the same for *Highway Patrol*, *Gunsmoke*, *Death Valley Days* and Bonanza. His final TV series credit was *Daniel Boone* in 1966 and over the final ten years of his career, he had roles in four lower budgeted films, including *Good Times*, starring Sonny and Cher.

Wright, Will (1894-1962) "Child Care" (Pete at Firehouse #7)

A former San Francisco newspaper reporter, Will Wright decided to switch careers and eventually made his way to Hollywood where he wound up with over 200 acting credits. He first worked with

Leave it to Beaver writers Joe Connelly and Bob Mosher on the *Amos 'n' Andy Show* in the episode "Counterfeiters Rent Basement." He also worked on that episode with future *Leave it to Beaver* actor John Hoyt ("Part-Time Genius," "Wally's New Suit," "Beaver's Accordion"). Will died of cancer in Hollywood at the age of sixty-eight.

Wyenn, Than (1919-2015) "Wally's Dinner Date" (The Waiter)

Than Wyenn began acting as a teenager and later studied with the great Lee Strasberg. Over the entirety of his acting career, although he worked with different directors, on different sets, working on shows that covered a variety of genres, working at a variety of studios, there remained one constant and that was his wife, Gertrude. At the time of his death, they had been married seventy-one years and had two children, Joel and Neil.

Now, about that career, his first acting credit came in 1949 when he played a cabbie in *The Undercover Man* which starred Glenn Ford as a treasury agent. Than had very few additional movie roles over his career, but a couple worth mentioning are his bit parts in Cecil B. DeMille's *The Ten Commandments* and Ron Howard's *Splash*. Of the almost 200 TV acting credits on his resume, many were on the top TV shows of whatever decade he was working. In the 1950s, he appeared on *Dragnet*, *Gunsmoke* and *Perry Mason*. In the 1960s, he appeared on *The Twilight Zone*, *The Alfred Hitchcock Hour*, *The Munsters, Rat Patrol* and *Get Smart*. The 1970s saw him working on *Night Gallery, Cannon, Lou Grant* and *The Six Million Dollar Man*. Then, in his final decade of work, he appeared on *Remington Steele, Quincy M.E., Newhart* and *Knight Rider*.

Another notable accomplishment for Than was that he was also one of the founders of the Yiddish Kinder Theater in Los Angeles.

Y

Young, Carleton G. (1907-1971) "Beaver and Gilbert" (John Gates)

Had a career in radio before moving permanently to movies and TV, working on shows like *The Count of Monte Cristo, The Whisperer* and *The Adventures of Ellery Queen* and many others. Early in his Hollywood career, he co-starred in the films *Queen of Burlesque* and *Hard, Fast and Beautiful!* About the same time, he also had a small role in *Bud Abbott and Lou Costello in Hollywood*. His first role in a television series was playing Dr. Henry Tully on *The Unexpected* in 1952. A few years later, he had a recurring role in Erle Stanley Gardner's *The Court of Last Resort*, a show that dramatized actual court cases of defendants found guilty, but where there may be a chance they were really innocent. When that series ended, his next role was as John Gates in *Leave it to Beaver*. After appearing as Gilbert's father, Young only worked in Hollywood for two more years, topping off his resume with a role on *Tales of Wells Fargo*.

Yount, John (b. 1947 or 1948) "The Clothing Drive" (Chuck)

His short career consisted of this role on *Leave it to Beaver* and appearing in one episode of *Alfred Hitchcock Presents*.

DIRECTORS
(Not alphabetical)

Hopper, Jerry (1907-1988) "It's a Small World"

Among Jerry Hopper's seventy-four credits are many TV westerns. Hailing from Guthrie, Oklahoma, he was most likely drawn to the genre because of his youth. In addition to directing the pilot episode of *Leave it to Beaver*, Hopper directed episodes of *Zane Grey Theater*, *Cimarron City*, *Laws of the Plainsman*, *Wichita Town*, *Overland Trail*, *Cheyenne*, *Bat Masterson*, *Tales of Well Fargo*, *Have Gun Will Travel*, Wagon *Train*, *Gunsmoke*, *Laredo*, and *The Virginian*. In World War II, Hopper was a combat photographer and after an injury in the South Pacific theater, was awarded a Purple Heart. Not limited to westerns after his lone *Leave it to Beaver* episode, he also worked on *Voyage to the Bottom of the Sea*, *Gilligan's Island*, *Perry Mason* and *The Fugitive*.

Tokar, Norman (1919-1979) 93 episodes

Not much is known about the early life of director Norman Tokar, who helmed almost 100 episodes of *Leave it to Beaver* during its first three seasons. Born in Newark, NJ two days before Thanksgiving in 1919, the son of a contractor,[188] one has to fast forward almost 20 years when Tokar, as an eighteen year old found work as an understudy to Ezra Stone's Henry Aldrich on the Clifford Goldsmith play, *What a Life*.[189] This play ran for 538 performances and eventually spun off the long running *Aldrich Family* radio show. One year later, Tokar made his Broadway debut playing the part of Irving Frankel in Richard Maibaum (screenwriter of multiple James Bond films) and Harry Clork's *See My Lawyer* at the Biltmore Theater on 47th Street. The show ran for a healthy 224 performances until April 1940. After this production, Tokar continued living in New York, performing small parts in many other plays including *Delicate Story*, *Lamented Life of Reilly*, *Sailor Beware*, *Days of Our Youth* and *The Magic Touch*.

     Tokar began his radio career on *The Aldrich Family* where after playing Henry's friend Willie Marshall, he took over for actor Ezra Stone, the longtime voice of Henry when Stone was drafted by the U.S. Army during World War II. Tokar remained in this role until he was called up to the U.S. Army Signal Corps in 1943.[190] Tokar not only played Henry's friend Willie Marshall and later the title role, but also wrote many of the radio scripts. It is safe to say that Norman Tokar's time with *The Aldrich Family* radio show was very influential in his later work with *Leave it to Beaver*. One could look at *The Aldrich Family* and see it as basically *Leave it to Beaver* without Wally and Beaver. From the wholesome and very intelligent father in Sam Aldrich who was awarded as radio's "outstanding father" by the National Father's Day Committee in 1942 to friends like Willie Marshall and Homer Brown. Those characters look much like Ward Cleaver, Lumpy Rutherford, Eddie Haskell and Larry Mondello. Additionally, as *Leave it to Beaver* was the first TV sitcom to look at life from a child's point of view, this was already the case with some radio shows, especially *The Aldrich Family*, even though Henry and his friends were older when they first appeared on radio, than the Cleaver kids were when they first appeared on TV.

     All *Leave it to Beaver* fans know Norman Tokar for his name appearing in the credits for basically all the episodes of the first three seasons. He was the director. He was the one responsible

---

[188] "The Aldrich Family." *Radio Album*. (New York: Dell Publishing, Winter 1942.) 41.
[189] Dunning, John. *On the Air: The Encyclopedia of Old-Time Radio*. (New York: Oxford University Press, 1998), 22.
[190] Ibid.

for the actors performing perfectly, or so that's what we see in the finished product. He could be a taskmaster at times and as Robert Mittelstaedt (the actor who played Charles Fredericks during the first two seasons) once quipped about Tokar, "He'd get angry with Whitey (Stan Fafara) when he wouldn't do what he was told. But that was before he (Tokar) found out Fafara was a little hard of hearing." Overall, Tokar was a much beloved director. Actress Pamela Beaird (Mary Ellen Rogers) said Tokar was great with the young actors. He was like a kid himself she mentioned, but he could be serious when he needed to be. She remembered him for wearing big dark rimmed glasses and just watching him would sometimes cause her and Tony Dow to bust up laughing before filming a scene together. His daughter Deborah said of her father, "He had a fabulous sense of humor."[191]

Tokar, after *Leave it to Beaver*, went on to direct many other television shows such as *The Tab Hunter Show*, *The Donna Reed Show* and *The Doris Day Show*. However, his biggest post-Beaver success came from his association with Walt Disney. His Disney directorial debut was with the adventure *Big Red* in 1962. He followed up with *Savage Same*, *Those Calloways*, *The Ugly Dachshund*. He had his biggest Disney hits in the 1970s with *Where the Red Fern Grows*, *The Apple Dumpling Gang*, *No Deposit No Return* and 1978's *The Cat from Outer Space*, his last film before his unexpected death at the age of 59.

Butler, David (1894-1979) 58 episodes

Directing ran in the Butler family. His father Fred Butler was a stage director and later became a director and actor in Hollywood, working in several silent pictures in the 1910s and early 1920s. The first film David Butler appeared in was *The Face at the Window* (1910), directed by famed director D.W. Griffith. He also worked with Griffith in other films, including *Birth of a Nation* where he played both a Union soldier and a Confederate soldier. Butler acted regularly in films until 1929 when he decided to go behind the camera, the place in Hollywood where he gained the most respect and success. His early years were spent at 20th Century Fox where he directed many Shirley Temple films. He then moved to Warner Brothers where he worked on a few Bob Hope movies (*Road to Morocco*, *They Got Me Covered*, *Caught in the Draft*, *The Princess and the Pirate*). After his last film for Warner Brothers in 1956, Butler went on to direct television shows until he retired in 1967. His first directorial work on TV was the time travel adventure show, *Captain Z-Ro* (1955-1956). It was just a few years later when he began directing various episodes of *Leave it to Beaver*. Ending his run on the show in 1963, he finished with fifty-eight episodes. While working on *LITB*, he also directed other shows including *Overland Trail*, *Bringing Up Buddy*, *The Deputy*, *Wagon Train*, *The Hathaways* and *Twilight Zone*.

Abbott, Norman (1922-2016) 43 episodes

The nephew of comedian Bud Abbott, Norman Abbott was raised by his uncle and his mother.[192] An actor at the beginning of his career in Hollywood, Norman Abbott, after his time in the Navy during WW II (as a member of the original Navy Seal team), went back to Hollywood and quickly began working toward what would become a very successful career in directing. His first taste of behind-the-scenes work occurred on the set of some Abbott and Costello films where he worked as the dialogue director. His first TV directorial work began with three episodes of *Stars of Jazz* in 1956. Two years later, he had his first interaction related to *Leave it to Beaver* when he directed six episodes of *The George Gobel Show*. George Gobel was part owner of Gomalco Productions which

[191] November 2022 correspondence with author.
[192] Saperstein, Pat. "Norman Abbott, Veteran Sitcom Director, Dies at 93" *Variety.com*. https://variety.com/2016/tv/news/norman-abbott-dead-dies-brady-bunch-bud-abbott-1201812235/

owned *Leave it to Beaver*. In two more years, he became a semi-regular director on *Leave it to Beaver*, directing forty-three episodes between 1960 and 1962. During that time, he also directed six episodes of another Connelly and Mosher production, *Ichabod and Me.*

After *Leave it to Beaver* finished its run, Abbott later directed multiple episodes of *The Munsters*, yet another Connelly and Mosher production. In the 1980s, he directed three episodes of *The New Leave it to Beaver*. One thing that is quite surprising is how young Abbott was when he first began directing *Leave it to Beaver*. He was only thirty-seven years old when he directed his first episode, *Wally's Orchid*. When actress Pamela Beaird Hensley, in a recent interview, was told of his age when he directed her in this episode, she was quite surprised, thinking he was a much older man. She had fond recollections of his direction for her on the set, especially in the scene where she's talking to Wally, telling him of her need to have an orchid. After *Leave it to Beaver*, Abbott continued to direct until 1989. One of his big claims to fame was helping create *Sugar Babies*, the Broadway comeback vehicle for Mickey Rooney in the late 1970s. A good man with great skills, these two things are not something always found in the same package, especially in Hollywood, but they were with Norman Abbott.

Beaumont, Hugh (1907-1982) 23 episodes

The only man listed in both the actor and director section; Hugh Beaumont began directing episodes during the third season of *Leave it to Beaver*. His directorial debut was "Wally and Alma," about six months after the beginning of season three. This occurred about six months after his mother-in-law suffered life threatening injuries in a car crash when the car she was in overturned about thirty miles south of Gillette, Wyoming and passed away from those injuries in a Cheyenne Wyoming hospital a few days later.[193] [194] His son Hunter was driving the family from Minnesota to Los Angeles when the one-car crash occurred. Every year, the family spent their summers in Minnesota. This year, there had been a change in the date when Hugh was needed back in Hollywood and instead of driving the family himself, he flew back and his son was tasked with driving the family back from Minnesota.[195] While it is only an assumption on my part, the move from Republic Studios to Universal may have necessitated a change in the shooting schedule, causing Hugh Beaumont to fly back to Hollywood instead of driving.

It may have always in the plans of Connelly and Mosher to have Hugh Beaumont direct episodes of *Leave it to Beaver*. Having him do so in season three may also have been due to what Jerry Mathers spoke of in his book *The World According to Beaver*. In his book, Jerry wrote that Hugh Beaumont was simply going through the motions of his role on the show in the months after the crash that took his mother-in-law's life. Whatever the reason for his directing beginning with S3 E25, "Wally and Alma," it was a good choice by the producers, as Beaumont clearly had a skill for getting the most out of actors in a scene and was a true professional.

In season three, he directed two episodes, the other was "Beaver's Bike," which aired the week following "Wally and Alma," but according to the production code, was filmed four weeks later. [196] In season four, Beaumont's directorial output increased to three episodes, and they were "Ward's Millions," "Wally and Dudley," and "Beaver's Rat." Season five saw that output go to six

---

[193] "Mrs. Anna Hohn" *Seward County Independent*, September 16. 1959.

[194] "Woman's Death Added to Wyoming Road Toll" *Billings Gazette*, September 20, 1959.

[195] Mathers, Cleaver. *The World According to Beaver.*

[196] This link will show the production codes for all episodes and although it may not be 100% correct, it is a good guide to the order in which the episodes were filmed.
https://en.wikipedia.org/wiki/List_of_Leave_It_to_Beaver_episodes

episodes and in the final season, Hugh Beaumont directed twelve episodes or almost one-third of the entire final season.

In the years after *Leave it to Beaver*, Beaumont never directed a TV show again, but he did spend a lot of time in community theater work, and sometimes that involved directing, something he enjoyed very much.

Neilson, James (1909-1979) "The Broken Window"

A prolific television director, James Neilson already had directed episodes on eighteen different shows before he was tapped to direct "The Broken Window" in season one of *Leave it to Beaver*. Neilson also directed one movie before directing Beaver. His lone movie was *Night Passage* starring Jimmy Stewart and Audie Murphy. Neilson directed the only episode in *Leave it to Beaver's* first season which was not directed by Norman Tokar. On an earlier Bob Mosher / Joe Connelly production, *The Ray Milland Show* (1953-1955), Neilson directed three episodes. After his lone *Leave it to Beaver* episode, Neilson went on to direct TV in all genres including many westerns, until he retired from Hollywood in 1973. Among those westerns were *Wagon Train*, *The Rifleman*, *Pony Express*, *Have Gun Will Travel*, *Bonanza* and *The Virginian*.

There were many other directors who worked on *Leave it to Beaver* that are not mentioned here in any biographical detail, they were: Earl Bellamy (4 episodes, 1960-1963), Gene Reynolds (3 episodes, 1960), Charles F. Haas (2 episodes, 1961-1963), Anton Leader (2 episodes, 1961-1962), Jeffrey Hayden (2 episodes, 1962) Andrew McCullough (1 episode, 1960), Bretaigne Windust (1 episode, 1960) and Dann Cahn (1 episode, 1961).

WRITERS

(Not alphabetical)

MacLane, Roland (1903-1984)

Writer Roland MacLane, the most prolific of all Leave it to Beaver writers (having written with partner Dick Conway, nearly one third of all the episodes) was born in Massachusetts in 1903. At the age of nineteen MacLane bravely journeyed by himself across the country to try his hand in Hollywood. His first work in Hollywood? He was a stuntman in silent pictures. Probably not wanting to risk life and limb, he eventually went into commercial art, becoming an art director in San Francisco before finally opening his own art store on Hollywood Boulevard. Owning an art store didn't particularly satisfy MacLane. He eventually landed a job as a newspaper reporter.[197]

By 1940, he was living in Glendale with his wife and two children and writing jokes for radio shows. He first broke into the business in this way because a friend told him he could make $5.00 a joke if they were used on a show. He moved onto writing radio scripts for shows like *My Friend Irma* and *The Edgar Bergen / Charlie McCarthy Show*. Bob Mosher and Joe Connelly were also writers Edgar Bergen at that time. Before *Leave it to Beaver*, MacLane had much success writing for *The Life of Riley* TV show and his talent is highlighted in the contrast shown in his *Leave it to Beaver* writing, as Riley featured a bumbling out of the loop father and Beaver featured a loving, intelligent, no-nonsense father.

According to MacLane's son in a 2015 interview, his father took the show very personally

---

[197] "Riley Writer Really Rambled." *The Pittsburgh Press*. March 18, 1956.

as many of the situations echoed his own family life with a loving wife who was affectionately called Mrs. Cleaver by his children's friends. The friends would even call his house and ask to speak to "the Beaver." And the most famous *Leave it to Beaver* episode, "In the Soup," was even inspired by a drive MacLane and his son took one day where they saw a Campbell's Soup billboard which had a cup of faux soup with steam coming out of the cup/bowl. His son asked, "Dad, do you think there's really soup in there?" That sparked a light in MacLane and voila, the most iconic episode of the most iconic of all classic TV shows was born.

MacLane's writing post-Beaver included *The Munsters*, *The Andy Griffith Show*, *The Donna Reed Show* and *Gilligan's Island*.

Conway, Dick (1914 -2003)

Dick Conway was the alphabetically superior in the dynamic writing duo of the Dick Conway / Roland MacLane. His name always appeared first in credits even though Conway was eleven years younger than MacLane. The duo began working together on TV in 1953 when they wrote an episode for *The Dennis Day Show* ("An Old Friend"). They continued working together on *The Life of Riley*, *How to Marry a Millionaire*, *Make Room for Daddy* and then their starring role as writers of one third of all *Leave it to Beaver* episodes.

After *Leave it to Beaver*, Conway and MacLane continued their partnership with episodes of *Gilligan's Island*, *The Munsters* and *The Donna Reed Show* with their last collaboration coming in a 1967 episode of *Off to See the Wizard*. Conway went on to write almost 100 episodes of *Petticoat Junction* and the 1970s saw him branch out into animation (*The All-New Superfriends Hour*) and drama (*Emergency!*, *The Life and Times of Grizzly Adams*).

It's safe to say, that *Leave it to Beaver* would not be nearly the show it was if not for the writing team of Dick Conway and Roland McLane.

Manhoff, Bill (1919-1974) "The Haircut," "Voodoo Magic," "Cleaning Up Beaver," "My Brother's Girl"

Bill Manhoff has three things in common with long time *Leave it to Beaver* director Norman Tokar. Like Tokar, Manhoff was instrumental in the first season of the situation comedy. They were both born in Newark. They also were both born in 1919. Manhoff wrote four of the funniest episodes of Leave it to Beaver's first season. Who cannot remember the hilarity of Beaver and Wally in, "The Haircut?" While only writing four episodes of *Leave it to Beaver*, Manhoff went on to write for a number of successful television programs in the 1960s and 1970s. The show where he enjoyed his most success was *The Real McCoys* for which he wrote nineteen episodes. Some of the other shows included *The Ann Southern Show*, *Petticoat Junction*, *Room 222*, *All in the Family*, *The Partridge Family* and *Sanford and Son*. In his one Broadway endeavor, he wrote *The Owl and the Pussycat* which ran for one year and over 400 performances. This show was later made into a feature adapted for film by screenwriter Buck Henry.

Ross, Bob (1908-1972) 13 episodes

The TV industry in Hollywood was a very insulated community in the 1950s. An example can be seen in the work of writer Bob Ross. A couple years before writing his first of thirteen episodes of *Leave it to Beaver*, Ross wrote an episode of *Professional Father* which starred Barbara Billingsley. This episode also featured three other future *Leave it to Beaver* actors, Beverly Washburn ("Blind Date Committee"), Phyllis Coates ("New Neighbors") and Joseph Kearns ("It's a Small World"). He also worked with *Leave it to Beaver* creators Joe Connelly and Bob Mosher on *The Amos 'n' Andy Show*. Then there's his connection with George Gobel. He wrote for *The George Gobel Show* and Gobel's production company produced *Leave it to Beaver* the first four years it aired. Ross went on after *Leave it to Beaver* to perform many duties on *The Andy Griffith Show* including script consulting, producing, and writing. When *The Andy Griffith Show* left the air, Ross created Mayberry R.F.D. which ran for seventy-eight episodes.

Diamond, Mel (1920-2002) "Wally's Girl Trouble" "The Perfume Salesmen" "Party Invitation"

One of the first TV writing jobs Mel Diamond found in Hollywood was his work for *Leave it to Beaver*. His only *Leave it to Beaver* scripts were written during season one. He wrote for quite a few shows after *Leave it to Beaver* including *The Ann Southern Show*, *The Many Loves of Dobie Gillis*, *The Bob Cummings Show* and *Bachelor Father* for which he wrote thirteen episodes, the most he wrote for any series. After a break in the mid-1960s, Diamond wrote one last episode in 1969 for *Here's Lucy*.

Gershman, Ben (1909-1995) "Wally's Girl Trouble" "The Perfume Salesmen" "Party Invitation"

In season one of *Leave it to Beaver*, Ben Gershman co-wrote three scripts with writer Mel Diamond. Gershman was a very accomplished TV writer before his contributions to *Leave it to Beaver*, having written forty-five scripts for *The Adventures of Ozzie and Harriet* show beginning in 1952. But for years before that, he had worked on the Ozzie and Harriet radio show. Working regularly on sitcoms into the early 1970s, Gershman had his most success with *The Andy Griffith Show*, *My Favorite Martian*, *Julia* and *The Brady Bunch*. His final work can be seen in the 1980 episode of *Diff'rent Strokes* titled "Small Claims Court."

Van Hartesveldt, Fran (1912-1970) "The Paper Route" "The Perfect Father")

While *Leave it to Beaver* fans may know Fran Van Haresveldt from his writing "The Paper Route," and "The Perfect Father," the world knows him from his most famous words ever uttered, "Think you can say 'Parkay' without lousing it up?"[198] These words were said to an aspiring actress named Betty White before she had a union card in Hollywood. She had just spoken to him in his office and basically was told she was out of luck when it came to getting a job because she first needed a union card. However, before she could become a member of the radio union (this was before TV was the big medium), she needed to have a set part on a show, a true Catch-22 situation. After being told the facts of life by Van Hartesveldt only moments earlier, she headed to the elevator. She walked in, dejected, pressed "1" and waited for the doors to close. As they did, none other than Mr. Encouragement reached in, preventing the doors from closing. He popped in and the unemployable Betty White stood in silence as they traversed to the first floor. As the door opened, a tinge of pity maybe, touched Van Hartesveldt's heart and he told Betty that he understood the situation she found herself in and agreed to let her say one word on the follow week's episode of *The Great Gildersleeve* show. That's all she would need to do to get a union card. He told her all she had to do was say the word, "Parkay" without messing it up. Well, she didn't mess it up and her career went on to be the ultimate definition of longevity.

He produced, directed and wrote radio shows such as *The Great Gildersleeve*, *The Aldrich Family*, *The Roy Rogers Show*, *Luke Slaughter of Tombstone* and others. However, his IMDB

---

[198] White, Betty. "Here We Go Again." Scribner, 1995, 21-22.

listing only shows he worked on two other television shows after *Beaver*, writing two episodes of *Tombstone Territory* and two episodes of *Bat Masterson*.

Leslie, Phil (1909-1988) "Beaver's Crush" "The Bank Account"

After a very successful career in radio working as the head writer for *Fibber McGee and Molly* for thirteen years and before that, writing for radio stars Bob Hope, Roy Rogers and Al Pierce, writer Phil Leslie went the only place he could after radio, television. His first attempt at TV writing was for *Leave it to Beaver*. He only wrote two episodes for *Leave it to Beaver* and they both aired in season one. Leslie went on to write for some of the most successful situation comedies of the 1960s. Just take a look at this amazing list: *Dennis the Menace*, *Petticoat Junction*, *The Beverly Hillbillies*, *The Donna Reed Show*, *Hazel*, *The Farmer's Daughter*, *Green Acres*, *The Addams Family*, *The Lucy Show*, *My Three Sons*, *Get Smart*, *Family Affair*, *Here's Lucy* and *The Brady Bunch*. Talk about writing for an entire generation of kids, that's what writer Phil Leslie did and he did it well.

Vollaerts, Hendrik (1918- 1988) "The Black Eye" "Part Time Genius"

Prolific over a number of different genres, Hendrik Vollaerts was talented enough to write one of the funniest episodes of *Leave it to Beaver*'s first season ("The Black Eye") and also write one of the most touching episodes of *Star Trek* ("For the World Is Hollow and I Have Touched The Sky"), arguably the best of that sci-fi show's third season. Additionally, Vollaerts wrote for *Voyage to the Bottom of the Sea* and even created a new villain for *Batman* named The Bookworm. Four years previous to writing his *Leave it to Beaver* episodes, he worked with Mosher and Connelly on their production, *The Ray Milland Show*. Vollaerts' final job in Hollywood was at age fifty-five when he wrote a script for the Hanna Barbera animated series *Devlin*. Hendrik Vollaerts passed away in Mission Viejo, CA at the age of 69 in 1988.

Nathan, Lydia (???- ???) "The Clubhouse"

Not much can be said about writer Lydia Nathan. She contributed stories to *Leave it to Beaver* and *Bachelor Father*. The *Bachelor Father* episode for which she is credited with the story idea was directed by Jerry Hopper, who also directed the pilot episode of *Leave it to Beaver* ("It's a Small World").

Goldsmith, Clifford (1899-1971) "Water Anyone?"

Goldsmith is best known for his writing the play *What a Life* in 1938 which introduced the popular Henry Aldrich character. Just a few years later, Goldsmith was one of the highest paid writers in Hollywood. In 1943, Time Magazine reported his salary was $3000 a week. *The Aldrich Family* was broadcast on radio from 1939 to 1953 and spawned eleven movies over that time and even a television show which lasted three years. After Aldrich, Goldsmith wrote occasionally for television on series such as *Dennis the Menace*, *The Donna Reed Show*, *The Patty Duke Show* and *The Flying Nun*.

Smith, Robert Paul (1915-1977) "Next Door Indians"

It'd be great to get a television credit just for suggesting a story and that's what happened with writer Robert Paul Smith. Already a successful novelist and playwright during the 1940s, he is probably best known for writing books on children doing nothing, such as *Where Did You Go? Out. What Did You Do? Nothing* and *How to Do Nothing with Nobody All Alone by Yourself*. He also co-wrote the play *The Tender Trap* with Max Schulman, creator of Dobie Gillis.

Patrick, John (1905-1995) "Music Lesson"

Probably one of the most successful of the *Leave it to Beaver* writers from season one. John Patrick contributed the story for "Music Lesson." This could've been a written outline of the story or a script. But in the early days of TV, there were many times writers weren't credited completely. This could've been one of those times. His track record up to this time was very impressive. He began writing radio scripts in the early 1930s for the radio program *Cecil and Sally* which originated in San Francisco and later was syndicated nationally. In addition to his radio work, he began writing plays and had his first big Broadway success with *The Hasty Heart* in 1945. By 1958 when he contributed his story to *Leave it to Beaver* producers Mosher and Connelly, Patrick had thirty-four writing credits, including many movie screenplays such as *Three Coins in the Fountain* and *Love is a Many-Splendored Thing*. Patrick won the Pulitzer Prize for Drama for his play *The Teahouse of the August Moon* in 1954 as well as two Tony Awards for the same play. After *Beaver*, Patrick went on to write more movies including *The World of Suzie Wong* and *The Shoes of the Fisherman*.

Whedon, John (1905-1991) "Beaver's Bad Day"

The Whedon family patriarch had a wonderful career in radio before moving into writing for TV. He wrote for various radio shows, but the highlight of his radio career was his tenure on *The Great Gildersleeve* show during the 1940s. In TV, he is best known for his work on *The Andy Griffith Show* and *The Dick Van Dyke show*. In season two of *Leave it to Beaver*, he also contributed the story for "The Grass is Always Greener," the better of his two Beaver contributions. John Whedon did much to entertain American audiences and does so today through his posterity. His son Tom Whedon and grandsons Joss, Jed and Zack Whedon have written scripts or created shows such as *Alice, Benson, It's a Living, The Golden Girls, Dollhouse, Buffy the Vampire Slayer, Angel, Parenthood, Roseanne, Southland, Deadwood, Agents of S.H.I.E.L.D.* and *Drop Dead Diva*.

Tibbles, George (1913-1987) 12 episodes

George Tibbles was a talented musician, composer, and scriptwriter. Although he wrote television scripts for some of best loved shows from the 1950s to the 1980s, he is probably best known for a song he wrote called, "The Woody Woodpecker Song," yes, that Woody Woodpecker. In 1948 this composition was nominated for an Academy Award in the best song category. He later composed the theme song for *The Charlie Weaver Show*, and the TV show *Pistols 'n' Petticoats*, a series he created in 1966. He wrote a majority of the scripts for two comedies starring Betty White, *Life with Elizabeth* (1952-1955) and *Date with the Angels* (1957-1958), and three episodes of *The Betty White Show* (1958). The 1960s saw a majority of his writing work done for *Dennis the Menace*, *Leave it to Beaver*, *Pistols 'n' Petticoats*, and *My Three Sons*, the show for which he wrote over 100 episodes from 1969-1972. Towards the end of his writing career in Hollywood, he worked regularly as either a scriptwriter or story consultant on *Hello Larry*, *One Day at a Time*, and *Charles in Charge*.

Dale Eunson (1904-2002) Katherine Eunson 12 episodes

Married scriptwriting team, working steadily from the early 1950s to 1969 together. The one show they are best known for is *Leave it to Beaver*, writing episodes for every season except the first one and a total of twelve. Among them are some of the best remembered of the series such as "Blind Date Committee," "Teacher Comes to Dinner," "The Hypnotist," "June's Birthday," and "Wally's Dinner Date." They also wrote for *How to Marry a Millionaire*, *Wagon Train*, *Father of the Bride*, and *Ironside*. After Katherine's death in 1970, Dale continued to write until 1977 and those shows included *Born Free*, *Little House on the Prairie*, and *The Waltons*.

Mathilde Ferro (1906-1990) and Theodore Ferro (1924-2003) 10 episodes

Along with Dale and Katherine Eunson, they were the second husband and wife writing team to work on *Leave it to Beaver*. They wrote ten episodes about the Cleaver family, and they were seen in seasons two, three, four and six. This husband-and-wife team also wrote for *Robert Montgomery Presents*, *Yancy Derringer*, *The Donna Reed Show*, *My Three Sons*, *Window on Main Street*, *Peyton Place and* their most prolific output coming on the soap operas *Days of Our Lives* and *General Hospital*.

Hoffman, Joseph (1909-1997) 6 episodes

A writer of many film screenplays from the 1930s to the mid-1950s, before writing for television. One of Joseph Hoffman's best screenplays was the Maureen O'Hara / Errol Flynn film *Against All Flags*. Most of his TV writing was done for three shows, *Leave it to Beaver*, *My Three Sons* and *Family Affair*. Of his *Beaver* episodes, most were written for season five. For season five, he wrote "Beaver's Laundry" and "Beaver the Babysitter." A few episodes after these aired, writer Bob Ross referenced Hoffman's film, *Against All Flags* in "Brother vs. Brother."

Other Writers

Here is a list of other writers who scripted episodes of *Leave it to Beaver*. These writers only have one or two episodes credited to them. Richard Baer, Ed James, Arthur Kober, Kenneth A. Enochs, Wilton Schiller, Lou Breslow, Allan Manings, Norman Tokar, Fred Shevin, Hugh Beaumont, Keith Fowler, Elon Packard, Norman Paul, Harry Winkler, Peggy Chantler Dick, William Cowley, Frank Gabrielson, Edward J. O'Connor, Jon Zimmer, Raphael Blau, Bob Fisher, Alan Lipscott, Ellis Marcus, Gwen Bagni, William Gargaro Jr.,and David Levinson.

For more information on the other writers and directors for which biographical details are not included, please visit http://leaveittobeaverbooks.com.

Author Note

Thank you for traversing with me back through time, to a simpler place with less worries and more fun. I hope you have enjoyed these pages filled with history, nostalgia and deep discussion into all things Leave it to Beaver. If you have, I hope you will review the book on Amazon.com or anywhere else you can leave a review. Please tell a friend about The World Famous Beaverpedia and take the book to get signed when you visit a cast member at an autograph show. Most of all, share your love for this TV show with others so we can help keep LITB popular for decades to come. Sincerely, Brian Humek, December 3, 2022

TV Show and Movie Index

U

V

People Index